Henry James

Henry James OM (15 April 1843 – 28 February 1916) was an American-British author regarded as a key transitional figure between literary realism and literary modernism, and is considered by many to be among the greatest novelists in the English language. He was the son of Henry James Sr. and the brother of renowned philosopher and psychologist William James and diarist Alice James.

He is best known for a number of novels dealing with the social and marital interplay between émigré Americans, English people, and continental Europeans. Examples of such novels include The Portrait of a Lady, The Ambassadors, and The Wings of the Dove. His later works were increasingly experimental. In describing the internal states of mind and social dynamics of his characters, James often made use of a style in which ambiguous or contradictory motives and impressions were overlaid or juxtaposed in the discussion of a character's psyche.(Source: Wikipedia)

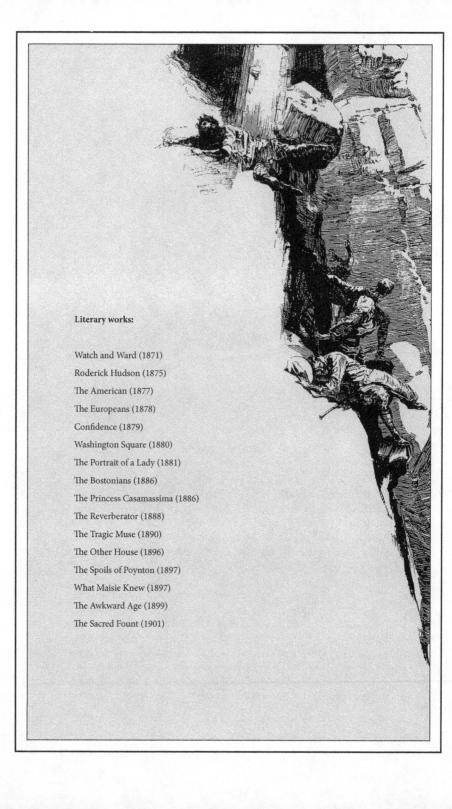

Literary works:

Watch and Ward (1871)

Roderick Hudson (1875)

The American (1877)

The Europeans (1878)

Confidence (1879)

Washington Square (1880)

The Portrait of a Lady (1881)

The Bostonians (1886)

The Princess Casamassima (1886)

The Reverberator (1888)

The Tragic Muse (1890)

The Other House (1896)

The Spoils of Poynton (1897)

What Maisie Knew (1897)

The Awkward Age (1899)

The Sacred Fount (1901)

THE
WORKS
OF
HENRY JAMES

VOL. 09 (OF 24)

PARTIAL PORTRAITS
PICTURE AND TEXT
RODERICK HUDSON

An Imprint of Moon Classics LLC

A Wholly Owned Subsidiary of Queenior LLC

A Melodragon Company

First Printing: 2020

ISBN 978-1-6627-1636-2 (Paperback)

ISBN 978-1-6627-1637-9 (Hardcover)

Published by Moon Classics

www.moonclassics.com

Contents

THE
WORKS
OF
HENRY JAMES
VOL. 09 (OF 24)

PARTIAL PORTRAITS

NOTICE

THE following attempts at literary portraiture originally appeared, with three exceptions, in American periodicals—The *Atlantic Monthly*, *The Century*, and *Harper's Weekly*. The paper on Emerson was contributed to *Macmillan's Magazine*, that on "The Art of Fiction" to *Longman's* and that on M. Guy de Maupassant to *The Fortnightly Review*. The reminiscences of Turgénieff were written immediately after his death, the article on Anthony Trollope on the same occasion, before the publication of his interesting Autobiography, and the appreciation of Alphonse Daudet before that of his three latest novels. The date affixed to the sketch of Robert Louis Stevenson is that of composition.

I. EMERSON

MR. ELLIOT CABOT has made a very interesting contribution to a class of books of which our literature, more than any other, offers admirable examples: he has given us a biography[1] intelligently and carefully composed. These two volumes are a model of responsible editing—I use that term because they consist largely of letters and extracts from letters: nothing could resemble less the manner in which the mere bookmaker strings together his frequently questionable pearls and shovels the heap into the presence of the public. Mr. Cabot has selected, compared, discriminated, steered an even course between meagreness and redundancy, and managed to be constantly and happily illustrative. And his work, moreover, strikes us as the better done from the fact that it stands for one of the two things that make an absorbing memoir a good deal more than for the other. If these two things be the conscience of the writer and the career of his hero, it is not difficult to see on which side the biographer of Emerson has found himself strongest. Ralph Waldo Emerson was a man of genius, but he led for nearly eighty years a life in which the sequence of events had little of the rapidity, or the complexity, that a spectator loves. There is something we miss very much as we turn these pages—something that has a kind of accidental, inevitable presence in almost any personal record—something that may be most definitely indicated under the name of colour. We lay down the book with a singular impression of paleness—an impression that comes partly from the tone of the biographer and partly from the moral complexion of his subject, but mainly from the vacancy of the page itself. That of Emerson's personal history is condensed into the single word Concord, and all the condensation in the world will not make it look rich. It presents a most continuous surface. Mr. Matthew Arnold, in his *Discourses in America*, contests Emerson's complete right to the title of a man of letters; yet letters surely were the very texture of his history. Passions, alternations, affairs, adventures had absolutely no part in it. It stretched itself out in enviable quiet—a quiet in which we hear the jotting of the pencil in the note-book. It is the very life for literature (I mean for one's own, not that of another): fifty years of residence in the home of one's forefathers, pervaded by reading, by walking in the woods and the daily addition of sentence to sentence.

If the interest of Mr. Cabot's pencilled portrait is incontestable and yet does not spring from variety, it owes nothing either to a source from which it might have borrowed much and which it is impossible not to regret a little that he has so completely neglected: I mean a greater reference to the social conditions in which Emerson moved, the company he lived in, the moral air he breathed. If his biographer had allowed himself a little more of the ironic touch, had put himself once in a way under the protection of Sainte-Beuve and had attempted something of a general picture, we should have felt that he only went with the occasion. I may overestimate the latent treasures of the field, but it seems to me there was distinctly an opportunity—an opportunity to make up moreover in some degree for the white tint of Emerson's career considered simply in itself. We know a man imperfectly until we know his society, and we but half know a society until we know its manners. This is especially true of a man of letters, for manners lie very close to literature. From those of the New England world in which Emerson's character formed itself Mr. Cabot almost averts his lantern, though we feel sure that there would have been delightful glimpses to be had and that he would have been in a position—that is that he has all the knowledge that would enable him— to help us to them. It is as if he could not trust himself, knowing the subject only too well. This adds to the effect of extreme discretion that we find in his volumes, but it is the cause of our not finding certain things, certain figures and scenes, evoked. What is evoked is Emerson's pure spirit, by a copious, sifted series of citations and comments. But we must read as much as possible between the lines, and the picture of the transcendental time (to mention simply one corner) has yet to be painted—the lines have yet to be bitten in. Meanwhile we are held and charmed by the image of Emerson's mind and the extreme appeal which his physiognomy makes to our art of discrimination. It is so fair, so uniform and impersonal, that its features are simply fine shades, the gradations of tone of a surface whose proper quality was of the smoothest and on which nothing was reflected with violence. It is a pleasure of the critical sense to find, with Mr. Cabot's extremely intelligent help, a notation for such delicacies.

We seem to see the circumstances of our author's origin, immediate and remote, in a kind of high, vertical moral light, the brightness of a society at once very simple and very responsible. The rare singleness that was in his nature (so that he was *all* the warning moral voice, without distraction or counter-solicitation), was also in the stock he sprang from, clerical for generations, on both sides, and clerical in the Puritan sense. His ancestors had lived long (for nearly two centuries) in the same corner of New England, and during that period had preached and studied and prayed and practised. It is impossible to imagine a spirit better prepared in advance to be exactly what it was—better educated for its office in its far-away unconscious beginnings. There is an inner satisfaction in seeing so straight, although so patient, a connection between the stem and the flower, and such a proof that when life wishes to produce something exquisite in quality she takes her measures many years in advance. A conscience like Emerson's could not have been turned off, as it were, from one generation to another: a succession of attempts, a long process of refining, was required. His perfection, in his own line, comes largely from the non-interruption of the process.

As most of us are made up of ill-assorted pieces, his reader, and Mr. Cabot's, envies him this transmitted unity, in which there was no mutual hustling or crowding of elements. It must have been a kind of luxury to be— that is to feel—so homogeneous, and it helps to account for his serenity, his power of acceptance, and that absence of personal passion which makes his private correspondence read like a series of beautiful circulars or expanded cards *pour prendre congé*. He had the equanimity of a result; nature had taken care of him and he had only to speak. He accepted himself as he accepted others, accepted everything; and his absence of eagerness, or in other words his modesty, was that of a man with whom it is not a question of success, who has nothing invested or at stake. The investment, the stake, was that of the race, of all the past Emersons and Bulkeleys and Waldos. There is much that makes us smile, to-day, in the commotion produced by his secession from the mild Unitarian pulpit: we wonder at a condition of opinion in which any utterance of his should appear to be wanting in superior piety—in the essence of good instruction. All that is changed: the great difference has become the infinitely small, and we admire a state of society in which scandal and schism took on no darker hue; but there is even yet a sort of drollery in the spectacle of a body of people among whom the author of *The American Scholar* and of the Address of 1838 at the Harvard Divinity College passed for profane, and who failed to see that he only gave his plea for the spiritual life the advantage of a brilliant expression. They were so provincial as to think that brilliancy came ill-recommended, and they were shocked at his ceasing to care for the prayer and the sermon. They might have perceived that he *was* the prayer and the sermon: not in the least a seculariser, but in his own subtle insinuating way a sanctifier.

Of the three periods into which his life divides itself, the first was (as in the case of most men) that of movement, experiment and selection—that of effort too and painful probation. Emerson had his message, but he was a good while looking for his form—the form which, as he himself would have said, he never completely found and of which it was rather characteristic of him that his later years (with their growing refusal to give him the *word*), wishing to attack him in his most vulnerable point, where his tenure was least complete, had in some degree the effect of despoiling him. It all sounds rather bare and stern, Mr. Cabot's account of his youth and early manhood, and we get an impression of a terrible paucity of alternatives. If he would be neither a farmer nor a trader he could "teach school"; that was the main resource and a part of the general educative process of the young New Englander who proposed to devote himself to the things of the mind. There was an advantage in the nudity, however, which was that, in Emerson's case at least, the things of the mind did get themselves admirably well considered. If it be his great distinction and his special sign that he had a more vivid conception of the moral life than any one else, it is probably not fanciful to say that he owed it in part to the limited way in which he saw our capacity for living illustrated. The plain, God-fearing, practical society which surrounded him was not fertile in variations: it had great intelligence and energy, but it moved altogether in the straightforward direction. On three occasions later—three journeys to Europe—he was introduced to a more complicated world; but his spirit, his moral taste, as it were, abode always within the undecorated walls of his youth. There he could dwell with that ripe unconsciousness of evil which is one of the most beautiful signs by which we know him. His early writings are full of quaint animadversion upon the vices of the place and time, but there is something charmingly vague, light and general in the arraignment. Almost the worst he can say is that these vices are negative and that his fellow-townsmen are not heroic. We feel that his first impressions were gathered in a community from which misery and extravagance, and either extreme, of any sort, were equally absent. What the life of New England fifty years ago offered to the observer was the common lot, in a kind of achromatic picture, without particular intensifications. It was from this table of the usual, the merely typical joys and sorrows that he proceeded to generalise—a fact that accounts in some degree for a certain inadequacy and thinness in his enumerations. But it helps to account also for his direct, intimate vision of the soul itself—not in its emotions, its contortions and perversions, but in its passive, exposed, yet healthy form. He knows the nature of man and the long tradition of its dangers; but we feel that whereas he can put his finger on the remedies, lying for the most part, as they do, in the deep recesses of virtue, of the spirit, he has only a kind of hearsay, uninformed acquaintance with the disorders. It would require some ingenuity, the reader may say too much, to trace closely this correspondence between his genius and the frugal, dutiful, happy but decidedly lean Boston of the past, where there was a great deal of will but very little fulcrum—like a ministry without an opposition.

The genius itself it seems to me impossible to contest—I mean the genius for seeing character as a real and supreme thing. Other writers have arrived at a more complete expression: Wordsworth and Goethe, for instance, give one a sense of having found their form, whereas with Emerson we never lose the sense that he is still seeking it. But no one has had so steady and constant, and above all so natural, a vision of what we require and what we are capable of in the way of aspiration and independence. With Emerson it is ever the special capacity for moral experience—always that and only that. We have the impression, somehow, that life had never bribed him to look at anything but the soul; and indeed in the world in which he grew up and lived the bribes and lures, the beguilements and prizes, were few. He was in an admirable position for showing, what he constantly endeavoured to show, that the prize was within. Any one who in New England at that time could do that was sure of success, of listeners and sympathy: most of all, of course, when it was a question of doing it with such a divine persuasiveness. Moreover, the way in which Emerson did it added to the charm—by word of mouth, face to face, with a rare, irresistible voice and a beautiful mild, modest authority. If Mr. Arnold is struck with the limited degree in which he was a man of letters I suppose it is because he is more struck with his having been, as it were, a man of lectures. But the lecture surely was never more purged of its grossness—the quality in it that suggests a strong light and a big brush—than as it issued from Emerson's lips; so far from being a vulgarisation, it was simply the esoteric made audible, and instead of treating the few as the many, after the usual fashion of gentlemen on platforms, he treated the many as the few. There was probably no other society at that time in which he would have got so many persons to understand that; for we think the better of his audience as we read him, and wonder where else people would have had so much moral attention to give. It is to be remembered however that during the winter of 1847-48, on the occasion of his second visit to England, he found many listeners in London and in provincial cities. Mr. Cabot's volumes are full of evidence of the satisfactions he offered, the delights and revelations he may be said to have promised, to a race which had to seek its entertainment, its rewards and consolations, almost exclusively in the moral world. But his own writings are fuller still; we find an instance almost wherever we open them.

"All these great and transcendent properties are ours.... Let us find room for this great guest in our small houses.... Where the heart is, there the muses, there the gods sojourn, and not in any geography of fame. Massachusetts, Connecticut River, and Boston Bay, you think paltry places, and the ear loves names of foreign and classic topography. But here we are, and if we will tarry a little we may come to learn that here is best.... The Jerseys were handsome enough ground for Washington to tread, and London streets for the feet of Milton.... That country is fairest which is inhabited by the noblest minds."

We feel, or suspect, that Milton is thrown in as a hint that the London streets are no such great place, and it all sounds like a sort of pleading consolation against bleakness.

The beauty of a hundred passages of this kind in Emerson's pages is that they are effective, that they do come home, that they rest upon insight and not upon ingenuity, and that if they are sometimes obscure it is never with the obscurity of paradox. We seem to see the people turning out into the snow after hearing them, glowing with a finer glow than even the climate could give and fortified for a struggle with overshoes and the east wind.

"Look to it first and only, that fashion, custom, authority, pleasure, and money, are nothing to you, are not as bandages over your eyes, that you cannot see; but live with the privilege of the immeasurable mind. Not too anxious to visit periodically all families and each family in your parish connection, when you meet one of these men or women be to them a divine man; be to them thought and virtue; let their timid aspirations find in you a friend; let their trampled instincts be genially tempted out in your atmosphere; let their doubts know that you have doubted, and their wonder feel that you have wondered."

When we set against an exquisite passage like that, or like the familiar sentences that open the essay on History ("He that is admitted to the right of reason is made freeman of the whole estate. What Plato has thought, he may think; what a saint has felt, he may feel; what at any time has befallen any man, he can understand"); when we compare the letters, cited by Mr. Cabot, to his wife from Springfield, Illinois (January 1853) we feel that his spiritual tact needed to be very just, but that if it was so it must have brought a blessing.

"Here I am in the deep mud of the prairies, misled I fear into this bog, not by a will-of-the-wisp, such as shine in bogs, but by a young New Hampshire editor, who over-estimated the strength of both of us, and fancied I should glitter in the prairie and draw the prairie birds and waders. It rains and thaws incessantly, and if we step off the short street we go up to the shoulders, perhaps, in mud. My chamber is a cabin; my fellow-boarders are legislators.... Two or three governors or ex-governors live in the house.... I cannot command daylight and solitude for study or for more than a scrawl."
...

And another extract:—

21

"A cold, raw country this, and plenty of night-travelling and arriving at four in the morning to take the last and worst bed in the tavern. Advancing day brings mercy and favour to me, but not the sleep.... Mercury 15° below zero.... I find well-disposed, kindly people among these sinewy farmers of the North, but in all that is called cultivation they are only ten years old."

He says in another letter (in 1860), "I saw Michigan and its forests and the Wolverines pretty thoroughly;" and on another page Mr. Cabot shows him as speaking of his engagements to lecture in the West as the obligation to "wade, and freeze, and ride, and run, and suffer all manner of indignities." This was not New England, but as regards the country districts throughout, at that time, it was a question of degree. Certainly never was the fine wine of philosophy carried to remoter or queerer corners: never was a more delicate diet offered to "two or three governors, or ex-governors," living in a cabin. It was Mercury, shivering in a mackintosh, bearing nectar and ambrosia to the gods whom he wished those who lived in cabins to endeavour to feel that they might be.

I have hinted that the will, in the old New England society, was a clue without a labyrinth; but it had its use, nevertheless, in helping the young talent to find its mould. There were few or none ready-made: tradition was certainly not so oppressive as might have been inferred from the fact that the air swarmed with reformers and improvers. Of the patient, philosophic manner in which Emerson groped and waited, through teaching the young and preaching to the adult, for his particular vocation, Mr. Cabot's first volume gives a full and orderly account. His passage from the Unitarian pulpit to the lecture-desk was a step which at this distance of time can hardly help appearing to us short, though he was long in making it, for even after ceasing to have a parish of his own he freely confounded the two, or willingly, at least, treated the pulpit as a platform. "The young people and the mature hint at odium and the aversion of faces, to be presently encountered in society," he writes in his journal in 1838; but in point of fact the quiet drama of his abdication was not to include the note of suffering. The Boston world might feel disapproval, but it was far too kindly to make this sentiment felt as a weight: every element of martyrdom was there but the important ones of the cause and the persecutors. Mr. Cabot marks the lightness of the penalties of dissent; if they were light in somewhat later years for the transcendentalists and fruit-eaters they could press but little on a man of Emerson's distinction, to whom, all his life, people went not to carry but to ask the right word. There was no consideration to give up, he could not have been one of the dingy if he had tried; but what he did renounce in 1838 was a material profession. He was "settled," and his indisposition to administer the communion unsettled him. He calls the whole business, in writing to Carlyle, "a tempest in our washbowl"; but it had the effect of forcing him to seek a new source of income. His wants were few and his view of life severe, and this came to him, little by little, as he was able to extend the field in which he read his discourses. In 1835, upon his second marriage, he took up his habitation at Concord, and his life fell into the shape it was, in a general way, to keep for the next half-century. It is here that we cannot help regretting that Mr. Cabot had not found it possible to treat his career a little more pictorially. Those fifty years of Concord—at least the earlier part of them—would have been a subject bringing into play many odd figures, many human incongruities: they would have abounded in illustrations of the primitive New England character, especially during the time of its queer search for something to expend itself upon. Objects and occupations have multiplied since then, and now there is no lack; but fifty years ago the expanse was wide and free, and we get the impression of a conscience gasping in the void, panting for sensations, with something of the movement of the gills of a landed fish. It would take a very fine point to sketch Emerson's benignant, patient, inscrutable countenance during the various phases of this democratic communion; but the picture, when complete, would be one of the portraits, half a revelation and half an enigma, that suggest and fascinate. Such a striking personage as old Miss Mary Emerson, our author's aunt, whose high intelligence and temper were much of an influence in his earlier years, has a kind of tormenting representative value: we want to see her from head to foot, with her frame and her background; having (for we happen to have it), an impression that she was a very remarkable specimen of the transatlantic Puritan stock, a spirit that would have dared the devil. We miss a more liberal handling, are tempted to add touches of our own, and end by convincing ourselves that Miss Mary Moody Emerson, grim intellectual virgin and daughter of a hundred ministers, with her local traditions and her combined love of empire and of speculation, would have been an inspiration for a novelist. Hardly less so the charming Mrs. Ripley, Emerson's life-long friend and neighbour, most delicate and accomplished of women, devoted to Greek and to her house, studious, simple and dainty—an admirable example of the old-fashioned New England lady. It was a freak of Miss Emerson's somewhat sardonic humour to give her once a broomstick to carry across Boston Common (under the pretext of a "moving"), a task accepted with docility but making of the victim the most benignant witch ever equipped with that utensil.

These ladies, however, were very private persons and not in the least of the reforming tribe: there are others who would have peopled Mr. Cabot's page to whom he gives no more than a mention. We must add that it is open to him to say that their features have become faint and indistinguishable to-day without more research than the question is apt to be worth: they are embalmed—in a collective way—the apprehensible part of them, in Mr. Frothingham's clever *History of Transcendentalism in New England*. This must be admitted to be true of even so lively a "factor," as we say nowadays, as the imaginative, talkative, intelligent and finally Italianised and shipwrecked Margaret Fuller: she is now one of the dim, one of Carlyle's "then-celebrated" at most. It seemed indeed as if Mr. Cabot rather grudged her a due place in the record of the company that Emerson kept, until we came across the delightful letter he quotes toward the end of his first volume—a letter interesting both as a specimen of inimitable, imperceptible edging away, and as an illustration of the curiously generalised way, as if with an implicit protest against personalities, in which his intercourse, epistolary and other, with his friends was conducted. There is an extract from a letter to his aunt on the occasion of the death of a deeply-loved brother (his own) which reads like a passage from some fine old chastened essay on the vanity of earthly hopes: strangely unfamiliar, considering the circumstances. Courteous and humane to the furthest possible point, to the point of an almost profligate surrender of his attention, there was no familiarity in him, no personal avidity. Even his letters to his wife are courtesies, they are not familiarities. He had only one style, one manner, and he had it for everything—even for himself, in his notes, in his journals. But he had it in perfection for Miss Fuller; he retreats, smiling and flattering, on tiptoe, as if he were advancing. "She ever seems to crave," he says in his journal, "something which I have not, or have not for her." What he had was doubtless not what she craved, but the letter in question should be read to see how the modicum was administered. It is only between the lines of such a production that we read that a part of her effect upon him was to bore him; for his system was to practise a kind of universal passive hospitality—he aimed at nothing less. It was only because he was so deferential that he could be so detached; he had polished his aloofness till it reflected the image of his solicitor. And this was not because he was an "uncommunicating egotist," though he amuses himself with saying so to Miss Fuller: egotism is the strongest of passions, and he was altogether passionless. It was because he had no personal, just as he had almost no physical wants. "Yet I plead not guilty to the malice prepense. 'Tis imbecility, not contumacy, though perhaps somewhat more odious. It seems very just, the irony with which you ask whether you may not be trusted and promise such docility. Alas, we will all promise, but the prophet loiters." He would not say even to himself that she bored him; he had denied himself the luxury of such easy and obvious short cuts. There is a passage in the lecture (1844) called "Man the Reformer," in which he hovers round and round the idea that the practice of trade, in certain conditions likely to beget an underhand competition, does not draw forth the nobler parts of character, till the reader is tempted to interrupt him with, "Say at once that it is impossible for a gentleman!"

So he remained always, reading his lectures in the winter, writing them in the summer, and at all seasons taking wood-walks and looking for hints in old books.

"Delicious summer stroll through the pastures.... On the steep park of Conantum I have the old regret—is all this beauty to perish? Shall none re-make this sun and wind; the sky-blue river; the river-blue sky; the yellow meadow, spotted with sacks and sheets of cranberry-gatherers; the red bushes; the iron-gray house, just the colour of the granite rocks; the wild orchard?"

His observation of Nature was exquisite—always the direct, irresistible impression.

25

"The hawking of the wild geese flying by night; the thin note of the companionable titmouse in the winter day; the fall of swarms of flies in autumn, from combats high in the air, pattering down on the leaves like rain; the angry hiss of the wood-birds; the pine throwing out its pollen for the benefit of the next century." ... (*Literary Ethics.*)

I have said there was no familiarity in him, but he was familiar with woodland creatures and sounds. Certainly, too, he was on terms of free association with his books, which were numerous and dear to him; though Mr. Cabot says, doubtless with justice, that his dependence on them was slight and that he was not "intimate" with his authors. They did not feed him but they stimulated; they were not his meat but his wine—he took them in sips. But he needed them and liked them; he had volumes of notes from his reading, and he could not have produced his lectures without them. He liked literature as a thing to refer to, liked the very names of which it is full, and used them, especially in his later writings, for purposes of ornament, to dress the dish, sometimes with an unmeasured profusion. I open *The Conduct of Life* and find a dozen on the page. He mentions more authorities than is the fashion to-day. He can easily say, of course, that he follows a better one—that of his well-loved and irrepressibly allusive Montaigne. In his own bookishness there is a certain contradiction, just as there is a latent incompleteness in his whole literary side. Independence, the return to nature, the finding out and doing for one's self, was ever what he most highly recommended; and yet he is constantly reminding his readers of the conventional signs and consecrations—of what other men have done. This was partly because the independence that he had in his eye was an independence without ill-nature, without rudeness (though he likes that word), and full of gentle amiabilities, curiosities and tolerances; and partly it is a simple matter of form, a literary expedient, confessing its character—on the part of one who had never really mastered the art of composition—of continuous expression. Charming to many a reader, charming yet ever slightly droll, will remain Emerson's frequent invocation of the "scholar": there is such a friendly vagueness and convenience in it. It is of the scholar that he expects all the heroic and uncomfortable things, the concentrations and relinquishments, that make up the noble life. We fancy this personage looking up from his book and arm-chair a little ruefully and saying, "Ah, but why *me* always and only? Why so much of me, and is there no one else to share the responsibility?" "Neither years nor books have yet availed to extirpate a prejudice then rooted in me [when as a boy he first saw the graduates of his college assembled at their anniversary], that a scholar is the favourite of heaven and earth, the excellency of his country, the happiest of men."

In truth, by this term he means simply the cultivated man, the man who has had a liberal education, and there is a voluntary plainness in his use of it—speaking of such people as the rustic, or the vulgar, speak of those who have a tincture of books. This is characteristic of his humility—that humility which was nine-tenths a plain fact (for it is easy for persons who have at bottom a great fund of indifference to be humble), and the remaining tenth a literary habit. Moreover an American reader may be excused for finding in it a pleasant sign of that prestige, often so quaintly and indeed so extravagantly acknowledged, which a connection with literature carries with it among the people of the United States. There is no country in which it is more freely admitted to be a distinction—*the* distinction; or in which so many persons have become eminent for showing it even in a slight degree. Gentlemen and ladies are celebrated there on this ground who would not on the same ground, though they might on another, be celebrated anywhere else. Emerson's own tone is an echo of that, when he speaks of the scholar—not of the banker, the great merchant, the legislator, the artist—as the most distinguished figure in the society about him. It is because he has most to give up that he is appealed to for efforts and sacrifices. "Meantime I know that a very different estimate of the scholar's profession prevails in this country," he goes on to say in the address from which I last quoted (the *Literary Ethics*), "and the importunity with which society presses its claim upon young men tends to pervert the views of the youth in respect to the culture of the intellect." The manner in which that is said represents, surely, a serious mistake: with the estimate of the scholar's profession which then prevailed in New England Emerson could have had no quarrel; the ground of his lamentation was another side of the matter. It was not a question of estimate, but of accidental practice. In 1838 there were still so many things of prime material necessity to be done that reading was driven to the wall; but the reader was still thought the cleverest, for he found time as well as intelligence. Emerson's own situation sufficiently indicates it. In what other country, on sleety winter nights, would provincial and bucolic populations have gone forth in hundreds for the cold comfort of a literary discourse? The distillation anywhere else would certainly have appeared too thin, the appeal too special. But for many years the American people of the middle regions, outside of a few cities, had in the most rigorous seasons no other recreation. A gentleman, grave or gay, in a bare room, with a manuscript, before a desk, offered the reward of toil, the refreshment of pleasure, to the young, the middle-aged and the old of both sexes. The hour was brightest, doubtless, when the gentleman was gay, like Doctor Oliver Wendell Holmes. But Emerson's gravity never sapped his career, any more than it chilled the regard in which he was held among those who were particularly his own people. It was impossible to be more honoured and cherished, far and near, than he was during his long residence in Concord, or more looked upon as the principal gentleman in the place. This was conspicuous to the writer of these remarks on the occasion of the curious, sociable, cheerful public funeral made for him in 1883 by all the countryside, arriving, as for the last honours to the first citizen, in trains, in waggons, on foot, in multitudes. It was a popular manifestation, the most striking I have ever seen provoked by the death of a man of letters.

If a picture of that singular and very illustrative institution the old American lecture-system would have constituted a part of the filling-in of the ideal memoir of Emerson, I may further say, returning to the matter for a moment, that such a memoir would also have had a chapter for some of those Concord-haunting figures which are not so much interesting in themselves as interesting because for a season Emerson thought them so. And the pleasure of that would be partly that it would push us to inquire how interesting he did really think them. That is, it would bring up the question of his inner reserves and scepticisms, his secret ennuis and ironies, the way he sympathised for courtesy and then, with his delicacy and generosity, in a world after all given much to the literal, let his courtesy pass for adhesion—a question particularly attractive to those for whom he has, in general, a fascination. Many entertaining problems of that sort present themselves for such readers: there is something indefinable for them in the mixture of which he was made—his fidelity as an interpreter of the so-called transcendental spirit and his freedom from all wish for any personal share in the effect of his ideas. He drops them, sheds them, diffuses them, and we feel as if there would be a grossness in holding him to anything so temporal as a responsibility. He had the advantage, for many years, of having the question of application assumed for him by Thoreau, who took upon himself to be, in the concrete, the sort of person that Emerson's "scholar" was in the abstract, and who paid for it by having a shorter life than that fine adumbration. The application, with Thoreau, was violent and limited (it became a matter of prosaic detail, the non-payment of taxes, the non-wearing of a necktie, the preparation of one's food one's self, the practice of a rude sincerity—all things not of the essence), so that, though he wrote some beautiful pages, which read like a translation of Emerson into the sounds of the field and forest and which no one who has ever loved nature in New England, or indeed anywhere, can fail to love, he suffers something of the *amoindrissement* of eccentricity. His master escapes that reduction altogether. I call it an advantage to have had such a pupil as Thoreau; because for a mind so much made up of reflection as Emerson's everything comes under that head which prolongs and reanimates the process—produces the return, again and yet again, on one's impressions. Thoreau must have had this moderating and even chastening effect. It did not rest, moreover, with him alone; the advantage of which I speak was not confined to Thoreau's case. In 1837 Emerson (in his journal) pronounced Mr. Bronson Alcott the most extraordinary man and the highest genius of his time: the sequence of which was that for more than forty years after that he had the gentleman living but half a mile away. The opportunity for the return, as I have called it, was not wanting.

His detachment is shown in his whole attitude toward the transcendental movement—that remarkable outburst of Romanticism on Puritan ground, as Mr. Cabot very well names it. Nothing can be more ingenious, more sympathetic and charming, than Emerson's account and definition of the matter in his lecture (of 1842) called "The Transcendentalist"; and yet nothing is more apparent from his letters and journals than that he regarded any such label or banner as a mere tiresome flutter. He liked to taste but not to drink—least of all to become intoxicated. He liked to explain the transcendentalists but did not care at all to be explained by them: a doctrine "whereof you know I am wholly guiltless," he says to his wife in 1842, "and which is spoken of as a known and fixed element, like salt or meal. So that I have to begin with endless disclaimers and explanations: 'I am not the man you take me for.'" He was never the man any one took him for, for the simple reason that no one could possibly take him for the elusive, irreducible, merely gustatory spirit for which he took himself.

"It is a sort of maxim with me never to harp on the omnipotence of limitations. Least of all do we need any suggestion of checks and measures; as if New England were anything else.... Of so many fine people it is true that being so much they ought to be a little more, and missing that are naught. It is a sort of King Renè period; there is no doing, but rare thrilling prophecy from bands of competing minstrels."

That is his private expression about a large part of a ferment in regard to which his public judgment was that

"That indeed constitutes a new feature in their portrait, that they are the most exacting and extortionate critics.... These exacting children advertise us of our wants. There is no compliment, no smooth speech with them; they pay you only this one compliment of insatiable expectation; they aspire, they severely exact, and if they only stand fast in this watch-tower, and stand fast unto the end, and without end, then they are terrible friends, whereof poet and priest cannot but stand in awe; and what if they eat clouds and drink wind, they have not been without service to the race of man."

That was saying the best for them, as he always said it for everything; but it was the sense of their being "bands of competing minstrels" and their camp being only a "measure and check," in a society too sparse for a synthesis, that kept him from wishing to don their uniform. This was after all but a misfitting imitation of his natural wear, and what he would have liked was to put that off—he did not wish to button it tighter. He said the best for his friends of the Dial, of Fruitlands and Brook Farm, in saying that they were fastidious and critical; but he was conscious in the next breath that what there was around them to be criticised was mainly a negative. Nothing is more perceptible to-day than that their criticism produced no fruit—that it was little else than a very decent and innocent recreation—a kind of Puritan carnival. The New England world was for much the most part very busy, but the Dial and Fruitlands and Brook Farm were the amusement of the leisure-class. Extremes meet, and as in older societies that class is known principally by its connection with castles and carriages, so at Concord it came, with Thoreau and Mr. W. H. Channing, out of the cabin and the wood-lot.

Emerson was not moved to believe in their fastidiousness as a productive principle even when they directed it upon abuses which he abundantly recognised. Mr. Cabot shows that he was by no means one of the professional abolitionists or philanthropists—never an enrolled "humanitarian."

"We talk frigidly of Reform until the walls mock us. It is that of which a man should never speak, but if he have cherished it in his bosom he should steal to it in darkness, as an Indian to his bride.... Does he not do more to abolish slavery who works all day steadily in his own garden, than he who goes to the abolition meeting and makes a speech? He who does his own work frees a slave."

I must add that even while I transcribe these words there comes to me the recollection of the great meeting in the Boston Music Hall, on the first day of 1863, to celebrate the signing by Mr. Lincoln of the proclamation freeing the Southern slaves—of the momentousness of the occasion, the vast excited multitude, the crowded platform and the tall, spare figure of Emerson, in the midst, reading out the stanzas that were published under the name of the Boston Hymn. They are not the happiest he produced for an occasion—they do not compare with the verses on the "embattled farmers," read at Concord in 1857, and there is a certain awkwardness in some of them. But I well remember the immense effect with which his beautiful voice pronounced the lines—

> "Pay ransom to the owner
>
> And fill the bag to the brim.
>
> Who is the owner? The slave is owner,

And ever was. Pay him!" And Mr. Cabot chronicles the fact that the *gran' rifiuto*—the great backsliding of Mr. Webster when he cast his vote in Congress for the Fugitive Slave Law of 1850—was the one thing that ever moved him to heated denunciation. He felt Webster's apostasy as strongly as he had admired his genius. "Who has not helped to praise him? Simply he was the one American of our time whom we could produce as a finished work of nature." There is a passage in his journal (not a rough jotting, but, like most of the entries in it, a finished piece of writing), which is admirably descriptive of the wonderful orator and is moreover one of the very few portraits, or even personal sketches, yielded by Mr. Cabot's selections. It shows that he could observe the human figure and "render" it to good purpose.

"His splendid wrath, when his eyes become fire, is good to see, so intellectual it is—the wrath of the fact and the cause he espouses, and not at all personal to himself.... These village parties must be dish-water to him, yet he shows himself just good-natured, just nonchalant enough; and he has his own way, without offending any one or losing any ground.... His expensiveness seems necessary to him; were he too prudent a Yankee it would be a sad deduction from his magnificence. I only wish he would not truckle [to the slave-holders]. I do not care how much he spends."

I doubtless appear to have said more than enough, yet I have passed by many of the passages I had marked for transcription from Mr. Cabot's volumes. There is one, in the first, that makes us stare as we come upon it, to the effect that Emerson "could see nothing in Shelley, Aristophanes, Don Quixote, Miss Austen, Dickens." Mr. Cabot adds that he rarely read a novel, even the famous ones (he has a point of contact here as well as, strangely enough, on two or three other sides with that distinguished moralist M. Ernest Renan, who, like Emerson, was originally a dissident priest and cannot imagine why people should write works of fiction); and thought Dante "a man to put into a museum, but not into your house; another Zerah Colburn; a prodigy of imaginative function, executive rather than contemplative or wise." The confession of an insensibility ranging from Shelley to Dickens and from Dante to Miss Austen and taking Don Quixote and Aristophanes on the way, is a large allowance to have to make for a man of letters, and may appear to confirm but slightly any claim of intellectual hospitality and general curiosity put forth for him. The truth was that, sparely constructed as he was and formed not wastefully, not with material left over, as it were, for a special function, there were certain chords in Emerson that did not vibrate at all. I well remember my impression of this on walking with him in the autumn of 1872 through the galleries of the Louvre and, later that winter, through those of the Vatican: his perception of the objects contained in these collections was of the most general order. I was struck with the anomaly of a man so refined and intelligent being so little spoken to by works of art. It would be more exact to say that certain chords were wholly absent; the tune was played, the tune of life and literature, altogether on those that remained. They had every wish to be equal to their office, but one feels that the number was short—that some notes could not be given. Mr. Cabot makes use of a singular phrase when he says, in speaking of Hawthorne, for several years our author's neighbour at Concord and a little—a very little we gather—his companion, that Emerson was unable to read his novels—he thought them "not worthy of him." This is a judgment odd almost to fascination—we circle round it and turn it over and over; it contains so elusive an ambiguity. How highly he must have esteemed the man of whose genius *The House of the Seven Gables* and *The Scarlet Letter* gave imperfectly the measure, and how strange that he should not have been eager to read almost anything that such a gifted being might have let fall! It was a rare accident that made them live almost side by side so long in the same small New England town, each a fruit of a long Puritan stem, yet with such a difference of taste. Hawthorne's vision was all for the evil and sin of the world; a side of life as to which Emerson's eyes were thickly bandaged. There were points as to which the latter's conception of right could be violated, but he had no great sense of wrong—a strangely limited one, indeed, for a moralist—no sense of the dark, the foul, the base. There were certain complications in life which he never suspected. One asks one's self whether that is why he did not care for Dante and Shelley and Aristophanes and Dickens, their works containing a considerable reflection of human perversity. But that still leaves the indifference to Cervantes and Miss Austen unaccounted for.

It has not, however, been the ambition of these remarks to account for everything, and I have arrived at the end without even pointing to the grounds on which Emerson justifies the honours of biography, discussion and illustration. I have assumed his importance and continuance, and shall probably not be gainsaid by those who read him. Those who do not will hardly rub him out. Such a book as Mr. Cabot's subjects a reputation to a test—leads people to look it over and hold it up to the light, to see whether it is worth keeping in use or even putting away in a cabinet. Such a revision of Emerson has no relegating consequences. The result of it is once more the impression that he serves and will not wear out, and that indeed we cannot afford to drop him. His instrument makes him precious. He did something better than any one else; he had a particular faculty, which has not been surpassed, for speaking to the soul in a voice of direction and authority. There have been many spiritual voices appealing, consoling, reassuring, exhorting, or even denouncing and terrifying, but none has had just that firmness and just that purity. It penetrates further, it seems to go back to the roots of our feelings, to where conduct and manhood begin; and moreover, to us to-day, there is something in it that says that it is connected somehow with the virtue of the world, has wrought and achieved, lived in thousands of minds, produced a mass of character and life. And there is this further sign of Emerson's singular power, that he is a striking exception to the general rule that writings live in the last resort by their form; that they owe a large part of their fortune to the art with which they have been composed. It is hardly too much, or too little, to say of Emerson's writings in general that they were not composed at all. Many and many things are beautifully said; he had felicities, inspirations, unforgettable phrases; he had frequently an exquisite eloquence.

"O my friends, there are resources in us on which we have not yet drawn. There are men who rise refreshed on hearing a threat; men to whom a crisis which intimidates and paralyses the majority—demanding not the faculties of prudence and thrift, but comprehension, immovableness, the readiness of sacrifice, come graceful and beloved as a bride.... But these are heights that we can scarce look up to and remember without contrition and shame. Let us thank God that such things exist."

None the less we have the impression that that search for a fashion and a manner on which he was always engaged never really came to a conclusion; it draws itself out through his later writings—it drew itself out through his later lectures, like a sort of renunciation of success. It is not on these, however, but on their predecessors, that his reputation will rest. Of course the way he spoke was the way that was on the whole most convenient to him; but he differs from most men of letters of the same degree of credit in failing to strike us as having achieved a style. This achievement is, as I say, usually the bribe or toll-money on the journey to posterity; and if Emerson goes his way, as he clearly appears to be doing, on the strength of his message alone, the case will be rare, the exception striking, and the honour great.

1887.

II. THE LIFE OF GEORGE ELIOT

THE writer of these pages has observed that the first question usually asked in relation to Mr. Cross's long-expected biography is whether the reader has not been disappointed in it. The inquirer is apt to be disappointed if the question be answered in the negative. It may as well be said, therefore, at the threshold of the following remarks, that such is not the feeling with which this particular reader laid down the book. The general feeling about it will depend very much on what has been looked for; there was probably, in advance, a considerable belief that we were to be treated to "revelations." I know not exactly why it should have been, but certain it is that the announcement of a biography of George Eliot has been construed more or less as a promise that we were to be admitted behind the scenes, as it were, of her life. No such result has taken place. We look at the drama from the point of view usually allotted to the public, and the curtain is lowered whenever it suits the biographer. The most "intimate" pages in the book are those in which the great novelist notes her derangements of health and depression of spirits. This history, to my sense, is quite as interesting as it might have been; that is, it is of the deepest interest, and one misses nothing that is characteristic or essential except perhaps a few more examples of the *vis comica* which made half the fortune of *Adam Bede* and *Silas Marner*. There is little that is absent that it would have been in Mr. Cross's power to give us. George Eliot's letters and journals are only a partial expression of her spirit, but they are evidently as full an expression as it was capable of giving itself when she was not wound up to the epic pitch. They do not explain her novels; they reflect in a singularly limited degree the process of growth of these great works; but it must be added that even a superficial acquaintance with the author was sufficient to assure one that her rich and complicated mind did not overflow in idle confidences. It was benignant and receptive in the highest degree, and nothing could have been more gracious than the manner of its intercourse; but it was deeply reserved and very far from egotistical, and nothing could have been less easy or agreeable to it, I surmise, than to attempt to tell people how, for instance, the plot of *Romola* got itself constructed or the character of Grandcourt got itself observed. There are critics who refuse to the delineator of this gentleman the title of a genius; who say that she had only a great talent overloaded with a great store of knowledge. The label, the epithet, matters little, but it is certain that George Eliot had this characteristic of the mind *possessed*: that the creations which brought her renown were of the incalculable kind, shaped themselves in mystery, in some intellectual back-shop or secret crucible, and were as little as possible implied in the aspect of her life. There is nothing more singular or striking in Mr. Cross's volumes than the absence of any indication, up to the time the *Scenes from Clerical Life* were published, that Miss Evans was a likely person to have written them; unless it be the absence of any indication, after they were published, that the deeply-studious, concentrated, home-keeping Mrs. Lewes was a likely person to have produced their successors. I know very well that there is no such thing in general as the air of the novelist, which it behoves those who practise this art to put on so that they may be recognised in public places; but there is such a thing as the air of the sage, the scholar, the philosopher, the votary of abstractions and of the lore of the ages, and in this pale but rich *Life* that is the face that is presented.

The plan on which it is composed is, so far as I know, without precedent, but it is a plan that could have occurred only to an "outsider" in literature, if I may venture to apply this term to one who has executed a literary task with such tact and success. The regular *littérateur*, hampered by tradition, would, I think, have lacked the boldness, the artless artfulness, of conjoining in the same text selected morsels of letters and journals, so as to form a continuous and multifarious *talk*, on the writer's part, punctuated only by marginal names and dates and divisions into chapters. There is something a little violent in the system, in spite of our feeling that it has been applied with a supple hand; but it was probably the best that Mr. Cross could have adopted, and it served especially well his purpose of appearing only as an arranger, or rather of not appearing at all. The modesty, the good taste, the self-effacement of the editorial element in the book are, in a word, complete, and the clearness and care of arrangement, the accuracy of reference, leave nothing to be desired. The form Mr. Cross has chosen, or invented, becomes, in the application, highly agreeable, and his rule of omission (for we have, almost always, only parts and passages of letters) has not prevented his volumes from being as copious as we could wish. George Eliot was not a great letter-writer, either in quantity or quality; she had neither the spirit, the leisure, nor the lightness of mind to conjure with the epistolary pen, and after her union with George Henry Lewes her disposition to play with it was further damped by his quick activity in her service. Letter-writing was part of the trouble he saved her; in this as in other ways he interposed between the world and his sensitive companion. The difference is striking between her habits in this respect and those of Madame George Sand, whose correspondence has lately been collected into six closely-printed volumes which testify afresh to her extraordinary energy and facility. Madame Sand, however, indefatigable producer as she was, was not a woman of study; she lived from day to day, from hand to mouth (intellectually), as it were, and had no general plan of life and culture. Her English compeer took the problem of production more seriously; she distilled her very substance into the things she gave the world. There was therefore so much the less of it left for casual utterance.

It was not till Marian Evans was past thirty, indeed, that she became an author by profession, and it may accordingly be supposed that her early letters are those which take us most into her confidence. This is true of those written when she was on the threshold of womanhood, which form a very full expression of her feelings at the time. The drawback here is that the feelings themselves are rather wanting in interest—one may almost say in amiability. At the age of twenty Marian Evans was a deeply religious young woman, whose faith took the form of a narrow evangelicism. Religious, in a manner, she remained to the end of her life, in spite of her adoption of a scientific explanation of things; but in the year 1839 she thought it ungodly to go to concerts and to read novels. She writes to her former governess that she can "only sigh" when she hears of the "marrying and giving in marriage that is constantly transacted;" expresses enjoyment of Hannah More's letters ("the contemplation of so blessed a character as hers is very salutary"); wishes that she "might be more useful in her own obscure and lowly station" ("I feel myself to be a mere cumberer of the ground"), that she "might seek to be sanctified wholly." These first fragments of her correspondence, first glimpses of her mind, are very curious; they have nothing in common with the later ones but the deep seriousness of the tone. Serious, of course, George Eliot continued to be to the end; the sense of moral responsibility, of the sadness and difficulty of life, was the most inveterate part of her nature. But the provincial strain in the letters from which I have quoted is very marked: they reflect a meagreness and grayness of outward circumstance; have a tinge as of Dissent in a small English town, where there are brick chapels in back streets. This was only a moment in her development; but there is something touching in the contrast between such a state of mind and that of the woman before whom, at middle age, all the culture of the world unrolled itself, and towards whom fame and fortune, and an activity which at the earlier period she would have thought very profane, pressed with rapidity. In 1839, as I have said, she thought very meanly of the art in which she was to attain such distinction. "I venture to believe that the same causes which exist in my own breast to render novels and romances pernicious have their counterpart in every fellow-creature.... The weapons of Christian warfare were never sharpened at the forge of romance." The style of these pietistic utterances is singularly strenuous and hard; the light and familiar are absent from them, and I think it is not too much to say that they show scarcely a single premonitory ray of the genius which had *Silas Marner* in reserve. This dryness was only a phase, indeed; it was speedily dispelled by more abundant showers of emotion— by the overflow of perception. Premonitory rays are still absent, however, after her first asceticism passes away—a change apparently co-incident with her removal from the country to the pleasant old town of Coventry, where all American pilgrims to midland shrines go and murmur Tennyson on the bridge. After the evangelical note began to fade it was still the desire for faith (a faith which could reconcile human affection with some of the unamiable truths of science), still the religious idea that coloured her thought; not the love of human life as a spectacle, nor the desire to spread the wings of the artist. It must be remembered, though, that during these years, if she was not stimulating prophecy in any definite form she was inhaling those impressions which were to make her first books so full of the delightful midland quality, the air of old-fashioned provincialism. The first piece of literary work she attempted (and she brought it to the best conclusion), was a translation of Strauss's *Life of Jesus*, which she began in 1844, when she was not yet twenty-five years of age; a task which indicates not only the persistence of her religious preoccupations, as well as the higher form they took, but the fact that with the limited facilities afforded by her life at that time she had mastered one of the most difficult of foreign languages and the vocabulary of a German exegetist. In 1841 she thought it wrong to encourage novels, but in 1847 she confesses to reading George Sand with great delight. There is no exhibition in Mr. Cross's pages of the steps by which she passed over to a position of tolerant scepticism; but the details of the process are after all of minor importance: the essential fact is that the change was predetermined by the nature of her mind.

The great event of her life was of course her acquaintance with George Henry Lewes. I say "of course," because this relation had an importance even more controlling than the publication and success of her first attempt at fiction, inasmuch as it was in consequence of Mr. Lewes's friendly urgency that she wrote the *Scenes of Clerical Life*. She met him for the first time in London, in the autumn of 1851; but it was not till the summer of 1854 that the connection with him began (it was marked to the world by their going to spend together several months in Germany, where he was bent on researches for his *Life of Goethe*), which was to become so much closer than many formal marriages and to last till his death in 1878. The episode of Miss Evans's life in London during these three years was already tolerably well known. She had become by this time a professional literary woman, and had regular work as assistant editor of the *Westminster Review*, to which she gave her most conscientious attention. Her accomplishments now were wide. She was a linguist, a copious reader, an earnest student of history and philosophy. She wrote much for her magazine as well as solicited articles from others, and several of her contributions are contained in the volume of essays published after her death—essays of which it is fair to say that they give but a faint intimation of her latent powers. George Henry Lewes was a versatile, hard-working journalist, with a tendency, apparently, of the drifting sort; and after having been made acquainted with each other by Mr. Herbert Spencer, the pair commingled their sympathies and their efforts. Her letters, at this season, contain constant mention of Lewes (one allusion to the effect that he "has quite won my regard, after having had a good deal of my vituperation"); she takes an interest in his health and corrects his proofs for him when he is absent. It was impossible for Mr. Lewes to marry, as he had a wife living, from whom he was separated. He had also three children, of whom the care did not devolve upon their mother. The union Miss Evans formed with him was a deliberate step, of which she accepted all the consequences. These consequences were excellent, so far as the world is at liberty to judge, save in an important particular. This particular is the fact that her false position, as we may call it, produced upon George Eliot's life a certain effect of sequestration which was not favourable to social freedom, or to freedom of observation, and which excited on the part of her companion a protecting, sheltering, fostering, precautionary attitude—the assumption that they lived in special, in abnormal conditions. It would be too much to say that George Eliot had not the courage of the situation she had embraced, but she had, at least, not the levity, the indifference; she was unable, in the premises, to be sufficiently superficial. Her deep, strenuous, much-considering mind, of which the leading mark is the capacity for a sort of luminous brooding, fed upon the idea of her irregularity with an intensity which doubtless only her magnificent intellectual activity and Lewes's brilliancy and ingenuity kept from being morbid. The fault of most of her work is the absence of spontaneity, the excess of reflection; and by her action in 1854 (which seemed superficially to be of the sort usually termed reckless), she committed herself to being nothing if not reflective, to cultivating a kind of compensatory earnestness. Her earnestness, her educated conscience, her exalted sense of responsibility, were coloured by her peculiar position; they committed her to a plan of life, of study, in which the accidental, the unexpected, were too little allowed for, and this is what I mean by speaking of her sequestration. If her relations with the world had been easier, in a word, her books would have been less difficult. Mr. Cross, very justly, merely touches upon this question of her forming a tie which was deprived of the sanction of the law; but he gives a portion of a letter written to Mrs. Bray more than a year after it had begun, which sufficiently indicates the serenity of her resolution. Repentance, of course, she never had—the success of her experiment was too rare and complete for that; and I do not mean that her attitude was ever for a moment apologetic. On the contrary, it was only too superabundantly confirmatory. Her effort was to pitch her life ever in the key of the superior wisdom that made her say to Mrs. Bray, in the letter of September 1855, "That any unworldly, unsuperstitious person who is sufficiently acquainted with the realities of life can pronounce my relation to Mr. Lewes immoral, I can only understand when I remember how subtle and complex are the influences that mould opinion." I need not attempt to project the light of criticism on this particular case of conscience; there remains ever, in the mutual relations of intelligent men and women, an element which is for themselves alone to consider. One reflection, however, forces itself upon the mind: if the connection had not taken place we should have lost the spectacle and influence of one of the most successful partnerships presented to us in the history of human affection. There has been much talk about George Eliot's "example," which is not to be deprecated so long as it is remembered that in speaking of the example of a woman of this value we can only mean example for good. Exemplary indeed in her long connection with George Henry Lewes were the qualities on which beneficent intimacy rests.

She was thirty-seven years old when the *Scenes from Clerical Life* were published, but this work opened wide for her the door of success, and fame and fortune came to her rapidly. Her union with Lewes had been a union of poverty: there is a sentence in her journal, of the year 1856, which speaks of their ascending certain cliffs called the Tors, at Ilfracombe, "only twice; for a tax of 3d. per head was demanded for this luxury, and we could not afford a sixpenny walk very frequently." The incentive to writing *Amos Barton* seems to have been mainly pecuniary. There was an urgent need to make money, and it appears to have been agreed between the pair that there was at least no harm in the lady's trying her hand at a story. Lewes professed a belief that she would really do something in this line, while she, more sceptical, reserved her judgment till after the test. The *Scenes from Clerical Life* were therefore pre-eminently an empirical work of fiction. With the sending of the first episode to the late Mr. John Blackwood for approval, there opened a relation between publisher and author which lasted to the end, and which was probably more genial and unclouded than any in the annals of literature, as well as almost unprecedentedly lucrative to both parties. This first book of George Eliot's has little of the usual air of a first book, none of the crudity of an early attempt; it was not the work of a youthful person, and one sees that the material had been long in her mind. The ripeness, the pathos, a sort of considered quality, are as striking to-day as when *Amos Barton* and *Janet's Repentance* were published, and enable us to understand that people should have asked themselves with surprise, at that time, who it was, in the midst of them, that had been taking notes so long and so wisely without giving a sign. *Adam Bede*, written rapidly, appeared in 1859, and George Eliot found herself a consummate novelist without having suspected it. The book was an immense, a brilliant success, and from this moment the author's life took its definite and final direction. She accepted the great obligations which to her mind belonged to a person who had the ear of the public, and her whole effort thenceforth was highly to respond to them—to respond to them by teaching, by vivid moral illustration and even by direct exhortation. It is striking that from the first her conception of the novelist's task is never in the least as the game of art. The most interesting passage in Mr. Cross's volumes is to my sense a simple sentence in a short entry in her journal in the year 1859, just after she had finished the first volume of *The Mill on the Floss* (the original title of which, by the way, had been *Sister Maggie*): "We have just finished reading aloud Père Goriot, a hateful book." That Balzac's masterpiece should have elicited from her only this remark, at a time, too, when her mind might have been opened to it by her own activity of composition, is significant of so many things that the few words are, in the whole *Life*, those I should have been most sorry to lose. Of course they are not all George Eliot would have had to say about Balzac, if some other occasion than a simple jotting in a diary had presented itself. Still, what even a jotting may *not* have said after a first perusal of *Le Père Goriot* is eloquent; it illuminates the author's general attitude with regard to the novel, which, for her, was not primarily a picture of life, capable of deriving a high value from its form, but a moralised fable, the last word of a philosophy endeavouring to teach by example.

This is a very noble and defensible view, and one must speak respectfully of any theory of work which would produce such fruit as *Romola* and *Middlemarch*. But it testifies to that side of George Eliot's nature which was weakest—the absence of free æsthetic life (I venture this remark in the face of a passage quoted from one of her letters in Mr. Cross's third volume); it gives the hand, as it were, to several other instances that may be found in the same pages. "My function is that of the *æsthetic*, not the doctrinal teacher; the rousing of the nobler emotions, which make mankind desire the social right, not the prescribing of special measures, concerning which the artistic mind, however strongly moved by social sympathy, is often not the best judge." That is the passage referred to in my parenthetic allusion, and it is a good general description of the manner in which George Eliot may be said to have acted on her generation; but the "artistic mind," the possession of which it implies, existed in her with limitations remarkable in a writer whose imagination was so rich. We feel in her, always, that she proceeds from the abstract to the concrete; that her figures and situations are evolved, as the phrase is, from her moral consciousness, and are only indirectly the products of observation. They are deeply studied and massively supported, but they are not *seen*, in the irresponsible plastic way. The world was, first and foremost, for George Eliot, the moral, the intellectual world; the personal spectacle came after; and lovingly humanly as she regarded it we constantly feel that she cares for the things she finds in it only so far as they are types. The philosophic door is always open, on her stage, and we are aware that the somewhat cooling draught of ethical purpose draws across it. This constitutes half the beauty of her work; the constant reference to ideas may be an excellent source of one kind of reality—for, after all, the secret of seeing a thing well is not necessarily that you see nothing else. Her preoccupation with the universe helped to make her characters strike you as also belonging to it; it raised the roof, widened the area, of her æsthetic structure. Nothing is finer, in her genius, than the combination of her love of general truth and love of the special case; without this, indeed, we should not have heard of her as a novelist, for the passion of the special case is surely the basis of the story-teller's art. All the same, that little sign of all that Balzac failed to suggest to her showed at what perils the special case got itself considered. Such dangers increased as her activity proceeded, and many judges perhaps hold that in her ultimate work, in *Middlemarch* and *Daniel Deronda* (especially the latter), it ceased to be considered at all. Such critics assure us that Gwendolen and Grandcourt, Deronda and Myra, are not concrete images, but disembodied types, pale abstractions, signs and symbols of a "great lesson." I give up

Deronda and Myra to the objector, but Grandcourt and Gwendolen seem to me to have a kind of superior reality; to be, in a high degree, what one demands of a figure in a novel, planted on their legs and complete.

The truth is, perception and reflection, at the outset, divided George Eliot's great talent between them; but as time went on circumstances led the latter to develop itself at the expense of the former—one of these circumstances being apparently the influence of George Henry Lewes. Lewes was interested in science, in cosmic problems; and though his companion, thanks to the original bent of her versatile, powerful mind, needed no impulse from without to turn herself to speculation, yet the contagion of his studies pushed her further than she would otherwise have gone in the direction of scientific observation, which is but another form of what I have called reflection. Her early novels are full of natural as distinguished from systematic observation, though even in them it is less the dominant note, I think, than the love of the "moral," the reaction of thought in the face of the human comedy. They had observation sufficient, at any rate, to make their fortune, and it may well be said that that is enough for any novel. In *Silas Marner*, in *Adam Bede*, the quality seems gilded by a sort of autumn haze, an afternoon light, of meditation, which mitigates the sharpness of portraiture. I doubt very much whether the author herself had a clear vision, for instance, of the marriage of Dinah Morris to Adam, or of the rescue of Hetty from the scaffold at the eleventh hour. The reason of this may be, indeed, that her perception was a perception of nature much more than of art, and that these particular incidents do not belong to nature (to my sense at least); by which I do not mean that they belong to a very happy art. I cite them, on the contrary, as an evidence of artistic weakness; they are a very good example of the view in which a story must have marriages and rescues in the nick of time, as a matter of course. I must add, in fairness to George Eliot, that the marriage of the nun-like Dinah, which shocks the reader, who sees in it a base concession, was a *trouvaille* of Lewes's and is a small sign of that same faulty judgment in literary things which led him to throw his influence on the side of her writing verse—verse which is *all* reflection, with direct, vivifying vision, or emotion, remarkably absent.

It is a part of this same limitation of the pleasure she was capable of taking in the fact of representation for itself that the various journals and notes of her visits to the Continent are, though by no means destitute of the tempered enjoyment of foreign sights which was as near as she ever came to rapture, singularly vague in expression on the subject of the general and particular spectacle—the life and manners, the works of art. She enumerates diligently all the pictures and statues she sees, and the way she does so is a proof of her active, earnest intellectual habits; but it is rarely apparent that they have said much to her, or that what they have said is one of their deeper secrets. She is capable of writing, after coming out of the great chapel of San Lorenzo, in Florence, that "the world-famous statues of Michael Angelo on the tombs ... remained to us as affected and exaggerated in the original as in copies and casts." That sentence startles one, on the part of the author of *Romola*, and that Mr. Cross should have printed it is a commendable proof of his impartiality.

It was in *Romola*, precisely, that the equilibrium I spoke of just now was lost, and that reflection began to weigh down the scale. *Romola* is pre-eminently a study of the human conscience in an historical setting which is studied almost as much, and few passages in Mr. Cross's volumes are more interesting than those relating to the production of this magnificent romance. George Eliot took all her work with a noble seriousness, but into none of it did she throw herself with more passion. It drained from her as much as she gave to it, and none of her writing ploughed into her, to use her biographer's expression, so deeply. She told him that she began it a young woman and finished it an old one. More than any of her novels it was evolved, as I have said, from her moral consciousness—a moral consciousness encircled by a prodigious amount of literary research. Her literary ideal was at all times of the highest, but in the preparation of *Romola* it placed her under a control absolutely religious. She read innumerable books, some of them bearing only remotely on her subject, and consulted without stint contemporary records and documents. She neglected nothing that would enable her to live, intellectually, in the period she had undertaken to describe. We know, for the most part, I think, the result. *Romola* is on the whole the finest thing she wrote, but its defects are almost on the scale of its beauties. The great defect is that, except in the person of Tito Melema, it does not seem positively to live. It is overladen with learning, it smells of the lamp, it tastes just perceptibly of pedantry. In spite of its want of blood, however, it assuredly will survive in men's remembrance, for the finest pages in it belong to the finest part of our literature. It is on the whole a failure, but such a failure as only a great talent can produce; and one may say of it that there are many great "hits" far less interesting than such a mistake. A twentieth part of the erudition would have sufficed, would have given us the feeling and colour of the time, if there had been more of the breath of the Florentine streets, more of the faculty of optical evocation, a greater saturation of the senses with the elements of the adorable little city. The difficulty with the book, for the most part, is that it is not Italian; it has always seemed to me the most Germanic of the author's productions. I cannot imagine a German writing (in the way of a novel) anything half so good; but if I could imagine it I should suppose *Romola* to be very much the sort of picture he would achieve—the sort of medium through which he would show us how, by the Arno-side, the fifteenth century came to an end. One of the sources of interest in the book is that, more than any of its companions, it indicates how much George Eliot proceeded by reflection and research; how little important, comparatively, she thought that same breath of the streets. It carries to a maximum the in-door quality.

The most definite impression produced, perhaps, by Mr. Cross's volumes (by the second and third) is that of simple success—success which had been the result of no external accidents (unless her union with Lewes be so denominated), but was involved in the very faculties nature had given her. All the elements of an eventual happy fortune met in her constitution. The great foundation, to begin with, was there—the magnificent mind, vigorous, luminous, and eminently sane. To her intellectual vigour, her immense facility, her exemption from cerebral lassitude, her letters and journals bear the most copious testimony. Her daily stint of arduous reading and writing was of the largest. Her ability, as one may express it in the most general way, was astonishing, and it belonged to every season of her long and fruitful career. Her passion for study encountered no impediment, but was able to make everything feed and support it. The extent and variety of her knowledge is by itself the measure of a capacity which triumphed wherever it wished. Add to this an immense special talent which, as soon as it tries its wings, is found to be adequate to the highest, longest flights and brings back great material rewards. George Eliot of course had drawbacks and difficulties, physical infirmities, constant liabilities to headache, dyspepsia, and other illness, to deep depression, to despair about her work; but these jolts of the chariot were small in proportion to the impetus acquired, and were hardly greater than was necessary for reminding her of the secret of all ambitious workers in the field of art—that effort, effort, always effort, is the only key to success. Her great furtherance was that, intensely intellectual being as she was, the life of affection and emotion was also widely open to her. She had all the initiation of knowledge and none of its dryness, all the advantages of judgment and all the luxuries of feeling. She had an imagination which enabled her to sit at home with book and pen, and yet enter into the life of other generations; project herself into Warwickshire ale-houses and Florentine symposia, reconstitute conditions utterly different from her own. Toward the end she triumphed over the great impossible; she reconciled the greatest sensibility with the highest serenity. She succeeded in guarding her pursuits from intrusion; in carrying out her habits; in sacrificing her work as little as possible; in leading, in the midst of a society united in conspiracies to interrupt and vulgarise, an independent, strenuously personal life. People who had the honour of penetrating into the sequestered precinct of the Priory—the house in London in which she lived from 1863 to 1880—remember well a kind of sanctity in the place, an atmosphere of stillness and concentration, something that suggested a literary temple.

It was part of the good fortune of which I speak that in Mr. Lewes she had found the most devoted of caretakers, the most jealous of ministers, a companion through whom all business was transacted. The one drawback of this relation was that, considering what she attempted, it limited her experience too much to itself; but for the rest it helped her in a hundred ways—it saved her nerves, it fortified her privacy, it protected her leisure, it diminished the friction of living. His admiration of her work was of the largest, though not always, I think, truly discriminating, and he surrounded her with a sort of temperate zone of independence—independence of everything except him and her own standards. Nervous, sensitive, delicate in every way in which genius is delicate (except, indeed, that she had a robust reason), it was a great thing for her to have accident made rare and exposure mitigated; and to this result Lewes, as the administrator of her fame, admirably contributed. He filtered the stream, giving her only the clearer water. The accident of reading reviews of one's productions, especially when they are bad, is, for the artist of our day, one of the most frequent; and Mr. Lewes, by keeping these things out of her way, enabled her to achieve what was perhaps the highest form of her success—an inaccessibility to the newspaper. "It is remarkable to me," she writes in 1876, "that I have entirely lost my *personal* melancholy. I often, of course, have melancholy thoughts about the destinies of my fellow creatures, but I am never in that *mood* of sadness which used to be my frequent visitant even in the midst of external happiness." Her later years, coloured by this accumulated wisdom, when she had taken her final form before the world and had come to be regarded more and more as a teacher and philosopher, are full of suggestion to the critic, but I have exhausted my limited space. There is a certain coldness in them perhaps—the coldness that results from most of one's opinions being formed, one's mind made up, on many great subjects; from the degree, in a word, to which "culture" had taken the place of the more primitive processes of experience.

"Ah, les livres, ils nous débordent, ils nous étouffent—nous périssons par les livres!" That cry of a distinguished French novelist (there is no harm in mentioning M. Alphonse Daudet), which fell upon the ear of the present writer some time ago, represents as little as possible the emotion of George Eliot confronted with literatures and sciences. M. Alphonse Daudet went on to say that, to his mind, the personal impression, the effort of direct observation, was the most precious source of information for the novelist; that nothing could take its place; that the effect of books was constantly to check and pervert this effort; that a second-hand, third-hand, tenth-hand, impression was constantly tending to substitute itself for a fresh perception; that we were ending by seeing everything through literature instead of through our own senses; and that in short literature was rapidly killing literature. This view has immense truth on its side, but the case would be too simple if, on one side or the other, there were only one way of finding out. The effort of the novelist is to find out, to know, or at least to see, and no one, in the nature of things, can less afford to be indifferent to sidelights. Books are themselves, unfortunately, an expression of human passions. George Eliot had no doubts, at any rate; if impressionism, before she laid down her pen, had already begun to be talked about, it would have made no difference with her—she would have had no desire to pass for an impressionist.

There is one question we cannot help asking ourselves as we close this record of her life; it is impossible not to let our imagination wander in the direction of what turn her mind or her fortune might have taken if she had never met George Henry Lewes, or never cast her lot with his. It is safe to say that, in one way or another, in the long run, her novels would have got themselves written, and it is possible they would have been more natural, as one may call it, more familiarly and casually human. Would her development have been less systematic, more irresponsible, more personal, and should we have had more of *Adam Bede* and *Silas Marner* and less of *Romola* and *Middlemarch*? The question, after all, cannot be answered, and I do not push it, being myself very grateful for *Middlemarch* and *Romola*. It is as George Eliot does actually present herself that we must judge her—a condition that will not prevent her from striking us as one of the noblest, most beautiful minds of our time. This impression bears the reader company throughout these letters and notes. It is impossible not to feel, as we close them, that she was an admirable being. They are less brilliant, less entertaining, than we might have hoped; they contain fewer "good things" and have even a certain grayness of tone, something measured and subdued, as of a person talking without ever raising her voice. But there rises from them a kind of fragrance of moral elevation; a love of justice, truth, and light; a large, generous way of looking at things; and a constant effort to hold high the torch in the dusky spaces of man's conscience. That is how we see her during the latter years of her life: frail, delicate, shivering a little, much fatigued and considerably spent, but still meditating on what could be acquired and imparted; still living, in the intelligence, a freer, larger life than probably had ever been the portion of any woman. To her own sex her memory, her example, will remain of the highest value; those of them for whom the "development" of woman is the hope of the future ought to erect a monument to George Eliot. She helped on the cause more than any one, in proving how few limitations are of necessity implied in the feminine organism. She went so far that such a distance seems enough, and in her effort she sacrificed no tenderness, no grace. There is much talk to-day about things being "open to women"; but George Eliot showed that there is nothing that is closed. If we criticise her novels we must remember that her nature came first and her work afterwards, and that it is not remarkable they should not resemble the productions, say, of Alexandre Dumas. What *is* remarkable, extraordinary—and the process remains inscrutable and mysterious—is that this quiet, anxious, sedentary, serious, invalidical English lady, without animal spirits, without adventures or sensations, should have made us believe that nothing in the world was alien to her; should have produced such rich, deep, masterly pictures of the multiform life of man.

1885.

III. DANIEL DERONDA: A CONVERSATION

THEODORA, one day early in the autumn, sat on her verandah with a piece of embroidery, the design of which she made up as she proceeded, being careful, however, to have a Japanese screen before her, to keep her inspiration at the proper altitude. Pulcheria, who was paying her a visit, sat near her with a closed book, in a paper cover, in her lap. Pulcheria was playing with the pug-dog, rather idly, but Theodora was stitching, steadily and meditatively. "Well," said Theodora, at last, "I wonder what he accomplished in the East." Pulcheria took the little dog into her lap and made him sit on the book. "Oh," she replied, "they had tea-parties at Jerusalem—exclusively of ladies—and he sat in the midst and stirred his tea and made high-toned remarks. And then Mirah sang a little, just a little, on account of her voice being so weak. Sit still, Fido," she continued, addressing the little dog, "and keep your nose out of my face. But it's a nice little nose, all the same," she pursued, "a nice little short snub nose and not a horrid big Jewish nose. Oh, my dear, when I think what a collection of noses there must have been at that wedding!" At this moment Constantius steps upon the verandah from within, hat and stick in hand and his shoes a trifle dusty. He has some distance to come before he reaches the place where the ladies are sitting, and this gives Pulcheria time to murmur, "Talk of snub noses!" Constantius is presented by Theodora to Pulcheria, and he sits down and exclaims upon the admirable blueness of the sea, which lies in a straight band across the green of the little lawn; comments too upon the pleasure of having one side of one's verandah in the shade. Soon Fido, the little dog, still restless, jumps off Pulcheria's lap and reveals the book, which lies title upward. "Oh," says Constantius, "you have been finishing *Daniel Deronda*?" Then follows a conversation which it will be more convenient to present in another form.

Theodora. Yes, Pulcheria has been reading aloud the last chapters to me. They are wonderfully beautiful.

Constantius (after a moment's hesitation). Yes, they are very beautiful. I am sure you read well, Pulcheria, to give the fine passages their full value.

Theodora. She reads well when she chooses, but I am sorry to say that in some of the fine passages of this last book she took quite a false tone. I couldn't have read them aloud myself; I should have broken down. But Pulcheria—would you really believe it?—when she couldn't go on it was not for tears, but for—the contrary.

Constantius. For smiles? Did you really find it comical? One of my objections to *Daniel Deronda* is the absence of those delightfully humorous passages which enlivened the author's former works.

Pulcheria. Oh, I think there are some places as amusing as anything in *Adam Bede* or *The Mill on the Floss*: for instance where, at the last, Deronda wipes Gwendolen's tears and Gwendolen wipes his.

Constantius. Yes, I know what you mean. I can understand that situation presenting a slightly ridiculous image; that is, if the current of the story don't swiftly carry you past.

Pulcheria. What do you mean by the current of the story? I never read a story with less current. It is not a river; it is a series of lakes. I once read of a group of little uneven ponds resembling, from a bird's-eye view, a looking-glass which had fallen upon the floor and broken, and was lying in fragments. That is what *Daniel Deronda* would look like, on a bird's-eye view.

Theodora. Pulcheria found that comparison in a French novel. She is always reading French novels.

Constantius. Ah, there are some very good ones.

Pulcheria (perversely). I don't know; I think there are some very poor ones.

Constantius. The comparison is not bad, at any rate. I know what you mean by *Daniel Deronda* lacking current. It has almost as little as *Romola*.

Pulcheria. Oh, *Romola* is unpardonably slow; it is a kind of literary tortoise.

Constantius. Yes, I know what you mean by that. But I am afraid you are not friendly to our great novelist.

Theodora. She likes Balzac and George Sand and other impure writers.

Constantius. Well, I must say I understand that.

Pulcheria. My favourite novelist is Thackeray, and I am extremely fond of Miss Austen.

Constantius. I understand that too. You read over *The Newcomes* and *Pride and Prejudice.*

Pulcheria. No, I don't read them over now; I think them over. I have been making visits for a long time past to a series of friends, and I have spent the last six months in reading *Daniel Deronda* aloud. Fortune would have it that I should always arrive by the same train as the new number. I am accounted a frivolous, idle creature; I am not a disciple in the new school of embroidery, like Theodora; so I was immediately pushed into a chair and the book thrust into my hand, that I might lift up my voice and make peace between all the impatiences that were snatching at it. So I may claim at least that I have read every word of the work. I never skipped.

Theodora. I should hope not, indeed!

Constantius. And do you mean that you really didn't enjoy it?

Pulcheria. I found it protracted, pretentious, pedantic.

Constantius. I see; I can understand that.

Theodora. Oh, you understand too much! This is the twentieth time you have used that formula.

Constantius. What will you have? You know I must try to understand; it's my trade.

Theodora. He means he writes reviews. Trying not to understand is what I call that trade!

Constantius. Say then I take it the wrong way; that is why it has never made my fortune. But I do try to understand; it is my—my—(He pauses.)

Theodora. I know what you want to say. Your strong side.

Pulcheria. And what is his weak side?

Theodora. He writes novels.

Constantius. I have written *one.* You can't call that a side. It's a little facet, at the most.

Pulcheria. You talk as if you were a diamond. I should like to read it— not aloud!

Constantius. You can't read it softly enough. But you, Theodora, you didn't find our book too "protracted"?

Theodora. I should have liked it to continue indefinitely, to keep coming out always, to be one of the regular things of life.

Pulcheria. Oh, come here, little dog! To think that *Daniel Deronda* might be perpetual when you, little short-nosed darling, can't last at the most more than nine or ten years!

Theodora. A book like *Daniel Deronda* becomes part of one's life; one lives in it, or alongside of it. I don't hesitate to say that I have been living in this one for the last eight months. It is such a complete world George Eliot builds up; it is so vast, so much-embracing! It has such a firm earth and such an ethereal sky. You can turn into it and lose yourself in it.

Pulcheria. Oh, easily, and die of cold and starvation!

Theodora. I have been very near to poor Gwendolen and very near to that sweet Mirah. And the dear little Meyricks also; I know them intimately well.

Pulcheria. The Meyricks, I grant you, are the best thing in the book.

Theodora. They are a delicious family; I wish they lived in Boston. I consider Herr Klesmer almost Shakespearean, and his wife is almost as good. I have been near to poor grand Mordecai——

Pulcheria. Oh, reflect, my dear; not too near!

Theodora. And as for Deronda himself I freely confess that I am consumed with a hopeless passion for him. He is the most irresistible man in the literature of fiction.

Pulcheria. He is not a man at all.

Theodora. I remember nothing more beautiful than the description of his childhood, and that picture of his lying on the grass in the abbey cloister, a beautiful seraph-faced boy, with a lovely voice, reading history and asking his Scotch tutor why the Popes had so many nephews. He must have been delightfully handsome.

Pulcheria. Never, my dear, with that nose! I am sure he had a nose, and I hold that the author has shown great pusillanimity in her treatment of it. She has quite shirked it. The picture you speak of is very pretty, but a picture is not a person. And why is he always grasping his coat-collar, as if he wished to hang himself up? The author had an uncomfortable feeling that she must make him do something real, something visible and sensible, and she hit upon that clumsy figure. I don't see what you mean by saying you have been *near* those people; that is just what one is not. They produce no illusion. They are described and analysed to death, but we don't see them nor hear them nor touch them. Deronda clutches his coat-collar, Mirah crosses her feet, Mordecai talks like the Bible; but that doesn't make real figures of them. They have no existence outside of the author's study.

Theodora. If you mean that they are nobly imaginative I quite agree with you; and if they say nothing to your own imagination the fault is yours, not theirs.

Pulcheria. Pray don't say they are Shakespearean again. Shakespeare went to work another way.

Constantius. I think you are both in a measure right; there is a distinction to be drawn. There are in *Daniel Deronda* the figures based upon observation and the figures based upon invention. This distinction, I know, is rather a rough one. There are no figures in any novel that are pure observation, and none that are pure invention. But either element may preponderate, and in those cases in which invention has preponderated George Eliot seems to me to have achieved at the best but so many brilliant failures.

Theodora. And are *you* turning severe? I thought you admired her so much.

Constantius. I defy any one to admire her more, but one must discriminate. Speaking brutally, I consider *Daniel Deronda* the weakest of her books. It strikes me as very sensibly inferior to *Middlemarch*. I have an immense opinion of *Middlemarch*.

Pulcheria. Not having been obliged by circumstances to read *Middlemarch* to other people, I didn't read it at all. I couldn't read it to myself. I tried, but I broke down. I appreciated Rosamond, but I couldn't believe in Dorothea.

Theodora (very gravely). So much the worse for you, Pulcheria. I have enjoyed *Daniel Deronda because* I had enjoyed *Middlemarch*. Why should you throw *Middlemarch* up against her? It seems to me that if a book is fine it is fine. I have enjoyed *Deronda* deeply, from beginning to end.

Constantius. I assure you, so have I. I can read nothing of George Eliot's without enjoyment. I even enjoy her poetry, though I don't approve of it. In whatever she writes I enjoy her intelligence; it has space and air, like a fine landscape. The intellectual brilliancy of *Daniel Deronda* strikes me as very great, in excess of anything the author has done. In the first couple of numbers of the book this ravished me. I delighted in its deep, rich English tone, in which so many notes seemed melted together.

Pulcheria. The tone is not English, it is German.

Constantius. I understand that—if Theodora will allow me to say so. Little by little I began to feel that I cared less for certain notes than for others. I say it under my breath—I began to feel an occasional temptation to skip. Roughly speaking, all the Jewish burden of the story tended to weary me; it is this part that produces the poor illusion which I agree with Pulcheria in finding. Gwendolen and Grandcourt are admirable—Gwendolen is a masterpiece. She is known, felt and presented, psychologically, altogether in the grand manner. Beside her and beside her husband—a consummate picture of English brutality refined and distilled (for Grandcourt is before all things brutal), Deronda, Mordecai and Mirah are hardly more than shadows. They and their fortunes are all improvisation. I don't say anything against improvisation. When it succeeds it has a surpassing charm. But it must succeed. With George Eliot it seems to me to succeed, but a little less than one would expect of her talent. The story of Deronda's life, his mother's story, Mirah's story, are quite the sort of thing one finds in George Sand. But they are really not so good as they would be in George Sand. George Sand would have carried it off with a lighter hand.

Theodora. Oh, Constantius, how can you compare George Eliot's novels to that woman's? It is sunlight and moonshine.

Pulcheria. I really think the two writers are very much alike. They are both very voluble, both addicted to moralising and philosophising *à tout bout de champ*, both inartistic.

Constantius. I see what you mean. But George Eliot is solid, and George Sand is liquid. When occasionally George Eliot liquefies—as in the history of Deronda's birth, and in that of Mirah—it is not to so crystalline a clearness as the author of *Consuelo* and *André*. Take Mirah's long narrative of her adventures, when she unfolds them to Mrs. Meyrick. It is arranged, it is artificial, *ancien jeu*, quite in the George Sand manner. But George Sand would have done it better. The false tone would have remained, but it would have been more persuasive. It would have been a fib, but the fib would have been neater.

Theodora. I don't think fibbing neatly a merit, and I don't see what is to be gained by such comparisons. George Eliot is pure and George Sand is impure; how can you compare them? As for the Jewish element in Deronda, I think it a very fine idea; it's a noble subject. Wilkie Collins and Miss Braddon would not have thought of it, but that does not condemn it. It shows a large conception of what one may do in a novel. I heard you say, the other day, that most novels were so trivial—that they had no general ideas. Here is a general idea, the idea interpreted by Deronda. I have never disliked the Jews as some people do; I am not like Pulcheria, who sees a Jew in every bush. I wish there were one; I would cultivate shrubbery. I have known too many clever and charming Jews; I have known none that were not clever.

Pulcheria. Clever, but not charming.

Constantius. I quite agree with you as to Deronda's going in for the Jews and turning out a Jew himself being a fine subject, and this quite apart from the fact of whether such a thing as a Jewish revival be at all a possibility. If it be a possibility, so much the better—so much the better for the subject, I mean.

Pulcheria. A la bonne heure!

Constantius. I rather suspect it is not a possibility; that the Jews in general take themselves much less seriously than that. They have other fish to fry. George Eliot takes them as a person outside of Judaism—æsthetically. I don't believe that is the way they take themselves.

Pulcheria. They have the less excuse then for keeping themselves so dirty.

Theodora. George Eliot must have known some delightful Jews.

Constantius. Very likely; but I shouldn't wonder if the most delightful of them had smiled a trifle, here and there, over her book. But that makes nothing, as Herr Klesmer would say. The subject is a noble one. The idea of depicting a nature able to feel and worthy to feel the sort of inspiration that takes possession of Deronda, of depicting it sympathetically, minutely and intimately—such an idea has great elevation. There is something very fascinating in the mission that Deronda takes upon himself. I don't quite know what it means, I don't understand more than half of Mordecai's rhapsodies, and I don't perceive exactly what practical steps could be taken. Deronda could go about and talk with clever Jews—not an unpleasant life.

Pulcheria. All that seems to me so unreal that when at the end the author finds herself confronted with the necessity of making him start for the East by the train, and announces that Sir Hugo and Lady Mallinger have given his wife "a complete Eastern outfit," I descend to the ground with a ludicrous jump.

Constantius. Unreal, if you please; that is no objection to it; it greatly tickles my imagination. I like extremely the idea of Mordecai believing, without ground of belief, that if he only wait, a young man on whom nature and society have centred all their gifts will come to him and receive from his hands the precious vessel of his hopes. It is romantic, but it is not vulgar romance; it is finely romantic. And there is something very fine in the author's own feeling about Deronda. He is a very liberal creation. He is, I think, a failure—a brilliant failure; if he had been a success I should call him a splendid creation. The author meant to do things very handsomely for him; she meant apparently to make a faultless human being.

Pulcheria. She made a dreadful prig.

Constantius. He *is* rather priggish, and one wonders that so clever a woman as George Eliot shouldn't see it.

Pulcheria. He has no blood in his body. His attitude at moments is like that of a high-priest in a *tableau vivant*.

Theodora. Pulcheria likes the little gentlemen in the French novels who take good care of their attitudes, which are always the same attitude, the attitude of "conquest"—of a conquest that tickles their vanity. Deronda has a contour that cuts straight through the middle of all that. He is made of a stuff that isn't dreamt of in their philosophy.

Pulcheria. Pulcheria likes very much a novel which she read three or four years ago, but which she has not forgotten. It was by Ivan Turgénieff, and it was called *On the Eve*. Theodora has read it, I know, because she admires Turgénieff, and Constantius has read it, I suppose, because he has read everything.

Constantius. If I had no reason but that for my reading, it would be small. But Turgénieff is my man.

Pulcheria. You were just now praising George Eliot's general ideas. The tale of which I speak contains in the portrait of the hero very much such a general idea as you find in the portrait of Deronda. Don't you remember the young Bulgarian student, Inssaroff, who gives himself the mission of rescuing his country from its subjection to the Turks? Poor man, if he had foreseen the horrible summer of 1876! His character is the picture of a race-passion, of patriotic hopes and dreams. But what a difference in the vividness of the two figures. Inssaroff is a man; he stands up on his feet; we see him, hear him, touch him. And it has taken the author but a couple of hundred pages—not eight volumes—to do it.

Theodora. I don't remember Inssaroff at all, but I perfectly remember the heroine, Helena. She is certainly most remarkable, but, remarkable as she is, I should never dream of calling her as wonderful as Gwendolen.

Constantius. Turgénieff is a magician, which I don't think I should call George Eliot. One is a poet, the other is a philosopher. One cares for the aspect of things and the other cares for the reason of things. George Eliot, in embarking with Deronda, took aboard, as it were, a far heavier cargo than Turgénieff with his Inssaroff. She proposed, consciously, to strike more notes.

Pulcheria. Oh, consciously, yes!

Constantius. George Eliot wished to show the possible picturesqueness—the romance, as it were—of a high moral tone. Deronda is a moralist, a moralist with a rich complexion.

Theodora. It is a most beautiful nature. I don't know anywhere a more complete, a more deeply analysed portrait of a great nature. We praise novelists for wandering and creeping so into the small corners of the mind. That is what we praise Balzac for when he gets down upon all fours to crawl through *Le Père Goriot* or *Les Parents Pauvres*. But I must say I think it a finer thing to unlock with as firm a hand as George Eliot some of the greater chambers of human character. Deronda is in a manner an ideal character, if you will, but he seems to me triumphantly married to reality. There are some admirable things said about him; nothing can be finer than those pages of description of his moral temperament in the fourth book—his elevated way of looking at things, his impartiality, his universal sympathy, and at the same time his fear of their turning into mere irresponsible indifference. I remember some of it verbally: "He was ceasing to care for knowledge—he had no ambition for practice—unless they could be gathered up into one current with his emotions."

Pulcheria. Oh, there is plenty about his emotions. Everything about him is "emotive." That bad word occurs on every fifth page.

Theodora. I don't see that it is a bad word.

Pulcheria. It may be good German, but it is poor English.

Theodora. It is not German at all; it is Latin. So, my dear!

Pulcheria. As I say, then, it is not English.

Theodora. This is the first time I ever heard that George Eliot's style was bad!

Constantius. It is admirable; it has the most delightful and the most intellectually comfortable suggestions. But it is occasionally a little too long-sleeved, as I may say. It is sometimes too loose a fit for the thought, a little baggy.

Theodora. And the advice he gives Gwendolen, the things he says to her, they are the very essence of wisdom, of warm human wisdom, knowing life and feeling it. "Keep your fear as a safeguard, it may make consequences passionately present to you." What can be better than that?

Pulcheria. Nothing, perhaps. But what can be drearier than a novel in which the function of the hero—young, handsome and brilliant—is to give didactic advice, in a proverbial form, to the young, beautiful and brilliant heroine?

Constantius. That is not putting it quite fairly. The function of Deronda is to make Gwendolen fall in love with him, to say nothing of falling in love himself with Mirah.

Pulcheria. Yes, the less said about that the better. All we know about Mirah is that she has delicate rings of hair, sits with her feet crossed, and talks like an article in a new magazine.

Constantius. Deronda's function of adviser to Gwendolen does not strike me as so ridiculous. He is not nearly so ridiculous as if he were lovesick. It is a very interesting situation—that of a man with whom a beautiful woman in trouble falls in love and yet whose affections are so preoccupied that the most he can do for her in return is to enter kindly and sympathetically into her position, pity her and talk to her. George Eliot always gives us something that is strikingly and ironically characteristic of human life; and what savours more of the essential crookedness of our fate than the sad cross-purposes of these two young people? Poor Gwendolen's falling in love with Deronda is part of her own luckless history, not of his.

Theodora. I do think he takes it to himself rather too little. No man had ever so little vanity.

Pulcheria. It is very inconsistent, therefore, as well as being extremely impertinent and ill-mannered, his buying back and sending to her her necklace at Leubronn.

Constantius. Oh, you must concede that; without it there would have been no story. A man writing of him, however, would certainly have made him more peccable. As George Eliot lets herself go, in that quarter, she becomes delightfully, almost touchingly, feminine. It is like her making Romola go to housekeeping with Tessa, after Tito Melema's death; like her making Dorothea marry Will Ladislaw. If Dorothea had married any one after her misadventure with Casaubon, she would have married a trooper.

Theodora. Perhaps some day Gwendolen will marry Rex.

Pulcheria. Pray, who is Rex?

Theodora. Why, Pulcheria, how can you forget?

Pulcheria. Nay, how can I remember? But I recall such a name in the dim antiquity of the first or second book. Yes, and then he is pushed to the front again at the last, just in time not to miss the falling of the curtain. Gwendolen will certainly not have the audacity to marry any one we know so little about.

Constantius. I have been wanting to say that there seems to me to be two very distinct elements in George Eliot—a spontaneous one and an artificial one. There is what she is by inspiration and what she is because it is expected of her. These two heads have been very perceptible in her recent writings; they are much less noticeable in her early ones.

Theodora. You mean that she is too scientific? So long as she remains the great literary genius that she is, how can she be too scientific? She is simply permeated with the highest culture of the age.

Pulcheria. She talks too much about the "dynamic quality" of people's eyes. When she uses such a phrase as that in the first sentence in her book she is not a great literary genius, because she shows a want of tact. There can't be a worse limitation.

Constantius. The "dynamic quality" of Gwendolen's glance has made the tour of the world.

Theodora. It shows a very low level of culture on the world's part to be agitated by a term perfectly familiar to all decently-educated people.

Pulcheria. I don't pretend to be decently educated; pray tell me what it means.

Constantius (promptly). I think Pulcheria has hit it in speaking of a want of tact. In the manner of the book, throughout, there is something that one may call a want of tact. The epigraphs in verse are a want of tact; they are sometimes, I think, a trifle more pretentious than really pregnant; the importunity of the moral reflections is a want of tact; the very diffuseness is a want of tact. But it comes back to what I said just now about one's sense of the author writing under a sort of external pressure. I began to notice it in *Felix Holt*; I don't think I had before. She strikes me as a person who certainly has naturally a taste for general considerations, but who has fallen upon an age and a circle which have compelled her to give them an exaggerated attention. She does not strike me as naturally a critic, less still as naturally a sceptic; her spontaneous part is to observe life and to feel it, to feel it with admirable depth. Contemplation, sympathy and faith—something like that,

I should say, would have been her natural scale. If she had fallen upon an age of enthusiastic assent to old articles of faith, it seems to me possible that she would have had a more perfect, a more consistent and graceful development, than she has actually had. If she had cast herself into such a current—her genius being equal—it might have carried her to splendid distances. But she has chosen to go into criticism, and to the critics she addresses her work; I mean the critics of the universe. Instead of feeling life itself, it is "views" upon life that she tries to feel.

Pulcheria. She is the victim of a first-class education. I am so glad!

Constantius. Thanks to her admirable intellect she philosophises very sufficiently; but meanwhile she has given a chill to her genius. She has come near spoiling an artist.

Pulcheria. She has quite spoiled one. Or rather I shouldn't say that, because there was no artist to spoil. I maintain that she is not an artist. An artist could never have put a story together so monstrously ill. She has no sense of form.

Theodora. Pray, what could be more artistic than the way that Deronda's paternity is concealed till almost the end, and the way we are made to suppose Sir Hugo is his father?

Pulcheria. And Mirah his sister. How does that fit together? I was as little made to suppose he was not a Jew as I cared when I found out he was. And his mother popping up through a trap-door and popping down again, at the last, in that scrambling fashion! His mother is very bad.

Constantius. I think Deronda's mother is one of the unvivified characters; she belongs to the cold half of the book. All the Jewish part is at bottom cold; that is my only objection. I have enjoyed it because my fancy often warms cold things; but beside Gwendolen's history it is like the empty half of the lunar disk beside the full one. It is admirably studied, it is imagined, it is understood, but it is not embodied. One feels this strongly in just those scenes between Deronda and his mother; one feels that one has been appealed to on rather an artificial ground of interest. To make Deronda's reversion to his native faith more dramatic and profound, the author has given him a mother who on very arbitrary grounds, apparently, has separated herself from this same faith and who has been kept waiting in the wing, as it were, for many acts, to come on and make her speech and say so. This moral situation of hers we are invited retrospectively to appreciate. But we hardly care to do so.

Pulcheria. I don't *see* the princess, in spite of her flame-coloured robe. Why should an actress and prima-donna care so much about religious matters?

Theodora. It was not only that; it was the Jewish race she hated, Jewish manners and looks. You, my dear, ought to understand that.

Pulcheria. I do, but I am not a Jewish actress of genius; I am not what Rachel was. If I were I should have other things to think about.

Constantius. Think now a little about poor Gwendolen.

Pulcheria. I don't care to think about her. She was a second-rate English girl who got into a flutter about a lord.

Theodora. I don't see that she is worse than if she were a first-rate American girl who should get into exactly the same flutter.

Pulcheria. It wouldn't be the same flutter at all; it wouldn't be any flutter. She wouldn't be afraid of the lord, though she might be amused at him.

Theodora. I am sure I don't perceive whom Gwendolen was afraid of. She was afraid of her misdeed—her broken promise—after she had committed it, and through that fear she was afraid of her husband. Well she might be! I can imagine nothing more vivid than the sense we get of his absolutely clammy selfishness.

Pulcheria. She was not afraid of Deronda when, immediately after her marriage and without any but the most casual acquaintance with him, she begins to hover about him at the Mallingers' and to drop little confidences about her conjugal woes. That seems to me very indelicate; ask any woman.

Constantius. The very purpose of the author is to give us an idea of the sort of confidence that *Deronda* inspired—its irresistible potency.

Pulcheria. A lay father-confessor—horrid!

Constantius. And to give us an idea also of the acuteness of Gwendolen's depression, of her haunting sense of impending trouble.

Theodora. It must be remembered that Gwendolen was in love with Deronda from the first, long before she knew it. She didn't know it, poor girl, but that was it.

Pulcheria. That makes the matter worse. It is very disagreeable to see her hovering and rustling about a man who is indifferent to her.

Theodora. He was not indifferent to her, since he sent her back her necklace.

Pulcheria. Of all the delicate attention to a charming girl that I ever heard of, that little pecuniary transaction is the most felicitous.

Constantius. You must remember that he had been *en rapport* with her at the gaming-table. She had been playing in defiance of his observation, and he, continuing to observe her, had been in a measure responsible for her loss. There was a tacit consciousness of this between them. You may contest the possibility of tacit consciousness going so far, but that is not a serious objection. You may point out two or three weak spots in detail; the fact remains that Gwendolen's whole history is vividly told. And see how the girl is known, inside out, how thoroughly she is felt and understood. It is the most *intelligent* thing in all George Eliot's writing, and that is saying much. It is so deep, so true, so complete, it holds such a wealth of psychological detail, it is more than masterly.

Theodora. I don't know where the perception of character has sailed closer to the wind.

Pulcheria. The portrait may be admirable, but it has one little fault. You don't care a straw for the original. Gwendolen is not an interesting girl, and when the author tries to invest her with a deep tragic interest she does so at the expense of consistency. She has made her at the outset too light, too flimsy; tragedy has no hold on such a girl.

Theodora. You are hard to satisfy. You said this morning that Dorothea was too heavy, and now you find Gwendolen too light. George Eliot wished to give us the perfect counterpart of Dorothea. Having made one portrait she was worthy to make the other.

Pulcheria. She has committed the fatal error of making Gwendolen vulgarly, pettily, drily selfish. She was *personally* selfish.

Theodora. I know nothing more personal than selfishness.

Pulcheria. I am selfish, but I don't go about with my chin out like that; at least I hope I don't. She was an odious young woman, and one can't care what becomes of her. When her marriage turned out ill she would have become still more hard and positive; to make her soft and appealing is very bad logic. The second Gwendolen doesn't belong to the first.

Constantius. She is perhaps at the first a little childish for the weight of interest she has to carry, a little too much after the pattern of the unconscientious young ladies of Miss Yonge and Miss Sewell.

Theodora. Since when it is forbidden to make one's heroine young? Gwendolen is a perfect picture of youthfulness—its eagerness, its presumption, its preoccupation with itself, its vanity and silliness, its sense of its own absoluteness. But she is extremely intelligent and clever, and therefore tragedy *can* have a hold upon her. Her conscience doesn't make the tragedy; that is an old story and, I think, a secondary form of suffering. It is the tragedy that makes her conscience, which then reacts upon it; and I can think of nothing more powerful than the way in which the growth of her conscience is traced, nothing more touching than the picture of its helpless maturity.

Constantius. That is perfectly true. Gwendolen's history is admirably typical—as most things are with George Eliot: it is the very stuff that human life is made of. What is it made of but the discovery by each of us that we are at the best but a rather ridiculous fifth wheel to the coach, after we have sat cracking our whip and believing that we are at least the coachman in person? We think we are the main hoop to the barrel, and we turn out to be but a very incidental splinter in one of the staves. The universe forcing itself with a slow, inexorable pressure into a narrow, complacent, and yet after all extremely sensitive mind, and making it ache with the pain of the process—that is Gwendolen's story. And it becomes completely characteristic in that her supreme perception of the fact that the world is whirling past her is in the disappointment not of a base but of an exalted passion. The very chance to embrace what the author is so fond of calling a "larger life" seems refused to her. She is punished for being narrow, and she is not allowed a chance to expand. Her finding Deronda pre-engaged to go to the East and stir up the race-feeling of the Jews strikes me as a wonderfully happy invention. The irony of the situation, for poor Gwendolen, is almost grotesque, and it makes one wonder whether the whole heavy structure of the Jewish question in the story was not built up by the author for the express purpose of giving its proper force to this particular stroke.

Theodora. George Eliot's intentions are extremely complex. The mass is for each detail and each detail is for the mass.

Pulcheria. She is very fond of deaths by drowning. Maggie Tulliver and her brother are drowned, Tito Melema is drowned, Mr. Grandcourt is drowned. It is extremely unlikely that Grandcourt should not have known how to swim.

Constantius. He did, of course, but he had a cramp. It served him right. I can't imagine a more consummate representation of the most detestable kind of Englishman—the Englishman who thinks it low to articulate. And in Grandcourt the type and the individual are so happily met: the type with its sense of the proprieties and the individual with his absence of all sense. He is the apotheosis of dryness, a human expression of the simple idea of the perpendicular.

Theodora. Mr. Casaubon, in *Middlemarch*, was very dry too; and yet what a genius it is that can give us two disagreeable husbands who are so utterly different!

Pulcheria. You must count the two disagreeable wives too—Rosamond Vincy and Gwendolen. They are very much alike. I know the author didn't mean it; it proves how common a type the worldly, *pincée*, selfish young woman seemed to her. They are both disagreeable; you can't get over that.

Constantius. There is something in that, perhaps. I think, at any rate, that the secondary people here are less delightful than in *Middlemarch*; there is nothing so good as Mary Garth and her father, or the little old lady who steals sugar, or the parson who is in love with Mary, or the country relatives of old Mr. Featherstone. Rex Gascoigne is not so good as Fred Vincy.

Theodora. Mr. Gascoigne is admirable, and Mrs. Davilow is charming.

Pulcheria. And you must not forget that you think Herr Klesmer "Shakespearean." Wouldn't "Wagnerian" be high enough praise?

Constantius. Yes, one must make an exception with regard to the Klesmers and the Meyricks. They are delightful, and as for Klesmer himself, and Hans Meyrick, Theodora may maintain her epithet. Shakespearean characters are characters that are born of the *overflow* of observation—characters that make the drama seem multitudinous, like life. Klesmer comes in with a sort of Shakespearean "value," as a painter would say, and so, in a different tone, does Hans Meyrick. They spring from a much-peopled mind.

Theodora. I think Gwendolen's confrontation with Klesmer one of the finest things in the book.

Constantius. It is like everything in George Eliot; it will bear thinking of.

Pulcheria. All that is very fine, but you cannot persuade me that *Deronda* is not a very ponderous and ill-made story. It has nothing that one can call a subject. A silly young girl and a solemn, sapient young man who doesn't fall in love with her! That is the *donnée* of eight monthly volumes. I call it very flat. Is that what the exquisite art of Thackeray and Miss Austen and Hawthorne has come to? I would as soon read a German novel outright.

Theodora. There is something higher than form—there is spirit.

Constantius. I am afraid Pulcheria is sadly æsthetic. She had better confine herself to Mérimée.

Pulcheria. I shall certainly to-day read over *La Double Méprise*.

Theodora. Oh, my dear, *y pensez-vous?*

Constantius. Yes, I think there is little art in *Deronda*, but I think there is a vast amount of life. In life without art you can find your account; but art without life is a poor affair. The book is full of the world.

Theodora. It is full of beauty and knowledge, and that is quite art enough for me.

Pulcheria (to the little dog). We are silenced, darling, but we are not convinced, are we? (The pug begins to bark.) No, we are not even silenced. It's a young woman with two bandboxes.

Theodora. Oh, it must be our muslins.

Constantius (rising to go). I see what you mean!

1876.

IV. ANTHONY TROLLOPE

WHEN, a few months ago, Anthony Trollope laid down his pen for the last time, it was a sign of the complete extinction of that group of admirable writers who, in England, during the preceding half century, had done so much to elevate the art of the novelist. The author of *The Warden*, of *Barchester Towers*, of *Framley Parsonage*, does not, to our mind, stand on the very same level as Dickens, Thackeray and George Eliot; for his talent was of a quality less fine than theirs. But he belonged to the same family—he had as much to tell us about English life; he was strong, genial and abundant. He published too much; the writing of novels had ended by becoming, with him, a perceptibly mechanical process. Dickens was prolific, Thackeray produced with a freedom for which we are constantly grateful; but we feel that these writers had their periods of gestation. They took more time to look at their subject; relatively (for to-day there is not much leisure, at best, for those who undertake to entertain a hungry public), they were able to wait for inspiration. Trollope's fecundity was prodigious; there was no limit to the work he was ready to do. It is not unjust to say that he sacrificed quality to quantity. Abundance, certainly, is in itself a great merit; almost all the greatest writers have been abundant. But Trollope's fertility was gross, importunate; he himself contended, we believe, that he had given to the world a greater number of printed pages of fiction than any of his literary contemporaries. Not only did his novels follow each other without visible intermission, overlapping and treading on each other's heels, but most of these works are of extraordinary length. *Orley Farm*, *Can You Forgive Her?*, *He Knew He Was Right*, are exceedingly voluminous tales. *The Way We Live Now* is one of the longest of modern novels. Trollope produced, moreover, in the intervals of larger labour a great number of short stories, many of them charming, as well as various books of travel, and two or three biographies. He was the great *improvvisatore* of these latter years. Two distinguished story-tellers of the other sex—one in France and one in England—have shown an extraordinary facility of composition; but Trollope's pace was brisker even than that of the wonderful Madame Sand and the delightful Mrs. Oliphant. He had taught himself to keep this pace, and had reduced his admirable faculty to a system. Every day of his life he wrote a certain number of pages of his current tale, a number sacramental and invariable, independent of mood and place. It was once the fortune of the author of these lines to cross the Atlantic in his company, and he has never forgotten the magnificent example of plain persistence that it was in the power of the eminent novelist to give on that occasion. The season was unpropitious, the vessel overcrowded, the voyage detestable; but Trollope shut himself up in his cabin every morning for a purpose which, on the part of a distinguished writer who was also an invulnerable sailor, could only be communion with the muse. He drove his pen as steadily on the tumbling ocean as in Montague Square; and as his voyages were many, it was his practice before sailing to come down to the ship and confer with the carpenter, who was instructed to rig up a rough writing-table in his small sea-chamber. Trollope has been accused of being deficient in imagination, but in the face of such a fact as that the charge will scarcely seem just. The power to shut one's eyes, one's ears (to say nothing of another sense), upon the scenery of a pitching Cunarder and open them upon the loves and sorrows of Lily Dale or the conjugal embarrassments of Lady Glencora Palliser, is certainly a faculty which could take to itself wings. The imagination that Trollope possessed he had at least thoroughly at his command. I speak of all this in order to explain (in part) why it was that, with his extraordinary gift, there was always in him a certain infusion of the common. He abused his gift, overworked it, rode his horse too hard. As an artist he never took himself seriously; many people will say this was why he was so delightful. The people who take themselves seriously are prigs and bores; and Trollope, with his perpetual "story," which was the only thing he cared about, his strong good sense, hearty good nature, generous appreciation of life in all its varieties, responds in perfection to a certain English ideal. According to that ideal it is rather dangerous to be explicitly or consciously an artist—to have a system, a doctrine, a form. Trollope, from the first, went in, as they say, for having as little form as possible; it is probably safe to affirm that he had no "views" whatever on the subject of novel-writing. His whole manner is that of a man who regards the practice as one of the more delicate industries, but has never troubled his head nor clogged his pen with theories about the nature of his business. Fortunately he was not obliged to do so, for he had an easy road to success; and his honest, familiar, deliberate way of treating his readers as if he were one of them, and shared their indifference to a general view, their limitations of knowledge, their love of a comfortable ending, endeared him to many persons in England and America. It is in the name of some chosen form that, of late years, things have been made most disagreeable for the novel-reader, who has been treated by several votaries of the new experiments in fiction to unwonted and bewildering sensations. With Trollope we were always safe; there were sure to be no new experiments.

His great, his inestimable merit was a complete appreciation of the usual. This gift is not rare in the annals of English fiction; it would naturally be found in a walk of literature in which the feminine mind has laboured so fruitfully. Women are delicate and patient observers; they hold their noses close, as it were, to the texture of life. They feel and perceive the real with a kind of personal tact, and their observations are recorded in a thousand delightful volumes. Trollope, therefore, with his eyes comfortably fixed on the familiar, the actual, was far from having invented a new category; his great distinction is that in resting there his vision took in so much of the field. And then he *felt* all daily and immediate things as well as saw them; felt them in a simple, direct, salubrious way, with their sadness, their gladness, their charm, their comicality, all their obvious and measurable meanings. He never wearied of the pre-established round of English customs—never needed a respite or a change—was content to go on indefinitely watching the life that surrounded him, and holding up his mirror to it. Into this mirror the public, at first especially, grew very fond of looking—for it saw itself reflected in all the most credible and supposable ways, with that curiosity that people feel to know how they look when they are represented, "just as they are," by a painter who does not desire to put them into an attitude, to drape them for an effect, to arrange his light and his accessories. This exact and on the whole becoming image, projected upon a surface without a strong intrinsic tone, constitutes mainly the entertainment that Trollope offered his readers. The striking thing to the critic was that his robust and patient mind had no particular bias, his imagination no light of its own. He saw things neither pictorially and grotesquely like Dickens; nor with that combined disposition to satire and to literary form which gives such "body," as they say of wine, to the manner of Thackeray; nor with anything of the philosophic, the transcendental cast—the desire to follow them to their remote relations—which we associate with the name of George Eliot. Trollope had his elements of fancy, of satire, of irony; but these qualities were not very highly developed, and he walked mainly by the light of his good sense, his clear, direct vision of the things that lay nearest, and his great natural kindness. There is something remarkably tender and friendly in his feeling about all human perplexities; he takes the good-natured, temperate, conciliatory view—the humorous view, perhaps, for the most part, yet without a touch of pessimistic prejudice. As he grew older, and had sometimes to go farther afield for his subjects, he acquired a savour of bitterness and reconciled himself sturdily to treating of the disagreeable. A more copious record of disagreeable matters could scarcely be imagined, for instance, than *The Way We Live Now*. But, in general, he has a wholesome mistrust of morbid analysis, an aversion to inflicting pain. He has an infinite love of detail, but his details are, for the most part, the innumerable items of the expected. When the French are disposed to pay a compliment to the English mind they are so good as to say that there is in it something remarkably *honnête*. If I might borrow this epithet without seeming to be patronising, I should apply it to the genius of Anthony Trollope. He represents in an eminent degree this natural decorum of the English spirit, and represents it all the better that there is not in him a grain of the mawkish or the prudish. He writes, he feels, he judges like a man, talking plainly and frankly about many things, and is by no means destitute of a certain saving grace of coarseness. But he has kept the purity of his imagination and held fast to old-fashioned reverences and preferences. He thinks it a sufficient objection to several topics to say simply that they are unclean. There was nothing in his theory of the story-teller's art that tended to convert the reader's or the writer's mind into a vessel for polluting things. He recognised the right of the vessel to protest, and would have regarded such a protest as conclusive. With a considerable turn for satire, though this perhaps is more evident in his early novels than in his later ones, he had as little as possible of the quality of irony. He never played with a subject, never juggled with the sympathies or the credulity of his reader, was never in the least paradoxical or mystifying. He sat down to his theme in a serious, business-like way, with his elbows on the table and his eye occasionally wandering to the clock.

To touch successively upon these points is to attempt a portrait, which I shall perhaps not altogether have failed to produce. The source of his success in describing the life that lay nearest to him, and describing it without any of those artistic perversions that come, as we have said, from a powerful imagination, from a cynical humour or from a desire to look, as George Eliot expresses it, for the suppressed transitions that unite all contrasts, the essence of this love of reality was his extreme interest in character. This is the fine and admirable quality in Trollope, this is what will preserve his best works in spite of those flatnesses which keep him from standing on quite the same level as the masters. Indeed this quality is so much one of the finest (to my mind at least), that it makes me wonder the more that the writer who had it so abundantly and so naturally should not have just that distinction which Trollope lacks, and which we find in his three brilliant contemporaries. If he was in any degree a man of genius (and I hold that he was), it was in virtue of this happy, instinctive perception of human varieties. His knowledge of the stuff we are made of, his observation of the common behaviour of men and women, was not reasoned nor acquired, not even particularly studied. All human doings deeply interested him, human life, to his mind, was a perpetual story; but he never attempted to take the so-called scientific view, the view which has lately found ingenious advocates among the countrymen and successors of Balzac. He had no airs of being able to tell you *why* people in a given situation would conduct themselves in a particular way; it was enough for him that he felt their feelings and struck the right note, because he had, as it were, a good ear. If he was a knowing psychologist he was so by grace; he was just and true without apparatus and without effort. He must have had a great taste for the moral question; he evidently believed that this is the basis of the interest of fiction. We must be careful, of course, in attributing convictions and opinions to Trollope, who, as I have said, had as little as possible of the pedantry of his art, and whose occasional chance utterances in regard to the object of the novelist and his means of achieving it are of an almost startling simplicity. But we certainly do not go too far in saying that he gave his practical testimony in favour of the idea that the interest of a work of fiction is great in proportion as the people stand on their feet. His great effort was evidently to make them stand so; if he achieved this result with as little as possible of a flourish of the hand it was nevertheless the measure of his success. If he had taken sides on the droll, bemuddled opposition between novels of character and novels of plot, I can imagine him to have said (except that he never expressed himself in epigrams), that he preferred the former class, inasmuch as character in itself is plot, while plot is by no means character. It is more safe indeed to believe that his great good sense would have prevented him from taking an idle controversy seriously. Character, in any sense in which we can get at it, is action, and action is plot, and any plot which hangs together, even if it pretend to interest us only in the fashion of a Chinese puzzle, plays upon our emotion, our suspense, by means of personal references. We care what happens to people only in proportion as we know what people are. Trollope's great apprehension of the real, which was what made him so interesting, came to him through his desire to satisfy us on this point—to tell us what certain people were and what they did in consequence of being so. That is the purpose of each of his tales; and if these things produce an illusion it comes from the gradual abundance of his testimony as to the temper, the tone, the passions, the habits, the moral nature, of a certain number of contemporary Britons.

His stories, in spite of their great length, deal very little in the surprising, the exceptional, the complicate; as a general thing he has no great story to tell. The thing is not so much a story as a picture; if we hesitate to call it a picture it is because the idea of composition is not the controlling one and we feel that the author would regard the artistic, in general, as a kind of affectation. There is not even much description, in the sense which the present votaries of realism in France attach to that word. The painter lays his scene in a few deliberate, not especially pictorial strokes, and never dreams of finishing the piece for the sake of enabling the reader to hang it up. The finish, such as it is, comes later, from the slow and somewhat clumsy accumulation of small illustrations. These illustrations are sometimes of the commonest; Trollope turns them out inexhaustibly, repeats them freely, unfolds them without haste and without rest. But they are all of the most obvious sort, and they are none the worse for that. The point to be made is that they have no great spectacular interest (we beg pardon of the innumerable love-affairs that Trollope has described), like many of the incidents, say, of Walter Scott and of Alexandre Dumas: if we care to know about them (as repetitions of a usual case), it is because the writer has managed, in his candid, literal, somewhat lumbering way, to tell us that about the men and women concerned which has already excited on their behalf the impression of life. It is a marvel by what homely arts, by what imperturbable button-holing persistence, he contrives to excite this impression. Take, for example, such a work as *The Vicar of Bullhampton*. It would be difficult to state the idea of this slow but excellent story, which is a capital example of interest produced by the quietest conceivable means. The principal persons in it are a lively, jovial, high-tempered country clergyman, a young woman who is in love with her cousin, and a small, rather dull squire who is in love with the young woman. There is no connection between the affairs of the clergyman and those of the two other persons, save that these two are the Vicar's friends. The Vicar gives countenance, for Christian charity's sake, to a young countryman who is suspected (falsely, as it appears), of murder, and also to the lad's sister, who is more than suspected of leading an immoral life. Various people are shocked at his indiscretion, but in the end he is shown to have been no worse a clergyman because he is a good fellow. A cantankerous nobleman, who has a spite against him, causes a Methodist conventicle to be erected at the gates of the vicarage; but afterward, finding that he has no title to the land used for this obnoxious purpose, causes the conventicle to be pulled down, and is reconciled with the parson, who accepts an invitation to stay at the castle. Mary Lowther, the heroine of *The Vicar of Bullhampton*, is sought in marriage by Mr. Harry Gilmore, to whose passion she is unable to respond; she accepts him, however, making him understand that she does not love him, and that her affections are fixed upon her kinsman, Captain Marrable, whom she would marry (and who would marry her), if he were not too poor to support a wife. If Mr. Gilmore will take her on these terms she will become his spouse; but she gives him all sorts of warnings. They are not superfluous; for, as Captain Marrable presently inherits a fortune, she throws over Mr. Gilmore, who retires to foreign lands, heart-broken, inconsolable. This is the substance of *The Vicar of Bullhampton*; the reader will see that it is not a very tangled skein. But if the interest is gradual it is extreme and constant, and it comes altogether from excellent portraiture. It is essentially a moral, a social interest. There is something masterly in the large-fisted grip with which, in work of this kind, Trollope handles his brush. The Vicar's nature is thoroughly analysed and rendered, and his monotonous friend the Squire, a man with limitations, but possessed and consumed by a genuine passion, is equally near the truth.

Trollope has described again and again the ravages of love, and it is wonderful to see how well, in these delicate matters, his plain good sense and good taste serve him. His story is always primarily a love-story, and a love-story constructed on an inveterate system. There is a young lady who has two lovers, or a young man who has two sweethearts; we are treated to the innumerable forms in which this predicament may present itself and the consequences, sometimes pathetic, sometimes grotesque, which spring from such false situations. Trollope is not what is called a colourist; still less is he a poet: he is seated on the back of heavy-footed prose. But his account of those sentiments which the poets are supposed to have made their own is apt to be as touching as demonstrations more lyrical. There is something wonderfully vivid in the state of mind of the unfortunate Harry Gilmore, of whom I have just spoken; and his history, which has no more pretensions to style than if it were cut out of yesterday's newspaper, lodges itself in the imagination in all sorts of classic company. He is not handsome, nor clever, nor rich, nor romantic, nor distinguished in any way; he is simply rather a dense, narrow-minded, stiff, obstinate, common-place, conscientious modern Englishman, exceedingly in love and, from his own point of view, exceedingly ill-used. He is interesting because he suffers and because we are curious to see the form that suffering will take in that particular nature. Our good fortune, with Trollope, is that the person put before us will have, in spite of opportunities not to have it, a certain particular nature. The author has cared enough about the character of such a person to find out exactly what it is. Another particular nature in *The Vicar of Bullhampton* is the surly, sturdy, sceptical old farmer Jacob Brattle, who doesn't want to be patronised by the parson, and in his dumb, dusky, half-brutal, half-spiritual melancholy, surrounded by domestic troubles, financial embarrassments and a puzzling world, declines altogether to be won over to clerical optimism. Such a figure as Jacob Brattle, purely episodical though it be, is an excellent English portrait. As thoroughly English, and the most striking thing in the book, is the combination, in the nature of Frank Fenwick—the delightful Vicar—of the patronising, conventional, clerical element with all sorts of manliness and spontaneity; the union, or to a certain extent the contradiction, of official and personal geniality. Trollope touches these points in a way that shows that he knows his man. Delicacy is not his great sign, but when it is necessary he can be as delicate as any one else.

I alighted, just now, at a venture, upon the history of Frank Fenwick; it is far from being a conspicuous work in the immense list of Trollope's novels. But to choose an example one must choose arbitrarily, for examples of almost anything that one may wish to say are numerous to embarrassment. In speaking of a writer who produced so much and produced always in the same way, there is perhaps a certain unfairness in choosing at all. As no work has higher pretensions than any other, there may be a certain unkindness in holding an individual production up to the light. "Judge me in the lump," we can imagine the author saying; "I have only undertaken to entertain the British public. I don't pretend that each of my novels is an organic whole." Trollope had no time to give his tales a classic roundness; yet there is (in spite of an extraordinary defect), something of that quality in the thing that first revealed him. *The Warden* was published in 1855. It made a great impression; and when, in 1857, *Barchester Towers* followed it, every one saw that English literature had a novelist the more. These were not the works of a young man, for Anthony Trollope had been born in 1815. It is remarkable to reflect, by the way, that his prodigious fecundity (he had published before *The Warden* three or four novels which attracted little attention), was enclosed between his fortieth and his sixty-seventh years. Trollope had lived long enough in the world to learn a good deal about it; and his maturity of feeling and evidently large knowledge of English life were for much in the effect produced by the two clerical tales. It was easy to see that he would take up room. What he had picked up, to begin with, was a comprehensive, various impression of the clergy of the Church of England and the manners and feelings that prevail in cathedral towns. This, for a while, was his speciality, and, as always happens in such cases, the public was disposed to prescribe to him that path. He knew about bishops, archdeacons, prebendaries, precentors, and about their wives and daughters; he knew what these dignitaries say to each other when they are collected together, aloof from secular ears. He even knew what sort of talk goes on between a bishop and a bishop's lady when the august couple are enshrouded in the privacy of the episcopal bedroom. This knowledge, somehow, was rare and precious. No one, as yet, had been bold enough to snatch the illuminating torch from the very summit of the altar. Trollope enlarged his field very speedily—there is, as I remember that work, as little as possible of the ecclesiastical in the tale of *The Three Clerks*, which came after *Barchester Towers*. But he always retained traces of his early divination of the clergy; he introduced them frequently, and he always did them easily and well. There is no ecclesiastical figure, however, so good as the first—no creation of this sort so happy as the admirable Mr. Harding. *The Warden* is a delightful tale, and a signal instance of Trollope's habit of offering us the spectacle of a character. A motive more delicate, more slender, as well as more charming, could scarcely be conceived. It is simply the history of an old man's conscience.

The good and gentle Mr. Harding, precentor of Barchester Cathedral, also holds the post of warden of Hiram's Hospital, an ancient charity where twelve old paupers are maintained in comfort. The office is in the gift of the bishop, and its emoluments are as handsome as the duties of the place are small. Mr. Harding has for years drawn his salary in quiet gratitude; but his moral repose is broken by hearing it at last begun to be said that the wardenship is a sinecure, that the salary is a scandal, and that a large part, at least, of his easy income ought to go to the pensioners of the hospital. He is sadly troubled and perplexed, and when the great London newspapers take up the affair he is overwhelmed with confusion and shame. He thinks the newspapers are right—he perceives that the warden is an overpaid and rather a useless functionary. The only thing he can do is to resign the place. He has no means of his own—he is only a quiet, modest, innocent old man, with a taste, a passion, for old church-music and the violoncello. But he determines to resign, and he does resign in spite of the sharp opposition of his friends. He does what he thinks right, and goes to live in lodgings over a shop in the Barchester High Street. That is all the story, and it has exceeding beauty. The question of Mr. Harding's resignation becomes a drama, and we anxiously wait for the catastrophe. Trollope never did anything happier than the picture of this sweet and serious little old gentleman, who on most of the occasions of life has shown a lamblike softness and compliance, but in this particular matter opposes a silent, impenetrable obstinacy to the arguments of the friends who insist on his keeping his sinecure—fixing his mild, detached gaze on the distance, and making imaginary passes with his fiddle-bow while they demonstrate his pusillanimity. The subject of *The Warden*, exactly viewed, is the opposition of the two natures of Archdeacon Grantley and Mr. Harding, and there is nothing finer in all Trollope than the vividness with which this opposition is presented. The archdeacon is as happy a portrait as the precentor—an image of the full-fed, worldly churchman, taking his stand squarely upon his rich temporalities, and regarding the church frankly as a fat social pasturage. It required the greatest tact and temperance to make the picture of Archdeacon Grantley stop just where it does. The type, impartially considered, is detestable, but the individual may be full of amenity. Trollope allows his archdeacon all the virtues he was likely to possess, but he makes his spiritual grossness wonderfully natural. No charge of exaggeration is possible, for we are made to feel that he is conscientious as well as arrogant, and expansive as well as hard. He is one of those figures that spring into being all at once, solidifying in the author's grasp. These two capital portraits are what we carry away from *The Warden*, which some persons profess to regard as our writer's masterpiece. We remember, while it was still something of a novelty, to have heard a judicious critic say that it had much of the charm of *The Vicar of Wakefield*. Anthony Trollope would not have accepted the compliment, and would not have wished this little tale to pass before several of its successors. He would have said, very justly, that it gives too small a measure of his knowledge of life. It has, however, a certain classic roundness, though, as we said a moment since, there is a blemish on its fair face. The chapter on Dr. Pessimist Anticant and Mr. Sentiment would be a mistake almost inconceivable if Trollope had not in other places taken pains to show us that for certain forms of satire (the more violent, doubtless), he had absolutely no gift. Dr. Anticant is a parody of Carlyle, and

Mr. Sentiment is an exposure of Dickens: and both these little *jeux d'esprit* are as infelicitous as they are misplaced. It was no less luckless an inspiration to convert Archdeacon Grantley's three sons, denominated respectively Charles James, Henry and Samuel, into little effigies of three distinguished English bishops of that period, whose well-known peculiarities are reproduced in the description of these unnatural urchins. The whole passage, as we meet it, is a sudden disillusionment; we are transported from the mellow atmosphere of an assimilated Barchester to the air of ponderous allegory.

I may take occasion to remark here upon a very curious fact—the fact that there are certain precautions in the way of producing that illusion dear to the intending novelist which Trollope not only habitually scorned to take, but really, as we may say, asking pardon for the heat of the thing, delighted wantonly to violate. He took a suicidal satisfaction in reminding the reader that the story he was telling was only, after all, a make-believe. He habitually referred to the work in hand (in the course of that work) as a novel, and to himself as a novelist, and was fond of letting the reader know that this novelist could direct the course of events according to his pleasure. Already, in *Barchester Towers*, he falls into this pernicious trick. In describing the wooing of Eleanor Bold by Mr. Arabin he has occasion to say that the lady might have acted in a much more direct and natural way than the way he attributes to her. But if she had, he adds, "where would have been my novel?" The last chapter of the same story begins with the remark, "The end of a novel, like the end of a children's dinner party, must be made up of sweetmeats and sugar-plums." These little slaps at credulity (we might give many more specimens) are very discouraging, but they are even more inexplicable; for they are deliberately inartistic, even judged from the point of view of that rather vague consideration of form which is the only canon we have a right to impose upon Trollope. It is impossible to imagine what a novelist takes himself to be unless he regard himself as an historian and his narrative as a history. It is only as an historian that he has the smallest *locus standi*. As a narrator of fictitious events he is nowhere; to insert into his attempt a back-bone of logic, he must relate events that are assumed to be real. This assumption permeates, animates all the work of the most solid story-tellers; we need only mention (to select a single instance), the magnificent historical tone of Balzac, who would as soon have thought of admitting to the reader that he was deceiving him, as Garrick or John Kemble would have thought of pulling off his disguise in front of the foot-lights. Therefore, when Trollope suddenly winks at us and reminds us that he is telling us an arbitrary thing, we are startled and shocked in quite the same way as if Macaulay or Motley were to drop the historic mask and intimate that William of Orange was a myth or the Duke of Alva an invention.

It is a part of this same ambiguity of mind as to what constitutes evidence that Trollope should sometimes endow his people with such fantastic names. Dr. Pessimist Anticant and Mr. Sentiment make, as we have seen, an awkward appearance in a modern novel; and Mr. Neversay Die, Mr. Stickatit, Mr. Rerechild and Mr. Fillgrave (the two last the family physicians), are scarcely more felicitous. It would be better to go back to Bunyan at once. There is a person mentioned in *The Warden* under the name of Mr. Quiverful—a poor clergyman, with a dozen children, who holds the living of Puddingdale. This name is a humorous allusion to his overflowing nursery, and it matters little so long as he is not brought to the front. But in *Barchester Towers*, which carries on the history of Hiram's Hospital, Mr. Quiverful becomes, as a candidate for Mr. Harding's vacant place, an important element, and the reader is made proportionately unhappy by the primitive character of this satiric note. A Mr. Quiverful with fourteen children (which is the number attained in *Barchester Towers*) is too difficult to believe in. We can believe in the name and we can believe in the children; but we cannot manage the combination. It is probably not unfair to say that if Trollope derived half his inspiration from life, he derived the other half from Thackeray; his earlier novels, in especial, suggest an honourable emulation of the author of *The Newcomes*. Thackeray's names were perfect; they always had a meaning, and (except in his absolutely jocose productions, where they were still admirable) we can imagine, even when they are most figurative, that they should have been borne by real people. But in this, as in other respects, Trollope's hand was heavier than his master's; though when he is content not to be too comical his appellations are sometimes fortunate enough. Mrs. Proudie is excellent, for Mrs. Proudie, and even the Duke of Omnium and Gatherum Castle rather minister to illusion than destroy it. Indeed, the names of houses and places, throughout Trollope, are full of colour.

I would speak in some detail of *Barchester Towers* if this did not seem to commit me to the prodigious task of appreciating each of Trollope's works in succession. Such an attempt as that is so far from being possible that I must frankly confess to not having read everything that proceeded from his pen. There came a moment in his vigorous career (it was even a good many years ago) when I renounced the effort to "keep up" with him. It ceased to seem obligatory to have read his last story; it ceased soon to be very possible to know which was his last. Before that, I had been punctual, devoted; and the memories of the earlier period are delightful. It reached, if I remember correctly, to about the publication of *He Knew He Was Right*; after which, to my recollection (oddly enough, too, for that novel was good enough to encourage a continuance of past favours, as the shopkeepers say), the picture becomes dim and blurred. The author of *Orley Farm* and *The Small House at Allington* ceased to produce individual works; his activity became a huge "serial." Here and there, in the vast fluidity, an organic particle detached itself. *The Last Chronicle of Barset*, for instance, is one of his most powerful things; it contains the sequel of the terrible history of Mr. Crawley, the starving curate—an episode full of that literally truthful pathos of which Trollope was so often a master, and which occasionally raised him quite to the level of his two immediate predecessors in the vivid treatment of English life—great artists whose pathetic effects were sometimes too visibly prepared. For the most part, however, he should be judged by the productions of the first half of his career; later the strong wine was rather too copiously watered. His practice, his acquired facility, were such that his hand went of itself, as it were, and the thing looked superficially like a fresh inspiration. But it was not fresh, it was rather stale; and though there was no appearance of effort, there was a fatal dryness of texture. It was too little of a new story and too much of an old one. Some of these ultimate compositions—*Phineas Redux* (*Phineas Finn* is much better), *The Prime Minister*, *John Caldigate*, *The American Senator*, *The Duke's Children*—betray the dull, impersonal rumble of the mill-wheel. What stands Trollope always in good stead (in addition to the ripe habit of writing), is his various knowledge of the English world—to say nothing of his occasionally laying under contribution the American. His American portraits, by the way (they are several in number), are always friendly; they hit it off more happily than the attempt to depict American character from the European point of view is accustomed to do: though, indeed, as we ourselves have not yet learned to represent our types very finely—are not apparently even very sure what our types are—it is perhaps not to be wondered at that transatlantic talent should miss the mark. The weakness of transatlantic talent in this particular is apt to be want of knowledge; but Trollope's knowledge has all the air of being excellent, though not intimate. Had he indeed striven to learn the way to the American heart? No less than twice, and possibly even oftener, has he rewarded the merit of a scion of the British aristocracy with the hand of an American girl. The American girl was destined sooner or later to make her entrance into British fiction, and Trollope's treatment of this complicated being is full of good humour and of that fatherly indulgence, that almost motherly sympathy, which characterises his attitude throughout toward the youthful feminine. He has not mastered all the springs of her delicate organism nor sounded all the mysteries of her conversation. Indeed, as regards these latter phenomena, he has observed a few of which he has been the sole observer. "I got to be thinking if any one of them should ask me to marry him," words attributed to Miss Boncassen, in *The Duke's Children*, have much more the note of English American than of American English. But, on the whole, in these matters Trollope does very well. His fund of acquaintance with his own country—and indeed with the world at large—was apparently inexhaustible, and it gives his novels a spacious, geographical quality which we should not know where to look for elsewhere in the same degree, and which is the sign of an extraordinary difference between such an horizon as his and the limited world-outlook, as the Germans would say, of the brilliant writers who practise the art of realistic fiction on the other side of the Channel. Trollope was familiar with all sorts and conditions of men, with the business of life, with affairs, with the great world of sport, with every component part of the ancient fabric of English society. He had travelled more than once all over the globe, and for him, therefore, the background of the human drama was a very extensive scene. He had none of the pedantry of the cosmopolite; he remained a sturdy and sensible middle-class Englishman. But his work is full of implied reference to the whole arena of modern vagrancy. He was for many years concerned in the management of the Post-Office; and we can imagine no experience more fitted to impress a man with the diversity of human relations. It is possibly from this source that he derived his fondness for transcribing the letters of his love-lorn maidens and other embarrassed persons. No contemporary story-teller deals so much in letters; the modern English epistle (very happily imitated, for the most part), is his unfailing resource.

There is perhaps little reason in it, but I find myself comparing this tone of allusion to many lands and many things, and whatever it brings us of easier respiration, with that narrow vision of humanity which accompanies the strenuous, serious work lately offered us in such abundance by the votaries of art for art who sit so long at their desks in Parisian *quatrièmes*. The contrast is complete, and it would be interesting, had we space to do so here, to see how far it goes. On one side a wide, good-humoured, superficial glance at a good many things; on the other a gimlet-like consideration of a few. Trollope's plan, as well as Zola's, was to describe the life that lay near him; but the two writers differ immensely as to what constitutes life and what constitutes nearness. For Trollope the emotions of a nursery-governess in Australia would take precedence of the adventures of a depraved *femme du monde* in Paris or London. They both undertake to do the same thing—to depict French and English manners; but the English writer (with his unsurpassed industry) is so occasional, so accidental, so full of the echoes of voices that are not the voice of the muse. Gustave Flaubert, Emile Zola, Alphonse Daudet, on the other hand, are nothing if not concentrated and sedentary. Trollope's realism is as instinctive, as inveterate as theirs; but nothing could mark more the difference between the French and English mind than the difference in the application, on one side and the other, of this system. We say system, though on Trollope's part it is none. He has no visible, certainly no explicit care for the literary part of the business; he writes easily, comfortably, and profusely, but his style has nothing in common either with the minute stippling of Daudet or the studied rhythms of Flaubert. He accepted all the common restrictions, and found that even within the barriers there was plenty of material. He attaches a preface to one of his novels—*The Vicar of Bullhampton*, before mentioned— for the express purpose of explaining why he has introduced a young woman who may, in truth, as he says, be called a "castaway"; and in relation to this episode he remarks that it is the object of the novelist's art to entertain the young people of both sexes. Writers of the French school would, of course, protest indignantly against such a formula as this, which is the only one of the kind that I remember to have encountered in Trollope's pages. It is meagre, assuredly; but Trollope's practice was really much larger than so poor a theory. And indeed any theory was good which enabled him to produce the works which he put forth between 1856 and 1869, or later. In spite of his want of doctrinal richness I think he tells us, on the whole, more about life than the "naturalists" in our sister republic. I say this with a full consciousness of the opportunities an artist loses in leaving so many corners unvisited, so many topics untouched, simply because I think his perception of character was naturally more just and liberal than that of the naturalists. This has been from the beginning the good fortune of our English providers of fiction, as compared with the French. They are inferior in audacity, in neatness, in acuteness, in intellectual vivacity, in the arrangement of material, in the art of characterising visible things. But they have been more at home in the moral world; as people say to-day they know their way about the conscience. This is the value of much of the work done by the feminine wing of the school—work which presents itself to French taste as deplorably thin and insipid. Much of it is exquisitely human, and that after all is a merit. As regards Trollope, one may perhaps characterise him best, in opposition to what I have ventured to call the sedentary school, by saying that he was a novelist who hunted the fox. Hunting was for years his most valued recreation, and I remember that when I made in his company the voyage of which I have spoken, he had timed his return from the Antipodes exactly so as to be able to avail himself of the first day on which it should be possible to ride to hounds. He "worked" the hunting-field largely; it constantly reappears in his novels; it was excellent material.

But it would be hard to say (within the circle in which he revolved) what material he neglected. I have allowed myself to be detained so long by general considerations that I have almost forfeited the opportunity to give examples. I have spoken of *The Warden* not only because it made his reputation, but because, taken in conjunction with *Barchester Towers*, it is thought by many people to be his highest flight. *Barchester Towers* is admirable; it has an almost

Thackerayan richness. Archdeacon Grantley grows more and more into life, and Mr. Harding is as charming as ever. Mrs. Proudie is ushered into a world in which she was to make so great an impression. Mrs. Proudie has become classical; of all Trollope's characters she is the most often referred to. She is exceedingly true; but I do not think she is quite so good as her fame, and as several figures from the same hand that have not won so much honour. She is rather too violent, too vixenish, too sour. The truly awful female bully—the completely fatal episcopal spouse—would have, I think, a more insidious form, a greater amount of superficial padding. The Stanhope family, in *Barchester Towers*, are a real *trouvaille*, and the idea of transporting the Signora Vesey-Neroni into a cathedral-town was an inspiration. There could not be a better example of Trollope's manner of attaching himself to character than the whole picture of Bertie Stanhope. Bertie is a delightful creation; and the scene in which, at the party given by Mrs. Proudie, he puts this majestic woman to rout is one of the most amusing in all the chronicles of Barset. It is perhaps permitted to wish, by the way, that this triumph had been effected by means intellectual rather than physical; though, indeed, if Bertie had not despoiled her of her drapery we should have lost the lady's admirable "Unhand it, sir!" Mr. Arabin is charming, and the henpecked bishop has painful truth; but Mr. Slope, I think, is a little too arrant a scamp. He is rather too much the old game; he goes too coarsely to work, and his clamminess and cant are somewhat overdone. He is an interesting illustration, however, of the author's dislike (at that period at least) of the bareness of evangelical piety. In one respect *Barchester Towers* is (to the best of our recollection) unique, being the only one of Trollope's novels in which the interest does not centre more or less upon a simple maiden in her flower. The novel offers us nothing in the way of a girl; though we know that this attractive object was to lose nothing by waiting. Eleanor Bold is a charming and natural person, but Eleanor Bold is not in her flower. After this, however, Trollope settled down steadily to the English girl; he took possession of her, and turned her inside out. He never made her a subject of heartless satire, as cynical fabulists of other lands have been known to make the shining daughters of those climes; he bestowed upon her the most serious, the most patient, the most tender, the most copious consideration. He is evidently always more or less in love with her, and it is a wonder how under these circumstances he should make her so objective, plant her so well on her feet. But, as I have said, if he was a lover, he was a paternal lover; as competent as a father who has had fifty daughters. He has presented the British maiden under innumerable names, in every station and in every emergency in life, and with every combination of moral and physical qualities. She is always definite and natural. She plays her part most properly. She has always health in her cheek and gratitude in her eye. She has not a touch of the morbid, and is delightfully tender, modest and fresh. Trollope's heroines have a strong family likeness, but it is a wonder how finely he discriminates between them. One feels, as one reads him, like a man with "sets" of female cousins. Such a person is inclined at first to lump each group together; but presently he finds that even in the groups there are subtle differences. Trollope's girls, for that matter, would make delightful cousins. He has scarcely drawn, that we can remember, a disagreeable damsel. Lady Alexandrina de Courcy is disagreeable, and so is Amelia Roper, and so are various provincial (and indeed metropolitan) spinsters, who set their caps at young clergymen and government clerks. Griselda Grantley was a stick; and considering that she was intended to be attractive, Alice Vavasor does not commend herself particularly to our affections. But the young women I have mentioned had ceased to belong to the blooming season; they had entered the bristling, or else the limp, period. Not that Trollope's more mature spinsters invariably fall into these extremes. Miss Thorne of Ullathorne, Miss Dunstable, Miss Mackenzie, Rachel Ray (if she may be called mature), Miss Baker and Miss Todd, in *The Bertrams*, Lady Julia Guest, who comforts poor John Eames: these and many other amiable figures rise up to contradict the idea. A gentleman who had sojourned in many lands was once asked by a lady (neither of these persons was English), in what country he had found the women most to his taste. "Well, in England," he replied. "In England?" the lady repeated. "Oh yes," said her interlocutor; "they are so affectionate!" The remark was fatuous, but it has the merit of describing Trollope's heroines. They are so affectionate. Mary Thorne, Lucy Robarts, Adela Gauntlet, Lily Dale, Nora Rowley, Grace Crawley, have a kind of clinging tenderness, a passive sweetness, which is quite in the old English tradition. Trollope's genius is not the genius of Shakespeare, but his heroines have something of the fragrance of Imogen and Desdemona. There are two little stories to which, I believe, his name has never been affixed, but which he is known to have written, that contain an extraordinarily touching representation of the passion of love in its most sensitive form. In *Linda Tressel* and *Nina Balatka* the vehicle is plodding prose, but the effect is none the less poignant. And in regard to this I may say that in a hundred places in Trollope the extremity of pathos is reached by the homeliest means. He often achieved a conspicuous intensity of the tragical. The long, slow process of the conjugal wreck of Louis Trevelyan and his wife (in *He Knew He Was Right*), with that rather lumbering movement which is often characteristic of Trollope, arrives at last at an impressive completeness of misery. It is the history of an accidental rupture between two stiff-necked and ungracious people—"the little rift within the lute"—which widens at last into a gulf of anguish. Touch is added to touch, one small, stupid, fatal aggravation to another; and as we gaze into the widening breach we wonder at the vulgar materials of which tragedy sometimes composes itself. I have always remembered the chapter called "Casalunga," toward the close of *He Knew He Was Right*, as a powerful picture of the insanity of stiff-neckedness. Louis Trevelyan, separated from his wife, alone, haggard, suspicious, unshaven, undressed, living in a desolate villa on a hill-top near Siena and returning doggedly to his fancied wrong, which he has nursed until it becomes an hallucination, is a picture worthy of Balzac. Here and in several other places Trollope has dared to be thoroughly logical; he has not sacrificed to conventional optimism; he has not been afraid of a misery which should be too much like life. He has had the same courage in the history of the wretched Mr. Crawley and in that of the much-to-be-pitied Lady Mason. In this latter episode he found an admirable subject. A quiet, charming, tender-souled English gentlewoman who (as I remember the story of *Orley Farm*) forges a codicil to a will in order to benefit her son, a young prig who doesn't appreciate immoral heroism, and who is suspected, accused, tried, and saved from conviction only by some turn of fortune that I forget; who is furthermore an object of high-bred, respectful, old-fashioned gallantry on the part of a neighbouring baronet, so that she sees herself dishonoured in his eyes as well as condemned in those of her boy: such a personage and such a situation would be sure to yield, under Trollope's handling, the last drop of their reality.

There are many more things to say about him than I am able to add to these very general observations, the limit of which I have already passed. It would be natural, for instance, for a critic who affirms that his principal merit is the portrayal of individual character, to enumerate several of the figures that he has produced. I have not done this, and I must ask the reader who is not acquainted with Trollope to take my assertion on trust; the reader who knows him will easily make a list for himself. No account of him is complete in which allusion is not made to his practice of carrying certain actors from one story to another—a practice which he may be said to have inherited from Thackeray, as Thackeray may be said to have borrowed it from Balzac. It is a great mistake, however, to speak of it as an artifice which would not naturally occur to a writer proposing to himself to make a general portrait of a society. He has to construct that society, and it adds to the illusion in any given case that certain other cases correspond with it. Trollope constructed a great many things—a clergy, an aristocracy, a middle-class, an administrative class, a little replica of the political world. His political novels are distinctly dull, and I confess I have not been able to read them. He evidently took a good deal of pains with his aristocracy; it makes its first appearance, if I remember right, in *Doctor Thorne*, in the person of the Lady Arabella de Courcy. It is difficult for us in America to measure the success of that picture, which is probably, however, not absolutely to the life. There is in *Doctor Thorne* and some other works a certain crudity of reference to distinctions of rank—as if people's consciousness of this matter were, on either side, rather inflated. It suggests a general state of tension. It is true that, if Trollope's consciousness had been more flaccid he would perhaps not have given us Lady Lufton and Lady Glencora Palliser. Both of these noble persons are as living as possible, though I see Lady Lufton, with her terror of Lucy Robarts, the best. There is a touch of poetry in the figure of Lady Glencora, but I think there is a weak spot in her history. The actual woman would have made a fool of herself to the end with Burgo Fitzgerald; she would not have discovered the merits of Plantagenet Palliser—or if she had, she would not have cared about them. It is an illustration of the business-like way in which Trollope laid out his work that he always provided a sort of underplot to alternate with his main story—a strain of narrative of which the scene is usually laid in a humbler walk of life. It is to his underplot that he generally relegates his vulgar people, his disagreeable young women; and I have often admired the perseverance with which he recounts these less edifying items. Now and then, it may be said, as in *Ralph the Heir*, the story appears to be all underplot and all vulgar people. These, however, are details. As I have already intimated, it is difficult to specify in Trollope's work, on account of the immense quantity of it; and there is sadness in the thought that this enormous mass does not present itself in a very portable form to posterity.

Trollope did not write for posterity; he wrote for the day, the moment; but these are just the writers whom posterity is apt to put into its pocket. So much of the life of his time is reflected in his novels that we must believe a part of the record will be saved; and the best parts of them are so sound and true and genial, that readers with an eye to that sort of entertainment will always be sure, in a certain proportion, to turn to them. Trollope will remain one of the most trustworthy, though not one of the most eloquent, of the writers who have helped the heart of man to know itself. The heart of man does not always desire this knowledge; it prefers sometimes to look at history in another way—to look at the manifestations without troubling about the motives. There are two kinds of taste in the appreciation of imaginative literature: the taste for emotions of surprise and the taste for emotions of recognition. It is the latter that Trollope gratifies, and he gratifies it the more that the medium of his own mind, through which we see what he shows us, gives a confident direction to our sympathy. His natural rightness and purity are so real that the good things he projects must be real. A race is fortunate when it has a good deal of the sort of imagination—of imaginative feeling— that had fallen to the share of Anthony Trollope; and in this possession our English race is not poor.

1883.

V. ROBERT LOUIS STEVENSON

I

IF there be a writer of our language at the present moment who has the effect of making us regret the extinction of the pleasant fashion of the literary portrait, it is certainly the bright particular genius whose name I have written at the head of these remarks. Mr. Stevenson fairly challenges portraiture, as we pass him on the highway of literature (if that be the road, rather than some wandering, sun-chequered by-lane, that he may be said to follow), just as the possible model, in local attire, challenges the painter who wanders through the streets of a foreign town looking for subjects. He gives us new ground to wonder why the effort to fix a face and figure, to seize a literary character and transfer it to the canvas of the critic, should have fallen into such discredit among us, and have given way, to the mere multiplication of little private judgment-seats, where the scales and the judicial wig, both of them considerable awry, and not rendered more august by the company of a vicious-looking switch, have taken the place, as the symbols of office, of the kindly, disinterested palette and brush. It has become the fashion to be effective at the expense of the sitter, to make some little point, or inflict some little dig, with a heated party air, rather than to catch a talent in the fact, follow its line, and put a finger on its essence: so that the exquisite art of criticism, smothered in grossness, finds itself turned into a question of "sides." The critic industriously keeps his score, but it is seldom to be hoped that the author, criminal though he may be, will be apprehended by justice through the handbills given out in the case; for it is of the essence of a happy description that it shall have been preceded by a happy observation and a free curiosity; and desuetude, as we may say, has overtaken these amiable, uninvidious faculties, which have not the glory of organs and chairs.

We hasten to add that it is not the purpose of these few pages to restore their lustre or to bring back the more penetrating vision of which we lament the disappearance. No individual can bring it back, for the light that we look at things by is, after all, made by all of us. It is sufficient to note, in passing, that if Mr. Stevenson had presented himself in an age, or in a country, of portraiture, the painters would certainly each have had a turn at him. The easels and benches would have bristled, the circle would have been close, and quick, from the canvas to the sitter, the rising and falling of heads. It has happened to all of us to have gone into a studio, a studio of pupils, and seen the thick cluster of bent backs and the conscious model in the midst. It has happened to us to be struck, or not to be struck, with the beauty or the symmetry of this personage, and to have made some remark which, whether expressing admiration or disappointment, has elicited from one of the attentive workers the exclamation, "Character, character is what he has!" These words may be applied to Mr. Robert Louis Stevenson; in the language of that art which depends most on direct observation, character, character is what he has. He is essentially a model, in the sense of a sitter; I do not mean, of course, in the sense of a pattern or a guiding light. And if the figures who have a life in literature may also be divided into two great classes, we may add that he is conspicuously one of the draped: he would never, if I may be allowed the expression, pose for the nude. There are writers who present themselves before the critic with just the amount of drapery that is necessary for decency; but Mr. Stevenson is not one of these—he makes his appearance in an amplitude of costume. His costume is part of the character of which I just now spoke; it never occurs to us to ask how he would look without it. Before all things he is a writer with a style—a model with a complexity of curious and picturesque garments. It is by the cut and the colour of this rich and becoming frippery—I use the term endearingly, as a painter might—that he arrests the eye and solicits the brush.

That is, frankly, half the charm he has for us, that he wears a dress and wears it with courage, with a certain cock of the hat and tinkle of the supererogatory sword; or in other words that he is curious of expression and regards the literary form not simply as a code of signals, but as the key-board of a piano, and as so much plastic material. He has that voice deplored, if we mistake not, by Mr. Herbert Spencer, a manner—a manner for manner's sake it may sometimes doubtless be said. He is as different as possible from the sort of writer who regards words as numbers, and a page as the mere addition of them; much more, to carry out our image, the dictionary stands for him as a wardrobe, and a proposition as a button for his coat. Mr. William Archer, in an article[2] so gracefully and ingeniously turned that the writer may almost be accused of imitating even while he deprecates, speaks of him as a votary of "lightness of touch," at any cost, and remarks that "he is not only philosophically content but deliberately resolved, that his readers shall look first to his manner, and only in the second place to his matter." I shall not attempt to gainsay this; I cite it rather, for the present, because it carries out our own sense. Mr. Stevenson delights in a style, and his own has nothing accidental or diffident; it is eminently conscious of its responsibilities, and meets them with a kind of gallantry—as if language were a pretty woman, and a person who proposes to handle it had of necessity to be something of a Don Juan. This bravery of gesture is a noticeable part of his nature, and it is rather odd that at the same time a striking feature of that nature should be an absence of care for things feminine. His books are for the most part books without women, and it is not women who fall most in love with them. But Mr. Stevenson does not need, as we may say, a petticoat to inflame him: a happy collocation of words will serve the purpose, or a singular image, or the bright eye of a passing conceit, and he will carry off a pretty paradox without so much as a scuffle. The tone of letters is in him—the tone of letters as distinct from that of philosophy, or of those industries whose uses are supposed to be immediate. Many readers, no doubt, consider that he carries it too far; they manifest an impatience for some glimpse of his moral message. They may be heard to ask what it is he proposes to demonstrate, with such a variety of paces and graces.

The main thing that he demonstrates, to our own perception, is that it is a delight to read him, and that he renews this delight by a constant variety of experiment. Of this anon, however; and meanwhile, it may be noted as a curious characteristic of current fashions that the writer whose effort is perceptibly that of the artist is very apt to find himself thrown on the defensive. A work of literature is a form, but the author who betrays a consciousness of the responsibilities involved in this circumstance not rarely perceives himself to be regarded as an uncanny personage. The usual judgment is that he may be artistic, but that he must not be too much so; that way, apparently, lies something worse than madness. This queer superstition has so successfully imposed itself, that the mere fact of having been indifferent to such a danger constitutes in itself an originality. How few they are in number and how soon we could name them, the writers of English prose, at the present moment, the quality of whose prose is personal, expressive, renewed at each attempt! The state of things that one would have expected to be the rule has become the exception, and an exception for which, most of the time, an apology appears to be thought necessary. A mill that grinds with regularity and with a certain commercial fineness—that is the image suggested by the manner of a good many of the fraternity. They turn out an article for which there is a demand, they keep a shop for a speciality, and the business is carried on in accordance with a useful, well-tested prescription. It is just because he has no speciality that Mr. Stevenson is an individual, and because his curiosity is the only receipt by which he produces. Each of his books is an independent effort—a window opened to a different view. *Doctor Jekyll and Mr. Hyde* is as dissimilar as possible from *Treasure Island*; *Virginibus Puerisque* has nothing in common with *The New Arabian Nights*, and I should never have supposed *A Child's Garden of Verses* to be from the hand of the author of *Prince Otto*.

Though Mr. Stevenson cares greatly for his phrase, as every writer should who respects himself and his art, it takes no very attentive reading of his volumes to show that it is not what he cares for most, and that he regards an expressive style only, after all, as a means. It seems to me the fault of Mr. Archer's interesting paper, that it suggests too much that the author of these volumes considers the art of expression as an end—an ingenious game of words. He finds that Mr. Stevenson is not serious, that he neglects a whole side of life, that he has no perception, and no consciousness, of suffering; that he speaks as a happy but heartless pagan, living only in his senses (which the critic admits to be exquisitely fine), and that in a world full of heaviness he is not sufficiently aware of the philosophic limitations of mere technical skill. In sketching these aberrations Mr. Archer himself, by the way, displays anything but ponderosity of hand. He is not the first reader, and he will not be the last, who shall have been irritated by Mr. Stevenson's jauntiness. That jauntiness is an essential part of his genius; but to my sense it ceases to be irritating—it indeed becomes positively touching and constitutes an appeal to sympathy and even to tenderness—when once one has perceived what lies beneath the dancing-tune to which he mostly moves. Much as he cares for his phrase, he cares more for life, and for a certain transcendently lovable part of it. He feels, as it seems to us, and that is not given to every one. This constitutes a philosophy which Mr. Archer fails to read between his lines—the respectable, desirable moral which many a reader doubtless finds that he neglects to point. He does not feel everything equally, by any manner of means; but his feelings are always his reasons. He regards them, whatever they may be, as sufficiently honourable, does not disguise them in other names or colours, and looks at whatever he meets in the brilliant candle-light that they shed. As in his extreme artistic vivacity he seems really disposed to try everything he has tried once, by way of a change, to be inhuman, and there is a hard glitter about *Prince Otto* which seems to indicate that in this case too he has succeeded, as he has done in most of the feats that he has attempted. But *Prince Otto* is even less like his other productions than his other productions are like each other.

The part of life which he cares for most is youth, and the direct expression of the love of youth is the beginning and the end of his message. His appreciation of this delightful period amounts to a passion, and a passion, in the age in which we live, strikes us on the whole as a sufficient philosophy. It ought to satisfy Mr. Archer, and there are writers who press harder than Mr. Stevenson, on whose behalf no such moral motive can be alleged. Mingled with this almost equal love of a literary surface, it represents a real originality. This combination is the keynote of Mr. Stevenson's faculty and the explanation of his perversities. The feeling of one's teens, and even of an earlier period (for the delights of crawling, and almost of the rattle, are embodied in *A Child's Garden of Verses*), and the feeling for happy turns— these, in the last analysis (and his sense of a happy turn is of the subtlest), are the corresponding halves of his character. If *Prince Otto* and *Doctor Jekyll* left me a clearer field for the assertion, I would say that everything he has written is a direct apology for boyhood; or rather (for it must be confessed that Mr. Stevenson's tone is seldom apologetic), a direct rhapsody on the age of heterogeneous pockets. Even members of the very numerous class who have held their breath over *Treasure Island* may shrug their shoulders at this account of the author's religion; but it is none the less a great pleasure—the highest reward of observation—to put one's hand on a rare illustration, and

Mr. Stevenson is certainly rare. What makes him so is the singular maturity of the expression that he has given to young sentiments: he judges them, measures them, sees them from the outside, as well as entertains them. He describes credulity with all the resources of experience, and represents a crude stage with infinite ripeness. In a word, he is an artist accomplished even to sophistication, whose constant theme is the unsophisticated. Sometimes, as in *Kidnapped*, the art is so ripe that it lifts even the subject into the general air: the execution is so serious that the idea (the idea of a boy's romantic adventures), becomes a matter of universal relations. What he prizes most in the boy's ideal is the imaginative side of it, the capacity for successful make-believe. The general freshness in which this is a part of the gloss seems to him the divinest thing in life; considerably more divine, for instance, than the passion usually regarded as the supremely tender one. The idea of making believe appeals to him much more than the idea of making love. That delightful little book of rhymes, the *Child's Garden*, commemorates from beginning to end the picturing, personifying, dramatising faculty of infancy—the view of life from the level of the nursery-fender. The volume is a wonder for the extraordinary vividness with which it reproduces early impressions: a child might have written it if a child could see childhood from the outside, for it would seem that only a child is really near enough to the nursery floor. And what is peculiar to Mr. Stevenson is that it is his own childhood he appears to delight in, and not the personal presence of little darlings. Oddly enough, there is no strong implication that he is fond of babies; he doesn't speak as a parent, or an uncle, or an educator—he speaks as a contemporary absorbed in his own game. That game is almost always a vision of dangers and triumphs, and if emotion, with him, infallibly resolves itself into memory, so memory is an evocation of throbs and thrills and suspense. He has given to the world the romance of boyhood, as others have produced that of the peerage and the police and the medical profession.

This amounts to saying that what he is most curious of in life is heroism—personal gallantry, if need be with a manner, or a banner, though he is also abundantly capable of enjoying it when it is artless. The delightful exploits of Jim Hawkins, in *Treasure Island*, are unaffectedly performed; but none the less "the finest action is the better for a piece of purple," as the author remarks in the paper on "The English Admirals" in *Virginibus Puerisque*, a paper of which the moral is, largely, that "we learn to desire a grand air in our heroes; and such a knowledge of the human stage as shall make them put the dots on their own i's, and leave us in no suspense as to when they mean to be heroic." The love of brave words as well as brave deeds—which is simply Mr. Stevenson's essential love of style—is recorded in this little paper with a charming, slightly sophistical ingenuity. "They served their guns merrily when it came to fighting, and they had the readiest ear for a bold, honourable sentiment of any class of men the world ever produced." The author goes on to say that most men of high destinies have even high-sounding names. Alan Breck, in *Kidnapped*, is a wonderful picture of the union of courage and swagger; the little Jacobite adventurer, a figure worthy of Scott at his best, and representing the highest point that Mr. Stevenson's talent has reached, shows us that a marked taste for tawdry finery—tarnished and tattered, some of it indeed, by ticklish occasions—is quite compatible with a perfectly high mettle. Alan Breck is at bottom a study of the love of glory, carried out with extreme psychological truth. When the love of glory is of an inferior order the reputation is cultivated rather than the opportunity; but when it is a pure passion the opportunity is cultivated for the sake of the reputation. Mr. Stevenson's kindness for adventurers extends even to the humblest of all, the mountebank and the strolling player, or even the pedlar whom he declares that in his foreign travels he is habitually taken for, as we see in the whimsical apology for vagabonds which winds up *An Inland Voyage*. The hungry conjurer, the gymnast whose *maillot* is loose, have something of the glamour of the hero, inasmuch as they too pay with their person. "To be even one of the outskirters of art leaves a fine stamp on a man's countenance.... That is the kind of thing that reconciles me to life: a ragged, tippling, incompetent old rogue, with the manners of a gentleman and the vanity of an artist, to keep up his self-respect!" What reconciles Mr. Stevenson to life is the idea that in the first place it offers the widest field that we know of for odd doings, and that in the second these odd doings are the best of pegs to hang a sketch in three lines or a paradox in three pages.

As it is not odd, but extremely usual, to marry, he deprecates that course in *Virginibus Puerisque*, the collection of short essays which is most a record of his opinions—that is, largely, of his likes and dislikes. It all comes back to his sympathy with the juvenile and that feeling about life which leads him to regard women as so many superfluous girls in a boy's game. They are almost wholly absent from his pages (the main exception is *Prince Otto*, though there is a Clara apiece in *The Rajah's Diamond* and *The Pavilion on the Links*), for they don't like ships and pistols and fights, they encumber the decks and require separate apartments, and, almost worst of all, have not the highest literary standard. Why should a person marry when he might be swinging a cutlass or looking for a buried treasure? Why should he waste at the nuptial altar precious hours in which he might be polishing periods? It is one of those curious and to my sense fascinating inconsistencies that we encounter in Mr. Stevenson's mind, that though he takes such an interest in the childish life he takes no interest in the fireside. He has an indulgent glance for it in the verses of the *Garden*, but to his view the normal child is the child who absents himself from the family-circle, in fact when he can, in imagination when he cannot, in the disguise of a buccaneer. Girls don't do this, and women are only grown-up girls, unless it be the delightful maiden, fit daughter of an imperial race, whom he commemorates in *An Inland Voyage*.

"A girl at school, in France, began to describe one of our regiments on parade to her French schoolmates; and as she went on, she told me, the recollection grew so vivid, she became so proud to be the countrywoman of such soldiers, that her voice failed her and she burst into tears. I have never forgotten that girl; and I think she very nearly deserves a statue. To call her a young lady, with all its niminy associations, would be to offer her an insult. She may rest assured of one thing; although she never should many a heroic general, never see any great or immediate result of her life, she will not have lived in vain for her native land."

There is something of that in Mr. Stevenson; when he begins to describe a British regiment on parade (or something of that sort), he too almost breaks down for emotion: which is why I have been careful to traverse the insinuation that he is primarily a chiseller of prose. If things had gone differently with him (I must permit myself this allusion to his personal situation, and I shall venture to follow it with two or three others), he might have been an historian of famous campaigns—a great painter of battle-pieces. Of course, however, in this capacity it would not have done for him to break down for emotion.

Although he remarks that marriage "is a field of battle and not a bed of roses," he points out repeatedly that it is a terrible renunciation and somehow, in strictness, incompatible even with honour—the sort of roving, trumpeting honour that appeals most to his sympathy. After that step,

"There are no more bye-path meadows where you may innocently linger, but the road lies long and straight and dusty to the grave.... You may think you had a conscience and believed in God; but what is a conscience to a wife?... To marry is to domesticate the Recording Angel. Once you are married, there is nothing left for you, not even suicide, but to be good.... How then, in such an atmosphere of compromise, to keep honour bright and abstain from base capitulations?... The proper qualities of each sex are eternally surprising to the other. Between the Latin and the Teuton races there are similar divergences, not to be bridged by the most liberal sympathy.... It is better to face the fact and know, when you marry, that you take into your life a creature of equal if unlike frailties; whose weak, human heart beats no more tunefully than yours."

If there be a grimness in that it is as near as Mr. Stevenson ever comes to being grim, and we have only to turn the page to find the corrective—something delicately genial, at least, if not very much less sad.

"The blind bow-boy who smiles upon us from the end of terraces in old Dutch gardens laughingly hurls his bird-bolts among a fleeting generation. But for as fast as ever he shoots, the game dissolves and disappears into eternity from under his falling arrows; this one is gone ere he is struck; the other has but time to make one gesture and give one passionate cry; and they are all the things of a moment."

That is an admission that though it is soon over, the great sentimental surrender is inevitable. And there is geniality too, still over the page (in regard to quite another matter), geniality, at least, for the profession of letters, in the declaration that there is

"One thing you can never make Philistine natures understand; one thing which yet lies on the surface, remains as unseizable to their wit as a high flight of metaphysics—namely, that the business of life is mainly carried on by the difficult art of literature, and according to a man's proficiency in that art shall be the freedom and fulness of his intercourse with other men."

Yet it is difficult not to believe that the ideal in which our author's spirit might most gratefully have rested would have been the character of the paterfamilias, when the eye falls on such a charming piece of observation as these lines about children in the admirable paper on *Child's Play*:

"If it were not for this perpetual imitation we should be tempted to fancy they despised us outright, or only considered us in the light of creatures brutally strong and brutally silly, among whom they condescended to dwell in obedience, like a philosopher at a barbarous court."

II

WE know very little about a talent till we know where it grew up, and it would halt terribly at the start, any account of the author of *Kidnapped* which should omit to insist promptly that he is a Scot of the Scots. Two facts, to my perception, go a great way to explain his composition: the first of which is that his boyhood was passed in the shadow of Edinburgh Castle, and the second that he came of a family that had set up great lights on the coast. His grandfather, his uncle, were famous constructors of lighthouses, and the name of the race is associated above all with the beautiful and beneficent tower of Skerryvore. We may exaggerate the way in which, in an imaginative youth, the sense of the "story" of things would feed upon the impressions of Edinburgh—though I suspect it would be difficult really to do so. The streets are so full of history and poetry, of picture and song, of associations springing from strong passions and strange characters, that, for our own part, we find ourselves thinking of an urchin going and coming there as we used to think (wonderingly, enviously), of the small boys who figured as supernumeraries, pages or imps, in showy scenes at the theatre: the place seems the background, the complicated "set" of a drama, and the children the mysterious little beings who are made free of the magic world. How must it not have beckoned on the imagination to pass and repass, on the way to school, under the Castle rock, conscious, acutely yet familiarly, of the gray citadel on the summit, lighted up with the tartans and bagpipes of Highland regiments? Mr. Stevenson's mind, from an early age, was furnished with the concrete Highlander, who must have had much of the effect that we nowadays call decorative. We have encountered somewhere a fanciful paper[3] of our author's, in which there is a reflection of half-holiday afternoons and, unless our own fancy plays us a trick, of lights red, in the winter dusk, in the high-placed windows of the old town—a delightful rhapsody on the penny sheets of figures for the puppet-shows of infancy, in life-like position and awaiting the impatient yet careful scissors. "If landscapes were sold," he says in *Travels with a Donkey*, "like the sheets of characters of my boyhood, one penny plain and twopence coloured, I should go the length of twopence every day of my life."

Indeed the colour of Scotland has entered into him altogether, and though, oddly enough, he has written but little about his native country, his happiest work shows, I think, that she has the best of his ability, the best of his ambition. *Kidnapped* (whose inadequate title I may deplore in passing) breathes in every line the feeling of moor and loch, and is the finest of his longer stories, and *Thrawn Janet*, a masterpiece in thirteen pages (lately republished in the volume of *The Merry Men*), is, among the shorter, the strongest in execution. The latter consists of a gruesome anecdote of the supernatural, related in the Scotch dialect, and the genuineness which this medium (at the sight of which, in general, the face of the reader grows long) wears in Mr. Stevenson's hands is a proof of how living the question of form always is to him, and what a variety of answers he has for it. It would never have occurred to us that the style of *Travels with a Donkey* or *Virginibus Puerisque* and the idiom of the parish of Balweary could be a conception of the same mind. If it be a good fortune for a genius to have had such a country as Scotland for its primary stuff, this is doubly the case when there has been a certain process of detachment, of extreme secularisation. Mr. Stevenson has been emancipated: he is, as we may say, a Scotchman of the world. None other, I think, could have drawn with such a mixture of sympathetic and ironical observation the character of the canny young Lowlander, David

Balfour, a good boy but an exasperating. *Treasure Island, The New Arabian Nights, Prince Otto, Doctor Jekyll and Mr. Hyde*, are not very directly founded on observation; but that quality comes in with extreme fineness as soon as the subject involves consideration of race.

I have been wondering whether there is something more than this that our author's pages would tell us about him, or whether that particular something is in the mind of an admirer because he happens to have had other lights on it. It has been possible for so acute a critic as Mr. William Archer to read pure high spirits and the gospel of the young man rejoicing in his strength and his matutinal cold bath between the lines of Mr. Stevenson's prose. And it is a fact that the note of a morbid sensibility is so absent from his pages, they contain so little reference to infirmity and suffering, that we feel a trick has really been played upon us on discovering by accident the actual state of the case with the writer who has indulged in the most enthusiastic allusion to the joy of existence. We must permit ourselves another mention of his personal situation, for it adds immensely to the interest of volumes through which there draws so strong a current of life, to know that they are not only the work of an invalid, but that they have largely been written in bed, in dreary "health-resorts," in the intervals of sharp attacks. There is almost nothing in them to lead us to guess this: the direct evidence indeed is almost all contained in the limited compass of *The Silverado Squatters*. In such a case, however, it is the indirect that is the most eloquent, and I know not where to look for that, unless in the paper called "Ordered South," and its companion "Aes Triplex," in *Virginibus Puerisque*. It is impossible to read "Ordered South" attentively without feeling that it is personal: the reflections it contains are from experience, not from fancy. The places and climates to which the invalid is carried to recover or to die are mainly beautiful, but

"In his heart of hearts he has to confess that [they are] not beautiful for him.... He is like an enthusiast leading about with him a stolid, indifferent tourist. There is some one by who is out of sympathy with the scene, and is not moved up to the measure of the occasion; and that some one is himself.... He seems to himself to touch things with muffled hands and to see them through a veil.... Many a white town that sits far out on the promontory, many a comely fold of wood on the mountain side, beckons and allures his imagination day after day, and is yet as inaccessible to his feet as the clefts and gorges of the clouds. The sense of distance grows upon him wonderfully; and after some feverish efforts and the fretful uneasiness of the first few days he falls contentedly in with the restrictions of his weakness.... He feels, if he is to be thus tenderly weaned from the passion of life, thus gradually inducted into the slumber of death, that when at last the end comes it will come quietly and fitly.... He will pray for Medea: when she comes let her either rejuvenate or slay."

The second of the short essays I have mentioned has a taste of mortality only because the purpose of it is to insist that the only sane behaviour is to leave death and the accidents that lead to it out of our calculations. Life "is a honeymoon with us all through, and none of the longest. Small blame to us if we give our whole hearts to this glowing bride of ours." The person who does so "makes a very different acquaintance with the world, keeps all his pulses going true and fast, and gathers impetus as he runs, until if he be running towards anything better than wildfire, he may shoot up and become a constellation in the end." Nothing can be more deplorable than to "forego all the issues of living in a parlour with a regulated temperature." Mr. Stevenson adds that as for those whom the gods love dying young, a man dies too young at whatever age he parts with life. The testimony of "Aes Triplex" to the author's own disabilities is after all very indirect. It consists mainly in the general protest not so much against the fact of extinction as against the theory of it. The reader only asks himself why the hero of *Travels with a Donkey*, the historian of Alan Breck, should think of these things. His appreciation of the active side of life has such a note of its own that we are surprised to find that it proceeds in a considerable measure from an intimate acquaintance with the passive. It seems too anomalous that the writer who has most cherished the idea of a certain free exposure should also be the one who has been reduced most to looking for it within, and that the figures of adventurers who, at least in our literature of to-day, are the most vivid, should be the most vicarious. The truth is, of course, that as the *Travels with a Donkey* and *An Inland Voyage* abundantly show, the author has a fund of reminiscences. He did not spend his younger years "in a parlour with a regulated temperature." A reader who happens to be aware of how much it has been his later fate to do so may be excused for finding an added source of interest—something indeed deeply and constantly touching—in this association of peculiarly restrictive conditions with the vision of high spirits and romantic accidents, of a kind of honourably picaresque career. Mr. Stevenson is, however, distinctly, in spite of his occasional practice of the gruesome, a frank optimist—an observer who not only loves life but does not shrink from the responsibility of recommending it. There is a systematic brightness in him which testifies to this and which is after all but one of the innumerable ingenuities of patience. What is remarkable in his case is that his productions should constitute an exquisite expression, a sort of whimsical gospel of enjoyment. The only difference between *An Inland Voyage* or *Travels with a Donkey* and *The New Arabian Nights* or *Treasure Island* or *Kidnapped*, is that in the later books the enjoyment is reflective (though it simulates spontaneity with singular art), whereas in the first two it is natural and, as it were, historical.

These little histories—the first volumes, if I mistake not, that introduced Mr. Stevenson to lovers of good writing—abound in charming illustrations of his disposition to look at the world as a not exactly refined but glorified, pacified Bohemia. They narrate the quest of personal adventure, on one occasion in a canoe on the Sambre and the Oise and on another at a donkey's tail over the hills and valleys of the Cévennes. I well remember that when I read them in their novelty, upwards of ten years ago, I seemed to see the author, unknown as yet to fame, jump before my eyes into a style. His steps in literature presumably had not been many; yet he had mastered his form—it had in these cases perhaps more substance than his matter—and a singular air of literary experience. It partly, though not completely, explains the phenomenon, that he had already been able to write the exquisite little story of *Will of the Mill*, published previously to *An Inland Voyage*, and republished to-day in the volume of *The Merry Men*, for in *Will of the Mill* there is something exceedingly rare, poetical and unexpected, with that most fascinating quality a work of imagination can have—a dash of alternative mystery as to its meaning, an air (the air of life itself), of half inviting, half defying you to interpret. This brief but finished composition stood in the same relation to the usual "magazine story" that a glass of Johannisberg occupies to a draught of table d'hôte *vin ordinaire*.

"One evening he asked the miller where the river went.... 'It goes out into the lowlands, and waters the great corn country, and runs through a sight of fine cities (so they say) where kings live all alone in great palaces, with a sentry walking up and down before the door. And it goes under bridges, with stone men upon them, looking down and smiling so curious at the water, and living folks leaning on their elbows on the wall and looking over too. And then it goes on and on, and down through marshes and sands, until at last it falls into the sea, where the ships are that bring tobacco and parrots from the Indies.'"

It is impossible not to open one's eyes at such a paragraph as that, especially if one has taken a common texture for granted. Will of the Mill spends his life in the valley through which the river runs, and through which, year after year, post-chaises and waggons and pedestrians, and once an army, "horse and foot, cannon and tumbrel, drum and standard," take their way, in spite of the dreams he once had of seeing the mysterious world, and it is not till death comes that he goes on his travels. He ends by keeping an inn, where he converses with many more initiated spirits; and though he is an amiable man he dies a bachelor, having broken off with more plainness than he would have used had he been less untravelled (of course he remains sadly provincial), his engagement to the parson's daughter. The story is in the happiest key and suggests all kinds of things: but what does it in particular represent? The advantage of waiting, perhaps—the valuable truth that, one by one, we tide over our impatiences. There are sagacious people who hold that if one does not answer a letter it ends by answering itself. So the sub-title of Mr. Stevenson's tale might be "The Beauty of Procrastination." If you do not indulge your curiosities your slackness itself makes at last a kind of rich element, and it comes to very much the same thing in the end. When it came to the point poor Will had not even the curiosity to marry; and the author leaves us in stimulating doubt as to whether he judges him too selfish or only too philosophic.

I find myself speaking of Mr. Stevenson's last volume (at the moment I write), before I have spoken, in any detail, of its predecessors: which I must let pass as a sign that I lack space for a full enumeration. I may mention two more of his productions as completing the list of those that have a personal reference. *The Silverado Squatters* describes a picnicking episode, undertaken on grounds of health, on a mountain-top in California; but this free sketch, which contains a hundred humorous touches, and in the figure of Irvine Lovelands one of Mr. Stevenson's most veracious portraits, is perhaps less vivid, as it is certainly less painful, than those other pages in which, some years ago, he commemorated the twelvemonth he spent in America—the history of a journey from New York to San Francisco in an emigrant train, performed as a sequel to a voyage across the Atlantic in the same severe conditions. He has never made his points better than in this half-humorous, half-tragical recital, nor given a more striking instance of his talent for reproducing the feeling of queer situations and contacts. It is much to be regretted that this little masterpiece had not been brought to light a second time, as also that he has not given the world (as I believe he came very near doing), his observations in the steerage of an Atlantic liner. If, as I say, our author has a taste for the impressions of Bohemia, he has been very consistent, and has not shrunk from going far afield in search of them. And as I have already been indiscreet, I may add that if it has been his fate to be converted in fact from the sardonic view of matrimony, this occurred under an influence which should have the particular sympathy of American readers. He went to California for his wife, and Mrs. Stevenson, as appears moreover by the title-page of his work, has had a hand—evidently a light and practised one—in *The Dynamiter*, the second series, characterised by a rich extravagance, of *The New Arabian Nights*. *The Silverado Squatters* is the history of a honeymoon, prosperous it would seem, putting Irvine Lovelands aside, save for the death of dog Chuchu "in his teens, after a life so shadowed and troubled, continually shaken with alarm and with the tear of elegant sentiment permanently in his eye."

Mr. Stevenson has a theory of composition in regard to the novel on which he is to be congratulated, as any positive and genuine conviction of this kind is vivifying so long as it is not narrow. The breath of the novelist's being is his liberty, and the incomparable virtue of the form he uses is that it lends itself to views innumerable and diverse, to every variety of illustration. There is certainly no other mould of so large a capacity. The doctrine of M. Zola himself, so jejune if literally taken, is fruitful, inasmuch as in practice he romantically departs from it. Mr. Stevenson does not need to depart, his individual taste being as much to pursue the romantic as his principle is to defend it. Fortunately, in England to-day, it is not much attacked. The triumphs that are to be won in the portrayal of the strange, the improbable, the heroic, especially as these things shine from afar in the credulous eye of youth, are his strongest, most constant incentive. On one happy occasion, in relating the history of *Doctor Jekyll*, he has seen them as they present themselves to a maturer vision. *Doctor Jekyll* is not a "boy's book," nor yet is *Prince Otto*; the latter, however, is not, like the former, an experiment in mystification—it is, I think, more than anything else, an experiment in style, conceived one summer's day when the author had given the reins to his high appreciation of Mr. George Meredith. It is perhaps the most literary of his works, but it is not the most natural. It is one of those coquetries, as we may call them for want of a better word, which may be observed in Mr. Stevenson's activity—a kind of artful inconsequence. It is easy to believe that if his strength permitted him to be a more abundant writer he would still more frequently play this eminently literary trick—that of dodging off in a new direction—upon those who might have fancied they knew all about him. I made the reflection, in speaking of *Will of the Mill*, that there is a kind of anticipatory malice in the subject of that fine story: as if the writer had intended to say to his reader "You will never guess, from the unction with which I describe the life of a man who never stirred five miles from home, that I am destined to make my greatest hits in treating of the rovers of the deep." Even here, however, the author's characteristic irony would have come in; for—the rare chances of life being what he most keeps his eye on—the uncommon belongs as much to the way the inquiring Will sticks to his door-sill as to the incident, say, of John Silver and his men, when they are dragging Jim Hawkins to his doom, hearing in the still woods of Treasure Island the strange hoot of the maroon.

The novelist who leaves the extraordinary out of his account is liable to awkward confrontations, as we are compelled to reflect in this age of newspapers and of universal publicity. The next report of the next divorce case (to give an instance) shall offer us a picture of astounding combinations of circumstance and behaviour, and the annals of any energetic race are rich in curious anecdote and startling example. That interesting compilation *Vicissitudes of Families* is but a superficial record of strange accidents: the family (taken of course in the long piece), is as a general thing a catalogue of odd specimens and tangled situations, and we must remember that the most singular products are those which are not exhibited. Mr. Stevenson leaves so wide a margin for the wonderful—it impinges with easy assurance upon the text—that he escapes the danger of being brought up by cases he has not allowed for. When he allows for Mr. Hyde he allows for everything, and one feels moreover that even if he did not wave so gallantly the flag of the imaginative and contend that the improbable is what has most character, he would still insist that we ought to make believe. He would say we ought to make believe that the extraordinary is the best part of life even if it were not, and to do so because the finest feelings—suspense, daring, decision, passion, curiosity, gallantry, eloquence, friendship—are involved in it, and it is of infinite importance that the tradition of these precious things should not perish. He would prefer, in a word, any day in the week, Alexandre Dumas to Honoré de Balzac, and it is indeed my impression that he prefers the author of *The Three Musketeers* to any novelist except Mr. George Meredith. I should go so far as to suspect that his ideal of the delightful work of fiction would be the adventures of Monte Cristo related by the author of *Richard Feverel*. There is some magnanimity in his esteem for Alexandre Dumas, inasmuch as in *Kidnapped* he has put into a fable worthy of that inventor a closeness of notation with which Dumas never had anything to do. He makes us say, Let the tradition live, by all means, since it was delightful; but at the same time he is the cause of our perceiving afresh that a tradition is kept alive only by something being added to it. In this particular case—in *Doctor Jekyll* and *Kidnapped*—Mr. Stevenson has added psychology.

The New Arabian Nights offer us, as the title indicates, the wonderful in the frankest, most delectable form. Partly extravagant and partly very specious, they are the result of a very happy idea, that of placing a series of adventures which are pure adventures in the setting of contemporary English life, and relating them in the placidly ingenuous tone of Scheherezade. This device is carried to perfection in *The Dynamiter*, where the manner takes on more of a kind of high-flown serenity in proportion as the incidents are more "steep." In this line *The Suicide Club* is Mr. Stevenson's greatest success, and the first two pages of it, not to mention others, live in the memory. For reasons which I am conscious of not being able to represent as sufficient, I find something ineffaceably impressive—something really haunting—in the incident of Prince Florizel and Colonel Geraldine, who, one evening in March, are "driven by a sharp fall of sleet into an Oyster Bar in the immediate neighbourhood of Leicester Square," and there have occasion to observe the entrance of a young man followed by a couple of commissionaires, each of whom carries a large dish of cream tarts under a cover—a young man who "pressed these confections on every one's acceptance with exaggerated courtesy." There is no effort at a picture here, but the imagination makes one of the lighted interior, the London sleet outside, the company that we guess, given the locality, and the strange politeness of the young man, leading on to circumstances stranger still. This is what may be called putting one in the mood for a story. But Mr. Stevenson's most brilliant stroke of that kind is the opening episode of *Treasure Island*, the arrival of the brown old seaman with the sabre-cut at the "Admiral Benbow," and the advent, not long after, of the blind sailor, with a green shade over his eyes, who comes tapping down the road, in quest of him, with his stick. *Treasure Island* is a "boy's book" in the sense that it embodies a boy's vision of the extraordinary, but it is unique in this, and calculated to fascinate the weary mind of experience, that what we see in it is not only the ideal fable but, as part and parcel of that, as it were, the young reader himself and his state of mind: we seem to read it over his shoulder, with an arm around his neck. It is all as perfect as a well-played boy's game, and nothing can exceed the spirit and skill, the humour and the open-air feeling with which the thing is kept at the palpitating pitch. It is not only a record of queer chances, but a study of young feelings: there is a moral side in it, and the figures are not puppets with vague faces. If Jim Hawkins illustrates successful daring, he does so with a delightful rosy good-boyishness and a conscious, modest liability to error. His luck is tremendous, but it does not make him proud, and his manner is refreshingly provincial and human. So is that, even more, of the admirable John Silver, one of the most picturesque and indeed in every way most genially presented villains in the whole literature of romance. He has a singularly distinct and expressive countenance, which of course turns out to be a grimacing mask. Never was a mask more knowingly, vividly painted. *Treasure Island* will surely become—it must already have become and will remain—in its way a classic: thanks to this indescribable mixture of the prodigious and the human, of surprising coincidences and familiar feelings. The language in which Mr. Stevenson has chosen to tell his story is an admirable vehicle for these feelings: with its humorous braveries and quaintnesses, its echoes of old ballads and yarns, it touches all kinds of sympathetic chords.

Is *Doctor Jekyll and Mr. Hyde* a work of high philosophic intention, or simply the most ingenious and irresponsible of fictions? It has the stamp of a really imaginative production, that we may take it in different ways; but I suppose it would generally be called the most serious of the author's tales. It deals with the relation of the baser parts of man to his nobler, of the capacity for evil that exists in the most generous natures; and it expresses these things in a fable which is a wonderfully happy invention. The subject is endlessly interesting, and rich in all sorts of provocation, and Mr. Stevenson is to be congratulated on having touched the core of it. I may do him injustice, but it is, however, here, not the profundity of the idea which strikes me so much as the art of the presentation—the extremely successful form. There is a genuine feeling for the perpetual moral question, a fresh sense of the difficulty of being good and the brutishness of being bad; but what there is above all is a singular ability in holding the interest. I confess that that, to my sense, is the most edifying thing in the short, rapid, concentrated story, which is really a masterpiece of concision. There is something almost impertinent in the way, as I have noticed, in which Mr. Stevenson achieves his best effects without the aid of the ladies, and *Doctor Jekyll* is a capital example of his heartless independence. It is usually supposed that a truly poignant impression cannot be made without them, but in the drama of Mr. Hyde's fatal ascendency they remain altogether in the wing. It is very obvious—I do not say it cynically—that they must have played an important part in his development. The gruesome tone of the tale is, no doubt, deepened by their absence: it is like the late afternoon light of a foggy winter Sunday, when even inanimate objects have a kind of wicked look. I remember few situations in the pages of mystifying fiction more to the purpose than the episode of Mr. Utterson's going to Doctor Jekyll's to confer with the butler when the Doctor is locked up in his laboratory, and the old servant, whose sagacity has hitherto encountered successfully the problems of the sideboard and the pantry, confesses that this time he is utterly baffled. The way the two men, at the door of the laboratory, discuss the identity of the mysterious personage inside, who has revealed himself in two or three inhuman glimpses to Poole, has those touches of which irresistible shudders are made. The butler's theory is that his master has been murdered, and that the murderer is in the room, personating him with a sort of clumsy diabolism. "Well, when that masked thing like a monkey jumped from among the chemicals and whipped into the cabinet, it went down my spine like ice." That is the effect upon the reader of most of the story. I say of most rather than of all, because the ice rather melts in the sequel, and I have some difficulty in accepting the business of the powders, which seems to me too explicit and explanatory. The powders constitute the machinery of the transformation, and it will probably have struck many readers that this uncanny process would be more conceivable (so far as one may speak of the conceivable in such a case), if the author had not made it so definite.

I have left Mr. Stevenson's best book to the last, as it is also the last he has given (at the present speaking) to the public—the tales comprising *The Merry Men* having already appeared; but I find that on the way I have anticipated some of the remarks that I had intended to make about it. That which is most to the point is that there are parts of it so fine as to suggest that the author's talent has taken a fresh start, various as have been the impulses in which it had already indulged, and serious the hindrances among which it is condemned to exert itself. There would have been a kind of perverse humility in his keeping up the fiction that a production so literary as *Kidnapped* is addressed to immature minds, and, though it was originally given to the world, I believe, in a "boy's paper," the story embraces every occasion that it meets to satisfy the higher criticism. It has two weak spots, which need simply to be mentioned. The cruel and miserly uncle, in the first chapters, is rather in the tone of superseded tradition, and the tricks he plays upon his

114

ingenuous nephew are a little like those of country conjurers. In these pages we feel that Mr. Stevenson is thinking too much of what a "boy's paper" is expected to contain. Then the history stops without ending, as it were; but I think I may add that this accident speaks for itself. Mr. Stevenson has often to lay down his pen for reasons that have nothing to do with the failure of inspiration, and the last page of David Balfour's adventures is an honourable plea for indulgence. The remaining five-sixths of the book deserve to stand by *Henry Esmond* as a fictive autobiography in archaic form. The author's sense of the English idiom of the last century, and still more of the Scotch, has enabled him to give a gallant companion to Thackeray's *tour de force*. The life, the humour, the colour of the central portions of *Kidnapped* have a singular pictorial virtue: these passages read like a series of inspired footnotes on some historic page. The charm of the most romantic episode in the world, though perhaps it would be hard to say why it is the most romantic, when it was associated with so much stupidity, is over the whole business, and the forlorn hope of the Stuarts is revived for us without evoking satiety. There could be no better instance of the author's talent for seeing the familiar in the heroic, and reducing the extravagant to plausible detail, than the description of Alan Breck's defence in the cabin of the ship and the really magnificent chapters of "The Flight in the Heather." Mr. Stevenson has in a high degree (and doubtless for good reasons of his own) what may be called the imagination of physical states, and this has enabled him to arrive at a wonderfully exact translation of the miseries of his panting Lowland hero, dragged for days and nights over hill and dale, through bog and thicket, without meat or drink or rest, at the tail of an Homeric Highlander. The great superiority of the book resides to my mind, however, in the fact that it puts two characters on their feet with admirable rectitude. I have paid my tribute to Alan Breck, and I can only repeat that he is a masterpiece. It is interesting to observe that though the man is extravagant, the author's touch exaggerates nothing: it is throughout of the most truthful, genial, ironical kind; full of penetration, but with none of the grossness of moralising satire. The figure is a genuine study, and nothing can be more charming than the way Mr. Stevenson both sees through it and admires it. Shall I say that he sees through David Balfour? This would be perhaps to under-estimate the density of that medium. Beautiful, at any rate,

115

is the expression which this unfortunate though circumspect youth gives to those qualities which combine to excite our respect and our objurgation in the Scottish character. Such a scene as the episode of the quarrel of the two men on the mountain-side is a real stroke of genius, and has the very logic and rhythm of life; a quarrel which we feel to be inevitable, though it is about nothing, or almost nothing, and which springs from exasperated nerves and the simple shock of temperaments. The author's vision of it has a profundity which goes deeper, I think, than *Doctor Jekyll*. I know of few better examples of the way genius has ever a surprise in its pocket—keeps an ace, as it were, up its sleeve. And in this case it endears itself to us by making us reflect that such a passage as the one I speak of is in fact a signal proof of what the novel can do at its best, and what nothing else can do so well. In the presence of this sort of success we perceive its immense value. It is capable of a rare transparency—it can illustrate human affairs in cases so delicate and complicated that any other vehicle would be clumsy. To those who love the art that Mr. Stevenson practises he will appear, in pointing this incidental moral, not only to have won a particular triumph, but to have given a delightful pledge.

1887.

VI. MISS WOOLSON

FLOODED as we have been in these latter days with copious discussion as to the admission of women to various offices, colleges, functions, and privileges, singularly little attention has been paid, by themselves at least, to the fact that in one highly important department of human affairs their cause is already gained—gained in such a way as to deprive them largely of their ground, formerly so substantial, for complaining of the intolerance of man. In America, in England, to-day, it is no longer a question of their admission into the world of literature: they are there in force; they have been admitted, with all the honours, on a perfectly equal footing. In America, at least, one feels tempted at moments to exclaim that they are in themselves the world of literature. In Germany and in France, in this line of production, their presence is less to be perceived. To speak only of the latter country, France has brought forth in the persons of Madame de Sévigné, Madame de Staël, and Madame Sand, three female writers of the first rank, without counting a hundred ladies to whom we owe charming memoirs and volumes of reminiscence; but in the table of contents of the *Revue des Deux Mondes*, that epitome of the literary movement (as regards everything, at least, but the famous doctrine, in fiction, of "naturalism"), it is rare to encounter the name of a female contributor. The covers of American and English periodicals tell a different story; in these monthly joints of the ladder of fame the ladies stand as thick as on the staircase at a crowded evening party.

There are, of course, two points of view from which this free possession of the public ear may be considered—as regards its effect upon the life of women, and as regards its effect upon literature. I hasten to add that I do not propose to consider either, and I touch on the general fact simply because the writer whose name I have placed at the head of these remarks happens to be a striking illustration of it. The work of Miss Constance Fenimore Woolson is an excellent example of the way the door stands open between the personal life of American women and the immeasurable world of print, and what makes it so is the particular quality that this work happens to possess. It breathes a spirit singularly and essentially conservative—the sort of spirit which, but for a special indication pointing the other way, would in advance seem most to oppose itself to the introduction into the feminine lot of new and complicating elements. Miss Woolson evidently thinks that lot sufficiently complicated, with the sensibilities which even in primitive ages women were acknowledged to possess; fenced in by the old disabilities and prejudices, they seem to her to have been by their very nature only too much exposed, and it would never occur to her to lend her voice to the plea for further exposure—for a revolution which should place her sex in the thick of the struggle for power. She sees it in preference surrounded certainly by plenty of doors and windows (she has not, I take it, a love of bolts and Oriental shutters), but distinctly on the private side of that somewhat evasive and exceedingly shifting line which divides human affairs into the profane and the sacred. Such is the turn of mind of the author of *Rodman the Keeper* and *East Angels*, and if it has not prevented her from writing books, from competing for the literary laurel, this is a proof of the strength of the current which to-day carries both sexes alike to that mode of expression.

Miss Woolson's first productions were two collections of short tales, published in 1875 and 1880, and entitled respectively *Castle Nowhere* and *Rodman the Keeper*. I may not profess an acquaintance with the former of these volumes, but the latter is full of interesting artistic work. Miss Woolson has done nothing better than the best pages in this succession of careful, strenuous studies of certain aspects of life, after the war, in Florida, Georgia and the Carolinas. As the fruit of a remarkable minuteness of observation and tenderness of feeling on the part of one who evidently did not glance and pass, but lingered and analysed, they have a high value, especially when regarded in the light of the *voicelessness* of the conquered and reconstructed South. Miss Woolson strikes the reader as having a compassionate sense of this pathetic dumbness—having perceived that no social revolution of equal magnitude had ever reflected itself so little in literature, remained so unrecorded, so unpainted and unsung. She has attempted to give an impression of this circumstance, among others, and a sympathy altogether feminine has guided her pen. She loves the whole region, and no daughter of the land could have handled its peculiarities more indulgently, or communicated to us more of the sense of close observation and intimate knowledge. Nevertheless it must be confessed that the picture, on the whole, is a picture of dreariness—of impressions that may have been gathered in the course of lonely afternoon walks at the end of hot days, when the sunset was wan, on the edge of rice-fields, dismal swamps, and other brackish inlets. The author is to be congratulated in so far as such expeditions may have been the source of her singularly exact familiarity with the "natural objects" of the region, including the negro of reality. She knows every plant and flower, every vague odour and sound, the song and flight of every bird, every tint of the sky and murmur of the forest, and she has noted scientifically the dialect of the freedmen. It is not too much to say that the negroes in *Rodman the Keeper* and in *East Angels* are a careful philological study, and that if Miss Woolson preceded Uncle Remus by a considerable interval, she may have the credit of the initiative—of having been the first to take their words straight from their lips.

No doubt that if in *East Angels*, as well as in the volume of tales, the sadness of Miss Woolson's South is more striking than its high spirits, this is owing somewhat to the author's taste in the way of subject and situation, and especially to her predilection for cases of heroic sacrifice—sacrifice sometimes unsuspected and always unappreciated. She is fond of irretrievable personal failures, of people who have had to give up even the memory of happiness, who love and suffer in silence, and minister in secret to the happiness of those who look over their heads. She is interested in general in secret histories, in the "inner life" of the weak, the superfluous, the disappointed, the bereaved, the unmarried. She believes in personal renunciation, in its frequency as well as its beauty. It plays a prominent part in each of her novels, especially in the last two, and the interest of *East Angels* at least is largely owing to her success in having made an extreme case of the virtue in question credible to the reader. Is it because this element is weaker in *Anne*, which was published in 1882, that *Anne* strikes me as the least happily composed of the author's works? The early chapters are charming and full of promise, but the story wanders away from them, and the pledge is not taken up. The reader has built great hopes upon Tita, but Tita vanishes into the vague, after putting him out of countenance by an infant marriage—an accident in regard to which, on the whole, throughout her stories, Miss Woolson shows perhaps an excessive indulgence. She likes the unmarried, as I have mentioned, but she likes marriages even better, and also sometimes hurries them forward in advance of the reader's exaction. The only complaint it would occur to me to make of *East Angels* is that Garda Thorne, whom we cannot think of as anything but a little girl, discounts the projects we have formed for her by marrying twice; and somehow the case is not bettered by the fact that nothing is more natural than that she should marry twice, unless it be that she should marry three times. We have perceived her, after all, from the first, to be peculiarly adapted to a succession of pretty widowhoods.

For the Major has an idea, a little fantastic perhaps, but eminently definite. This idea is the secret effort of an elderly woman to appear really as young to her husband as (owing to peculiar circumstances) he believed her to be when he married her. Nature helps her (she happens to preserve, late in life, the look of comparative youth), and art helps nature, and her husband's illusions, fostered by failing health and a weakened brain, help them both, so that she is able to keep on the mask till his death, when she pulls it off with a passionate cry of relief—ventures at last, gives herself the luxury, to be old. The sacrifice in this case has been the sacrifice of the maternal instinct, she having had a son, now a man grown, by a former marriage, who reappears after unsuccessful wanderings in far lands, and whom she may not permit herself openly to recognise. The sacrificial attitude is indeed repeated on the part of her step-daughter, who, being at last taken into Madam Carroll's confidence, suffers the young man—a shabby, compromising, inglorious acquaintance—to pass for her lover, thereby discrediting herself almost fatally (till the situation is straightened out), with the Rev. Frederick Owen, who has really been marked out by Providence for the character, and who cannot explain on any comfortable hypothesis her relations with the mysterious Bohemian. Miss Woolson's women in general are capable of these refinements of devotion and exaltations of conscience, and she has a singular talent for making our sympathies go with them. The conception of Madam Carroll is highly ingenious and original, and the small stippled portrait has a real fascination. It is the first time that a woman has been represented as painting her face, dyeing her hair, and "dressing young," out of tenderness for another:

the effort usually has its source in tenderness for herself. But Miss Woolson has done nothing of a neater execution than this fanciful figure of the little ringleted, white-frocked, falsely juvenile lady, who has the toilet-table of an actress and the conscience of a Puritan.

The author likes a glamour, and by minute touches and gentle, conciliatory arts, she usually succeeds in producing a valid one. If I had more space I should like to count over these cumulative strokes, in which a delicate manipulation of the real is mingled with an occasionally frank appeal to the romantic muse. But I can only mention two of the most obvious: one the frequency of her reference to the episcopal church as an institution giving a tone to American life (the sort of tone which it is usually assumed that we must seek in civilisations more permeated with ecclesiasticism); the other her fondness for family histories—for the idea of perpetuation of race, especially in the backward direction. I hasten to add that there is nothing of the crudity of sectarianism in the former of these manifestations, or of the dreariness of the purely genealogical passion in the latter; but none the less is it clear that Miss Woolson likes little country churches that are dedicated to saints not vulgarised by too much notoriety, that are dressed with greenery (and would be with holly if there were any), at Christmas and Easter; that have "rectors," well connected, who are properly garmented, and organists, slightly deformed if possible, and addicted to playing Gregorian chants in the twilight, who are adequately artistic; likes also generations that have a pleasant consciousness of a few warm generations behind them, screening them in from too bleak a past, from vulgar draughts in the rear. I know not whether for the most part we are either so Anglican or so long-descended as in Miss Woolson's pages we strike ourselves as being, but it is certain that as we read we protest but little against the soft impeachment. She represents us at least as we should like to be, and she does so with such discretion and taste that we have no fear of incurring ridicule by assent. She has a high sense of the picturesque; she cannot get on without a social atmosphere. Once, I think, she has looked for these things in the wrong place—at the country boarding-house denominated Caryl's, in *Anne*, where there must have been flies and grease in the dining-room, and the ladies must have been overdressed; but as a general thing her quest is remarkably happy. She stays at home, and yet gives us a sense of being "abroad"; she has a remarkable faculty of making the new world seem ancient. She succeeds in representing Far Edgerly, the mountain village in *For the Major*, as bathed in the precious medium I speak of. Where is it meant to be, and where was the place that gave her the pattern of it? We gather vaguely, though there are no negroes, that it is in the south; but this, after all, is a tolerably indefinite part of the United States. It is somewhere in the midst of forests, and yet it has as many idiosyncrasies as Mrs. Gaskell's *Cranford*, with added possibilities of the pathetic and the tragic. What new town is so composite? What composite town is so new? Miss Woolson anticipates these questions; that is she prevents us from asking them: we swallow Far Edgerly whole, or say at most, with a sigh, that if it couldn't have been like that it certainly ought to have been.

It is, however, in *East Angels* that she has been most successful in this feat of evoking a local tone, and this is a part of the general superiority of that very interesting work, which to my mind represents a long stride of her talent, and has more than the value of all else she has done. In *East Angels* the attempt to create an atmosphere has had, to a considerable degree, the benefit of the actual quality of things in the warm, rank peninsula which she has studied so exhaustively and loves so well. Miss Woolson found a tone in the air of Florida, but it is not too much to say that she has left it still more agreeably rich— converted it into a fine golden haze. Wonderful is the tact with which she has pressed it into the service of her story, draped the bare spots of the scene with it, and hung it there half as a curtain and half as a background. *East Angels* is a performance which does Miss Woolson the highest honour, and if her talent is capable, in another novel, of making an advance equal to that represented by this work in relation to its predecessors, she will have made a substantial contribution to our new literature of fiction. Long, comprehensive, copious, still more elaborate than her other elaborations, *East Angels* presents the interest of a large and well-founded scheme. The result is not flawless at every point, but the undertaking is of a fine, high kind, and, for the most part, the effect produced is thoroughly worthy of it. The author has, in other words, proposed to give us the complete natural history, as it were, of a group of persons collected, in a complicated relationship, in a little winter-city on a southern shore, and she has expended on her subject stores of just observation and an infinite deal of the true historical spirit. How much of this spirit and of artistic feeling there is in the book, only an attentive perusal will reveal. The central situation is a very interesting one, and is triumphantly treated, but I confess that what is most substantial to me in the book is the writer's general conception of her task, her general attitude of watching life, waiting upon it and trying to catch it in the fact. I know not what theories she may hold in relation to all this business, to what camp or league she may belong; my impression indeed would be that she is perfectly free—that she considers that though camps and leagues may be useful organisations for looking for the truth, it is not in their own bosom that it is usually to be found. However this may be, it is striking that, artistically, she has had a fruitful instinct in seeing the novel as a picture of the actual, of the characteristic—a study of human types and passions, of the evolution of personal relations. In *East Angels* she has gone much farther in this direction than in either of her other novels.

The book has, to my sense, two defects, which I may as well mention at once—two which are perhaps, however, but different faces of the same. One is that the group on which she has bent her lens strikes us as too detached, too isolated, too much on a desert island. Its different members go to and fro a good deal, to New York and to Europe, but they have a certain shipwrecked air, as of extreme dependence on each other, though surrounded with every convenience. The other fault is that the famous "tender sentiment" usurps among them a place even greater perhaps than that which it holds in life, great as the latter very admittedly is. I spoke just now of their complicated relationships, but the complications are almost exclusively the complications of love. Our impression is of sky and sand—the sky of azure, the sand of silver—and between them, conspicuous, immense, against the low horizon, the question of engagement and marriage. I must add that I do not mean to imply that this question is not, in the very nature of things, at any time and in any place, immense, or that in a novel it should be expected to lose its magnitude. I take it indeed that on such a simple shore as Miss Woolson has described, love (with the passions that flow from it), is almost inevitably the subject, and that the perspective is not really false. It is not that the people are represented as hanging together by that cord to an abnormal degree, but that, there being few accessories and circumstances, there is no tangle and overgrowth to disguise the effect. It is a question of effect, but it is characteristic of the feminine, as distinguished from the masculine hand, that in any portrait of a corner of human affairs the particular effect produced in *East Angels*, that of what we used to call the love-story, will be the dominant one. The love-story is a composition in which the elements are distributed in a particular proportion, and every tale which contains a great deal of love has not necessarily a title to the name. That title depends not upon how much love there may be, but upon how little of other things. In novels by men other things are there to a greater or less degree, and I therefore doubt whether a man may be said ever to have produced a work exactly belonging to the class in question. In men's novels, even of the simplest strain, there are still other references and other explanations; in women's, when they are of the category to which I allude, there are none but that one. And there is certainly much to be said for it.

In *East Angels* the sacrifice, as all Miss Woolson's readers know, is the great sacrifice of Margaret Harold, who immolates herself—there is no other word—deliberately, completely, and repeatedly, to a husband whose behaviour may as distinctly be held to have absolved her. The problem was a very interesting one, and worthy to challenge a superior talent—that of making real and natural a transcendent, exceptional act, representing a case in which the sense of duty is raised to exaltation. What makes Margaret Harold's behaviour exceptional and transcendent is that, in order to render the barrier between herself and the man who loves her, and whom she loves, absolutely insurmountable, she does her best to bring about his marriage, endeavours to put another woman into the frame of mind to respond to him in the event (possible, as she is a woman whom he has once appeared to love) of his attempting to console himself for a bitter failure. The care, the ingenuity, the precautions the author has exhibited, to make us accept Mrs. Harold in her integrity, are perceptible on every page, and they leave us finally no alternative but to accept her; she remains exalted, but she remains at the same time thoroughly sound. For it is not a simple question of cleverness of detail, but a question of the larger sort of imagination, and Margaret Harold would have halted considerably if her creator had not taken the supreme precaution of all, and conceived her from the germ as capable of a certain heroism—of clinging at the cost of a grave personal loss to an idea which she believes to be a high one, and taking such a fancy to it that she endeavours to paint it, by a refinement of magnanimity, with still richer hues. She is a picture, not of a woman indulging in a great spasmodic flight or moral *tour de force*, but of a nature bent upon looking at life from a high point of view, an attitude in which there is nothing abnormal, and which the author illustrates, as it were, by a test case. She has drawn Margaret with so close and firm and living a line that she seems to put us in the quandary, if we repudiate her, of denying that a woman *may* look at life from a high point of view. She seems to say to us: "Are there distinguished natures, or are there not? Very well, if there are, that's what they can do—they can try and provide for the happiness of others (when they adore them) even to their own injury." And we feel that we wish to be the first to agree that there *are* distinguished natures.

Garda Thorne is the next best thing in the book to Margaret, and she is indeed equally good in this, that she is conceived with an equal clearness. But Margaret produces her impression upon us by moving before us and doing certain things, whereas Garda is more explained, or rather she explains herself more, tells us more about herself. She says somewhere, or some one says of her, that she doesn't narrate, but in fact she does narrate a good deal, for the purpose of making the reader understand her. This the reader does, very constantly, and Garda is a brilliant success. I must not, however, touch upon the different parts of *East Angels*, because in a work of so much patience and conscience a single example carries us too far. I will only add that in three places in especial the author has been so well inspired as to give a definite pledge of high accomplishment in the future. One of these salient passages is the description of the closing days of Mrs. Thorne, the little starved yet ardent daughter of the Puritans, who has been condemned to spend her life in the land of the relaxed, and who, before she dies, pours out her accumulations of bitterness—relieves herself in a passionate confession of everything she has suffered and missed, of how she has hated the very skies and fragrances of Florida, even when, as a consistent Christian, thankful for every mercy, she has pretended most to appreciate them. Mrs. Thorne is the pathetic, tragic form of the type of which Mrs. Stowe's Miss Ophelia was the comic. In almost all of Miss Woolson's stories the New England woman is represented as regretting the wholesome austerities of the region of her birth. She reverts to them, in solemn hours, even when, like Mrs. Thorne, she may appear for a time to have been converted to mild winters. Remarkably fine is the account of the expedition undertaken by Margaret Harold and Evert Winthrop to look for Lanse in the forest, when they believe him, or his wife thinks there may be reason to believe him, to have been lost and overtaken by a storm. The picture of their paddling the boat by torchlight into the reaches of the river, more or less smothered in the pestilent jungle, with the personal drama, in the unnatural place, reaching an acute stage between them—this whole episode is in a high degree vivid, strange, and powerful. Lastly, Miss Woolson has risen altogether to the occasion in the scene in which Margaret "has it out," as it were, with Evert Winthrop, parts from him and, leaving him baffled and unsurpassably sore, gives him the measure of her determination to accept the necessity of her fate. These three episodes are not alike, yet they have, in the high finish of Miss Woolson's treatment of them, a family resemblance. Moreover, they all have the stamp which I spoke of at first—the stamp of the author's conservative feeling, the implication that for her the life of a woman is essentially an affair of private relations.

1887.

VII. ALPHONSE DAUDET

I

"THE novel of manners grows thick in England, and there are many reasons for it. In the first place it was born there, and a plant always flourishes in its own country." So wrote M. Taine, the French critic, many years ago. But those were the years of Dickens and Thackeray (as a prelude to a study of the latter of whom the remark was made); and the branch of literature mentioned by M. Taine has no longer, in the soil of our English-speaking genius, so strong a vitality. The French may bear the palm to-day in the representation of manners by the aid of fiction. Formerly, it was possible to oppose Balzac and Madame Sand to Dickens and Thackeray; but at present we have no one, either in England or in America, to oppose to Alphonse Daudet. The appearance of a new novel by this admirable genius is to my mind the most delightful literary event that can occur just now; in other words Alphonse Daudet is at the head of his profession. I say of his profession advisedly, for he belongs to our modern class of trained men of letters; he is not an occasional or a desultory poet; he is a novelist to his finger-tips—a soldier in the great army of constant producers. But such as he is, he is a master of his art, and I may as well say definitely that if I attempt to sketch in a few pages his literary countenance, it will be found that the portrait is from the hand of an admirer. We most of us feel that among the artists of our day certain talents have more to say to us and others less; we have our favourites, and we have our objects of indifference. The writer of these remarks has always had a sympathy for the author of the *Lettres de mon Moulin*; he began to read his novels with a prejudice in their favour. This prejudice sprang from the Letters aforesaid, which do not constitute a novel, but a volume of the lightest and briefest tales. They had, to my mind, an extraordinary charm; they put me quite on the side of Alphonse Daudet, whatever he might do in the future. One of the first things he did was to publish the history of *Fromont Jeune et Risler Aîné*. It is true that this work did not give me the pleasure that some of its successors have done, and though it has been crowned by the French Academy, I still think it weaker than *Les Rois en Exil* and *Numa Roumestan*. But I liked it better on a second reading than on a first; it contains some delightful things. After that came *Jack* and *Le Nabab*, and the two novels I have just mentioned, and that curious and interesting tale of *L'Evangéliste*, which appeared a few months since, and which proves that the author's genius, though on the whole he has pressed it hard, is still nervous, fresh, and young. Each of these things has been better than the last, with the exception, perhaps, of *L'Evangéliste*, which, to my taste, is not superior to *Numa Roumestan*. *Numa Roumestan* is a masterpiece; it is really a perfect work; it has no weakness, no roughness; it is a compact and harmonious whole. Daudet's other works have had their inequalities, their infirmities, certain places where, if you tapped them, they sounded hollow. His danger has always been a perceptible tendency to the factitious; sometimes he has fallen into the trap laid for him by a taste for superficial effects. In *Fromont Jeune*, for instance, it seems to me difficult to care much for the horrid little heroine herself, carefully as she is studied. She has been pursued, but she has not been caught, for she is not interesting (even for a *coquine*), not even human. She is a mechanical doll, with nothing for the imagination to take hold of. She is one more proof of the fact that it is difficult to give the air of consistency to vanity and depravity, though the portraiture of the vicious side of life would seem, from the pictorial point of view, to offer such attractions. The reader's quarrel with Sidonie Chèbe is not that she is bad, but that she is not *felt*, as the æsthetic people say. In *Jack* the hollow spot, as I have called it, is the episode of Doctor Rivals and his daughter Cécile, which reminds us of the more genial parts of Dickens. It is perhaps because to us readers of English speech the figure of the young girl, in a French novel, is almost always wanting in reality—seems to be thin and conventional; in any case poor Jack's love-affair, at the end of the book, does not produce the illusion of the rest of his touching history. In *Le Nabab* this artificial element is very considerable; it centres about the figure of Paul de Géry and embraces the whole group of M. Joyeuse and his blooming daughters, with their pretty attitudes—taking in also the very shadowy André Maranne, so touchingly re-united to his mother, who had lived for ten years with an Irish doctor to whom she was not married. In *Les Rois en Exil*, Tom Lévis and the diabolical Séphora seem to me purely fanciful creations, without any relation to reality;

they are the inferior part of the book. They are composed by a master of composition, and the comedian Tom is described with immense spirit, an art which speaks volumes as to a certain sort of Parisian initiation. But if this artistic and malignant couple are very clever water-colour, they are not really humanity. Ruffians and rascals have a certain moral nature, as well as the better-behaved; but in the case I have mentioned M. Daudet fails to put his finger upon it. The same with Madame Autheman, the evil genius of poor Eline Ebsen, in the *L'Evangéliste*. She seems to me terribly, almost grotesquely, void. She is an elaborate portrait of a fanatic of Protestantism, a bigot to the point of monstrosity, cold-blooded, implacable, cruel. The figure is painted with Alphonse Daudet's inimitable art; no one that handles the pen to-day is such a pictorial artist as he. But Madame Autheman strikes me as quite automatic; psychologically she is a blank. One does not see the operation of her character. She must have had a soul, and a very curious one. It was a great opportunity for a piece of spiritual portraiture; but we know nothing about Madame Autheman's inner springs, and I think we fail to believe in her. I should go so far as to say that we get little more of an inside view, as the phrase is, of Eline Ebsen; we are not shown the spiritual steps by which she went over to the enemy—vividly, admirably as the outward signs and consequences of this disaster are depicted. The logic of the matter is absent in both cases, and it takes all the magic of the author's legerdemain to prevent us from missing it. These things, however, are exceptions, and the tissue of each of his novels is, for all the rest, really pure gold. No one has such grace, such lightness and brilliancy of execution; it is a fascination to see him at work. The beauty of *Numa Roumestan* is that it has no hollow places; the idea and the picture melt everywhere into one. Emile Zola, criticising the work in a very friendly spirit, speaks of the episode of Hortense Le Quesnoy and the Provençal *tambourinaire* as a false note, and declares that it wounds his sense of delicacy. Valmajour is a peasant of the south of France; he is young, handsome, wears a costume, and is a master of the rustic fife and tambourine— instruments that are much appreciated in his part of the country. Mademoiselle Le Quesnoy, living in Paris, daughter of a distinguished member of the French judiciary—"le premier magistrat de France"—young, charming, imaginative, romantic, marked out for a malady of the chest, and with a certain innocent perversity of mind, sees him play before an applauding crowd in the old Roman arena at Nîmes, and forthwith conceives a secret, a singular but not, under the circumstances, an absolutely unnatural passion for him. He comes up to Paris to seek his fortune at the "variety" theatres, where his feeble and primitive music quite fails to excite enthusiasm. The young girl, reckless and impulsive, and full of sympathy with his mortification, writes him in three words (upon one of her little photographs) an assurance of her devotion; and this innocent missive, falling soon into the hands of his rapacious and exasperated sister (a wonderful figure, one of the most living that has ever come from Daudet's pen), becomes a source of infinite alarm to the family of Mademoiselle Le Quesnoy, who see her compromised, calumniated and black-mailed, and finally of complete humiliation to poor Hortense herself, now fallen into a rapid consumption, and cured of her foolish infatuation by a nearer view of the vain and ignorant Valmajour. An agent of the family recovers the photograph (with the aid of ten thousand francs), and the young girl, with the bitter taste of her disappointment still in her soul, dies in her flower.

This little story, as I say, is very shocking to M. Zola, who cites it as an example of the folly of a departure from consistent realism. What is observed, says M. Zola, on the whole very justly, is strong; what is invented is always weak, especially what is invented to please the ladies. "See in this case," he writes, "all the misery of invented episodes. This love of Hortense, with which the author has doubtless wished to give the impression of something touching, produces a discomfort, as if it were a violation of nature. It is therefore the pages written for the ladies that are repulsive—even to a man accustomed to the saddest dissections of the human corpse." I am not of M. Zola's opinion—delightful as it would be to be of that opinion when M. Zola's sense of propriety is ruffled. The incident of Hortense and Valmajour is not (to my sense) a blot upon *Numa Roumestan*; on the contrary, it is perfectly conceivable, and is treated with admirable delicacy. "This romantic stuff," says M. Zola, elsewhere, "is as painful as a pollution. That a young girl should lose her head over a tenor, that may be explained, for she loves the operatic personage in the interpreter. She has before her a young man sharpened and refined by life, elegant, having at least certain appearances of talent and intelligence. But this tambourinist, with his drum and penny-whistle, this village dandy, a poor devil who doesn't even know how to speak! No, life has not such cruelties as that, I protest, I who certainly, as a general thing, am not accustomed to give ground before human aberrations!" This objection was worth making; but I should look at the matter in another way. It seems to me much more natural that a girl of the temper and breeding that M. Daudet has described should take a momentary fancy to a prepossessing young rustic, bronzed by the sun of Provence (even if it be conceded that his soul was vulgar), than that she should fasten her affections upon a "lyric artist," suspected of pomatum and paint, and illuminated by the footlights. These are points which it is vain to discuss, however, both because they are delicate and because they are details. I have come so far simply from a desire to justify my high admiration of *Numa Roumestan*. But Emile Zola, again, has expressed this feeling more felicitously than I can hope to do. "This, moreover, is a very slight blemish in a work which I regard as one of those, of all Daudet's productions, that is most personal to himself. He has put his whole nature into it, helped by his southern temperament, having only to make large draughts upon his innermost recollections and sensations. I do not think that he has hitherto reached such an intensity either of irony or of geniality.... Happy the books which arrive in this way, at the hour of the complete maturity of a talent! They are simply the widest unfolding of an artist's nature; they have in happy equilibrium the qualities of observation and the qualities of style. For Alphonse Daudet *Numa Roumestan* will mark this interfusion of a temperament and a subject that are made for each other, the perfect plenitude of a work which the writer exactly fills."

II

As I say, however, these are details, and I have touched them prematurely. Alphonse Daudet is a charmer, and the effect of his brilliant, friendly, indefinable genius is to make it difficult, in speaking of him, to take things in their order or follow a plan. In writing of him some time ago, in another place, I so far lost my head as to remark, with levity, that he was "a great little novelist." The diminutive epithet then, I must now say, was nothing more than a term of endearment, the result of an irresistible impulse to express a sense of personal fondness. This kind of feeling is difficult to utter in English, and the utterance of it, so far as this is possible, is not thought consistent with the dignity of a critic. If we were talking French, nothing would be simpler than to say that Alphonse Daudet is adorable, and have done with it. But this resource is denied me, and I must arrive at my meaning by a series of circumlocutions. I am not able even to say that he is very "personal"; that epithet, so valuable in the vocabulary of French literary criticism, has, when applied to the talent of an artist, a meaning different from the sense in which we use it. "A novelist so personal and so penetrating," says Emile Zola, speaking of the author of *Numa Roumestan*. That phrase, in English, means nothing in particular; so that I must add to it that the charm of Daudet's talent comes from its being charged to an extraordinary degree with his temperament, his feelings, his instincts, his natural qualities. This, of course, is a charm, in a style, only when nature has been generous. To Alphonse Daudet she has been exceptionally so; she has placed in his hand an instrument of many chords. A delicate, nervous organisation, active and indefatigable in spite of its delicacy, and familiar with emotion of almost every kind, equally acquainted with pleasure and with pain; a light, quick, joyous, yet reflective, imagination, a faculty of seeing images, making images, at every turn, of conceiving everything in the visible form, in the plastic spirit; an extraordinary sensibility to all the impressions of life and a faculty of language which is in perfect harmony with his wonderful fineness of perception— these are some of the qualities of which he is the happy possessor, and which make his equipment for the work he has undertaken exceedingly rich. There are others besides; but enumerations are ponderous, and we should avoid that danger in speaking of a genius whose lightness of touch never belies itself. His elder brother, who has not his talent, has written a little book about him in which the word *modernité* perpetually occurs. M. Ernest Daudet, in *Mon Frère et Moi*, insists upon his possession of the qualities expressed by this barbarous substantive, which is so indispensable to the new school. Alphonse Daudet is, in truth, very modern; he has all the newly-developed, the newly-invented, perceptions. Nothing speaks so much to his imagination as the latest and most composite things, the refinements of current civilisation, the most delicate shades of the actual. It is scarcely too much to say that (especially in the Parisian race), modern manners, modern nerves, modern wealth, and modern improvements, have engendered a new sense, a sense not easily named nor classified, but recognisable in all the most characteristic productions of contemporary art. It is partly physical, partly moral, and the shortest way to describe it is to say that it is a more analytic consideration of appearances. It is known by its tendency to resolve its discoveries into pictorial form. It sees the connection between feelings and external conditions, and it expresses such relations as they have not been expressed hitherto. It deserves to win victories, because it has opened its eyes well to the fact that the magic of the arts of representation lies in their appeal to the associations awakened by things. It traces these associations into the most unlighted corners of our being, into the most devious paths of experience. The appearance of things is constantly more complicated as the world grows older, and it needs a more and more patient art, a closer notation, to divide it into its parts. Of this art Alphonse Daudet has a wonderfully large allowance, and that is why I say that he is peculiarly modern. It is very true that his manner is not the manner of patience—though he must always have had a great deal of that virtue in the preparation of his work. The new school of fiction in France is based very much on the taking of notes; the library of the great Flaubert, of the brothers de Goncourt, of Emile Zola, and of the writer of whom I speak, must have been in a large measure a library of memorandum-books. This of course only puts the patience back a stage or two. In composition Daudet proceeds by quick, instantaneous vision, by the happiest divination, by catching the idea as it suddenly springs up before him with a whirr of wings. What he mainly sees is the great surface of life and the parts that lie near the surface. But life is, immensely, a matter of surface, and if our emotions in general are interesting, the *form* of those emotions has the merit of being the most definite thing about them. Like most French imaginative writers (judged, at least, from the English standpoint), he is much less concerned with the moral, the metaphysical world, than with the sensible. We proceed usually from the former to the latter, while the French reverse the process. Except in politics, they are uncomfortable in the presence of abstractions, and lose no time in reducing them to the concrete. But even the concrete, for them, is a field for poetry, which brings us to the fact that the delightful thing in Daudet's talent is the inveterate poetical touch. This is what mainly distinguishes him from the other lights of the realistic school—modifies so completely in his case the hardness of consistent realism. There is something very hard, very dry, in Flaubert, in Edmond de Goncourt, in the robust Zola; but there is something very soft in Alphonse Daudet. "Benevolent nature," says Zola, "has placed him at that exquisite point where poetry ends and reality begins." That is happily said; Daudet's great characteristic is this mixture of the sense of the real with the sense of the beautiful. His imagination is constantly at play with his theme; it has a horror of the literal, the limited; it sees an object in all its intermingled relations—on its sentimental, its pathetic, its comical, its pictorial side. Flaubert, in whom Alphonse Daudet would probably recognise to a certain degree a literary paternity, is far from being a simple realist; but he was destitute of this sense of the beautiful, destitute of facility and grace. He had, to take its place, a sense of the strange, the grotesque, to which *Salammbo, La Tentation de Saint-Antoine,* his indescribable posthumous novel of *Bouvard et Pécuchet,* abundantly testify. The talent of the brothers Goncourt strikes us as a talent that was associated originally with a sense of beauty; but we receive an impression that this feeling has been perverted and warped. It has ceased to be natural and free; it has become morbid and peevish, has turned mainly to curiosity and mannerism. And these two authors are capable, during a whole book (as in *Germinie Lacerteux* or *La Fille Elisa*), of escaping from its influence altogether. No one would probably ever think of accusing Emile Zola of having a perception of the beautiful. He has an illimitable, and at times a very valuable, sense of the ugly, of the unclean; but when he addresses himself to the poetic aspect of things, as in *La Faute de l'Abbé Mouret,* he is apt to have terrible misadventures.

III

It is for the expressive talents that we feel an affection, and Daudet is eminently expressive. His manner is the manner of talk, and if the talk is sincere, that makes a writer touch us. Daudet expresses many things; but he most frequently expresses himself—his own temper in the presence of life, his own feeling on a thousand occasions. This personal note is especially to be observed in his earlier productions—in the *Lettres de mon Moulin*, the *Contes du Lundi, Le Petit Chose*; it is also very present in the series of prefaces which he has undertaken to supply to the octavo edition of his works. In these prefaces he gives the history of each successive book—relates the circumstances under which it was written. These things are ingenuously told, but what we are chiefly conscious of in regard to them, is that Alphonse Daudet must express himself. His brother informs us that he is writing his memoirs, and this will have been another opportunity for expression. Ernest Daudet, as well (as I have mentioned), has attempted to express him. *Mon Frère et Moi* is one of those productions which it is difficult for an English reader to judge in fairness: it is so much more confidential than we, in public, ever venture to be. The French have, on all occasions, the courage of their emotion, and M. Ernest Daudet's leading emotion is a boundless admiration for his junior. He lays it before us very frankly and gracefully—not, on the whole, indiscreetly; and I have no quarrel whatever with his volume, for it contains a considerable amount of information on a very interesting subject. Indirectly, indeed, as well as directly, it helps us to a knowledge of his brother. Alphonse Daudet was born in Provence; he comes of an expansive, a confidential race. His style is impregnated with the southern sunshine, and his talent has the sweetness of a fruit that has grown in the warm, open air. He has the advantage of being a Provençal converted, as it were—of having a southern temperament and a northern reason. We know what he thinks of the southern temperament— *Numa Roumestan* is a vivid exposition of that. "*Gau de carriero, doulou d'oustau*," as the Provençal has it; "*joie de rue, douleur de maison*—joy in the street and pain in the house"—that proverb, says Alphonse Daudet, describes and formulates a whole race. It has given him the subject of an admirable story, in which he has depicted with equal force and tenderness the amiable weaknesses, the mingled violence and levity of the children of the clime of the fig and olive. He has put before us, above all, their mania for talk, their irrepressible chatter, the qualities that, with them, render all passion, all purpose, inordinately vocal. Himself a complete "*produit du Midi*," like the famille Mèfre in *Numa Roumestan*, he has achieved the feat of becoming objective to his own vision, getting outside of his ingredients and judging them. This he has done by the aid of his Parisianised conscience, his exquisite taste, and that finer wisdom which resides in the artist, from whatever soil he springs. Successfully as he has done it, however, he has not done it so well but that he too does not show a little of the heightened colour, the super-abundant statement, the restless movement of his compatriots. He is nothing if not demonstrative; he is always in a state of feeling; he has not a very definite ideal of reserve. It must be added that he is a man of genius, and that genius never spends its capital; that he is an artist, and that an artist always has a certain method and order. But it remains characteristic of his origin that the author of *Numa Roumestan*, one of the happiest and most pointed of satires, should have about him the aroma of some of the qualities satirised. There are passages in his tales and in his prefaces that are genuine "produits du Midi," and his brother's account of him could only have been written by a Provençal brother.

To be *personnel* to that point, transparent, effusive, gushing, to give one's self away in one's books, has never been, and will never be, the ideal of us of English speech; but that does not prevent our enjoying immensely, when we meet it, a happy example of this alien spirit. For myself, I am free to confess, half my affection for Alphonse Daudet comes from the fact that he writes in a way in which I would not write even if I could. There are certain kinds of feeling and observation, certain impressions and ideas, to which we are rather ashamed to give a voice, and yet are ashamed not to have in our scale. In these matters Alphonse Daudet renders us a great service: he expresses such things on our behalf. I may add that he usually does it much better than the cleverest of us could do even if we were to try. I have said that he is a Provençal converted, and I should do him a great injustice if I did not dwell upon his conversion. His brother relates the circumstances under which he came up to Paris, at the age of twenty (in a threadbare overcoat and a pair of india-rubbers), to seek his literary fortune. His beginnings were difficult, his childhood had been hard, he was familiar with poverty and disaster. He had no adventitious aid to success—his whole fortune consisted in his exquisite organisation. But Paris was to be, artistically, a mine of wealth to him, and of all the anxious and eager young spirits who, on the battle-field of uncarpeted *cinquièmes*, have laid siege to the indifferent city, none can have felt more deeply conscious of the mission to take possession of it. Alphonse Daudet, at the present hour, is in complete possession of Paris; he knows it, loves it; uses it; he has assimilated it to its last particle. He has made of it a Paris of his own—a Paris like a vast crisp water-colour, one of the water-colours of the school of Fortuny. The French have a great advantage in the fact that they admire their capital very much as if it were a foreign city. Most of their artists, their men of letters, have come up from the provinces, and well as they may learn to know the metropolis, it never ceases to be a spectacle, a wonder, a fascination for them. This comes partly from the intrinsic brilliancy and interest of the place, partly from the poverty of provincial life, and partly from the degree to which the faculty of appreciation is developed in Frenchmen of the class of which I speak. To Daudet, at any rate, the familiar aspects of Paris are endlessly pictorial, and part of the charm of his novels (for those who share his relish for that huge flower of civilisation) is in the way he recalls it, evokes it, suddenly presents it, in parts or as a whole, to our senses. The light, the sky, the feeling of the air, the odours of the streets, the look of certain vistas, the silvery, muddy Seine, the cool, grey tone of colour, the physiognomy of particular quarters, the whole Parisian expression, meet you suddenly in his pages, and remind you again and again that if he paints with a pen he writes with a brush. I remember that when I read *Le Nabab* and *Les Rois en Exil* for the first time, I said to myself that this was the *article de Paris* in supreme perfection, and that no reader could understand such productions who had not had a copious experience of the scene. It is certain, at any rate, that those books have their full value only for minds more or less Parisianised; half their meaning, their magic, their subtlety of intention is liable to be lost. It may be said that this is a great limitation—that the works of the best novelists may be understood by all the world. There is something in that; but I know not, all the same, whether the fact I indicate be a great limitation. It is certainly a very illustrative quality. Daudet has caught the tone of a particular pitch of manners; he applies it with the lightest, surest hand, and his picture shines and lives. The most generalised representation of life cannot do more than that.

I shrink very much from speaking of systems, in relation to such a genius as this: I should incline to believe that Daudet's system is simply to be as vivid as he can. Emile Zola has a system—at least he says so; but I do not remember, on the part of the author of *Numa Roumestan*, the smallest technical profession of faith. Nevertheless, he has taken a line, as we say, and his line is to sail as close as possible to the actual. The life of Paris being his subject, his attempt, most frequently, is to put his finger upon known examples; so that he has been accused of portraying individuals instead of portraying types. There are few of his figures to which the name of some celebrity of the day has not been attached. The Nabob is François Bravais; the Duc de Mora is the Duc de Morny. The Irish Doctor Jenkins is an English physician who flourished in Paris from such a year to such another; people are still living (wonderful to say), who took his little pills *à base arsénicale*. Félicia Ruys is Mademoiselle Sarah Bernhardt; Constance Crenmitz is Madame Taglioni; the Queen of Illyria is the Queen of Naples; the Prince of Axel is the Prince of Orange; Tom Lévis is an English house-agent (*not* in the Rue Royale, but hard by); Elysée Méraut is a well-known journalist, and Doctor Bouchereau a well-known surgeon. Such is the key, we are told, to these ingenious mystifications, and to many others which I have not the space to mention. It matters little, to my mind, whether in each case the cap fits the supposed model; for nothing is more evident than that Alphonse Daudet has proposed to himself to represent not only the people but the persons of his time. The conspicuity of certain individuals has added to the force with which they speak to his imagination. His taste is for salient figures, and he has said to himself that there is no greater proof of being salient than being known. The temptation to "put people into a book" is a temptation of which every writer of fiction knows something, and I hold that to succumb to it is not only legitimate but inevitable. Putting people into books is what the novelist lives upon; the question in the matter is the question of delicacy, for according to that delicacy the painter conjures away recognition or insists upon it. Daudet has been accused of the impertinence of insisting, and I believe that two or three of his portraits have provoked a protest. He is charged with ingratitude for having produced an effigy of the Duke of Morny, who had been his benefactor, and employed him as a secretary. Such a matter as this is between M. Daudet and his conscience, and I am far from pretending to pronounce upon it. The uninitiated reader can only say that the figure is a very striking one—such a picture as (it may be imagined) the Duc de Morny would not be displeased to have inspired. It may fairly be conceded, however, that Daudet is much more an observer than an inventor. The invented parts of his tales, like the loves of Jack and of Paul de Géry and the machinations of Madame Autheman (the theological vampire of *L'Evangéliste*, to whom I shall return for a moment), are the vague, the ineffective as well as the romantic parts. (I remember that in reading *Le Nabab*, it was not very easy to keep Paul de Géry and André Maranne apart.) It is the real—the transmuted real—that he gives us best; the fruit of a process that adds to observation what a kiss adds to a greeting. The joy, the excitement of recognition, are keen, even when the object recognised is dismal. They are part of his spirit—part of his way of seeing things. *L'Evangéliste* is the saddest story conceivable; but it is lighted, throughout, by the author's irrepressibly humorous view of the conditions in which its successive elements present themselves, and by the extraordinary vivacity with which, in his hands, narration and description proceed. His humour is of the finest; it is needless to say that it is never violent nor vulgar. It is a part of the high spirits—the animal spirits, I should say, if the phrase had not an association of coarseness—that accompany the temperament of his race; and it is stimulated by the perpetual entertainment which so rare a visual faculty naturally finds in the spectacle of life, even while encountering there a multitude of distressing things. Daudet's gaiety is a part of his poetry, and his poetry is a part of everything he touches. There is little enough gaiety in the subject of *Jack*, and yet the whole story is told with a smile. To complete the charm of the thing, the smile is full of feeling. Here and there it becomes an immense laugh, and the result is a delightful piece of drollery. *Les Aventures Prodigieuses de Tartarin de Tarascon* contains all his high spirits; it is one of his few stories in which laughter and tears are not intermingled.

This little tale, which is one of his first, is, like *Numa Roumestan*, a satire on a southern foible. Tartarin de Tarascon is an excellent man who inhabits the old town on the Rhone over which the palace of the good King René keeps guard; he has not a fault in the world except an imagination too vivid. He is liable to visions, to hallucinations; the desire that a thing shall happen speedily resolves itself into the belief that the thing will happen—then that it is happening—then that it *has* happened. Tartarin accordingly presents himself to the world (and to himself) as a gentleman to whom all wonders are familiar; his experience blooms with supposititious flowers. The coveted thing for a man of his romantic mould is that he shall be the bravest of the brave, and he passes his life in a series of heroic exploits, in which, as you listen to him, it is impossible not to believe. He passes over from Marseilles to Algiers, where his adventures deepen to a climax, and where he has a desperate flirtation with the principal ornament of the harem of a noble Arab. The lady proves at the end to be a horribly improper little Frenchwoman, and poor Tartarin, abused and disabused, returns to Tarascon to meditate on what might have been. Nothing could be more charming than the light comicality of the sketch, which fills a small volume. This is the most mirthful, the most completely diverting of all Daudet's tales; but the same element, in an infinitely subtler form, runs through the others. The essence of it is the wish to please, and this brings me back to the point to which I intended to return. The wish to please is the quality by which Daudet persuades his readers most; it is this that elicits from them that friendliness, that confession that they are charmed, of which I spoke at the beginning of these remarks. It gives a sociability to his manner, in spite of the fact that he describes all sorts of painful and odious things. This contradiction is a part of his originality. He has no pretension to being simple, he is perfectly conscious of being complex, and in nothing is he more modern than in this expressive and sympathetic smile—the smile of the artist, the sceptic, the man of the world—with which he shows us the miseries and cruelties of life. It is singular that we should like him for that—and doubtless many people do not, or think they do not. What they really dislike, I believe, is the things he relates, which are often lamentable.

IV

THE first of these were slight and simple, and for the most part cheerful; little anecdotes and legends of Provence, impressions of an artist's holidays in that strange, bare, lovely land, and of wanderings further afield, in Corsica and Algeria; sketches of Paris during the siege; incidents of the invasion, the advent of the Prussian rule in other parts of the country. In all these things there is *la note émue*, the smile which is only a more synthetic sign of being moved. And then such grace of form, such lightness of touch, such alertness of observation! Some of the chapters of the *Lettres de mon Moulin* are such perfect vignettes, that the brief treatment of small subjects might well have seemed, at first, Alphonse Daudet's appointed work. He had almost invented a manner, and it was impossible to do better than he the small piece, or even the passage. Glimpses, reminiscences, accidents, he rendered them with the brilliancy of a violinist improvising on a sudden hint. The *Lettres de mon Moulin*, moreover, are impregnated with the light, with the fragrance of a Provençal summer; the rosemary and thyme are in the air as we read, the white rocks and the grey foliage stretch away to an horizon of hills—the Alpilles, the little Alps—on which colour is as iridescent as the breast of a dove. The Provence of Alphonse Daudet is a delightful land; even when the mistral blows there it has a music in its whistle. Emile Zola has protested against this; he too is of Provençal race, he passed his youth in the old Languedoc, and he intimates that his fanciful friend throws too much sweetness into the picture. It is beyond contradiction that Daudet, like Tartarin de Tarascon and Numa Roumestan, exaggerates a little; he sees with great intensity, and is very sensitive to agreeable impressions. *Le Petit Chose*, his first long story, reads to-day like the attempt of a beginner, and of a beginner who had read and enjoyed Dickens. I risk this allusion to the author of *Copperfield* in spite of a conviction that Alphonse Daudet must be tired of hearing that he imitates him. It is not imitation; there is nothing so gross as imitation in the length and breadth of Daudet's work; but it is conscious sympathy, for there is plenty of that. There are pages in his tales which seem to say to us that at one moment of his life Dickens had been a revelation to him—pages more particularly in *Le Petit Chose*, in *Fromont Jeune* and in *Jack*. The heroine of the first of these works (a very shadowy personage) is never mentioned but as the "black eyes"; some one else is always spoken of as the *dame de grand mérite*; the heroine's father, who keeps a flourishing china-shop, never opens his mouth without saying "C'est le cas de le dire." These are harmless, they are indeed sometimes very happy, Dickensisms. We make no crime of them to M. Daudet, who must have felt as intelligently as he has felt everything else the fascinating form of the English novelist's drollery. *Fromont Jeune et Risler Aîné* is a study

141

of life in the old quarter of the Marais, the Paris of the seventeenth century, whose stately *hôtels* have been invaded by the innumerable activities of modern trade. When I say a study, I use the word with all those restrictions with which it must be applied to a genius who is truthful without being literal, and who has a pair of butterfly's wings attached to the back of his observation. If sub-titles were the fashion to-day, the right one for *Fromont Jeune* would be—*or the Dangers of Partnership*. The action takes place for the most part in a manufactory of wall-papers, and the persons in whom the author seeks to interest us are engaged in this useful industry. There are delightful things in the book, but, as I intimated at the beginning of these remarks, there are considerable inequalities. The pages that made M. Daudet's fortune—for it was with *Fromont Jeune* that his fortune began—are those which relate to the history of M. Delobelle, the superannuated tragedian, his long-suffering wife, and his exquisite lame daughter, who makes butterflies and humming-birds for ladies' head-dresses. This eccentric and pathetic household was an immense hit, and Daudet has never been happier than in the details of the group. Delobelle himself, who has not had an engagement for ten years, and who never will have one again, but who holds none the less that it is his duty not to leave the stage, "not to give up the theatre," though his platonic passion is paid for by the weary eyesight of his wife and daughter, who sit up half the night attaching bead-eyes to little stuffed animals—the blooming and sonorous Delobelle, ferociously selfish and fantastically vain, under the genial forms of melodrama, is a beautiful representation of a vulgarly factitious nature. The book revealed a painter; all the descriptive passages, the pictorial touches, had the truest felicity. No one better than Daudet gives what we call the feeling of a place. The story illustrates, among other things, the fact that a pretty little woman who is consumed with the lowest form of vanity, and unimpeded in her operations by the possession of a heart, may inflict an unlimited amount of injury upon people about her, if she only have the opportunity. The case is well demonstrated, and Sidonie Chèbe is an elaborate study of flimsiness; her papery quality, as I may call it, her rustling dryness, are effectively rendered. But I think there is a limit to the interest which the English-speaking reader of French novels can take to-day in the adventures of a lady who leads the life of Madame Sidonie. In the first place he has met her again and again—he knows exactly what she will do and say in every situation; and in the second there always seems to him to be in her vices, her disorders, an element of the conventional. There is a receipt among French novelists for making little high-heeled reprobates. However this may be, he has at least a feeling that at night all cats are grey, and that the particular tint of depravity of a woman whose nature has the shallowness of a sanded floor is not a very important *constatation*. Daudet has expended much ingenuity in endeavouring to hit the particular tint of Sidonie; he has wished to make her a type—the type of the daughter of small unsuccessful shopkeepers (narrow-minded and self-complacent to imbecility), whose corruption comes from the examples, temptations, opportunities of a great city, as well as from her impure blood and the infection of the meanest associations. But what all this illustrates was not worth illustrating.

The early chapters of *Jack* are admirable; the later ones suffer a little, I think, from the story being drawn out too much, like an accordion when it wishes to be plaintive. Jack is a kind of younger brother of the Petit Chose, though he takes the troubles of life rather more stoutly than that delicate and diminutive hero; a poor boy with a doting and disreputable mother, whose tenderness is surpassed by her frivolity, and who sacrifices her son to the fantastic egotism of an unsuccessful man of letters with whom she passes several years of her life. She is another study of *coquinerie*—she is another shade; but she is a more apprehensible figure than Sidonie Chèbe—she is, indeed, a very admirable portrait. The success of the book, however, is the figure of her lover, that is of her protector and bully, the unrecognised genius aforesaid, author of *Le Fils de Faust*, an uncirculated dramatic poem in the manner of Goethe, and centre of a little group of *ratés*—a collection of dead-beats, as we say to-day, as pretentious, as impotent, as envious and as bilious as himself. He conceives a violent hatred of the offspring of his amiable companion, and the subject of *Jack* is the persecution of the boy by this monstrous charlatan. This persecution is triumphantly successful; the youthful hero dies on the threshold of manhood, broken down by his tribulations and miseries: he has been thrown upon the world to earn his bread, and among other things seeks a livelihood as a stoker on an Atlantic steamer. Jack has been taken young, and though his nature is gentle and tender, his circumstances succeed in degrading him. He is reduced at the end to a kind of bewildered brutishness. The story is simply the history of a juvenile martyrdom, pityingly, expansively told, and I am afraid that Mr. Charles Dudley Warner, who, in writing lately about "Modern Fiction,"[4] complains of the abuse of pathetic effects in that form of composition, would find little to commend in this brilliant paraphrase of suffering. Mr. Warner's complaint is eminently just, and the fault of *Jack* is certainly the abuse of pathos. Mr. Warner does not mention Alphonse Daudet by name, but it is safe to assume that in his reflections upon the perversity of those writers who will not make a novel as comfortable as one's stockings, or as pretty as a Christmas card, he was thinking of the author of so many uncompromising *dénouements*. It is true that this probability is diminished by the fact that when he remarks that surely "the main object in the novel is to entertain," he appears to imply that the writers who furnish his text are faithless to this duty. It is possible he would not have made that implication if he had had in mind the productions of a story-teller who has the great peculiarity of being "amusing," as the old-fashioned critics say, even when he touches the source of tears. The word entertaining has two or three shades of meaning; but in whatever sense it is used I may say, in parenthesis, that I do not agree with Mr. Warner's description of the main object of the novel. I should put the case differently: I should say that the main object of the novel is to represent life. I cannot understand any other motive for interweaving imaginary incidents, and I do not perceive any other measure of the value of such combinations. The *effect* of a novel—the effect of any work of art—is to entertain; but that is a very different thing. The success of a work of art, to my mind, may be measured by the degree to which it produces a certain illusion; that illusion makes it appear to us for the time that we have lived another life—that we have had a miraculous enlargement of experience. The greater the art the greater the miracle, and the more certain also the fact that we have been entertained—in the best meaning of that word, at least, which signifies that we have been living at the expense of some one else. I am perfectly aware that to say the object of a novel is to represent life does not bring the question to a point so fine as to be uncomfortable for any one. It is of the greatest importance that there should be a very free appreciation of such a question, and the definition I have hinted at gives plenty of scope for that. For, after all, may not people differ infinitely as to what constitutes life—what constitutes representation? Some people, for instance, hold that Miss Austen deals with life, that Miss Austen represents. Others attribute these achievements to the accomplished Ouida. Some people find that illusion, that enlargement of experience, that miracle of living at the expense of others, of which I have spoken, in the novels of Alexandre Dumas. Others revel in them in the pages of Mr. Howells.

V

M. DAUDET'S unfortunate Jack, at any rate, lives altogether at his own cost—that of his poor little juvenile constitution, and of his innocent affections and aspirations. He is sent to the horrible Gymnase Moronval, where he has no beguiling works of fiction to read. The Gymnase Moronval is a Dotheboys' Hall in a Parisian "passage"—a very special class of academy. Nothing could be more effective than Daudet's picture of this horrible institution, with its bankrupt and exasperated proprietors, the greasy penitentiary of a group of unremunerative children whose parents and guardians have found it convenient to forget them. The episode of the wretched little hereditary monarch of an African tribe who has been placed there for a royal education, and who, livid with cold, short rations, and rough usage, and with his teeth chattering with a sense of dishonour, steals away and wanders in the streets of Paris, and then, recaptured and ferociously punished, surrenders his little dusky soul in the pestilential dormitory of the establishment—all this part of the tale is a masterpiece of vivid description. We seem to assist at the terrible soirées where the *ratés* exhibit their talents (M. Moronval is of course a *raté*), and where the wife of the principal, a very small woman with a very big head and a very high forehead, expounds the wonderful Méthode-Décostère (invented by herself and designated by her maiden name), for pronouncing the French tongue with elegance. My criticism of this portion of the book, and indeed of much of the rest of it, would be that the pathetic element is too intentional, too *voulu*, as the French say. And I am not sure that the reader enters into the author's reason for making Charlotte, Jack's mother, a woman of the class that we do not specify in American magazines. She is an accommodating idiot, but her good nature is unfortunately not consecutive, and she consents, at the instigation of the diabolical d'Argenton, to her child's being brought up like a pauper. D'Argenton, like Delobelle, is a study of egotism pushed to the grotesque; but the portrait is still more complete, and some of the details are inimitable. As regards the infatuated Charlotte, who sacrifices her child to the malignity of her lover, I repeat that certain of the features of her character appear to me a mistake, judged in relation to the effect that the author wishes to produce. He wishes to show us all that the boy loses in being disinherited—if I may use that term with respect to a situation in which there is nothing to inherit. But his loss is not great when we consider that his mother had, after all, very little to give him. She had divested herself of important properties. Bernard Jansoulet, in *Le Nabab*, is not, like the two most successful figures that Daudet has previously created, a representation of full-blown selfishness. The unhappy nabab is generous to a fault; he is the most good-natured and free-handed of men, and if he has made use of all sorts of means to build up his enormous fortune, he knows an equal number of ways of spending it. This voluminous tale had an immense success; it seemed to show that Daudet had found his manner, a manner that was perfectly new and remarkably ingenious. As I have said, it held up the mirror to contemporary history, and attempted to complete for us, by supplementary revelations, those images which are projected by the modern newspaper and the album of photographs. *Les Rois en Exil* is an historical novel of this pattern, in which the process is applied with still more spirit. In these two works Daudet enlarged his canvas surprisingly, and showed his ability to deal with a multitude of figures.

The distance traversed artistically from the little anecdotes of the *Lettres de mon Moulin* to the complex narrative of *Le Nabab* and its successor, are like the transformation—often so rapid—of a slim and charming young girl into a blooming and accomplished woman of the world. The author's style had taken on bone and muscle, and become conscious of treasures of nervous agility. I have left myself no space to speak of these things in detail, and it was not part of my purpose to examine Daudet's novels piece by piece; but I may say that it is the items, the particular touches, that make the value of writing of this kind. I am not concerned to defend the process, the system, so far as there is a system; but I cannot open either *Le Nabab* or *Les Rois en Exil*, cannot rest my eyes upon a page, without being charmed by the brilliancy of execution. It is difficult to give an idea, by any general terms, of Daudet's style—a style which defies convention, tradition, homogeneity, prudence, and sometimes even syntax, gathers up every patch of colour, every colloquial note, that will help to illustrate, and moves eagerly, lightly, triumphantly along, like a clever woman in the costume of an eclectic age. There is nothing classic in this mode of expression; it is not the old-fashioned drawing in black and white. It never rests, never is satisfied, never leaves the idea sitting half-draped, like patience on a monument; it is always panting, straining, fluttering, trying to add a little more, to produce the effect which shall make the reader see with his eyes, or rather with the marvellous eyes of Alphonse Daudet. *Le Nabab* is full of episodes which are above all pages of execution, triumphs of translation. The author has drawn up a list of the Parisian solemnities and painted the portrait—or given a summary—of each of them. The opening day at the Salon, a funeral at Père-la-Chaise, a debate in the Chamber of Deputies, the *première* of a new play at a favourite theatre, furnish him with so many opportunities for his gymnastics of observation. I should like to say how rich and entertaining I think the figure of Jansoulet, the robust and good-natured son of his own works (originally a dock-porter at Marseilles), who, after amassing a fabulous number of millions in selling European luxuries on commission to the Bey of Tunis, comes to Paris to try to make his social fortune as he has already made his financial, and after being a nine-days' wonder, a public joke, and the victim of his boundless hospitality; after being flattered by charlatans, rifled by adventurers, belaboured by newspapers, and "exploited" to the last penny of his coffers and the last pulsation of his vanity by every one who comes near him, dies of apoplexy in his box at the theatre, while the public hoots him for being unseated for electoral frauds in the Chamber of Deputies, where for a single mocking hour he has tasted the sweetness of political life. I should like to say, too, that however much or however little the Duc de Mora may resemble the Duc de Morny, the character depicted by Daudet is a wonderful study of that modern passion, the love of "good form." The chapter that relates the death of the Duke, and describes the tumult, the confusion, of his palace, the sudden extinction of the rapacious interests that crowd about him, and to which the collapse of his splendid security comes as the first breath of a revolution—this chapter is famous, and gives the fullest measure of what Daudet can do when he fairly warms to his work.

Les Rois en Exil, however, has a greater perfection; it is simpler, more equal, and it contains much more of the beautiful. In *Le Nabab* there are various lacunæ and a certain want of logic; it is not a sustained narrative, but a series of almost diabolically clever pictures. But the other book has more largeness of line—a fine tragic movement which deepens and presses to the catastrophe. Daudet had observed that several dispossessed monarchs had taken up their residence in the French capital—some of them waiting and plotting for a restoration, and chafing under their disgrace; others indifferent, resigned, relieved, eager to console themselves with the pleasures of Paris. It occurred to him to suppose a drama in which these exalted personages should be the actors, and which, unlike either of his former productions, should have a pure and noble heroine. He was conscious of a dauntless little imagination, the idea of making kings and queens talk among themselves had no terror for him; he had faith in his good taste, in his exquisite powers of divination. The success is worthy of the spirit—the gallant artistic spirit—in which it was invoked. *Les Rois en Exil* is a finished picture. He has had, it is true, to simplify his subject a good deal to make it practicable; the court of the king and queen of Illyria, in the suburb of Saint-Mandé, is a little too much like a court in a fairy-tale. But the amiable depravity of Christian, in whom conviction, resolution, ambition, are hopelessly dead, and whose one desire is to enjoy Paris with the impunity of a young man about town; the proud, serious, concentrated nature of Frederica, who believes ardently in her royal function, and lives with her eyes fixed on the crown, which she regards as a symbol of duty; both of these conceptions do M. Daudet the utmost honour, and prove that he is capable of handling great situations—situations which have a depth of their own, and do not depend for their interest on amusing accidents. It takes perhaps some courage to say so, but the feelings, the passions, the view of life, of royal personages, differ essentially from those of common mortals; their education, their companions, their traditions, their exceptional position, take sufficient care of that. Alphonse Daudet has comprehended the difference; and I scarcely know, in the last few years, a straighter flight of imagination. The history of the queen of Illyria is a tragedy. Her husband sells his birthright for a few millions of francs, and rolls himself in the Parisian gutter; her child perishes from poverty of blood; she herself dries up in her despair. There is nothing finer in all Daudet than the pages, at the end of the book, which describe her visits to the great physician Bouchereau, when she takes her poor half-blind child by the hand, and (wishing an opinion unbiassed by the knowledge of her rank) goes to sit in his waiting-room like one of the vulgar multitude. Wonderful are the delicacy, the verity, the tenderness of these pages; we always point to them to justify our predilection. But we must stop pointing. We will not say more of *Numa Roumestan* than we have already said; for it is better to pass so happy a work by than to speak of it inadequately. We will only repeat that we delight in *Numa Roumestan*. Alphonse Daudet's last book is a novelty at the time I write; *L'Evangéliste* has been before the public but a month or two. I will say but little of it, partly because my opportunity is already over, and partly because I have found that, for a fair judgment of one of Daudet's works, the book should be read a second time, after a certain interval has elapsed. This interval has not brought round my second perusal of *L'Evangéliste*. My first suggests that with all the author's present mastery of his resources the book has a grave defect. It is not that the story is painful; that is a defect only when the sources of this element are not, as I may say, abundant. It treats of a young girl (a Danish Protestant) who is turned to stone by a Medusa of Calvinism, the sombre and fanatical wife of a great Protestant banker. Madame Autheman persuades Eline Ebsen to wash her hands of the poor old mother with whom up to this moment she has lived in the closest affection, and go forth into strange countries to stir up the wicked to conversion. The excellent Madame Ebsen, bewildered, heart-broken, desperate, terrified at the imagined penalties of her denunciation of the rich and powerful bigot (so that she leaves her habitation and hides in a household of small mechanics to escape from them—one of the best episodes in the book), protests, struggles, goes down on her knees in vain; then, at last, stupefied and exhausted, desists, looks for the last time at her inexorable, impenetrable daughter, who has hard texts on her lips and no recognition in her eye, and who lets her pass away, without an embrace, for ever. The incident in itself is perfectly conceivable: many well-meaning persons have held human relationships cheap in the face of a religious call. But Daudet's weakness has been simply a want of acquaintance with his subject. Proposing to himself to describe a particular phase of French Protestantism, he has "got up" certain of his facts with commendable zeal; but he has not felt nor understood the matter, has looked at it solely from the outside, sought to make it above all things grotesque and extravagant. Into these excesses it doubtless frequently falls; but there is a general human verity which regulates even the most stubborn wills, the most perverted lives; and of this saving principle the author, in quest of striking pictures, has rather lost his grasp. His pictures are striking, as a matter of course; but to us readers of Protestant race, familiar with the large, free, salubrious life which the children of that faith have carried with them over the globe, there is almost a kind of drollery in these fearsome pictures of the Protestant temperament. The fact is that M. Daudet has not (to my belief) any natural understanding of the religious passion; he has a quick perception of many things, but that province of the human mind cannot be *fait de chic*—experience, there, is the only explorer. Madame Autheman is not a real bigot; she is simply a dusky effigy, she is undemonstrated. Eline Ebsen is not a victim, inasmuch as she is but half alive, and victims are victims only in virtue of being thoroughly sentient. I do not easily perceive her spiritual joints. All the human part of the book, however, has the author's habitual felicity; and the reader of these remarks knows what I hold that to be. It may seem to him, indeed, that in making the concession I made just above—in saying that Alphonse Daudet's insight fails him when he begins to take the soul into account—I partly retract some of the admiration I have expressed for him. For that amounts, after all, to saying that he has no high imagination, and, as a consequence, no ideas. It is very true, I am afraid, that he has not a great number of ideas. There are certain things he does not conceive—certain forms that never appear to him. Imaginative writers of the first order always give us an impression that they have a kind of philosophy. We should be embarrassed to put our finger on Daudet's philosophy. "And yet you have praised him so much," we fancy we hear it urged; "you have praised him as if he were one of the very first." All that is very true, and yet we take nothing back. Determinations of rank are a delicate matter, and it is sufficient priority for an author that one likes him immensely. Daudet is bright, vivid, tender; he has an intense artistic life. And then he is so free. For the spirit that moves slowly, going carefully from point to point, not sure whether this or that or the other will "do," the sight of such freedom is delightful.

1883.

VIII. GUY DE MAUPASSANT

I

THE first artists, in any line, are doubtless not those whose general ideas about their art are most often on their lips—those who most abound in precept, apology, and formula and can best tell us the reasons and the philosophy of things. We know the first usually by their energetic practice, the constancy with which they apply their principles, and the serenity with which they leave us to hunt for their secret in the illustration, the concrete example. None the less it often happens that a valid artist utters his mystery, flashes upon us for a moment the light by which he works, shows us the rule by which he holds it just that he should be measured. This accident is happiest, I think, when it is soonest over; the shortest explanations of the products of genius are the best, and there is many a creator of living figures whose friends, however full of faith in his inspiration, will do well to pray for him when he sallies forth into the dim wilderness of theory. The doctrine is apt to be so much less inspired than the work, the work is often so much more intelligent than the doctrine. M. Guy de Maupassant has lately traversed with a firm and rapid step a literary crisis of this kind; he has clambered safely up the bank at the further end of the morass. If he has relieved himself in the preface to *Pierre et Jean*, the last-published of his tales, he has also rendered a service to his friends; he has not only come home in a recognisable plight, escaping gross disaster with a success which even his extreme good sense was far from making in advance a matter of course, but he has expressed in intelligible terms (that by itself is a ground of felicitation) his most general idea, his own sense of his direction. He has arranged, as it were, the light in which he wishes to sit. If it is a question of attempting, under however many disadvantages, a sketch of him, the critic's business therefore is simplified: there will be no difficulty in placing him, for he himself has chosen the spot, he has made the chalk-mark on the floor.

I may as well say at once that in dissertation M. de Maupassant does not write with his best pen; the philosopher in his composition is perceptibly inferior to the story-teller. I would rather have written half a page of *Boule de Suif* than the whole of the introduction to Flaubert's *Letters to Madame Sand*; and his little disquisition on the novel in general, attached to that particular example of it which he has just put forth,[5] is considerably less to the point than the masterpiece which it ushers in. In short, as a commentator M. de Maupassant is slightly common, while as an artist he is wonderfully rare. Of course we must, in judging a writer, take one thing with another, and if I could make up my mind that M. de Maupassant is weak in theory, it would almost make me like him better, render him more approachable, give him the touch of softness that he lacks, and show us a human flaw. The most general quality of the author of *La Maison Tellier* and *Bel-Ami*, the impression that remains last, after the others have been accounted for, is an essential hardness— hardness of form, hardness of nature; and it would put us more at ease to find that if the fact with him (the fact of execution) is so extraordinarily definite and adequate, his explanations, after it, were a little vague and sentimental. But I am not sure that he must even be held foolish to have noticed the race of critics: he is at any rate so much less foolish than several of that fraternity. He has said his say concisely and as if he were saying it once for all. In fine, his readers must be grateful to him for such a passage as that in which he remarks that whereas the public at large very legitimately says to a writer, "Console me, amuse me, terrify me, make me cry, make me dream, or make me think," what the sincere critic says is, "Make me something fine in the form that shall suit you best, according to your temperament." This seems to me to put into a nutshell the whole question of the different classes of fiction, concerning which there has recently been so much discourse. There are simply as many different kinds as there are persons practising the art, for if a picture, a tale, or a novel be a direct impression of life (and that surely constitutes its interest and value), the impression will vary according to the plate that takes it, the particular structure and mixture of the recipient.

I am not sure that I know what M. de Maupassant means when he says, The critic shall appreciate the result only according to the nature of the effort; he has no right to concern himself with tendencies." The second clause of that observation strikes me as rather in the air, thanks to the vagueness of the last word. But our author adds to the definiteness of his contention when he goes on to say that any form of the novel is simply a vision of the world from the standpoint of a person constituted after a certain fashion, and that it is therefore absurd to say that there is, for the novelist's use, only one reality of things. This seems to me commendable, not as a flight of metaphysics, hovering over bottomless gulfs of controversy, but, on the contrary, as a just indication of the vanity of certain dogmatisms. The particular way we see the world is our particular illusion about it, says M. de Maupassant, and this illusion fits itself to our organs and senses; our receptive vessel becomes the furniture of *our* little plot of the universal consciousness.

"How childish, moreover, to believe in reality, since we each carry our own in our thought and in our organs. Our eyes, our ears, our sense of smell, of taste, differing from one person to another, create as many truths as there are men upon earth. And our minds, taking instruction from these organs, so diversely impressed, understand, analyse, judge, as if each of us belonged to a different race. Each one of us, therefore, forms for himself an illusion of the world, which is the illusion poetic, or sentimental, or joyous, or melancholy, or unclean, or dismal, according to his nature. And the writer has no other mission than to reproduce faithfully this illusion, with all the contrivances of art that he has learned and has at his command. The illusion of beauty, which is a human convention! The illusion of ugliness, which is a changing opinion! The illusion of truth, which is never immutable! The illusion of the ignoble, which attracts so many! The great artists are those who make humanity accept their particular illusion. Let us, therefore, not get angry with any one theory, since every theory is the generalised expression of a temperament asking itself questions."

What is interesting in this is not that M. de Maupassant happens to hold that we have no universal measure of the truth, but that it is the last word on a question of art from a writer who is rich in experience and has had success in a very rare degree. It is of secondary importance that our impression should be called, or not called, an illusion; what is excellent is that our author has stated more neatly than we have lately seen it done that the value of the artist resides in the clearness with which he gives forth that impression. His particular organism constitutes a *case*, and the critic is intelligent in proportion as he apprehends and enters into that case. To quarrel with it because it is not another, which it could not possibly have been without a wholly different outfit, appears to M. de Maupassant a deplorable waste of time. If this appeal to our disinterestedness may strike some readers as chilling (through their inability to conceive of any other form than the one they like—a limitation excellent for a reader but poor for a judge), the occasion happens to be none of the best for saying so, for M. de Maupassant himself precisely presents all the symptoms of a "case" in the most striking way, and shows us how far the consideration of them may take us. Embracing such an opportunity as this, and giving ourselves to it freely, seems to me indeed to be a course more fruitful in valid conclusions, as well as in entertainment by the way, than the more common method of establishing one's own premises. To make clear to ourselves those of the author of *Pierre et Jean*—those to which he is committed by the very nature of his mind—is an attempt that will both stimulate and repay curiosity. There is no way of looking at his work less dry, less academic, for as we proceed from one of his peculiarities to another, the whole horizon widens, yet without our leaving firm ground, and we see ourselves landed, step by step, in the most general questions—those explanations of things which reside in the race, in the society. Of course there are cases and cases, and it is the salient ones that the disinterested critic is delighted to meet.

What makes M. de Maupassant salient is two facts: the first of which is that his gifts are remarkably strong and definite, and the second that he writes directly *from* them, as it were: holds the fullest, the most uninterrupted—I scarcely know what to call it—the boldest communication with them. A case is poor when the cluster of the artist's sensibilities is small, or they themselves are wanting in keenness, or else when the personage fails to admit them—either through ignorance, or diffidence, or stupidity, or the error of a false ideal—to what may be called a legitimate share in his attempt. It is, I think, among English and American writers that this latter accident is most liable to occur; more than the French we are apt to be misled by some convention or other as to the sort of feeler we *ought* to put forth, forgetting that the best one will be the one that nature happens to have given us. We have doubtless often enough the courage of our opinions (when it befalls that we have opinions), but we have not so constantly that of our perceptions. There is a whole side of our perceptive apparatus that we in fact neglect, and there are probably many among us who would erect this tendency into a duty. M. de Maupassant neglects nothing that he possesses; he cultivates his garden with admirable energy; and if there is a flower you miss from the rich parterre, you may be sure that it could not possibly have been raised, his mind not containing the soil for it. He is plainly of the opinion that the first duty of the artist, and the thing that makes him most useful to his fellow-men, is to master his instrument, whatever it may happen to be.

His own is that of the senses, and it is through them alone, or almost alone, that life appeals to him; it is almost alone by their help that he describes it, that he produces brilliant works. They render him this great assistance because they are evidently, in his constitution, extraordinarily alive; there is scarcely a page in all his twenty volumes that does not testify to their vivacity. Nothing could be further from his thought than to disavow them and to minimise their importance. He accepts them frankly, gratefully, works them, rejoices in them. If he were told that there are many English writers who would be sorry to go with him in this, he would, I imagine, staring, say that that is about what was to have been expected of the Anglo-Saxon race, or even that many of them probably could not go with him if they would. Then he would ask how our authors can be so foolish as to sacrifice such a *moyen*, how they can afford to, and exclaim, "They must be pretty works, those they produce, and give a fine, true, complete account of life, with such omissions, such lacunæ!" M. de Maupassant's productions teach us, for instance, that his sense of smell is exceptionally acute—as acute as that of those animals of the field and forest whose subsistence and security depend upon it. It might be thought that he would, as a student of the human race, have found an abnormal development of this faculty embarrassing, scarcely knowing what to do with it, where to place it. But such an apprehension betrays an imperfect conception of his directness and resolution, as well as of his constant economy of means. Nothing whatever prevents him from representing the relations of men and women as largely governed by the scent of the parties. Human life in his pages (would this not be the most general description he would give of it?) appears for the most part as a sort of concert of odours, and his people are perpetually engaged, or he is engaged on their behalf, in sniffing up and distinguishing them, in some pleasant or painful exercise of the nostril. "If everything in life speaks to the nostril, why on earth shouldn't we say so?" I suppose him to inquire; "and what a proof of the empire of poor conventions and hypocrisies, *chez vous autres*, that you should pretend to describe and characterise, and yet take no note (or so little that it comes to the same thing) of that essential sign!"

Not less powerful is his visual sense, the quick, direct discrimination of his eye, which explains the singularly vivid concision of his descriptions. These are never prolonged nor analytic, have nothing of enumeration, of the quality of the observer, who counts the items to be sure he has made up the sum. His eye *selects* unerringly, unscrupulously, almost impudently—catches the particular thing in which the character of the object or the scene resides, and, by expressing it with the artful brevity of a master, leaves a convincing, original picture. If he is inveterately synthetic, he is never more so than in the way he brings this hard, short, intelligent gaze to bear. His vision of the world is for the most part a vision of ugliness, and even when it is not, there is in his easy power to generalise a certain absence of love, a sort of bird's-eye-view contempt. He has none of the superstitions of observation, none of our English indulgences, our tender and often imaginative superficialities. If he glances into a railway carriage bearing its freight into the Parisian suburbs of a summer Sunday, a dozen dreary lives map themselves out in a flash.

"There were stout ladies in farcical clothes, those middle-class goodwives of the *banlieue* who replace the distinction they don't possess by an irrelevant dignity; gentlemen weary of the office, with sallow faces and twisted bodies, and one of their shoulders a little forced up by perpetual bending at work over a table. Their anxious, joyless faces spoke moreover of domestic worries, incessant needs for money, old hopes finally shattered; for they all belonged to the army of poor threadbare devils who vegetate frugally in a mean little plaster house, with a flower-bed for a garden." ...

Even in a brighter picture, such as the admirable vignette of the drive of Madame Tellier and her companions, the whole thing is an impression, as painters say nowadays, in which the figures are cheap. The six women at the station clamber into a country cart and go jolting through the Norman landscape to the village.

"But presently the jerky trot of the nag shook the vehicle so terribly that the chairs began to dance, tossing up the travellers to right, to left, with movements like puppets, scared grimaces, cries of dismay suddenly interrupted by a more violent bump. They clutched the sides of the trap, their bonnets turned over on to their backs, or upon the nose or the shoulder; and the white horse continued to go, thrusting out his head and straightening the little tail, hairless like that of a rat, with which from time to time he whisked his buttocks. Joseph Rivet, with one foot stretched upon the shaft, the other leg bent under him, and his elbows very high, held the reins and emitted from his throat every moment a kind of cluck which caused the animal to prick up his ears and quicken his pace. On either side of the road the green country stretched away. The colza, in flower, produced in spots a great carpet of undulating yellow, from which there rose a strong, wholesome smell, a smell penetrating and pleasant, carried very far by the breeze. In the tall rye the cornflowers held up their little azure heads, which the women wished to pluck; but M. Rivet refused to stop. Then, in some place, a whole field looked as if it were sprinkled with blood, it was so crowded with poppies. And in the midst of the great level, taking colour in this fashion from the flowers of the soil, the trap passed on with the jog of the white horse, seeming itself to carry a nosegay of richer hues; it disappeared behind the big trees of a farm, to come out again where the foliage stopped and parade afresh through the green and yellow crops, pricked with red or blue, its blazing cartload of women, which receded in the sunshine."

As regards the other sense, the sense *par excellence*, the sense which we scarcely mention in English fiction, and which I am not very sure I shall be allowed to mention in an English periodical, M. de Maupassant speaks for that, and of it, with extraordinary distinctness and authority. To say that it occupies the first place in his picture is to say too little; it covers in truth the whole canvas, and his work is little else but a report of its innumerable manifestations. These manifestations are not, for him, so many incidents of life; they are life itself, they represent the standing answer to any question that we may ask about it. He describes them in detail, with a familiarity and a frankness which leave nothing to be added; I should say with singular truth, if I did not consider that in regard to this article he may be taxed with a certain exaggeration. M. de Maupassant would doubtless affirm that where the empire of the sexual sense is concerned, no exaggeration is possible: nevertheless it may be said that whatever depths may be discovered by those who dig for them, the impression of the human spectacle for him who takes it as it comes has less analogy with that of the monkeys' cage than this admirable writer's account of it. I speak of the human spectacle as we Anglo-Saxons see it—as we Anglo-Saxons pretend we see it, M. de Maupassant would possibly say.

At any rate, I have perhaps touched upon this peculiarity sufficiently to explain my remark that his point of view is almost solely that of the senses. If he is a very interesting case, this makes him also an embarrassing one, embarrassing and mystifying for the moralist. I may as well admit that no writer of the day strikes me as equally so. To find M. de Maupassant a lion in the path—that may seem to some people a singular proof of want of courage; but I think the obstacle will not be made light of by those who have really taken the measure of the animal. We are accustomed to think, we of the English faith, that a cynic is a living advertisement of his errors, especially in proportion as he is a thorough-going one; and M. de Maupassant's cynicism, unrelieved as it is, will not be disposed of off-hand by a critic of a competent literary sense. Such a critic is not slow to perceive, to his no small confusion, that though, judging from usual premises, the author of *Bel-Ami* ought to be a warning, he somehow is not. His baseness, as it pervades him, ought to be written all over him; yet somehow there are there certain aspects—and those commanding, as the house-agents say—in which it is not in the least to be perceived. It is easy to exclaim that if he judges life only from the point of view of the senses, many are the noble and exquisite things that he must leave out. What he leaves out has no claim to get itself considered till after we have done justice to what he takes in. It is this positive side of M. de Maupassant that is most remarkable—the fact that his literary character is so complete and edifying. "Auteur à peu près irréprochable dans un genre qui ne l'est pas," as that excellent critic M. Jules Lemaître says of him, he disturbs us by associating a conscience and a high standard with a temper long synonymous, in our eyes, with an absence of scruples. The situation would be simpler certainly if he were a bad writer; but none the less it is possible, I think, on the whole, to circumvent him, even without attempting to prove that after all he is one.

The latter part of his introduction to *Pierre et Jean* is less felicitous than the beginning, but we learn from it—and this is interesting—that he regards the analytic fashion of telling a story, which has lately begotten in his own country some such remarkable experiments (few votaries as it has attracted among ourselves), as very much less profitable than the simple epic manner which "avoids with care all complicated explanations, all dissertations upon motives, and confines itself to making persons and events pass before our eyes." M. de Maupassant adds that in his view "psychology should be hidden in a book, as it is hidden in reality under the facts of existence. The novel conceived in this manner gains interest, movement, colour, the bustle of life." When it is a question of an artistic process, we must always mistrust very sharp distinctions, for there is surely in every method a little of every other method. It is as difficult to describe an action without glancing at its motive, its moral history, as it is to describe a motive without glancing at its practical consequence. Our history and our fiction are what we do; but it surely is not more easy to determine where what we do begins than to determine where it ends—notoriously a hopeless task. Therefore it would take a very subtle sense to draw a hard and fast line on the borderland of explanation and illustration. If psychology be hidden in life, as, according to M. de Maupassant, it should be in a book, the question immediately comes up, "From whom is it hidden?" From some people, no doubt, but very much less from others; and all depends upon the observer, the nature of one's observation, and one's curiosity. For some people motives, reasons, relations, explanations, are a part of the very surface of the drama, with the footlights beating full upon them. For me an act, an incident, an attitude, may be a sharp, detached, isolated thing, of which I give a full account in saying that in such and such a way it came off. For you it may be hung about with implications, with relations, and conditions as necessary to help you to recognise it as the clothes of your friends are to help you know them in the street. You feel that they would seem strange to you without petticoats and trousers.

M. de Maupassant would probably urge that the right thing is to know, or to guess, how events come to pass, but to say as little about it as possible. There are matters in regard to which he feels the importance of being explicit, but that is not one of them. The contention to which I allude strikes me as rather arbitrary, so difficult is it to put one's finger upon the reason why, for instance, there should be so little mystery about what happened to Christiane Andermatt, in *Mont-Oriol*, when she went to walk on the hills with Paul Brétigny, and so much, say, about the forces that formed her for that gentleman's convenience, or those lying behind any other odd collapse that our author may have related. The rule misleads, and the best rule certainly is the tact of the individual writer, which will adapt itself to the material as the material comes to him. The cause we plead is ever pretty sure to be the cause of our idiosyncrasies, and if M. de Maupassant thinks meanly of "explanations," it is, I suspect, that they come to him in no great affluence. His view of the conduct of man is so simple as scarcely to require them; and indeed so far as they are needed he *is*, virtually, explanatory. He deprecates reference to motives, but there is one, covering an immense ground in his horizon, as I have already hinted, to which he perpetually refers. If the sexual impulse be not a moral antecedent, it is none the less the wire that moves almost all M. de Maupassant's puppets, and as he has not hidden it, I cannot see that he has eliminated analysis or made a sacrifice to discretion. His pages are studded with that particular analysis; he is constantly peeping behind the curtain, telling us what he discovers there. The truth is that the admirable system of simplification which makes his tales so rapid and so concise (especially his shorter ones, for his novels in some degree, I think, suffer from it), strikes us as not in the least a conscious intellectual effort, a selective, comparative process. He tells us all he knows, all he suspects, and if these things take no account of the moral nature of man, it is because he has no window looking in that direction, and not because artistic scruples have compelled him to close it up. The very compact mansion in which he dwells presents on that side a perfectly dead wall.

This is why, if his axiom that you produce the effect of truth better by painting people from the outside than from the inside has a large utility, his example is convincing in a much higher degree. A writer is fortunate when his theory and his limitations so exactly correspond, when his curiosities may be appeased with such precision and promptitude. M. de Maupassant contends that the most that the analytic novelist can do is to put himself—his own peculiarities—into the costume of the figure analysed. This may be true, but if it applies to one manner of representing people who are not ourselves, it applies also to any other manner. It is the limitation, the difficulty of the novelist, to whatever clan or camp he may belong. M. de Maupassant is remarkably objective and impersonal, but he would go too far if he were to entertain the belief that he has kept himself out of his books. They speak of him eloquently, even if it only be to tell us how easy—how easy, given his talent of course—he has found this impersonality. Let us hasten to add that in the case of describing a character it is doubtless more difficult to convey the impression of something that is not one's self (the constant effort, however delusive at bottom, of the novelist), than in the case of describing some object more immediately visible. The operation is more delicate, but that circumstance only increases the beauty of the problem.

On the question of style our author has some excellent remarks; we may be grateful indeed for every one of them, save an odd reflection about the way to "become original" if we happen not to be so. The recipe for this transformation, it would appear, is to sit down in front of a blazing fire, or a tree in a plain, or any object we encounter in the regular way of business, and remain there until the tree, or the fire, or the object, whatever it be, become different for us from all other specimens of the same class. I doubt whether this system would always answer, for surely the resemblance is what we wish to discover, quite as much as the difference, and the best way to preserve it is not to look for something opposed to it. Is not this indication of the road to take to become, as a writer, original touched with the same fallacy as the recommendation about eschewing analysis? It is the only *naïveté* I have encountered in M. de Maupassant's many volumes. The best originality is the most unconscious, and the best way to describe a tree is the way in which it has struck us. "Ah, but we don't always know how it has struck us," the answer to that may be, "and it takes some time and ingenuity—much fasting and prayer—to find out." If we do not know, it probably has not struck us very much: so little indeed that our inquiry had better be relegated to that closed chamber of an artist's meditations, that sacred back kitchen, which no *a priori* rule can light up. The best thing the artist's adviser can do in such a case is to trust him and turn away, to let him fight the matter out with his conscience. And be this said with a full appreciation of the degree in which M. de Maupassant's observations on the whole question of a writer's style, at the point we have come to to-day, bear the stamp of intelligence and experience. His own style is of so excellent a tradition that the presumption is altogether in favour of what he may have to say.

He feels oppressively, discouragingly, as many another of his countrymen must have felt—for the French have worked their language as no other people have done—the penalty of coming at the end of three centuries of literature, the difficulty of dealing with an instrument of expression so worn by friction, of drawing new sounds from the old familiar pipe. "When we read, so saturated with French writing as we are that our whole body gives us the impression of being a paste made of words, do we ever find a line, a thought, which is not familiar to us, and of which we have not had at least a confused presentiment?" And he adds that the matter is simple enough for the writer who only seeks to amuse the public by means already known; he attempts little, and he produces "with confidence, in the candour of his mediocrity," works which answer no question and leave no trace. It is he who wants to do more than this that has less and less an easy time of it. Everything seems to him to have been done, every effect produced, every combination already made. If he be a man of genius, his trouble is lightened, for mysterious ways are revealed to him, and new combinations spring up for him even after novelty is dead. It is to the simple man of taste and talent, who has only a conscience and a will, that the situation may sometimes well appear desperate; he judges himself as he goes, and he can only go step by step over ground where every step is already a footprint.

If it be a miracle whenever there is a fresh tone, the miracle has been wrought for M. de Maupassant. Or is he simply a man of genius to whom short cuts have been disclosed in the watches of the night? At any rate he has had faith—religion has come to his aid; I mean the religion of his mother tongue, which he has loved well enough to be patient for her sake. He has arrived at the peace which passeth understanding, at a kind of conservative piety. He has taken his stand on simplicity, on a studied sobriety, being persuaded that the deepest science lies in that direction rather than in the multiplication of new terms, and on this subject he delivers himself with superlative wisdom. "There is no need of the queer, complicated, numerous, and Chinese vocabulary which is imposed on us to-day under the name of artistic writing, to fix all the shades of thought; the right way is to distinguish with an extreme clearness all those modifications of the value of a word which come from the place it occupies. Let us have fewer nouns, verbs and adjectives of an almost imperceptible sense, and more different phrases variously constructed, ingeniously cast, full of the science of sound and rhythm. Let us have an excellent general form rather than be collectors of rare terms." M. de Maupassant's practice does not fall below his exhortation (though I must confess that in the foregoing passage he makes use of the detestable expression "stylist," which I have not reproduced). Nothing can exceed the masculine firmness, the quiet force of his own style, in which every phrase is a close sequence, every epithet a paying piece, and the ground is completely cleared of the vague, the ready-made and the second-best. Less than any one to-day does he beat the air; more than any one does he hit out from the shoulder.

II

He has produced a hundred short tales and only four regular novels; but if the tales deserve the first place in any candid appreciation of his talent it is not simply because they are so much the more numerous: they are also more characteristic; they represent him best in his originality, and their brevity, extreme in some cases, does not prevent them from being a collection of masterpieces. (They are very unequal, and I speak of the best.) The little story is but scantily relished in England, where readers take their fiction rather by the volume than by the page, and the novelist's idea is apt to resemble one of those old-fashioned carriages which require a wide court to turn round. In America, where it is associated pre-eminently with Hawthorne's name, with Edgar Poe's, and with that of Mr. Bret Harte, the short tale has had a better fortune. France, however, has been the land of its great prosperity, and M. de

Maupassant had from the first the advantage of addressing a public accustomed to catch on, as the modern phrase is, quickly. In some respects, it may be said, he encountered prejudices too friendly, for he found a tradition of indecency ready made to his hand. I say indecency with plainness, though my indication would perhaps please better with another word, for we suffer in English from a lack of roundabout names for the *conte leste*—that element for which the French, with their *grivois*, their *gaillard*, their *égrillard*, their *gaudriole*, have so many convenient synonyms. It is an honoured tradition in France that the little story, in verse or in prose, should be liable to be more or less obscene (I can think only of that alternative epithet), though I hasten to add that among literary forms it does not monopolise the privilege. Our uncleanness is less producible—at any rate it is less produced.

For the last ten years our author has brought forth with regularity these condensed compositions, of which, probably, to an English reader, at a first glance, the most universal sign will be their licentiousness. They really partake of this quality, however, in a very differing degree, and a second glance shows that they may be divided into numerous groups. It is not fair, I think, even to say that what they have most in common is their being extremely *lestes*. What they have most in common is their being extremely strong, and after that their being extremely brutal. A story may be obscene without being brutal, and *vice versâ*, and M. de Maupassant's contempt for those interdictions which are supposed to be made in the interest of good morals is but an incident—a very large one indeed—of his general contempt. A pessimism so great that its alliance with the love of good work, or even with the calculation of the sort of work that pays best in a country of style, is, as I have intimated, the most puzzling of anomalies (for it would seem in the light of such sentiments that nothing is worth anything), this cynical strain is the sign of such gems of narration as *La Maison Tellier, L'Histoire d'une Fille de Ferme, L'Ane, Le Chien, Mademoiselle Fifi, Monsieur Parent, L'Héritage, En Famille, Le Baptême, Le Père Amable*. The author fixes a hard eye on some small spot of human life, usually some ugly, dreary, shabby, sordid one, takes up the particle, and squeezes it either till it grimaces or till it bleeds. Sometimes the grimace is very droll, sometimes the wound is very horrible; but in either case the whole thing is real, observed, noted, and represented, not an invention

165

or a castle in the air. M. de Maupassant sees human life as a terribly ugly business relieved by the comical, but even the comedy is for the most part the comedy of misery, of avidity, of ignorance, helplessness, and grossness. When his laugh is not for these things, it is for the little *saletés* (to use one of his own favourite words) of luxurious life, which are intended to be prettier, but which can scarcely be said to brighten the picture. I like *La Bête à Maître Belhomme*, *La Ficelle*, *Le Petit Fût*, *Le Cas de Madame Luneau*, *Tribuneaux Rustiques*, and many others of this category much better than his anecdotes of the mutual confidences of his little *marquises* and *baronnes*.

Not counting his novels for the moment, his tales may be divided into the three groups of those which deal with the Norman peasantry, those which deal with the *petit employé* and small shopkeeper, usually in Paris, and the miscellaneous, in which the upper walks of life are represented, and the fantastic, the whimsical, the weird, and even the supernatural, figure as well as the unexpurgated. These last things range from *Le Horla* (which is not a specimen of the author's best vein—the only occasion on which he has the weakness of imitation is when he strikes us as emulating Edgar Poe) to *Miss Harriet*, and from *Boule de Suif* (a triumph) to that almost inconceivable little growl of Anglophobia, *Découverte*—inconceivable I mean in its irresponsibility and ill-nature on the part of a man of M. de Maupassant's distinction; passing by such little perfections as *Petit Soldat*, *L'Abandonné*, *Le Collier* (the list is too long for complete enumeration), and such gross imperfections (for it once in a while befalls our author to go woefully astray), as *La Femme de Paul*, *Châli*, *Les Sœurs Rondoli*. To these might almost be added as a special category the various forms in which M. de Maupassant relates adventures in railway carriages. Numerous, to his imagination, are the pretexts for enlivening fiction afforded by first, second, and third class compartments; the accidents (which have nothing to do with the conduct of the train) that occur there constitute no inconsiderable part of our earthly transit.

It is surely by his Norman peasant that his tales will live; he knows this worthy as if he had made him, understands him down to the ground, puts him on his feet with a few of the freest, most plastic touches. M. de Maupassant does not admire him, and he is such a master of the subject that it would ill become an outsider to suggest a revision of judgment. He is a part of the contemptible furniture of the world, but on the whole, it would appear, the most grotesque part of it. His caution, his canniness, his natural astuteness, his stinginess, his general grinding sordidness, are as unmistakable as that quaint and brutish dialect in which he expresses himself, and on which our author plays like a virtuoso. It would be impossible to demonstrate with a finer sense of the humour of the thing the fatuities and densities of his ignorance, the bewilderments of his opposed appetites, the overreachings of his caution. His existence has a gay side, but it is apt to be the barbarous gaiety commemorated in *Farce Normande*, an anecdote which, like many of M. de Maupassant's anecdotes, it is easier to refer the reader to than to repeat. If it is most convenient to place *La Maison Tellier* among the tales of the peasantry, there is no doubt that it stands at the head of the list. It is absolutely unadapted to the perusal of ladies and young persons, but it shares this peculiarity with most of its fellows, so that to ignore it on that account would be to imply that we must forswear M. de Maupassant altogether, which is an incongruous and insupportable conclusion. Every good story is of course both a picture and an idea, and the more they are interfused the better the problem is solved. In *La Maison Tellier* they fit each other to perfection; the capacity for sudden innocent delights latent in natures which have lost their innocence is vividly illustrated by the singular scenes to which our acquaintance with Madame and her staff (little as it may be a thing to boast of), successively introduces us. The breadth, the freedom, and brightness of all this give the measure of the author's talent, and of that large, keen way of looking at life which sees the pathetic and the droll, the stuff of which the whole piece is made, in the queerest and humblest patterns. The tone of *La Maison Tellier* and the few compositions which closely resemble it, expresses M. de Maupassant's nearest approach to geniality. Even here, however, it is the geniality of the showman exhilarated by the success with which he feels that he makes his mannikins (and especially his womankins) caper and squeak, and who after the performance tosses them into their box with the irreverence of a practised hand. If the pages of the author of *Bel-Ami* may be searched almost in vain for a manifestation of the sentiment of respect, it is naturally not by Mme. Tellier and her charges that we must look most to see it called forth; but they are among the things that please him most.

Sometimes there is a sorrow, a misery, or even a little heroism, that he handles with a certain tenderness (*Une Vie* is the capital example of this), without insisting on the poor, the ridiculous, or, as he is fond of saying, the bestial side of it. Such an attempt, admirable in its sobriety and delicacy, is the sketch, in *L'Abandonné*, of the old lady and gentleman, Mme. de Cadour and M. d'Apreval, who, staying with the husband of the former at a little watering-place on the Normandy coast, take a long, hot walk on a summer's day, on a straight, white road, into the interior, to catch a clandestine glimpse of a young farmer, their illegitimate son. He has been pensioned, he is ignorant of his origin, and is a common-place and unconciliatory rustic. They look at him, in his dirty farmyard, and no sign passes between them; then they turn away and crawl back, in melancholy silence, along the dull French road. The manner in which this dreary little occurrence is related makes it as large as a chapter of history. There is tenderness in *Miss Harriet*, which sets forth how an English old maid, fantastic, hideous, sentimental, and tract-distributing, with a smell of india-rubber, fell in love with an irresistible French painter, and drowned herself in the well because she saw him kissing the maid-servant; but the figure of the lady grazes the farcical. Is it because we know Miss Harriet (if we are not mistaken in the type the author has had in his eye) that we suspect the good spinster was not so weird and desperate, addicted though her class may be, as he says, to "haunting all the *tables d'hôte* in Europe, to spoiling Italy, poisoning Switzerland, making the charming towns of the Mediterranean uninhabitable, carrying everywhere their queer little manias, their *mœurs de vestales pétrifiées*, their indescribable garments, and that odour of india-rubber which makes one think that at night they must be slipped into a case?" What would Miss Harriet have said to M. de Maupassant's friend, the hero of the *Découverte*, who, having married a little Anglaise because he thought she was charming when she spoke broken French, finds she is very flat as she becomes more fluent, and has nothing more urgent than to denounce her to a gentleman he meets on the steamboat, and to relieve his wrath in ejaculations of "Sales Anglais"?

M. de Maupassant evidently knows a great deal about the army of clerks who work under government, but it is a terrible tale that he has to tell of them and of the *petit bourgeois* in general. It is true that he has treated the *petit bourgeois* in *Pierre et Jean* without holding him up to our derision, and the effort has been so fruitful, that we owe to it the work for which, on the whole, in the long list of his successes, we are most thankful. But of *Pierre et Jean*, a production neither comic nor cynical (in the degree, that is, of its predecessors), but serious and fresh, I will speak anon. In *Monsieur Parent, L'Héritage, En Famille, Une Partie de Campagne, Promenade*, and many other pitiless little pieces, the author opens the window wide to his perception of everything mean, narrow, and sordid. The subject is ever the struggle for existence in hard conditions, lighted up simply by more or less *polissonnerie*. Nothing is more striking to an Anglo-Saxon reader than the omission of all the other lights, those with which our imagination, and I think it ought to be said our observation, is familiar, and which our own works of fiction at any rate do not permit us to forget: those of which the most general description is that they spring from a certain mixture of good-humour and piety—piety, I mean, in the civil and domestic sense quite as much as in the religious. The love of sport, the sense of decorum, the necessity for action, the habit of respect, the absence of irony, the pervasiveness of childhood, the expansive tendency of the race, are a few of the qualities (the analysis might, I think, be pushed much further) which ease us off, mitigate our tension and irritation, rescue us from the nervous exasperation which is almost the commonest element of life as depicted by M. de Maupassant. No doubt there is in our literature an immense amount of conventional blinking, and it may be questioned whether pessimistic representation in M. de Maupassant's manner do not follow his particular original more closely than our perpetual quest of pleasantness (does not Mr. Rider Haggard make even his African carnage pleasant?) adheres to the lines of the world we ourselves know.

Fierce indeed is the struggle for existence among even our pious and good-humoured millions, and it is attended with incidents as to which after all little testimony is to be extracted from our literature of fiction. It must never be forgotten that the optimism of that literature is partly the optimism of women and of spinsters; in other words the optimism of ignorance as well as of delicacy. It might be supposed that the French, with their mastery of the *arts d'agrément*, would have more consolations than we, but such is not the account of the matter given by the new generation of painters. To the

French we seem superficial, and we are certainly open to the reproach; but none the less even to the infinite majority of readers of good faith there will be a wonderful want of correspondence between the general picture of *Bel-Ami*, of *Mont-Oriol*, of *Une Vie*, *Yvette* and *En Famille*, and our own vision of reality. It is an old impression of course that the satire of the French has a very different tone from ours; but few English readers will admit that the feeling of life is less in ours than in theirs. The feeling of life is evidently, *de part et d'autre*, a very different thing. If in ours, as the novel illustrates it, there are superficialities, there are also qualities which are far from being negatives and omissions: a large imagination and (is it fatuous to say?) a large experience of the positive kind. Even those of our novelists whose manner is most ironic pity life more and hate it less than M. de Maupassant and his great initiator Flaubert. It comes back I suppose to our good-humour (which may apparently also be an artistic force); at any rate, we have reserves about our shames and our sorrows, indulgences and tolerances about our Philistinism, forbearances about our blows, and a general friendliness of conception about our possibilities, which take the cruelty from our self-derision and operate in the last resort as a sort of tribute to our freedom. There is a horrible, admirable scene in *Monsieur Parent*, which is a capital example of triumphant ugliness. The harmless gentleman who gives his name to the tale has an abominable wife, one of whose offensive attributes is a lover (unsuspected by her husband), only less impudent than herself. M. Parent comes in from a walk with his little boy, at dinner-time, to encounter suddenly in his abused, dishonoured, deserted home, convincing proof of her misbehaviour. He waits and waits dinner for her, giving her the benefit of every doubt; but when at last she enters, late in the evening, accompanied by the partner of her guilt, there is a tremendous domestic concussion. It is to the peculiar vividness of this scene that I allude, the way we hear it and see it, and its most repulsive details are evoked for us: the sordid confusion, the vulgar noise, the disordered table and ruined dinner, the shrill insolence of the wife, her brazen mendacity, the scared inferiority of the lover, the mere momentary heroics of the weak husband, the scuffle and somersault, the eminently unpoetic justice with which it all ends.

170

When Thackeray relates how Arthur Pendennis goes home to take pot-luck with the insolvent Newcomes at Boulogne, and how the dreadful Mrs. Mackenzie receives him, and how she makes a scene, when the frugal repast is served, over the diminished mutton-bone, we feel that the notation of that order of misery goes about as far as we can bear it. But this is child's play to the history of M. and Mme. Caravan and their attempt, after the death (or supposed death) of the husband's mother, to transfer to their apartment before the arrival of the other heirs certain miserable little articles of furniture belonging to the deceased, together with the frustration of the manœuvre not only by the grim resurrection of the old woman (which is a sufficiently fantastic item), but by the shock of battle when a married daughter and her husband appear. No one gives us like M. de Maupassant the odious words exchanged on such an occasion as that: no one depicts with so just a hand the feelings of small people about small things. These feelings are very apt to be "fury"; that word is of strikingly frequent occurrence in his pages. *L'Héritage* is a drama of private life in the little world of the Ministère de la Marine—a world, according to M. de Maupassant, of dreadful little jealousies and ineptitudes. Readers of a robust complexion should learn how the wretched M. Lesable was handled by his wife and her father on his failing to satisfy their just expectations, and how he comported himself in the singular situation thus prepared for him. The story is a model of narration, but it leaves our poor average humanity dangling like a beaten rag.

Where does M. de Maupassant find the great multitude of his detestable women? or where at least does he find the courage to represent them in such colours? Jeanne de Lamare, in *Une Vie*, receives the outrages of fate with a passive fortitude; and there is something touching in Mme. Roland's *âme tendre de caissière*, as exhibited in *Pierre et Jean*. But for the most part M. de Maupassant's heroines are a mixture of extreme sensuality and extreme mendacity. They are a large element in that general disfigurement, that *illusion de l'ignoble, qui attire tant d'êtres*, which makes the perverse or the stupid side of things the one which strikes him first, which leads him, if he glances at a group of nurses and children sunning themselves in a Parisian square, to notice primarily the *yeux de brute* of the nurses; or if he speaks of the longing for a taste of the country which haunts the shopkeeper fenced in behind his counter, to identify it as the *amour bête de la nature*; or if he has occasion to put the boulevards before us on a summer's evening, to seek his effect in these terms: "The city, as hot as a stew, seemed to sweat in the suffocating night. The drains puffed their pestilential breath from their mouths of granite, and the underground kitchens poured into the streets, through their low windows, the infamous miasmas of their dishwater and old sauces." I do not contest the truth of such indications, I only note the particular selection and their seeming to the writer the most *apropos*.

Is it because of the inadequacy of these indications when applied to the long stretch that M. de Maupassant's novels strike us as less complete, in proportion to the talent expended upon them, than his *contes* and *nouvelles*? I make this invidious distinction in spite of the fact that *Une Vie* (the first of the novels in the order of time) is a remarkably interesting experiment, and that *Pierre et Jean* is, so far as my judgment goes, a faultless production. *Bel-Ami* is full of the bustle and the crudity of life (its energy and expressiveness almost bribe one to like it), but it has the great defect that the physiological explanation of things here too visibly contracts the problem in order to meet it. The world represented is too special, too little inevitable, too much to take or to leave as we like—a world in which every man is a cad and every woman a harlot. M. de Maupassant traces the career of a finished blackguard who succeeds in life through women, and he represents him primarily as succeeding in the profession of journalism. His colleagues and his mistresses are as depraved as himself, greatly to the injury of the ironic idea, for the real force of satire would have come from seeing him engaged and victorious with natures better than his own. It may be remarked that this was the case with the nature of Mme. Walter; but the reply to that is—hardly! Moreover the author's whole treatment of the episode of Mme. Walter is the thing on which his admirers have least to congratulate him. The taste of it is so atrocious, that it is difficult to do justice to the way it is made to stand out. Such an instance as this pleads with irresistible eloquence, as it seems to me, the cause of that salutary diffidence or practical generosity which I mentioned on a preceding page. I know not the English or American novelist who could have written this portion of the history of *Bel-Ami* if he would. But I also find it impossible to conceive of a member of that fraternity who would have written it if he could. The subject of *Mont-Oriol* is full of queerness to the English mind. Here again the picture has much more importance than the idea, which is simply that a gentleman, if he happen to be a low animal, is liable to love a lady very much less if she presents him with a pledge of their affection. It need scarcely be said that the lady and gentleman who in M. de Maupassant's pages exemplify this interesting truth are not united in wedlock—that is with each other.

M. de Maupassant tells us that he has imbibed many of his principles from Gustave Flaubert, from the study of his works as well as, formerly, the enjoyment of his words. It is in *Une Vie* that Flaubert's influence is most directly traceable, for the thing has a marked analogy with *L'Education Sentimentale*. That is, it is the presentation of a simple piece of a life (in this case a long piece), a series of observations upon an episode *quelconque*, as the French say, with the minimum of arrangement of the given objects. It is an excellent example of the way the impression of truth may be conveyed by that form, but it would have been a still better one if in his search for the effect of dreariness (the effect of dreariness may be said to be the subject of *Une Vie*, so far as the subject is reducible) the author had not eliminated excessively. He has arranged, as I say, as little as possible; the necessity of a "plot" has in no degree imposed itself upon him, and his effort has been to give the uncomposed, unrounded look of life, with its accidents, its broken rhythm, its queer resemblance to the famous description of "Bradshaw"—a compound of trains that start but don't arrive, and trains that arrive but don't start. It is almost an arrangement of the history of poor Mme. de Lamare to have left so many things out of it, for after all she is described in very few of the relations of life. The principal ones are there certainly; we see her as a daughter, a wife, and a mother, but there is a certain accumulation of secondary experience that marks any passage from youth to old age which is a wholly absent element in M. de Maupassant's narrative, and the suppression of which gives the thing a tinge of the arbitrary. It is in the power of this secondary experience to make a great difference, but nothing makes any difference for Jeanne de Lamare as M. de Maupassant puts her before us. Had she no other points of contact than those he describes?—no friends, no phases, no episodes, no chances, none of the miscellaneous *remplissage* of life? No doubt M. de Maupassant would say that he has had to select, that the most comprehensive enumeration is only a condensation, and that, in accordance with the very just principles enunciated in that preface to which I have perhaps too repeatedly referred, he has sacrificed what is uncharacteristic to what is characteristic. It characterises the career of this French country lady of fifty years ago that its long gray expanse should be seen as peopled with but five or six figures. The essence of the matter is that she was deceived in almost every affection, and that essence is given if the persons who deceived her are given.

The reply is doubtless adequate, and I have only intended my criticism to suggest the degree of my interest. What it really amounts to is that if the subject of this artistic experiment had been the existence of an English lady, even a very dull one, the air of verisimilitude would have demanded that she should have been placed in a denser medium. *Une Vie* may after all be only a testimony to the fact of the melancholy void of the coast of Normandy, even within a moderate drive of a great seaport, under the Restoration and Louis Philippe. It is especially to be recommended to those who are interested in the question of what constitutes a "story," offering as it does the most definite sequences at the same time that it has nothing that corresponds to the usual idea of a plot, and closing with an implication that finds us prepared. The picture again in this case is much more dominant than the idea, unless it be an idea that loneliness and grief are terrible. The picture, at any rate, is full of truthful touches, and the work has the merit and the charm that it is the most delicate of the author's productions and the least hard. In none other has he occupied himself so continuously with so innocent a figure as his soft, bruised heroine; in none other has he paid our poor blind human history the compliment (and this is remarkable, considering the flatness of so much of the particular subject) of finding it so little *bête*. He may think it, here, but comparatively he does not say it. He almost betrays a sense of moral things. Jeanne is absolutely passive, she has no moral spring, no active moral life, none of the edifying attributes of character (it costs her apparently as little as may be in the way of a shock, a complication of feeling, to discover, by letters, after her mother's death, that this lady has not been the virtuous woman she has supposed); but her chronicler has had to handle the immaterial forces of

174

patience and renunciation, and this has given the book a certain purity, in spite of two or three "physiological" passages that come in with violence—a violence the greater as we feel it to be a result of selection. It is very much a mark of M. de Maupassant that on the most striking occasion, with a single exception, on which his picture is not a picture of libertinage it is a picture of unmitigated suffering. Would he suggest that these are the only alternatives?

The exception that I here allude to is for *Pierre et Jean*, which I have left myself small space to speak of. Is it because in this masterly little novel there is a show of those immaterial forces which I just mentioned, and because Pierre Roland is one of the few instances of operative character that can be recalled from so many volumes, that many readers will place M. de Maupassant's latest production altogether at the head of his longer ones? I am not sure, inasmuch as after all the character in question is not extraordinarily distinguished, and the moral problem not presented in much complexity. The case is only relative. Perhaps it is not of importance to fix the reasons of preference in respect to a piece of writing so essentially a work of art and of talent. *Pierre et Jean* is the best of M. de Maupassant's novels mainly because M. de Maupassant has never before been so clever. It is a pleasure to see a mature talent able to renew itself, strike another note, and appear still young. This story suggests the growth of a perception that everything has not been said about the actors on the world's stage when they are represented either as helpless victims or as mere bundles of appetites. There is an air of responsibility about Pierre Roland, the person on whose behalf the tale is mainly told, which almost constitutes a pledge. An inquisitive critic may ask why in this particular case M. de Maupassant should have stuck to the *petit bourgeois*, the circumstances not being such as to typify that class more than another. There are reasons indeed which on reflection are perceptible; it was necessary that his people should be poor, and necessary even that to attenuate Madame Roland's misbehaviour she should have had the excuse of the contracted life of a shopwoman in the Rue Montmartre. Were the inquisitive critic slightly malicious as well, he might suspect the author of a fear that he should seem to give way to the *illusion du beau* if in addition to representing the little group in *Pierre et Jean* as persons of about the normal conscience he had also represented them as of the cultivated class. If they belong to the humble life this belittles and—I am still quoting the supposedly malicious critic—M. de Maupassant *must*, in one way or the other, belittle. To the English reader it will appear, I think, that Pierre and Jean are rather more of the cultivated class than two young Englishmen in the same social position. It belongs to the drama that the struggle of the elder brother—educated, proud, and acute—should be partly with the pettiness of his opportunities. The author's choice of a *milieu*, moreover, will serve to English readers as an example of how much more democratic contemporary French fiction is than that of his own country. The greater part of it—almost all the work of Zola and of Daudet, the best of Flaubert's novels, and the best of those of the brothers De Goncourt—treat of that vast, dim section of society which, lying between those luxurious walks on whose behalf there are easy presuppositions and that darkness of misery which, in addition to being picturesque, brings philanthropy also to the writer's aid, constitutes really, in extent and expressiveness, the substance of any nation. In England, where the fashion of fiction still sets mainly to the country house and the hunting-field, and yet more novels are published than anywhere else in the world, that thick twilight of mediocrity of condition has been little explored. May it yield triumphs in the years to come!

It may seem that I have claimed little for M. de Maupassant, so far as English readers are concerned with him, in saying that after publishing twenty improper volumes he has at last published a twenty-first, which is neither indecent nor cynical. It is not this circumstance that has led me to dedicate so many pages to him, but the circumstance that in producing all the others he yet remained, for those who are interested in these matters, a writer with whom it was impossible not to reckon. This is why I called him, to begin with, so many ineffectual names: a rarity, a "case," an embarrassment, a lion in the path. He is still in the path as I conclude these observations, but I think that in making them we have discovered a legitimate way round. If he is a master of his art and it is discouraging to find what low views are compatible with mastery, there is satisfaction, on the other hand in learning on what particular condition he holds his strange success. This condition, it seems to me, is that of having totally omitted one of the items of the problem, an omission which has made the problem so much easier that it may almost be described as a short cut to a solution. The question is whether it be a fair cut. M. de Maupassant has simply skipped the whole reflective part of his men and women—that reflective part which governs conduct and produces character. He may say that he does not see it, does not know it; to which the answer is, "So much the better for you, if you wish to describe life without it. The strings you pull are by so much the less numerous, and you can therefore pull those that remain with greater promptitude, consequently with greater firmness, with a greater air of knowledge." Pierre Roland, I repeat, shows a capacity for reflection, but I cannot think who else does, among the thousand figures who compete with him—I mean for reflection addressed to anything higher than the gratification of an instinct. We have an impression that M. d'Apreval and Madame de Cadour reflect, as they trudge back from their mournful excursion, but that indication is not pushed very far. An aptitude for this exercise is a part of disciplined manhood, and disciplined manhood M. de Maupassant has simply not attempted to represent. I can remember no instance in which he sketches any considerable capacity for conduct, and his women betray that capacity as little as his men. I am much mistaken if he has once painted a gentleman, in the English sense of the term. His gentlemen, like Paul Brétigny and Gontran de Ravenel, are guilty of the most extraordinary deflections. For those who are conscious of this element in life, look for it and like it, the gap will appear to be immense. It will lead them to say, "No wonder you have a contempt if that is the way you limit the field. No wonder you judge people roughly if that is the way you see them. Your work, on your premises, remains the admirable thing it is, but is your 'case' not adequately explained?"

The erotic element in M. de Maupassant, about which much more might have been said, seems to me to be explained by the same limitation, and explicable in a similar way wherever else its literature occurs in excess. The carnal side of man appears the most characteristic if you look at it a great deal; and you look at it a great deal if you do not look at the other, at the side by which he reacts against his weaknesses, his defeats. The more you look at the other, the less the whole business to which French novelists have ever appeared to English readers to give a disproportionate place—the business, as I may say, of the senses—will strike you as the only typical one. Is not this the most useful reflection to make in regard to the famous question of the morality, the decency, of the novel? It is the only one, it seems to me, that will meet the case as we find the case to-day. Hard and fast rules, *a priori* restrictions, mere interdictions (you shall not speak of this, you shall not look at that), have surely served their time, and will in the nature of the case never strike an energetic talent as anything but arbitrary. A healthy, living and growing art, full of curiosity and fond of exercise, has an indefeasible mistrust of rigid prohibitions. Let us then leave this magnificent art of the novelist to itself and to its perfect freedom, in the faith that one example is as good as another, and that our fiction will always be decent enough if it be sufficiently general. Let us not be alarmed at this prodigy (though prodigies are alarming) of M. de Maupassant, who is at once so licentious and so impeccable, but gird ourselves up with the conviction that another point of view will yield another perfection.

1888.

IX. IVAN TURGÉNIEFF

WHEN the mortal remains of Ivan Turgénieff were about to be transported from Paris for interment in his own country, a short commemorative service was held at the Gare du Nord. Ernest Renan and Edmond About, standing beside the train in which his coffin had been placed, bade farewell in the name of the French people to the illustrious stranger who for so many years had been their honoured and grateful guest. M. Renan made a beautiful speech, and M. About a very clever one, and each of them characterised, with ingenuity, the genius and the moral nature of the most touching of writers, the most lovable of men. "Turgénieff," said M. Renan, "received by the mysterious decree which marks out human vocations the gift which is noble beyond all others: he was born essentially impersonal." The passage is so eloquent that one must repeat the whole of it. "His conscience was not that of an individual to whom nature had been more or less generous: it was in some sort the conscience of a people. Before he was born he had lived for thousands of years; infinite successions of reveries had amassed themselves in the depths of his heart. No man has been as much as he the incarnation of a whole race: generations of ancestors, lost in the sleep of centuries, speechless, came through him to life and utterance."

I quote these lines for the pleasure of quoting them; for while I see what M. Renan means by calling Turgénieff impersonal, it has been my wish to devote to his delightful memory a few pages written under the impression of contact and intercourse. He seems to us impersonal, because it is from his writings almost alone that we of English, French and German speech have derived our notions—even yet, I fear, rather meagre and erroneous—of the Russian people. His genius for us is the Slav genius; his voice the voice of those vaguely-imagined multitudes whom we think of more and more to-day as waiting their turn, in the arena of civilisation, in the grey expanses of the North. There is much in his writings to encourage this view, and it is certain that he interpreted with wonderful vividness the temperament of his fellow-countrymen. Cosmopolite that he had become by the force of circumstances, his roots had never been loosened in his native soil. The ignorance with regard to Russia and the Russians which he found in abundance in the rest of Europe—and not least in the country he inhabited for ten years before his death—had indeed the effect, to a certain degree, to throw him back upon the deep feelings which so many of his companions were unable to share with him, the memories of his early years, the sense of wide Russian horizons, the joy and pride of his mother-tongue. In the collection of short pieces, so deeply interesting, written during the last few years of his life, and translated into German under the name of *Senilia*, I find a passage—it is the last in the little book—which illustrates perfectly this reactionary impulse: "In days of doubt, in days of anxious thought on the destiny of my native land, thou alone art my support and my staff, O great powerful Russian tongue, truthful and free! If it were not for thee how should man not despair at the sight of what is going on at home? But it is inconceivable that such a language has not been given to a great people." This Muscovite, home-loving note pervades his productions, though it is between the lines, as it were, that we must listen for it. None the less does it remain true that he was not a simple conduit or mouthpiece; the inspiration was his own as well as the voice. He was an individual, in other words, of the most unmistakable kind, and those who had the happiness to know him have no difficulty to-day in thinking of him as an eminent, responsible figure. This pleasure, for the writer of these lines, was as great as the pleasure of reading the admirable tales into which he put such a world of life and feeling: it was perhaps even greater, for it was not only with the pen that nature had given Turgénieff the power to express himself. He was the richest, the most delightful, of talkers, and his face, his person, his temper, the thoroughness with which he had been equipped for human intercourse, make in the memory of his friends an image which is completed, but not thrown into the shade, by his literary distinction. The whole image is tinted with sadness: partly because the element of melancholy in his nature was deep and constant—readers of his novels have no need to be told of that; and partly because, during the last years of his life, he had been condemned to suffer atrociously. Intolerable pain had been his portion for too many months before he died; his end was not a soft decline, but a deepening distress. But of brightness, of the faculty of enjoyment, he had also the large allowance usually made to first-rate men, and he was a singularly complete human being. The author of these pages had greatly admired his writings before having the fortune to make his acquaintance, and this privilege, when it presented itself, was highly illuminating. The man and the writer together occupied from that moment a very high place in his affection. Some time before knowing him I committed to print certain reflections which his tales had led me to make; and I may perhaps, therefore, without impropriety give them a supplement which shall have a more vivifying reference. It is almost irresistible to attempt to say, from one's own point of view, what manner of man he was.

It was in consequence of the article I just mentioned that I found reason to meet him, in Paris, where he was then living, in 1875. I shall never forget the impression he made upon me at that first interview. I found him adorable; I could scarcely believe that he would prove—that any man could prove—on nearer acquaintance so delightful as that. Nearer acquaintance only confirmed my hope, and he remained the most approachable, the most practicable, the least unsafe man of genius it has been my fortune to meet. He was so simple, so natural, so modest, so destitute of personal pretension and of what is called the consciousness of powers, that one almost doubted at moments whether he were a man of genius after all. Everything good and fruitful lay near to him; he was interested in everything; and he was absolutely without that eagerness of self-reference which sometimes accompanies great, and even small, reputations. He had not a particle of vanity; nothing whatever of the air of having a part to play or a reputation to keep up. His humour exercised itself as freely upon himself as upon other subjects, and he told stories at his own expense with a sweetness of hilarity which made his peculiarities really sacred in the eyes of a friend. I remember vividly the smile and tone of voice with which he once repeated to me a figurative epithet which Gustave Flaubert (of whom he was extremely fond) had applied to him—an epithet intended to characterise a certain expansive softness, a comprehensive indecision, which pervaded his nature, just as it pervades so many of the characters he has painted. He enjoyed Flaubert's use of this term, good-naturedly opprobrious, more even than Flaubert himself, and recognised perfectly the element of truth in it. He was natural to an extraordinary degree; I do not think I have ever seen his match in this respect, certainly not among people who bear, as he did, at the same time, the stamp of the highest cultivation. Like all men of a large pattern, he was composed of many different pieces; and what was always striking in him was the mixture of simplicity with the fruit of the most various observation. In the little article in which I had attempted to express my admiration for his works, I had been moved to say of him that he had the aristocratic temperament: a remark which in the light of further knowledge seemed to me singularly inane. He was not subject to any definition of that sort, and to say that he was democratic would be (though his political ideal was a democracy), to give an equally superficial account of him. He felt and understood the opposite sides of life; he was imaginative, speculative, anything but literal. He had not in his mind a grain of prejudice as large as the point of a needle, and people (there are many) who think this a defect would have missed it immensely in Ivan Serguéitch. (I give his name, without attempting the Russian orthography, as it was uttered by his friends when they addressed him in French.) Our Anglo-Saxon, Protestant, moralistic, conventional standards were far away from him, and he judged things with a freedom and spontaneity in which I found a perpetual refreshment. His sense of beauty, his love of truth and right, were the foundation of his nature; but half the charm of conversation with him was that one breathed an air in which cant phrases and arbitrary measurements simply sounded ridiculous.

I may add that it was not because I had written a laudatory article about his books that he gave me a friendly welcome; for in the first place my article could have very little importance for him, and in the second it had never been either his habit or his hope to bask in the light of criticism. Supremely modest as he was, I think he attached no great weight to what might happen to be said about him; for he felt that he was destined to encounter a very small amount of intelligent appreciation, especially in foreign countries. I never heard him even allude to any judgment which might have been passed upon his productions in England. In France he knew that he was read very moderately; the "demand" for his volumes was small, and he had no illusions whatever on the subject of his popularity. He had heard with pleasure that many intelligent persons in the United States were impatient for everything that might come from his pen; but I think he was never convinced, as one or two of the more zealous of these persons had endeavoured to convince him, that he could boast of a "public" in America. He gave me the impression of thinking of criticism as most serious workers think of it—that it is the amusement, the exercise, the subsistence of the critic (and, so far as this goes, of immense use); but that though it may often concern other readers, it does not much concern the artist himself. In comparison with all those things which the production of a considered work forces the artist little by little to say to himself, the remarks of the critic are vague and of the moment; and yet, owing to the large publicity of the proceeding, they have a power to irritate or discourage which is quite out of proportion to their use to the person criticised. It was not, moreover (if this explanation be not more gross than the spectre it is meant to conjure away), on account of any esteem which he accorded to my own productions (I used regularly to send them to him) that I found him so agreeable, for to the best of my belief he was unable to read them. As regards one of the first that I had offered him he wrote me a little note to tell me that a distinguished friend, who was his constant companion, had read three or four chapters aloud to him the evening before and that one of them was written *de main de maître*! This gave me great pleasure, but it was my first and last pleasure of the kind. I continued, as I say, to send him my fictions, because they were the only thing I had to give; but he never alluded to the rest of the work in question, which he evidently did not finish, and never gave any sign of having read its successors. Presently I quite ceased to expect this, and saw why it was (it interested me much), that my writings could not appeal to him. He cared, more than anything else, for the air of reality, and my reality was not to the purpose. I do not think my stories struck him as quite meat for men. The manner was more apparent than the matter; they were too *tarabiscoté*, as I once heard him say of the style of a book—had on the surface too many little flowers and knots of ribbon. He had read a great deal of English, and knew the language remarkably well—too well, I used often to think, for he liked to speak it with those to whom it was native, and, successful as the effort always was, it deprived him of the facility and raciness with which he expressed himself in French.

I have said that he had no prejudices, but perhaps after all he had one. I think he imagined it to be impossible to a person of English speech to converse in French with complete correctness. He knew Shakespeare thoroughly, and at one time had wandered far and wide in English literature. His opportunities for speaking English were not at all frequent, so that when the necessity (or at least the occasion) presented itself, he remembered the phrases he had encountered in books. This often gave a charming quaintness and an unexpected literary turn to what he said. "In Russia, in spring, if you enter a beechen grove"—those words come back to me from the last time I saw him. He continued to read English books and was not incapable of attacking the usual Tauchnitz novel. The English writer (of our day) of whom I remember to have heard him speak with most admiration was Dickens, of whose faults he was conscious, but whose power of presenting to the eye a vivid, salient figure he rated very high. In the young French school he was much interested; I mean, in the new votaries of realism, the grandsons of Balzac. He was a good friend of most of them, and with Gustave Flaubert, the most singular and most original of the group, he was altogether intimate. He had his reservations and discriminations, and he had, above all, the great back-garden of his Slav imagination and his Germanic culture, into which the door constantly stood open, and the grandsons of Balzac were not, I think, particularly free to accompany him. But he had much sympathy with their experiment, their general movement, and it was on the side of the careful study of life as the best line of the novelist that, as may easily be supposed, he ranged himself. For some of the manifestations of the opposite tradition he had a great contempt. This was a kind of emotion he rarely expressed, save in regard to certain public wrongs and iniquities; bitterness and denunciation seldom passed his mild lips. But I remember well the little flush of conviction, the seriousness, with which he once said, in allusion to a novel which had just been running through the *Revue des Deux Mondes*, "If I had written anything so bad as that, I should blush for it all my life."

His was not, I should say, predominantly, or even in a high degree, the artistic nature, though it was deeply, if I may make the distinction, the poetic. But during the last twelve years of his life he lived much with artists and men of letters, and he was eminently capable of kindling in the glow of discussion. He cared for questions of form, though not in the degree in which Flaubert and Edmond de Goncourt cared for them, and he had very lively sympathies. He had a great regard for Madame George Sand, the head and front of the old romantic tradition; but this was on general grounds, quite independent of her novels, which he never read, and which she never expected him, or apparently any one else, to read. He thought her character remarkably noble and sincere. He had, as I have said, a great affection for Gustave Flaubert, who returned it; and he was much interested in Flaubert's extraordinary attempts at bravery of form and of matter, knowing perfectly well when they failed. During those months which it was Flaubert's habit to spend in Paris, Turgénieff went almost regularly to see him on Sunday afternoon, and was so good as to introduce me to the author of *Madame Bovary*, in whom I saw many reasons for Turgénieff's regard. It was on these Sundays, in Flaubert's little salon, which, at the top of a house at the end of the Faubourg Saint-Honoré, looked rather bare and provisional, that, in the company of the other familiars of the spot, more than one of whom[6] have commemorated these occasions, Turgénieff's beautiful faculty of talk showed at its best. He was easy, natural, abundant, more than I can describe, and everything that he said was touched with the exquisite quality of his imagination. What was discussed in that little smoke-clouded room was chiefly questions of taste, questions of art and form; and the speakers, for the most part, were in æsthetic matters, radicals of the deepest dye. It would have been late in the day to propose among them any discussion of the relation of art to morality, any question as to the degree in which a novel might or might not concern itself with the teaching of a lesson. They had settled these preliminaries long ago, and it would have been primitive and incongruous to recur to them. The conviction that held them together was the conviction that art and morality are two perfectly different things, and that the former has no more to do with the latter than it has with astronomy or embryology. The only duty of a novel was to be well written; that merit included every other of which it was capable. This state of mind was never more apparent than one afternoon when *ces messieurs* delivered themselves on the subject of an incident which had just befallen one of them. *L'Assommoir* of Emile Zola had been discontinued in the journal through which it was running as a serial, in consequence of repeated protests from the subscribers. The subscriber, as a type of human imbecility, received a wonderful dressing, and the Philistine in general was roughly handled. There were gulfs of difference between Turgénieff and Zola, but Turgénieff, who, as I say, understood everything, understood Zola too, and rendered perfect justice to the high solidity of much of his work. His attitude, at such times, was admirable, and I could imagine nothing more genial or more fitted to give an idea of light, easy, human intelligence. No one could desire more than he that art should be art; always, ever, incorruptibly, art. To him this proposition would have seemed as little in need of proof, or susceptible of refutation, as the axiom that law should always be law or medicine always medicine. As much as any one he was prepared to take note of the fact that the demand for abdications and concessions never comes from artists themselves, but always from purchasers, editors, subscribers. I am pretty sure that his word about all this would have been that he could not quite see what was meant by the talk about novels being moral or the reverse; that a novel could no more propose to itself to be moral than a painting or a symphony, and that it was arbitrary to lay down a distinction between the numerous forms of art. He was the last man to be blind to their unity. I suspect that he would have said, in short, that distinctions were demanded in the interest of the moralists, and that the demand was indelicate, owing to their want of jurisdiction. Yet at the same time that I make this suggestion as to his state of mind I remember how little he struck me as bound by mere neatness of formula, how little there was in him of the partisan or the pleader. What he thought of the relation of art to life his stories, after all, show better than anything else. The immense variety of life was ever present to his mind, and he would never have argued the question I have just hinted at in the interest of particular liberties—the liberties that were apparently the dearest to his French *confrères*. It was this air that he carried about with him of feeling all the variety of life, of knowing strange and far-off things, of having an horizon in which the Parisian horizon—so familiar, so wanting in mystery, so perpetually *exploité*—easily lost itself, that distinguished him from these companions. He was not all there, as the phrase is; he had something behind, in reserve. It was Russia, of course, in a large measure; and, especially before the spectacle of what is going on there to-day, that was a large quantity. But so far as he was on the spot, he was an element of pure sociability.

I did not intend to go into these details immediately, for I had only begun to say what an impression of magnificent manhood he made upon me when I first knew him. That impression, indeed, always remained with me, even after it had been brought home to me how much there was in him of the quality of genius. He was a beautiful intellect, of course, but above all he was a delightful, mild, masculine figure. The combination of his deep, soft, lovable spirit, in which one felt all the tender parts of genius, with his immense, fair Russian physique, was one of the most attractive things conceivable. He had a frame which would have made it perfectly lawful, and even becoming, for him to be brutal; but there was not a grain of brutality in his composition. He had always been a passionate sportsman; to wander in the woods or the steppes, with his dog and gun, was the pleasure of his heart. Late in life he continued to shoot, and he had a friend in Cambridgeshire for the sake of whose partridges, which were famous, he used sometimes to cross the Channel. It would have been impossible to imagine a better representation of a Nimrod of the north. He was exceedingly tall, and broad and robust in proportion. His head was one of the finest, and though the line of his features was irregular, there was a great deal of beauty in his face. It was eminently of the Russian type—almost everything in it was wide. His expression had a singular sweetness, with a touch of Slav languor, and his eye, the kindest of eyes, was deep and melancholy. His hair, abundant and straight, was as white as silver, and his beard, which he wore trimmed rather short, was of the colour of his hair. In all his tall person, which was very striking wherever it appeared, there was an air of neglected strength, as if it had been a part of his modesty never to remind himself that he was strong. He used sometimes to blush like a boy of sixteen. He had very few forms and ceremonies, and almost as little manner as was possible to a man of his natural *prestance*. His noble appearance was in itself a manner; but whatever he did he did very simply, and he had not the slightest pretension to not being subject to rectification. I never saw any one receive it with less irritation. Friendly, candid, unaffectedly benignant, the impression that he produced most strongly and most generally was, I think, simply that of goodness.

When I made his acquaintance he had been living, since his removal from Baden-Baden, which took place in consequence of the Franco-Prussian war, in a large detached house on the hill of Montmartre, with his friends of many years, Madame Pauline Viardot and her husband, as his fellow-tenants. He occupied the upper floor, and I like to recall, for the sake of certain delightful talks, the aspect of his little green sitting-room, which has, in memory, the consecration of irrecoverable hours. It was almost entirely green, and the walls were not covered with paper, but draped in stuff. The *portières* were green, and there was one of those immense divans, so indispensable to Russians, which had apparently been fashioned for the great person of the master, so that smaller folk had to lie upon it rather than sit. I remember the white light of the Paris street, which came in through windows more or less blinded in their lower part, like those of a studio. It rested, during the first years that I went to see Turgénieff, upon several choice pictures of the modern French school, especially upon a very fine specimen of Théodore Rousseau, which he valued exceedingly. He had a great love of painting, and was an excellent critic of a picture. The last time I saw him—it was at his house in the country—he showed me half a dozen large copies of Italian works, made by a young Russian in whom he was interested, which he had, with characteristic kindness, taken into his own apartments in order that he might bring them to the knowledge of his friends. He thought them, as copies, remarkable; and they were so, indeed, especially when one perceived that the original work of the artist had little value. Turgénieff warmed to the work of praising them, as he was very apt to do; like all men of imagination he had frequent and zealous admirations. As a matter of course there was almost always some young Russian in whom he was interested, and refugees and pilgrims of both sexes were his natural clients. I have heard it said by persons who had known him long and well that these enthusiasms sometimes led him into error, that he was apt to *se monter la tête* on behalf of his protégés. He was prone to believe that he had discovered the coming Russian genius; he talked about his discovery for a month, and then suddenly one heard no more of it. I remember his once telling me of a young woman who had come to see him on her return from America, where she had been studying obstetrics at some medical college, and who, without means and without friends, was in want of help and of work. He accidentally learned that she had written something, and asked her to let him see it. She sent it to him, and it proved to be a tale in which certain phases of rural life were described with striking truthfulness. He perceived in the young lady a great natural talent; he sent her story off to Russia to be printed, with the conviction that it would make a great impression, and he expressed the hope of being able to introduce her to French readers. When I mentioned this to an old friend of Turgénieff he smiled, and said that we should not hear of her again, that Ivan Serguéitch had already discovered a great many surprising talents, which, as a general thing, had not borne the test. There was apparently some truth in this, and Turgénieff's liability to be deceived was too generous a weakness for me to hesitate to allude to it, even after I have insisted on the usual certainty of his taste. He was deeply interested in his young Russians; they were what interested him most in the world. They were almost always unhappy, in want and in rebellion against an order of things which he himself detested. The study of the Russian character absorbed and fascinated him, as all readers of his stories know. Rich, unformed, undeveloped, with all sorts of adumbrations, of qualities in a state of fusion, it stretched itself out as a mysterious expanse in which it was impossible as yet to perceive the relation between gifts and weaknesses. Of its weaknesses he was keenly conscious, and I once heard him express himself with an energy that did him honour and a frankness that even surprised me (considering that it was of his countrymen that he spoke), in regard to a weakness which he deemed the greatest of all—a weakness for which a man whose love of veracity was his strongest feeling would have least toleration. His young compatriots, seeking their fortune in foreign lands, touched his imagination and his pity, and it is easy to conceive that under the circumstances the impression they often made upon him may have had great intensity. The Parisian background, with its brilliant sameness, its absence of surprises (for those who have known it long), threw them into relief and made him see them as he saw the figures in his tales, in relations, in situations which brought them out. There passed before him in the course of time many wonderful Russian types. He told me once of his having been visited by a religious sect. The sect consisted of but two persons, one of whom was the object of worship and the other the worshipper. The divinity apparently was travelling about Europe in company with his prophet. They were intensely serious but it was very handy, as the term is, for each. The god had always his altar and the altar had (unlike some altars) always its god.

In his little green salon nothing was out of place; there were none of the odds and ends of the usual man of letters, which indeed Turgénieff was not; and the case was the same in his library at Bougival, of which I shall presently speak. Few books even were visible; it was as if everything had been put away. The traces of work had been carefully removed. An air of great comfort, an immeasurable divan and several valuable pictures—that was the effect of the place. I know not exactly at what hours Turgénieff did his work; I think he had no regular times and seasons, being in this respect as different as possible from Anthony Trollope, whose autobiography, with its candid revelation of intellectual economies, is so curious. It is my impression that in Paris Turgénieff wrote little; his times of production being rather those weeks of the summer that he spent at Bougival, and the period of that visit to Russia which he supposed himself to make every year. I say "supposed himself," because it was impossible to see much of him without discovering that he was a man of delays. As on the part of some other Russians whom I have known, there was something Asiatic in his faculty of procrastination. But even if one suffered from it a little one thought of it with kindness, as a part of his general mildness and want of rigidity. He went to Russia, at any rate, at intervals not infrequent, and he spoke of these visits as his best time for production. He had an estate far in the interior, and here, amid the stillness of the country and the scenes and figures which give such a charm to the *Memoirs of a Sportsman*, he drove his pen without interruption.

It is not out of place to allude to the fact that he possessed considerable fortune; this is too important in the life of a man of letters. It had been of great value to Turgénieff, and I think that much of the fine quality of his work is owing to it. He could write according to his taste and his mood; he was never pressed nor checked (putting the Russian censorship aside) by considerations foreign to his plan, and never was in danger of becoming a hack. Indeed, taking into consideration the absence of a pecuniary spur and that complicated indolence from which he was not exempt, his industry is surprising, for his tales are a long list. In Paris, at all events, he was always open to proposals for the midday breakfast. He liked to breakfast *au cabaret*, and freely consented to an appointment. It is not unkind to add that, at first, he never kept it. I may mention without reserve this idiosyncrasy of Turgénieff's, because in the first place it was so inveterate as to be very amusing—it amused not only his friends but himself; and in the second, he was as sure to come in the end as he was sure not to come in the beginning. After the appointment had been made or the invitation accepted, when the occasion was at hand, there arrived a note or a telegram in which Ivan Serguéitch excused himself, and begged that the meeting might be deferred to another date, which he usually himself proposed. For this second date still another was sometimes substituted; but if I remember no appointment that he exactly kept, I remember none that he completely missed. His friends waited for him frequently, but they never lost him. He was very fond of that wonderful Parisian *déjeûner*—fond of it I mean as a feast of reason. He was extremely temperate, and often ate no breakfast at all; but he found it a good hour for talk, and little, on general grounds, as one might be prepared to agree with him, if he was at the table one was speedily convinced. I call it wonderful, the *déjeûner* of Paris, on account of the assurance with which it plants itself in the very middle of the morning. It divides the day between rising and dinner so unequally, and opposes such barriers of repletion to any prospect of ulterior labours, that the unacclimated stranger wonders when the fertile French people do their work. Not the least wonderful part of it is that the stranger himself likes it, at last, and manages to piece together his day with the shattered fragments that survive. It was not, at any rate, when one had the good fortune to breakfast at twelve o'clock with Turgénieff that one was struck with its being an inconvenient hour. Any hour was convenient for meeting a human being who conformed so completely to one's idea of the best that human nature is capable of. There are places in Paris which I can think of only in relation to some occasion on which he was present, and when I pass them the particular things I heard him say there come back to me. There is a café in the Avenue de l'Opéra—a new, sumptuous establishment, with very deep settees, on the right as you leave the Boulevard—where I once had a talk with him, over an order singularly moderate, which was prolonged far into the afternoon, and in the course of which he was extraordinarily suggestive and interesting, so that my memory now reverts affectionately to all the circumstances. It evokes the grey damp of a Parisian December, which made the dark interior of the café look more and more rich and hospitable, while the light faded, the lamps were lit, the habitués came in to drink absinthe and play their afternoon game of dominoes, and we still lingered over our morning meal. Turgénieff talked almost exclusively about Russia, the nihilists, the remarkable figures that came to light among them, the curious visits he received, the dark prospects of his native land. When he was in the vein, no man could speak more to the imagination of his auditor. For myself, at least, at such times, there was something extraordinarily vivifying and stimulating in his talk, and I always left him in a state of "intimate" excitement, with a feeling that all sorts of valuable things had been suggested to me; the condition in which a man swings his cane as he walks, leaps lightly over gutters, and then stops, for no reason at all, to look, with an air of being struck, into a shop window where he sees nothing. I remember another symposium, at a restaurant on one of the corners of the little *place* in front of the Opéra Comique, where we were four, including Ivan Serguéitch, and the two other guests were also Russian, one of them uniting to the charm of this nationality the merit of a sex that makes the combination irresistible. The establishment had been a discovery of Turgénieff's—a discovery, at least, as far as our particular needs were concerned—and I remember that we hardly congratulated him on it. The dinner, in a low entresol, was not what it had been intended to be, but the talk was better even than our expectations. It was not about nihilism but about some more agreeable features of life, and I have no recollection of Turgénieff in a mood more spontaneous and charming. One of our friends had, when he spoke French, a peculiar way of sounding the word *adorable*, which was frequently on his lips, and I remember well his expressive prolongation of the *a* when, in speaking of the occasion afterwards, he applied this term to Ivan Serguéitch. I scarcely know, however, why I should drop into the detail of such reminiscences, and my excuse is but the desire that we all have, when a human relationship is closed, to save a little of it from the past—to make a mark which may stand for some of the happy moments of it.

Nothing that Turgénieff had to say could be more interesting than his talk about his own work, his manner of writing. What I have heard him tell of these things was worthy of the beautiful results he produced; of the deep purpose, pervading them all, to show us life itself. The germ of a story, with him, was never an affair of plot—that was the last thing he thought of: it was the representation of certain persons. The first form in which a tale appeared to him was as the figure of an individual, or a combination of individuals, whom he wished to see in action, being sure that such people must do something very special and interesting. They stood before him definite, vivid, and he wished to know, and to show, as much as possible of their nature. The first thing was to make clear to himself what he did know, to begin with; and to this end, he wrote out a sort of biography of each of his characters, and everything that they had done and that had happened to them up to the opening of the story. He had their *dossier*, as the French say, and as the police has of that of every conspicuous criminal. With this material in his hand he was able to proceed; the story all lay in the question, What shall I make them do? He always made them do things that showed them completely; but, as he said, the defect of his manner and the reproach that was made him was his want of "architecture"—in other words, of composition. The great thing, of course, is to have architecture as well as precious material, as Walter Scott had them, as Balzac had them. If one reads Turgénieff's stories with the knowledge that they were composed—or rather that they came into being—in this way, one can trace the process in every line. Story, in the conventional sense of the word—a fable constructed, like Wordsworth's phantom, "to startle and waylay"—there is as little as possible. The thing consists of the motions of a group of selected creatures, which are not the result of a preconceived action, but a consequence of the qualities of the actors. Works of art are produced from every possible point of view, and stories, and very good ones, will continue to be written in which the evolution is that of a dance—a series of steps the more complicated and lively the better, of course, determined from without and forming a figure. This figure will always, probably, find favour with many readers, because it reminds them enough, without reminding them too much, of life. On this opposition many young talents in France are ready to rend each other, for there is a numerous school on either side. We have not yet in England and America arrived at the point of treating such questions with passion, for we have not yet arrived at the point of feeling them intensely, or indeed, for that matter, of understanding them very well. It is not open to us as yet to discuss whether a novel had better be an excision from life or a structure built up of picture-cards, for we have not made up our mind as to whether life in general may be described. There is evidence of a good deal of shyness on this point—a tendency rather to put up fences than to jump over them. Among us, therefore, even a certain ridicule attaches to the consideration of such alternatives. But individuals may feel their way, and perhaps even pass unchallenged, if they remark that for them the manner in which Turgénieff worked will always seem the most fruitful. It has the immense recommendation that in relation to any human occurrence it begins, as it were, further back. It lies in its power to tell us the most about men and women. Of course it will but slenderly satisfy those numerous readers among whom the answer to this would be, "Hang it, we don't care a straw about men and women: we want a good story!"

And yet, after all, *Elena* is a good story, and *Lisa* and *Virgin Soil* are good stories. Reading over lately several of Turgénieff's novels and tales, I was struck afresh with their combination of beauty and reality. One must never forget, in speaking of him, that he was both an observer and a poet. The poetic element was constant, and it had great strangeness and power. It inspired most of the short things that he wrote during the last few years of his life, since the publication of *Virgin Soil*, things that are in the highest degree fanciful and exotic. It pervades the frequent little reveries, visions, epigrams of the *Senilia*. It was no part of my intention, here, to criticise his writings, having said my say about them, so far as possible, some years ago. But I may mention that in re-reading them I find in them all that I formerly found of two other elements—their richness and their sadness. They give one the impression of life itself, and not of an arrangement, a *réchauffé* of life. I remember Turgénieff's once saying in regard to Homais, the little Norman country apothecary, with his pedantry of "enlightened opinions," in *Madame Bovary*, that the great strength of such a portrait consisted in its being at once an individual, of the most concrete sort, and a type. This is the great strength of his own representations of character; they are so strangely, fascinatingly particular, and yet they are so recognisably general. Such a remark as that about Homais makes me wonder why it was that Turgénieff should have rated Dickens so high, the weakness of Dickens being in regard to just that point. If Dickens fail to live long, it will be because his figures are particular without being general; because they are individuals without being types; because we do not feel their continuity with the rest of humanity—see the matching of the pattern with the piece out of which all the creations of the novelist and the dramatist are cut. I often meant, but accidentally neglected, to put Turgénieff on the subject of Dickens again, and ask him to explain his opinion. I suspect that his opinion was in a large measure merely that Dickens diverted him, as well he might. That complexity of the pattern was in itself fascinating. I have mentioned Flaubert, and I will return to him simply to say that there was something very touching in the nature of the friendship that united these two men. It is much to the honour of Flaubert, to my sense, that he appreciated Ivan Turgénieff. There was a partial similarity between them. Both were large, massive men, though the Russian reached to a greater height than the Norman; both were completely honest and sincere, and both had the pessimistic element in their composition. Each had a tender regard for the other, and I think that I am neither incorrect nor indiscreet in saying that on Turgénieff's part this regard had in it a strain of compassion. There was something in Gustave Flaubert that appealed to such a feeling. He had failed, on the whole, more than he had succeeded, and the great machinery of erudition,—the great polishing process,—which he brought to bear upon his productions, was not accompanied with proportionate results. He had talent without having cleverness, and imagination without having fancy. His effort was heroic, but except in the case of *Madame Bovary*, a masterpiece, he imparted something to his works (it was as if he had covered them with metallic plates) which made them sink rather than sail. He had a passion for perfection of form and for a certain splendid suggestiveness of style. He wished to produce perfect phrases, perfectly interrelated, and as closely woven together as a suit of chain-mail. He looked at life altogether as an artist, and took his work with a seriousness that never belied itself. To write an admirable page—and his idea of what constituted an admirable page was transcendent— seemed to him something to live for. He tried it again and again, and he came very near it; more than once he touched it, for *Madame Bovary* surely will live. But there was something ungenerous in his genius. He was cold, and he would have given everything he had to be able to glow. There is nothing in his novels like the passion of Elena for Inssaroff, like the purity of Lisa, like the anguish of the parents of Bazaroff, like the hidden wound of Tatiana; and yet Flaubert yearned, with all the accumulations of his vocabulary, to touch the chord of pathos. There were some parts of his mind that did not "give," that did not render a sound. He had had too much of some sorts of experience and not enough of others. And yet this failure of an organ, as I may call it, inspired those who knew him with a kindness. If Flaubert was powerful and limited, there is something human, after all, and even rather august in a strong man who has not been able completely to express himself.

After the first year of my acquaintance with Turgénieff I saw him much less often. I was seldom in Paris, and sometimes when I was there he was absent. But I neglected no opportunity of seeing him, and fortune frequently assisted me. He came two or three times to London, for visits provokingly brief. He went to shoot in Cambridgeshire, and he passed through town in arriving and departing. He liked the English, but I am not sure that he liked London, where he had passed a lugubrious winter in 1870-71. I remember some of his impressions of that period, especially a visit that he had paid to a "bishopess" surrounded by her daughters, and a description of the cookery at the lodgings which he occupied. After 1876 I frequently saw him as an invalid. He was tormented by gout, and sometimes terribly besieged; but his account of what he suffered was as charming—I can apply no other word to it—as his description of everything else. He had so the habit of observation, that he perceived in excruciating sensations all sorts of curious images and analogies, and analysed them to an extraordinary fineness. Several times I found him at Bougival, above the Seine, in a very spacious and handsome chalet—a little unsunned, it is true—which he had built alongside of the villa occupied by the family to which, for years, his life had been devoted. The place is delightful; the two houses are midway up a long slope, which descends, with the softest inclination, to the river, and behind them the hill rises to a wooded crest. On the left, in the distance, high up and above an horizon of woods, stretches the romantic aqueduct of Marly. It is a very pretty domain. The last time I saw him, in November 1882, it was at Bougival. He had been very ill, with strange, intolerable symptoms, but he was better, and he had good hopes. They were not justified by the event. He got worse again, and the months that followed were cruel. His beautiful serene mind should not have been darkened and made acquainted with violence; it should have been able to the last to take part, as it had always done, in the decrees and mysteries of fate. At the moment I saw him, however, he was, as they say in London, in very good form, and my last impression of him was almost bright. He was to drive into Paris, not being able to bear the railway, and he gave me a seat in the carriage. For an hour and a half he constantly talked, and never better. When we got into the city I alighted on the boulevard extérieur, as we were to go in different directions. I bade him good-bye at the carriage window, and never saw him again. There was a kind of fair going on, near by, in the chill November air, beneath the denuded little trees of the Boulevard, and a Punch and Judy show, from which nasal sounds proceeded. I almost regret having accidentally to mix up so much of Paris with this perhaps too complacent enumeration of occasions, for the effect of it may be to suggest that Ivan Turgénieff had been Gallicised. But this was not the case; the French capital was an accident for him, not a necessity. It touched him at many points, but it let him alone at many others, and he had, with that great tradition of ventilation of the Russian mind, windows open into distances which stretched far beyond the *banlieue*. I have spoken of him from the limited point of view of my own acquaintance with him, and unfortunately left myself little space to allude to a matter which filled his existence a good deal more than the consideration of how a story should be written—his hopes and fears on behalf of his native land. He wrote fictions and dramas, but the great drama of his life was the struggle for a better state of things in Russia. In this drama he played a distinguished part, and the splendid obsequies that, simple and modest as he was, have unfolded themselves over his grave, sufficiently attest the recognition of it by his countrymen. His funeral, restricted and officialised, was none the less a magnificent "manifestation." I have read the accounts of it, however, with a kind of chill, a feeling in which assent to the honours paid him bore less part than it ought. All this pomp and ceremony seemed to lift him out of the range of familiar recollection, of valued reciprocity, into the majestic position of a national glory. And yet it is in the presence of this obstacle to social contact that those who knew and loved him must address their farewell to him now. After all, it is difficult to see how the obstacle can be removed. He was the most generous, the most tender, the most delightful, of men; his large nature overflowed with the love of justice: but he also was of the stuff of which glories are made.

1884.

X. GEORGE DU MAURIER

MANY years ago a small American child, who lived in New York and played in Union Square, which was then inclosed by a high railing and governed by a solitary policeman—a strange, superannuated, dilapidated functionary, carrying a little cane and wearing, with a very copious and very dirty shirt-front, the costume of a man of the world—a small American child was a silent devotee of *Punch*. Half an hour spent to-day in turning over the early numbers transports him quite as much to old New York as to the London of the first Crystal Palace and the years that immediately followed it. From about 1850 to 1855 he lived, in imagination, no small part of his time, in the world represented by the pencil of Leech. He pored over the pictures of the people riding in the Row, of the cabmen and the costermongers, of the little pages in buttons, of the bathing-machines at the sea-side, of the small boys in tall hats and Eton jackets, of the gentlemen hunting the fox, of the pretty girls in striped petticoats and coiffures of the shape of the mushroom. These things were the features of a world which he longed so to behold, that the familiar woodcuts (they were not so good in those days as they have become since) grew at last as real to him as the furniture of his home; and when he at present looks at the *Punch* of thirty years ago he finds in it an odd association of mediæval New York. He remembers that it was in such a locality, in that city, that he first saw such a picture: he recalls the fading light of the winter dusk, with the red fire and the red curtains in the background, in which more than once he was bidden to put down the last numbers of the humorous sheet and come to his tea. *Punch* was England; *Punch* was London; and England and London were at that time words of multifarious suggestion to this small American child. He liked much more to think of the British Empire than to indulge in the sports natural to his tender age, and many of his hours were spent in making mental pictures of the society of which the recurrent woodcuts offered him specimens and revelations. He had from year to year the prospect of really beholding this society (he heard every spring, from the earliest period, that his parents would go to Europe, and then he heard that they would not), and he had measured the value of the prospect with a keenness possibly premature. He knew the names of the London streets, of the theatres, of many of the shops: the dream of his young life was to take a walk in Kensington Gardens and go to Drury Lane to see a pantomime. There was a great deal in the old *Punch* about the pantomimes, and harlequins and columbines peopled the secret visions of this perverted young New Yorker. It was a mystic satisfaction to him that he had lived in Piccadilly when he was a baby; he remembered neither the period nor the place, but the name of the latter had a strange delight for him. It had been promised him that he should behold once more that romantic thoroughfare, and he did so by the time he was twelve years old. Then he found that if *Punch* had been London (as he lay on the hearth-rug inhaling the exotic fragrance of the freshly-arrived journal), London was *Punch* and something more. He remembers to-day vividly his impression of the London streets in the summer of 1855; they had an extraordinary look of familiarity, and every figure, every object he encountered, appeared to have been drawn by Leech. He has learned to know these things better since then; but his childish impression is subject to extraordinary revivals. The expansive back of an old lady getting into an omnibus, the attitude of a little girl bending from her pony in the park, the demureness of a maid-servant opening a street-door in Brompton, the top-heavy attitude of the small "Ameliar-Ann," as she stands planted with the baby in her arms on the corner of a Westminster slum, the coal-heavers, the cabmen, the publicans, the butcher-boys, the flunkeys, the guardsmen, the policemen (in spite of their change of uniform), are liable at this hour, in certain moods, to look more like sketchy tail-pieces than natural things. (There are moments indeed—not identical with those we speak of—in which certain figures, certain episodes, in the London streets, strike an even stranger, deeper note of reminiscence. They remind the American traveller of Hogarth: he may take a walk in Oxford Street—on some dirty winter afternoon—and find everything he sees Hogarthian.)

We know not whether the form of infantine nostalgia of which we speak is common, or was then common, among small Americans; but we are sure that, when fortune happens to favour it, it is a very delightful pain. In those days, in America, the manufacture of children's picture-books was an undeveloped industry; the best things came from London, and brought with them the aroma of a richer civilisation. The covers were so beautiful and shining, the paper and print so fine, the coloured illustrations so magnificent, that it was easy to see that over there the arts were at a very high point. The very name of the publisher on the title-page (the small boy we speak of always looked at that) had a thrilling and mystifying effect. But, above all, the contents were so romantic and delectable! There were things in the English story-books that one read as a child, just as there were things in *Punch*, that one couldn't have seen in New York, even if one had been fifty years old. The age had nothing to do with it; one had a conviction that they were not there to be seen—we can hardly say why. It is, perhaps, because the plates in the picture-books were almost always coloured; but it was evident that there was a great deal more colour in that other world. We remember well the dazzling tone of a little Christmas book by Leech, which was quite in the spirit of *Punch*, only more splendid, for the plates were plastered with blue and pink. It was called *Young Troublesome; or, Master Jacky's Holidays*, and it has probably become scarce to-day. It related the mischievous pranks of an Eton school-boy while at home for his Christmas vacation, and the exploit we chiefly recollect was his blacking with a burnt stick the immaculate calves of the footman who is carrying up some savoury dish to the banquet from which (in consequence of his age and his habits), Master Jacky is excluded. Master Jacky was so handsome, so brilliant, so heroic, so regardless of dangers and penalties, so fertile in resources; and those charming young ladies, his sisters, his cousins— the innocent victims of his high spirits—had such golden ringlets, such rosy cheeks, such pretty shoulders, such delicate blue sashes over such fresh muslin gowns. Master Jacky seemed to lead a life all illumined with rosy Christmas fire. A little later came Richard Doyle's delightful volume, giving the history of *Brown, Jones, and Robinson*, and it would be difficult to exaggerate the action of these remarkable designs in forming the taste of our fantastic little amateur. They told him, indeed, much less about England than about the cities of the continent; but that was not a drawback, for he could take in the continent too. Moreover, he felt that these three travellers were intensely British; they looked at everything from the London point of view, and it gave him an immense feeling of initiation to be able to share their susceptibilities.

Was there not also a delightful little picture at the end, which represented them as restored to British ground, each holding up a tankard of foaming ale, with the boots, behind them, rolling their battered portmanteaux into the inn? This seemed somehow to commemorate one's own possible arrival in old England, even though it was not likely that overflowing beer would be a feature of so modest an event; just as all the rest of it was a foretaste of Switzerland, of the Rhine, of North Italy, which after this would find one quite prepared. We are sorry to say that when, many years later, we ascended, for the first time, to the roof of Milan Cathedral, what we first thought of was not the "waveless plain of Lombardy" nor the beauty of the edifice, but the "little London snob" whom Brown, Jones, and Robinson saw writing his name on one of the pinnacles of the church. We had our preferences in this genial trio. We adored little Jones, the artist—if memory doesn't betray us (we haven't seen the book for twenty years), and Jones *was* the artist. It is difficult to say why we adored him, but it was certainly the dream of our life at that foolish period to make his acquaintance. We did so, in fact, not very long after. We were taken in due course to Europe, and we met him on a steamboat on the Lake of Geneva. There was no introduction, we had no conversation, but he was the Jones we had prefigured and loved. Thackeray's Christmas books (*The Rose and the Ring* apart—it dates from 1854) came before this: we remember them in our earliest years. They, too, were of the family of *Punch*—which is my excuse for this superfluity of preface—and they were a revelation of English manners. "English manners," for a child, could of course only mean certain individual English figures—the figures in *Our Street*, in *Doctor Birch and his Young Friends* (we were glad we were not of the number), in *Mrs. Perkins's Ball*. In the first of these charming little volumes there is a pictorial exposition of the reason why the nurse-maids in *Our Street* like Kensington Gardens. When in the course of time we were taken to walk in those lovely shades, we looked about us for a simpering young woman and an insinuating soldier on a bench, with a bawling baby sprawling on the path hard by, and we were not slow to discover the group.

Many people in the United States, and doubtless in other countries, have gathered their knowledge of English life almost entirely from *Punch*, and it would be difficult to imagine a more abundant, and on the whole a more accurate, informant. The accumulated volumes of this periodical contain evidence on a multitude of points of which there is no mention in the serious works—not even in the novels—of the day. The smallest details of social habit are depicted there, and the oddities of a race of people in whom oddity is strangely compatible with the dominion of convention. That the ironical view of these things is given does not injure the force of the testimony, for the irony of *Punch*, strangely enough, has always been discreet, even delicate. It is a singular fact that, though taste is not supposed to be the strong point of the English mind, this eminently representative journal has rarely been guilty of a violation of decorum. The taste of *Punch*, like its good-humour, has known very few lapses. The *London Charivari*—we remember how difficult it was (in 1853) to arrive at the right pronunciation—has in this respect very little to envy its Parisian original. English comedy is coarse, French comedy is fine— that would be the general assumption, certainly, on the part of a French critic. But a comparison between the back volumes of the *Charivari* and the back volumes of *Punch* would make it necessary to modify this formula. English humour is simple, innocent, plain, a trifle insipid, apt to sacrifice to the graces, to the proprieties; but if *Punch* be our witness English humour is not coarse. We are fortunately not obliged to declare just now what French humour appears to be—in the light of the *Charivari*, the *Journal Amusant*, the *Journal Pour Rire*. A Frenchman may say, in perfect good faith, that (to his sense) English drollery has doubtless every merit but that of being droll. French drollery, he may say, is salient, saltatory; whereas the English comic effort has little freedom of wing. The French, in these matters, like a great deal of salt; whereas the English, who spice their food very highly and have a cluster of sharp condiments on the table, take their caricatures comparatively mild. *Punch*, in short, is for the family—*Punch* may be sent up to the nursery. This surely may be admitted; and it is the fact that *Punch* is for the family that constitutes its high value. The family is, after all, the people; and a satirical sheet which holds up the mirror to this institution can hardly fail to be instructive. "Yes, if it hold the mirror up impartially," we can imagine the foreign critic to rejoin; "but in these matters the British caricaturist is not to be trusted. He slurs over a great deal—he omits a great deal more. He must, above all things, be proper; and there is a whole side of life which, in spite of his Juvenalian pretensions, he never touches at all." We must allow the foreign critic his supposed retort, without taking space to answer back—we may imagine him to be a bit of a "naturalist"—and admit that it is perhaps because they are obliged to be proper that Leech and Du Maurier give us, on the whole, such a cleanly, healthy, friendly picture of English manners. Such sustained and inveterate propriety is in itself a great force; it takes in a good deal, as well as leaves out. The general impression that we derive from the long series of *Punch* is a very cheerful and favourable one; it speaks of a vigorous, good-humoured, much-civilised people. The good-humour is, perhaps, the most striking point—not only the good-humour of the artist who represents the scene, but that of the figures engaged in it. The difference is remarkable in this respect between *Punch* and the French comic papers. The wonderful Cham, who for so many years contributed to those sheets, had an extraordinary sense of the ludicrous and a boundless stock of facetious invention. He was strangely expressive; he could place a figure before you, in the most violent action, with half a dozen strokes of his pencil. But his people were like wild-cats and scorpions. The temper of the French *bourgeoisie*, as represented by Cham, is a thing to make one take to one's heels. They perpetually tear and rend each other, show their teeth and their claws, kick each other down-stairs, and pitch each other from windows. All this is in the highest degree farcical and grotesque; but at bottom it is almost horrible. (It must be admitted that Cham and his wonderful colleague, Daumier, are much more horrible than Gavarni, who was admirably real, and at the same time capable of beauty and grace. Gavarni's women are charming; those of Cham and Daumier are monsters.) There is nothing, or almost nothing, of the horrible in *Punch*. The author of these remarks has a friend whom he has heard more than once maintain the too-ingenious thesis that the caricatures of Cham prove the French to be a cruel people; the same induction could, at least, never be made, even in an equal spirit of paradox, from the genial pages of *Punch*. "If *Punch* is never horrible, it is because *Punch* is always superficial, for life is full of the horrible"—so we may imagine our naturalistic objector to go on. However this may be, *Punch* is fortunate in having fallen on so smooth a surface. English life, as depicted by Leech and Du Maurier, and by that admirable Charles Keene—the best-humoured perhaps of the three, whose talent is so great that we have always wondered why it is not more comprehensive—is a compound of several very wholesome tastes: the love of the country, the love of action, the love of a harmless joke within the limits of due reverence, the love of sport, of horses and dogs, of family life, of children, of horticulture. With this there are a few other tastes of a less innocent kind— the love of ardent spirits, for instance, or of punching people's heads—or even the love of a lord. In Leech's drawings, country life plays a great part; his landscapes, in their extreme sketchiness, are often admirable. He gave in a few strokes the look of the hunting-field in winter—the dark damp slopes, the black dense hedges, the low thick sky. He was very general; he touched on everything, sooner or later; but he enjoyed his sporting subjects more than anything else. In this he was thoroughly English. No close observer of that people can fail to perceive that the love of sport is the thing that binds them most closely together, and in which they have the greatest number of feelings in common. Leech depicted, with infinite vividness, the accidents of the chase and of the fishing-season; and his treatment of the horse in especial contributed greatly to his popularity. He understood the animal, he knew him intimately, he loved him; and he drew him as if he knew how to ride as well as to draw. The English forgive a great deal to those who ride well; and this is doubtless why the badness of some of the sporting subjects that have appeared in *Punch* since Leech's death has been tolerated: the artist has been presumed to have a good seat. Leech never made a mistake; he did well whatever he did; and it must be remembered that for many years he furnished the political cartoon to *Punch*, as well as the smaller drawings. He was always amusing, always full of sense and point, always intensely English. His foreigner is always an inferior animal—his Frenchman is the Frenchman of Leicester Square, the Frenchman whom the Exhibition of 1851 revealed to the people of London. His point is perfectly perceptible—it is never unduly fine. His children are models of ruddy, chubby, shy yet sturdy British babyhood; and nothing could be nicer than his young women. The English maiden, in Leech, is emphatically a nice girl; modest and fresh, simple and blooming, and destined evidently for use as much as for ornament. In those early days to which we referred at the beginning of this article we were deeply in love with the young ladies of Leech, and we have never ceased to admire the simple art with which he made these hastily designed creatures conform unerringly to the English type. They have English eyes and English cheeks, English figures, English hands and feet, English ringlets, English petticoats. Leech was extremely observant, but he had not a strong imagination; he had a sufficient, but not a high sense of beauty; his ideal of the beautiful had nothing of the unattainable; it was simply a *résumé* of the fresh faces he saw about him. The great thing, however, was that he was a natural, though not in the least an analytic or an exact, draughtsman; his little figures live and move; many of his little scenes are stamped on the memory. I have spoken of his representations of the country, but his town-pictures are numerous and capital. He knew his London, and his sketches of the good people of that metropolis are as happy as his episodes in the drawing-room and the hunting-field. He was admirably broad and free; and no one in his line has had more than he the knack of giving what is called a general effect. He conveys at times the look of the London streets—the colour, the temperature, the damp blackness. He does the winter weather to perfection. Long before I had seen it I was acquainted, through his sketches, with the aspect of Baker Street in December. Out of such a multitude of illustrations it is difficult to choose; the two volumes of *Sketches of Life and Character*, transferred from *Punch*, are a real museum. But I recall, for instance, the simple little sketch of the worthy man up to his neck in bed on a January morning, to whom, on the other side of the door, the prompt housemaid, with her hammer in her hand, announces that "I have just broken the ice in your bath, sir." The black cold dawn, the very smell of the early chill, that raw sootiness of the London winter air, the red nose of the housemaid, the unfashionable street seen through the window—impart a peculiar vividness to the small inky-looking woodcut.

We have said too much about Leech, however, and the purpose of these remarks is not to commemorate his work. *Punch*, for the last fifteen years, has been, artistically speaking, George du Maurier. (We ought, perhaps, before this, to have said that none of our observations are to be taken as applying to the letterpress of the comic journal, which has probably never been fully appreciated in America.) It has employed other talents than his—notably Charles Keene, who is as broad, as jovial, as English (half his jokes are against Scotchmen) as Leech, but whose sense of the beautiful, the delicate, is inferior even to Leech's. But for a great many people, certainly in America, Du Maurier has long been, as I say, the successor of Leech, the embodiment of the pictorial spirit of *Punch*. Shut up in the narrow limits of black and white, without space, without colour, without the larger opportunities, Du Maurier has nevertheless established himself as an exquisite talent and a genuine artist. He is not so much of a laugher as Leech—he deals in the smile rather than the laugh—but he is a much deeper observer, and he carries his drawing infinitely further. He has not Leech's animal spirits; a want of boyishness, a tendency to reflection, to lowness of tone, as his own Postlethwaite would say, is perhaps his limitation. But his seriousness—if he be too serious—is that of the satirist as distinguished from the simple joker; and if he reflects, he does so in the literal sense of the word—holds up a singularly polished and lucid mirror to the drama of English society. More than twenty years ago, when he began to draw in *Once a Week*—that not very long-lived periodical which set out on its career with a high pictorial standard—it was apparent that the careful young artist who finished his designs very highly and signed them with a French name, stood very much upon his own feet. The earliest things of his that we know have the quality which has made him distinguished to-day—the union of a great sense of beauty with a great sense of reality. It was apparent from the first that this was not a simple and uniform talent, but a gift that had sprung from a combination of sources. It is important to remember, in speaking of Du Maurier—who is one of the pillars of the British journal *par excellence*—that he has French blood in his veins. George du Maurier, as we understand his history, was born in England, of a French father and an English mother, but was removed to France in his early years and educated according to the customs of that country. Later, however, he returned to England; and it would not be difficult for a careful student of his drawings to guess that England is the land of his predilection. He has drawn a great many French figures, but he has drawn them as one who knows them rather than as one who loves them. He has perhaps been, as the phrase is, a little hard upon the French; at any rate, he has been decidedly easy for the English. The latter are assuredly a very handsome race; but if we were to construct an image of them from the large majority of Du Maurier's drawings we should see before us a people of gods and goddesses. This does not alter the fact that there is a very Gallic element in some of Du Maurier's gifts—his fineness of perception, his remarkable power of specifying types, his taste, his grace, his lightness, a certain refinement of art. It is hard to imagine that a talent so remarkable should not have given early evidences; but in spite of such evidences Du Maurier was, on the threshold of manhood, persuaded by those to whom it was his duty to listen to turn his attention, as Mrs. Micawber says, to chemistry. He pursued this science without enthusiasm, though he had for some time a laboratory of his own. Before long, however, the laboratory was converted into a studio. His talent insisted on its liberty, and he committed himself to the plastic. He studied this charming element in Paris, at Düsseldorf; he began to work in London. This period of his life was marked by a great calamity, which has left its trace on his career and his work, and which it is needful to mention in order to speak with any fairness of these things. Abruptly, without a warning, his eyesight partly forsook him, and his activity was cruelly threatened. It is a great pleasure, in alluding to this catastrophe, to be able to speak of it as a signal example of difficulty vanquished. George du Maurier was condemned to many dark days, at the end of which he learned that he should have to carry on his task for the rest of his life with less than half a man's portion of the sense most valuable to the artist. The beautiful work that he has produced in such abundance for so many years has been achieved under restrictions of vision which might well have made any work impossible. It is permitted, accordingly, to imagine that if the artist had had the usual resources, we should not at the present moment have to consider him simply as an accomplished draughtsman in black and white. It is impossible to look at many of his drawings without perceiving that they are full of the art of the painter, and that the form they have taken, charming as it has been, is arbitrary and inadequate.

John Leech died on 27th October 1864, and the first sketches in *Punch* that we recognise as Du Maurier's appeared in that year. The very earliest that we have detected belong, indeed, to 5th December 1863. These beginnings are slight and sketchy head-pieces and vignettes; the first regular "picture" (with a legend beneath it) that we remember is of the date of 11th June 1864. It represents a tipsy waiter (or college servant) on a staircase, where he has smashed a trayful of crockery. We perceive nothing else of importance for some time after this, but suddenly his hand appears again in force, and from the summer of 1865 its appearances are frequent. The finish and delicacy, the real elegance of these early drawings, are extreme: the hand was already the hand of a brilliant executant. No such manner as this had hitherto been seen in *Punch*. By the time one had recognised that it was not a happy accident, but an accomplished habit, it had become the great feature, the "attraction," of the comic journal. *Punch* had never before suspected that it was so artistic; had never taken itself, in such matters, so seriously. Much the larger part of Du Maurier's work has been done for *Punch*, but he has designed as well many illustrations for books. The most charming of these perhaps are the drawings he executed in 1868 for a new edition of Thackeray's *Esmond*, which had been preceded several years before by a set of designs for Mrs. Gaskell's *Wives and Daughters*, first ushered into the world as a serial in the *Cornhill*. To the *Cornhill* for many years Du Maurier has every month contributed an illustration; he has reproduced every possible situation that is likely to be encountered in the English novel of manners; he has interpreted pictorially innumerable flirtations, wooings, philanderings, ruptures. The interest of the English novel of manners is frequently the interest of the usual; the situations presented to the artist are apt to lack superficial strangeness. A lady and gentleman sitting in a drawing-room, a lady and a gentleman going out to walk, a sad young woman watching at a sick-bed, a handsome young man lighting a cigarette—this is the range of incident through which the designer is called upon to move. But in these drawing-room and flower-garden episodes the artist is thoroughly at home; he accepts of course the material that is given him, but we fancy him much more easily representing quiet, harmonious things than depicting deeds of violence. It is a noticeable fact that in *Punch*, where he has his liberty, he very seldom represents such deeds. His occasional departures from this habit are of a sportive and fantastic sort, in which he ceases to pretend to be real: like the dream of the timorous Jenkins (15th February 1868), who sees himself hurled to destruction by a colossal foreshortened cab-horse. Du Maurier's fantastic—we speak of the extreme manifestations of it—is always admirable, ingenious, unexpected, pictorial; so much so, that we have often wondered that he should not have cultivated this vein more largely. As a general thing, however, in these excursions into the impossible it is some *charming* impossibility that he offers us—a picture of some happy contrivance which would make life more diverting: such as the playing of lawn-tennis on skates (on a lawn of ice), or the faculty on the part of young men on bicycles of carrying their sweethearts behind them on a pillion. We recommend the reader to turn to *Punch's Almanac* for 1865, in which two brilliant full-page illustrations represent the "Probable Results of the Acclimatisation Society." Nothing could be fuller of delicate fancy and of pictorial facility than this prophecy of the domestication in the London streets, and by the Serpentine of innumerable strange beasts—giraffes, ostriches, zebras, kangaroos, hippopotami, elephants, lions, panthers. Speaking of strange beasts, the strangest of all perhaps is the wonderful big dog who has figured of late years in Du Maurier's drawings, and who has probably passed with many persons as a kind of pictorial caprice. He is depicted as of such super-canine proportions, quite overshadowing and dwarfing the amiable family to whom he is represented as belonging, that he might be supposed to be another illustration of the artist's turn for the heroic in the graceful. But, as it happens, he is not an invention, but a portrait—the portrait of a magnificent original, a literally gigantic St. Bernard, the property of the artist—the biggest, the handsomest, the most benignant of all domesticated shaggy things.

We think we are safe in saying that those ruder forms of incongruity which as a general thing constitute the stock-in-trade of the caricaturist fail to commend themselves to this particular satirist. He is too fond of the beautiful—his great passion is for the lovely; not for what is called ideal beauty, which is usually a matter of not very successful guess-work, but for loveliness observed in the life and manners around him, and reproduced with a generous desire to represent it as usual. The French express a certain difference better than we; they talk of those who see *en beau* and those who see *en laid*. Du Maurier is as highly developed an example as we could desire of the former tendency—just as Cham and Daumier are examples of the latter; just, too, if we may venture to select instances from the staff of *Punch*, as Charles Keene and Linley Sambourne are examples of the latter. Du Maurier can see ugliness wonderfully well when he has a strong motive for looking for it, as witness so many of the figures in his crusade against the "æsthetic" movement. Who could be uglier than Maudle and Postlethwaite and all the other apparitions from "passionate Brompton"? Who could have more bulging foreheads, more protuberant eyes, more retreating jaws, more sloping shoulders, more objectionable hair, more of the signs generally of personal debility? To say, as we said just now, that Du Maurier carries his specification of types very far is to say mainly that he defines with peculiar completeness his queer people, his failures, his grotesques. But it strikes us that it is just this vivid and affectionate appreciation of beauty that makes him do such justice to the eccentrics. We have heard his ugly creations called malignant—compared (to their disadvantage) with similar figures in Leech. Leech, it was said, is always good-natured and jovial, even in the excesses of caricature; whereas his successor (with a much greater brilliancy of execution) betrays, in dealing with the oddities of the human family, a taint of "French ferocity." We think the discrimination fallacious; and it is only because we do not believe Du Maurier's reputation for amiability to be really in danger that we do not hasten to defend him from the charge of ferocity—French or English. The fact is he attempts discriminations that Leech never dreamt of. Leech's characterisations are all simple, whereas Du Maurier's are extremely complicated. He would like every one to be tall and straight and fair, to have a well-cut mouth and chin, a well-poised head, well-shaped legs, an air of nobleness, of happy development. He perceives, however, that nature plays us some dreadful tricks, and he measures her departure from these beautiful conditions with extreme displeasure. He regrets it with all the force of his appreciation of the beautiful, and he feels the strongest desire to indicate the culpability of the aberration. He has an artistic æsthetic need to make ugly people as ugly as they are; he holds that such serious facts should not be superficially treated. And then, besides that, his fancy finds a real entertainment in the completeness, in the perfection, of certain forms of facial queerness. No one has rendered like Du Maurier the ridiculous little people who crop up in the interstices of that huge and complicated London world. We have no such finished types as these in America. If the English find us all a little odd, oddity, in American society, never ripens and rounds itself off so perfectly as in some of these products of a richer tradition. All those English terms of characterisation which exist in America at the most only as precarious exotics, but which are on every one's lips in England—the snob, the cad, the prig, the duffer—Du Maurier has given us a thousand times the figure they belong to. No one has done the "duffer" so well; there are a hundred variations of the countenance of Mr. McJoseph, the gentleman commemorated in *Punch* on the 19th August 1876; or the even happier physiognomy of the other gentleman who on the 2d November 1872 says to a lady that he "never feels safe from the British snob till he is south of the Danube," and to whom the lady retorts, "And what do the South Danubians say?" This personage is in profile: his face is fat, complacent, cautious; his hair and whiskers have as many curves and flourishes as the signature of a writing-master; he is an incarnation of certain familiar elements of English life—"the great middle class," the Philistinism, the absence of irony, the smugness and literalism. Du Maurier is full of soft irony: he has that infusion of it which is indispensable to an artistic nature, and we may add that in this respect he seems to us more French than English. This quality has helped him immensely to find material in the so-called æsthetic movement of the last few years. None of his duffers have been so good as his æsthetic duffers. But of this episode we must wait a little to speak. The point that, for the moment, we wished to make is, that he has a peculiar perception of the look of breeding, of race; and that, left to himself, as it were, he would ask nothing better than to make it the prerogative of all his characters. Only he is not left to himself. For, looking about into the world he perceives Sir Gorgius Midas and Mr. McJoseph, and the whole multitude of the vulgar who have not been cultivated like orchids and race-horses. But his extreme inclination to give his figures the benefit of the supposition that most people have the feelings of gentlemen makes him, as we began by saying, a very happy interpreter of those frequent works of fiction of which the action goes on for the most part in the drawing-room of the British country house. Every drawing-room, unfortunately, is not a home of the graces; but for the artist, given such an apartment, a group of quiet, well-shaped people is more or less implied. The "fashionable novel," as it flourished about 1830, is no more; and its extinction is not to be regretted. We believe it was rarely accompanied with illustrations; but if it were to be revived Du Maurier would be the man to make the pictures—the pictures of people rather slim and still, with long necks and limbs so straight that they look stiff, who might be treated with the amount of derision justified (if the fashionable novel of 1830 is to be believed) by their passion for talking bad French.

We have been looking over the accumulations of *Punch* for the last twenty years, and Du Maurier's work, which during this long period is remarkably abundant and various, has given us more impressions than we can hope to put into form. The result of sitting for several hours at such a banquet of drollery, of poring over so many caricatures, of catching the point of so many jokes, is a kind of indigestion of the visual sense. This is especially the case if one happens to be liable to confusions and lapses of memory. Every picture, every pleasantry, drives the last out of the mind, and even the figures we recall best get mixed up with another story than their own. The early drawings, as a general thing, are larger than the late ones; we believe that the artist was obliged to make them large in order to make them at all. (They were then photographed, much reduced, upon the block; and it is impossible to form an idea of the delicacy of Du Maurier's work without having seen the designs themselves, which are in pen and ink.) As the years have gone on the artist has apparently been able to use a shorter stroke, there has been less need of reducing it, and the full-page picture has become more rare. The wealth of execution was sometimes out of proportion to the jest beneath the cut; the joke might be as much or as little of a joke as one would, the picture was at any rate before all things a picture. What could be more charming than the drawing (24th October 1868) of the unconscious Oriana and the ingenious Jones? It is a real work of art, a thing to have had the honours of colour, and of the "line" at the Academy; and that the artist should have been able to give it to us for threepence, on the reverse of a printed page, is a striking proof of his affluence. The unconscious Oriana—she is drawn very large— sits in the foreground, in the shadow of some rocks that ornament the sands at a bathing-place. Her beautiful hair falls over her shoulders (she has been taking her bath, and has hung her tresses out to dry), and her charming eyes are bent upon the second volume of a novel. The beach stretches away into the distance—with all the expression of space; and here the ingenious Jones carries out his little scheme of catching a portrait of the object—an object profoundly indifferent—of his adoration. He pretends to sit to an itinerant photographer, and apparently places himself in the line of the instrument, which in reality, thanks to a private understanding with the artist, is focussed upon the figure of his mistress. There is not much landscape in Du Maurier—the background is almost always an interior; but whenever he attempts an out-of-door scene he does it admirably. What could be prettier and at the same time more real than the big view (9th September 1876) of the low tide on Scarborough sands? We forget the joke, but we remember the scene—two or three figures, with their backs to us, leaning over a terrace or balcony in the foreground, and looking down at the great expanse of the uncovered beach, which is crowded with the activities of a populous bathing-place. The bathers, the walkers, the machines, the horses, the dogs, are seen with distinctness—a multitude of little black points—as under a magnifying glass; the whole place looks vast and swarming, and the particular impression the artist wished to convey is thoroughly caught. The particular impression—that is the great point with Du Maurier; his intention is never vague; he likes to specify the place, the hour, the circumstances. We forget the joke, but we remember the scene. This may easily happen, as one looks over Du Maurier's work; we frankly confess that though he often amuses us, he never strikes us primarily as a joker. It is not the exuberance of his humour but the purity of his line that arrests us, and we think of him much less as a purveyor of fun than as a charming draughtsman who has been led by circumstances to cultivate a vein of pleasantry. At every turn we find the fatal gift of beauty, by which we mean that his people are so charming that their prettiness throws the legend into the shade. Beauty comes so easily to him that he lavishes it with unconscious freedom. If he represents Angelina reprimanding the housemaid, it is ten to one that Angelina will be a Juno and the housemaid a Hebe. Whatever be the joke, this element of grace almost makes the picture serious. The point of course is not that Angelina should be lovely, but that the housemaid should be ridiculous; and you feel that if you should call the artist's attention to this he would reply: "I am really very sorry, but she is the plainest woman I can make—for the money!" This is what happens throughout—his women (and we may add his children) being monotonously, incorrigibly fair. He is exceedingly fond of children; he has represented them largely at every age and in every attitude; but we can scarcely recall an instance of his making them anything but beautiful. They are always delightful—they are the nicest children in the world. They say droll things, but they never do ugly ones, and their whole child-world is harmonious and happy. We might have referred that critic whom we quoted above, who observed in Du Maurier's manner the element of "ferocity," to the leniency of his treatment of the rising generation. The children of Cham are little monsters; so are Daumier's; and the infants of Gavarni, with a grace of their own, like everything he drew, are simply rather diminutive and rather more sophisticated adults. Du Maurier is fond of large families, of the picturesqueness of the British nursery; he is a votary of the *culte du bébé* and has never a happier touch than when he represents a blooming brood walking out in gradations of size. The pretty points of children are intimately known to him, and he throws them into high relief; he understands, moreover, the infant wardrobe as well as the infant mind. His little boys and girls are "turned out" with a completeness which has made the despair of many an American mother. It may perhaps appear invidious to say that the little girls are even nicer than the little boys, but this is no more than natural, with the artist's delicate appreciation of female loveliness. It begins, to his vision, in the earliest periods and goes on increasing till it is embodied in the stature of those slim Junos of whom we have spoken.

It is easy to see that Du Maurier is of the eminently justifiable opinion that nothing in the world is so fair as the fairness of fair women; and if so many of his women are fair, it is to be inferred that he has a secret for drawing out their advantages. This secret, indeed, is simply that fineness of perception of which we have already had occasion to speak and to which it is necessary so often to refer. He is evidently of the opinion that almost any woman has beauty if you look at her in the right way—carefully enough, intelligently enough; and that *a fortiori* the exceptionally handsome women contain treasures of plasticity. Feminine line and surface, curves of shoulder, stretches of arm, turns of head, undulations of step, are matters of attentive study to him; and his women have for the most part the art of looking as if they excelled in amiability as much as in contour. We know a gentleman who, on being requested to inscribe himself on one of those formidable folios kept in certain houses, in which you indite the name of your favourite flower, favourite virtue, favourite historical character, wrote, in the compartment dedicated to the "three favourite qualities in a woman" the simple words: "Grace. Grace. Grace." Du Maurier might have been this gentleman, for his women are inveterately and imperturbably graceful. We have heard people complain of it; complain too that they all look alike, that they are always sisters—all products of a single birth. They have indeed a mutual resemblance; but when once the beautiful type has been found, we see no reason why, from a restless love of change, the artist should depart from it. We should feel as if Du Maurier had been fickle and faithless if he were suddenly to cease to offer us the tall, tranquil persons he understands so well. They have an inestimable look of repose, a kind of Greek serenity. There is a figure in a cut of which we have forgotten both the "point" and the date (we mention it at hazard—it is one in a hundred), which only needed to be modelled in clay to be a truly "important" creation. A couple of children address themselves to a youthful aunt, who leans her hand upon a toilet-table, presenting her back, clothed in a loose gown, not gathered in at the waist, to the spectator. Her charming pose, the way her head slowly turns, the beautiful folds of her robe, make her look more like a statuette in a museum than like a figure in *Punch*. We have forgotten what the children are saying, but we remember her charming attitude, which is a capital example of the love of beauty for beauty's sake. It is the same bias as the characteristic of the poet.

The intention of these remarks has been supposed to be rather a view of Du Maurier in his relation to English society than a technical estimate of his powers—a line of criticism to which we may already appear unduly to have committed ourselves. He is predominantly a painter of social as distinguished from popular life, and when the other day he collected some of his drawings into a volume he found it natural to give them the title of *English Society at Home*. He looks at the luxurious classes more than at the people, though he by no means ignores the humours of humble life. His consideration of the peculiarities of costermongers and "cadgers" is comparatively perfunctory, as he is too fond of civilisation and of the higher refinements of the grotesque. His colleague, the frank and objective Keene, has a more natural familiarity with the British populace. There is a whole side of English life at which Du Maurier scarcely glances—the great sporting element, which supplies half of their gaiety and all their conversation to millions of her Majesty's subjects. He is shy of the turf and of the cricket-field; he only touches here and there upon the river; but he has made "society" completely his own—he has sounded its depths, explored its mysteries, discovered and divulged its secrets. His observation of these things is extraordinarily acute, and his illustrations, taken together, form a complete comedy of manners, in which the same personages constantly reappear, so that we have the sense, indispensable to keenness of interest, of tracing their adventures to a climax. So many of the conditions of English life are spectacular (and to American eyes even romantic) that Du Maurier has never been at a loss for subjects. He may have been at a loss for his joke—we hardly see how he could fail to be, at the rate at which he has been obliged to produce; but we repeat that to ourselves the joke is the least part of the affair. We mean that he is never at a loss for scenes. English society makes scenes all round him, and he has only to look to see the most charming combinations, which at the same time have the merit that you can always take the satirical view of them. He sees, for instance, the people in the Park; the crowd that gathers under the trees on June afternoons to watch the spectacle of the Row, with the slow, solemn jostle of the drive going on behind it. Such a spectacle as this may be vain and unprofitable to a mind bent upon higher business, but it is full of material for the artist, who finds a fund of inspiration in the thousand figures, faces, types, accidents, attitudes. The way people stand and sit, the way they stroll and pause, the way they lean over the rail to talk to one of the riders, the way they stare and yawn and bore themselves—these things are charming to Du Maurier, who always reproduces the *act* with wonderful fidelity. This we should bear in mind, having spoken above of his aversion to the violent. He has indeed a preference for quiet and gradual movements. But it is not in the least because he is not able to make the movement definite. No one represents a particular attitude better than he; and it is not too much to say that the less flagrant the attitude, the more latent its intention, the more successfully he represents it.

The postures people take while they are waiting for dinner, while they are thinking what to say, while they are pretending to listen to music, while they are making speeches they don't mean; the thousand strange and dreary expressions (of face and figure) which the detached mind may catch at any moment in wandering over a collection of people who are supposed to be amusing themselves in a superior manner—all this is entirely familiar to Du Maurier; he renders it with inimitable fidelity. His is the detached mind—he takes refuge in the divine independence of art. He reproduces to the life the gentleman who is looking with extraordinary solemnity at his boots, the lady who is gazing with sudden rapture at the ceiling, the grimaces of fifty people who would be surprised at their reflection if the mirror were suddenly to be presented to them. In such visions as these of course the comical mingles with the beautiful, and fond as Du Maurier is of the beautiful, it is sometimes heroically sacrificed. At any rate the comic effect is (in the drawing) never missed. The legend that accompanies it may sometimes appear to be wanting in the grossest drollery, but the expression of the figures is always such that you must say: "How he has hit it!" This is the kind of comedy in which Du Maurier excels—the comedy of those social relations in which the incongruities are pressed beneath the surface, so that the picture has need of a certain amount of explanation. The explanation is often rather elaborate—in many cases one may almost fancy that the image came first and the motive afterward. That is, it looks as if the artist, having seen a group of persons in certain positions, had said to himself: "They must—or at least they *may*—be saying so and so;" and then had represented these positions and affixed the interpretation. He passes over none of those occasions on which society congregates—the garden-party, the picnic, the flower-show, the polo-match (though he has not much cultivated the humours of sport, he has represented polo more than once, and he has done ample justice to lawn-tennis, just as he did it, years ago, to the charming, dawdling, "spooning" tedium of croquet, which he depicted as played only by the most adorable young women, with the most diminutive feet); but he introduces us more particularly to indoors entertainments—to the London dinner-party in all those variations which cover such a general sameness; to the afternoon tea, to the fashionable "squash," to the late and suffocating "small and early," to the scientific *conversazione*, to the evening with a little music. His musical parties are numerous and admirable—he has exposed in perfection the weak points of those entertainments: the infatuated tenor, bawling into the void of the public indifference; the air of lassitude that pervades the company; the woe-begone look of certain faces; the false and overacted attention of certain others; the young lady who is wishing to

217

sing, and whose mamma is glaring at the young lady who *is* singing; the bristling heads of foreigners of the professional class, which stand out against the sleekness of British respectability.

Du Maurier understands the foreigner as no caricaturist has done hitherto; and we hasten to add that his portraits of continental types are never caricatures. They are serious studies, in which the idiosyncrasies of the race in question are vividly presented. His Germans would be the best if his French folk were not better still; but he has rendered most happily the aspect—and indeed the very temperament—of the German pianist. He has not often attempted the American; and the American reader who turns over the back volumes of *Punch* and encounters the cartoons, born under an evil star, in which, during the long weary years of the War, the obedient pencil of Mr. Tenniel contributed at the expense of the American physiognomy to the gaiety of nations, will not perhaps regret that Du Maurier should have avoided this particular field of portraiture. It is not, however, that he has not occasionally been inspired by the American girl, whom he endows with due prettiness, as in the case of the two transatlantic young ladies who, in the presence of a fine Alpine view, exclaim to a British admirer: "My! ain't it rustic?" As for the French, he knows them intimately, as he has a right to do. He thinks better of the English of course; but his Frenchman is a very different affair from the Frenchman of Leech—the Frenchman who is sea-sick (as if it were the appanage of his race alone!) on the Channel steamer. In such a matter as this Du Maurier is really psychological; he is versed in the qualities which illustrate the difference of race. He accentuates first of course the physical variation; he contrasts—with a subtlety which may not at first receive all the credit it deserves—the long, fair English body, inclined to the bony, the lean, the angular, with the short, plump French personality, in which the neck is rarely a feature, in which the stomach is too much of one, in which the calves of the legs grow fat, in which in the women several of the joints, the wrists, the shape of the hand, are apt to be charming. Some of his happiest drawings are reminiscences of a midsummer sojourn at a French watering-place. We have long been in the habit of looking for *Punch* with peculiar impatience at this season of the year. When the artist goes to France he takes his big dog with him, and he has more than once commemorated the effect of this impressive member of a quiet English family upon the Norman and Breton populations. There have appeared at this time certain anecdotic pictures of English travellers in French towns—in shops, markets, tramcars—in which some of the deeper disparities of the two peoples have been (under the guise of its being all a joke) very sufficiently exposed. Du Maurier on the whole does justice to the French; his English figures, in these international tableaux, by no means always come off best. When the English family of many persons troops into the *charcutier's* or the perfumer's and stands planted there— mute, inexpressive, perpendicular—the demonstrations, the professions, the abundant speech of the neat, plump, insinuating *boutiquière* are a well-intended tribute to the high civilisation of her country. Du Maurier has done the "low" foreigner of the London (or of his native) streets—the foreigner whose unspeakable baseness prompts the Anglo-Saxon observer to breathe the Pharisee's vow of thanks that he is not as these people are; but, as we have seen, he has done the low Englishman quite as well—the 'Arry of the London music-halls, the companion of 'Andsome 'Arriet and Mr. Belville. Du Maurier's rendering of 'Arry's countenance, with its bloated purple bloom, of 'Arry's figure, carriage and costume—of his deportment at the fancy fair, where the professional beauties solicit his custom—is a triumph of exactitude. One of the most poignant of the drawings that illustrate his ravages in our civilisation is the large design which a year or two ago represented the narrow canal beneath the Bridge of Sighs. The hour is evening, and the period is the detested date at which the penny-steamer was launched upon the winding water-ways of the loveliest city in the world. The odious little vessel, belching forth a torrent of black smoke, passes under the covered arch which connects the ducal palace with the ducal prison. 'Andsome 'Arriet and Mr. Belville (personally conducted) are of course on board, and 'Arriet remarks that the Bridge of Sighs isn't much of a size after all. To which her companion rejoins that it has been immortalised by Byron, any way—"'im as wrote 'Our Boys,' you know." This fragment of dialogue expresses concisely the arguments both for and against the importation of the cheap and nasty into Venetian waters.

Returning for a moment to Du Maurier's sketches of the French, we must recall the really interesting design in which, at a child's party at the Casino of a *station balnéaire*, a number of little natives are inviting a group of

English children to dance. The French children have much the better manners; they make their little bows with a smile, they click their heels together and crook their little arms as they offer them to their partners. The sturdy British infants are dumb, mistrustful, vaguely bewildered. Presently you perceive that in the very smart attire of the gracious little Gauls *everything is wrong*—their high heels, their poor little legs, at once too bare and too much covered, their superfluous sashes and scarfs. The small English are invested in plain Jerseys and knickerbockers. The whole thing is a pearl of observation, of reflection. Let us recall also the rebuke administered to M. Dubois, the distinguished young man of science who, just arrived from Paris and invited to dine by the Duke of Stilton, mentions this latter fact in apology for being late to a gentleman to whose house he goes on leaving the Duke's. This gentleman, assisted by Mr. Grigsby (both of them specimens of the snob-philistine whom Du Maurier has brought to such perfection), reprehends him in a superior manner for his rashness, reminds him that in England it is "not usual for a professional man" to allude in that promiscuous manner to having dined with a duke—a privilege which Grigsby characterises "the perfection of consummate achievement." The advantage is here with poor M. Dubois, who is a natural and sympathetic figure, a very *gentil* little Frenchman. The advantage is doubtless also with Mlle. Serrurier and her mother, though Mademoiselle is not very pretty, in a scene in which, just after the young lady has been singing at Mrs. Ponsonby de Tomkyns's, the clever Mrs. Ponsonby plays her off on the Duchess (as an inducement to come to another party) and then plays the Duchess off on the little vocalist and her mother, who, in order to secure the patronage of the Duchess, promise to come to the entertainment in question. The clever Mrs. Ponsonby thus gets both the Duchess and the vocalist for nothing. The broad-faced French girl, with small, salient eyes, her countenance treated in the simplest and surest manner, is a capital specimen of Du Maurier's skill in race-portraiture; and though they may be a knowing couple in their way, we are sure that she and her mamma are incapable of the machinations of Mrs. Ponsonby de Tomkyns.

This lady is a real creation. She is an incident of one of the later phases of Du Maurier's activity—a child of the age which has also produced Mrs. Cimabue Brown and Messrs. Maudle and Postlethwaite. She is not one of the heroines of the æsthetic movement, though we may be sure she dabbles in that movement so far as it pays to do so. Mrs. Ponsonby de Tomkyns is a little of everything, in so far as anything pays. She is always on the lookout, she never misses an opportunity. She is not a specialist, for that cuts off too many opportunities, and the æsthetic people have the *tort*, as the French say, to be specialists. No, Mrs. Ponsonby de Tomkyns is—what shall we call her?—well, she is the modern social spirit. She is prepared for everything; she is ready to take advantage of everything; she would invite Mr. Bradlaugh to dinner if she thought the Duchess would come to meet him. The Duchess is her great achievement—she never lets go of her Duchess. She is young, very nice-looking, slim, graceful, indefatigable. She tires poor Ponsonby completely out; she can keep going for hours after poor Ponsonby is reduced to stupefaction. This unfortunate husband is indeed almost always stupefied. He is not, like his wife, a person of imagination. She leaves him far behind, though he is so inconvertible that if she were a less superior person he would have been a sad encumbrance. He always figures in the corner of the scenes in which she distinguishes herself, separated from her by something like the gulf that separated Caliban from Ariel. He has his hands in his pockets, his head poked forward; what is going on is quite beyond his comprehension. He vaguely wonders what his wife will do next; her manœuvres quite transcend him. Mrs. Ponsonby de Tomkyns always succeeds. She is never at fault; she is as quick as the instinct of self-preservation. She is the little London lady who is determined to be a greater one. She pushes, pushes, gently but firmly—always pushes. At last she arrives. It is true that she had only the other day, on 29th June 1882, a considerable failure; we refer the reader to the little incident of Madame Gaminot, in the *Punch* for that date. But she will recover from it; she has already recovered from it. She is not even afraid of Sir Gorgius Midas—of the dreadful Midas junior. She pretends to think Lady Midas the most elegant of women; when it is necessary to flatter, she lays it on as with a trowel. She hesitates at nothing; she is very modern. If she doesn't take the æsthetic line more than is necessary, she finds it necessary to take it a little; for if we are to believe Du Maurier, the passion for strange raiment and blue china has during the last few years made ravages in the London world. We may be sure that Mrs. Ponsonby de Tomkyns has an array of fragile disks attached to her walls, and that she can put in a word about Botticelli at the right moment. She is far, however, from being a representative of æstheticism, for her hair is very neatly arranged, and her dress looks French and superficial.

In Mrs. Cimabue Brown we see the priestess of the æsthetic cult, and this lady is on the whole a different sort of person. She knows less about duchesses, but she knows more about dados. Du Maurier's good-natured "chaff" of the eccentricities of the plastic sense so newly and so strangely awakened in England has perhaps been the most brilliant episode of his long connection with *Punch*. He has invented Mrs. Cimabue Brown—he has invented Maudle and Postlethwaite. These remarkable people have had great success in America, and have contributed not a little to the curiosity felt in that country on the subject of the English Renascence. Strange rumours and legends in relation to this great movement had made their way across the Atlantic; the sayings and doings of a mysterious body of people, devotees of the lovely and the precious, living in goodly houses and walking in gracious garments, were repeated and studied in our simpler civilisation. There has not been as yet an American Renascence, in spite of the taste for "sincere" sideboards and fragments of crockery. American interiors are perhaps to-day as "gracious" as English; but the movement in the United States has stopped at household furniture, has not yet set its mark upon speech and costume— much less upon the human physiognomy. Du Maurier of course has lent a good deal of his own fame to the vagaries he depicts; but it is certain that the new æsthetic life has had a good deal of reality. A great many people have discovered themselves to be fitted for it both by nature and by grace; so that noses and chins, facial angles of every sort shaped according to this higher rule have become frequent in London society. This reaction of taste upon nature is really a marvel, and the miracle has not been repeated in America, nor so far as we know upon the continent of Europe. The love of Botticelli has actually remoulded the features of several persons. London, for many seasons, was full of Botticelli women, with wan cheeks and weary eyes, enveloped in mystical, crumpled robes. Their language was apt to correspond with their faces; they talked in strange accents, with melancholy murmurs and cadences. They announced a gospel of joy, but their expression, their manners, were joyless. These peculiarities did not cross the ocean; for somehow the soil of the western world was not as yet prepared for them. American ladies were even heard to declare that there was something in their constitution that would prevent their ever dressing like that. They had another ideal; they were committed to the whalebone. But meanwhile, as I say, there was something irritating, fascinating, mystifying in the light thrown on the subject by *Punch*. It seemed to many persons to be desired that we too should have a gospel of joy; American life was not particularly "gracious," and if only the wind could be made to blow from the æsthetic quarter a great many dry places would be refreshed. These desires perhaps have subsided; for *Punch* of late has rather neglected the Renascence. Mrs. Cimabue Brown is advancing in years, and Messrs. Maudle and Postlethwaite have been through all their paces. The new æsthetic life, in short, shows signs of drawing to a close, after having, as many people tell us, effected a revolution in English taste—having at least, if not peopled the land with beauty, made certain consecrated forms of ugliness henceforth impossible.

The whole affair has been very curious and, we think, very characteristic of the English mind. The same episode fifty times repeated—a hundred "revolutions of taste," accompanied with an infinite expenditure of money—would fail to convince certain observant and possibly too sceptical strangers that the English are an æsthetic people. They have not a spontaneous artistic life; their taste is a matter of conscience, reflection, duty, and the writer who in our time has appealed to them most eloquently on behalf of art has rested his plea on moral standards—has talked exclusively of right and wrong. It is impossible to live much among them, to be a spectator of their habits, their manners, their arrangements, without perceiving that the artistic point of view is the last that they naturally take. The sense of manner is not part of their constitution. They arrive at it, as they have arrived at so many things, because they are ambitious, resolute, enlightened, fond of difficulties; but there is always a strange element either of undue apology or of exaggerated defiance in their attempts at the cultivation of beauty. They carry on their huge broad back a nameless mountain of conventions and prejudices, a dusky cloud of inaptitudes and fears, which casts a shadow upon the frank and confident practice of art. The consequence of all this is that their revivals of taste are even stranger than the abuses they are meant to correct. They are violent, voluntary, mechanical; wanting in grace, in tact, in the sense of humour and of proportion. A genuine artist like Du Maurier could not fail to perceive all this, and to perceive also that it gave him a capital opportunity. None of his queer people are so queer as some of these perverted votaries of joy. "Excuse me, it is not a Botticelli—before a Botticelli I am dumb," one of them says to a poor plain man who shows him a picture which has been attributed to that master. We have said already, and repeated, that Du Maurier has a great deal of irony—the irony of the thorough-going artist and of the observer who has a strain of foreign blood in his veins. There are certain pretensions that such a mind can never take seriously; in the artist there is of necessity, as it appears to us, a touch of the democrat—though, perhaps, he is as unlikely to have more than a certain dose of this disposition as he is to be wholly without it. Some of his drawings seem to us to have for the public he addresses a stinging democratic meaning; like the adventure of M. Dubois (of whom we have spoken), who had had the inconvenience of dining with a duke; or the reply of the young man to whom Miss Midas remarks that he is the first commoner she has ever danced with: "And why is it the commoners have avoided you so?"—or the response of the German *savant* to Mrs. Lyon Hunter, who invites him to dine, without his wife, though she is on his arm, to meet various great ladies whom she enumerates: "And pray, do you think they would not be respectable company for my wife?" Du Maurier possesses in perfection the independence of the genuine artist in the presence of a hundred worldly superstitions and absurdities. We have said, however, that the morality, so to speak, of his drawings was a subordinate question: what we wished to insist upon is their completeness, their grace, their beauty, their rare pictorial character. It is an accident that the author of such things should not have been a painter—that he has not been an ornament of the English school. Indeed, with the restrictions to which he has so well accommodated himself, he is such an ornament. No English artistic work in these latter years has, in our opinion, been more exquisite in quality.

1883.

XI. THE ART OF FICTION

I SHOULD not have affixed so comprehensive a title to these few remarks, necessarily wanting in any completeness upon a subject the full consideration of which would carry us far, did I not seem to discover a pretext for my temerity in the interesting pamphlet lately published under this name by Mr. Walter Besant. Mr. Besant's lecture at the Royal Institution—the original form of his pamphlet—appears to indicate that many persons are interested in the art of fiction, and are not indifferent to such remarks, as those who practise it may attempt to make about it. I am therefore anxious not to lose the benefit of this favourable association, and to edge in a few words under cover of the attention which Mr. Besant is sure to have excited. There is something very encouraging in his having put into form certain of his ideas on the mystery of story-telling.

It is a proof of life and curiosity—curiosity on the part of the brotherhood of novelists as well as on the part of their readers. Only a short time ago it might have been supposed that the English novel was not what the French call *discutable*. It had no air of having a theory, a conviction, a consciousness of itself behind it—of being the expression of an artistic faith, the result of choice and comparison. I do not say it was necessarily the worse for that: it would take much more courage than I possess to intimate that the form of the novel as Dickens and Thackeray (for instance) saw it had any taint of incompleteness. It was, however, *naïf* (if I may help myself out with another French word); and evidently if it be destined to suffer in any way for having lost its *naïveté* it has now an idea of making sure of the corresponding advantages. During the period I have alluded to there was a comfortable, good-humoured feeling abroad that a novel is a novel, as a pudding is a pudding, and that our only business with it could be to swallow it. But within a year or two, for some reason or other, there have been signs of returning animation—the era of discussion would appear to have been to a certain extent opened. Art lives upon discussion, upon experiment, upon curiosity, upon variety of attempt, upon the exchange of views and the comparison of standpoints; and there is a presumption that those times when no one has anything particular to say about it, and has no reason to give for practice or preference, though they may be times of honour, are not times of development—are times, possibly even, a little of dulness. The successful application of any art is a delightful spectacle, but the theory too is interesting; and though there is a great deal of the latter without the former I suspect there has never been a genuine success that has not had a latent core of conviction. Discussion, suggestion, formulation, these things are fertilising when they are frank and sincere. Mr. Besant has set an excellent example in saying what he thinks, for his part, about the way in which fiction should be written, as well as about the way in which it should be published; for his view of the "art," carried on into an appendix, covers that too. Other labourers in the same field will doubtless take up the argument, they will give it the light of their experience, and the effect will surely be to make our interest in the novel a little more what it had for some time threatened to fail to be—a serious, active, inquiring interest, under protection of which this delightful study may, in moments of confidence, venture to say a little more what it thinks of itself.

It must take itself seriously for the public to take it so. The old superstition about fiction being "wicked" has doubtless died out in England; but the spirit of it lingers in a certain oblique regard directed toward any story which does not more or less admit that it is only a joke. Even the most jocular novel feels in some degree the weight of the proscription that was formerly directed against literary levity: the jocularity does not always succeed in passing for orthodoxy. It is still expected, though perhaps people are ashamed to say it, that a production which is after all only a "make-believe" (for what else is a "story"?) shall be in some degree apologetic—shall renounce the pretension of attempting really to represent life. This, of course, any sensible, wide-awake story declines to do, for it quickly perceives that the tolerance granted to it on such a condition is only an attempt to stifle it disguised in the form of generosity. The old evangelical hostility to the novel, which was as explicit as it was narrow, and which regarded it as little less favourable to our immortal part than a stage-play, was in reality far less insulting. The only reason for the existence of a novel is that it does attempt to represent life. When it relinquishes this attempt, the same attempt that we see on the canvas of the painter, it will have arrived at a very strange pass. It is not expected of the picture that it will make itself humble in order to be forgiven; and the analogy between the art of the painter and the art of the novelist is, so far as I am able to see, complete. Their inspiration is the same, their process (allowing for the different quality of the vehicle), is the same, their success is the same. They may learn from each other, they may explain and sustain each other. Their cause is the same, and the honour of one is the honour of another. The Mahometans think a picture an unholy thing, but it is a long time since any Christian did, and it is therefore the more odd that in the Christian mind the traces (dissimulated though they may be) of a suspicion of the sister art should linger to this day. The only effectual way to lay it to rest is to emphasise the analogy to which I just alluded—to insist on the fact that as the picture is reality, so the novel is history. That is the only general description (which does it justice) that we may give of the novel. But history also is allowed to represent life; it is not, any more than painting, expected to apologise. The subject-matter of fiction is stored up likewise in documents and records, and if it will not give itself away, as they say in California, it must speak with assurance, with the tone of the historian. Certain accomplished novelists have a habit of giving themselves away which must often bring tears to the eyes of people who take their fiction seriously. I was lately struck, in reading over many pages of Anthony Trollope, with his want of discretion in this particular. In a digression, a parenthesis or an aside, he concedes to the reader that he and this trusting friend are only "making believe." He admits that the events he narrates have not really happened, and that he can give his narrative any turn the reader may like best. Such a betrayal of a sacred office seems to me, I confess, a terrible crime; it is what I mean by the attitude of apology, and it shocks me every whit as much in Trollope as it would have shocked me in Gibbon or Macaulay. It implies that the novelist is less occupied in looking for the truth (the truth, of course I mean, that he assumes, the premises that we must grant him, whatever they may be), than the historian, and in doing so it deprives him at a stroke of all his standing-room. To represent and illustrate the past, the actions of men, is the task of either writer, and the only difference that I can see is, in proportion as he succeeds, to the honour of the novelist, consisting as it does in his having more difficulty in collecting his evidence, which is so far from being purely literary. It seems to me to give him a great character, the fact that he has at once so much in common with the philosopher and the painter; this double analogy is a magnificent heritage.

It is of all this evidently that Mr. Besant is full when he insists upon the fact that fiction is one of the *fine* arts, deserving in its turn of all the honours and emoluments that have hitherto been reserved for the successful profession of music, poetry, painting, architecture. It is impossible to insist too much on so important a truth, and the place that Mr. Besant demands for the work of the novelist may be represented, a trifle less abstractly, by saying that he demands not only that it shall be reputed artistic, but that it shall be reputed very artistic indeed. It is excellent that he should have struck this note, for his doing so indicates that there was need of it, that his proposition may be to many people a novelty. One rubs one's eyes at the thought; but the rest of Mr. Besant's essay confirms the revelation. I suspect in truth that it would be possible to confirm it still further, and that one would not be far wrong in saying that in addition to the people to whom it has never occurred that a novel ought to be artistic, there are a great many others who, if this principle were urged upon them, would be filled with an indefinable mistrust. They would find it difficult to explain their repugnance, but it would operate strongly to put them on their guard. "Art," in our Protestant communities, where so many things have got so strangely twisted about, is supposed in certain circles to have some vaguely injurious effect upon those who make it an important consideration, who let it weigh in the balance. It is assumed to be opposed in some mysterious manner to morality, to amusement, to instruction. When it is embodied in the work of the painter (the sculptor is another affair!) you know what it is: it stands there before you, in the honesty of pink and green and a gilt frame; you can see the worst of it at a glance, and you can be on your guard. But when it is introduced into literature it becomes more insidious—there is danger of its hurting you before you know it. Literature should be either instructive or amusing, and there is in many minds an impression that these artistic preoccupations, the search for form, contribute to neither end, interfere indeed with both. They are too frivolous to be edifying, and too serious to be diverting; and they are moreover priggish and paradoxical and superfluous. That, I think, represents the manner in which the latent thought of many people who read novels as an exercise in skipping would explain itself if it were to become articulate. They would argue, of course, that a novel ought to be "good," but they would interpret this term in a fashion of their own, which indeed would vary considerably from one critic to another. One would say that being good means representing virtuous and aspiring characters, placed in prominent positions; another would say that it depends on a "happy ending," on a distribution at the last of prizes, pensions, husbands, wives, babies, millions, appended paragraphs, and cheerful remarks. Another still would say that it means being full of incident and movement, so that we shall wish to jump ahead, to see who was the mysterious stranger, and if the stolen will was ever found, and shall not be distracted from this pleasure by any tiresome analysis or "description." But they would all agree that the "artistic" idea would spoil some of their fun. One would hold it accountable for all the description, another would see it revealed in the absence of sympathy. Its hostility to a happy ending would be evident, and it might even in some cases render any ending at all impossible. The "ending" of a novel is, for many persons, like that of a good dinner, a course of dessert and ices, and the artist in fiction is regarded as a sort of meddlesome doctor who forbids agreeable aftertastes. It is therefore true that this conception of Mr. Besant's of the novel as a superior form encounters not only a negative but a positive indifference. It matters little that as a work of art it should really be as little or as much of its essence to supply happy endings, sympathetic characters, and an objective tone, as if it were a work of mechanics: the association of ideas, however incongruous, might easily be too much for it if an eloquent voice were not sometimes raised to call attention to the fact that it is at once as free and as serious a branch of literature as any other.

Certainly this might sometimes be doubted in presence of the enormous number of works of fiction that appeal to the credulity of our generation, for it might easily seem that there could be no great character in a commodity so quickly and easily produced. It must be admitted that good novels are much compromised by bad ones, and that the field at large suffers discredit from overcrowding. I think, however, that this injury is only superficial, and that the superabundance of written fiction proves nothing against the principle itself.

It has been vulgarised, like all other kinds of literature, like everything else to-day, and it has proved more than some kinds accessible to vulgarisation. But there is as much difference as there ever was between a good novel and a bad one: the bad is swept with all the daubed canvases and spoiled marble into some unvisited limbo, or infinite rubbish-yard beneath the back-windows of the world, and the good subsists and emits its light and stimulates our desire for perfection. As I shall take the liberty of making but a single criticism of Mr. Besant, whose tone is so full of the love of his art, I may as well have done with it at once. He seems to me to mistake in attempting to say so definitely beforehand what sort of an affair the good novel will be. To indicate the danger of such an error as that has been the purpose of these few pages; to suggest that certain traditions on the subject, applied *a priori*, have already had much to answer for, and that the good health of an art which undertakes so immediately to reproduce life must demand that it be perfectly free. It lives upon exercise, and the very meaning of exercise is freedom. The only obligation to which in advance we may hold a novel, without incurring the accusation of being arbitrary, is that it be interesting. That general responsibility rests upon it, but it is the only one I can think of. The ways in which it is at liberty to accomplish this result (of interesting us) strike me as innumerable, and such as can only suffer from being marked out or fenced in by prescription. They are as various as the temperament of man, and they are successful in proportion as they reveal a particular mind, different from others. A novel is in its broadest definition a personal, a direct impression of life: that, to begin with, constitutes its value, which is greater or less according to the intensity of the impression. But there will be no intensity at all, and therefore no value, unless there is freedom to feel and say. The tracing of a line to be followed, of a tone to be taken, of a form to be filled out, is a limitation of that freedom and a suppression of the very thing that we are most curious about. The form, it seems to me, is to be appreciated after the fact: then the author's choice has been made, his standard has been indicated; then we can follow lines and directions and compare tones and resemblances. Then in a word we can enjoy one of the most charming of pleasures, we can estimate quality, we can apply the test of execution. The execution belongs to the author alone; it is what is most personal to him, and we measure him by that. The advantage, the luxury, as well as the torment and responsibility of the novelist, is that there is no limit to what he may attempt as an executant—no limit to his possible experiments, efforts, discoveries, successes. Here it is especially that he works, step by step, like his brother of the brush, of whom we may always say that he has painted his picture in a manner best known to himself. His manner is his secret, not necessarily a jealous one. He cannot disclose it as a general thing if he would; he would be at a loss to teach it to others. I say this with a due recollection of having insisted on the community of method of the artist who paints a picture and the artist who writes a novel. The painter *is* able to teach the rudiments of his practice, and it is possible, from the study of good work (granted the aptitude), both to learn how to paint and to learn how to write. Yet it remains true, without injury to the *rapprochement*, that the literary artist would be obliged to say to his pupil much more than the other, "Ah, well, you must do it as you can!" It is a question of degree, a matter of delicacy. If there are exact sciences, there are also exact arts, and the grammar of painting is so much more definite that it makes the difference.

I ought to add, however, that if Mr. Besant says at the beginning of his essay that the "laws of fiction may be laid down and taught with as much precision and exactness as the laws of harmony, perspective, and proportion," he mitigates what might appear to be an extravagance by applying his remark to "general" laws, and by expressing most of these rules in a manner with which it would certainly be unaccommodating to disagree. That the novelist must write from his experience, that his "characters must be real and such as might be met with in actual life;" that "a young lady brought up in a quiet country village should avoid descriptions of garrison life," and "a writer whose friends and personal experiences belong to the lower middle-class should carefully avoid introducing his characters into society;" that one should enter one's notes in a common-place book; that one's figures should be clear in outline; that making them clear by some trick of speech or of carriage is a bad method, and "describing them at length" is a worse one; that English Fiction should have a "conscious moral purpose;" that "it is almost impossible to estimate too highly the value of careful workmanship—that is, of style;" that "the most important point of all is the story," that "the story is everything": these are principles with most of which it is surely impossible not to sympathise.

That remark about the lower middle-class writer and his knowing his place is perhaps rather chilling; but for the rest I should find it difficult to dissent from any one of these recommendations. At the same time, I should find it difficult positively to assent to them, with the exception, perhaps, of the injunction as to entering one's notes in a common-place book. They scarcely seem to me to have the quality that Mr. Besant attributes to the rules of the novelist—the "precision and exactness" of "the laws of harmony, perspective, and proportion." They are suggestive, they are even inspiring, but they are not exact, though they are doubtless as much so as the case admits of: which is a proof of that liberty of interpretation for which I just contended. For the value of these different injunctions—so beautiful and so vague—is wholly in the meaning one attaches to them. The characters, the situation, which strike one as real will be those that touch and interest one most, but the measure of reality is very difficult to fix. The reality of Don Quixote or of Mr. Micawber is a very delicate shade; it is a reality so coloured by the author's vision that, vivid as it may be, one would hesitate to propose it as a model: one would expose one's self to some very embarrassing questions on the part of a pupil. It goes without saying that you will not write a good novel unless you possess the sense of reality; but it will be difficult to give you a recipe for calling that sense into being. Humanity is immense, and reality has a myriad forms; the most one can affirm is that some of the flowers of fiction have the odour of it, and others have not; as for telling you in advance how your nosegay should be composed, that is another affair. It is equally excellent and inconclusive to say that one must write from experience; to our supposititious aspirant such a declaration might savour of mockery. What kind of experience is intended, and where does it begin and end? Experience is never limited, and it is never complete; it is an immense sensibility, a kind of huge spider-web of the finest silken threads suspended in the chamber of consciousness, and catching every airborne particle in its tissue. It is the very atmosphere of the mind; and when the mind is imaginative—much more when it happens to be that of a man of genius—it takes to itself the faintest hints of life, it converts the very pulses of the air into revelations. The young lady living in a village has only to be a damsel upon whom nothing is lost to make it quite unfair (as it seems to me) to declare to her that she shall have nothing to say about the military. Greater miracles have been seen than that, imagination assisting, she should speak the truth about some of these gentlemen. I remember an English novelist, a woman of genius, telling me that she was much commended for the impression she had managed to give in one of her tales of the nature and way of life of the French Protestant youth. She had been asked where she learned so much about this recondite being, she had been congratulated on her peculiar opportunities. These opportunities consisted in her having once, in Paris, as she ascended a staircase, passed an open door where, in the household of a *pasteur*, some of the young Protestants were seated at table round a finished meal. The glimpse made a picture; it lasted only a moment, but that moment was experience. She had got her direct personal impression, and she turned out her type. She knew what youth was, and what Protestantism; she also had the advantage of having seen what it was to be French, so that she converted these ideas into a concrete image and produced a reality. Above all, however, she was blessed with the faculty which when you give it an inch takes an ell, and which for the artist is a much greater source of strength than any accident of residence or of place in the social scale. The power to guess the unseen from the seen, to trace the implication of things, to judge the whole piece by the pattern, the condition of feeling life in general so completely that you are well on your way to knowing any particular corner of it—this cluster of gifts may almost be said to constitute experience, and they occur in country and in town, and in the most differing stages of education. If experience consists of impressions, it may be said that impressions *are* experience, just as (have we not seen it?) they are the very air we breathe. Therefore, if I should certainly say to a novice, "Write from experience and experience only," I should feel that this was rather a tantalising monition if I were not careful immediately to add, "Try to be one of the people on whom nothing is lost!"

I am far from intending by this to minimise the importance of exactness—of truth of detail. One can speak best from one's own taste, and I may therefore venture to say that the air of reality (solidity of specification) seems to me to be the supreme virtue of a novel—the merit on which all its other merits (including that conscious moral purpose of which Mr. Besant speaks) helplessly and submissively depend. If it be not there they are all as nothing, and if these be there, they owe their effect to the success with which the author has produced the illusion of life. The cultivation of this success, the study of this exquisite process, form, to my taste, the beginning and the end of the art of the novelist. They are his inspiration, his despair, his reward, his torment, his delight. It is here in very truth that he competes with life; it is here that he competes with his brother the painter in *his* attempt to render the look of things, the look that conveys their meaning, to catch the colour, the relief, the expression, the surface, the substance of the human spectacle. It is in regard to this that Mr. Besant is well inspired when he bids him take notes. He cannot possibly take too many, he cannot possibly take enough. All life solicits him, and to "render" the simplest surface, to produce the most momentary illusion, is a very complicated business. His case would be easier, and the rule would be more exact, if Mr. Besant had been able to tell him what notes to take. But this, I fear, he can never learn in any manual; it is the business of his life. He has to take a great many in order to select a few, he has to work them up as he can, and even the guides and philosophers who might have most to say to him must leave him alone when it comes to the application of precepts, as we leave the painter in communion with his palette. That his characters "must be clear in outline," as Mr. Besant says—he feels that down to his boots; but how he shall make them so is a secret between his good angel and himself. It would be absurdly simple if he could be taught that a great deal of "description" would make them so, or that on the contrary the absence of description and the cultivation of dialogue, or the absence of dialogue and the multiplication of "incident," would rescue him from his difficulties. Nothing, for instance, is more possible than that he be of a turn of mind for which this odd, literal opposition of description and dialogue, incident and description, has little meaning and light. People often talk of these things as if they had a kind of internecine distinctness, instead of melting into each other at every breath, and being intimately associated parts of one general effort of expression. I cannot imagine composition existing in a series of blocks, nor conceive, in any novel worth discussing at all, of a passage of description that is not in its intention narrative, a passage of dialogue that is not in its intention descriptive, a touch of truth of any sort that does not partake of the nature of incident, or an incident that derives its interest from any other source than the general and only source of the success of a work of art—that of being illustrative. A novel is a living thing, all one and continuous, like any other organism, and in proportion as it lives will it be found, I think, that in each of the parts there is something of each of the other parts. The critic who over the close texture of a finished work shall pretend to trace a geography of items will mark some frontiers as artificial, I fear, as any that have been known to history. There is an old-fashioned distinction between the novel of character and the novel of incident which must have cost many a smile to the intending fabulist who was keen about his work. It appears to me as little to the point as the equally celebrated distinction between the novel and the romance—to answer as little to any reality. There are bad novels and good novels, as there are bad pictures and good pictures; but that is the only distinction in which I see any meaning, and I can as little imagine speaking of a novel of character as I can imagine speaking of a picture of character. When one says picture one says of character, when one says novel one says of incident, and the terms may be transposed at will. What is character but the determination of incident? What is incident but the illustration of character? What is either a picture or a novel that is *not* of character? What else do we seek in it and find in it? It is an incident for a woman to stand up with her hand resting on a table and look out at you in a certain way; or if it be not an incident I think it will be hard to say what it is. At the same time it is an expression of character. If you say you don't see it (character in *that—allons donc!*), this is exactly what the artist who has reasons of his own for thinking he *does* see it undertakes to show you. When a young man makes up his mind that he has not faith enough after all to enter the church as he intended, that is an incident, though you may not hurry to the end of the chapter to see whether perhaps he doesn't change once more. I do not say that these are extraordinary or startling incidents. I do not pretend to estimate the degree of interest proceeding from them, for this will depend upon the skill of the painter. It sounds almost puerile to say that some incidents are intrinsically much more important than others, and I need not take this precaution after having professed my sympathy for the major ones in remarking that the only classification of the novel that I can understand is into that which has life and that which has it not.

The novel and the romance, the novel of incident and that of character—these clumsy separations appear to me to have been made by critics and readers for their own convenience, and to help them out of some of their occasional queer predicaments, but to have little reality or interest for the producer, from whose point of view it is of course that we are attempting to consider the art of fiction. The case is the same with another shadowy category which Mr. Besant apparently is disposed to set up—that of the "modern English novel"; unless indeed it be that in this matter he has fallen into an accidental confusion of standpoints. It is not quite clear whether he intends the remarks in which he alludes to it to be didactic or historical. It is as difficult to suppose a person intending to write a modern English as to suppose him writing an ancient English novel: that is a label which begs the question. One writes the novel, one paints the picture, of one's language and of one's time, and calling it modern English will not, alas! make the difficult task any easier. No more, unfortunately, will calling this or that work of one's fellow-artist a romance—unless it be, of course, simply for the pleasantness of the thing, as for instance when Hawthorne gave this heading to his story of *Blithedale*. The French, who have brought the theory of fiction to remarkable completeness, have but one name for the novel, and have not attempted smaller things in it, that I can see, for that. I can think of no obligation to which the "romancer" would not be held equally with the novelist; the standard of execution is equally high for each. Of course it is of execution that we are talking—that being the only point of a novel that is open to contention. This is perhaps too often lost sight of, only to produce interminable confusions and cross-purposes. We must grant the artist his subject, his idea, his *donnée*: our criticism is applied only to what he makes of it. Naturally I do not mean that we are bound to like it or find it interesting: in case we do not our course is perfectly simple—to let it alone. We may believe that of a certain idea even the most sincere novelist can make nothing at all, and the event may perfectly justify our belief; but the failure will have been a failure to execute, and it is in the execution that the fatal weakness is recorded. If we pretend to respect the artist at all, we must allow him his freedom of choice, in the face, in particular cases, of innumerable presumptions that the choice will not fructify. Art derives a considerable part of its beneficial exercise from flying in the face of presumptions, and some of the most interesting experiments of which it is capable are hidden in the bosom of common things. Gustave Flaubert has written a story about the devotion of a servant-girl to a parrot, and the production, highly finished as it is, cannot on the whole be called a success. We are perfectly free to find it flat, but I think it might have been interesting; and I, for my part, am extremely glad he should have written it; it is a contribution to our knowledge of what can be done—or what cannot. Ivan Turgénieff has written a tale about a deaf and dumb serf and a lap-dog, and the thing is touching, loving, a little masterpiece. He struck the note of life where Gustave Flaubert missed it—he flew in the face of a presumption and achieved a victory.

Nothing, of course, will ever take the place of the good old fashion of "liking" a work of art or not liking it: the most improved criticism will not abolish that primitive, that ultimate test. I mention this to guard myself from the accusation of intimating that the idea, the subject, of a novel or a picture, does not matter. It matters, to my sense, in the highest degree, and if I might put up a prayer it would be that artists should select none but the richest. Some, as I have already hastened to admit, are much more remunerative than others, and it would be a world happily arranged in which persons intending to treat them should be exempt from confusions and mistakes. This fortunate condition will arrive only, I fear, on the same day that critics become purged from error. Meanwhile, I repeat, we do not judge the artist with fairness unless we say to him, "Oh, I grant you your starting-point, because if I did not I should seem to prescribe to you, and heaven forbid I should take that responsibility. If I pretend to tell you what you must not take, you will call upon me to tell you then what you must take; in which case I shall be prettily caught. Moreover, it isn't till I have accepted your data that I can begin to measure you. I have the standard, the pitch; I have no right to tamper with your flute and then criticise your music. Of course I may not care for your idea at all; I may think it silly, or stale, or unclean; in which case I wash my hands of you altogether. I may content myself with believing that you will not have succeeded in being interesting, but I shall, of course, not attempt to demonstrate it, and you will be as indifferent to me as I am to you. I needn't remind you that there are all sorts of tastes: who can know it better? Some people, for excellent reasons, don't like to read about carpenters; others, for reasons even better, don't like to read about courtesans. Many object to Americans. Others (I believe they are mainly editors and publishers) won't look at Italians. Some readers don't like quiet subjects; others don't like bustling ones. Some enjoy a complete illusion, others the consciousness of large concessions. They choose their novels accordingly, and if they don't care about your idea they won't, *a fortiori*, care about your treatment."

So that it comes back very quickly, as I have said, to the liking: in spite of M. Zola, who reasons less powerfully than he represents, and who will not reconcile himself to this absoluteness of taste, thinking that there are certain things that people ought to like, and that they can be made to like. I am quite at a loss to imagine anything (at any rate in this matter of fiction) that people *ought* to like or to dislike. Selection will be sure to take care of itself, for it has a constant motive behind it. That motive is simply experience. As people feel life, so they will feel the art that is most closely related to it. This closeness of relation is what we should never forget in talking of the effort of the novel. Many people speak of it as a factitious, artificial form, a product of ingenuity, the business of which is to alter and arrange the things that surround us, to translate them into conventional, traditional moulds. This, however, is a view of the matter which carries us but a very short way, condemns the art to an eternal repetition of a few familiar *clichés*, cuts short its development, and leads us straight up to a dead wall. Catching the very note and trick, the strange irregular rhythm of life, that is the attempt whose strenuous force keeps Fiction upon her feet. In proportion as in what she offers us we see life *without* rearrangement do we feel that we are touching the truth; in proportion as we see it *with* rearrangement do we feel that we are being put off with a substitute, a compromise and convention. It is not uncommon to hear an extraordinary assurance of remark in regard to this matter of rearranging, which is often spoken of as if it were the last word of art. Mr. Besant seems to me in danger of falling into the great error with his rather unguarded talk about "selection." Art is essentially selection, but it is a selection whose main care is to be typical, to be inclusive. For many people art means rose-coloured window-panes, and selection means picking a bouquet for Mrs. Grundy. They will tell you glibly that artistic considerations have nothing to do with the disagreeable, with the ugly; they will rattle off shallow commonplaces about the province of art and the limits of art till you are moved to some wonder in return as to the province and the limits of ignorance. It appears to me that no one can ever have made a seriously artistic attempt without becoming conscious of an immense increase—a kind of revelation—of freedom. One perceives in that case—by the light of a heavenly ray—that the province of art is all life, all feeling, all observation, all vision. As Mr. Besant so justly intimates, it is all experience. That is a sufficient answer to those who maintain that it must not touch the sad things of life, who stick into its divine unconscious bosom little prohibitory inscriptions on the end of sticks, such as we see in public gardens—"It is forbidden to walk on the grass; it is forbidden to touch the flowers; it is not allowed to introduce dogs or to remain after dark; it is requested to keep to the right." The young aspirant in the line of fiction whom we continue to imagine will do nothing without taste, for in that case his freedom would be of little use to him; but the first advantage of his taste will be to reveal to him the absurdity of the little sticks and tickets. If he have taste, I must add, of course he will have ingenuity, and my disrespectful reference to that quality just now was not meant to imply that it is useless in fiction. But it is only a secondary aid; the first is a capacity for receiving straight impressions.

Mr. Besant has some remarks on the question of "the story" which I shall not attempt to criticise, though they seem to me to contain a singular ambiguity, because I do not think I understand them. I cannot see what is meant by talking as if there were a part of a novel which is the story and part of it which for mystical reasons is not—unless indeed the distinction be made in a sense in which it is difficult to suppose that any one should attempt to convey anything. "The story," if it represents anything, represents the subject, the idea, the *donnée* of the novel; and there is surely no "school"—Mr. Besant speaks of a school—which urges that a novel should be all treatment and no subject. There must assuredly be something to treat; every school is intimately conscious of that. This sense of the story being the idea, the starting-point, of the novel, is the only one that I see in which it can be spoken of as something different from its organic whole; and since in proportion as the work is successful the idea permeates and penetrates it, informs and animates it, so that every word and every punctuation-point contribute directly to the expression, in that proportion do we lose our sense of the story being a blade which may be drawn more or less out of its sheath. The story and the novel, the idea and the form, are the needle and thread, and I never heard of a guild of tailors who recommended the use of the thread without the needle, or the needle without the thread. Mr. Besant is not the only critic who may be observed to have spoken as if there were certain things in life which constitute stories, and certain others which do not. I find the same odd implication in an entertaining article in the *Pall Mall Gazette*, devoted, as it happens, to Mr. Besant's lecture. "The story is the thing!" says this graceful writer, as if with a tone of opposition to some other idea. I should think it was, as every painter who, as the time for "sending in" his picture looms in the distance, finds himself still in quest of a subject—as every belated artist not fixed about his theme will heartily agree. There are some subjects which speak to us and others which do not, but he would be a clever man who should undertake to give a rule—an index expurgatorius—by which the story and the no-story should be known apart. It is impossible (to me at least) to imagine any such rule which shall not be altogether arbitrary. The writer in the *Pall Mall* opposes the delightful (as I suppose) novel of *Margot la Balafrée* to certain tales in which "Bostonian nymphs" appear to have "rejected English dukes for psychological reasons." I am not acquainted with the romance just designated, and can scarcely forgive the *Pall Mall* critic for not mentioning the name of the author, but the title appears to refer to a lady who may have received a scar in some heroic adventure. I am inconsolable at not being acquainted with this episode, but am utterly at a loss to see why it is a story when the rejection (or acceptance) of a duke is not, and why a reason, psychological or other, is not a subject when a cicatrix is. They are all particles of the multitudinous life with which the novel deals, and surely no dogma which pretends to make it lawful to touch the one and unlawful to touch the other will stand for a moment on its feet. It is the special picture that must stand or fall, according as it seem to possess truth or to lack it. Mr. Besant does not, to my sense, light up the subject by intimating that a story must, under penalty of not being a story, consist of "adventures." Why of adventures more than of green spectacles? He mentions a category of impossible things, and among them he places "fiction without adventure." Why without adventure, more than without matrimony, or celibacy, or parturition, or cholera, or hydropathy, or Jansenism? This seems to me to bring the novel back to the hapless little *rôle* of being an artificial, ingenious thing—bring it down from its large, free character of an immense and exquisite correspondence with life. And what *is* adventure, when it comes to that, and by what sign is the listening pupil to recognise it? It is an adventure—an immense one—for me to write this little article; and for a Bostonian nymph to reject an English duke is an adventure only less stirring, I should say, than for an English duke to be rejected by a Bostonian nymph. I see dramas within dramas in that, and innumerable points of view. A psychological reason is, to my imagination, an object adorably pictorial; to catch the tint of its complexion—I feel as if that idea might inspire one to Titianesque efforts. There are few things more exciting to me, in short, than a psychological reason, and yet, I protest, the novel seems to me the most magnificent form of art. I have just been reading, at the same time, the delightful story of *Treasure Island*, by Mr. Robert Louis Stevenson and, in a manner less consecutive, the last tale from M. Edmond de Goncourt, which is entitled *Chérie*. One of these works treats of murders, mysteries, islands of dreadful renown, hairbreadth escapes, miraculous coincidences and buried doubloons. The other treats of a little French girl who lived in a fine house in Paris, and died of wounded sensibility because no one would marry her. I call *Treasure Island* delightful, because it appears to me to have succeeded wonderfully in what it attempts; and I venture to bestow no epithet upon *Chérie*, which strikes me as having failed deplorably in what it attempts—that is in tracing the development of the moral consciousness of a child. But one of these productions strikes me as exactly as much of a novel as the other, and as having a "story" quite as much. The moral consciousness of a child is as much a part of life as the islands of the Spanish Main, and the one sort of geography seems to me to have those "surprises" of which Mr. Besant speaks quite as much as the other. For myself (since it comes back in the last resort, as I say, to the preference of the individual), the picture of the child's experience has the advantage that I can at successive steps (an immense luxury, near to the "sensual pleasure" of which Mr. Besant's critic in the *Pall Mall* speaks) say Yes or No, as it may be, to what the artist puts before me. I have been a child in fact, but I have been on a quest for a buried treasure only in supposition, and it is a simple accident that with M. de Goncourt I should have for the most part to say No. With George Eliot, when she painted that country with a far other intelligence, I always said Yes.

The most interesting part of Mr. Besant's lecture is unfortunately the briefest passage—his very cursory allusion to the "conscious moral purpose" of the novel. Here again it is not very clear whether he be recording a fact or laying down a principle; it is a great pity that in the latter case he should not have developed his idea. This branch of the subject is of immense importance, and Mr. Besant's few words point to considerations of the widest reach, not to be lightly disposed of. He will have treated the art of fiction but superficially who is not prepared to go every inch of the way that these considerations will carry him. It is for this reason that at the beginning of these remarks I was careful to notify the reader that my reflections on so large a theme have no pretension to be exhaustive. Like Mr. Besant, I have left the question of the morality of the novel till the last, and at the last I find I have used up my space. It is a question surrounded with difficulties, as witness the very first that meets us, in the form of a definite question, on the threshold. Vagueness, in such a discussion, is fatal, and what is the meaning of your morality and your conscious moral purpose? Will you not define your terms and explain how (a novel being a picture) a picture can be either moral or immoral? You wish to paint a moral picture or carve a moral statue: will you not tell us how you would set about it? We are discussing the Art of Fiction; questions of art are questions (in the widest sense) of execution; questions of morality are quite another affair, and will you not let us see how it is that you find it so easy to mix them up? These things are so clear to Mr. Besant that he has deduced from them a law which he sees embodied in English Fiction, and which is "a truly admirable thing and a great cause for congratulation." It is a great cause for congratulation indeed when such thorny problems become as smooth as silk. I may add that in so far as Mr. Besant perceives that in point of fact English Fiction has addressed itself preponderantly to these delicate questions he will appear to many people to have made a vain discovery. They will have been positively struck, on the contrary, with the moral timidity of the usual English novelist; with his (or with her) aversion to face the difficulties with which on every side the treatment of reality bristles. He is apt to be extremely shy (whereas the picture that Mr. Besant draws is a picture of boldness), and the sign of his work, for the most part, is a cautious silence on certain subjects. In the English novel (by which of course I mean the American as well), more than in any other, there is a traditional difference between that which people know and that which they agree to admit that they know, that which they see and that which they speak of, that which they feel to be a part of life and that which they allow to enter into literature. There is the great difference, in short, between what they talk of in conversation and what they talk of in print. The essence of moral energy is to survey the whole field, and I should directly reverse Mr. Besant's remark and say not that the English novel has a purpose, but that it has a diffidence. To what degree a purpose in a work of art is a source of corruption I shall not attempt to inquire; the one that seems to me least dangerous is the purpose of making a perfect work. As for our novel, I may say lastly on this score that as we find it in England to-day it strikes me as addressed in a large degree to "young people," and that this in itself constitutes a presumption that it will be rather shy. There are certain things which it is generally agreed not to discuss, not even to mention, before young people. That is very well, but the absence of discussion is not a symptom of the moral passion. The purpose of the English novel—"a truly admirable thing, and a great cause for congratulation"—strikes me therefore as rather negative.

There is one point at which the moral sense and the artistic sense lie very near together; that is in the light of the very obvious truth that the deepest quality of a work of art will always be the quality of the mind of the producer. In proportion as that intelligence is fine will the novel, the picture, the statue partake of the substance of beauty and truth. To be constituted of such elements is, to my vision, to have purpose enough. No good novel will ever proceed from a superficial mind; that seems to me an axiom which, for the artist in fiction, will cover all needful moral ground: if the youthful aspirant take it to heart it will illuminate for him many of the mysteries of "purpose." There are many other useful things that might be said to him, but I have come to the end of my article, and can only touch them as I pass. The critic in the *Pall Mall Gazette*, whom I have already quoted, draws attention to the danger, in speaking of the art of fiction, of generalising. The danger that he has in mind is rather, I imagine, that of particularising, for there are some comprehensive remarks which, in addition to those embodied in Mr Besant's suggestive lecture, might without fear of misleading him be addressed to the ingenuous student. I should remind him first of the magnificence of the form that is open to him, which offers to sight so few restrictions and such innumerable opportunities. The other arts, in comparison, appear confined and hampered; the various conditions under which they are exercised are so rigid and definite. But the only condition that I can think of attaching to the composition of the novel is, as I have already said, that it be sincere. This freedom is a splendid privilege, and the first lesson of the young novelist is to learn to be worthy of it. "Enjoy it as it deserves," I should say to him; "take possession of it, explore it to its utmost extent, publish it, rejoice in it. All life belongs to you, and do not listen either to those who would shut you up into corners of it and tell you that it is only here and there that art inhabits, or to those who would persuade you that this heavenly messenger wings her way outside of life altogether, breathing a superfine air, and turning away her head from the truth of things. There is no impression of life, no manner of seeing it and feeling it, to which the plan of the novelist may not offer a place; you have only to remember that talents so dissimilar as those of Alexandre Dumas and Jane Austen, Charles Dickens and Gustave Flaubert have worked in this field with equal glory. Do not think too much about optimism and pessimism; try and catch the colour of life itself. In France to-day we see a prodigious effort (that of Emile Zola, to whose solid and serious work no explorer of the capacity of the novel can allude without respect), we see an extraordinary effort vitiated by a spirit of pessimism on a narrow basis. M. Zola is magnificent, but he strikes an English reader as ignorant; he has an air of working in the dark; if he had as much light as energy, his results would be of the highest value. As for the aberrations of a shallow optimism, the ground (of English fiction especially) is strewn with their brittle particles as with broken glass. If you must indulge in conclusions, let them have the taste of a wide knowledge. Remember that your first duty is to be as complete as possible—to make as perfect a work. Be generous and delicate and pursue the prize."

1884.

PICTURE AND TEXT

NOTE

Two of the following papers were originally published, with illustrations, in Harper's Magazine and the title of one of them—the first of titles has been altered from "Our Artists in Europe." The other, the article on Mr. Sargent, was accompanied by reproductions of several of his portraits. The notice of Mr. Abbey and that of Mr. Reinhart appeared in Harper's Weekly. That of Mr. Alfred Parsons figured as an introduction to the catalogue of an exhibition of his pictures. The sketch of Daumier was first contributed to *The Century*, and "After the Play" to *The New Review*.

BLACK AND WHITE

If there be nothing new under the sun there are some things a good deal less old than others. The illustration of books, and even more of magazines, may be said to have been born in our time, so far as variety and abundance are the signs of it; or born, at any rate, the comprehensive, ingenious, sympathetic spirit in which we conceive and practise it.

If the centuries are ever arraigned at some bar of justice to answer in regard to what they have given, of good or of bad, to humanity, our interesting age (which certainly is not open to the charge of having stood with its hands in its pockets) might perhaps do worse than put forth the plea of having contributed a fresh interest in "black and white." The claim may now be made with the more confidence from the very evident circumstance that this interest is far from exhausted. These pages are an excellent place for such an assumption. In Harper they have again and again, as it were, illustrated the illustration, and they constitute for the artist a series of invitations, provocations and opportunities. They may be referred to without arrogance in support of the contention that the limits of this large movement, with all its new and rare refinement, are not yet in sight.

I

It is on the contrary the constant extension that is visible, with the attendant circumstances of multiplied experiment and intensified research—circumstances that lately pressed once more on the attention of the writer of these remarks on his finding himself in the particular spot which history will perhaps associate most with the charming revival. A very old English village, lying among its meadows and hedges, in the very heart of the country, in a hollow of the green hills of Worcestershire, is responsible directly and indirectly for some of the most beautiful work in black and white with which I am at liberty to concern myself here; in other words, for much of the work of Mr. Abbey and Mr. Alfred Parsons. I do not mean that Broadway has told these gentlemen all they know (the name, from which the American reader has to brush away an incongruous association, may as well be written first as last); for Mr. Parsons, in particular, who knows everything that can be known about English fields and flowers, would have good reason to insist that the measure of his large landscape art is a large experience. I only suggest that if one loves Broadway and is familiar with it, and if a part of that predilection is that one has seen Mr. Abbey and Mr. Parsons at work there, the pleasant confusion takes place of itself; one's affection for the wide, long, grass-bordered vista of brownish gray cottages, thatched, latticed, mottled, mended, ivied, immemorial, grows with the sense of its having ministered to other minds and transferred itself to other recipients; just as the beauty of many a bit in many a drawing of the artists I have mentioned is enhanced by the sense, or at any rate by the desire, of recognition. Broadway and much of the land about it are in short the perfection of the old English rural tradition, and if they do not underlie all the combinations by which (in their pictorial accompaniments to rediscovered ballads, their vignettes to story or sonnet) these particular talents touch us almost to tears, we feel at least that they *would* have sufficed: they cover the scale.

In regard, however, to the implications and explications of this perfection of a village, primarily and to be just, Broadway is, more than any one else. Mr.

Frank Millet. Mr. Laurence Hutton discovered but Mr. Millet appropriated it: its sweetness was wasted until he began to distil and bottle it. He disinterred the treasure, and with impetuous liberality made us sharers in his fortune. His own work, moreover, betrays him, as well as the gratitude of participants, as I could easily prove if it did not perversely happen that he has commemorated most of his impressions in color. That excludes them from the small space here at my command; otherwise I could testify to the identity of old nooks and old objects, those that constitute both out-of-door and in-door furniture.

In such places as Broadway, and it is part of the charm of them to American eyes, the sky looks down on almost as many "things" as the ceiling, and "things" are the joy of the illustrator. Furnished apartments are useful to the artist, but a furnished country is still more to his purpose. A ripe midland English region is a museum of accessories and specimens, and is sure, under any circumstances, to contain the article wanted. This is the great recommendation of Broadway; everything in it is convertible. Even the passing visitor finds himself becoming so; the place has so much character that it rubs off on him, and if in an old garden—an old garden with old gates and old walls and old summer-houses—he lies down on the old grass (on an immemorial rug, no doubt), it is ten to one but that he will be converted. The little oblong sheaves of blank paper with elastic straps are fluttering all over the place. There is portraiture in the air and composition in the very accidents. Everything is a subject or an effect, a "bit" or a good thing. It is always some kind of day; if it be not one kind it is another. The garden walls, the mossy roofs, the open doorways and brown interiors, the old-fashioned flowers, the bushes in figures, the geese on the green, the patches, the jumbles, the glimpses, the color, the surface, the general complexion of things, have all a value, a reference and an application. If they are a matter of appreciation, that is why the gray-brown houses are perhaps more brown than gray, and more yellow than either. They are various things in turn, according to lights and days and needs. It is a question of color (all consciousness at Broadway is that), but the irresponsible profane are not called upon to settle the tint.

It is delicious to be at Broadway and to *be* one of the irresponsible profane—not to have to draw. The single street is in the grand style, sloping slowly upward to the base of the hills for a mile, but you may enjoy it without a carking care as to how to "render" the perspective. Everything is stone except the general greenness—a charming smooth local stone, which looks as if it had been meant for great constructions and appears even in dry weather to have been washed and varnished by the rain. Half-way up the road, in the widest place, where the coaches used to turn (there were many of old, but the traffic of Broadway was blown to pieces by steam, though the destroyer has not come nearer than half a dozen miles), a great gabled mansion, which was once a manor or a house of state, and is now a rambling inn, stands looking at a detached swinging sign which is almost as big as itself—a very grand sign, the "arms" of an old family, on the top of a very tall post. You will find something very like the place among Mr. Abbey's delightful illustrations to, "She Stoops to Conquer." When the September day grows dim and some of the windows glow, you may look out, if you like, for Tony Lumpkin's red coat in the doorway or imagine Miss Hardcastle's quilted petticoat on the stair.

II

It is characteristic of Mr. Frank Millet's checkered career, with opposites so much mingled in it, that such work as he has done for Harper should have had as little in common as possible with midland English scenery. He has been less a producer in black and white than a promoter and, as I may say, a protector of such production in others; but none the less the back volumes of Harper testify to the activity of his pencil as well as to the variety of his interests. There was a time when he drew little else but Cossacks and Orientals, and drew them as one who had good cause to be vivid. Of the young generation he was the first to know the Russian plastically, especially the Russian soldier, and he had paid heavily for his acquaintance. During the Russo-Turkish war he was correspondent in the field (with the victors) of the New York *Herald* and the London *Daily News*—a capacity in which he made many out-of-the-way, many precious, observations. He has seen strange countries—the East and the South and the West and the North—and practised many arts. To the London *Graphic*, in 1877 he sent striking sketches from the East, as well as capital prose to the journals I have mentioned. He has always been as capable of writing a text for his own sketches as of making sketches for the text of others. He has made pictures without words and words without pictures. He has written some very clever ghost-stories, and drawn and painted some very immediate realities. He has lately given himself up to these latter objects, and discovered that they have mysteries more absorbing than any others. I find in Harper, in 1885. "A Wild-goose Chase" through North Germany and Denmark, in which both pencil and pen are Mr. Millet's, and both show the natural and the trained observer.

He knows the art-schools of the Continent, the studios of Paris, the "dodges" of Antwerp, the subjects, the models of Venice, and has had much æsthetic as well as much personal experience. He has draped and distributed Greek plays at Harvard, as well as ridden over Balkans to post pressing letters, and given publicity to English villages in which susceptible Americans may get the strongest sensations with the least trouble to themselves. If the trouble in each case will have been largely his, this is but congruous with the fact that he has not only found time to have a great deal of history himself, but has suffered himself to be converted by others into an element—beneficent I should call it if discretion did not forbid me—of *their* history. Springing from a very old New England stock, he has found the practice of art a wonderful antidote, in his own language, "for belated Puritanism." He is very modern, in the sense of having tried many things and availed himself of all of the facilities of his time; but especially on this ground of having fought out for himself the battle of the Puritan habit and the æsthetic experiment. His experiment was admirably successful from the moment that the Puritan levity was forced to consent to its becoming a serious one. In other words, if Mr. Millet is artistically interesting to-day (and to the author of these remarks he is highly so), it is because he is a striking example of what the typical American quality can achieve.

He began by having an excellent pencil, because as a thoroughly practical man he could not possibly have had a weak one. But nothing is more remunerative to follow than the stages by which "faculty" in general (which is what I mean by the characteristic American quality) has become the particular faculty; so that if in the artist's present work one recognizes— recognizes even fondly—the national handiness, it is as handiness regenerate and transfigured. The American adaptiveness has become a Dutch finish. The only criticism I have to make is of the preordained paucity of Mr. Millet's drawings; for my mission is not to speak of his work in oils, every year more important (as was indicated by the brilliant interior with figures that greeted the spectator in so friendly a fashion on the threshold of the Royal Academy exhibition of 1888), nor to say that it is illustration too—illustration of any old-fashioned song or story that hums in the brain or haunts the memory— nor even to hint that the admirable rendering of the charming old objects with which it deals (among which I include the human face and figure in dresses unfolded from the lavender of the past), the old surfaces and tones, the stuffs and textures, the old mahogany and silver and brass—the old sentiment too, and the old picture-making vision—are in the direct tradition of Terburg and De Hoogh and Metzu.

III

There is no paucity about Mr. Abbey as a virtuoso in black and white, and if one thing more than another sets the seal upon the quality of his work, it is the rare abundance in which it is produced. It is not a frequent thing to find combinations infinite as well as exquisite. Mr. Abbey has so many ideas, and the gates of composition have been opened so wide to him, that we cultivate his company with a mixture of confidence and excitement. The readers of Harper have had for years a great deal of it, and they will easily recognize the feeling I allude to—the expectation of familiarity in variety. The beautiful art and taste, the admirable execution, strike the hour with the same note; but the figure, the scene, is ever a fresh conception. Never was ripe skill less mechanical, and never was the faculty of perpetual evocation less addicted to prudent economies. Mr. Abbey never saves for the next picture, yet the next picture will be as expensive as the last. His whole career has been open to the readers of Harper, so that what they may enjoy on any particular occasion is not only the talent, but a kind of affectionate sense of the history of the talent, That history is, from the beginning, in these pages, and it is one of the most interesting and instructive, just as the talent is one of the richest and the most sympathetic in the art-annals of our generation. I may as well frankly declare that I have such a taste for Mr. Abbey's work that I cannot affect a judicial tone about it. Criticism is appreciation or it is nothing, and an intelligence of the matter in hand is recorded more substantially in a single positive sign of such appreciation than in a volume of sapient objections for objection's sake—the cheapest of all literary commodities. Silence is the perfection of disapproval, and it has the great merit of leaving the value of speech, when the moment comes for it, unimpaired.

Accordingly it is important to translate as adequately as possible the positive side of Mr. Abbey's activity. None to-day is more charming, and none helps us more to take the large, joyous, observant, various view of the business of art. He has enlarged the idea of illustration, and he plays with it in a hundred spontaneous, ingenious ways. "Truth and poetry" is the motto legibly stamped upon his pencil-case, for if he has on the one side a singular sense of the familiar, salient, importunate facts of life, on the other they reproduce themselves in his mind in a delightfully qualifying medium. It is this medium that the fond observer must especially envy Mr. Abbey, and that a literary observer will envy him most of all.

Such a hapless personage, who may have spent hours in trying to produce something of the same result by sadly different means, will measure the difference between the roundabout, faint descriptive tokens of respectable prose and the immediate projection of the figure by the pencil. A charming story-teller indeed he would be who should write as Mr. Abbey draws. However, what is style for one art is style for other, so blessed is the fraternity that binds them together, and the worker in words may take a lesson from the picture-maker of "She Stoops to Conquer." It is true that what the verbal artist would like to do would be to find out the secret of the pictorial, to drink at the same fountain. Mr. Abbey is essentially one of those who would tell us if he could, and conduct us to the magic spring; but here he is in the nature of the case helpless, for the happy *ambiente* as the Italians call it, in which his creations move is exactly the thing, as I take it, that he can least give an account of. It is a matter of genius and imagination—one of those things that a man determines for himself as little as he determines the color of his eyes. How, for instance, can Mr. Abbey explain the manner in which he directly *observes* figures, scenes, places, that exist only in the fairy-land of his fancy? For the peculiar sign of his talent is surely this observation in the remote. It brings the remote near to us, but such a complicated journey as it must first have had to make! Remote in time (in differing degrees), remote in place, remote in feeling, in habit, and in their ambient air, are the images that spring from his pencil, and yet all so vividly, so minutely, so consistently seen! Where does he see them, where does he find them, how does he catch them, and in what language does he delightfully converse with them? In what mystic recesses of space does the revelation descend upon him?

The questions flow from the beguiled but puzzled admirer, and their tenor sufficiently expresses the claim I make for the admirable artist when I say that his truth is interfused with poetry. He spurns the literal and yet superabounds in the characteristic, and if he makes the strange familiar he makes the familiar just strange enough to be distinguished. Everything is so human, so humorous and so caught in the act, so buttoned and petticoated and gartered, that it might be round the corner; and so it is—but the corner is the corner of another world. In that other world Mr. Abbey went forth to dwell in extreme youth, as I need scarcely be at pains to remind those who have followed him in Harper. It is not important here to give a catalogue of his contributions to that journal: turn to the back volumes and you will meet him at every step. Every one remembers his young, tentative, prelusive illustrations to Herrick, in which there are the prettiest glimpses, guesses and foreknowledge of the effects he was to make completely his own. The Herrick was done mainly, if I mistake not, before he had been to England, and it remains, in the light of this fact, a singularly touching as well as a singularly promising performance. The eye of sense in such a case had to be to a rare extent the mind's eye, and this convertibility of the two organs has persisted.

From the first and always that other world and that qualifying medium in which I have said that the human spectacle goes on for Mr. Abbey have been a county of old England which is not to be found in any geography, though it borders, as I have hinted, on the Worcestershire Broadway. Few artistic phenomena are more curious than the congenital acquaintance of this perverse young Philadelphian with that mysterious locality. It is there that he finds them all—the nooks, the corners, the people, the clothes, the arbors and gardens and teahouses, the queer courts of old inns, the sun-warmed angles of old parapets. I ought to have mentioned for completeness, in addition to his pictures to Goldsmith and to the scraps of homely British song (this latter class has contained some of his most exquisite work), his delicate drawing's for Mr. William Black's *Judith Shakespeare*. And in relation to that distinguished name—I don't mean Mr. Black's—it is a comfort, if I may be allowed the expression, to know that (as, to the best of my belief, I violate no confidence in saying) he is even now engaged in the great work of illustrating the comedies. He is busy with "The Merchant of Venice;" he is up to his neck in studies, in rehearsals. Here again, while in prevision I admire the result, what I can least refrain from expressing is a sort of envy of the process, knowing what it is with Mr. Abbey and what explorations of the delightful it entails—arduous, indefatigable, till the end seems almost smothered in the means (such material complications they engender), but making one's daily task a thing of beauty and honor and beneficence.

IV

Even if Mr. Alfred Parsons were not a masterly contributor to the pages of Harper, it would still be almost inevitable to speak of him after speaking of Mr. Abbey, for the definite reason (I hope that in giving it I may not appear to invade too grossly the domain of private life) that these gentlemen are united in domestic circumstance as well as associated in the nature of their work. In London, in the relatively lucid air of Campden Hill, they dwell together, and their beautiful studios are side by side. However, there is a reason for commemorating Mr. Parsons' work which has nothing to do with the accidental—the simple fact that that work forms the richest illustration of the English landscape that is offered us to-day. Harper has for a long time past been full of Mr. Alfred Parsons, who has made the dense, fine detail of his native land familiar in far countries, amid scenery of a very different type. This is what the modern illustration can do when the ripeness of the modern sense is brought to it and the wood-cutter plays with difficulties as the brilliant Americans do to-day, following his original at a breakneck pace. An illusion is produced which, in its very completeness, makes one cast an uneasy eye over the dwindling fields that are still left to conquer. Such art as Alfred Parsons'— such an accomplished translation of local aspects, translated in its turn by cunning hands and diffused by a wonderful system of periodicity through vast and remote communities, has, I confess, in a peculiar degree, the effect that so many things have in this age of multiplication—that of suppressing intervals and differences and making the globe seem alarmingly small. Vivid and repeated evocations of English rural things—the meadows and lanes, the sedgy streams, the old orchards and timbered houses, the stout, individual, insular trees, the flowers under the hedge and in it and over it, the sweet rich country seen from the slope, the bend of the unformidable river, the actual romance of the castle against the sky, the place on the hill-side where the gray church begins to peep (a peaceful little grassy path leads up to it over a stile)—all this brings about a terrible displacement of the very objects that make pilgrimage a passion, and hurries forward that ambiguous advantage which I don't envy our grandchildren, that of knowing all about everything in advance, having trotted round the globe annually in the magazines and lost the bloom of personal experience. It is a part of the general abolition of mystery with which we are all so complacently busy today. One would like to retire to another planet with a box of Mr. Parsons' drawings, and be homesick there for the pleasant places they commemorate.

There are many things to be said about his talent, some of which are not the easiest in the world to express. I shall not, however, make them more difficult by attempting to catalogue his contributions in these pages. A turning of the leaves of Harper brings one constantly face to face with him, and a systematic search speedily makes one intimate. The reader will remember the beautiful Illustrations to Mr. Blackmore's novel of *Springhaven*, which were interspersed with striking figure-pieces from the pencil of that very peculiar pictorial humorist Mr. Frederick Barnard, who, allowing for the fact that he always seems a little too much to be drawing for Dickens and that the footlights are the illumination of his scenic world, has so remarkable a sense of English types and attitudes, costumes and accessories, in what may be called the great-coat-and-gaiters period—the period when people were stiff with riding and wicked conspiracies went forward in sanded provincial inn-parlors. Mr. Alfred Parsons, who is still conveniently young, waked to his first vision of pleasant material in the comprehensive county of Somerset—a capital centre of impression for a painter of the bucolic. He has been to America; he has even reproduced with remarkable discrimination and truth some of the way-side objects of that country, not making them look in the least like their English equivalents, if equivalents they may be said to have. Was it there that Mr. Parsons learned so well how Americans would like England to appear? I ask this idle question simply because the England of his pencil, and not less of his brush (of his eminent brush there would be much to say), is exactly the England that the American imagination, restricted to itself, constructs from the poets, the novelists, from all the delightful testimony it inherits. It was scarcely to have been supposed possible that the native point of view would embrace and observe so many of the things that the more or less famished outsider is, in vulgar parlance, "after." In other words (though I appear to utter a foolish paradox), the danger might have been that Mr. Parsons knew his subject too well to feel it—to feel it, I mean, *à l'Américaine*. He is as tender of it as if he were vague about it, and as certain of it as if he were *blasé*.

But after having wished that his country should be just so, we proceed to discover that it is in fact not a bit different. Between these phases of our consciousness he is an unfailing messenger. The reader will remember how often he has accompanied with pictures the text of some amiable paper describing a pastoral region—Warwickshire or Surrey. Devonshire or the Thames. He will remember his exquisite designs for certain of Wordsworth's sonnets. A sonnet of Wordsworth is a difficult thing to illustrate, but Mr. Parsons' ripe taste has shown him the way. Then there are lovely morsels from his hand associated with the drawings of his friend Mr. Abbey—head-pieces, tailpieces, vignettes, charming combinations of flower and foliage, decorative clusters of all sorts of pleasant rural emblems. If he has an inexhaustible feeling for the country in general, his love of the myriad English flowers is perhaps the fondest part of it. He draws them with a rare perfection, and always—little definite, delicate, tremulous things as they are—with a certain nobleness. This latter quality, indeed. I am prone to find in all his work, and I should insist on it still more if I might refer to his important paintings. So composite are the parts of which any distinguished talent is made up that we have to feel our way as we enumerate them; and yet that very ambiguity is a challenge to analysis and to characterization. This "nobleness" on Mr. Parsons' part is the element of style—something large and manly, expressive of the total character of his facts. His landscape is the landscape of the male vision, and yet his touch is full of sentiment, of curiosity and endearment. These things, and others besides, make him the most interesting, the most living, of the new workers in his line. And what shall I say of the other things besides? How can I take precautions enough to say that among the new workers, deeply English as he is, there is comparatively something French in his manner? Many people will like him because they see in him—or they think they do—a certain happy mean. Will they not fancy they catch him taking the middle way between the unsociable French *étude* and the old-fashioned English "picture"? If one of these extremes is a desert, the other, no doubt, is an oasis still more vain. I have a recollection of productions of Mr. Alfred Parsons' which might have come from a Frenchman who was in love with English river-sides. I call to mind no studies—if he has made any—of French scenery; but if I did they would doubtless appear English enough. It is the fashion among sundry to maintain that the English landscape is of no use for *la peinture sérieuse*, that it is wanting in technical accent and is in general too storytelling, too self-conscious and dramatic also too lumpish and stodgy, of a green—*d'un vert bête*—which, when reproduced, looks like that of the chromo. Certain it is that there are many hands which are not to be trusted with it, and taste and integrity have been known to go down before it. But Alfred Parsons may be pointed to as one who has made the luxuriant and lovable things of his own country almost as "serious" as those familiar objects—the pasture and the poplar—which, even when infinitely repeated by the great school across the Channel, strike us as but meagre morsels of France.

V

In speaking of Mr. George H. Boughton, A.R.A., I encounter the same difficulty as with Mr. Millet: I find the window closed through which alone almost it is just to take a view of his talent. Mr. Boughton is a painter about whom there is little that is new to tell to-day, so conspicuous and incontestable is his achievement, the fruit of a career of which the beginning was not yesterday. He is a draughtsman and an illustrator only on occasion and by accident. These accidents have mostly occurred, however, in the pages of Harper, and the happiest of them will still be fresh in the memory of its readers. In the *Sketching Rambles in Holland* Mr. Abbey was a participant (as witness, among many things, the admirable drawing of the old Frisian woman bent over her Bible in church, with the heads of the burghers just visible above the rough archaic pew-tops—a drawing opposite to page 112 in the handsome volume into which these contributions were eventually gathered together); but most of the sketches were Mr. Boughton's, and the charming, amusing text is altogether his, save in the sense that it commemorates his companion's impressions as well as his own—the delightful, irresponsible, visual, sensual, pictorial, capricious impressions of a painter in a strange land, the person surely whom at particular moments one would give most to be. If there be anything happier than the impressions of a painter, it is the impressions of two, and the combination is set forth with uncommon spirit and humor in this frank record of the innocent lust of the eyes. Mr. Boughton scruples little, in general, to write as well as to draw, when the fancy takes him; to write in the manner of painters, with the bold, irreverent, unconventional, successful brush. If I were not afraid of the patronizing tone I would say that there is little doubt that if as a painter he had not had to try to write in character, he would certainly have made a characteristic writer. He has the most enviable "finds," not dreamed of in timid literature, yet making capital descriptive prose. Other specimens of them may be encountered in two or three Christmas tales, signed with the name whose usual place is the corner of a valuable canvas.

If Mr. Boughton is in this manner not a simple talent, further complications and reversions may be observed in him, as, for instance, that having reverted from America, where he spent his early years, back to England, the land of his origin, he has now in a sense oscillated again from the latter to the former country. He came to London one day years ago (from Paris, where he had been eating nutritively of the tree of artistic knowledge), in order to re-embark on the morrow for the United States; but that morrow never came—it has never come yet. Certainly now it never *can* come, for the country that Mr. Boughton left behind him in his youth is no longer there; the "old New York" is no longer a port to sail to, unless for phantom ships. In imagination, however, the author of "The Return of the *Mayflower*" has several times taken his way back; he has painted with conspicuous charm and success various episodes of the early Puritan story. He was able on occasion to remember vividly enough the low New England coast and the thin New England air. He has been perceptibly an inventor, calling into being certain types of face and dress, certain tones and associations of color (all in the line of what I should call subdued harmonies if I were not afraid of appearing to talk a jargon), which people are hungry for when they acquire "a Boughton," and which they can obtain on no other terms. This pictorial element in which he moves is made up of divers delicate things, and there would be a roughness in attempting to unravel the tapestry. There is old English, and old American, and old Dutch in it, and a friendly, unexpected new Dutch too—an ingredient of New Amsterdam—a strain of Knickerbocker and of Washington Irving. There is an admirable infusion of landscape in it, from which some people regret that Mr. Boughton should ever have allowed himself to be distracted by his importunate love of sad-faced, pretty women in close-fitting coifs and old silver-clasped cloaks. And indeed, though his figures are very "tender," his landscape is to my sense tenderer still. Moreover, Mr. Boughton bristles, not aggressively, but in the degree of a certain conciliatory pertinacity, with contradictious properties. He lives in one of the prettiest and most hospitable houses in London, but the note of his work is the melancholy of rural things, of lonely people and of quaint, far-off legend and refrain. There is a delightful ambiguity of period and even of clime in him, and he rejoices in that inability to depict the modern which is the most convincing sign of the contemporary.

He has a genius for landscape, yet he abounds in knowledge of every sort of ancient fashion of garment; the buckles and button-holes, the very shoe-ties, of the past are dear to him. It is almost always autumn or winter in his pictures. His horizons are cold, his trees are bare (he does the bare tree beautifully), and his draperies lined with fur; but when he exhibits himself directly, as in the fantastic "Rambles" before mentioned, contagious high spirits are the clearest of his showing. Here he appears as an irrepressible felicitous sketcher, and I know no pleasanter record of the joys of sketching, or even of those of simply looking. Théophile Gautier himself was not more inveterately addicted to this latter wanton exercise. There ought to be a pocket edition of Mr. Boughton's book, which would serve for travellers in other countries too, give them the point of view and put them in the mood. Such a blessing, and such a distinction too, is it to have an eye. Mr. Boughton's, in his good-humored Dutch wanderings, holds from morning till night a sociable, graceful revel. From the moment it opens till the moment it closes, its day is a round of adventures. His jolly pictorial narrative, reflecting every glint of October sunshine and patch of russet shade, tends to confirm us afresh in the faith that the painter's life is the best life, the life that misses fewest impressions.

VI

Mr. Du Maurier has a brilliant history, but it must be candidly recognized that it is written or drawn mainly in an English periodical. It is only during the last two or three years that the most ironical of the artists of *Punch* has exerted himself for the entertainment of the readers of Harper; but I seem to come too late with any commentary on the nature of his satire or the charm of his execution. When he began to appear in Harper he was already an old friend, and for myself I confess I have to go through rather a complicated mental operation to put into words what I think of him. What does a man think of the language he has learned to speak? He judges it only while he is learning. Mr. Du Maurier's work, in regard to the life it embodies, is not so much a thing we see as one of the conditions of seeing. He has interpreted for us for so many years the social life of England that the interpretation has become the text itself. We have accepted his types, his categories, his conclusions, his sympathies and his ironies, It is not given to all the world to thread the mazes of London society, and for the great body of the disinherited, the vast majority of the Anglo-Saxon public. Mr. Du Maurier's representation is the thing represented. Is the effect of it to nip in the bud any remote yearning for personal participation? I feel tempted to say yes, when I think of the follies, the flatnesses, the affectations and stupidities that his teeming pencil has made vivid. But that vision immediately merges itself in another—a panorama of tall, pleasant, beautiful people, placed in becoming attitudes, in charming gardens, in luxurious rooms, so that I can scarcely tell which is the more definite, the impression satiric or the impression plastic.

This I take to be a sign that Mr. Du Maurier knows how to be general and has a conception of completeness. The world amuses him, such queer things go on in it; but the part that amuses him most is certain lines of our personal structure. That amusement is the brightest; the other is often sad enough. A sharp critic might accuse Mr. Du Maurier of lingering too complacently on the lines in question; of having a certain ideal of "lissome" elongation to which the promiscuous truth is sometimes sacrificed. But in fact this artist's P truth never pretends to be promiscuous; it is avowedly select and specific. What he depicts is so preponderantly the "tapering" people that the remainder of the picture, in a notice as brief as the present, may be neglected. If his *dramatis personæ* are not all the tenants of drawing-rooms, they are represented at least in some relation to these. 'Arry and his friends at the fancy fair are in society for the time; the point of introducing them is to show how the contrast intensifies them. Of late years Mr. Du Maurier has perhaps been a little too docile to the muse of elegance; the idiosyncrasies of the "masher" and the high girl with elbows have beguiled him into occasional inattention to the doings of the short and shabby. But his career has been long and rich, and I allude, in such words, but to a moment of it.

The moral of it—I refer to the artistic one—seen altogether, is striking and edifying enough. What Mr. Du Maurier has attempted to do is to give, in a thousand interrelated drawings, a general satiric picture of the social life of his time and country. It is easy to see that through them "an increasing purpose runs;" they all hang together and refer to each other—complete, confirm, correct, illuminate each other. Sometimes they are not satiric: satire is not pure charm, and the artist has allowed himself to "go in" for pure charm. Sometimes he has allowed himself to go in for pure fantasy, so that satire (which should hold on to the mane of the real) slides off the other side of the runaway horse. But he remains, on the whole, pencil in hand, a wonderfully copious and veracious historian of his age and his civilization.

VII

I have left Mr. Reinhart to the last because of his importance, and now this very importance operates as a restriction and even as a sort of reproach to me. To go well round him at a deliberate pace would take a whole book. With Mr. Abbey, Mr. Reinhart is the artist who has contributed most abundantly to Harper; his work, indeed, in quantity, considerably exceeds Mr. Abbey's. He is the observer of the immediate, as Mr. Abbey is that of the considerably removed, and the conditions he asks us to accept are less expensive to the imagination than those of his colleague. He is, in short, the vigorous, racy *prosateur* of that human comedy of which Mr. Abbey is the poet. He illustrates the modern sketch of travel, the modern tale—the poor little "quiet," psychological, conversational modern tale, which I often think the artist invited to represent it to the eye must hate, unless he be a very intelligent master, little, on a superficial view, would there appear to be in it to represent. The superficial view is, after all, the natural one for the picture-maker. A talent of the first order, however, only wants to be set thinking, as a single word will often make it. Mr. Reinhart at any rate, triumphs; whether there be life or not in the little tale itself, there is unmistakable life in his version of it. Mr. Reinhart deals in that element purely with admirable frankness and vigor. He is not so much suggestive as positively and sharply representative. His facility, his agility, his universality are a truly stimulating sight. He asks not too many questions of his subject, but to those he does ask he insists upon a thoroughly intelligible answer. By his universality I mean perhaps as much as anything else his admirable drawing; not precious, as the æsthetic say, nor pottering, as the vulgar, but free, strong and secure, which enables him to do with the human figure at a moment's notice anything that any occasion may demand. It gives him an immense range, and I know not how to express (it is not easy) my sense of a certain capable indifference that is in him otherwise than by saying that he would quite as soon do one thing as another.

For it is true that the admirer of his work rather misses in him that intimation of a secret preference which many strong draughtsmen show, and which is not absent, for instance (I don't mean the secret, but the intimation), from the beautiful doings of Mr. Abbey. It is extremely present in Mr. Du Maurier's work, just as it was visible, less elusively, in that of John Leech, his predecessor in *Punch*. Mr. Abbey has a haunting type; Du Maurier has a haunting type. There was little perhaps of the haunted about Leech, but we know very well how he wanted his pretty girls, his British swell, and his "hunting men" to look. He betrayed a predilection; he had his little ideal. That an artist may be a great force and not have a little ideal, the scarcely too much to be praised Charles Keene is there (I mean he is in *Punch*) to show us. He has not a haunting type—not he—and I think that no one has yet discovered how he would have liked his pretty girls to look. He has kept the soft conception too much to himself—he has not trifled with the common truth by letting it appear. This common truth, in its innumerable combinations, is what Mr. Rein-hart also shows us (with of course infinitely less of a *parti pris* of laughing at it), though, as I must hasten to add, the female face and form in his hands always happen to take on a much lovelier cast than in Mr. Keene's. These things with him, however, are not a private predilection, an artist's dream. Mr. Reinhart is solidly an artist, but I doubt whether as yet he dreams, and the absence of private predilections makes him seem a little hard. He is sometimes rough with our average humanity, and especially rough with the feminine portion of it. He usually represents American life, in which that portion is often spoken of as showing to peculiar advantage. But Mr. Reinhart sees it generally, as very *bourgeois*. His good ladies are apt to be rather thick and short, rather huddled and plain. I shouldn't mind it so much if they didn't look so much alive. They are incontestably possible. The long, brilliant series of drawings he made to accompany Mr. Charles Dudley Warner's papers on the American watering-places form a rich *bourgeois* epic, which imaginations haunted by a type must accept with philosophy, for the sketches in question will have carried the tale, and all sorts of irresistible illusion with it, to the four corners of the earth. Full of observation and reality, of happy impressionism, taking all things as they come, with many a charming picture of youthful juxtaposition, they give us a sense, to which nothing need be added, of the energy of Mr. Reinhart's pencil. They are a final collection of pictorial notes on the manners and customs, the aspects and habitats, in July and August, of the great American democracy; of which, certainly, taking one thing with another, they give a very comfortable, cheerful account. But they confirm that analytic view of which I have ventured to give a hint—the view of Mr. Reinhart as an artist of immense capacity who yet somehow doesn't care. I must add that this aspect of him is modified, in the one case very gracefully, in the other by the operation of a sort of constructive humor, remarkably strong, in his illustrations of Spanish life and his sketches of the Berlin political world.

His fashion of remaining outside, as it were, makes him (to the analyst) only the more interesting, for the analyst, if he have any critical life in him, will be prone to wonder *why* he doesn't care, and whether matters may not be turned about in such a way as that he should, with the consequence that his large capacity would become more fruitful still. Mr. Reinhart is open to the large appeal of Paris, where he lives—as is evident from much of his work—where he paints, and where, in crowded exhibitions, reputation and honors have descended upon him. And yet Paris, for all she may have taught him, has not given him the mystic sentiment—about which I am perhaps writing nonsense. Is it nonsense to say that, being very much an incarnation of the modern international spirit (he might be a Frenchman in New York were he not an American in Paris), the moral of his work is possibly the inevitable want of finality, of intrinsic character, in that sweet freedom? Does the cosmopolite necessarily pay for his freedom by a want of function—the impersonality of not being representative? Must one be a little narrow to have a sentiment, and very local to have a quality, or at least a style; and would the missing type, if I may mention it yet again, haunt our artist—who is somehow, in his rare instrumental facility, outside of quality and style—a good deal more if he were not, amid the mixture of associations and the confusion of races, liable to fall into vagueness as to what types are? He can do anything he likes; by which I mean he can do wonderfully even the things he doesn't like. But he strikes me as a force not yet fully used.

EDWIN A. ABBE

Nothing is more interesting in the history of an artistic talent than the moment at which its "elective affinity" declares itself, and the interest is great in proportion as the declaration is unmistakable. I mean by the elective affinity of a talent its climate and period of preference, the spot on the globe or in the annals of mankind to which it most fondly attaches itself, to which it reverts incorrigibly, round which it revolves with a curiosity that is insatiable, from which in short it draws its strongest inspiration. A man may personally inhabit a certain place at a certain time, but in imagination he may be a perpetual absentee, and to a degree worse than the worst Irish landlord, separating himself from his legal inheritance not only by mountains and seas, but by centuries as well. When he is a man of genius these perverse predilections become fruitful and constitute a new and independent life, and they are indeed to a certain extent the sign and concomitant of genius. I do not mean by this that high ability would always rather have been born in another country and another age, but certainly it likes to choose, it seldom fails to react against imposed conditions. If it accepts them it does so because it likes them for themselves; and if they fail to commend themselves it rarely scruples to fly away in search of others. We have witnessed this flight in many a case; I admit that if we have sometimes applauded it we have felt at other moments that the discontented, undomiciled spirit had better have stayed at home.

Mr. Abbey has gone afield, and there could be no better instance of a successful fugitive and a genuine affinity, no more interesting example of selection—selection of field and subject—operating by that insight which has the precocity and certainty of an instinct. The domicile of Mr. Abbey's genius is the England of the eighteenth century; I should add that the palace of art which he has erected there commands—from the rear, as it were—various charming glimpses of the preceding age. The finest work he has yet done is in his admirable illustrations, in Harper's Magazine, to "She Stoops to Conquer," but the promise that he would one day do it was given some years ago in his delightful volume of designs to accompany Herrick's poems; to which we may add, as supplementary evidence, his drawings for Mr. William Black's novel of *Judith Shakespeare.*

Mr. Abbey was born in Philadelphia in 1852, and manifesting his brilliant but un-encouraged aptitudes at a very early age, came in 1872 to New York to draw for Harper's WEEKLY. Other views than this, if I have been correctly Informed, had been entertained for his future—a fact that provokes a smile now that his manifest destiny has been, or is in course of being, so very neatly accomplished. The spirit of modern aesthetics did not, at any rate, as I understand the matter, smile upon his cradle, and the circumstance only increases the interest of his having had from the earliest moment the clearest artistic vision.

It has sometimes happened that the distinguished draughtsman or painter has been born in the studio and fed, as it were, from the palette, but in the great majority of cases he has been nursed by the profane, and certainly, on the doctrine of mathematical chances, a Philadelphia genius would scarcely be an exception. Mr. Abbey was fortunate, however, in not being obliged to lose time; he learned how to swim by jumping into deep water. Even if he had not known by instinct how to draw, he would have had to perform the feat from the moment that he found himself attached to the "art department" of a remarkably punctual periodical. In such a periodical the events of the day are promptly reproduced; and with the morrow so near the day is necessarily a short one—too short for gradual education. Such a school is not, no doubt, the ideal one, but in fact it may have a very happy influence. If a youth is to give an account of a scene with his pencil at a certain hour—to give it, as it were, or perish—he will have become conscious, in the first place, of a remarkable incentive to observe it. so that the roughness of the foster-mother who imparts the precious faculty of quick, complete observation is really a blessing in disguise. To say that it was simply under this kind of pressure that Mr. Abbey acquired the extraordinary refinement which distinguishes his work in black and white is doubtless to say too much; but his admirers may be excused, in view of the beautiful result, for almost wishing, on grounds of patriotism, to make the training, or the absence of training, responsible for as much as possible. For as no artistic genius that our country has produced is more delightful than Mr. Abbey's, so, surely, nothing could be more characteristically American than that it should have formed itself in the conditions that happened to be nearest at hand, with the crowds, streets and squares, the railway stations and telegraph poles, the wondrous sign-boards and triumphant bunting, of New York for the source of its inspiration, and with a big hurrying printing-house for its studio. If to begin the practice of art in these conditions was to incur the danger of being crude, Mr. Abbey braved it with remarkable success. At all events, if he went neither I through the mill of Paris nor through that of Munich, the writer of these lines more than consoles himself for the accident. His talent is unsurpassably fine, and yet we reflect with complacency that he picked it up altogether at home. If he is highly distinguished he is irremediably native, and (premising always that I speak mainly of his work in black and white) it is difficult to see, as we look, for instance, at the admirable series of his drawings for "She Stoops to Conquer," what more Paris or Munich could have done for him. There is a certain refreshment in meeting an American artist of the first order who is not a pupil of Gérôme or of Cabanel.

Of course, I hasten to add, we must make our account with the fact that, as I began with remarking, the great development of Mr. Abbey's powers has taken place amid the brown old accessories of a country where that eighteenth century which he presently marked for his own are more profusely represented than they have the good-fortune to be in America, and consequently limit our contention to the point that his talent itself was already formed when this happy initiation was opened to it. He went to England for the first time in 1878. but it was not all at once that he fell into the trick, so irresistible for an artist doing his special work, of living there, I must forbid myself every impertinent conjecture, but it may be respectfully assumed that Mr. Abbey rather drifted into exile than committed himself to it with malice prepense. The habit, at any rate, to-day appears to be confirmed, and, to express it roughly, he is surrounded by the utensils and conveniences that he requires. During these years, until the recent period when he began to exhibit at the water-color exhibitions, his work has been done principally for Harper's Magazine, and the record of it is to be found in the recent back volumes. I shall not take space to tell it over piece by piece, for the reader who turns to the Magazine will have no difficulty in recognizing it. It has a distinction altogether its own; there is always poetry, humor, charm, in the idea, and always infinite grace and security in the execution.

As I have intimated, Mr. Abbey never deals with the things and figures of to-day; his imagination must perform a wide backward journey before it can take the air. But beyond this modern radius it breathes with singular freedom and naturalness. At a distance of fifty years it begins to be at home; it expands and takes possession; it recognizes its own. With all his ability, with all his tact, it would be impossible to him, we conceive, to illustrate a novel of contemporary manners; he would inevitably throw it back to the age of hair-powder and post-chaises. The coats and trousers, the feminine gear, the chairs and tables of the current year, the general aspect of things immediate and familiar, say nothing to his mind, and there are other interpreters to whom he is quite content to leave them. He shows no great interest even in the modern face, if there be a modern face apart from a modern setting; I am not sure what he thinks of its complications and refinements of expression, but he has certainly little relish for its *banal*, vulgar mustache, its prosaic, mercantile whisker, surmounting the last new thing in shirt-collars. Dear to him is the physiognomy of clean-shaven periods, when cheek and lip and chin, abounding in line and surface, had the air of soliciting the pencil. Impeccable as he is in drawing, he likes a whole face, with reason, and likes a whole figure; the latter not to the exclusion of clothes, in which he delights, but as the clothes of our great-grandfathers helped it to be seen. No one has ever understood breeches and stockings better than he, or the human leg, that delight of the draughtsman, as the costume of the last century permitted it to be known. The petticoat and bodice of the same period have as little mystery for him, and his women and girls have altogether the poetry of a by-gone manner and fashion. They are not modern heroines, with modern nerves and accomplishments, but figures of remembered song and story, calling up visions of spinet and harpsichord that have lost their music today, high-walled gardens that have ceased to bloom, flowered stuffs that are faded, locks of hair that are lost, love-letters that are pale. By which I don't mean that they are vague and spectral, for Mr. Abbey has in the highest degree the art of imparting life, and he gives it in particular to his well-made, blooming maidens. They live in a world in which there is no question of their passing Harvard or other examinations, but they stand very firmly on their quaintly-shod feet. They are exhaustively "felt," and eminently qualified to attract the opposite sex, which is not the case with ghosts, who, moreover, do not wear the most palpable petticoats of quilted satin, nor sport the most delicate fans, nor take generally the most ingratiating attitudes.

The best work that Mr. Abbey has done is to be found in the succession of illustrations to "She Stoops to Conquer;" here we see his happiest characteristics and—till he does something still more brilliant—may take his full measure. No work in black and white in our time has been more truly artistic, and certainly no success more unqualified. The artist has given us an evocation of a social state to its smallest details, and done it with an unsurpassable lightness of touch. The problem was in itself delightful—the accidents and incidents (granted a situation *de comédie*) of an old, rambling, wainscoted, out-of-the-way English country-house, in the age of Goldsmith. Here Mr. Abbey is in his element—given up equally to unerring observation and still more infallible divination. The whole place, and the figures that come and go in it, live again, with their individual look, their peculiarities, their special signs and oddities. The spirit of the dramatist has passed completely into the artist's sense, but the spirit of the historian has done so almost as much. Tony Lumpkin is, as we say nowadays, a document, and Miss Hardcastle embodies the results of research. Delightful are the humor and quaintness and grace of all this, delightful the variety and the richness of personal characterization, and delightful, above all, the drawing. It is impossible to represent with such vividness unless, to begin with, one sees; and it is impossible to see unless one wants to very much, or unless, in other words, one has a great love. Mr. Abbey has evidently the tenderest affection for just the old houses and the old things, the old faces and voices, the whole irrevocable human scene which the genial hand of Goldsmith has passed over to him, and there is no inquiry about them that he is not in a position to answer. He is intimate with the buttons of coats and the buckles of shoes: he knows not only exactly what his people wore, but exactly how they wore it, and how they felt when they had it on. He has sat on the old chairs and sofas, and rubbed against the old wainscots, and leaned over the old balusters. He knows every mended place in Tony Lumpkin's stockings, and exactly how that ingenuous youth leaned back on the spinet, with his thick, familiar thumb out, when he presented his inimitable countenance, with a grin, to Mr. Hastings, after he had set his fond mother a-whimpering. (There is nothing in the whole series, by-the-way, better indicated than the exquisitely simple, half-bumpkin, half-vulgar expression of Tony's countenance and smile in this scene, unless it be the charming arch yet modest face of Miss Hardcastle, lighted by the candle she carries, as, still holding the door by which she comes in, she is challenged by young Mar-low to relieve his bewilderment as to where he really is and what *she* really is.) In short, if we have all seen "She Stoops to Conquer" acted, Mr. Abbey has had the better fortune of seeing it off the stage; and it is noticeable how happily he has steered clear of the danger of making his people theatrical types—mere masqueraders and wearers of properties. This is especially the case with his women, who have not a hint of the conventional paint and patches, simpering with their hands in the pockets of aprons, but are taken from the same originals from which Goldsmith took them.

If it be asked on the occasion of this limited sketch of Mr. Abbey's powers where, after all, he did learn to draw so perfectly, I know no answer but to say that he learned it in the school in which he learned also to paint (as he has been doing in these latest years, rather tentatively at first, but with greater and greater success)—the school of his own personal observation. His drawing is the drawing of direct, immediate, solicitous study of the particular case, without tricks or affectations or any sort of cheap subterfuge, and nothing can exceed the charm of its delicacy, accuracy and elegance, its variety and freedom, its clear, frank solution of difficulties. If for the artist it be the foundation of every joy to know exactly what he wants (as I hold it is indeed), Mr. Abbey is, to all appearance, to be constantly congratulated. And I apprehend that he would not deny that it is a good-fortune for him to have been able to arrange his life so that his eye encounters in abundance the particular cases of which I speak. Two or three years ago, at the Institute of Painters in Water-colors, in London, he exhibited an exquisite picture of a peaceful old couple sitting in the corner of a low, quiet, ancient room, in the waning afternoon, and listening to their daughter as she stands up in the middle and plays the harp to them. They are Darby and Joan, with all the poetry preserved; they sit hand in hand, with bent, approving heads, and the deep recess of the window looking into the garden (where we may be sure there are yew-trees clipped into the shape of birds and beasts), the panelled room, the quaintness of the fireside, the old-time provincial expression of the scene, all belong to the class of effects which Mr. Abbey understands supremely well. So does the great russet wall and high-pitched mottled roof of the rural almshouse which figures in the admirable water-color picture that he exhibited last spring. A group of remarkably pretty countrywomen have been arrested in front of it by the passage of a young soldier—a raw recruit in scarlet tunic and white ducks, somewhat prematurely conscious of military glory. He gives them the benefit of the goose-step as he goes; he throws back his head and distends his fingers, presenting to the ladies a back expressive of more consciousness of his fine figure than of the lovely mirth that the artist has depicted in their faces. Lovely is their mirth indeed, and lovely are they altogether. Mr. Abbey has produced nothing more charming than this bright knot of handsome, tittering daughters of burghers, in their primeval pelisses and sprigged frocks. I have, however, left myself no space to go into the question of his prospective honors as a painter, to which everything now appears to point, and I have mentioned the two pictures last exhibited mainly because they illustrate the happy opportunities with which he has been able to surround himself. The sweet old corners he appreciates, the russet walls of moss-grown charities, the lowbrowed nooks of manor, cottage and parsonage, the fresh complexions that flourish in green, pastoral countries where it rains not a little—every item in this line that seems conscious of its pictorial use appeals to Mr. Abbey not in vain. He might have been a grandson of Washington Irving, which is a proof of what I have already said, that none of the young American workers in the same field have so little as he of that imperfectly assimilated foreignness of suggestion which is sometimes regarded as the strength, but which is also in some degree the weakness, of the pictorial effort of the United States. His execution is as sure of itself as if it rested upon infinite Parisian initiation, but his feeling can best be described by saying that it is that of our own dear mother-tongue. If the writer speaks when he writes, and the draughtsman speaks when he draws. Mr. Abbey, in expressing himself with his pencil, certainly speaks pure English, He reminds us to a certain extent of Meissonier, especially the Meissonier of the illustrations to that charming little volume of the *Conies Rémois*, and the comparison is highly to his advantage in the matter of freedom, variety, ability to represent movement (Meissonier's figures are stock-still), and facial expression—above all, in the handling of the female personage, so rarely attempted by the French artist. But he differs from the latter signally in the fact that though he shares his sympathy as to period and costume, his people are of another race and tradition, and move in a world locally altogether different. Mr. Abbey is still young, he is full of ideas and intentions, and the work he has done may, in view of his time of life, of his opportunities and the singular completeness of his talent, be regarded really as a kind of foretaste and prelude. It can hardly fail that he will do better things still, when everything is so favorable. Life itself is his subject, and that is always at his door. The only obstacle, therefore, that can be imagined in Mr. Abbey's future career is a possible embarrassment as to what to choose. He has hitherto chosen so well, however, that this obstacle will probably not be insuperable.

CHARLES S. REINHART

We Americans are accused of making too much ado about our celebrities, of being demonstratively conscious of each step that we take in the path of progress; and the accusation has its ground doubtless in this sense, that it is possible among us to-day to become a celebrity on unprecedentedly easy terms. This, however, at the present hour is the case all the world over, and it is difficult to see where the standard of just renown remains so high that the first stone may be cast. It is more and more striking that the machinery of publicity is so enormous, so constantly growing and so obviously destined to make the globe small, in relation of the objects, famous or obscure, which cover it, that it procures for the smallest facts and the most casual figures a reverberation to be expected only in the case of a world-conqueror. The newspaper and the telegram constitute a huge sounding-board, which has, every day and every hour, to be made to vibrate, to be fed with items, and the diffusion of the items takes place on a scale out of any sort of proportion to their intrinsic importance. The crackle of common things is transmuted into thunder—a thunder perhaps more resounding in America than elsewhere for the reason that the sheet of tin shaken by the Jupiter of the Press has been cut larger. But the difference is only of degree, not of kind; and if the system we in particular have brought to perfection would seem to be properly applied only to Alexanders and Napoleons, it is not striking that these adequate subjects present themselves even in other countries. The end of it all surely no man can see, unless it be that collective humanity is destined to perish from a rupture of its tympanum. That is a theme for a later hour, and meanwhile perhaps it is well not to be too frightened. Some of the items I just spoke of are, after all, larger than others; and if, as a general thing, it is a mistake to pull up our reputations to see how they are growing, there are some so well grown that they will bear it, and others of a hardy stock even while they are tender. We may feel, for instance, comparatively little hesitation in extending an importunate hand towards the fine young sapling of which Mr. Reinhart is one of the branches. It is a plant of promise, which has already flowered profusely and the fragrance of which it would be affectation not to to notice. Let us notice it, then, with candor, for it has all the air of being destined to make the future sweeter. The plant in question is of course simply the art of illustration in black and white, to which American periodical literature has, lately given such an impetus and which has returned the good office by conferring a great distinction on our magazines. In its new phase the undertaking has succeeded; and it is not always that fortune descends upon so deserving a head. Two or three fine talents in particular have helped it to succeed, and Mr. Reinhart is not the least conspicuous of these. It would be idle for a writer in Harper to pretend to any diffidence of appreciation of his work: for the pages are studded, from many years back, with the record of his ability. Mr. Rein-hart took his first steps and made his first hits in Harper, which owes him properly a portrait in return for so much portraiture. I may exaggerate the charm and the importance of the modern illustrative form, may see in it a capacity of which it is not yet itself wholly conscious, but if I do so Mr. Reinhart is partly responsible for the aberration. Abundant, intelligent, interpretative work in black and white is, to the sense of the writer of these lines, one of the pleasantest things of the time, having only to rise to the occasion to enjoy a great future. This idea, I confess, is such as to lead one to write not only sympathetically but pleadingly about the artists to whom one looks for confirmation of it. If at the same time as we commemorate what they have done we succeed in enlarging a little the conception of what they may yet do, we shall be repaid even for having exposed ourselves as fanatics— fanatics of the general manner, I mean, not of particular representatives of it.

May not this fanaticism, in a particular case, rest upon a sense of the resemblance between the general chance, as it may be called, of the draughtsman in black and white, with contemporary life for his theme, and the opportunity upon which the literary artist brings another form to bear? The forms are different, though with analogies; but the field is the same—the immense field of contemporary life observed for an artistic purpose. There is nothing so interesting as that, because it is ourselves; and no artistic problem is so charming as to arrive, either in a literary or a plastic form, at a close and direct notation of what we observe. If one has attempted some such exploit in a literary form, one cannot help having a sense of union and comradeship with those who have approached the question with the other instrument. This will be especially the case if we happen to have appreciated that instrument even to envy. We may as well say it outright, we envy it quite unspeakably in the hands of Mr. Reinhart and in those of Mr. Abbey. There is almost no limit to the service to which we can imagine it to be applied, and we find ourselves wishing that these gentlemen may be made adequately conscious of all the advantages it represents. We wonder whether they really *are* so; we are disposed even to assume that they are not, in order to join the moral, to insist on the lesson. The master whom we have mentally in view Mr. Reinhart is a near approach to him may be, if he will only completely know it, so prompt, so copious, so universal—so "all there," as we say nowadays, and indeed so all everywhere. There is only too much to see, too much to do, and his process is the one that comes nearest to minimizing the quantity. He can touch so many things, he can go from one scene to another, he can sound a whole concert of notes while the painter is setting up his easel. The painter is majestic, dignified, academic, important, superior, anything you will; but he is, in the very nature of the case, only occasional. He is "serious," but he is comparatively clumsy: he is a terrible time getting under way, and he has to sacrifice so many subjects while he is doing one. The illustrator makes one immense sacrifice, of course—that of color; but with it he purchases a freedom which enables him to attack ever so many ideas. It is by variety and numerosity that he commends himself to his age, and it is for these qualities that his age commends him to the next. The twentieth century, the latter half of it, will, no doubt, have its troubles, but it will have a great compensatory luxury, that of seeing the life of a hundred years before much more vividly than we—even happy we—see the life of a hundred years ago. But for this our illustrators must do their best, appreciate the endless capacity of their form. It is to the big picture what the short story is to the novel.

It is doubtless too much, I hasten to add, to ask Mr. Reinhart, for instance, to work to please the twentieth century. The end will not matter if he pursues his present very prosperous course of activity, for it is assuredly the fruitful vein, the one I express the hope to see predominant, the portrayal of the manners, types and aspects that surround us. Mr. Reinhart has reached that happy period of life when a worker is in full possession of his means, when he has done for his chosen instrument everything he can do in the way of forming it and rendering it complete and flexible, and has the fore only to apply it with freedom, confidence and success. These, to our sense, are the golden hours of an artist's life; happier even than the younger time when the future seemed infinite in the light of the first rays of glory, the first palpable hits. The very sense that the future is *not* unlimited and that opportunity is at its high-water-mark gives an intensity to the enjoyment of maturity. Then the acquired habit of "knowing how" must simplify the problem of execution and leave the artist free to think only of his purpose, as befits a real creator. Mr. Reinhart is at the enviable stage of knowing in perfection how; he has arrived at absolute facility and felicity. The machine goes of itself; it is no longer necessary to keep lifting the cover and pouring in the oil of fond encouragement: all the attention may go to the idea and the subject. It may, however, remain very interesting to others to know how the faculty was trained, the pipe was tuned. The early phases of such a process have a relative importance even when, at the lime (so gradual are many beginnings and so obscure man a morrow) they may have appeared neither delightful nor profitable. They are almost always to be summed up in the single precious word practice. This word represents, at any rate, Mr. Reinhart's youthful history, and the profusion in which, though no doubt occasionally disguised, the boon was supplied to him in the offices of Harper's Magazine. There is nothing so innate that it has not also to be learned, for the best part of any aptitude is the capacity to increase it.

Mr. Reinhart's experience began to accumulate very early, for at Pittsburgh, where he was born, he was free to draw to his heart's content. There was no romantic attempt, as I gather, to nip him in the bud. On the contrary, he was despatched with almost prosaic punctuality to Europe, and was even encouraged to make himself at home in Munich. Munich, in his case, was a *pis-aller* for Paris, where it would have been his preference to study when he definitely surrendered, as it were, to his symptoms. He went to Paris, but Paris seemed blocked and complicated, and Munich presented advantages which, if not greater, were at least easier to approach. Mr. Reinhart passe through the mill of the Bavarian school, and when it had turned him out with its characteristic polish he came back to America with a very substantial stock to dispose of. It would take a chapter by itself if we were writing a biography, this now very usual episode of the return of the young American from the foreign conditions in which he has learned his professional language, and his position in face of the community that he addresses in a strange idiom. There has to be a prompt adjustment between ear and voice, if the interlocutor is not to seem to himself to be intoning in the void. There is always an inner history in all this, as well as an outer one—such, however, as it would take much space to relate. Mr. Reinhart's more or less alienated accent fell, by good-fortune, on a comprehending listener. He had made a satirical drawing, in the nature of the "cartoon" of a comic journal, on a subject of the hour, and addressed it to the editor of *Harper's Weekly*. The drawing was not published—the satire was perhaps not exactly on the right note—but the draughtsman was introduced. Thus began, by return of post, as it were, and with preliminaries so few that they could not well have been less, a connection of many years. If I were writing a biography another chapter would come in here—a curious, almost a pathetic one; for the course of things is so rapid in this country that the years of Mr. Reinhart's apprenticeship to pictorial journalism, positively recent as they are, already are almost prehistoric. To-morrow, at least, the complexion of that time, its processes, ideas and standards, together with some of the unsophisticated who carried them out, will belong to old New York. A certain mollifying dimness rests upon them now, and their superseded brilliancy gleams through it but faintly. It is a lively span for Mr. Reinhart to have been at once one of the unsophisticated and one of the actually modern.

That portion of his very copious work to which, more particularly. I apply the latter term, has been done for Harper's Magazine. During these latter years it has come, like so much of American work to-day, from beyond the seas. Whether or not that foreign language of which I just spoke never became, in New York, for this especial possessor of it, a completely convenient medium of conversation, is more than I can say; at any rate Mr. Reinhart eventually reverted to Europe and settled in Paris. Paris had seemed rather inhospitable to him in his youth, but he has now fitted his key to the lock. It would be satisfactory to be able to express scientifically the reasons why, as a general thing, the American artist, as well as his congener of many another land, carries on his function with less sense of resistance in that city than elsewhere. He likes Paris best, but that is not scientific. The difference is that though theoretically the production of pictures is recognized in America and in England, in Paris it is recognized both theoretically and practically. And I do not mean by this simply that pictures are bought—for they are not, predominantly, as it happens—but that they are more presupposed. The plastic is implied in the French conception of things, and the studio is as natural a consequence of it as the post-office is of letter-writing. Vivid representation is the genius of the French language and the need of the French mind. The people have invented more aids to it than any other, and as these aids make up a large part of the artist's life, he feels his best home to be in the place where he finds them most. He may begin to quarrel with that home on the day a complication is introduced by the question of *what* he shall represent—a totally different consideration from that of the method; but for Mr. Reinhart this question has not yet offered insoluble difficulties. He represents everything—he has accepted so general an order. So long as his countrymen flock to Paris and pass in a homogeneous procession before his eyes, there is not the smallest difficulty in representing *them*. When the case requires that they shall be taken in connection with their native circumstances and seen in their ambient air, he is prepared to come home and give several months to the task, as on the occasion of Mr. Dudley Warner's history of a tour among the watering-places, to which he furnished so rich and so curious a pictorial accompaniment. Sketch-book in hand, he betakes himself, according to need, to Germany, to England, to Italy, to Spain. The readers of Harper will have forgotten his admirable pictorial notes on the political world at Berlin, so rich and close in characterization. To the *Spanish Vistas* of Mr. G. P. Lathrop he contributed innumerable designs, delightful notes of an artist's quest of the sketchable, many of which are singularly full pictures. The "Soldiers Playing Dominoes" at a café is a powerful page of life. Mr. Reinhart has, of course, interpreted many a fictive scene—he has been repeatedly called upon to make the novel and the story visible. This he energetically and patiently does; though of course we are unable to say whether the men and women he makes us see are the very people whom the authors have seen. That is a thing that, in any case, one will never know; besides, the authors who don't see vaguely are apt to see perversely. The story-teller has, at any rate, the comfort with Mr. Reinhart that his drawings are constructive and have the air of the actual. He likes to represent character—he rejoices in the specifying touch.

The evidence of this is to be found also in his pictures, for I ought already to have mentioned that, for these many years (they are beginning to be many), he has indulged in the luxury of color. It is not probable that he regards himself in the first place as an illustrator, in the sense to which the term is usually restricted. He is a very vigorous and various painter, and at the Salon a constant and conspicuous exhibitor. He is fond of experiments, difficulties and dangers, and I divine that it would be his preference to be known best by his painting, in which he handles landscape with equal veracity. It is a pity that the critic is unable to contend with him on such a point without appearing to underestimate that work. Mr. Reinhart has so much to show for his preference that I am conscious of its taking some assurance to say that I am not sure he is right. This would be the case even if he had nothing else to show than the admirable picture entitled "Washed Ashore" ("Un Epave ") which made such an impression in the Salon of 1887. It represents the dead body of an unknown man whom the tide has cast up, lying on his back, feet forward, disfigured, dishonored by the sea. A small group of villagers are collected near it, divided by the desire to look and the fear to see. A gendarme, official and responsible, his uniform contrasting with the mortal disrepair of the victim, takes down in his note-book the *procès-verbal* of the incident, and an old sailor, pointing away with a stiffened arm, gives him the benefit of what *he* knows about the matter. Plain, pitying, fish-wives, hushed, with their shawls in their mouths, hang back, as if from a combination too solemn—the mixture of death and the law. Three or four men seem to be glad it isn't they. The thing is a masterpiece of direct representation, and has wonderfully the air of something seen, found without being looked for. Excellently composed but not artificial, deeply touching but not sentimental, large, close and sober, this important work gives the full measure of Mr. Reinhart's great talent and constitutes a kind of pledge. It may be perverse on my part to see in it the big banknote, as it were, which may be changed into a multitude of gold and silver pieces. I cannot, however, help doing so. "Washed Ashore" is painted as only a painter paints, but I irreverently translate it into its equivalent in "illustrations"—half a hundred little examples, in black and white, of the same sort of observation. For this observation, immediate, familiar, sympathetic, human, and not involving a quest of style for which color is really indispensable, is a mistress at whose service there is no derogation in placing one's self. To do little things instead of big *may* be a derogation; a great deal will depend upon the way the little things are done. Besides, no work of art is absolutely little. I grow bold and even impertinent as I think of the way Mr. Rein-hart might scatter the smaller coin. At any rate, whatever proportion his work in this line may bear to the rest, it is to be hoped that nothing will prevent him from turning out more and more to play the rare faculty that produces it. His studies of American *moeurs* in association with Mr. Warner went so far on the right road that we would fain see him make all the rest of the journey. They made us ask straightway for more, and were full of intimations of what was behind. They showed what there is to see—what there is to guess. Let him carry the same inquiry further, let him carry it all the way. It would be serious work and would abound in reality; it would help us, as it were, to know what we are talking about. In saying this I feel how much I confirm the great claims I just made for the revival of illustration.

ALFRED PARSONS

It would perhaps be extravagant to pretend, in this embarrassed age, that Merry England is still intact; but it would be strange if the words "happy England" should not rise to the lips of the observer of Mr. Alfred Parsons' numerous and delightful studies of the gardens, great and small, of his country. They surely have a representative value in more than the literal sense, and might easily minister to the quietest complacency of patriotism. People whose criticism is imaginative will see in them a kind of compendium of what, in home things, is at once most typical and most enviable; and, going further, they will almost wish that such a collection might be carried by slow stages round the globe, to kindle pangs in the absent and passions in the alien. As it happens to be a globe the English race has largely peopled, we can measure the amount of homesickness that would be engendered on the way. In fact, one doubts whether the sufferer would even need to be of English strain to attach the vision of home to the essentially lovable places that Mr. Parsons depicts. They seem to generalize and typify the idea, so that every one may feel, in every case, that he has a sentimental property in the scene. The very sweetness of its reality only helps to give it that story-book quality which persuades us we have known it in youth.

And yet such scenes may well have been constructed for the despair of the Colonial; for they remind us, at every glance, of that perfection to which there is no short cut—not even "unexampled prosperity "—and to which time is the only guide. Mr. Parsons' pictures speak of many complicated things, but (in what they tell us of his subjects) they speak most of duration. Such happy nooks have grown slowly, such fortunate corners have had a history; and their fortune has been precisely that they have had time to have it comfortably, have not been obliged to try for character without it.

Character is their strong point and the most expensive of all ingredients. Mr. Parsons' portraiture seizes every shade of it, seizes it with unfailing sympathy. He is doubtless clever enough to paint rawness when he must, but he has an irrepressible sense of ripeness. Half the ripeness of England—half the religion, one might almost say—is in its gardens; they are truly pious foundations. It is doubtless because there are so many of them that the country seems so finished, and the sort of care they demand is an intenser deliberation, which passes into the national temper. One must have lived in other lands to observe fully how large a proportion of this one is walled in for growing flowers. The English love of flowers is inveterate; it is the most, unanimous protest against the grayness of some of the conditions, and it should receive justice from those who accuse the race of taking its pleasure too sadly. A good garden is an organized revel, and there is no country in which there are so many.

Mr. Parsons had therefore only to choose, at his leisure, and one might heartily have envied him the process, scarcely knowing which to prefer of all the pleasant pilgrimages that would make up such a quest. He had, fortunately, the knowledge which could easily lead to more, and a career of discovery behind him. He knew the right times for the right things, and the right things for the right places. He had innumerable memories and associations; he had painted up and down the land and looked over many walls. He had followed the bounty of the year from month to month and from one profusion to another. To follow it with him, in this admirable series, is to see that he is master of the subject. There will be no lack of confidence on the part of those who have already perceived, in much of Mr. Parsons' work, a supreme illustration of all that is widely nature-loving in the English interest in the flower. No sweeter submission to mastery can be imagined than the way the daffodils, under his brush (to begin at the beginning), break out into early April in the lovely drawings of Stourhead. One of the most charming of these—a corner of an old tumbled-up place in Wiltshire, where many things have come and gone—represents that moment of transition in which contrast is so vivid as to make it more dramatic than many plays—the very youngest throb of spring, with the brown slope of the foreground coming back to consciousness in pale lemon-colored patches and, on the top of the hill, against the still cold sky, the equally delicate forms of the wintry trees. By the time these forms have thickened, the expanses of daffodil will have become a mass of bluebells. All the daffodil pictures have a rare loveliness, but especially those that deal also with the earlier fruit-blossom, the young plum-trees in Berkshire orchards. Here the air is faintly pink, and the painter makes us feel the little *blow* in the thin blue sky. The spring, fortunately, is everybody's property and, in the language of all the arts, the easiest word to conjure with. It is therefore partly Mr. Parsons' good-luck that we enjoy so his rendering of these phases; but on the other hand we look twice when it's a case of meddling with the exquisite, and if he inspires us with respect it is because we feel that he has been deeply initiated. No one knows better the friendly reasons for our stopping, when chatting natives pronounce the weather "foine," at charming casual corners of old villages, where grassy ways cross each other and timbered houses bulge irregularly and there are fresh things behind crooked palings; witness the little vision of Blewbury, in Berkshire, reputedly of ancient British origin, with a road all round it and only footways within. No one, in the Herefordshire orchards, masses the white cow-parsley in such profusion under the apple blossoms; or makes the whitewashed little damson-trees look so innocently responsible and charming on the edge of the brook over which the planks are laid for the hens. Delightful, in this picture, is the sense of the clean spring day, after rain, with the blue of the sky washed faint. Delightful is the biggish view (one of the less numerous oil-pictures) of the Somersetshire garden, where that peculiarly English look of the open-air room is produced by the stretched carpet of the turf and the firm cushions of the hedges, and a pair of proprietors, perhaps happier than they know, are putting in an afternoon among their tulips, under the flushed apple-trees whose stems are so thin and whose brims so heavy. Are the absorbed couple, at any rate, aware of the surprising degree to which the clustered ruddy roofs of the next small town, over the hedge, off at the left, may remind the fanciful spectator of the way he has seen little dim Italian cities look on their hill-tops? The whole thing, in this subject, has the particular English note to which Mr. Parsons repeatedly testifies, the nook quality, the air of a land and a life so infinitely subdivided that they produce a thousand pleasant privacies. The painter moves with the months and finds, after the earliest things, the great bed of pansies in the angle of the old garden at Sutton, in which, for felicity of position and perfect pictorial service rendered—to say nothing of its polygonal, pyramidal roof—the ancient tool-house, or tea-house, is especially to be commended.

Very far descended is such a corner as this, very full of reference to vanished combinations and uses; and the artist communicates to us a feeling for it that makes us wish disinterstedly it may be still as long preserved.

He finds in June, at Blackdown, the blaze of the yellow azalea-bush, or in another spot the strong pink of the rhododendron, beneath the silver firs that deepen the blue of the sky. He finds the Vicarage Walk, at King's Langley, a smother of old-fashioned flowers—a midsummer vista for the figures of a happy lady and a lucky dog. He finds the delicious huddle of the gabled, pigeon-haunted roof of a certain brown old building at Frame, with poppies and gladiolus and hollyhock crowding the beautiful foreground. He finds—apparently in the same place—the tangle of the hardy flowers that come while the roses are still in bloom, with the tall blue larkspurs standing high among them. He finds the lilies, white and red, at Broadway, and the poppies, which have dropped most of their petals—apparently to let the roses, which are just coming out, give *their* grand party. Their humility is rewarded by the artist's admirable touch in the little bare poppy-heads that nod on their flexible pins.

But I cannot go on to say everything that such a seeker, such a discoverer, as Mr. Parsons finds—the less that the purpose of these limited remarks is to hint at our own *trouvailles*. A view of the field, at any rate, would be incomplete without such specimens as the three charming oil-pictures which commemorate Holme Lacey. There are gardens and gardens, and these represent the sort that are always spoken of in the plural and most arrogate the title. They form, in England, a magnificent collection, and if they abound in a quiet assumption of the grand style it must be owned that they frequently achieve it. There are people to be found who enjoy them, and it is not, at any rate, when Mr. Parsons deals with them that we have an opening for strictures. As we look at the blaze of full summer in the brilliantly conventional parterres we easily credit the tale of the 40,000 plants it takes to fill the beds. More than this, we like the long paths of turf that stretch between splendid borders, recalling the frescoed galleries of a palace; we like the immense hedges, whose tops are high against the sky. While we are liking, we like perhaps still better, since they deal with a very different order, the two water-colors from the dear little garden at Winchelsea—especially the one in which the lady takes he ease in her hammock (on a sociable, shady terrace, from which the ground drops), and looks at red Rye, across the marshes. Another garden where a contemplative hammock would be in order is the lovely canonical plot at Salisbury, with the everlasting spire above it tinted in the summer sky—unless, in the same place, you should choose to hook yourself up by the grassy bank of the Avon, at the end of the lawn, with the meadows, the cattle, the distant willows across the river, to look at.

Three admirable water-colors are devoted by Mr. Parsons to the perceptible dignity of Gravetye, in Sussex, the dignity of very serious gardens, entitled to ceremonious consideration, Few things in England can show a greater wealth of bloom than the wide flowery terrace immediately beneath the gray, gabled house, where tens of thousands of tea-roses, in predominant possession, have, in one direction, a mass of high yews for a background. They divide their province with the carnations and pansies: a wilder ness of tender petals ignorant of anything rougher than the neighborhood of the big unchanged medley of tall yuccas and saxifrage, with miscellaneous filling-in, in the picture which presents the charming house in profile. The artist shows us later, in September, at Gravetye, the pale violet multitude of the Michaelmas daisies; another I great bunch, or bank, of which half masks and greatly beautifies the rather bare yellow cottage at Broadway. This brings us on to the autumn, if I count as autumnal the admirable large water-color of a part of a garden at Shiplake, with the second bloom of the roses and a glimpse of a turn of the Thames. This exquisite picture expresses to perfection the beginning of the languor of the completed season—with its look of warm rest, of doing nothing, in the cloudless sky. To the same or a later moment belongs the straight walk at Fladbury—the old rectory garden by the Avon, with its Irish yews and the red lady in her chair; also the charming water-color of young, slim apple-trees, full of fruit (this must be October), beneath an admirable blue and white sky. Still later comes the big pear-tree that has turned, among barer boughs, to flame-color, and, in another picture, the very pale russet of the thinned cherry-trees, standing, beneath a grayish sky, above a foreshortened slope. Last of all we have, in oils, December and a hard frost in a bare apple-orchard, indented with a deep gully which makes the place somehow a subject and which, in fact, three or four years ago, made it one for a larger picture by Mr. Parsons, full of truth and style.

This completes his charming story of the life of the English year, told in a way that convinces us of his intimate acquaintance with it. Half the interest of Mr. Parsons' work is in the fact that he paints from a full mind and from a store of assimilated knowledge. In every touch of nature that he communicates to us we feel something of the thrill of the whole—we feel the innumerable relations, the possible variations of the particular objects. This makes his manner serious and masculine—rescues it from the thinness of tricks and the coquetries of *chic*. We walk with him on a firm earth, we taste the tone of the air and seem to take nature and the climate and all the complicated conditions by their big general hand. The painter's manner, in short, is one with the study of things—his talent is a part of their truth. In this happy series we seem to see still more how that talent was formed, how his rich motherland has been, from the earliest observation, its nurse and inspirer. He gives back to her all the good she has done him.

JOHN S. SARGENT

I was on the point of beginning this sketch of the work of an artist to whom distinction has come very early in life by saying, in regard to the degree to which the subject of it enjoys the attention of the public, that no American painter has hitherto won himself such recognition from the expert; but I find myself pausing at the start as on the edge of a possible solecism. Is Mr. Sargent in very fact an American painter? The proper answer to such a question is doubtless that we shall be well advised to pretend it, and the reason of this is simply that we have an excellent opportunity. Born in Europe, he has also spent his life in Europe, but none the less the burden of proof would rest with those who should undertake to show that he is a European. Moreover he has even on the face of it this great symptom of an American origin, that in the line of his art he might easily be mistaken for a Frenchman. It sounds like a paradox, but it is a very simple truth, that when to-day we look for "American art" we find it mainly in Paris. When we find it out of Paris, we at least find a great deal of Paris in it. Mr. Sargent came up to the irresistible city in his twentieth year, from Florence, where in 1856 he had been born of American parents and where his fortunate youth had been spent. He entered immediately the studio of Caro-lus Duran, and revealed himself in 1877, at the age of twenty-two, in the portrait of that master—-a fine model in more than one sense of the word. He was already in possession of a style; and if this style has gained both in finish and in assurance, it has not otherwise varied. As he saw and "rendered" ten years ago, so he sees and renders to-day; and I may add that there is no present symptom of his passing into another manner.

Those who have appreciated his work most up to the present time articulate no wish for a change, so completely does that work seem to them, in its kind, the exact translation of his thought, the exact "fit" of his artistic temperament. It is difficult to imagine a young painter less in the dark about his own ideal, more lucid and more responsible from the first about what he desires. In an altogether exceptional degree does he give us the sense that the intention and the art of carrying it out are for him one and the same thing. In the brilliant portrait of Carolus Duran, which he was speedily and strikingly to surpass, he gave almost the full measure of this admirable peculiarity, that perception with him is already by itself a kind of execution. It is likewise so, of course, with many another genuine painter; but in Sargent's case the process by which the object seen resolves itself into the object pictured is extraordinarily immediate. It is as if painting were pure tact of vision, a simple manner of feeling.

From the time of his first successes at the Salon he was hailed, I believe, as a recruit of high value to the camp of the Impressionists, and to-day he is for many people most conveniently pigeon-holed under that head. It is not necessary to protest against the classification if this addition always be made to it, that Mr. Sargent's impressions happen to be worthy of record. This is by no means inveterately the case with those of the ingenuous artists who most rejoice in the title in question. To render the impression of an object may be a very fruitful effort, but it is not necessarily so; that will depend upon what, I won't say the object, but the impression, may have been. The talents engaged in this school lie, not unjustly, as it seems to me under the suspicion of seeking the solution of their problem exclusively in simplification. If a painter works for other eyes as well as his own he courts a certain danger in this direction—that of being arrested by the cry of the spectator: "Ah! but excuse me; I myself take more impressions than that" We feel a synthesis not to be an injustice only when it is rich. Mr. Sargent simplifies, I think, but he simplifies with style, and his impression is the finest form of his energy.

His work has been almost exclusively in portraiture, and it has been his fortune to paint more women than men; therefore he has had but a limited opportunity to reproduce that generalized grand air with which his view of certain figures of gentlemen invests the model, which is conspicuous in the portrait of Carolus Duran and of which his splendid "Docteur Pozzi," the distinguished Paris surgeon (a work not sent to the Salon), is an admirable example. In each of these cases the model has been of a gallant pictorial type, one of the types which strike us as made for portraiture (which is by no means the way of all), as especially appears, for instance, in the handsome hands and frilled wrists of M. Carolus, whose cane rests in his fine fingers as if it were the hilt of a rapier. The most brilliant of all Mr. Sargent's productions is the portrait of a young lady, the magnificent picture which he exhibited in 1881; and if it has mainly been his fortune since to commemorate the fair faces of women, there is no ground for surprise at this sort of success on the part of one who had given so signal a proof of possessing the secret of the particular aspect that the contemporary lady (of any period) likes to wear in the eyes of posterity. Painted when he was but four-and-twenty years of age, the picture by which Mr. Sargent was represented at the Salon of 1881 is a performance which may well have made any critic of imagination rather anxious about his future. In common with the superb group of the children of Mr. Edward Boit, exhibited two years later, it offers the slightly "uncanny" spectacle of a talent which on the very threshold of its career has nothing more to learn. It is not simply precocity in the guise of maturity—a phenomenon we very often meet, which deceives us only for an hour; it is the freshness of youth combined with the artistic experience, really felt and assimilated, of generations. My admiration for this deeply distinguished work is such that I am perhaps in danger of overstating its merits; but it is worth taking into account that to-day, after several years' acquaintance with them, these merits seem to me more and more to justify enthusiasm. The picture has this sign of productions of the first order, that its style clearly would save it if everything else should change—our measure of its value of resemblance, its expression of character, the fashion of dress, the particular associations it evokes. It is not only a portrait, but a picture, and it arouses even in the profane spectator something of the painter's sense, the joy of engaging also, by sympathy, in the solution of the artistic problem. There are works of which it is sometimes said that they are painters' pictures (this description is apt to be intended invidiously), and the production of which I speak has the good-fortune at once to belong to this class and to give the "plain man" the kind of pleasure that the plain man looks for.

The young lady, dressed in black satin, stands upright, with her right hand bent back, resting on her waist, while the other, with the arm somewhat extended, offers to view a single white flower. The dress. stretched at the hips over a sort of hoop, and ornamented in front, where it opens on a velvet petticoat with large satin bows, has an old-fashioned air, as if it had been worn by some demure princess who might have sat for Velasquez. The hair, of which the arrangement is odd and charming, is disposed in two or three large curls fastened at one side over the temple with a comb. Behind the figure is the vague faded sheen, exquisite in tone, of a silk curtain, light, undefined, and losing itself at the bottom. The face is young, candid and peculiar. Out of these few elements the artist has constructed a picture which it is impossible to forget, of which the most striking characteristic is its simplicity, and yet which overflows with perfection. Painted with extraordinary breadth and freedom, so that surface and texture are interpreted by the lightest hand, it glows with life, character and distinction, and strikes us as the most complete—with one exception perhaps—of the author's productions. I know not why this representation of a young girl in black, engaged in the casual gesture of holding up a flower, should make so ineffaceable an impression and tempt one to become almost lyrical in its praise; but I remember that, encountering the picture unexpectedly in New York a year or two after it had been exhibited in Paris, it seemed to me to have acquired an extraordinary general value, to stand for more artistic truth than it would be easy to formulate. The language of painting, the tongue in which, exclusively, Mr. Sargent expresses himself, is a medium into which a considerable part of the public, for the simple an excellent reason that they don't understand it, will doubtless always be reluctant and unable to follow him.

Two years before he exhibited the young lady in black, in 1879, Mr. Sargent had spent several months in Spain, and here, even more than he had already been, the great Velasquez became the god of his idolatry. No scenes are more delightful to the imagination than those in which we figure youth and genius confronted with great examples, and if such matters did not belong to the domain of private life we might entertain ourselves with reconstructing the episode of the first visit to the museum of Madrid, the shrine of the painter of Philip IV., of a young Franco-American worshipper of the highest artistic sensibility, expecting a supreme revelation and prepared to fall on his knees. It is evident that Mr. Sargent fell on his knees and that in this attitude he passed a considerable part of his sojourn in Spain. He is various and experimental; if I am not mistaken, he sees each work that he produces in a light of its own, not turning off successive portraits according to some well-tried receipt which has proved useful in the case of their predecessors; nevertheless there is one idea that pervades them all, in a different degree, and gives them a family resemblance—the idea that it would be inspiring to know just how Velasquez would have treated the theme. We can fancy that on each occasion Mr. Sargent, as a solemn preliminary, invokes him as a patron saint. This is not, in my intention, tantamount to saying that the large canvas representing the contortions of a dancer in the lamp-lit room of a *posada*, which he exhibited on his return from Spain, strikes me as having come into the world under the same star as those compositions of the great Spaniard which at Madrid alternate with his royal portraits. This singular work, which has found an appreciative home in Boston, has the stamp of an extraordinary energy and facility—of an actual scene, with its accidents and peculiarities caught, as distinguished from a composition where arrangement and invention have played their part. It looks like life, but it looks also, to my view, rather like a perversion of life, and has the quality of an enormous "note" or memorandum, rather than of a representation. A woman in a voluminous white silk dress and a black mantilla pirouettes in the middle of a dusky room, to the accompaniment of her own castanets and that of a row of men and women who sit in straw chairs against the whitewashed wall and thrum upon guitar and tambourine or lift other castanets into the air. She appears almost colossal, and the twisted and inflated folds of her long dress increase her volume. She simpers, in profile, with a long chin, while she slants back at a dangerous angle, and the lamplight (it proceeds from below, as if she were on a big platform) makes a strange play in her large face. In the background the straight line of black-clad, black-hatted, white-shirted musicians projects shadows against the wall, on which placards, guitars, and dirty finger-marks display themselves. The merit of this production is that the air of reality is given in it with remarkable breadth and boldness; its defect it is difficult to express save by saying that it makes the spectator vaguely uneasy and even unhappy—an accident the more to be regretted as a lithe, inspired female figure, given up to the emotion of the dance, is not intrinsically a displeasing object. "El Jaleo" sins, in my opinion, in the direction of ugliness, and, independently of the fact that the heroine is circling round incommoded by her petticoats, has a want of serenity.

This is not the defect of the charming, dusky, white-robed person who, in the Tangerine subject exhibited at the Salon of 1880 (the fruit of an excursion to the African coast at the time of the artist's visit to Spain), stands on a rug, under a great white Moorish arch, and from out of the shadows of the large drapery, raised pentwise by her hands, which covers her head, looks down, with painted eyes and brows showing above a bandaged mouth, at the fumes of a beautiful censer or chafing-dish placed on the carpet. I know not who this stately Mahometan may be, nor in what mysterious domestic or religious rite she may be engaged; but in her muffled contemplation and her pearl-colored robes, under her plastered arcade which shines in the Eastern light, she transports and torments us. The picture is exquisite, a radiant effect of white upon white, of similar but discriminated tones. In dividing the honor that Mr. Sargent has won by his finest work between the portrait of the young lady of 1881 and the group of four little girls which was painted in 1882 and exhibited with the success it deserved the following year, I must be careful to give the latter picture not too small a share. The artist has done nothing more felicitous and interesting than this view of a rich dim, rather generalized French interior (the perspective of a hall with a shining floor, where screens and tall Japanese vases shimmer and loom), which encloses the life and seems to form the happy play-world of a family of charming children. The treatment is eminently unconventional, and there is none of the usual symmetrical balancing of the figures in the foreground. The place is regarded as a whole; it is a scene, a comprehensive impression; yet none the less do the little figures in their white pinafores (when was the pinafore ever painted with that power and made so poetic?) detach themselves and live with a personal life. Two of the sisters stand hand in hand at the back, in the delightful, the almost equal, company of a pair of immensely tall emblazoned jars, which overtop them and seem also to partake of the life of the picture; the splendid porcelain and the aprons of the children shine together, while a mirror in the brown depth behind them catches the light. Another little girl presents herself, with abundant tresses and slim legs, her hands behind her, quite to the left; and the youngest, nearest to the spectator, sits on the floor and plays with her doll. The naturalness of the composition, the loveliness of the complete effect, the light, free' security of the execution, the sense it gives us as of assimilated secrets and of instinct and knowledge playing together— all this makes the picture as astonishing a work on the part of a young man of twenty-six as the portrait of 1881 was astonishing on the part of a young man of twenty-four.

It is these remarkable encounters that justify us in writing almost prematurely of a career which is not yet half unfolded. Mr. Sargent is sometimes accused of a want of "finish," but if finish means the last word of expressiveness of touch, "The Hall with the Four Children," as we may call it, may-stand as a permanent reference on this point. If the picture of the Spanish dancer illustrates, as it seems to me to do, the latent dangers of the Impressionist practice, so this finer performance shows what victories it may achieve. And in relation to the latter I must repeat what I said about the young lady with the flower, that this is the sort of work which, when produced in youth, leads the attentive spectator to ask unanswerable questions. He finds himself murmuring, "Yes, but what is left?" and even wondering whether it be an advantage to an artist to obtain early in life such possession of his means that the struggle with them, discipline, *tâtonnement*, cease to exist for him. May not this breed an irresponsibility of cleverness, a wantonness, an irreverence—what is vulgarly termed a "larkiness"—on the part of the youthful genius who has, as it were, all his fortune in his pocket? Such are the possibly superfluous broodings of those who are critical even in their warmest admirations and who sometimes suspect that it may be better for an artist to have a certain part of his property invested in unsolved difficulties. When this is not the case, the question with regard to his future simplifies itself somewhat portentously. "What will he do with it?" we ask, meaning by the pronoun the sharp, completely forged weapon. It becomes more purely a question of responsibility, and we hold him altogether to a higher account. This is the case with Mr. Sargent; he knows so much about the art of painting that he perhaps does not fear emergencies quite enough, and that having knowledge to spare he may be tempted to play with it and waste it. Various, curious, as we have called him, he occasionally tries experiments which seem to arise from the mere high spirits of his brush, and runs risks little courted by the votaries of the literal, who never expose their necks to escape from the common. For the literal and the common he has the smallest taste; when he renders an object into the language of painting his translation is a generous paraphrase.

As I have intimated, he has painted little but portraits; but he has painted very many of these, and I shall not attempt in so few pages to give a catalogue of his works. Every canvas that has come from his hands has not figured at the Salon; some of them have seen the light at other exhibitions in Paris; some of them in London (of which city Mr. Sargent is now an inhabitant), at the Royal Academy and the Grosvenor Gallery. If he has been mainly represented by portraits there are two or three little subject-pictures of which I retain a grateful memory. There stands out in particular, as a pure gem, a small picture exhibited at the Grosvenor, representing a small group of Venetian girls of the lower class, sitting in gossip together one summer's day in the big, dim hall of a shabby old palazzo. The shutters let in a clink of light; the scagliola pavement gleams faintly in it; the whole place is bathed in a kind of transparent shade. The girls are vaguely engaged in some very humble household work; they are counting turnips or stringing onions, and these small vegetables, enchantingly painted, look as valuable as magnified pearls. The figures are extraordinarily natural and vivid; wonderfully light and fine is the touch by which the painter evokes the small familiar Venetian realities (he has handled them with a vigor altogether peculiar in various other studies which I have not space to enumerate), and keeps the whole thing free from that element of humbug which has ever attended most attempts to reproduce the idiosyncrasies of Italy. I am, however, drawing to the end of my remarks without having mentioned a dozen of those brilliant triumphs in the field of portraiture with which Mr. Sargent's name is preponderantly associated. I jumped from his "Carolus Duran" to the masterpiece of 1881 without speaking of the charming "Madame Pailleron" of 1879, or the picture of this lady's children the following year. Many, or rather most, of Mr. Sargent's sitters have been French, and he has studied the physiognomy of this nation so attentively that a little of it perhaps remains in the brush with which to-day, more than in his first years, he represents other types. I have alluded to his superb "Docteur Pozzi," to whose very handsome, still youthful head and slightly artificial posture he has given so fine a French cast that he might be excused if he should, even on remoter pretexts, find himself reverting to it. This gentleman stands up in his brilliant red dressing-gown with the *prestance* of a princely Vandyck. I should like to commemorate the portrait of a lady of a certain age and of an equally certain interest of appearance—a lady in black, with black hair, a black hat and a vast feather, which was displayed at that entertaining little annual exhibition of the "Mirlitons," in the Place Vendôme. With the exquisite modelling of its face (no one better than Mr. Sargent understands the beauty that resides in exceeding fineness), this head remains in my mind as a masterly rendering of the look of experience—such experience as may be attributed to a woman slightly faded and eminently distinguished. Subject and treatment in this valuable piece are of an equal interest, and in the latter there is an element of positive sympathy which is not always in a high degree the sign of Mr. Sargent's work. What shall I say of the remarkable canvas which, on the occasion of the Salon of 1884, brought the critics about our artist's ears, the already celebrated portrait of "Madame G.?" It is an experiment of a highly original kind, and the painter has had in the case, in regard to what Mr. Ruskin would call the "rightness" of his attempt, the courage of his opinion. A contestable beauty, according to Parisian fame, the lady stands upright beside a table on which her right arm rests, with her body almost fronting the spectator and her face in complete profile. She wears an entirely sleeveless dress of black satin, against which her admirable left arm detaches itself; the line of her harmonious profile has a sharpness which Mr. Sargent does not always seek, and the crescent of Diana, an ornament in diamonds, rests on her singular head. This work had not the good-fortune to please the public at large, and I believe it even excited a kind of unreasoned scandal—an idea sufficiently amusing in the light of some of the manifestations of the plastic effort to which, each year, the Salon stands sponsor. This superb picture, noble in conception and masterly in line, gives to the figure represented something of the high relief of the profiled images on great friezes. It is a work to take or to leave, as the phrase is, and one in regard to which the question of liking or disliking comes promptly to be settled. The author has never gone further in being boldly and consistently himself.

Two of Mr. Sargent's recent productions have been portraits of American ladies whom it must have been a delight to paint; I allude to those of Lady

Playfair and Mrs. Henry White, both of which were seen in the Royal Academy of 1885, and the former subsequently in Boston, where it abides. These things possess, largely, the quality which makes Mr. Sargent so happy as a painter of women—a quality which can best be expressed by a reference to what it is not, to the curiously literal, prosaic, sexless treatment to which, in the commonplace work that looks down at us from the walls of almost all exhibitions, delicate feminine elements have evidently so often been sacrificed. Mr. Sargent handles these elements with a special feeling for them, and they borrow a kind of noble intensity from his brush. This intensity is not absent from the two portraits I just mentioned, that of Lady Playfair and that of Mrs. Henry White; it looks out at us from the erect head and frank animation of the one, and the silvery sheen and shimmer of white satin and white lace which form the setting of the slim tall-ness of the other. In the Royal Academy of 1886 Mr. Sargent was represented by three important canvases, all of which reminded the spectator of how much the brilliant effect he produces in an English exhibition arises from a certain appearance that he has of looking down from a height, a height of cleverness, a sensible giddiness of facility, at the artistic problems of the given case. Sometimes there is even a slight impertinence in it; that, doubtless, was the impression of many of the people who passed, staring, with an ejaculation, before the triumphant group of the three Misses V. These young ladies, seated in a row, with a room much foreshortened for a background, and treated with a certain familiarity of frankness, excited in London a chorus of murmurs not dissimilar to that which it had been the fortune of the portrait exhibited in 1884 to elicit in Paris, and had the further privilege of drawing forth some prodigies of purblind criticism. Works of this character are a genuine service; after the short-lived gibes of the profane have subsided, they are found to have cleared the air. They remind people that the faculty of taking a direct, independent, unborrowed impression is not altogether lost.

In this very rapid review I have accompanied Mr. Sargent to a very recent date. If I have said that observers encumbered with a nervous temperament may at any moment have been anxious about his future, I have it on my conscience to add that the day has not yet come for a complete extinction of this anxiety. Mr. Sargent is so young, in spite of the place allotted to him in these pages, so often a record of long careers and uncontested triumphs that, in spite also of the admirable works he has already produced, his future is the most valuable thing he has to show. We may still ask ourselves what he will do with it, while we indulge the hope that he will see fit to give successors to the two pictures which I have spoken of emphatically as his finest. There is no greater work of art than a great portrait—a truth to be constantly taken to heart by a painter holding in his hands the weapon that Mr. Sargent wields. The gift that he possesses he possesses completely—the immediate perception of the end and of the means. Putting aside the question of the subject (and to a great portrait a common sitter will doubtless not always contribute), the highest result is achieved when to this element of quick perception a certain faculty of brooding reflection is added. I use this name for want of a better, and I mean the quality in the light of which the artist sees deep into his subject, undergoes it, absorbs it, discovers in it new things that were not on the surface, becomes patient with it, and almost reverent, and, in short, enlarges and humanizes the technical problem.

HONORÉ DAUMIER

AS we attempt, at the present day, to write the history of everything, it would be strange if we had happened to neglect the annals of caricature; for the very essence of the art of Cruikshank and Gavarni, of Daumier and Leech, is to be historical; and every one knows how addicted is this great science to discoursing about itself. Many industrious seekers, in England and France, have ascended the stream of time to the source of the modern movement of pictorial satire. The stream of time is in this case mainly the stream of journalism; for social and political caricature, as the present century has practised it, is only journalism made doubly vivid.

The subject indeed is a large one, if we reflect upon it, for many people would tell us that journalism is the greatest invention of our age. If this rich affluent has shared the great fortune of the general torrent, so, on other sides, it touches the fine arts, touches manners, touches morals. All this helps to account for its inexhaustible life; journalism is the criticism of the moment *at* the moment, and caricature is that criticism at once simplified and intensified by a plastic form. We know the satiric image as periodical, and above all as punctual—the characteristics of the printed sheet with which custom has at last inveterately associated it.

This, by-the-way, makes us wonder considerably at the failure of caricature to achieve, as yet, a high destiny in America—a failure which might supply an occasion for much explanatory discourse, much searching of the relations of things. The newspaper has been taught to flourish among us as it flourishes nowhere else, and to flourish moreover on a humorous and irreverent basis; yet it has never taken to itself this helpful concomitant of an unscrupulous spirit and a quick periodicity. The explanation is probably that it needs an old society to produce ripe caricature. The newspaper thrives in the United States, but journalism languishes; for the lively propagation of news is one thing and the large interpretation of it is another. A society has to be old before it becomes critical, and it has to become critical before it can take pleasure in the reproduction of its incongruities by an instrument as impertinent as the indefatigable crayon. Irony, scepticism, pessimism are, in any particular soil, plants of gradual growth, and it is in the art of caricature that they flower most aggressively. Furthermore they must be watered by education—I mean by the education of the eye and hand—all of which things take time. The soil must be rich too, the incongruities must swarm. It is open to doubt whether a pure democracy is very liable to make this particular satiric return upon itself; for which it would seem tha' certain social complications are indispensable. These complications are supplied from the moment a democracy becomes, as we may say, impure from its own point of view; from the moment variations and heresies, deviations or perhaps simple affirmations of taste and temper begin to multiply within it. Such things afford a *point d'appui*; for it is evidently of the essence of caricature to be reactionary. We hasten to add that its satiric force varies immensely in kind and in degree according to the race, or to the individual talent, that takes advantage of it.

I used just now the term pessimism; but that was doubtless in a great measure because I have been turning over a collection of the extraordinarily vivid drawings of Honoré Daumier. The same impression would remain with me, no doubt, if I had been consulting an equal quantity of the work of Gavarni the wittiest, the most literary and most acutely profane of all chartered mockers with the pencil. The feeling of disrespect abides in all these things, the expression of the spirit for which humanity is definable primarily by its weaknesses. For Daumier these weaknesses are altogether ugly and grotesque, while for Gavarni they are either basely graceful or touchingly miserable; but the vision of them in both cases is close and direct. If, on the other hand, we look through a dozen volumes of the collection of *Punch* we get an equal impression of hilarity, but we by no means get an equal impression of irony. Certainly the pages of *Punch* do not reek with pessimism; their "criticism of life" is gentle and forbearing. Leech is positively optimistic; there is at any rate nothing infinite in his irreverence; it touches bottom as soon as it approaches the pretty woman or the nice girl. It is such an apparition as this that really, in Gavarni, awakes the scoffer. Du Maurier is as graceful as Gavarni, but his sense of beauty conjures away almost everything save our minor vices. It is in the exploration of our major ones that Gavarni makes his principal discoveries of charm or of absurdity of attitude. None the less, of course, the general inspiration of both artists is the same: the desire to try the innumerable different ways in which the human subject may *not* be taken seriously.

If this view of that subject, in its plastic manifestations, makes history of a sort, it will not in general be of a kind to convert those persons who find history sad reading. The writer of the present lines remained unconverted, lately, on an occasion on which many cheerful influences were mingled with his impression. They were of a nature to which he usually does full justice, even overestimating perhaps their charm of suggestion; but, at the hour I speak of, the old Parisian quay, the belittered print-shop, the pleasant afternoon, the glimpse of the great Louvre on the other side of the Seine, in the interstices of the sallow *estampes* suspended in window and doorway— all these elements of a rich actuality availed only to mitigate, without transmuting, that general vision of a high, cruel pillory which pieced itself together as I drew specimen after specimen from musty portfolios. I had been passing the shop when I noticed in a small *vitrine*, let into the embrasure of the doorway, half a dozen soiled, striking lithographs, which it took no more than a first glance to recognize as the work of Daumier. They were only old pages of the *Charivari*, torn away from the text and rescued from the injury of time; and they were accompanied with an inscription to the effect that many similar examples of the artist were to be seen within. To become aware of this circumstance was to enter the shop and to find myself promptly surrounded with bulging; *cartons* and tattered relics. These relics—crumpled leaves of the old comic journals of the period from 1830 to 1855—are neither rare nor expensive; but I happened to have lighted on a particularly copious collection, and I made the most of my small good-fortune, in order to transmute it, if possible, into a sort of compensation for my having missed unavoidably, a few months before, the curious exhibition "de la Caricature Moderne" held for several weeks just at hand, in the École des Beaux-Arts.

Daumier was said to have appeared there in considerable force; and it was a loss not to have had that particular opportunity of filling one's mind with him.

There was perhaps a perversity in having wished to do so, strange, indigestible stuff of contemplation as he might appear to be; but the perversity had had an honorable growth. Daumier's great days were in the reign of Louis-Philippe; but in the early years of the Second Empire he still plied his coarse and formidable pencil. I recalled, from a juvenile consciousness, the last failing strokes of it. They used to impress me in Paris, as a child, with their abnormal blackness as well as with their grotesque, magnifying movement, and there was something in them that rather scared a very immature admirer. This small personage, however, was able to perceive later, when he was unfortunately deprived of the chance of studying them, that there were various things in them besides the power to excite a vague alarm. Daumier was perhaps a great artist; at all events unsatisfied curiosity increased in proportion to that possibility.

The first complete satisfaction of it was really in the long hours that I spent in the little shop on the quay. There I filled my mind with him, and there too, at no great cost, I could make a big parcel of these cheap reproductions of his work. This work had been shown in the Ecole des Beaux-Arts as it came from his hand; M. Champfleury, his biographer, his cataloguer and devotee, having poured forth the treasures of a precious collection, as I suppose they would be called in the case of an artist of higher flights. It was only as he was seen by the readers of the comic journals of his day that I could now see him; but I tried to make up for my want of privilege by prolonged immersion. I was not able to take home all the portfolios from the shop on the quay, but I took home what I could, and I went again to turn over the superannuated piles. I liked looking at them on the spot; I seemed still surrounded by the artist's vanished Paris and his extinct Parisians. Indeed no quarter of the delightful city probably shows, on the whole, fewer changes from the aspect it wore during the period of Louis-Philippe, the time when it will ever appear to many of its friends to have been most delightful. The long line of the quay is unaltered, and the rare charm of the river. People came and went in the shop: it is a wonder how many, in the course of an hour, may lift the latch even of an establishment that pretends to no great business. What was all this small, sociable, contentious life but the great Daumier's subject-matter? He was the painter of the Parisian bourgeois, and the voice of the bourgeois was in the air.

M. Champfleury has given a summary of Daumier's career in his smart little *Histoire e la Caricature Moderne,* a record not at all abundant in personal detail. The biographer has told his story better perhaps in his careful catalogue of the artist's productions, the first sketch of which is to be found in *L'Art* for 1878. This copious list is Daumier's real history; his life cannot have been a very different business from his work. I read in the interesting publication of M. Grand-Carteret (*Les Moeurs et la Caricature en France* 1888) that our artist produced nearly 4000 lithographs and a thousand drawings on wood, up to the time when failure of eyesight compelled him to rest. This is not the sort of activity that leaves a man much time for independent adventures, and Daumier was essentially of the type, common in France, of the specialist so immersed in his specialty that he can be painted in only one attitude—a general circumstance which perhaps helps to account for the paucity, in that country, of biography, in our English sense of the word, in proportion to the superabundance of criticism.

Honoré Daumier was born at Marseilles February 26th, 1808; he died on the 11th of the same month, 1879. His main activity, however, was confined to the earlier portion of a career of almost exactly seventy-one years, and I find it affirmed in Vapereau's *Dictionnaire des Contemporains* that he became completely blind between 1850 and 1860. He enjoyed a pension from the State of 2400 francs; but what relief from misery could mitigate a quarter of a century of darkness for a man who had looked out at the world with such vivifying eyes? His father had followed the trade of a glazier, but was otherwise vocal than in the emission of the rich street-cry with which we used all to be familiar, and which has vanished with so many other friendly pedestrian notes. The elder Daumier wrought verses as well as window-panes, and M. Champfleury has disinterred a small volume published by him in 1823. The merit of his poetry is not striking; but he was able to transmit the artistic nature to his son, who, becoming promptly conscious of it, made the inevitable journey to Paris in search of fortune.

The young draughtsman appeared to have missed at first the way to this boon; inasmuch as in the year 1832 he found himself condemned to six months' imprisonment for a lithograph disrespectful to Louis-Philippe. This drawing had appeared in the *Caricature*, an organ of pictorial satire founded in those days by one Philipon, with the aid of a band of young mockers to whom he gave ideas and a direction, and several others, of whom Gavarni, Henry Monnier, Decamps, Grandville, were destined to make themselves a place. M. Eugène Montrosier, in a highly appreciative article on Daumier in *L'Art* for 1878, says that this same Philipon was *le journalisme fait homme*; which did not prevent him—rather in fact fostered such a result—from being perpetually in delicate relations with the government. He had had many horses killed under him, and had led a life of attacks, penalties, suppressions and resurrections. He subsequently established the *Charivari* and launched a publication entitled *L'Association Lithographique Mensuelle*, which brought to light much of Daumier's early work. The artist passed rapidly from seeking his way to finding it, and from an ineffectual to a vigorous form.

In this limited compass and in the case of such a quantity of production it is almost impossible to specify—difficult to pick dozens of examples out of thousands. Daumier became more and more the political spirit of the *Charivari*, or at least the political pencil, for M. Philipon, the breath of whose nostrils was opposition—one perceives from here the little bilious, bristling, ingenious, insistent man—is to be credited with a suggestive share in any enterprise in which he had a hand. This pencil played over public life, over the sovereign, the ministers, the deputies, the peers, the judiciary, the men and the measures, the reputations and scandals of the moment, with a strange, ugly, extravagant, but none the less sane and manly vigor. Daumier's sign is strength above all, and in turning over his pages to-day there is no intensity of force that the careful observer will not concede to him. It is perhaps another matter to assent to the proposition, put forth by his greatest admirers among his countrymen, that he is the first of all caricaturists. To the writer of this imperfect sketch he remains considerably less interesting than Gavarni; and/or a particular reason, which it is difficult to express otherwise than by saying that he is too simple. Simplicity was not Gavarni's fault, and indeed to a large degree it was Daumier's merit. The single grossly ridiculous or almost hauntingly characteristic thing which his figures represent is largely the reason why they still represent life and an unlucky reality years after the names attached to them have parted with a vivifying power. Such vagueness has overtaken them, for the most part, and to such a thin reverberation have they shrunk, the persons and the affairs which were then so intensely sketchable. Daumier handled them with a want of ceremony which would have been brutal were it not for the element of science in his work, making them immense and unmistakable in their drollery, or at least in their grotesqueness; for the term drollery suggests gayety, and Daumier is anything but gay. *Un rude peintre de moeurs*, M. Champfleury calls him; and the phrase expresses his extreme breadth of treatment.

Of the victims of his "rudeness" M. Thiers is almost the only one whom the present generation may recognize without a good deal of reminding, and indeed his hand is relatively light in delineating this personage of few inches and many episodes. M. Thiers must have been dear to the caricaturist, for he belonged to the type that was easy to "do;" it being well known that these gentlemen appreciate public characters in direct proportion to their saliency of feature. When faces are reducible to a few telling strokes their wearers are overwhelmed with the honors of publicity; with which, on the other hand, nothing is more likely to interfere than the possession of a countenance neatly classical. Daumier had only to give M. Thiers the face of a clever owl, and the trick was played. Of course skill was needed to individualize the symbol, but that is what caricaturists propose to themselves. Of how well he succeeded the admirable plate of the lively little minister in a "new dress"—tricked out in the uniform of a general of the First Republic—is a sufficient illustration. The bird of night is not an acute bird, but how the artist has presented the image of a selected specimen! And with what a life-giving pencil the whole figure is put on its feet, what intelligent drawing, what a rich, free stroke! The allusions conveyed in it are to such forgotten things that it is strange to think the personage was, only the other year, still contemporaneous; that he might have been met, on a fine day, taking a few firm steps in a quiet part of the Champs Élysées, with his footman carrying a second overcoat and looking doubly tall behind him. In whatever attitude Daumier depicts him, planted as a tiny boxing-master at the feet of the virtuous colossus in a blouse (whose legs are apart, like those of the Rhodian), in whom the artist represents the People, to watch the match that is about to come off between Ratapoil and M. Berryer, or even in the act of lifting the "parricidal" club of a new repressive law to deal a blow at the Press, an effulgent, diligent, sedentary muse (this picture, by the way, is a perfect specimen of the simple and telling in political caricature)—however, as I say, he takes M. Thiers, there is always a rough indulgence in his crayon, as if he were grateful to him for lending himself so well. He invented Ratapoil as he appropriated Robert Macaire, and as a caricaturist he never fails to put into circulation, when he can, a character to whom he may attribute as many as possible of the affectations or the vices of the day. Robert Macaire, an imaginative, a romantic rascal, was the hero of a highly successful melodrama written for Frederick Lemaitre; but Daumier made him the type of the swindler at large in an age of feverish speculation—the projector of showy companies, the advertiser of worthless shares. There is a whole series of drawings descriptive of his exploits, a hundred masterly plates which, according to M. Champfleury, consecrated Daumier's reputation. The subject, the legend, was in most cases, still according to M. Champfleury, suggested by Philipon. Sometimes it was very witty; as for instance when Bertrand, the muddled acolyte or scraping second fiddle of the hero, objects, in relation to a brilliant scheme which he has just developed, with the part Bertrand is to play, that there are constables in the country, and he promptly replies, "Constables? So much the better—they'll take the shares!" Ratapoil was an evocation of the same general character, but with a difference of *nuance*—the ragged political bully, or hand-to-mouth demagogue, with the smashed tall hat, cocked to one side, the absence of linen, the club half-way up his sleeve, the swagger and pose of being gallant for the people. Ratapoil abounds in the promiscuous drawings that I have looked over, and is always very strong and living, with a considerable element of the sinister, so often in Daumier an accompaniment of the comic. There is an admirable page—it brings the idea down to 1851—in which a sordid but astute peasant, twirling his thumbs on his stomach and looking askance, allows this political adviser to urge upon him in a whisper that there is not a minute to lose—to lose for action, of course—if he wishes to keep his wife, his house, his field, his heifer and his calf. The canny scepticism in the ugly, half-averted face of the typical rustic who considerably suspects his counsellor is indicated by a few masterly strokes.

This is what the student of Daumier recognizes as his science, or, if the word has a better grace, his art. It is what has kept life in his work so long after so many of the occasions of it have been swept into darkness. Indeed, there is no such commentary on renown as the "back numbers" of a comic journal. They show us that at certain moments certain people were eminent, only to make us unsuccessfully try to remember what they were eminent *for*. And the comparative obscurity (comparative, I mean, to the talent of the caricaturist) overtakes even the most justly honored names. M. Berryer was a splendid speaker and a public servant of real distinction and the highest utility; yet the fact that to-day his name is on few men's lips seems to be emphasized by this other fact that we continue to pore over Daumier, in whose plates we happen to come across him. It reminds one afresh how Art is an embalmer, a magician, whom we can never speak too fair. People duly impressed with this truth are sometimes laughed at for their superstitious tone, which is pronounced, according to the fancy of the critic, mawkish, maudlin or hysterical. But it is really difficult to see how any reiteration of the importance of art can overstate the plain facts. It prolongs, it preserves, it consecrates, it raises from the dead. It conciliates, charms, bribes posterity; and it murmurs to mortals, as the old French poet sang to his mistress, "You will be fair only so far as I have said so." When it whispers even to the great, "You depend upon me, and I can do more for you, in the long-run, than any one else," it is scarcely too proud. It puts method and power and the strange, real, mingled air of things into Daumier's black sketchiness, so full of the technical *gras*, the "fat" which French critics commend and which we have no word to express. It puts power above all, and the effect which he best achieves, that of a certain simplification of the attitude or the gesture to an almost symbolic generality. His persons represent only one thing, but they insist tremendously on that, and their expression of it abides with us, unaccompanied with timid detail. It may really be said that they represent only one class—the old and ugly; so that there is proof enough of a special faculty in his having played such a concert, lugubrious though it be, on a single chord. It has been made a reproach to him, says M. Grand-Carteret, that "his work is lacking in two capital elements—*la jeunesse et la femme*;" and the commentator resents his being made to suffer for the deficiency—"as if an artist could be at the same time deep, comic, graceful and pretty; as if all those who have a real value had not created for themselves a form to which they remain confined and a type which they reproduce in all its variations, as soon as they have touched the æsthetic ideal that has been their dream. Assuredly humanity, as this great painter saw it, could not be beautiful; one asks one's self what maiden in her teens, a pretty face, would have done in the midst of these good, plain folk, stunted and elderly, with faces like wrinkled apples. A simple accessory most of the time, woman is for him merely a termagant or a blue-stocking who has turned the corner."

When the eternal feminine, for Daumier appears in neither of these forms he sees it in Madame Chaboulard or Madame Fribochon, the old snuff-taking, gossiping portress, in a nightcap and shuffling *savates*, relating or drinking in the wonderful and the intimate. One of his masterpieces represents three of these dames, lighted by a guttering candle, holding their heads together to discuss the fearful earthquake at Bordeaux, the consequence of the government's allowing the surface of the globe to be unduly dug out in California. The representation of confidential imbecility could not go further. When a man leaves out so much of life as Daumier—youth and beauty and the charm of woman and the loveliness of childhood and the manners of those social groups of whom it may most be said that they *have* manners— when he exhibits a deficiency on this scale it might seem that the question was not to be so easily disposed of as in the very non-apologetic words I have just quoted. All the same (and I confess it is singular), we may feel what Daumier omitted and yet not be in the least shocked by the claim of predominance made for him. It is impossible to spend a couple of hours over him without assenting to this claim, even though there may be a weariness in such a panorama of ugliness and an inevitable reaction from it. This anomaly, and the challenge to explain it which appears to proceed from him, render him, to my sense, remarkably interesting. The artist whose idiosyncrasies, whose limitations, if you will, make us question and wonder, in the light of his fame, has an element of fascination not attaching to conciliatory talents. If M. Eugene Montrosier may say of him without scandalizing us that such and such of his drawings belong to the very highest art, it is interesting (and Daumier profits by the interest) to put one's finger on the reason we are not scandalized.

I think this reason is that, on the whole he is so peculiarly serious. This may seem an odd ground of praise for a jocose draughtsman, and of course what I mean is that his comic force is serious—a very different thin from the absence of comedy. This essential sign of the caricaturist may surely be anything it will so long as it is there. Daumier's figures are almost always either foolish, fatuous politicians or frightened, mystified bourgeois; yet they help him to give us a strong sense of the nature of man. They are some times so serious that they are almost tragic the look of the particular pretension, combined with inanity, is carried almost to madness. There is a magnificent drawing of the series of "Le Public du Salon," old classicists looking up, horrified and scandalized, at the new romantic work of 1830, in which the faces have an appalling gloom of mystification and platitude. We feel that Daumier reproduces admirably the particular life that he sees, because it is the very medium in which he moves. He has no wide horizon; the absolute bourgeois hems him in, and he is a bourgeois himself, without poetic ironies, to whom a big cracked mirror has been given. His thick, strong, manly touch stands, in every way, for so much knowledge. He used to make little images, in clay and in wax (many of them still exist), of the persons he was in the habit of representing, so that they might constantly seem to be "sitting" for him. The caricaturist of that day had not the help of the ubiquitous photograph. Daumier painted actively, as well, in his habitation, all dedicated to work, on the narrow island of St. Louis, where the Seine divides and where the monuments of old Paris stand thick, and the types that were to his purpose pressed close upon him. He had not far to go to encounter the worthy man, in the series of "Les Papas," who is reading the evening paper at the café with so amiable and placid a credulity, while his unnatural little boy, opposite to him, finds sufficient entertainment in the much-satirized *Constitutionnel*. The bland absorption of the papa, the face of the man who believes everything he sees in the newspaper, is as near as Daumier often comes to positive gentleness of humor. Of the same family is the poor gentleman, in "Actualités," seen, in profile, under a doorway where he has taken refuge from a torrent of rain, who looks down at his neat legs with a sort of speculative contrition and says. "To think of my having just ordered two pairs of white trousers." The *tout petit bourgeois* palpitates in both these sketches.

I must repeat that it is absurd to pick half a dozen at hazard, out of five thousand; yet a few selections are the only way to call attention to his strong drawing. This has a virtuosity of its own, for all its hit-or-miss appearance. Whatever he touches—the nude, in the swimming-baths on the Seine, the intimations of landscape, when his *petits rentiers* go into the suburbs for a Sunday—acquires relief and character, Docteur Véron, a celebrity of the reign of Louis-Philippe, a Mæcenas of the hour, a director of the opera, author of the *Mémoires d'un Bourgeois de Paris*—this temporary "illustration," who appears to have been almost indecently ugly, would not be vivid to us to-day had not Daumier, who was often effective at his expense, happened to have represented him, in some crisis of his career, as a sort of naked inconsolable Vitellius. He renders the human body with a cynical sense of its possible flabbiness and an intimate acquaintance with its structure. "Une Promenade Conjugale," in the series of "Tout ce qu'on voudra," portrays a hillside, on a summer afternoon, on which a man has thrown himself on his back to rest, with his arms locked under his head. His fat, full-bosomed, middle-aged wife, under her parasol, with a bunch of field-flowers in her hand, looks down at him patiently and seems to say, "Come, my dear, get up." There is surely no great point in this; the only point is life, the glimpse of the little snatch of poetry in prose. It is a matter of a few broad strokes of the crayon; yet the pleasant laziness of the man, the idleness of the day, the fragment of homely, familiar dialogue, the stretch of the field with a couple of trees merely suggested, have a communicative truth.

I perhaps exaggerate all this, and in insisting upon the merit of Daumier may appear to make light of the finer accomplishment of several more modern talents, in England and France, who have greater ingenuity and subtlety and have carried qualities of execution so, much further. In looking at this complicated younger work, which has profited so by experience and comparison, it is inevitable that we should perceive it to be infinitely more cunning. On the other hand Daumier, moving in his contracted circle, has an impressive depth. It comes back to his strange seriousness. He is a draughtsman by race, and if he has not extracted the same brilliancy from training, or perhaps even from effort and experiment, as some of his successors, does not his richer satiric and sympathetic feeling more than make up the difference?

However this question may be answered, some of his drawings belong to the class of the unforgetable. It may be a perversity of prejudice, but even the little cut of the "Connoisseurs," the group of gentlemen collected round a picture and criticising it in various attitudes of sapience and sufficiency, appears to me to have the strength that abides. The criminal in the dock, the flat-headed murderer, bending over to speak to his advocate, who turns a whiskered, professional, anxious head to caution and remind him. tells a large, terrible story and awakes a recurrent shudder. We see the gray court-room, we feel the personal suspense and the immensity of justice. The "Saltimbanques," reproduced in *L'Art* for 1878, is a page of tragedy, the finest of a cruel series. M. Eugène Montrosier says of it that "The drawing is masterly, incomparably firm, the composition superb, the general impression quite of the first order." It exhibits a pair of lean, hungry mountebanks, a clown and a harlequin beating the drum and trying a comic attitude to attract the crowd, at a fair, to a poor booth in front of which a painted canvas, offering to view a simpering fat woman, is suspended. But the crowd doesn't come, and the battered tumblers, with their furrowed cheeks, go through their pranks in the void. The whole thing is symbolic and full of grim-ness, imagination and pity. It is the sense that we shall find in him, mixed with his homelier extravagances, an element prolific in indications of this order that draws us back to Daumier.

AFTER THE PLAY

The play was not over when the curtain fell, four months ago; it was continued in a supplementary act or epilogue which took place immediately afterwards. "Come home to tea," Florentia said to certain friends who had stopped to speak to her in the lobby of the little theatre in Soho—they had been present at a day performance by the company of the Theatre Libre, transferred for a week from Paris; and three of these—Auberon and Dorriforth, accompanying Amicia—turned up so expeditiously that the change of scene had the effect of being neatly executed. The short afterpiece—it was in truth very slight—began with Amicia's entrance and her declaration that she would never again go to an afternoon performance: it was such a horrid relapse into the real to find it staring at you through the ugly daylight on coming out of the blessed fictive world.

Dorriforth. Ah, you touch there on one of the minor sorrows of life. That's an illustration of the general change that comes to pass in us as we grow older, if we have ever loved the stage: the fading of the glamour and the mystery that surround it.

Auberon. Do you call it a minor sorrow? It's one of the greatest. And nothing can mitigate it.

Amicia. Wouldn't it be mitigated a little if the stage were a trifle better? You must remember how that has changed.

Auberon. Never, never: it's the same old stage. The change is in ourselves.

Florentia. Well, I never would have given an evening to what we have just seen. If one could have put it in between luncheon and tea, well enough. But one's evenings are too precious.

Dorriforth. Note that—it's very important.

Florentia. I mean too precious for that sort of thing.

Auberon. Then you didn't sit spellbound by the little history of the Due d'Enghien?

Florentia. I sat yawning. Heavens, what a piece!

Amicia. Upon my word I liked it. The last act made me cry.

Dorriforth. Wasn't it a curious, interesting specimen of some of the things that are worth trying: an attempt to sail closer to the real?

Auberon. How much closer? The fiftieth part of a point—it isn't calculable.

Florentia. It was just like any other play—I saw no difference. It had neither a plot, nor a subject, nor dialogue, nor situations, nor scenery, nor costumes, nor acting.

Amicia. Then it was hardly, as you say, just like any other play.

Auberon. Florentia should have said like any other *bad* one. The only way it differed seemed to be that it was bad in theory as well as in fact.

Amicia. It's a *morceau de vie*, as the French say.

Auberon. Oh, don't begin on the French!

Amicia. It's a French experiment—*que voulez-vous?*

Auberon. English experiments will do.

Dorriforth. No doubt they would—if there *were* any. But I don't see them.

Amicia. Fortunately: think what some of them might be! Though Florentia saw nothing I saw many things in this poor little shabby "Due d'Enghien," coming over to our roaring London, where the dots have to be so big on the i's, with its barely audible note of originality. It appealed to me, touched me, offered me a poignant suggestion of the way things happen in life.

Auberon. In life they happen clumsily, stupidly, meanly. One goes to the theatre just for the refreshment of seeing them happen in another way—in symmetrical, satisfactory form, with unmistakable effect and just at the right moment.

Dorriforth. It shows how the same cause may produce the most diverse consequences. In this truth lies the only hope of art.

Auberon. Oh, art, art—don't talk about art!

Amicia. Mercy, we must talk about something!

Dorriforth. Auberon hates generalizations. Nevertheless I make bold to say that we go to the theatre in the same spirit in which we read a novel, some of us to find one thing and some to find another; and according as we look for the particular thing we find it.

Auberon. That's a profound remark.

Florentia. We go to find amusement: that, surely, is what we all go for.

Amicia. There's such a diversity in our idea of amusement.

Auberon. Don't you impute to people more ideas than they have?

Dorriforth. Ah, one must do that or one couldn't talk about them. We go to be interested; to be absorbed, beguiled and to lose ourselves, to give ourselves up, in short, to a charm.

Florentia. And the charm is the strange, the extraordinary.

Amicia. Ah, speak for yourself! The charm is the recognition of what we know, what we feel.

Dorriforth. See already how you differ.

"SO!"

What we surrender ourselves to is the touch of nature, the sense of life.

Amicia. The first thing is to believe.

Florentia. The first thing, on the contrary, is to *dis*believe.

Auberon. Lord, listen to them!

Dorriforth. The first thing is to folio—to care.

Florentia. I read a novel, I go to the theatre, to forget.

Amicia. To forget what?

Florentia. To forget life; to thro myself into something more beautiful more exciting: into fable and romance.

Dorriforth. The attraction of fable and romance is that it's about *us*, about you and me—or people whose power to suffer and to enjoy is the same as ours. In other words, we *live* their experience, for the time, and that's hardly escaping from life.

Florentia. I'm not at all particular as to what you call it. Call it an escape from the common, the prosaic, the immediate.

Dorriforth. You couldn't put it better. That's the life that art, with Auberon's permission, gives us; that's the distinction it confers. This is why the greatest commonness is when our guide turns out a vulgar fellow—the angel, as we had supposed him, who has taken us by the hand. Then what becomes of our escape?

Florentia. It's precisely then that I complain of him. He leads us into foul and dreary places—into flat and foolish deserts.

Dorriforth. He leads us into his own mind, his own vision of things: that's the only place into which the poet *can* lead us. It's there that he finds "As You Like It," it is there that he finds "Comus," or "The Way of the World," or the Christmas pantomime. It is when he betrays us, after he has got us in and locked the door, when he can't keep from us that we are in a bare little hole and that there are no pictures on the walls, it is then that the immediate and the foolish overwhelm us.

Amicia. That's what I liked in the piece we have been looking at. There was an artistic intention, and the little room wasn't bare: there was sociable company in it. The actors were very humble aspirants, they were common—

Auberon. Ah, when the French give their mind to that—!

Amicia. Nevertheless they struck me as recruits to an interesting cause, which as yet (the house was so empty) could confer neither money nor glory. They had the air, poor things, of working for love.

Auberon. For love of what?

Amicia. Of the whole little enterprise—the idea of the Théâtre Libre.

Florentia. Gracious, what you see in things! Don't you suppose they were paid?

Amicia. I know nothing about it. I liked their shabbiness—they had only what was indispensable in the way of dress and scenery. That often pleases me: the imagination, in certain cases, is more finely persuaded by the little than by the much.

Dorriforth. I see what Amicia means.

Florentia. I'll warrant you do, and a great deal more besides.

Dorriforth. When the appointments are meagre and sketchy the responsibility that rests upon the actors becomes a still more serious thing, and the spectator's observation of the way they rise to it a pleasure more intense. The face and the voice are more to the purpose than acres of painted canvas, and a touching intonation, a vivid gesture or two, than an army of supernumeraries.

Auberon. Why not have everything—the face, the voice, the touching intonations, the vivid gestures, the acres of painted canvas, *and* the army of supernumeraries? Why not use bravely and intelligently every resource of which the stage disposes? What else was Richard Wagner's great theory, in producing his operas at Bayreuth?

Dorriforth. Why not, indeed? That would be the ideal. To have the picture complete at the same time the figures do their part in producing the particular illusion required—what a perfection and what a joy! I know no answer to that save the aggressive, objectionable fact. Simply look at the stage of to-day and observe that these two branches of the matter never do happen to go together. There is evidently a corrosive principle in the large command of machinery and decorations—a germ of perversion and corruption. It gets the upperhand—it becomes the master. It is so much less easy to get good actors than good scenery and to represent a situation by the delicacy of personal art than by "building it in" and having everything real. Surely there is no reality worth a farthing, on the stage, but what the actor gives, and only when he has learned his business up to the hilt need he concern himself with his material accessories. He hasn't a decent respect for his art unless he be ready to render his part as if the whole illusion depended on that alone and the accessories didn't exist. The acting is everything or it's nothing. It ceases to be everything as soon as something else becomes very important. This is the case, to-day, on the London stage: something else is very important. The public have been taught to consider it so: the clever machinery has ended by operating as a bribe and a blind. Their sense of the rest of the matter has gone to the dogs, as you may perceive when you hear a couple of occupants of the stalls talking, in a tone that excites your curiosity, about a performance that's "splendid."

Amicia. Do you ever hear the occupants of the stalls talking? Never, in the *entr'actes*, have I detected, on their lips, a criticism or a comment.

Dorriforth. Oh, they say "splendid"—distinctly! But a question or two reveals that their reference is vague: they don't themselves know whether they mean the art of the actor or that of the stage-carpenter.

Auberon. Isn't that confusion a high result of taste? Isn't it what's called a feeling for the *ensemble?* The artistic effect, as a whole, is so welded together that you can't pick out the parts.

Dorriforth. Precisely; that's what it is in the best cases, and some examples are wonderfully clever.

Florentia. Then what fault do you find? Dorriforth. Simply this—that the whole is a pictorial whole, not a dramatic one. There is something indeed that you can't pick out, for the very good reason that—in any serious sense of the word—it isn't there.

Florentia. The public has taste, then, if it recognizes and delights in a fine picture.

Dorriforth. I never said it hadn't, so far as that goes. The public likes to be amused, and small blame to it. It isn't very particular about the means, but it has rather a preference for amusements that I believes to be "improving," other things being equal. I don't think it's either very intelligent or at all opinionated, the dear old public it takes humbly enough what is given it and it doesn't cry for the moon. It has an idea that fine scenery is an appeal to its nobler part, and that it shows a nice critical sense in preferring it to poor. That's a real intellectual flight, for the public.

Auberon. Very well, its preference is right, and why isn't that a perfectly legitimate state of things?

Dorriforth. Why isn't it? It distinctly *is!* Good scenery and poor acting are better than poor scenery with the same sauce. Only it becomes then another matter: we are no longer talking about the drama.

Auberon. Very likely that's the future of the drama, in London—an immense elaboration of the picture.

Dorriforth. My dear fellow, you take the words out of my mouth. An immense elaboration of the picture and an immense sacrifice of everything else: it would take very little more to persuade me that that will be the only formula for our children. It's all right, when once we have buried our dead. I have no doubt that the scenic part of the art, remarkable as some of its achievements already appear to us, is only in its infancy, and that we are destined to see wonders done that we now but faintly conceive. The probable extension of the mechanical arts is infinite. "Built in," forsooth! We shall see castles and cities and mountains and rivers built in. Everything points that way; especially the constitution of the contemporary multitude. It is huge and good-natured and common. It likes big, unmistakable, knock-down effects; it likes to get its money back in palpable, computable change. It's in a tremendous hurry, squeezed together, with a sort of generalized gape, and the last thing it expects of you is that you will spin things fine. You can't portray a character, alas, or even, vividly, any sort of human figure, unless, in some degree, you do that. Therefore the theatre, inevitably accommodating itself, will be at last a landscape without figures. I mean, of course, without figures that count. There will be little illustrations of costume stuck about—dressed manikins; but they'll have nothing to say: they won't even go through the form of speech.

Amicia. What a hideous prospect!

Dorriforth. Not necessarily, for we shall have grown used to it: we shall, as I say, have buried our dead. To-day it's cruel, because our old ideals are only dying, they are *in extremis*, they are virtually defunct, but they are above-ground—we trip and stumble on them. We shall eventually lay them tidily away. This is a bad moment, because it's a moment of transition, and we still *miss* the old superstition, the bravery of execution, the eloquence of the lips, the interpretation of character. We miss these things, of course, in proportion as the ostensible occasion for them is great; we miss them particularly, for instance, when the curtain rises on Shakespeare. Then we are conscious of a certain divine dissatisfaction, of a yearning for that which isn't. But we shall have got over this discomfort on the day when we have accepted the ostensible occasion as merely and frankly ostensible, and the real one as having nothing to do with it.

Florentia. I don't follow you. As I'm one of the squeezed, gaping public, I must be dense and vulgar. You do, by-the-way, immense injustice to that body. They do care for character—care much for it. Aren't they perpetually talking about the actor's conception of it?

Dorriforth. Dear lady, what better proof can there be of their ineptitude, and that painted canvas and real water are the only things they understand? The vanity of wasting time over that!

Auberon. Over what?

Dorriforth. The actor's conception of a part. It's the refuge of observers who are no observers and critics who are no critics. With what on earth have we to do save his execution?

Florentia. I don't in the least agree with you.

Amicia. Are you very sure, my poor Dorriforth?

326

Auberon. Give him rope and he'll hang himself.

Dorriforth. It doesn't need any great license to ask who in the world holds in his bosom the sacred secret of the right conception. All the actor can do is to give us his. We must take that one for granted, we make him a present of it. He must impose his conception upon us—

Auberon (interrupting). I thought you said we accepted it.

Dorriforth. Impose it upon our *attention*. clever Auberon. It is because we accept his idea that he must repay us by making it vivid, by showing us how valuable it is. We give him a watch: he must show us what time it keeps. He winds it up, that is he executes the conception, and his execution is what we criticise, if we be so moved. Can anything be more absurd than to hear people discussing the conception of a part of which the execution doesn't exist—the idea of a character which never arrives at form? Think what it is, that form, as an accomplished actor may give it to us, and admit that we have enough to do to hold him to this particular honor.

Auberon. Do you mean to say you don't think some conceptions are better than some others?

Dorriforth. Most assuredly, some are better: the proof of the pudding is in the eating. The best are those which yield the most points, which have the largest face; those, in other words, that are the most demonstrable, or, in other words still, the most actable. The most intelligent performer is he who recognizes most surely this "actable" and distinguishes in it the more from the less. But we are so far from being in possession of a subjective pattern to which we have a right to hold him that he is entitled directly to contradict any such absolute by presenting us with different versions of the same text, each completely colored, completely consistent with itself. Every actor in whom the artistic life is strong must often feel the challenge to do that. I should never think, for instance, of contesting an actress's right to represent Lady Macbeth as a charming, insinuating woman, if she really sees the figure that way. I may be surprised at such a vision; but so far from being scandalized, I am positively thankful for the extension of knowledge, of pleasure, that she is able to open to me.

Auberon. A reading, as they say, either commends itself to one's sense of truth or it doesn't. In the one case—

Dorriforth. In the one case I recognize—even—or especially—when the presumption may have been against the particular attempt, a consummate illustration of what art can do. In the other I moralize indulgently upon human rashness.

Florentia. You have an assurance *à taute épreuve*; but you are deplorably superficial. There is a whole group of plays and a whole category of acting to which your generalizations quite fail to apply. Help me, Auberon.

Auberon. You're easily exhausted. I suppose she means that it's far from true everywhere that the scenery is everything. It may be true—I don't say it is!—of two or three good-natured playhouses in London. It isn't true—how can it be?—of the provincial theatres or of the others in the capital. Put it even that they would be all scenery if they could; they can't, poor things—so they have to provide acting.

Dorriforth. They have to, fortunately; but what do we hear of it?

Florentia. How do you mean, what do we hear of it?

Dorriforth. In what trumpet of fame does it reach us? They do what they can, the performers Auberon alludes to, and they are brave souls. But I am speaking of the conspicuous cases, of the exhibitions that draw.

Florentia. There is good acting that draws; one could give you names and places.

Dorriforth. I have already guessed those you mean. But when it isn't too much a matter of the paraphernalia it is too little a matter of the play. A play nowadays is a rare bird. I should like to see ¦ one. **Florentia.** There are lots of them, all the while—the newspapers talk about them. People talk about them at dinners.

Dorriforth. What do they say about them?

Florentia. The newspapers?

Dorriforth. No, I don't care for *them*. The people at dinners.

Florentia. Oh. they don't say anything in particular.

Dorriforth. Doesn't that seem to show the effort isn't very suggestive?

Amicia. The conversation at dinners certainly isn't.

Dorriforth. I mean our contemporary drama. To begin with, you can't find it there's no text.

Florentia. No text?

Auberon. So much the better!

Dorriforth. So much the better if there is to be no criticism. There is only a dirt prompter's book. One can't put one's hand upon it; one doesn't know what one is discussing. There is no "authority"—nothing is ever published.

Amicia. The pieces wouldn't bear that.

Dorriforth. It would be a small ordeal to resist—if there were anything in them. Look at the novels!

Amicia. The text is the French *brochure*. The "adaptation" is unprintable.

Dorriforth. That's where it's so wrong, It ought at least to be as good as the original.

Auberon. Aren't there some "rights" to protect—some risk of the play being stolen if it's published?

Dorriforth. There may be—I don't know. Doesn't that only prove how little important we regard the drama as being, and how little seriously we take it, if we won't even trouble ourselves to bring about decent civil conditions for its existence? What have we to do with the French *brochure?* how does that help us to represent our own life, our manners, our customs, our ideas, our English types, our English world? Such a field for comedy, for tragedy, for portraiture, for satire, as they all make–such subjects as they would yield! Think of London alone—what a matchless hunting-ground for the satirist— the most magnificent that ever was. If the occasion always produced the man London would have produced an Aristophanes. But somehow it doesn't.

Florentia. Oh, types and ideas, Aristophanes and satire—!

Dorriforth. I'm too ambitious, you mean? I shall presently show you that I'm not ambitious at all. Everything makes against that—I am only reading the signs.

Auberon. The plays are arranged to be as English as possible: they are altered, they are fitted.

Dorriforth. Fitted? Indeed they are, and to the capacity of infants. They are in too many cases made vulgar, puerile, barbarous. They are neither fish nor flesh, and with all the point that's left out and all the naïveté that's put in, they cease to place before us any coherent appeal or any recognizable society.

Auberon. They often make good plays to act, all the same.

Dorriforth. They may; but they don't make good plays to see or to hear. The theatre consists of two things, *que diable*—of the stage and the drama, and I don't see how you can have it unless you have both, or how you can have either unless you have the other. They are the two blades of a pair of scissors.

Auberon. You are very unfair to native talent. There are lots of *strictly original* plays—

Amicia. Yes, they put that expression on the posters.

Auberon. I don't know what they put on the posters; but the plays are written and acted—produced with great success.

Dorriforth. Produced—partly. A play isn't fully produced until it is in a form in which you can refer to it. We have to talk in the air. I can refer to my Congreve, but I can't to my Pinero. {*}

* *Since the above was written several of Mr. Pinero's plays have been published.*

Florentia. The authors are not bound to publish them if they don't wish.

Dorriforth. Certainly not, nor are they in that case bound to insist on one's not being a little vague about them. They are perfectly free to withhold them; they may have very good reasons for it, and I can imagine some that would be excellent and worthy of all respect. But their withholding them is one of the signs.

Auberon. What signs?

Dorriforth. Those I just spoke of—those we are trying to read together. The signs that ambition and desire are folly, that the sun of the drama has set, that the matter isn't worth talking about, that it has ceased to be an interest for serious folk, and that everything—everything, I mean, that's anything—is over. The sooner we recognize it the sooner to sleep, the sooner we get clear of misleading illusions and are purged of the bad blood that disappointment makes. It's a pity, because the theatre—after every allowance is made—*might* have been a fine thing. At all events it was a pleasant—it was really almost a noble—dream. *Requiescat!*

Florentia. I see nothing to confirm your absurd theory. I delight in the play; more people than ever delight in it with me; more people than ever go to it, and there are ten theatres in London where there were two of old.

Dorriforth. Which is what was to demonstrated. Whence do they derive their nutriment?

Auberon. Why, from the enormous public.

Dorriforth. My dear fellow, I'm not talking of the box-office. What wealth of dramatic, of histrionic production have we to meet that enormous demand? There will be twenty theatres ten years hence where there are ten to-day, and there will be, no doubt, ten times as many people "delighting in them," like Florentla. But it won't alter the fact that our dream will have been dreamed. Florentia said a word when we came in which alone speaks volumes.

Florentia. What was my word?

331

Auberon. You are sovereignly unjust to native talent among the actors—I leave the dramatists alone. There are many who do excellent, independent work; strive for perfection, completeness—in short, the things we want.

Dorriforth. I am not in the least unjust to them—I only pity them: they have so little to put *sous la dent*. It must seem to them at times that no one will work for them, that they are likely to starve for parts—forsaken of gods and men.

Florentia. If they work, then, in solitude and sadness, they have the more honor, and one should recognize more explicitly their great merit.

Dorriforth. Admirably said. Their laudable effort is precisely the one little loop-hole that I see of escape from the general doom. Certainly we must try to enlarge it—that small aperture into the blue. We must fix our eyes on it and make much of it, exaggerate it, do anything with it that may contribute to restore a working faith. Precious that must be to the sincere spirits on the stage who are conscious of all the other things—formidable things—that rise against them.

Amicia. What other things do you mean?

Dorriforth. Why, for one thing, the grossness and brutality of London, with its scramble, its pressure, its hustle of engagements, of preoccupations, its long distances, its late hours, its nightly dinners, its innumerable demands on the attention, its general congregation of influences fatal to the isolation, to the punctuality, to the security, of the dear old playhouse spell. When Florentia said in her charming way—

Florentia. Here's my dreadful speech at last.

Dorriforth. When you said that you went to the Théâtre Libre in the afternoon because you couldn't spare an evening, I recognized the death-knell of the drama. *Time*, the very breath of its nostrils, is lacking. Wagner was clever to go to leisurely Bayreuth among the hills—the Bayreuth of spacious days, a paradise of "development."

Talk to a London audience of "development!" The long runs would, if necessary, put the whole question into a nutshell. Figure to yourself, for then the question is answered, how an intelligent actor must loathe them, and what a cruel negation he must find in them of the artistic life, the life of which the very essence is variety of practice, freshness of experiment, and to feel that one must do many things in turn to do any one of them completely.

Auberon. I don't in the least understand your *acharnement*, in view of the vagueness of your contention.

Dorriforth. My *acharnement* is your little joke, and my contention is a little lesson in philosophy.

Florentia. I prefer a lesson in taste. I had one the other night at the "Merry Wives."

Dorriforth. If you come to that, so did I!

Amicia. So she does spare an evening sometimes.

Florentia. It was all extremely quiet and comfortable, and I don't in the least recognize Dorriforth's lurid picture of the dreadful conditions. There was no scenery—at least not too much; there was just enough, and it was very pretty, and it was in its place.

Dorriforth. And what else was there?

Florentia. There was very good acting.

Amicia. I also went, and I thought it all, for a sportive, wanton thing, quite painfully ugly.

Auberon. Uglier than that ridiculous black room, with the invisible people groping about in it, of your precious "Duc d'Enghien?"

Dorriforth. The black room is doubtless not the last word of art, but it struck me as a successful application of a happy idea. The contrivance was perfectly simple—a closer night effect than is usually attempted, with a few guttering candles, which threw high shadows over the bare walls, on the table of the court-martial. Out of the gloom came the voices and tones of the distinguishable figures, and it is perhaps a fancy of mine that it made them—given the situation, of course—more impressive and dramatic.

Auberon. You rail against scenery, but what could belong more to the order of things extraneous to what you perhaps a little priggishly call the delicacy of personal art than the arrangement you are speaking of?

Dorriforth. I was talking of the abuse of scenery. I never said anything so idiotic as that the effect isn't helped by an appeal to the eye and an adumbration of the whereabouts.

Auberon. But where do you draw the line and fix the limit? What is the exact dose?

Dorriforth. It's a question of taste and tact.

Florentia. And did you find taste and tact in that coal-hole of the Théâtre Libre?

Dorriforth. Coal-hole is again your joke. I found a strong impression in it—an impression of the hurried, extemporized cross-examination, by night, of an impatient and mystified prisoner, whose dreadful fate had been determined in advance, who was to be shot, high-handedly, in the dismal dawn. The arrangement didn't worry and distract me: it was simplifying, intensifying. It gave, what a judicious *mise-en-scène* should always do, the essence of the matter, and left the embroidery to the actors.

Florentia. At the "Merry Wives," where you could see your hand before your face, I could make out the embroidery.

Dorriforth. Could you, under Falstaff's pasteboard cheeks and the sad disfigurement of his mates? There was no excess of scenery, Auberon says. Why, Falstaff's very person was nothing *but* scenery. A false face, a false figure, false hands, false legs—scarcely a square inch on which the irrepressible humor of the rogue could break into illustrative touches. And he is so human, so expressive, of so rich a physiognomy. One would rather Mr. Beerbohm Tree should have played the part in his own clever, elegant slimness—-that would at least have represented life. A Falstaff all "make-up" is an opaque substance.

This seems to me an example of what the rest still more suggested, that in dealing with a production like the "Merry Wives" really the main quality to put forward is discretion. You must resolve such a production, as a thing represented, into a tone that the imagination can take an aesthetic pleasure in. Its grossness must be transposed, as it were, to a fictive scale, a scale of fainter tints and generalized signs. A filthy, eruptive, realistic Bardolph and Pistol overlay the romantic with the literal. Relegate them and blur them, to the eye; let their blotches be constructive and their raggedness relative.

Amicia. Ah, it was *so* ugly!

Dorriforth. What a pity then, after all, there wasn't more painted canvas to divert you! Ah, decidedly, the theatre of the future must be that.

Florentia. Please remember your theory that our life's a scramble, and suffer me to go and dress for dinner.

1889.

RODERICK HUDSON

CHAPTER I. Rowland

Mallet had made his arrangements to sail for Europe on the first of September, and having in the interval a fortnight to spare, he determined to spend it with his cousin Cecilia, the widow of a nephew of his father. He was urged by the reflection that an affectionate farewell might help to exonerate him from the charge of neglect frequently preferred by this lady. It was not that the young man disliked her; on the contrary, he regarded her with a tender admiration, and he had not forgotten how, when his cousin had brought her home on her marriage, he had seemed to feel the upward sweep of the empty bough from which the golden fruit had been plucked, and had then and there accepted the prospect of bachelorhood. The truth was, that, as it will be part of the entertainment of this narrative to exhibit, Rowland Mallet had an uncomfortably sensitive conscience, and that, in spite of the seeming paradox, his visits to Cecilia were rare because she and her misfortunes were often uppermost in it. Her misfortunes were three in number: first, she had lost her husband; second, she had lost her money (or the greater part of it); and third, she lived at Northampton, Massachusetts. Mallet's compassion was really wasted, because Cecilia was a very clever woman, and a most skillful counter-plotter to adversity. She had made herself a charming home, her economies were not obtrusive, and there was always a cheerful flutter in the folds of her crape. It was the consciousness of all this that puzzled Mallet whenever he felt tempted to put in his oar. He had money and he had time, but he never could decide just how to place these gifts gracefully at Cecilia's service. He no longer felt like marrying her: in these eight years that fancy had died a natural death. And yet her extreme cleverness seemed somehow to make charity difficult and patronage impossible. He would rather chop off his hand than offer her a check, a piece of useful furniture, or a black silk dress; and yet there was some sadness in seeing such a bright, proud woman living in such a small, dull way. Cecilia had, moreover, a turn for sarcasm, and her smile, which was her pretty feature, was never so pretty as when her sprightly phrase had a lurking scratch in it. Rowland remembered that, for him, she was all smiles, and suspected, awkwardly, that he ministered not a little to her sense of the irony of things. And in truth, with his means, his leisure, and his opportunities, what had he done? He had an unaffected suspicion of his uselessness. Cecilia, meanwhile, cut out her own dresses, and was personally giving her little girl the education of a princess.

This time, however, he presented himself bravely enough; for in the way of activity it was something definite, at least, to be going to Europe and to be meaning to spend the winter in Rome. Cecilia met him in the early dusk at the gate of her little garden, amid a studied combination of floral perfumes. A rosy widow of twenty-eight, half cousin, half hostess, doing the honors of an odorous cottage on a midsummer evening, was a phenomenon to which the young man's imagination was able to do ample justice. Cecilia was always gracious, but this evening she was almost joyous. She was in a happy mood, and Mallet imagined there was a private reason for it—a reason quite distinct from her pleasure in receiving her honored kinsman. The next day he flattered himself he was on the way to discover it.

For the present, after tea, as they sat on the rose-framed porch, while Rowland held his younger cousin between his knees, and she, enjoying her situation, listened timorously for the stroke of bedtime, Cecilia insisted on talking more about her visitor than about herself.

"What is it you mean to do in Europe?" she asked, lightly, giving a turn to the frill of her sleeve—just such a turn as seemed to Mallet to bring out all the latent difficulties of the question.

"Why, very much what I do here," he answered. "No great harm."

"Is it true," Cecilia asked, "that here you do no great harm? Is not a man like you doing harm when he is not doing positive good?"

"Your compliment is ambiguous," said Rowland.

"No," answered the widow, "you know what I think of you. You have a particular aptitude for beneficence. You have it in the first place in your character. You are a benevolent person. Ask Bessie if you don't hold her more gently and comfortably than any of her other admirers."

"He holds me more comfortably than Mr. Hudson," Bessie declared, roundly.

Rowland, not knowing Mr. Hudson, could but half appreciate the eulogy, and Cecilia went on to develop her idea. "Your circumstances, in the second place, suggest the idea of social usefulness. You are intelligent, you are well-informed, and your charity, if one may call it charity, would be discriminating. You are rich and unoccupied, so that it might be abundant. Therefore, I say, you are a person to do something on a large scale. Bestir yourself, dear Rowland, or we may be taught to think that virtue herself is setting a bad example."

"Heaven forbid," cried Rowland, "that I should set the examples of virtue! I am quite willing to follow them, however, and if I don't do something on the grand scale, it is that my genius is altogether imitative, and that I have not recently encountered any very striking models of grandeur. Pray, what shall I do? Found an orphan asylum, or build a dormitory for Harvard College? I am not rich enough to do either in an ideally handsome way, and I confess that, yet awhile, I feel too young to strike my grand coup. I am holding myself ready for inspiration. I am waiting till something takes my fancy irresistibly. If inspiration comes at forty, it will be a hundred pities to have tied up my money-bag at thirty."

"Well, I give you till forty," said Cecilia. "It 's only a word to the wise, a notification that you are expected not to run your course without having done something handsome for your fellow-men."

Nine o'clock sounded, and Bessie, with each stroke, courted a closer embrace. But a single winged word from her mother overleaped her successive intrenchments. She turned and kissed her cousin, and deposited an irrepressible tear on his moustache. Then she went and said her prayers to her mother: it was evident she was being admirably brought up. Rowland, with the permission of his hostess, lighted a cigar and puffed it awhile in silence. Cecilia's interest in his career seemed very agreeable. That Mallet was without vanity I by no means intend to affirm; but there had been times when, seeing him accept, hardly less deferentially, advice even more peremptory than the

341

widow's, you might have asked yourself what had become of his vanity. Now, in the sweet-smelling starlight, he felt gently wooed to egotism. There was a project connected with his going abroad which it was on his tongue's end to communicate. It had no relation to hospitals or dormitories, and yet it would have sounded very generous. But it was not because it would have sounded generous that poor Mallet at last puffed it away in the fumes of his cigar. Useful though it might be, it expressed most imperfectly the young man's own personal conception of usefulness. He was extremely fond of all the arts, and he had an almost passionate enjoyment of pictures. He had seen many, and he judged them sagaciously. It had occurred to him some time before that it would be the work of a good citizen to go abroad and with all expedition and secrecy purchase certain valuable specimens of the Dutch and Italian schools as to which he had received private proposals, and then present his treasures out of hand to an American city, not unknown to aesthetic fame, in which at that time there prevailed a good deal of fruitless aspiration toward an art-museum. He had seen himself in imagination, more than once, in some mouldy old saloon of a Florentine palace, turning toward the deep embrasure of the window some scarcely-faded Ghirlandaio or Botticelli, while a host in reduced circumstances pointed out the lovely drawing of a hand. But he imparted none of these visions to Cecilia, and he suddenly swept them away with the declaration that he was of course an idle, useless creature, and that he would probably be even more so in Europe than at home. "The only thing is," he said, "that there I shall seem to be doing something. I shall be better entertained, and shall be therefore, I suppose, in a better humor with life. You may say that that is just the humor a useless man should keep out of. He should cultivate discontentment. I did a good many things when I was in Europe before, but I did not spend a winter in Rome. Every one assures me that this is a peculiar refinement of bliss; most people talk about Rome in the same way. It is evidently only a sort of idealized form of loafing: a passive life in Rome, thanks to the number and the quality of one's impressions, takes on a very respectable likeness to activity. It is still lotus-eating, only you sit down at table, and the lotuses are served up on rococo china. It 's all very well, but I have a distinct prevision of this—that if Roman life does n't do something substantial to make you happier, it increases tenfold your liability to moral misery. It seems to me a rash thing for a sensitive soul deliberately to cultivate its sensibilities by rambling too often among the ruins of the Palatine, or riding too often in the shadow of the aqueducts. In such recreations the chords of feeling grow tense, and after-life, to spare your intellectual nerves, must play upon them with a touch as dainty as the tread of Mignon when she danced her egg-dance."

"I should have said, my dear Rowland," said Cecilia, with a laugh, "that your nerves were tough, that your eggs were hard!"

"That being stupid, you mean, I might be happy? Upon my word I am not. I am clever enough to want more than I 've got. I am tired of myself, my own thoughts, my own affairs, my own eternal company. True happiness, we are told, consists in getting out of one's self; but the point is not only to get out—you must stay out; and to stay out you must have some absorbing errand. Unfortunately, I 've got no errand, and nobody will trust me with one. I want to care for something, or for some one. And I want to care with a certain ardor; even, if you can believe it, with a certain passion. I can't just now feel ardent and passionate about a hospital or a dormitory. Do you know I sometimes think that I 'm a man of genius, half finished? The genius has been left out, the faculty of expression is wanting; but the need for expression remains, and I spend my days groping for the latch of a closed door."

"What an immense number of words," said Cecilia after a pause, "to say you want to fall in love! I 've no doubt you have as good a genius for that as any one, if you would only trust it."

"Of course I 've thought of that, and I assure you I hold myself ready. But, evidently, I 'm not inflammable. Is there in Northampton some perfect epitome of the graces?"

"Of the graces?" said Cecilia, raising her eyebrows and suppressing too distinct a consciousness of being herself a rosy embodiment of several. "The household virtues are better represented. There are some excellent girls, and there are two or three very pretty ones. I will have them here, one by one, to tea, if you like."

"I should particularly like it; especially as I should give you a chance to see, by the profundity of my attention, that if I am not happy, it 's not for want of taking pains."

Cecilia was silent a moment; and then, "On the whole," she resumed, "I don't think there are any worth asking. There are none so very pretty, none so very pleasing."

"Are you very sure?" asked the young man, rising and throwing away his cigar-end.

"Upon my word," cried Cecilia, "one would suppose I wished to keep you for myself. Of course I am sure! But as the penalty of your insinuations, I shall invite the plainest and prosiest damsel that can be found, and leave you alone with her."

Rowland smiled. "Even against her," he said, "I should be sorry to conclude until I had given her my respectful attention."

This little profession of ideal chivalry (which closed the conversation) was not quite so fanciful on Mallet's lips as it would have been on those of many another man; as a rapid glance at his antecedents may help to make the reader perceive. His life had been a singular mixture of the rough and the smooth. He had sprung from a rigid Puritan stock, and had been brought up to think much more intently of the duties of this life than of its privileges and pleasures. His progenitors had submitted in the matter of dogmatic theology to the relaxing influences of recent years; but if Rowland's youthful consciousness was not chilled by the menace of long punishment for brief transgression, he had at least been made to feel that there ran through all things a strain of right and of wrong, as different, after all, in their complexions, as the texture, to the spiritual sense, of Sundays and week-days. His father was a chip of the primal Puritan block, a man with an icy smile and a stony frown. He had always bestowed on his son, on principle, more frowns than smiles, and if the lad had not been turned to stone himself, it was because nature had blessed him, inwardly, with a well of vivifying waters. Mrs. Mallet had been a Miss Rowland, the daughter of a retired sea-captain, once famous on the ships that sailed from Salem and Newburyport. He had brought to port many a cargo which crowned the edifice of fortunes already almost colossal, but he had also done a little sagacious trading on his own account, and he was able to retire, prematurely for so sea-worthy a maritime organism, upon a pension of his own providing. He was to be seen for a year on the Salem wharves, smoking the best tobacco and eying the seaward horizon with an inveteracy which superficial minds interpreted as a sign of repentance. At last, one evening, he disappeared beneath it, as he had often done before; this time, however, not as a commissioned navigator, but simply as an amateur of an observing turn likely to prove oppressive to the officer in command of the vessel. Five months later his place at home knew him again, and made the acquaintance also of a handsome, blonde young woman, of redundant contours, speaking a foreign tongue. The foreign tongue proved, after much conflicting research, to be the idiom of Amsterdam, and the young woman, which was stranger still, to be Captain Rowland's wife. Why he had gone forth so suddenly across the seas to marry her, what had happened between them before, and whether—though it was of questionable propriety for a good citizen to espouse a young person of mysterious origin, who did her hair in fantastically elaborate plaits, and in whose appearance "figure" enjoyed such striking predominance—he would not have had a heavy weight on his conscience if he had remained an irresponsible bachelor; these questions and many others, bearing with varying degrees of immediacy on the subject, were much propounded but scantily answered, and this history need not be charged with resolving them. Mrs. Rowland, for so handsome a woman, proved a tranquil neighbor and an excellent housewife. Her extremely fresh complexion, however, was always suffused with an air of apathetic homesickness, and she played her part in American society chiefly by having the little squares of brick pavement in front of her dwelling scoured and polished as nearly as possible into the likeness of Dutch tiles. Rowland Mallet remembered having seen her, as a child—an immensely stout, white-faced lady, wearing a high cap of very stiff tulle, speaking English with a formidable accent, and suffering from dropsy. Captain Rowland was a little bronzed and wizened man, with eccentric opinions. He advocated the creation of a public promenade along the sea, with arbors and little green tables for the consumption of beer, and a platform, surrounded by Chinese lanterns, for dancing. He especially desired the town library to be opened on Sundays, though, as he never entered it on week-days, it was easy to turn the proposition into ridicule. If, therefore, Mrs. Mallet was a woman of an exquisite moral tone, it was not that she had inherited her temper from an ancestry with a turn for casuistry. Jonas Mallet, at the time of his marriage, was conducting with silent shrewdness a small, unpromising business. Both his shrewdness and his silence increased with his years, and at the close of his life he was an extremely well-dressed, well-brushed gentleman, with a frigid gray eye, who said little to anybody, but of whom everybody said that he had a very handsome fortune. He was not a sentimental father, and the roughness I just now spoke of in Rowland's life dated from his early boyhood. Mr. Mallet, whenever he looked at his son, felt extreme compunction at having made a fortune. He remembered that the fruit had not dropped ripe from the tree into his own mouth, and determined it should be no fault of his if the boy was corrupted by luxury. Rowland, therefore, except for a good deal of expensive instruction in foreign tongues and abstruse sciences, received the education of a poor man's son. His fare was plain, his temper familiar with the discipline of patched trousers, and his habits marked by an exaggerated simplicity which it really cost a good deal of money to preserve unbroken. He was kept in the country for months together, in the midst of servants who had strict injunctions to see that he suffered no serious harm, but were as strictly forbidden to wait upon him. As no school could be found conducted on principles sufficiently rigorous, he was attended at home by a master who set a high price on the understanding that he was to illustrate the beauty of abstinence not only by precept but by example. Rowland passed for a child of ordinary parts, and certainly, during his younger years, was an excellent imitation of a boy who had inherited nothing whatever that was to make life easy. He was passive, pliable, frank, extremely slow at his books, and inordinately fond of trout-fishing. His hair, a memento of his Dutch ancestry, was of the fairest shade of yellow, his complexion absurdly rosy, and his measurement around the waist, when he was about ten years old, quite alarmingly large. This, however, was but an episode in his growth; he became afterwards a fresh-colored, yellow-bearded man, but he was never accused of anything worse than a tendency to corpulence. He emerged from childhood a simple, wholesome, round-eyed lad, with no suspicion that a less roundabout course might have been taken to make him happy, but with a vague sense that his young experience was not a fair sample of human freedom, and that he was to make a great many discoveries. When he was about fifteen, he achieved a momentous one. He ascertained that his mother was a saint. She had always been a very distinct presence in his life, but so ineffably gentle a one that his sense was fully opened to it only by the danger of losing her. She had an illness which for many months was liable at any moment to terminate fatally, and during her long-arrested convalescence she removed the mask which she had worn for years by her husband's order. Rowland spent his days at her side and felt before long as if he had made a new friend. All his impressions at this period were commented and interpreted at leisure in the future, and it was only then that he understood that his mother had been for fifteen years a perfectly unhappy woman. Her marriage had been an immitigable error which she had spent her life in trying to look straight in the face. She found nothing to oppose to her husband's will of steel but the appearance of absolute compliance; her spirit sank, and she lived for a while in a sort of helpless moral torpor. But at last, as her child emerged from babyhood, she began to feel a certain charm in patience, to discover the uses of ingenuity, and to learn that, somehow or other, one can always arrange one's life. She cultivated from this time forward a little private plot of sentiment, and it was of this secluded precinct that, before her death, she gave her son the key. Rowland's allowance at college was barely sufficient to maintain him decently, and as soon as he graduated, he was taken into his father's counting-house, to do small drudgery on a proportionate salary. For three years he earned his living as regularly as the obscure functionary in fustian who swept the office. Mr. Mallet was consistent, but the perfection of his consistency was known only on his death. He left but a third of his property to his son, and devoted the remainder to various public institutions and local charities. Rowland's third was an easy competence, and he never felt a moment's jealousy of his fellow-pensioners; but when one of the establishments which had figured most advantageously in his father's will bethought itself to affirm the existence of a later instrument, in which it had been still more handsomely treated, the young man felt a sudden passionate need to repel the claim by process of law. There was a lively tussle, but he gained his case; immediately after which he made, in another quarter, a donation of the contested sum. He cared nothing for the money, but he had felt an angry desire to protest against a destiny which seemed determined to be exclusively salutary. It seemed to him that he would bear a little spoiling. And yet he treated himself to a very modest quantity, and submitted without reserve to the great national discipline which began in 1861. When the Civil War broke out he immediately obtained a commission, and did his duty for three long years as a citizen soldier. His duty was obscure, but he never lost a certain private satisfaction in remembering that on two or three occasions it had been performed with something of an ideal precision. He had disentangled himself from business, and after the war he felt a profound disinclination to tie the knot again. He had no desire to make money, he had money enough; and although he knew, and was frequently reminded, that a young man is the better for a fixed occupation, he could discover no moral advantage in driving a lucrative trade. Yet few young men of means and leisure ever made less of a parade of idleness, and indeed idleness in any degree could hardly be laid at the door of a young man who took life in the serious, attentive, reasoning fashion of our friend. It often seemed to Mallet that he wholly lacked the prime requisite of a graceful flaneur—the simple, sensuous, confident relish of pleasure. He had frequent fits of extreme melancholy, in which he declared that he was neither fish nor flesh nor good red herring. He was neither an irresponsibly contemplative nature nor a sturdily practical one, and he was forever looking in vain for the uses of the things that please and the charm of the things that sustain. He was an awkward mixture of strong moral impulse and restless aesthetic curiosity, and yet he would have made a most ineffective reformer and a very indifferent artist. It seemed to him that the glow of happiness must be found either in action, of some immensely solid kind, on behalf of an idea, or in producing a masterpiece in one of the arts. Oftenest, perhaps, he wished he were a vigorous young man of genius, without a penny. As it was, he could only buy pictures, and not paint them; and in the way of action, he had to content himself with making a rule to render scrupulous moral justice to handsome examples of it in others. On the whole, he had an incorruptible modesty. With his blooming complexion and his serene gray eye, he felt the friction of existence more than was suspected; but he asked no allowance on grounds of temper, he assumed that fate had treated him inordinately well and that he had no excuse for taking an ill-natured view of life, and he undertook constantly to believe that all women were fair, all men were brave, and the world was a delightful place of sojourn, until the contrary had been distinctly proved.

Cecilia's blooming garden and shady porch had seemed so friendly to repose and a cigar, that she reproached him the next morning with indifference to her little parlor, not less, in its way, a monument to her ingenious taste. "And by the way," she added as he followed her in, "if I refused last night to show you a pretty girl, I can at least show you a pretty boy."

She threw open a window and pointed to a statuette which occupied the place of honor among the ornaments of the room. Rowland looked at it a moment and then turned to her with an exclamation of surprise. She gave him a rapid glance, perceived that her statuette was of altogether exceptional merit, and then smiled, knowingly, as if this had long been an agreeable certainty.

"Who did it? where did you get it?" Rowland demanded.

"Oh," said Cecilia, adjusting the light, "it 's a little thing of Mr. Hudson's."

"And who the deuce is Mr. Hudson?" asked Rowland. But he was absorbed; he lost her immediate reply. The statuette, in bronze, something less than two feet high, represented a naked youth drinking from a gourd. The attitude was perfectly simple. The lad was squarely planted on his feet, with his legs a little apart; his back was slightly hollowed, his head thrown back, and both hands raised to support the rustic cup. There was a loosened fillet of wild flowers about his head, and his eyes, under their drooped lids, looked straight into the cup. On the base was scratched the Greek word $\Delta\iota\psi\alpha$, Thirst. The figure might have been some beautiful youth of ancient fable,—Hylas or Narcissus, Paris or Endymion. Its beauty was the beauty of natural movement; nothing had been sought to be represented but the perfection of an attitude. This had been most attentively studied, and it was exquisitely rendered. Rowland demanded more light, dropped his head on this side and that, uttered vague exclamations. He said to himself, as he had said more than once in the Louvre and the Vatican, "We ugly mortals, what beautiful creatures we are!" Nothing, in a long time, had given him so much pleasure. "Hudson—Hudson," he asked again; "who is Hudson?"

"A young man of this place," said Cecilia.

"A young man? How old?"

"I suppose he is three or four and twenty."

"Of this place, you say—of Northampton, Massachusetts?"

"He lives here, but he comes from Virginia."

"Is he a sculptor by profession?"

"He 's a law-student."

Rowland burst out laughing. "He has found something in Blackstone that I never did. He makes statues then simply for his pleasure?"

Cecilia, with a smile, gave a little toss of her head. "For mine!"

"I congratulate you," said Rowland. "I wonder whether he could be induced to do anything for me?"

"This was a matter of friendship. I saw the figure when he had modeled it in clay, and of course greatly admired it. He said nothing at the time, but a week ago, on my birthday, he arrived in a buggy, with this. He had had it cast at the foundry at Chicopee; I believe it 's a beautiful piece of bronze. He begged me to accept."

"Upon my word," said Mallet, "he does things handsomely!" And he fell to admiring the statue again.

"So then," said Cecilia, "it 's very remarkable?"

"Why, my dear cousin," Rowland answered, "Mr. Hudson, of Virginia, is an extraordinary—" Then suddenly stopping: "Is he a great friend of yours?" he asked.

"A great friend?" and Cecilia hesitated. "I regard him as a child!"

"Well," said Rowland, "he 's a very clever child. Tell me something about him: I should like to see him."

Cecilia was obliged to go to her daughter's music-lesson, but she assured Rowland that she would arrange for him a meeting with the young sculptor. He was a frequent visitor, and as he had not called for some days it was likely he would come that evening. Rowland, left alone, examined the statuette at his leisure, and returned more than once during the day to take another look at it. He discovered its weak points, but it wore well. It had the stamp of genius. Rowland envied the happy youth who, in a New England village, without aid or encouragement, without models or resources, had found it so easy to produce a lovely work.

In the evening, as he was smoking his cigar on the veranda, a light, quick step pressed the gravel of the garden path, and in a moment a young man made his bow to Cecilia. It was rather a nod than a bow, and indicated either that he was an old friend, or that he was scantily versed in the usual social forms. Cecilia, who was sitting near the steps, pointed to a neighboring chair, but the young man seated himself abruptly on the floor at her feet, began to fan himself vigorously with his hat, and broke out into a lively objurgation upon the hot weather. "I 'm dripping wet!" he said, without ceremony.

"You walk too fast," said Cecilia. "You do everything too fast."

"I know it, I know it!" he cried, passing his hand through his abundant dark hair and making it stand out in a picturesque shock. "I can't be slow if I try. There 's something inside of me that drives me. A restless fiend!"

Cecilia gave a light laugh, and Rowland leaned forward in his hammock. He had placed himself in it at Bessie's request, and was playing that he was her baby and that she was rocking him to sleep. She sat beside him, swinging the hammock to and fro, and singing a lullaby. When he raised himself she pushed him back and said that the baby must finish its nap. "But I want to see the gentleman with the fiend inside of him," said Rowland.

"What is a fiend?" Bessie demanded. "It 's only Mr. Hudson."

"Very well, I want to see him."

"Oh, never mind him!" said Bessie, with the brevity of contempt.

"You speak as if you did n't like him."

"I don't!" Bessie affirmed, and put Rowland to bed again.

The hammock was swung at the end of the veranda, in the thickest shade of the vines, and this fragment of dialogue had passed unnoticed. Rowland submitted a while longer to be cradled, and contented himself with listening to Mr. Hudson's voice. It was a soft and not altogether masculine organ, and was pitched on this occasion in a somewhat plaintive and pettish key. The young man's mood seemed fretful; he complained of the heat, of the dust, of a shoe that hurt him, of having gone on an errand a mile to the other side of the town and found the person he was in search of had left Northampton an hour before.

"Won't you have a cup of tea?" Cecilia asked. "Perhaps that will restore your equanimity."

"Aye, by keeping me awake all night!" said Hudson. "At the best, it 's hard enough to go down to the office. With my nerves set on edge by a sleepless night, I should perforce stay at home and be brutal to my poor mother."

"Your mother is well, I hope."

"Oh, she 's as usual."

"And Miss Garland?"

"She 's as usual, too. Every one, everything, is as usual. Nothing ever happens, in this benighted town."

"I beg your pardon; things do happen, sometimes," said Cecilia. "Here is a dear cousin of mine arrived on purpose to congratulate you on your statuette." And she called to Rowland to come and be introduced to Mr. Hudson. The young man sprang up with alacrity, and Rowland, coming forward to shake hands, had a good look at him in the light projected from the parlor window. Something seemed to shine out of Hudson's face as a warning against a "compliment" of the idle, unpondered sort.

"Your statuette seems to me very good," Rowland said gravely. "It has given me extreme pleasure."

"And my cousin knows what is good," said Cecilia. "He 's a connoisseur."

Hudson smiled and stared. "A connoisseur?" he cried, laughing. "He 's the first I 've ever seen! Let me see what they look like;" and he drew Rowland nearer to the light. "Have they all such good heads as that? I should like to model yours."

"Pray do," said Cecilia. "It will keep him a while. He is running off to Europe."

"Ah, to Europe!" Hudson exclaimed with a melancholy cadence, as they sat down. "Happy man!"

But the note seemed to Rowland to be struck rather at random, for he perceived no echo of it in the boyish garrulity of his later talk. Hudson was a tall, slender young fellow, with a singularly mobile and intelligent face. Rowland was struck at first only with its responsive vivacity, but in a short time he perceived it was remarkably handsome. The features were admirably chiseled and finished, and a frank smile played over them as gracefully as a breeze among flowers. The fault of the young man's whole structure was an excessive want of breadth. The forehead, though it was high and rounded, was narrow; the jaw and the shoulders were narrow; and the result was an air of insufficient physical substance. But Mallet afterwards learned that this fair, slim youth could draw indefinitely upon a mysterious fund of nervous force, which outlasted and outwearied the endurance of many a sturdier temperament. And certainly there was life enough in his eye to furnish an immortality! It was a generous dark gray eye, in which there came and went a sort of kindling glow, which would have made a ruder visage striking, and which gave at times to Hudson's harmonious face an altogether extraordinary beauty. There was to Rowland's sympathetic sense a slightly pitiful disparity between the young sculptor's delicate countenance and the shabby gentility of his costume. He was dressed for a visit—a visit to a pretty woman. He was clad from head to foot in a white linen suit, which had never been remarkable for the felicity of its cut, and had now quite lost that crispness which garments of this complexion can as ill spare as the back-scene of a theatre the radiance of the footlights. He wore a vivid blue cravat, passed through a ring altogether too splendid to be valuable; he pulled and twisted, as he sat, a pair of yellow kid gloves; he emphasized his conversation with great dashes and flourishes of a light, silver-tipped walking-stick, and he kept constantly taking off and putting on one of those slouched sombreros which are the traditional property of the Virginian or Carolinian of romance. When this was on, he was very picturesque, in spite of his mock elegance; and when it was off, and he sat nursing it and turning it about and not knowing what to do with it, he could hardly be said to be awkward. He evidently had a natural relish for brilliant accessories, and appropriated what came to his hand. This was visible in his talk, which abounded in the florid and sonorous. He liked words with color in them.

Rowland, who was but a moderate talker, sat by in silence, while Cecilia, who had told him that she desired his opinion upon her friend, used a good deal of characteristic finesse in leading the young man to expose himself. She perfectly succeeded, and Hudson rattled away for an hour with a volubility in which boyish unconsciousness and manly shrewdness were singularly combined. He gave his opinion on twenty topics, he opened up an endless budget of local gossip, he described his repulsive routine at the office of Messrs. Striker and Spooner, counselors at law, and he gave with great felicity and gusto an account of the annual boat-race between Harvard and Yale, which he had lately witnessed at Worcester. He had looked at the straining oarsmen and the swaying crowd with the eye of the sculptor. Rowland was a good deal amused and not a little interested. Whenever Hudson uttered some peculiarly striking piece of youthful grandiloquence, Cecilia broke into a long, light, familiar laugh.

"What are you laughing at?" the young man then demanded. "Have I said anything so ridiculous?"

"Go on, go on," Cecilia replied. "You are too delicious! Show Mr. Mallet how Mr. Striker read the Declaration of Independence."

Hudson, like most men with a turn for the plastic arts, was an excellent mimic, and he represented with a great deal of humor the accent and attitude of a pompous country lawyer sustaining the burden of this customary episode of our national festival. The sonorous twang, the see-saw gestures, the odd pronunciation, were vividly depicted. But Cecilia's manner, and the young man's quick response, ruffled a little poor Rowland's paternal conscience. He wondered whether his cousin was not sacrificing the faculty of reverence in her clever protege to her need for amusement. Hudson made no serious rejoinder to Rowland's compliment on his statuette until he rose to go. Rowland wondered whether he had forgotten it, and supposed that the oversight was a sign of the natural self-sufficiency of genius. But Hudson stood a moment before he said good night, twirled his sombrero, and hesitated for the first time. He gave Rowland a clear, penetrating glance, and then, with a wonderfully frank, appealing smile: "You really meant," he asked, "what you said a while ago about that thing of mine? It is good—essentially good?"

"I really meant it," said Rowland, laying a kindly hand on his shoulder. "It is very good indeed. It is, as you say, essentially good. That is the beauty of it."

Hudson's eyes glowed and expanded; he looked at Rowland for some time in silence. "I have a notion you really know," he said at last. "But if you don't, it does n't much matter."

"My cousin asked me to-day," said Cecilia, "whether I supposed you knew yourself how good it is."

Hudson stared, blushing a little. "Perhaps not!" he cried.

"Very likely," said Mallet. "I read in a book the other day that great talent in action—in fact the book said genius—is a kind of somnambulism. The artist performs great feats, in a dream. We must not wake him up, lest he should lose his balance."

"Oh, when he 's back in bed again!" Hudson answered with a laugh. "Yes, call it a dream. It was a very happy one!"

"Tell me this," said Rowland. "Did you mean anything by your young Water-drinker? Does he represent an idea? Is he a symbol?"

Hudson raised his eyebrows and gently scratched his head. "Why, he 's youth, you know; he 's innocence, he 's health, he 's strength, he 's curiosity. Yes, he 's a good many things."

"And is the cup also a symbol?"

"The cup is knowledge, pleasure, experience. Anything of that kind!"

"Well, he 's guzzling in earnest," said Rowland.

Hudson gave a vigorous nod. "Aye, poor fellow, he 's thirsty!" And on this he cried good night, and bounded down the garden path.

"Well, what do you make of him?" asked Cecilia, returning a short time afterwards from a visit of investigation as to the sufficiency of Bessie's bedclothes.

"I confess I like him," said Rowland. "He 's very immature,—but there 's stuff in him."

"He 's a strange being," said Cecilia, musingly.

"Who are his people? what has been his education?" Rowland asked.

"He has had no education, beyond what he has picked up, with little trouble, for himself. His mother is a widow, of a Massachusetts country family, a little timid, tremulous woman, who is always on pins and needles about her son. She had some property herself, and married a Virginian gentleman of good estates. He turned out, I believe, a very licentious personage, and made great havoc in their fortune. Everything, or almost everything, melted away, including Mr. Hudson himself. This is literally true, for he drank himself to death. Ten years ago his wife was left a widow, with scanty means and a couple of growing boys. She paid her husband's debts as best she could, and came to establish herself here, where by the death of a charitable relative she had inherited an old-fashioned ruinous house. Roderick, our friend, was her pride and joy, but Stephen, the elder, was her comfort and support. I remember him, later; he was an ugly, sturdy, practical lad, very different from his brother, and in his way, I imagine, a very fine fellow. When the war broke out he found that the New England blood ran thicker in his veins than the

Virginian, and immediately obtained a commission. He fell in some Western battle and left his mother inconsolable. Roderick, however, has given her plenty to think about, and she has induced him, by some mysterious art, to abide, nominally at least, in a profession that he abhors, and for which he is about as fit, I should say, as I am to drive a locomotive. He grew up a la grace de Dieu, and was horribly spoiled. Three or four years ago he graduated at a small college in this neighborhood, where I am afraid he had given a good deal more attention to novels and billiards than to mathematics and Greek. Since then he has been reading law, at the rate of a page a day. If he is ever admitted to practice I 'm afraid my friendship won't avail to make me give him my business. Good, bad, or indifferent, the boy is essentially an artist— an artist to his fingers' ends."

"Why, then," asked Rowland, "does n't he deliberately take up the chisel?"

"For several reasons. In the first place, I don't think he more than half suspects his talent. The flame is smouldering, but it is never fanned by the breath of criticism. He sees nothing, hears nothing, to help him to self-knowledge. He 's hopelessly discontented, but he does n't know where to look for help. Then his mother, as she one day confessed to me, has a holy horror of a profession which consists exclusively, as she supposes, in making figures of people without their clothes on. Sculpture, to her mind, is an insidious form of immorality, and for a young man of a passionate disposition she considers the law a much safer investment. Her father was a judge, she has two brothers at the bar, and her elder son had made a very promising beginning in the same line. She wishes the tradition to be perpetuated. I 'm pretty sure the law won't make Roderick's fortune, and I 'm afraid it will, in the long run, spoil his temper."

"What sort of a temper is it?"

"One to be trusted, on the whole. It is quick, but it is generous. I have known it to breathe flame and fury at ten o'clock in the evening, and soft, sweet music early on the morrow. It 's a very entertaining temper to observe. I, fortunately, can do so dispassionately, for I 'm the only person in the place he has not quarreled with."

357

"Has he then no society? Who is Miss Garland, whom you asked about?"

"A young girl staying with his mother, a sort of far-away cousin; a good plain girl, but not a person to delight a sculptor's eye. Roderick has a goodly share of the old Southern arrogance; he has the aristocratic temperament. He will have nothing to do with the small towns-people; he says they 're 'ignoble.' He cannot endure his mother's friends—the old ladies and the ministers and the tea-party people; they bore him to death. So he comes and lounges here and rails at everything and every one."

This graceful young scoffer reappeared a couple of evenings later, and confirmed the friendly feeling he had provoked on Rowland's part. He was in an easier mood than before, he chattered less extravagantly, and asked Rowland a number of rather naif questions about the condition of the fine arts in New York and Boston. Cecilia, when he had gone, said that this was the wholesome effect of Rowland's praise of his statuette. Roderick was acutely sensitive, and Rowland's tranquil commendation had stilled his restless pulses. He was ruminating the full-flavored verdict of culture. Rowland felt an irresistible kindness for him, a mingled sense of his personal charm and his artistic capacity. He had an indefinable attraction—the something divine of unspotted, exuberant, confident youth. The next day was Sunday, and Rowland proposed that they should take a long walk and that Roderick should show him the country. The young man assented gleefully, and in the morning, as Rowland at the garden gate was giving his hostess Godspeed on her way to church, he came striding along the grassy margin of the road and out-whistling the music of the church bells. It was one of those lovely days of August when you feel the complete exuberance of summer just warned and checked by autumn. "Remember the day, and take care you rob no orchards," said Cecilia, as they separated.

The young men walked away at a steady pace, over hill and dale, through woods and fields, and at last found themselves on a grassy elevation studded with mossy rocks and red cedars. Just beneath them, in a great shining curve, flowed the goodly Connecticut. They flung themselves on the grass and tossed stones into the river; they talked like old friends. Rowland lit a cigar, and Roderick refused one with a grimace of extravagant disgust. He thought them vile things; he did n't see how decent people could tolerate them. Rowland was amused, and wondered what it was that made this ill-mannered speech seem perfectly inoffensive on Roderick's lips. He belonged to the race of mortals, to be pitied or envied according as we view the matter, who are not held to a strict account for their aggressions. Looking at him as he lay stretched in the shade, Rowland vaguely likened him to some beautiful, supple, restless, bright-eyed animal, whose motions should have no deeper warrant than the tremulous delicacy of its structure, and be graceful even when they were most inconvenient. Rowland watched the shadows on Mount Holyoke, listened to the gurgle of the river, and sniffed the balsam of the pines. A gentle breeze had begun to tickle their summits, and brought the smell of the mown grass across from the elm-dotted river meadows. He sat up beside his companion and looked away at the far-spreading view. It seemed to him beautiful, and suddenly a strange feeling of prospective regret took possession of him. Something seemed to tell him that later, in a foreign land, he would remember it lovingly and penitently.

"It 's a wretched business," he said, "this practical quarrel of ours with our own country, this everlasting impatience to get out of it. Is one's only safety then in flight? This is an American day, an American landscape, an American atmosphere. It certainly has its merits, and some day when I am shivering with ague in classic Italy, I shall accuse myself of having slighted them."

Roderick kindled with a sympathetic glow, and declared that America was good enough for him, and that he had always thought it the duty of an honest citizen to stand by his own country and help it along. He had evidently thought nothing whatever about it, and was launching his doctrine on the inspiration of the moment. The doctrine expanded with the occasion, and he declared that he was above all an advocate for American art. He did n't see why we should n't produce the greatest works in the world. We were the biggest people, and we ought to have the biggest conceptions. The biggest conceptions of course would bring forth in time the biggest performances. We had only to be true to ourselves, to pitch in and not be afraid, to fling Imitation overboard and fix our eyes upon our National Individuality. "I declare," he cried, "there 's a career for a man, and I 've twenty minds to decide, on the spot, to embrace it—to be the consummate, typical, original, national American artist! It 's inspiring!"

Rowland burst out laughing and told him that he liked his practice better than his theory, and that a saner impulse than this had inspired his little Water-drinker. Roderick took no offense, and three minutes afterwards was talking volubly of some humbler theme, but half heeded by his companion, who had returned to his cogitations. At last Rowland delivered himself of the upshot of these. "How would you like," he suddenly demanded, "to go to Rome?"

Hudson stared, and, with a hungry laugh which speedily consigned our National Individuality to perdition, responded that he would like it reasonably well. "And I should like, by the same token," he added, "to go to Athens, to Constantinople, to Damascus, to the holy city of Benares, where there is a golden statue of Brahma twenty feet tall."

"Nay," said Rowland soberly, "if you were to go to Rome, you should settle down and work. Athens might help you, but for the present I should n't recommend Benares."

"It will be time to arrange details when I pack my trunk," said Hudson.

"If you mean to turn sculptor, the sooner you pack your trunk the better."

"Oh, but I 'm a practical man! What is the smallest sum per annum, on which one can keep alive the sacred fire in Rome?"

"What is the largest sum at your disposal?"

Roderick stroked his light moustache, gave it a twist, and then announced with mock pomposity: "Three hundred dollars!"

"The money question could be arranged," said Rowland. "There are ways of raising money."

"I should like to know a few! I never yet discovered one."

"One consists," said Rowland, "in having a friend with a good deal more than he wants, and not being too proud to accept a part of it."

Roderick stared a moment and his face flushed. "Do you mean—do you mean?".... he stammered. He was greatly excited.

Rowland got up, blushing a little, and Roderick sprang to his feet. "In three words, if you are to be a sculptor, you ought to go to Rome and study the antique. To go to Rome you need money. I 'm fond of fine statues, but unfortunately I can't make them myself. I have to order them. I order a dozen from you, to be executed at your convenience. To help you, I pay you in advance."

Roderick pushed off his hat and wiped his forehead, still gazing at his companion. "You believe in me!" he cried at last.

"Allow me to explain," said Rowland. "I believe in you, if you are prepared to work and to wait, and to struggle, and to exercise a great many virtues. And then, I 'm afraid to say it, lest I should disturb you more than I should help you. You must decide for yourself. I simply offer you an opportunity."

Hudson stood for some time, profoundly meditative. "You have not seen my other things," he said suddenly. "Come and look at them."

"Now?"

"Yes, we 'll walk home. We 'll settle the question."

He passed his hand through Rowland's arm and they retraced their steps. They reached the town and made their way along a broad country street, dusky with the shade of magnificent elms. Rowland felt his companion's arm trembling in his own. They stopped at a large white house, flanked with melancholy hemlocks, and passed through a little front garden, paved with moss-coated bricks and ornamented with parterres bordered with high box hedges. The mansion had an air of antiquated dignity, but it had seen its best days, and evidently sheltered a shrunken household. Mrs. Hudson, Rowland was sure, might be seen in the garden of a morning, in a white apron and a pair of old gloves, engaged in frugal horticulture. Roderick's studio was behind, in the basement; a large, empty room, with the paper peeling off the walls. This represented, in the fashion of fifty years ago, a series of small fantastic landscapes of a hideous pattern, and the young sculptor had presumably torn it away in great scraps, in moments of aesthetic exasperation. On a board in a corner was a heap of clay, and on the floor, against the wall, stood some dozen medallions, busts, and figures, in various stages of completion. To exhibit them Roderick had to place them one by one on the end of a long packing-box, which served as a pedestal. He did so silently, making no explanations, and looking at them himself with a strange air of quickened curiosity. Most of the things were portraits; and the three at which he looked longest were finished busts. One was a colossal head of a negro, tossed back, defiant, with distended nostrils; one was the portrait of a young man whom Rowland immediately perceived, by the resemblance, to be his deceased brother; the last represented a gentleman with a pointed nose, a long, shaved upper lip, and a tuft on the end of his chin. This was a face peculiarly unadapted to sculpture; but as a piece of modeling it was the best, and it was admirable. It reminded Rowland in its homely veracity, its artless artfulness, of the works of the early Italian Renaissance. On the pedestal was cut the name—Barnaby Striker, Esq. Rowland remembered that this was the appellation of the legal luminary from whom his companion had undertaken to borrow a reflected ray, and although in the bust there was naught flagrantly set down in malice, it betrayed, comically to one who could relish the secret, that the features of the original had often been scanned with an irritated eye. Besides these there were several rough studies of the nude, and two or three figures of a fanciful kind. The most noticeable (and it had singular beauty) was a small modeled design for a sepulchral monument; that, evidently, of Stephen Hudson. The young soldier lay sleeping eternally, with his hand on his sword, like an old crusader in a Gothic cathedral.

Rowland made no haste to pronounce; too much depended on his judgment. "Upon my word," cried Hudson at last, "they seem to me very good."

And in truth, as Rowland looked, he saw they were good. They were youthful, awkward, and ignorant; the effort, often, was more apparent than the success. But the effort was signally powerful and intelligent; it seemed to Rowland that it needed only to let itself go to compass great things. Here and there, too, success, when grasped, had something masterly. Rowland turned to his companion, who stood with his hands in his pockets and his hair very much crumpled, looking at him askance. The light of admiration was in Rowland's eyes, and it speedily kindled a wonderful illumination on Hudson's handsome brow. Rowland said at last, gravely, "You have only to work!"

"I think I know what that means," Roderick answered. He turned away, threw himself on a rickety chair, and sat for some moments with his elbows on his knees and his head in his hands. "Work—work?" he said at last, looking up, "ah, if I could only begin!" He glanced round the room a moment and his eye encountered on the mantel-shelf the vivid physiognomy of Mr. Barnaby Striker. His smile vanished, and he stared at it with an air of concentrated enmity. "I want to begin," he cried, "and I can't make a better beginning than this! Good-by, Mr. Striker!" He strode across the room, seized a mallet that lay at hand, and before Rowland could interfere, in the interest of art if not of morals, dealt a merciless blow upon Mr. Striker's skull. The bust cracked into a dozen pieces, which toppled with a great crash upon the floor. Rowland relished neither the destruction of the image nor his companion's look in working it, but as he was about to express his displeasure the door opened and gave passage to a young girl. She came in with a rapid step and startled face, as if she had been summoned by the noise. Seeing the heap of shattered clay and the mallet in Roderick's hand, she gave a cry of horror. Her voice died away when she perceived that Rowland was a stranger, but she murmured reproachfully, "Why, Roderick, what have you done?"

Roderick gave a joyous kick to the shapeless fragments. "I 've driven the money-changers out of the temple!" he cried.

The traces retained shape enough to be recognized, and she gave a little moan of pity. She seemed not to understand the young man's allegory, but yet to feel that it pointed to some great purpose, which must be an evil one, from being expressed in such a lawless fashion, and to perceive that Rowland was in some way accountable for it. She looked at him with a sharp, frank mistrust, and turned away through the open door. Rowland looked after her with extraordinary interest.

CHAPTER II. Roderick

Early on the morrow Rowland received a visit from his new friend. Roderick was in a state of extreme exhilaration, tempered, however, by a certain amount of righteous wrath. He had had a domestic struggle, but he had remained master of the situation. He had shaken the dust of Mr. Striker's office from his feet.

"I had it out last night with my mother," he said. "I dreaded the scene, for she takes things terribly hard. She does n't scold nor storm, and she does n't argue nor insist. She sits with her eyes full of tears that never fall, and looks at me, when I displease her, as if I were a perfect monster of depravity. And the trouble is that I was born to displease her. She does n't trust me; she never has and she never will. I don't know what I have done to set her against me, but ever since I can remember I have been looked at with tears. The trouble is," he went on, giving a twist to his moustache, "I 've been too absurdly docile. I 've been sprawling all my days by the maternal fireside, and my dear mother has grown used to bullying me. I 've made myself cheap! If I 'm not in my bed by eleven o'clock, the girl is sent out to explore with a lantern. When I think of it, I fairly despise my amiability. It 's rather a hard fate, to live like a saint and to pass for a sinner! I should like for six months to lead Mrs. Hudson the life some fellows lead their mothers!"

"Allow me to believe," said Rowland, "that you would like nothing of the sort. If you have been a good boy, don't spoil it by pretending you don't like it. You have been very happy, I suspect, in spite of your virtues, and there are worse fates in the world than being loved too well. I have not had the pleasure of seeing your mother, but I would lay you a wager that that is the trouble. She is passionately fond of you, and her hopes, like all intense hopes, keep trembling into fears." Rowland, as he spoke, had an instinctive vision of how such a beautiful young fellow must be loved by his female relatives.

Roderick frowned, and with an impatient gesture, "I do her justice," he cried. "May she never do me less!" Then after a moment's hesitation, "I 'll tell you the perfect truth," he went on. "I have to fill a double place. I have to be my brother as well as myself. It 's a good deal to ask of a man, especially when he has so little talent as I for being what he is not. When we were both young together I was the curled darling. I had the silver mug and the biggest piece of pudding, and I stayed in-doors to be kissed by the ladies while he made mud-pies in the garden and was never missed, of course. Really, he was worth fifty of me! When he was brought home from Vicksburg with a piece of shell in his skull, my poor mother began to think she had n't loved him enough. I remember, as she hung round my neck sobbing, before his coffin, she told me that I must be to her everything that he would have been. I swore in tears and in perfect good faith that I would, but naturally I have not kept my promise. I have been utterly different. I have been idle, restless, egotistical, discontented. I have done no harm, I believe, but I have done no good. My brother, if he had lived, would have made fifty thousand dollars and put gas and water into the house. My mother, brooding night and day on her bereavement, has come to fix her ideal in offices of that sort. Judged by that standard I 'm nowhere!"

Rowland was at loss how to receive this account of his friend's domestic circumstances; it was plaintive, and yet the manner seemed to him over-trenchant. "You must lose no time in making a masterpiece," he answered; "then with the proceeds you can give her gas from golden burners."

"So I have told her; but she only half believes either in masterpiece or in proceeds. She can see no good in my making statues; they seem to her a snare of the enemy. She would fain see me all my life tethered to the law, like a browsing goat to a stake. In that way I 'm in sight. 'It 's a more regular occupation!' that 's all I can get out of her. A more regular damnation! Is it a fact that artists, in general, are such wicked men? I never had the pleasure of knowing one, so I could n't confute her with an example. She had the advantage of me, because she formerly knew a portrait-painter at Richmond, who did her miniature in black lace mittens (you may see it on the parlor table), who used to drink raw brandy and beat his wife. I promised her that, whatever I might do to my wife, I would never beat my mother, and that as for brandy, raw or diluted, I detested it. She sat silently crying for an hour, during which I expended treasures of eloquence. It 's a good thing to have to reckon up one's intentions, and I assure you, as I pleaded my cause, I was most agreeably impressed with the elevated character of my own. I kissed her solemnly at last, and told her that I had said everything and that she must make the best of it. This morning she has dried her eyes, but I warrant you it is n't a cheerful house. I long to be out of it!"

"I 'm extremely sorry," said Rowland, "to have been the prime cause of so much suffering. I owe your mother some amends; will it be possible for me to see her?"

"If you 'll see her, it will smooth matters vastly; though to tell the truth she 'll need all her courage to face you, for she considers you an agent of the foul fiend. She does n't see why you should have come here and set me by the ears: you are made to ruin ingenuous youths and desolate doting mothers. I leave it to you, personally, to answer these charges. You see, what she can't forgive—what she 'll not really ever forgive—is your taking me off to Rome. Rome is an evil word, in my mother's vocabulary, to be said in a whisper, as you 'd say 'damnation.' Northampton is in the centre of the earth and Rome far away in outlying dusk, into which it can do no Christian any good to penetrate. And there was I but yesterday a doomed habitue of that repository of every virtue, Mr. Striker's office!"

"And does Mr. Striker know of your decision?" asked Rowland.

"To a certainty! Mr. Striker, you must know, is not simply a good-natured attorney, who lets me dog's-ear his law-books. He's a particular friend and general adviser. He looks after my mother's property and kindly consents to regard me as part of it. Our opinions have always been painfully divergent, but I freely forgive him his zealous attempts to unscrew my head-piece and set it on hind part before. He never understood me, and it was useless to try to make him. We speak a different language—we 're made of a different clay. I had a fit of rage yesterday when I smashed his bust, at the thought of all the bad blood he had stirred up in me; it did me good, and it 's all over now. I don't hate him any more; I 'm rather sorry for him. See how you 've improved me! I must have seemed to him wilfully, wickedly stupid, and I 'm sure he only tolerated me on account of his great regard for my mother. This morning I grasped the bull by the horns. I took an armful of law-books that have been gathering the dust in my room for the last year and a half, and presented myself at the office. 'Allow me to put these back in their places,' I said. 'I shall never have need for them more—never more, never more, never more!' 'So you 've learned everything they contain?' asked Striker, leering over his spectacles. 'Better late than never.' 'I 've learned nothing that you can teach me,' I cried. 'But I shall tax your patience no longer. I 'm going to be a sculptor. I 'm going to Rome. I won't bid you good-by just yet; I shall see you again. But I bid good-by here, with rapture, to these four detested walls—to this living tomb! I did n't know till now how I hated it! My compliments to Mr. Spooner, and my thanks for all you have not made of me!'"

"I 'm glad to know you are to see Mr. Striker again," Rowland answered, correcting a primary inclination to smile. "You certainly owe him a respectful farewell, even if he has not understood you. I confess you rather puzzle me. There is another person," he presently added, "whose opinion as to your new career I should like to know. What does Miss Garland think?"

Hudson looked at him keenly, with a slight blush. Then, with a conscious smile, "What makes you suppose she thinks anything?" he asked.

"Because, though I saw her but for a moment yesterday, she struck me as a very intelligent person, and I am sure she has opinions."

The smile on Roderick's mobile face passed rapidly into a frown. "Oh, she thinks what I think!" he answered.

Before the two young men separated Rowland attempted to give as harmonious a shape as possible to his companion's scheme. "I have launched you, as I may say," he said, "and I feel as if I ought to see you into port. I am older than you and know the world better, and it seems well that we should voyage a while together. It 's on my conscience that I ought to take you to Rome, walk you through the Vatican, and then lock you up with a heap of clay. I sail on the fifth of September; can you make your preparations to start with me?"

Roderick assented to all this with an air of candid confidence in his friend's wisdom that outshone the virtue of pledges. "I have no preparations to make," he said with a smile, raising his arms and letting them fall, as if to indicate his unencumbered condition. "What I am to take with me I carry here!" and he tapped his forehead.

"Happy man!" murmured Rowland with a sigh, thinking of the light stowage, in his own organism, in the region indicated by Roderick, and of the heavy one in deposit at his banker's, of bags and boxes.

When his companion had left him he went in search of Cecilia. She was sitting at work at a shady window, and welcomed him to a low chintz-covered chair. He sat some time, thoughtfully snipping tape with her scissors; he expected criticism and he was preparing a rejoinder. At last he told her of Roderick's decision and of his own influence in it. Cecilia, besides an extreme surprise, exhibited a certain fine displeasure at his not having asked her advice.

"What would you have said, if I had?" he demanded.

"I would have said in the first place, 'Oh for pity's sake don't carry off the person in all Northampton who amuses me most!' I would have said in the second place, 'Nonsense! the boy is doing very well. Let well alone!'"

"That in the first five minutes. What would you have said later?"

"That for a man who is generally averse to meddling, you were suddenly rather officious."

Rowland's countenance fell. He frowned in silence. Cecilia looked at him askance; gradually the spark of irritation faded from her eye.

"Excuse my sharpness," she resumed at last. "But I am literally in despair at losing Roderick Hudson. His visits in the evening, for the past year, have kept me alive. They have given a silver tip to leaden days. I don't say he is of a more useful metal than other people, but he is of a different one. Of course, however, that I shall miss him sadly is not a reason for his not going to seek his fortune. Men must work and women must weep!"

"Decidedly not!" said Rowland, with a good deal of emphasis. He had suspected from the first hour of his stay that Cecilia had treated herself to a private social luxury; he had then discovered that she found it in Hudson's lounging visits and boyish chatter, and he had felt himself wondering at last whether, judiciously viewed, her gain in the matter was not the young man's loss. It was evident that Cecilia was not judicious, and that her good sense, habitually rigid under the demands of domestic economy, indulged itself with a certain agreeable laxity on this particular point. She liked her young friend just as he was; she humored him, flattered him, laughed at him, caressed him—did everything but advise him. It was a flirtation without the benefits of a flirtation. She was too old to let him fall in love with her, which might have done him good; and her inclination was to keep him young, so that the nonsense he talked might never transgress a certain line. It was quite conceivable that poor Cecilia should relish a pastime; but if one had philanthropically embraced the idea that something considerable might be made of Roderick, it was impossible not to see that her friendship was not what might be called tonic. So Rowland reflected, in the glow of his new-born sympathy. There was a later time when he would have been grateful if Hudson's susceptibility to the relaxing influence of lovely women might have been limited to such inexpensive tribute as he rendered the excellent Cecilia.

"I only desire to remind you," she pursued, "that you are likely to have your hands full."

"I 've thought of that, and I rather like the idea; liking, as I do, the man. I told you the other day, you know, that I longed to have something on my hands. When it first occurred to me that I might start our young friend on the path of glory, I felt as if I had an unimpeachable inspiration. Then I remembered there were dangers and difficulties, and asked myself whether I had a right to step in between him and his obscurity. My sense of his really having the divine flame answered the question. He is made to do the things that humanity is the happier for! I can't do such things myself, but when I see a young man of genius standing helpless and hopeless for want of capital, I feel—and it 's no affectation of humility, I assure you—as if it would give at least a reflected usefulness to my own life to offer him his opportunity."

"In the name of humanity, I suppose, I ought to thank you. But I want, first of all, to be happy myself. You guarantee us at any rate, I hope, the masterpieces."

"A masterpiece a year," said Rowland smiling, "for the next quarter of a century."

"It seems to me that we have a right to ask more: to demand that you guarantee us not only the development of the artist, but the security of the man."

Rowland became grave again. "His security?"

"His moral, his sentimental security. Here, you see, it 's perfect. We are all under a tacit compact to preserve it. Perhaps you believe in the necessary turbulence of genius, and you intend to enjoin upon your protege the importance of cultivating his passions."

"On the contrary, I believe that a man of genius owes as much deference to his passions as any other man, but not a particle more, and I confess I have a strong conviction that the artist is better for leading a quiet life. That is what I shall preach to my protege, as you call him, by example as well as by precept. You evidently believe," he added in a moment, "that he will lead me a dance."

"Nay, I prophesy nothing. I only think that circumstances, with our young man, have a great influence; as is proved by the fact that although he has been fuming and fretting here for the last five years, he has nevertheless managed to make the best of it, and found it easy, on the whole, to vegetate. Transplanted to Rome, I fancy he 'll put forth a denser leafage. I should like vastly to see the change. You must write me about it, from stage to stage. I hope with all my heart that the fruit will be proportionate to the foliage. Don't think me a bird of ill omen; only remember that you will be held to a strict account."

"A man should make the most of himself, and be helped if he needs help," Rowland answered, after a long pause. "Of course when a body begins to expand, there comes in the possibility of bursting; but I nevertheless approve of a certain tension of one's being. It 's what a man is meant for. And then I believe in the essential salubrity of genius—true genius."

"Very good," said Cecilia, with an air of resignation which made Rowland, for the moment, seem to himself culpably eager. "We 'll drink then to-day at dinner to the health of our friend."

* * *

Having it much at heart to convince Mrs. Hudson of the purity of his intentions, Rowland waited upon her that evening. He was ushered into a large parlor, which, by the light of a couple of candles, he perceived to be very meagrely furnished and very tenderly and sparingly used. The windows were open to the air of the summer night, and a circle of three persons was temporarily awed into silence by his appearance. One of these was Mrs. Hudson, who was sitting at one of the windows, empty-handed save for the pocket-handkerchief in her lap, which was held with an air of familiarity with its sadder uses. Near her, on the sofa, half sitting, half lounging, in the attitude of a visitor outstaying ceremony, with one long leg flung over the other and a large foot in a clumsy boot swinging to and fro continually, was a lean, sandy-haired gentleman whom Rowland recognized as the original of the portrait of Mr. Barnaby Striker. At the table, near the candles, busy with a substantial piece of needle-work, sat the young girl of whom he had had a moment's quickened glimpse in Roderick's studio, and whom he had learned to be Miss Garland, his companion's kinswoman. This young lady's limpid, penetrating gaze was the most effective greeting he received. Mrs. Hudson rose with a soft, vague sound of distress, and stood looking at him shrinkingly and waveringly, as if she were sorely tempted to retreat through the open window. Mr. Striker swung his long leg a trifle defiantly. No one, evidently, was used to offering hollow welcomes or telling polite fibs. Rowland introduced himself; he had come, he might say, upon business.

"Yes," said Mrs. Hudson tremulously; "I know—my son has told me. I suppose it is better I should see you. Perhaps you will take a seat."

With this invitation Rowland prepared to comply, and, turning, grasped the first chair that offered itself.

"Not that one," said a full, grave voice; whereupon he perceived that a quantity of sewing-silk had been suspended and entangled over the back, preparatory to being wound on reels. He felt the least bit irritated at the curtness of the warning, coming as it did from a young woman whose countenance he had mentally pronounced interesting, and with regard to

371

whom he was conscious of the germ of the inevitable desire to produce a responsive interest. And then he thought it would break the ice to say something playfully urbane.

"Oh, you should let me take the chair," he answered, "and have the pleasure of holding the skeins myself!"

For all reply to this sally he received a stare of undisguised amazement from Miss Garland, who then looked across at Mrs. Hudson with a glance which plainly said: "You see he 's quite the insidious personage we feared." The elder lady, however, sat with her eyes fixed on the ground and her two hands tightly clasped. But touching her Rowland felt much more compassion than resentment; her attitude was not coldness, it was a kind of dread, almost a terror. She was a small, eager woman, with a pale, troubled face, which added to her apparent age. After looking at her for some minutes Rowland saw that she was still young, and that she must have been a very girlish bride. She had been a pretty one, too, though she probably had looked terribly frightened at the altar. She was very delicately made, and Roderick had come honestly by his physical slimness and elegance. She wore no cap, and her flaxen hair, which was of extraordinary fineness, was smoothed and confined with Puritanic precision. She was excessively shy, and evidently very humble-minded; it was singular to see a woman to whom the experience of life had conveyed so little reassurance as to her own resources or the chances of things turning out well. Rowland began immediately to like her, and to feel impatient to persuade her that there was no harm in him, and that, twenty to one, her son would make her a well-pleased woman yet. He foresaw that she would be easy to persuade, and that a benevolent conversational tone would probably make her pass, fluttering, from distrust into an oppressive extreme of confidence. But he had an indefinable sense that the person who was testing that strong young eyesight of hers in the dim candle-light was less readily beguiled from her mysterious feminine preconceptions. Miss Garland, according to Cecilia's judgment, as Rowland remembered, had not a countenance to inspire a sculptor; but it seemed to Rowland that her countenance might fairly inspire a man who was far from being a sculptor. She was not pretty, as the eye of habit judges prettiness, but when you made the observation you somehow failed to set it down against her, for you had already passed from measuring contours to tracing meanings. In Mary Garland's face there were many possible ones, and they gave you the more to think about that it was not—like Roderick Hudson's, for instance—a quick and mobile face, over which expression flickered like a candle in a wind. They followed each other slowly, distinctly, gravely, sincerely, and you might almost have fancied that, as they came and went, they gave her a sort of pain. She was tall and slender, and had an air of maidenly strength and decision. She had a broad forehead and dark eyebrows, a trifle thicker than those of classic beauties; her gray eye was clear but not brilliant, and her features were perfectly irregular. Her mouth was large, fortunately for the principal grace of her physiognomy was her smile, which displayed itself with magnificent amplitude. Rowland, indeed, had not yet seen her smile, but something assured him that her rigid gravity had a radiant counterpart. She wore a scanty white dress, and had a nameless rustic air which would have led one to speak of her less as a young lady than as a young woman. She was evidently a girl of a great personal force, but she lacked pliancy. She was hemming a kitchen towel with the aid of a large steel thimble. She bent her serious eyes at last on her work again, and let Rowland explain himself.

"I have become suddenly so very intimate with your son," he said at last, addressing himself to Mrs. Hudson, "that it seems just I should make your acquaintance."

"Very just," murmured the poor lady, and after a moment's hesitation was on the point of adding something more; but Mr. Striker here interposed, after a prefatory clearance of the throat.

"I should like to take the liberty," he said, "of addressing you a simple question. For how long a period of time have you been acquainted with our young friend?" He continued to kick the air, but his head was thrown back and his eyes fixed on the opposite wall, as if in aversion to the spectacle of Rowland's inevitable confusion.

"A very short time, I confess. Hardly three days."

"And yet you call yourself intimate, eh? I have been seeing Mr. Roderick daily these three years, and yet it was only this morning that I felt as if I had at last the right to say that I knew him. We had a few moments' conversation in my office which supplied the missing links in the evidence. So that now I do venture to say I 'm acquainted with Mr. Roderick! But wait three years, sir, like me!" and Mr. Striker laughed, with a closed mouth and a noiseless shake of all his long person.

Mrs. Hudson smiled confusedly, at hazard; Miss Garland kept her eyes on her stitches. But it seemed to Rowland that the latter colored a little. "Oh, in three years, of course," he said, "we shall know each other better. Before many years are over, madam," he pursued, "I expect the world to know him. I expect him to be a great man!"

Mrs. Hudson looked at first as if this could be but an insidious device for increasing her distress by the assistance of irony. Then reassured, little by little, by Rowland's benevolent visage, she gave him an appealing glance and a timorous "Really?"

But before Rowland could respond, Mr. Striker again intervened. "Do I fully apprehend your expression?" he asked. "Our young friend is to become a great man?"

"A great artist, I hope," said Rowland.

"This is a new and interesting view," said Mr. Striker, with an assumption of judicial calmness. "We have had hopes for Mr. Roderick, but I confess, if I have rightly understood them, they stopped short of greatness. We should n't have taken the responsibility of claiming it for him. What do you say, ladies? We all feel about him here—his mother, Miss Garland, and myself—as if his merits were rather in the line of the"—and Mr. Striker waved his hand with a series of fantastic flourishes in the air—"of the light ornamental!" Mr. Striker bore his recalcitrant pupil a grudge, but he was evidently trying both to be fair and to respect the susceptibilities of his companions. But he was unversed in the mysterious processes of feminine emotion. Ten minutes before, there had been a general harmony of sombre views; but on hearing Roderick's limitations thus distinctly formulated to a stranger, the two ladies mutely protested. Mrs. Hudson uttered a short, faint sigh, and Miss Garland raised her eyes toward their advocate and visited him with a short, cold glance.

"I 'm afraid, Mrs. Hudson," Rowland pursued, evading the discussion of Roderick's possible greatness, "that you don't at all thank me for stirring up your son's ambition on a line which leads him so far from home. I suspect I have made you my enemy."

Mrs. Hudson covered her mouth with her finger-tips and looked painfully perplexed between the desire to confess the truth and the fear of being impolite. "My cousin is no one's enemy," Miss Garland hereupon declared, gently, but with that same fine deliberateness with which she had made Rowland relax his grasp of the chair.

"Does she leave that to you?" Rowland ventured to ask, with a smile.

"We are inspired with none but Christian sentiments," said Mr. Striker; "Miss Garland perhaps most of all. Miss Garland," and Mr. Striker waved his hand again as if to perform an introduction which had been regrettably omitted, "is the daughter of a minister, the granddaughter of a minister, the sister of a minister." Rowland bowed deferentially, and the young girl went on with her sewing, with nothing, apparently, either of embarrassment or elation at the promulgation of these facts. Mr. Striker continued: "Mrs. Hudson, I see, is too deeply agitated to converse with you freely. She will allow me to address you a few questions. Would you kindly inform her, as exactly as possible, just what you propose to do with her son?"

The poor lady fixed her eyes appealingly on Rowland's face and seemed to say that Mr. Striker had spoken her desire, though she herself would have expressed it less defiantly. But Rowland saw in Mr. Striker's many-wrinkled light blue eye, shrewd at once and good-natured, that he had no intention of defiance, and that he was simply pompous and conceited and sarcastically compassionate of any view of things in which Roderick Hudson was regarded in a serious light.

"Do, my dear madam?" demanded Rowland. "I don't propose to do anything. He must do for himself. I simply offer him the chance. He 's to study, to work—hard, I hope."

"Not too hard, please," murmured Mrs. Hudson, pleadingly, wheeling about from recent visions of dangerous leisure. "He 's not very strong, and I 'm afraid the climate of Europe is very relaxing."

"Ah, study?" repeated Mr. Striker. "To what line of study is he to direct his attention?" Then suddenly, with an impulse of disinterested curiosity on his own account, "How do you study sculpture, anyhow?"

"By looking at models and imitating them."

"At models, eh? To what kind of models do you refer?"

"To the antique, in the first place."

"Ah, the antique," repeated Mr. Striker, with a jocose intonation. "Do you hear, madam? Roderick is going off to Europe to learn to imitate the antique."

"I suppose it 's all right," said Mrs. Hudson, twisting herself in a sort of delicate anguish.

"An antique, as I understand it," the lawyer continued, "is an image of a pagan deity, with considerable dirt sticking to it, and no arms, no nose, and no clothing. A precious model, certainly!"

"That 's a very good description of many," said Rowland, with a laugh.

"Mercy! Truly?" asked Mrs. Hudson, borrowing courage from his urbanity.

"But a sculptor's studies, you intimate, are not confined to the antique," Mr. Striker resumed. "After he has been looking three or four years at the objects I describe"—

"He studies the living model," said Rowland.

"Does it take three or four years?" asked Mrs. Hudson, imploringly.

"That depends upon the artist's aptitude. After twenty years a real artist is still studying."

"Oh, my poor boy!" moaned Mrs. Hudson, finding the prospect, under every light, still terrible.

"Now this study of the living model," Mr. Striker pursued. "Inform Mrs. Hudson about that."

"Oh dear, no!" cried Mrs. Hudson, shrinkingly.

"That too," said Rowland, "is one of the reasons for studying in Rome. It 's a handsome race, you know, and you find very well-made people."

"I suppose they 're no better made than a good tough Yankee," objected Mr. Striker, transposing his interminable legs. "The same God made us."

"Surely," sighed Mrs. Hudson, but with a questioning glance at her visitor which showed that she had already begun to concede much weight to his opinion. Rowland hastened to express his assent to Mr. Striker's proposition.

Miss Garland looked up, and, after a moment's hesitation: "Are the Roman women very beautiful?" she asked.

Rowland too, in answering, hesitated; he was looking straight at the young girl. "On the whole, I prefer ours," he said.

She had dropped her work in her lap; her hands were crossed upon it, her head thrown a little back. She had evidently expected a more impersonal answer, and she was dissatisfied. For an instant she seemed inclined to make a rejoinder, but she slowly picked up her work in silence and drew her stitches again.

Rowland had for the second time the feeling that she judged him to be a person of a disagreeably sophisticated tone. He noticed too that the kitchen towel she was hemming was terribly coarse. And yet his answer had a resonant inward echo, and he repeated to himself, "Yes, on the whole, I prefer ours."

"Well, these models," began Mr. Striker. "You put them into an attitude, I suppose."

"An attitude, exactly."

"And then you sit down and look at them."

"You must not sit too long. You must go at your clay and try to build up something that looks like them."

"Well, there you are with your model in an attitude on one side, yourself, in an attitude too, I suppose, on the other, and your pile of clay in the middle, building up, as you say. So you pass the morning. After that I hope you go out and take a walk, and rest from your exertions."

"Unquestionably. But to a sculptor who loves his work there is no time lost. Everything he looks at teaches or suggests something."

"That 's a tempting doctrine to young men with a taste for sitting by the hour with the page unturned, watching the flies buzz, or the frost melt on the window-pane. Our young friend, in this way, must have laid up stores of information which I never suspected!"

"Very likely," said Rowland, with an unresentful smile, "he will prove some day the completer artist for some of those lazy reveries."

This theory was apparently very grateful to Mrs. Hudson, who had never had the case put for her son with such ingenious hopefulness, and found herself disrelishing the singular situation of seeming to side against her own flesh and blood with a lawyer whose conversational tone betrayed the habit of cross-questioning.

"My son, then," she ventured to ask, "my son has great—what you would call great powers?"

"To my sense, very great powers."

Poor Mrs. Hudson actually smiled, broadly, gleefully, and glanced at Miss Garland, as if to invite her to do likewise. But the young girl's face remained serious, like the eastern sky when the opposite sunset is too feeble to make it glow. "Do you really know?" she asked, looking at Rowland.

"One cannot know in such a matter save after proof, and proof takes time. But one can believe."

"And you believe?"

"I believe."

But even then Miss Garland vouchsafed no smile. Her face became graver than ever.

"Well, well," said Mrs. Hudson, "we must hope that it is all for the best."

Mr. Striker eyed his old friend for a moment with a look of some displeasure; he saw that this was but a cunning feminine imitation of resignation, and that, through some untraceable process of transition, she was now taking more comfort in the opinions of this insinuating stranger than in his own tough dogmas. He rose to his feet, without pulling down his waistcoat, but with a wrinkled grin at the inconsistency of women. "Well, sir, Mr. Roderick's powers are nothing to me," he said, "nor no use he makes of them. Good or bad, he 's no son of mine. But, in a friendly way, I 'm glad to hear so fine an account of him. I 'm glad, madam, you 're so satisfied with the prospect. Affection, sir, you see, must have its guarantees!" He paused a moment, stroking his beard, with his head inclined and one eye half-closed, looking at Rowland. The look was grotesque, but it was significant, and it puzzled Rowland more than it amused him. "I suppose you 're a very brilliant young man," he went on, "very enlightened, very cultivated, quite up to the mark in the fine arts and all that sort of thing. I 'm a plain, practical old boy, content to follow an honorable profession in a free country. I did n't go off to the Old World to learn my business; no one took me by the hand; I had to grease my wheels myself, and, such as I am, I 'm a self-made man, every inch of me! Well, if our young friend is booked for fame and fortune, I don't suppose his going to Rome will stop him. But, mind you, it won't help him such a long way, either. If you have undertaken to put him through, there 's a thing or two you 'd better remember. The crop we gather depends upon the seed we sow. He may be the biggest genius of the age: his potatoes won't come up without his hoeing them. If he takes things so almighty easy as—well, as one or two young fellows of genius I 've had under my eye—his produce will never gain the prize. Take the word for it of a man who has made his way inch by inch, and does n't believe that we 'll wake up to find our work done

379

because we 've lain all night a-dreaming of it; anything worth doing is devilish hard to do! If your young protajay finds things easy and has a good time and says he likes the life, it 's a sign that—as I may say—you had better step round to the office and look at the books. That 's all I desire to remark. No offense intended. I hope you 'll have a first-rate time."

Rowland could honestly reply that this seemed pregnant sense, and he offered Mr. Striker a friendly hand-shake as the latter withdrew. But Mr. Striker's rather grim view of matters cast a momentary shadow on his companions, and Mrs. Hudson seemed to feel that it necessitated between them some little friendly agreement not to be overawed.

Rowland sat for some time longer, partly because he wished to please the two women and partly because he was strangely pleased himself. There was something touching in their unworldly fears and diffident hopes, something almost terrible in the way poor little Mrs. Hudson seemed to flutter and quiver with intense maternal passion. She put forth one timid conversational venture after another, and asked Rowland a number of questions about himself, his age, his family, his occupations, his tastes, his religious opinions. Rowland had an odd feeling at last that she had begun to consider him very exemplary, and that she might make, later, some perturbing discovery. He tried, therefore, to invent something that would prepare her to find him fallible. But he could think of nothing. It only seemed to him that Miss Garland secretly mistrusted him, and that he must leave her to render him the service, after he had gone, of making him the object of a little firm derogation. Mrs. Hudson talked with low-voiced eagerness about her son.

"He 's very lovable, sir, I assure you. When you come to know him you 'll find him very lovable. He 's a little spoiled, of course; he has always done with me as he pleased; but he 's a good boy, I 'm sure he 's a good boy. And every one thinks him very attractive: I 'm sure he 'd be noticed, anywhere. Don't you think he 's very handsome, sir? He features his poor father. I had another—perhaps you 've been told. He was killed." And the poor little lady bravely smiled, for fear of doing worse. "He was a very fine boy, but very different from Roderick. Roderick is a little strange; he has never been an easy boy. Sometimes I feel like the goose—was n't it a goose, dear?" and startled by the audacity of her comparison she appealed to Miss Garland—"the goose, or the hen, who hatched a swan's egg. I have never been able to give him what he needs. I have always thought that in more—in more brilliant circumstances he might find his place and be happy. But at the same time I was afraid of the world for him; it was so large and dangerous and dreadful. No doubt I know very little about it. I never suspected, I confess, that it contained persons of such liberality as yours."

Rowland replied that, evidently, she had done the world but scanty justice. "No," objected Miss Garland, after a pause, "it is like something in a fairy tale."

"What, pray?"

"Your coming here all unknown, so rich and so polite, and carrying off my cousin in a golden cloud."

If this was badinage Miss Garland had the best of it, for Rowland almost fell a-musing silently over the question whether there was a possibility of irony in that transparent gaze. Before he withdrew, Mrs. Hudson made him tell her again that Roderick's powers were extraordinary. He had inspired her with a clinging, caressing faith in his wisdom. "He will really do great things," she asked, "the very greatest?"

"I see no reason in his talent itself why he should not."

"Well, we 'll think of that as we sit here alone," she rejoined. "Mary and I will sit here and talk about it. So I give him up," she went on, as he was going. "I 'm sure you 'll be the best of friends to him, but if you should ever forget him, or grow tired of him, or lose your interest in him, and he should come to any harm or any trouble, please, sir, remember"—And she paused, with a tremulous voice.

"Remember, my dear madam?"

"That he is all I have—that he is everything—and that it would be very terrible."

"In so far as I can help him, he shall succeed," was all Rowland could say. He turned to Miss Garland, to bid her good night, and she rose and put out her hand. She was very straightforward, but he could see that if she was too modest to be bold, she was much too simple to be shy. "Have you no charge to lay upon me?" he asked—to ask her something.

She looked at him a moment and then, although she was not shy, she blushed. "Make him do his best," she said.

Rowland noted the soft intensity with which the words were uttered. "Do you take a great interest in him?" he demanded.

"Certainly."

"Then, if he will not do his best for you, he will not do it for me." She turned away with another blush, and Rowland took his leave.

He walked homeward, thinking of many things. The great Northampton elms interarched far above in the darkness, but the moon had risen and through scattered apertures was hanging the dusky vault with silver lamps. There seemed to Rowland something intensely serious in the scene in which he had just taken part. He had laughed and talked and braved it out in self-defense; but when he reflected that he was really meddling with the simple stillness of this little New England home, and that he had ventured to disturb so much living security in the interest of a far-away, fantastic hypothesis, he paused, amazed at his temerity. It was true, as Cecilia had said, that for an unofficious man it was a singular position. There stirred in his mind an odd feeling of annoyance with Roderick for having thus peremptorily enlisted his sympathies. As he looked up and down the long vista, and saw the clear white houses glancing here and there in the broken moonshine, he could almost have believed that the happiest lot for any man was to make the most of life in some such tranquil spot as that. Here were kindness, comfort, safety, the warning voice of duty, the perfect hush of temptation. And as Rowland looked along the arch of silvered shadow and out into the lucid air of the American night, which seemed so doubly vast, somehow, and strange and nocturnal, he felt like declaring that here was beauty too—beauty sufficient for an artist not to starve upon it. As he stood, lost in the darkness, he presently heard a rapid tread on the other side of the road, accompanied by a loud, jubilant whistle, and in a moment a figure emerged into an open gap of moonshine. He had no difficulty in recognizing Hudson, who was presumably returning from a visit to Cecilia. Roderick stopped suddenly and stared up at the moon, with his face vividly illuminated. He broke out into a snatch of song:—

"The splendor falls on castle walls And snowy summits old in story!"

And with a great, musical roll of his voice he went swinging off into the darkness again, as if his thoughts had lent him wings. He was dreaming of the inspiration of foreign lands,—of castled crags and historic landscapes. What a pity, after all, thought Rowland, as he went his own way, that he should n't have a taste of it!

It had been a very just remark of Cecilia's that Roderick would change with a change in his circumstances. Rowland had telegraphed to New York for another berth on his steamer, and from the hour the answer came Hudson's spirits rose to incalculable heights. He was radiant with good-humor, and his kindly jollity seemed the pledge of a brilliant future. He had forgiven his old enemies and forgotten his old grievances, and seemed every way reconciled to a world in which he was going to count as an active force. He was inexhaustibly loquacious and fantastic, and as Cecilia said, he had suddenly become so good that it was only to be feared he was going to start not for Europe but for heaven. He took long walks with Rowland, who felt more and more the fascination of what he would have called his giftedness. Rowland returned several times to Mrs. Hudson's, and found the two ladies doing their best to be happy in their companion's happiness. Miss Garland, he thought, was succeeding better than her demeanor on his first visit had promised. He tried to have some especial talk with her, but her extreme reserve forced him to content himself with such response to his rather urgent overtures as might be extracted from a keenly attentive smile. It must be confessed, however, that if the response was vague, the satisfaction was great, and that Rowland, after his second visit, kept seeing a lurking reflection of this smile in the most unexpected places. It seemed strange that she should please him so well at so slender a cost, but please him she did, prodigiously, and his pleasure had a quality altogether new to him. It made him restless, and a trifle melancholy; he walked about absently, wondering and wishing. He wondered, among other things, why fate should have condemned him to make the acquaintance of a girl whom he would make a sacrifice to know better, just as he was leaving the country for years. It seemed to him that he was turning his back on a chance of happiness—happiness of a sort of which the slenderest germ should be cultivated. He asked himself whether, feeling as he did, if he had only himself to please, he would give up his journey and—wait. He had Roderick to please now, for whom disappointment would be cruel; but he said to himself that certainly, if there were no Roderick in the case, the ship should sail without him. He asked Hudson several questions about his cousin, but Roderick, confidential on most points, seemed to have reasons of his own for being reticent on this one. His measured answers quickened Rowland's curiosity, for Miss Garland, with her own irritating half-suggestions, had only to be a subject of guarded allusion in others to become intolerably interesting. He learned from Roderick that she was the daughter of a country minister, a far-away cousin of his mother, settled in another part of the State; that she was one of a half-a-dozen daughters, that the family was very poor, and that she had come a couple of months before to pay his mother a long visit. "It is to be a very long one now," he said, "for it is settled that she is to remain while I am away."

The fermentation of contentment in Roderick's soul reached its climax a few days before the young men were to make their farewells. He had been sitting with his friends on Cecilia's veranda, but for half an hour past he had said nothing. Lounging back against a vine-wreathed column and gazing idly at the stars, he kept caroling softly to himself with that indifference to ceremony for which he always found allowance, and which in him had a sort of pleading grace. At last, springing up: "I want to strike out, hard!" he exclaimed. "I want to do something violent, to let off steam!"

"I 'll tell you what to do, this lovely weather," said Cecilia. "Give a picnic. It can be as violent as you please, and it will have the merit of leading off our emotion into a safe channel, as well as yours."

Roderick laughed uproariously at Cecilia's very practical remedy for his sentimental need, but a couple of days later, nevertheless, the picnic was given. It was to be a family party, but Roderick, in his magnanimous geniality, insisted on inviting Mr. Striker, a decision which Rowland mentally applauded. "And we 'll have Mrs. Striker, too," he said, "if she 'll come, to keep my mother in countenance; and at any rate we 'll have Miss Striker—the divine Petronilla!" The young lady thus denominated formed, with Mrs. Hudson, Miss Garland, and Cecilia, the feminine half of the company. Mr. Striker presented himself, sacrificing a morning's work, with a magnanimity greater even than Roderick's, and foreign support was further secured in the person of Mr. Whitefoot, the young Orthodox minister. Roderick had chosen the feasting-place; he knew it well and had passed many a summer afternoon there, lying at his length on the grass and gazing at the blue undulations of the horizon. It was a meadow on the edge of a wood, with mossy rocks protruding through the grass and a little lake on the other side. It was a cloudless August day; Rowland always remembered it, and the scene, and everything that was said and done, with extraordinary distinctness. Roderick surpassed himself in friendly jollity, and at one moment, when exhilaration was at the highest, was seen in Mr. Striker's high white hat, drinking champagne from a broken tea-cup to Mr. Striker's health. Miss Striker had her father's pale blue eye; she was dressed as if she were going to sit for her photograph, and remained for a long time with Roderick on a little promontory overhanging the lake. Mrs. Hudson sat all day with a little meek, apprehensive smile. She was afraid of an "accident," though unless Miss Striker (who indeed was a little of a romp) should push Roderick into the lake, it was hard to see what accident could occur. Mrs. Hudson was as neat and crisp and uncrumpled at the end of the festival as at the beginning. Mr. Whitefoot, who but a twelvemonth later became a convert to episcopacy and was already cultivating a certain conversational sonority, devoted himself to Cecilia. He had a little book in his pocket, out of which he read to her at intervals, lying stretched at her feet, and it was a lasting joke with Cecilia, afterwards, that she would never tell what Mr. Whitefoot's little book had been. Rowland had placed himself near Miss Garland, while the feasting went forward on the grass. She wore a so-called gypsy hat—a little straw hat, tied down over her ears, so as to cast her eyes into shadow, by a ribbon passing outside of it. When the company dispersed, after lunch, he proposed to her to take a stroll in the wood. She hesitated a moment and looked toward Mrs. Hudson, as if for permission to leave her. But Mrs. Hudson was listening to Mr. Striker, who sat gossiping to her with relaxed magniloquence, his waistcoat unbuttoned and his hat on his nose.

"You can give your cousin your society at any time," said Rowland. "But me, perhaps, you 'll never see again."

"Why then should we wish to be friends, if nothing is to come of it?" she asked, with homely logic. But by this time she had consented, and they were treading the fallen pine-needles.

"Oh, one must take all one can get," said Rowland. "If we can be friends for half an hour, it 's so much gained."

"Do you expect never to come back to Northampton again?"

"'Never' is a good deal to say. But I go to Europe for a long stay."

"Do you prefer it so much to your own country?"

"I will not say that. But I have the misfortune to be a rather idle man, and in Europe the burden of idleness is less heavy than here."

She was silent for a few minutes; then at last, "In that, then, we are better than Europe," she said. To a certain point Rowland agreed with her, but he demurred, to make her say more.

"Would n't it be better," she asked, "to work to get reconciled to America, than to go to Europe to get reconciled to idleness?"

"Doubtless; but you know work is hard to find."

"I come from a little place where every one has plenty," said Miss Garland. "We all work; every one I know works. And really," she added presently, "I look at you with curiosity; you are the first unoccupied man I ever saw."

"Don't look at me too hard," said Rowland, smiling. "I shall sink into the earth. What is the name of your little place?"

"West Nazareth," said Miss Garland, with her usual sobriety. "It is not so very little, though it 's smaller than Northampton."

"I wonder whether I could find any work at West Nazareth," Rowland said.

"You would not like it," Miss Garland declared reflectively. "Though there are far finer woods there than this. We have miles and miles of woods."

"I might chop down trees," said Rowland. "That is, if you allow it."

"Allow it? Why, where should we get our firewood?" Then, noticing that he had spoken jestingly, she glanced at him askance, though with no visible diminution of her gravity. "Don't you know how to do anything? Have you no profession?"

Rowland shook his head. "Absolutely none."

"What do you do all day?"

"Nothing worth relating. That 's why I am going to Europe. There, at least, if I do nothing, I shall see a great deal; and if I 'm not a producer, I shall at any rate be an observer."

"Can't we observe everywhere?"

"Certainly; and I really think that in that way I make the most of my opportunities. Though I confess," he continued, "that I often remember there are things to be seen here to which I probably have n't done justice. I should like, for instance, to see West Nazareth."

She looked round at him, open-eyed; not, apparently, that she exactly supposed he was jesting, for the expression of such a desire was not necessarily facetious; but as if he must have spoken with an ulterior motive. In fact, he had spoken from the simplest of motives. The girl beside him pleased him unspeakably, and, suspecting that her charm was essentially her own and not reflected from social circumstance, he wished to give himself the satisfaction of contrasting her with the meagre influences of her education. Miss Garland's second movement was to take him at his word. "Since you are free to do as you please, why don't you go there?"

"I am not free to do as I please now. I have offered your cousin to bear him company to Europe, he has accepted with enthusiasm, and I cannot retract."

"Are you going to Europe simply for his sake?"

Rowland hesitated a moment. "I think I may almost say so."

Miss Garland walked along in silence. "Do you mean to do a great deal for him?" she asked at last.

"What I can. But my power of helping him is very small beside his power of helping himself."

For a moment she was silent again. "You are very generous," she said, almost solemnly.

"No, I am simply very shrewd. Roderick will repay me. It 's an investment. At first, I think," he added shortly afterwards, "you would not have paid me that compliment. You distrusted me."

She made no attempt to deny it. "I did n't see why you should wish to make Roderick discontented. I thought you were rather frivolous."

"You did me injustice. I don't think I 'm that."

"It was because you are unlike other men—those, at least, whom I have seen."

"In what way?"

"Why, as you describe yourself. You have no duties, no profession, no home. You live for your pleasure."

"That 's all very true. And yet I maintain I 'm not frivolous."

"I hope not," said Miss Garland, simply. They had reached a point where the wood-path forked and put forth two divergent tracks which lost themselves in a verdurous tangle. Miss Garland seemed to think that the difficulty of choice between them was a reason for giving them up and turning back. Rowland thought otherwise, and detected agreeable grounds for preference in the left-hand path. As a compromise, they sat down on a fallen log. Looking about him, Rowland espied a curious wild shrub, with a spotted crimson leaf; he went and plucked a spray of it and brought it to Miss

Garland. He had never observed it before, but she immediately called it by its name. She expressed surprise at his not knowing it; it was extremely common. He presently brought her a specimen of another delicate plant, with a little blue-streaked flower. "I suppose that 's common, too," he said, "but I have never seen it—or noticed it, at least." She answered that this one was rare, and meditated a moment before she could remember its name. At last she recalled it, and expressed surprise at his having found the plant in the woods; she supposed it grew only in open marshes. Rowland complimented her on her fund of useful information.

"It 's not especially useful," she answered; "but I like to know the names of plants as I do those of my acquaintances. When we walk in the woods at home—which we do so much—it seems as unnatural not to know what to call the flowers as it would be to see some one in the town with whom we were not on speaking terms."

"Apropos of frivolity," Rowland said, "I 'm sure you have very little of it, unless at West Nazareth it is considered frivolous to walk in the woods and nod to the nodding flowers. Do kindly tell me a little about yourself." And to compel her to begin, "I know you come of a race of theologians," he went on.

"No," she replied, deliberating; "they are not theologians, though they are ministers. We don't take a very firm stand upon doctrine; we are practical, rather. We write sermons and preach them, but we do a great deal of hard work beside."

"And of this hard work what has your share been?"

"The hardest part: doing nothing."

"What do you call nothing?"

"I taught school a while: I must make the most of that. But I confess I did n't like it. Otherwise, I have only done little things at home, as they turned up."

"What kind of things?"

"Oh, every kind. If you had seen my home, you would understand."

Rowland would have liked to make her specify; but he felt a more urgent need to respect her simplicity than he had ever felt to defer to the complex circumstance of certain other women. "To be happy, I imagine," he contented himself with saying, "you need to be occupied. You need to have something to expend yourself upon."

"That is not so true as it once was; now that I am older, I am sure I am less impatient of leisure. Certainly, these two months that I have been with Mrs. Hudson, I have had a terrible amount of it. And yet I have liked it! And now that I am probably to be with her all the while that her son is away, I look forward to more with a resignation that I don't quite know what to make of."

"It is settled, then, that you are to remain with your cousin?"

"It depends upon their writing from home that I may stay. But that is probable. Only I must not forget," she said, rising, "that the ground for my doing so is that she be not left alone."

"I am glad to know," said Rowland, "that I shall probably often hear about you. I assure you I shall often think about you!" These words were half impulsive, half deliberate. They were the simple truth, and he had asked himself why he should not tell her the truth. And yet they were not all of it; her hearing the rest would depend upon the way she received this. She received it not only, as Rowland foresaw, without a shadow of coquetry, of any apparent thought of listening to it gracefully, but with a slight movement of nervous deprecation, which seemed to betray itself in the quickening of her step. Evidently, if Rowland was to take pleasure in hearing about her, it would have to be a highly disinterested pleasure. She answered nothing, and Rowland too, as he walked beside her, was silent; but as he looked along the shadow-woven wood-path, what he was really facing was a level three years of disinterestedness. He ushered them in by talking composed civility until he had brought Miss Garland back to her companions.

He saw her but once again. He was obliged to be in New York a couple of days before sailing, and it was arranged that Roderick should overtake him at the last moment. The evening before he left Northampton he went to say farewell to Mrs. Hudson. The ceremony was brief. Rowland soon perceived that the poor little lady was in the melting mood, and, as he dreaded her tears, he compressed a multitude of solemn promises into a silent hand-shake and took his leave. Miss Garland, she had told him, was in the back-garden with Roderick: he might go out to them. He did so, and as he drew near he heard Roderick's high-pitched voice ringing behind the shrubbery. In a moment, emerging, he found Miss Garland leaning against a tree, with her cousin before her talking with great emphasis. He asked pardon for interrupting them, and said he wished only to bid her good-by. She gave him her hand and he made her his bow in silence. "Don't forget," he said to Roderick, as he turned away. "And don't, in this company, repent of your bargain."

"I shall not let him," said Miss Garland, with something very like gayety. "I shall see that he is punctual. He must go! I owe you an apology for having doubted that he ought to." And in spite of the dusk Rowland could see that she had an even finer smile than he had supposed.

Roderick was punctual, eagerly punctual, and they went. Rowland for several days was occupied with material cares, and lost sight of his sentimental perplexities. But they only slumbered, and they were sharply awakened. The weather was fine, and the two young men always sat together upon deck late into the evening. One night, toward the last, they were at the stern of the great ship, watching her grind the solid blackness of the ocean into phosphorescent foam. They talked on these occasions of everything conceivable, and had the air of having no secrets from each other. But it was on Roderick's conscience that this air belied him, and he was too frank by nature, moreover, for permanent reticence on any point.

"I must tell you something," he said at last. "I should like you to know it, and you will be so glad to know it. Besides, it 's only a question of time; three months hence, probably, you would have guessed it. I am engaged to Mary Garland."

Rowland sat staring; though the sea was calm, it seemed to him that the ship gave a great dizzying lurch. But in a moment he contrived to answer coherently: "Engaged to Miss Garland! I never supposed—I never imagined"—

"That I was in love with her?" Roderick interrupted. "Neither did I, until this last fortnight. But you came and put me into such ridiculous good-humor that I felt an extraordinary desire to tell some woman that I adored her. Miss Garland is a magnificent girl; you know her too little to do her justice. I have been quietly learning to know her, these past three months, and have been falling in love with her without being conscious of it. It appeared, when I spoke to her, that she had a kindness for me. So the thing was settled. I must of course make some money before we can marry. It 's rather droll, certainly, to engage one's self to a girl whom one is going to leave the next day, for years. We shall be condemned, for some time to come, to do a terrible deal of abstract thinking about each other. But I wanted her blessing on my career and I could not help asking for it. Unless a man is unnaturally selfish he needs to work for some one else than himself, and I am sure I shall run a smoother and swifter course for knowing that that fine creature is waiting, at Northampton, for news of my greatness. If ever I am a dull companion and over-addicted to moping, remember in justice to me that I am in love and that my sweetheart is five thousand miles away."

Rowland listened to all this with a sort of feeling that fortune had played him an elaborately-devised trick. It had lured him out into mid-ocean and smoothed the sea and stilled the winds and given him a singularly sympathetic comrade, and then it had turned and delivered him a thumping blow in mid-chest. "Yes," he said, after an attempt at the usual formal congratulation, "you certainly ought to do better—with Miss Garland waiting for you at Northampton."

Roderick, now that he had broken ground, was eloquent and rung a hundred changes on the assurance that he was a very happy man. Then at last, suddenly, his climax was a yawn, and he declared that he must go to bed. Rowland let him go alone, and sat there late, between sea and sky.

CHAPTER III. Rome

One warm, still day, late in the Roman autumn, our two young men were sitting beneath one of the high-stemmed pines of the Villa Ludovisi. They had been spending an hour in the mouldy little garden-house, where the colossal mask of the famous Juno looks out with blank eyes from that dusky corner which must seem to her the last possible stage of a lapse from Olympus. Then they had wandered out into the gardens, and were lounging away the morning under the spell of their magical picturesqueness. Roderick declared that he would go nowhere else; that, after the Juno, it was a profanation to look at anything but sky and trees. There was a fresco of Guercino, to which Rowland, though he had seen it on his former visit to Rome, went dutifully to pay his respects. But Roderick, though he had never seen it, declared that it could n't be worth a fig, and that he did n't care to look at ugly things. He remained stretched on his overcoat, which he had spread on the grass, while Rowland went off envying the intellectual comfort of genius, which can arrive at serene conclusions without disagreeable processes. When the latter came back, his friend was sitting with his elbows on his knees and his head in his hands. Rowland, in the geniality of a mood attuned to the mellow charm of a Roman villa, found a good word to say for the Guercino; but he chiefly talked of the view from the little belvedere on the roof of the casino, and how it looked like the prospect from a castle turret in a fairy tale.

"Very likely," said Roderick, throwing himself back with a yawn. "But I must let it pass. I have seen enough for the present; I have reached the top of the hill. I have an indigestion of impressions; I must work them off before I go in for any more. I don't want to look at any more of other people's works, for a month—not even at Nature's own. I want to look at Roderick Hudson's. The result of it all is that I 'm not afraid. I can but try, as well as the rest of them! The fellow who did that gazing goddess yonder only made an experiment. The other day, when I was looking at Michael Angelo's Moses, I was seized with a kind of defiance—a reaction against all this mere passive enjoyment of grandeur. It was a rousing great success, certainly, that rose there before me, but somehow it was not an inscrutable mystery, and it seemed to me, not perhaps that I should some day do as well, but that at least I might!"

"As you say, you can but try," said Rowland. "Success is only passionate effort."

"Well, the passion is blazing; we have been piling on fuel handsomely. It came over me just now that it is exactly three months to a day since I left Northampton. I can't believe it!"

"It certainly seems more."

"It seems like ten years. What an exquisite ass I was!"

"Do you feel so wise now?"

"Verily! Don't I look so? Surely I have n't the same face. Have n't I a different eye, a different expression, a different voice?"

"I can hardly say, because I have seen the transition. But it 's very likely. You are, in the literal sense of the word, more civilized. I dare say," added Rowland, "that Miss Garland would think so."

"That 's not what she would call it; she would say I was corrupted."

Rowland asked few questions about Miss Garland, but he always listened narrowly to his companion's voluntary observations.

"Are you very sure?" he replied.

"Why, she 's a stern moralist, and she would infer from my appearance that I had become a cynical sybarite." Roderick had, in fact, a Venetian watch-chain round his neck and a magnificent Roman intaglio on the third finger of his left hand.

"Will you think I take a liberty," asked Rowland, "if I say you judge her superficially?"

"For heaven's sake," cried Roderick, laughing, "don't tell me she 's not a moralist! It was for that I fell in love with her, and with rigid virtue in her person."

"She is a moralist, but not, as you imply, a narrow one. That 's more than a difference in degree; it 's a difference in kind. I don't know whether I ever mentioned it, but I admire her extremely. There is nothing narrow about her but her experience; everything else is large. My impression of her is of a person of great capacity, as yet wholly unmeasured and untested. Some day or other, I 'm sure, she will judge fairly and wisely of everything."

"Stay a bit!" cried Roderick; "you 're a better Catholic than the Pope. I shall be content if she judges fairly of me—of my merits, that is. The rest she must not judge at all. She 's a grimly devoted little creature; may she always remain so! Changed as I am, I adore her none the less. What becomes of all our emotions, our impressions," he went on, after a long pause, "all the material of thought that life pours into us at such a rate during such a memorable three months as these? There are twenty moments a week—a day, for that matter, some days—that seem supreme, twenty impressions that seem ultimate, that appear to form an intellectual era. But others come treading on their heels and sweeping them along, and they all melt like water into water and settle the question of precedence among themselves. The curious thing is that the more the mind takes in, the more it has space for, and that all one's ideas are like the Irish people at home who live in the different corners of a room, and take boarders."

"I fancy it is our peculiar good luck that we don't see the limits of our minds," said Rowland. "We are young, compared with what we may one day be. That belongs to youth; it is perhaps the best part of it. They say that old people do find themselves at last face to face with a solid blank wall, and stand thumping against it in vain. It resounds, it seems to have something beyond it, but it won't move! That 's only a reason for living with open doors as long as we can!"

"Open doors?" murmured Roderick. "Yes, let us close no doors that open upon Rome. For this, for the mind, is eternal summer! But though my doors may stand open to-day," he presently added, "I shall see no visitors. I want to pause and breathe; I want to dream of a statue. I have been working hard for three months; I have earned a right to a reverie."

Rowland, on his side, was not without provision for reflection, and they lingered on in broken, desultory talk. Rowland felt the need for intellectual rest, for a truce to present care for churches, statues, and pictures, on even better grounds than his companion, inasmuch as he had really been living Roderick's intellectual life the past three months, as well as his own. As he looked back on these full-flavored weeks, he drew a long breath of satisfaction, almost of relief. Roderick, thus far, had justified his confidence and flattered his perspicacity; he was rapidly unfolding into an ideal brilliancy. He was changed even more than he himself suspected; he had stepped, without faltering, into his birthright, and was spending money, intellectually, as lavishly as a young heir who has just won an obstructive lawsuit. Roderick's glance and voice were the same, doubtless, as when they enlivened the summer dusk on Cecilia's veranda, but in his person, generally, there was an indefinable expression of experience rapidly and easily assimilated. Rowland had been struck at the outset with the instinctive quickness of his observation and his free appropriation of whatever might serve his purpose. He had not been, for instance, half an hour on English soil before he perceived that he was dressed like a rustic, and he had immediately reformed his toilet with the most unerring tact. His appetite for novelty was insatiable, and for everything characteristically foreign, as it presented itself, he had an extravagant greeting; but in half an hour the novelty had faded, he had guessed the secret, he had plucked out the heart of the mystery and was clamoring for a keener sensation. At the end of a month, he presented, mentally, a puzzling spectacle to his companion. He had caught, instinctively, the key-note of the old world. He observed and enjoyed, he criticised and rhapsodized, but though all things interested him and many delighted him, none surprised him; he had divined their logic and measured their proportions, and referred them infallibly to their categories. Witnessing the rate at which he did intellectual execution on the general spectacle of European life, Rowland at moments felt vaguely uneasy for the future; the boy was living too fast, he would have said, and giving alarming pledges to ennui in his later years. But we must live as our pulses are timed, and Roderick's struck the hour very often. He was, by imagination, though he never became in manner, a natural man of the world; he had intuitively, as an artist, what one may call the historic consciousness.

He had a relish for social subtleties and mysteries, and, in perception, when occasion offered him an inch he never failed to take an ell. A single glimpse of a social situation of the elder type enabled him to construct the whole, with all its complex chiaroscuro, and Rowland more than once assured him that he made him believe in the metempsychosis, and that he must have lived in European society, in the last century, as a gentleman in a cocked hat and brocaded waistcoat. Hudson asked Rowland questions which poor Rowland was quite unable to answer, and of which he was equally unable to conceive where he had picked up the data. Roderick ended by answering them himself, tolerably to his satisfaction, and in a short time he had almost turned the tables and become in their walks and talks the accredited source of information. Rowland told him that when he turned sculptor a capital novelist was spoiled, and that to match his eye for social detail one would have to go to Honore de Balzac. In all this Rowland took a generous pleasure; he felt an especial kindness for his comrade's radiant youthfulness of temperament. He was so much younger than he himself had ever been! And surely youth and genius, hand in hand, were the most beautiful sight in the world. Roderick added to this the charm of his more immediately personal qualities. The vivacity of his perceptions, the audacity of his imagination, the picturesqueness of his phrase when he was pleased,—and even more when he was displeased,—his abounding good-humor, his candor, his unclouded frankness, his unfailing impulse to share every emotion and impression with his friend; all this made comradeship a pure felicity, and interfused with a deeper amenity their long evening talks at cafe doors in Italian towns.

They had gone almost immediately to Paris, and had spent their days at the Louvre and their evenings at the theatre. Roderick was divided in mind as to whether Titian or Mademoiselle Delaporte was the greater artist. They had come down through France to Genoa and Milan, had spent a fortnight in Venice and another in Florence, and had now been a month in Rome. Roderick had said that he meant to spend three months in simply looking, absorbing, and reflecting, without putting pencil to paper. He looked indefatigably, and certainly saw great things—things greater, doubtless, at times, than the intentions of the artist. And yet he made few false steps and wasted little time in theories of what he ought to like and to dislike. He judged instinctively and passionately, but never vulgarly. At Venice, for a couple of days, he had half a fit of melancholy over the pretended discovery that he had missed his way, and that the only proper vestment of plastic conceptions was the coloring of Titian and Paul Veronese. Then one morning the two young men had themselves rowed out to Torcello, and Roderick lay back for a couple of hours watching a brown-breasted gondolier making superb muscular movements, in high relief, against the sky of the Adriatic, and at the end jerked himself up with a violence that nearly swamped the gondola, and declared that the only thing worth living for was to make a colossal bronze and set it aloft in the light of a public square. In Rome his first care was for the Vatican; he went there again and again. But the old imperial and papal city altogether delighted him; only there he really found what he had been looking for from the first—the complete antipodes of Northampton. And indeed Rome is the natural home of those spirits with which we just now claimed fellowship for Roderick—the spirits with a deep relish for the artificial element in life and the infinite superpositions of history. It is the immemorial city of convention. The stagnant Roman air is charged with convention; it colors the yellow light and deepens the chilly shadows. And in that still recent day the most impressive convention in all history was visible to men's eyes, in the Roman streets, erect in a gilded coach drawn by four black horses. Roderick's first fortnight was a high aesthetic revel. He declared that Rome made him feel and understand more things than he could express: he was sure that life must have there, for all one's senses, an incomparable fineness; that more interesting things must happen to one than anywhere else. And he gave Rowland to understand that he meant to live freely and largely, and be as interested as occasion demanded. Rowland saw no reason to regard this as a menace of dissipation, because, in the first place, there was in all dissipation, refine it as one might, a grossness which would disqualify it for Roderick's favor, and because, in the second, the young sculptor was a man to regard all things in the light of his art, to hand over his passions to his genius to be dealt with, and to find that he could live largely enough without exceeding the circle of wholesome curiosity. Rowland took immense satisfaction in his companion's deep impatience to make something of all his impressions. Some of these indeed found their way into a channel which did not lead to statues, but it was none the less a safe one. He wrote frequent long letters to Miss Garland; when Rowland went with him to post them he thought wistfully of the fortune of the great loosely-written missives, which cost Roderick unconscionable sums in postage. He received punctual answers of a more frugal form, written in a clear, minute hand, on paper vexatiously thin. If Rowland was present when they came, he turned away and thought of other things—or tried to. These were the only moments when his sympathy halted, and they were brief. For the rest he let the days go by unprotestingly, and enjoyed Roderick's serene efflorescence as he would have done a beautiful summer sunrise. Rome, for the past month, had been delicious. The annual descent of the Goths had not yet begun, and sunny leisure seemed to brood over the city.

Roderick had taken out a note-book and was roughly sketching a memento of the great Juno. Suddenly there was a noise on the gravel, and the young men, looking up, saw three persons advancing. One was a woman of middle age, with a rather grand air and a great many furbelows. She looked very hard at our friends as she passed, and glanced back over her shoulder, as if to hasten the step of a young girl who slowly followed her. She had such an expansive majesty of mien that Rowland supposed she must have some proprietary right in the villa and was not just then in a hospitable mood. Beside her walked a little elderly man, tightly buttoned in a shabby black coat, but with a flower in his lappet, and a pair of soiled light gloves. He was a grotesque-looking personage, and might have passed for a gentleman of the old school, reduced by adversity to playing cicerone to foreigners of distinction. He had a little black eye which glittered like a diamond and rolled about like a ball of quicksilver, and a white moustache, cut short and stiff, like a worn-out brush. He was smiling with extreme urbanity, and talking in a low, mellifluous voice to the lady, who evidently was not listening to him. At a considerable distance behind this couple strolled a young girl, apparently of about twenty. She was tall and slender, and dressed with extreme elegance; she led by a cord a large poodle of the most fantastic aspect. He was combed and decked like a ram for sacrifice; his trunk and haunches were of the most transparent pink, his fleecy head and shoulders as white as jeweler's cotton, and his tail and ears ornamented with long blue ribbons. He stepped along stiffly and solemnly beside his mistress, with an air of conscious elegance. There was something at first slightly ridiculous in the sight of a young lady gravely appended to an animal of these incongruous attributes, and Roderick, with his customary frankness, greeted the spectacle with a confident smile. The young girl perceived it and turned her face full upon him, with a gaze intended apparently to enforce greater deference. It was not deference, however, her face provoked, but startled, submissive admiration; Roderick's smile fell dead, and he sat eagerly staring. A pair of extraordinary dark blue eyes, a mass of dusky hair over a low forehead, a blooming oval of perfect purity, a flexible lip, just touched with disdain, the step and carriage of a tired princess—these were the general features of his vision. The young lady was walking slowly and letting her long dress rustle over the gravel; the young men had time to see her distinctly before she averted her face and went her way. She left a vague, sweet perfume behind her as she passed.

"Immortal powers!" cried Roderick, "what a vision! In the name of transcendent perfection, who is she?" He sprang up and stood looking after her until she rounded a turn in the avenue. "What a movement, what a manner, what a poise of the head! I wonder if she would sit to me."

"You had better go and ask her," said Rowland, laughing. "She is certainly most beautiful."

"Beautiful? She 's beauty itself—she 's a revelation. I don't believe she is living—she 's a phantasm, a vapor, an illusion!"

"The poodle," said Rowland, "is certainly alive."

"Nay, he too may be a grotesque phantom, like the black dog in Faust."

"I hope at least that the young lady has nothing in common with Mephistopheles. She looked dangerous."

"If beauty is immoral, as people think at Northampton," said Roderick, "she is the incarnation of evil. The mamma and the queer old gentleman, moreover, are a pledge of her reality. Who are they all?"

"The Prince and Princess Ludovisi and the principessina," suggested Rowland.

"There are no such people," said Roderick. "Besides, the little old man is not the papa." Rowland smiled, wondering how he had ascertained these facts, and the young sculptor went on. "The old man is a Roman, a hanger-on of the mamma, a useful personage who now and then gets asked to dinner. The ladies are foreigners, from some Northern country; I won't say which."

"Perhaps from the State of Maine," said Rowland.

"No, she 's not an American, I 'll lay a wager on that. She 's a daughter of this elder world. We shall see her again, I pray my stars; but if we don't, I shall have done something I never expected to—I shall have had a glimpse of ideal beauty." He sat down again and went on with his sketch of the Juno, scrawled away for ten minutes, and then handed the result in silence to Rowland. Rowland uttered an exclamation of surprise and applause. The drawing represented the Juno as to the position of the head, the brow, and the broad fillet across the hair; but the eyes, the mouth, the physiognomy were a vivid portrait of the young girl with the poodle. "I have been wanting a subject," said Roderick: "there 's one made to my hand! And now for work!"

They saw no more of the young girl, though Roderick looked hopefully, for some days, into the carriages on the Pincian. She had evidently been but passing through Rome; Naples or Florence now happily possessed her, and she was guiding her fleecy companion through the Villa Reale or the Boboli Gardens with the same superb defiance of irony. Roderick went to work and spent a month shut up in his studio; he had an idea, and he was not to rest till he had embodied it. He had established himself in the basement of a huge, dusky, dilapidated old house, in that long, tortuous, and preeminently Roman street which leads from the Corso to the Bridge of St. Angelo. The black archway which admitted you might have served as the portal of the Augean stables, but you emerged presently upon a mouldy little court, of which the fourth side was formed by a narrow terrace, overhanging the Tiber. Here, along the parapet, were stationed half a dozen shapeless fragments of sculpture, with a couple of meagre orange-trees in terra-cotta tubs, and an oleander that never flowered. The unclean, historic river swept beneath; behind were dusky, reeking walls, spotted here and there with hanging rags and flower-pots in windows; opposite, at a distance, were the bare brown banks of the stream, the huge rotunda of St. Angelo, tipped with its seraphic statue, the dome of St. Peter's, and the broad-topped pines of the Villa Doria. The place was crumbling and shabby and melancholy, but the river was delightful, the rent was a trifle, and everything was picturesque. Roderick was in the best humor with his quarters from the first, and was certain that the working mood there would be intenser in an hour than in twenty years of Northampton. His studio was a huge, empty room with a vaulted ceiling, covered with vague, dark traces of an old fresco, which Rowland, when he spent an hour with his friend, used to stare at vainly for some surviving coherence of floating draperies and clasping arms. Roderick had lodged himself economically in the same quarter. He occupied a fifth floor on the Ripetta, but he was only at home to sleep, for when he was not at work he was either lounging in Rowland's more luxurious rooms or strolling through streets and churches and gardens.

Rowland had found a convenient corner in a stately old palace not far from the Fountain of Trevi, and made himself a home to which books and pictures and prints and odds and ends of curious furniture gave an air of leisurely permanence. He had the tastes of a collector; he spent half his afternoons ransacking the dusty magazines of the curiosity-mongers, and often made his way, in quest of a prize, into the heart of impecunious Roman households, which had been prevailed upon to listen—with closed doors and an impenetrably wary smile—to proposals for an hereditary "antique." In the evening, often, under the lamp, amid dropped curtains and the scattered gleam of firelight upon polished carvings and mellow paintings, the two friends sat with their heads together, criticising intaglios and etchings, water-color drawings and illuminated missals. Roderick's quick appreciation of every form of artistic beauty reminded his companion of the flexible temperament of those Italian artists of the sixteenth century who were indifferently painters and sculptors, sonneteers and engravers. At times when he saw how the young sculptor's day passed in a single sustained pulsation, while his own was broken into a dozen conscious devices for disposing of the hours, and intermingled with sighs, half suppressed, some of them, for conscience' sake, over what he failed of in action and missed in possession—he felt a pang of something akin to envy. But Rowland had two substantial aids for giving patience the air of contentment: he was an inquisitive reader and a passionate rider. He plunged into bulky German octavos on Italian history, and he spent long afternoons in the saddle, ranging over the grassy desolation of the Campagna. As the season went on and the social groups began to constitute themselves, he found that he knew a great many people and that he had easy opportunity for knowing others. He enjoyed a quiet corner of a drawing-room beside an agreeable woman, and although the machinery of what calls itself society seemed to him to have many superfluous wheels, he accepted invitations and made visits punctiliously, from the conviction that the only way not to be overcome by the ridiculous side of most of such observances is to take them with exaggerated gravity. He introduced Roderick right and left, and suffered him to make his way himself—an enterprise for which Roderick very soon displayed an all-sufficient capacity. Wherever he went he made, not exactly what is called a favorable impression, but what, from a practical point of view, is better—a puzzling one. He took to evening parties as a duck to water, and before the winter was half over was the most freely and frequently discussed young man in the heterogeneous foreign colony. Rowland's theory of his own duty was to let him run his course and play his cards, only holding himself ready to point out shoals and pitfalls, and administer a friendly propulsion through tight places. Roderick's manners on the precincts of the Pincian were quite the same as his manners on Cecilia's veranda: that is, they were no manners at all. But it remained as true as before that it would have been impossible, on the whole, to violate ceremony with less of lasting offense. He interrupted, he contradicted, he spoke to people he had never seen, and left his social creditors without the smallest conversational interest on their loans; he lounged and yawned, he talked loud when he should have talked low, and low when he should have talked loud. Many people, in consequence, thought him insufferably conceited, and declared that he ought to wait till he had something to show for his powers, before he assumed the airs of a spoiled celebrity. But to Rowland and to most friendly observers this judgment was quite beside the mark, and the young man's undiluted naturalness was its own justification. He was impulsive, spontaneous, sincere; there were so many people at dinner-tables and in studios who were not, that it seemed worth while to allow this rare specimen all possible freedom of action. If Roderick took the words out of your mouth when you were just prepared to deliver them with the most effective accent, he did it with a perfect good conscience and with no pretension of a better right to being heard, but simply because he was full to overflowing of his own momentary thought and it sprang from his lips without asking leave. There were persons who waited on your periods much more deferentially, who were a hundred times more capable than Roderick of a reflective impertinence. Roderick received from various sources, chiefly feminine, enough finely-adjusted advice to have established him in life as an embodiment of the proprieties, and he received it, as he afterwards listened to criticisms on his statues, with unfaltering candor and good-humor. Here and there, doubtless, as he went, he took in a reef in his sail; but he was too adventurous a spirit to be successfully tamed, and he remained at most points the florid, rather strident young Virginian whose serene inflexibility had been the despair of Mr. Striker. All this was what friendly commentators (still chiefly feminine) alluded to when they spoke of his delightful freshness, and critics of harsher sensibilities (of the other sex) when they denounced his damned impertinence. His appearance enforced these impressions—his handsome face, his radiant, unaverted eyes, his childish, unmodulated voice. Afterwards, when those who loved him were in tears, there was something in all this unspotted comeliness that seemed to lend a mockery to the causes of their sorrow.

Certainly, among the young men of genius who, for so many ages, have gone up to Rome to test their powers, none ever made a fairer beginning than Roderick. He rode his two horses at once with extraordinary good fortune; he established the happiest modus vivendi betwixt work and play. He wrestled all day with a mountain of clay in his studio, and chattered half the night away in Roman drawing-rooms. It all seemed part of a kind of divine facility. He was passionately interested, he was feeling his powers; now that they had thoroughly kindled in the glowing aesthetic atmosphere of Rome, the ardent young fellow should be pardoned for believing that he never was to see the end of them. He enjoyed immeasurably, after the chronic obstruction of home, the downright act of production. He kept models in his studio till they dropped with fatigue; he drew, on other days, at the Capitol and the Vatican, till his own head swam with his eagerness, and his limbs stiffened with the cold. He had promptly set up a life-sized figure which he called an "Adam," and was pushing it rapidly toward completion. There were naturally a great many wiseheads who smiled at his precipitancy, and cited him as one more example of Yankee crudity, a capital recruit to the great army of those who wish to dance before they can walk. They were right, but Roderick was right too, for the success of his statue was not to have been foreseen; it partook, really, of the miraculous. He never surpassed it afterwards, and a good judge here and there has been known to pronounce it the finest piece of sculpture of our modern era. To Rowland it seemed to justify superbly his highest hopes of his friend, and he said to himself that if he had invested his happiness in fostering a genius, he ought now to be in possession of a boundless complacency. There was something especially confident and masterly in the artist's negligence of all such small picturesque accessories as might serve to label his figure to a vulgar apprehension. If it represented the father of the human race and the primal embodiment of human sensation, it did so in virtue of its look of balanced physical perfection, and deeply, eagerly sentient vitality. Rowland, in fraternal zeal, traveled up to Carrara and selected at the quarries the most magnificent block of marble he could find, and when it came down to Rome, the two young men had a "celebration." They drove out to Albano, breakfasted boisterously (in their respective measure) at the inn, and lounged away the day in the sun on the top of Monte Cavo. Roderick's head was full of ideas for other works, which he described with infinite spirit and eloquence, as vividly as if they were ranged on their pedestals before him. He had an indefatigable fancy; things he saw in the streets, in the country, things he heard and read, effects he saw just missed or half-expressed in the works of others, acted upon his mind as a kind of challenge, and he was terribly restless until, in some form or other, he had taken up the glove and set his lance in rest.

The Adam was put into marble, and all the world came to see it. Of the criticisms passed upon it this history undertakes to offer no record; over many of them the two young men had a daily laugh for a month, and certain of the formulas of the connoisseurs, restrictive or indulgent, furnished Roderick with a permanent supply of humorous catch-words. But people enough spoke flattering good-sense to make Roderick feel as if he were already half famous. The statue passed formally into Rowland's possession, and was paid for as if an illustrious name had been chiseled on the pedestal. Poor Roderick owed every franc of the money. It was not for this, however, but because he was so gloriously in the mood, that, denying himself all breathing-time, on the same day he had given the last touch to the Adam, he began to shape the rough contour of an Eve. This went forward with equal rapidity and success. Roderick lost his temper, time and again, with his models, who offered but a gross, degenerate image of his splendid ideal; but his ideal, as he assured Rowland, became gradually such a fixed, vivid presence, that he had only to shut his eyes to behold a creature far more to his purpose than the poor girl who stood posturing at forty sous an hour. The Eve was finished in a month, and the feat was extraordinary, as well as the statue, which represented an admirably beautiful woman. When the spring began to muffle the rugged old city with its clambering festoons, it seemed to him that he had done a handsome winter's work and had fairly earned a holiday. He took a liberal one, and lounged away the lovely Roman May, doing nothing. He looked very contented; with himself, perhaps, at times, a trifle too obviously. But who could have said without good reason? He was "flushed with triumph;" this classic phrase portrayed him, to Rowland's sense. He would lose himself in long reveries, and emerge from them with a quickened smile and a heightened color. Rowland grudged him none of his smiles, and took an extreme satisfaction in his two statues. He had the Adam and the Eve transported to his own apartment, and one warm evening in May he gave a little dinner in honor of the artist. It was small, but Rowland had meant it should be very agreeably composed. He thought over his friends and chose four. They were all persons with whom he lived in a certain intimacy.

One of them was an American sculptor of French extraction, or remotely, perhaps, of Italian, for he rejoiced in the somewhat fervid name of Gloriani. He was a man of forty, he had been living for years in Paris and in Rome, and he now drove a very pretty trade in sculpture of the ornamental and fantastic sort. In his youth he had had money; but he had spent it recklessly, much of it scandalously, and at twenty-six had found himself obliged to make capital of his talent. This was quite inimitable, and fifteen years of indefatigable exercise had brought it to perfection. Rowland admitted its power, though it gave him very little pleasure; what he relished in the man was the extraordinary vivacity and frankness, not to call it the impudence, of his ideas. He had a definite, practical scheme of art, and he knew at least what he meant. In this sense he was solid and complete. There were so many of the aesthetic fraternity who were floundering in unknown seas, without a notion of which way their noses were turned, that Gloriani, conscious and compact, unlimitedly intelligent and consummately clever, dogmatic only as to his own duties, and at once gracefully deferential and profoundly indifferent to those of others, had for Rowland a certain intellectual refreshment quite independent of the character of his works. These were considered by most people to belong to a very corrupt, and by many to a positively indecent school. Others thought them tremendously knowing, and paid enormous prices for them; and indeed, to be able to point to one of Gloriani's figures in a shady corner of your library was tolerable proof that you were not a fool. Corrupt things they certainly were; in the line of sculpture they were quite the latest fruit of time. It was the artist's opinion that there is no essential difference between beauty and ugliness; that they overlap and intermingle in a quite inextricable manner; that there is no saying where one begins and the other ends; that hideousness grimaces at you suddenly from out of the very bosom of loveliness, and beauty blooms before your eyes in the lap of vileness; that it is a waste of wit to nurse metaphysical distinctions, and a sadly meagre entertainment to caress imaginary lines; that the thing to aim at is the expressive, and the way to reach it is by ingenuity; that for this purpose everything may serve, and that a consummate work is a sort of hotch-potch of the pure and the impure, the graceful and the grotesque. Its prime duty is to amuse, to puzzle, to fascinate, to savor of a complex imagination. Gloriani's statues were florid and meretricious; they looked like magnified goldsmith's work. They were extremely elegant, but they had no charm for Rowland. He never bought one, but Gloriani was such an honest fellow, and withal was so deluged with orders, that this made no difference in their friendship. The artist might have passed for a Frenchman. He was a great talker, and a very picturesque one; he was almost bald; he had a small, bright eye, a broken nose, and a moustache with waxed ends. When sometimes he received you at his lodging, he introduced you to a lady with a plain face whom he called Madame Gloriani—which she was not.

Rowland's second guest was also an artist, but of a very different type. His friends called him Sam Singleton; he was an American, and he had been in Rome a couple of years. He painted small landscapes, chiefly in water-colors: Rowland had seen one of them in a shop window, had liked it extremely, and, ascertaining his address, had gone to see him and found him established in a very humble studio near the Piazza Barberini, where, apparently, fame and fortune had not yet found him out. Rowland took a fancy to him and bought several of his pictures; Singleton made few speeches, but was grateful. Rowland heard afterwards that when he first came to Rome he painted worthless daubs and gave no promise of talent. Improvement had come, however, hand in hand with patient industry, and his talent, though of a slender and delicate order, was now incontestable. It was as yet but scantily recognized, and he had hard work to live. Rowland hung his little water-colors on the parlor wall, and found that, as he lived with them, he grew very fond of them. Singleton was a diminutive, dwarfish personage; he looked like a precocious child. He had a high, protuberant forehead, a transparent brown eye, a perpetual smile, an extraordinary expression of modesty and patience. He listened much more willingly than he talked, with a little fixed, grateful grin; he blushed when he spoke, and always offered his ideas in a sidelong fashion, as if the presumption were against them. His modesty set them off, and they were eminently to the point. He was so perfect an example of the little noiseless, laborious artist whom chance, in the person of a moneyed patron, has never taken by the hand, that Rowland would have liked to befriend him by stealth. Singleton had expressed a fervent admiration for Roderick's productions, but had not yet met the young master. Roderick was lounging against the chimney-piece when he came in, and Rowland presently introduced him. The little water-colorist stood with folded hands, blushing, smiling, and looking up at him as if Roderick were himself a statue on a pedestal. Singleton began to murmur something about his pleasure, his admiration; the desire to make his compliment smoothly gave him a kind of grotesque formalism. Roderick looked down at him surprised, and suddenly burst into a laugh. Singleton paused a moment and then, with an intenser smile, went on: "Well, sir, your statues are beautiful, all the same!"

Rowland's two other guests were ladies, and one of them, Miss Blanchard, belonged also to the artistic fraternity. She was an American, she was young, she was pretty, and she had made her way to Rome alone and unaided. She lived alone, or with no other duenna than a bushy-browed old serving-woman, though indeed she had a friendly neighbor in the person of a certain Madame Grandoni, who in various social emergencies lent her a protecting wing, and had come with her to Rowland's dinner. Miss Blanchard had a little money, but she was not above selling her pictures. These represented generally a bunch of dew-sprinkled roses, with the dew-drops very highly finished, or else a wayside shrine, and a peasant woman, with her back turned, kneeling before it. She did backs very well, but she was a little weak in faces. Flowers, however, were her speciality, and though her touch was a little old-fashioned and finical, she painted them with remarkable skill. Her pictures were chiefly bought by the English. Rowland had made her acquaintance early in the winter, and as she kept a saddle horse and rode a great deal, he had asked permission to be her cavalier. In this way they had become almost intimate. Miss Blanchard's name was Augusta; she was slender, pale, and elegant looking; she had a very pretty head and brilliant auburn hair, which she braided with classical simplicity. She talked in a sweet, soft voice, used language at times a trifle superfine, and made literary allusions. These had often a patriotic strain, and Rowland had more than once been irritated by her quotations from Mrs. Sigourney in the cork-woods of Monte Mario, and from Mr. Willis among the ruins of Veii. Rowland was of a dozen different minds about her, and was half surprised, at times, to find himself treating it as a matter of serious moment whether he liked her or not. He admired her, and indeed there was something admirable in her combination of beauty and talent, of isolation and tranquil self-support. He used sometimes to go into the little, high-niched, ordinary room which served her as a studio, and find her working at a panel six inches square, at an open casement, profiled against the deep blue Roman sky. She received him with a meek-eyed dignity that made her seem like a painted saint on a church window, receiving the daylight in all her being. The breath of reproach passed her by with folded wings. And yet Rowland wondered why he did not like her better. If he failed, the reason was not far to seek. There was another woman whom he liked better, an image in his heart which refused to yield precedence.

On that evening to which allusion has been made, when Rowland was left alone between the starlight and the waves with the sudden knowledge that Mary Garland was to become another man's wife, he had made, after a while, the simple resolution to forget her. And every day since, like a famous philosopher who wished to abbreviate his mourning for a faithful servant, he had said to himself in substance—"Remember to forget Mary Garland." Sometimes it seemed as if he were succeeding; then, suddenly, when he was least expecting it, he would find her name, inaudibly, on his lips, and seem to see her eyes meeting his eyes. All this made him uncomfortable, and seemed to portend a possible discord. Discord was not to his taste; he shrank from imperious passions, and the idea of finding himself jealous of an unsuspecting friend was absolutely repulsive. More than ever, then, the path of duty was to forget Mary Garland, and he cultivated oblivion, as we may say, in the person of Miss Blanchard. Her fine temper, he said to himself, was a trifle cold and conscious, her purity prudish, perhaps, her culture pedantic. But since he was obliged to give up hopes of Mary Garland, Providence owed him a compensation, and he had fits of angry sadness in which it seemed to him that to attest his right to sentimental satisfaction he would be capable of falling in love with a woman he absolutely detested, if she were the best that came in his way. And what was the use, after all, of bothering about a possible which was only, perhaps, a dream? Even if Mary Garland had been free, what right had he to assume that he would have pleased her? The actual was good enough. Miss Blanchard had beautiful hair, and if she was a trifle old-maidish, there is nothing like matrimony for curing old-maidishness.

Madame Grandoni, who had formed with the companion of Rowland's rides an alliance which might have been called defensive on the part of the former and attractive on that of Miss Blanchard, was an excessively ugly old lady, highly esteemed in Roman society for her homely benevolence and her shrewd and humorous good sense. She had been the widow of a German archaeologist, who had come to Rome in the early ages as an attaché of the Prussian legation on the Capitoline. Her good sense had been wanting on but a single occasion, that of her second marriage. This occasion was certainly a momentous one, but these, by common consent, are not test cases. A couple of years after her first husband's death, she had accepted the hand and the name of a Neapolitan music-master, ten years younger than herself, and with no fortune but his fiddle-bow. The marriage was most unhappy, and the

Maestro Grandoni was suspected of using the fiddle-bow as an instrument of conjugal correction. He had finally run off with a prima donna assoluta, who, it was to be hoped, had given him a taste of the quality implied in her title. He was believed to be living still, but he had shrunk to a small black spot in Madame Grandoni's life, and for ten years she had not mentioned his name. She wore a light flaxen wig, which was never very artfully adjusted, but this mattered little, as she made no secret of it. She used to say, "I was not always so ugly as this; as a young girl I had beautiful golden hair, very much the color of my wig." She had worn from time immemorial an old blue satin dress, and a white crape shawl embroidered in colors; her appearance was ridiculous, but she had an interminable Teutonic pedigree, and her manners, in every presence, were easy and jovial, as became a lady whose ancestor had been cup-bearer to Frederick Barbarossa. Thirty years' observation of Roman society had sharpened her wits and given her an inexhaustible store of anecdotes, but she had beneath her crumpled bodice a deep-welling fund of Teutonic sentiment, which she communicated only to the objects of her particular favor. Rowland had a great regard for her, and she repaid it by wishing him to get married. She never saw him without whispering to him that Augusta Blanchard was just the girl.

It seemed to Rowland a sort of foreshadowing of matrimony to see Miss Blanchard standing gracefully on his hearth-rug and blooming behind the central bouquet at his circular dinner-table. The dinner was very prosperous and Roderick amply filled his position as hero of the feast. He had always an air of buoyant enjoyment in his work, but on this occasion he manifested a good deal of harmless pleasure in his glory. He drank freely and talked bravely; he leaned back in his chair with his hands in his pockets, and flung open the gates of his eloquence. Singleton sat gazing and listening open-mouthed, as if Apollo in person were talking. Gloriani showed a twinkle in his eye and an evident disposition to draw Roderick out. Rowland was rather regretful, for he knew that theory was not his friend's strong point, and that it was never fair to take his measure from his talk.

"As you have begun with Adam and Eve," said Gloriani, "I suppose you are going straight through the Bible." He was one of the persons who thought Roderick delightfully fresh.

"I may make a David," said Roderick, "but I shall not try any more of the Old Testament people. I don't like the Jews; I don't like pendulous noses. David, the boy David, is rather an exception; you can think of him and treat him as a young Greek. Standing forth there on the plain of battle between the contending armies, rushing forward to let fly his stone, he looks like a beautiful runner at the Olympic games. After that I shall skip to the New Testament. I mean to make a Christ."

"You 'll put nothing of the Olympic games into him, I hope," said Gloriani.

"Oh, I shall make him very different from the Christ of tradition; more—more"—and Roderick paused a moment to think. This was the first that Rowland had heard of his Christ.

"More rationalistic, I suppose," suggested Miss Blanchard.

"More idealistic!" cried Roderick. "The perfection of form, you know, to symbolize the perfection of spirit."

"For a companion piece," said Miss Blanchard, "you ought to make a Judas."

"Never! I mean never to make anything ugly. The Greeks never made anything ugly, and I 'm a Hellenist; I 'm not a Hebraist! I have been thinking lately of making a Cain, but I should never dream of making him ugly. He should be a very handsome fellow, and he should lift up the murderous club with the beautiful movement of the fighters in the Greek friezes who are chopping at their enemies."

"There 's no use trying to be a Greek," said Gloriani. "If Phidias were to come back, he would recommend you to give it up. I am half Italian and half French, and, as a whole, a Yankee. What sort of a Greek should I make? I think the Judas is a capital idea for a statue. Much obliged to you, madame, for the suggestion. What an insidious little scoundrel one might make of him, sitting there nursing his money-bag and his treachery! There can be a great deal of expression in a pendulous nose, my dear sir, especially when it is cast in green bronze."

"Very likely," said Roderick. "But it is not the sort of expression I care for. I care only for perfect beauty. There it is, if you want to know it! That 's as good a profession of faith as another. In future, so far as my things are not positively beautiful, you may set them down as failures. For me, it 's either that or nothing. It 's against the taste of the day, I know; we have really lost the faculty to understand beauty in the large, ideal way. We stand like a race with shrunken muscles, staring helplessly at the weights our forefathers easily lifted. But I don't hesitate to proclaim it—I mean to lift them again! I mean to go in for big things; that 's my notion of my art. I mean to do things that will be simple and vast and infinite. You 'll see if they won't be infinite! Excuse me if I brag a little; all those Italian fellows in the Renaissance used to brag. There was a sensation once common, I am sure, in the human breast—a kind of religious awe in the presence of a marble image newly created and expressing the human type in superhuman purity. When Phidias and Praxiteles had their statues of goddesses unveiled in the temples of the AEgean, don't you suppose there was a passionate beating of hearts, a thrill of mysterious terror? I mean to bring it back; I mean to thrill the world again! I mean to produce a Juno that will make you tremble, a Venus that will make you swoon!"

"So that when we come and see you," said Madame Grandoni, "we must be sure and bring our smelling-bottles. And pray have a few soft sofas conveniently placed."

"Phidias and Praxiteles," Miss Blanchard remarked, "had the advantage of believing in their goddesses. I insist on believing, for myself, that the pagan mythology is not a fiction, and that Venus and Juno and Apollo and Mercury used to come down in a cloud into this very city of Rome where we sit talking nineteenth century English."

"Nineteenth century nonsense, my dear!" cried Madame Grandoni. "Mr. Hudson may be a new Phidias, but Venus and Juno—that 's you and I—arrived to-day in a very dirty cab; and were cheated by the driver, too."

"But, my dear fellow," objected Gloriani, "you don't mean to say you are going to make over in cold blood those poor old exploded Apollos and Hebes."

413

"It won't matter what you call them," said Roderick. "They shall be simply divine forms. They shall be Beauty; they shall be Wisdom; they shall be Power; they shall be Genius; they shall be Daring. That 's all the Greek divinities were."

"That 's rather abstract, you know," said Miss Blanchard.

"My dear fellow," cried Gloriani, "you 're delightfully young."

"I hope you 'll not grow any older," said Singleton, with a flush of sympathy across his large white forehead. "You can do it if you try."

"Then there are all the Forces and Mysteries and Elements of Nature," Roderick went on. "I mean to do the Morning; I mean to do the Night! I mean to do the Ocean and the Mountains; the Moon and the West Wind. I mean to make a magnificent statue of America!"

"America—the Mountains—the Moon!" said Gloriani. "You 'll find it rather hard, I 'm afraid, to compress such subjects into classic forms."

"Oh, there 's a way," cried Roderick, "and I shall think it out. My figures shall make no contortions, but they shall mean a tremendous deal."

"I 'm sure there are contortions enough in Michael Angelo," said Madame Grandoni. "Perhaps you don't approve of him."

"Oh, Michael Angelo was not me!" said Roderick, with sublimity. There was a great laugh; but after all, Roderick had done some fine things.

Rowland had bidden one of the servants bring him a small portfolio of prints, and had taken out a photograph of Roderick's little statue of the youth drinking. It pleased him to see his friend sitting there in radiant ardor, defending idealism against so knowing an apostle of corruption as Gloriani, and he wished to help the elder artist to be confuted. He silently handed him the photograph.

"Bless me!" cried Gloriani, "did he do this?"

"Ages ago," said Roderick.

Gloriani looked at the photograph a long time, with evident admiration.

"It 's deucedly pretty," he said at last. "But, my dear young friend, you can't keep this up."

"I shall do better," said Roderick.

"You will do worse! You will become weak. You will have to take to violence, to contortions, to romanticism, in self-defense. This sort of thing is like a man trying to lift himself up by the seat of his trousers. He may stand on tiptoe, but he can't do more. Here you stand on tiptoe, very gracefully, I admit; but you can't fly; there 's no use trying."

"My 'America' shall answer you!" said Roderick, shaking toward him a tall glass of champagne and drinking it down.

Singleton had taken the photograph and was poring over it with a little murmur of delight.

"Was this done in America?" he asked.

"In a square white wooden house at Northampton, Massachusetts," Roderick answered.

"Dear old white wooden houses!" said Miss Blanchard.

"If you could do as well as this there," said Singleton, blushing and smiling, "one might say that really you had only to lose by coming to Rome."

"Mallet is to blame for that," said Roderick. "But I am willing to risk the loss."

The photograph had been passed to Madame Grandoni. "It reminds me," she said, "of the things a young man used to do whom I knew years ago, when I first came to Rome. He was a German, a pupil of Overbeck and a votary of spiritual art. He used to wear a black velvet tunic and a very low shirt collar; he had a neck like a sickly crane, and let his hair grow down to his shoulders. His name was Herr Schafgans. He never painted anything so profane as a man taking a drink, but his figures were all of the simple and slender and angular pattern, and nothing if not innocent—like this one of yours. He would not have agreed with Gloriani any more than you. He used to come and see me very often, and in those days I thought his tunic and his long neck infallible symptoms of genius. His talk was all of gilded aureoles and beatific visions; he lived on weak wine and biscuits, and wore a lock of Saint Somebody's hair in a little bag round his neck. If he was not a Beato Angelico, it was not his own fault. I hope with all my heart that Mr. Hudson will do the fine things he talks about, but he must bear in mind the history of dear Mr. Schafgans as a warning against high-flown pretensions. One fine day this poor young man fell in love with a Roman model, though she had never sat to him, I believe, for she was a buxom, bold-faced, high-colored creature, and he painted none but pale, sickly women. He offered to marry her, and she looked at him from head to foot, gave a shrug, and consented. But he was ashamed to set up his menage in Rome. They went to Naples, and there, a couple of years afterwards, I saw him. The poor fellow was ruined. His wife used to beat him, and he had taken to drinking. He wore a ragged black coat, and he had a blotchy, red face. Madame had turned washerwoman and used to make him go and fetch the dirty linen. His talent had gone heaven knows where! He was getting his living by painting views of Vesuvius in eruption on the little boxes they sell at Sorrento."

"Moral: don't fall in love with a buxom Roman model," said Roderick. "I 'm much obliged to you for your story, but I don't mean to fall in love with any one."

Gloriani had possessed himself of the photograph again, and was looking at it curiously. "It 's a happy bit of youth," he said. "But you can't keep it up—you can't keep it up!"

The two sculptors pursued their discussion after dinner, in the drawing-room. Rowland left them to have it out in a corner, where Roderick's Eve stood over them in the shaded lamplight, in vague white beauty, like the guardian angel of the young idealist. Singleton was listening to Madame Grandoni, and Rowland took his place on the sofa, near Miss Blanchard. They had a good deal of familiar, desultory talk. Every now and then Madame Grandoni looked round at them. Miss Blanchard at last asked Rowland certain questions about Roderick: who he was, where he came from, whether it was true, as she had heard, that Rowland had discovered him and brought him out at his own expense. Rowland answered her questions; to the last he gave a vague affirmative. Finally, after a pause, looking at him, "You 're very generous," Miss Blanchard said. The declaration was made with a certain richness of tone, but it brought to Rowland's sense neither delight nor confusion. He had heard the words before; he suddenly remembered the grave sincerity with which Miss Garland had uttered them as he strolled with her in the woods the day of Roderick's picnic. They had pleased him then; now he asked Miss Blanchard whether she would have some tea.

When the two ladies withdrew, he attended them to their carriage. Coming back to the drawing-room, he paused outside the open door; he was struck by the group formed by the three men. They were standing before Roderick's statue of Eve, and the young sculptor had lifted up the lamp and was showing different parts of it to his companions. He was talking ardently, and the lamplight covered his head and face. Rowland stood looking on, for the group struck him with its picturesque symbolism. Roderick, bearing the lamp and glowing in its radiant circle, seemed the beautiful image of a genius which combined sincerity with power. Gloriani, with his head on one side, pulling his long moustache and looking keenly from half-closed eyes at the lighted marble, represented art with a worldly motive, skill unleavened by faith, the mere base maximum of cleverness. Poor little Singleton, on the other side, with his hands behind him, his head thrown back, and his eyes following devoutly the course of Roderick's elucidation, might pass for an embodiment of aspiring candor, with feeble wings to rise on. In all this, Roderick's was certainly the beau role.

Gloriani turned to Rowland as he came up, and pointed back with his thumb to the statue, with a smile half sardonic, half good-natured. "A pretty thing—a devilish pretty thing," he said. "It 's as fresh as the foam in the milk-pail. He can do it once, he can do it twice, he can do it at a stretch half a dozen times. But—but—"

He was returning to his former refrain, but Rowland intercepted him. "Oh, he will keep it up," he said, smiling, "I will answer for him."

Gloriani was not encouraging, but Roderick had listened smiling. He was floating unperturbed on the tide of his deep self-confidence. Now, suddenly, however, he turned with a flash of irritation in his eye, and demanded in a ringing voice, "In a word, then, you prophesy that I am to fail?"

Gloriani answered imperturbably, patting him kindly on the shoulder. "My dear fellow, passion burns out, inspiration runs to seed. Some fine day every artist finds himself sitting face to face with his lump of clay, with his empty canvas, with his sheet of blank paper, waiting in vain for the revelation to be made, for the Muse to descend. He must learn to do without the Muse! When the fickle jade forgets the way to your studio, don't waste any time in tearing your hair and meditating on suicide. Come round and see me, and I will show you how to console yourself."

"If I break down," said Roderick, passionately, "I shall stay down. If the Muse deserts me, she shall at least have her infidelity on her conscience."

"You have no business," Rowland said to Gloriani, "to talk lightly of the Muse in this company. Mr. Singleton, too, has received pledges from her which place her constancy beyond suspicion." And he pointed out on the wall, near by, two small landscapes by the modest water-colorist.

The sculptor examined them with deference, and Singleton himself began to laugh nervously; he was trembling with hope that the great Gloriani would be pleased. "Yes, these are fresh too," Gloriani said; "extraordinarily fresh! How old are you?"

"Twenty-six, sir," said Singleton.

"For twenty-six they are famously fresh. They must have taken you a long time; you work slowly."

"Yes, unfortunately, I work very slowly. One of them took me six weeks, the other two months."

"Upon my word! The Muse pays you long visits." And Gloriani turned and looked, from head to foot, at so unlikely an object of her favors. Singleton smiled and began to wipe his forehead very hard. "Oh, you!" said the sculptor; "you 'll keep it up!"

A week after his dinner-party, Rowland went into Roderick's studio and found him sitting before an unfinished piece of work, with a hanging head and a heavy eye. He could have fancied that the fatal hour foretold by Gloriani had struck. Roderick rose with a sombre yawn and flung down his tools. "It 's no use," he said, "I give it up!"

"What is it?"

"I have struck a shallow! I have been sailing bravely, but for the last day or two my keel has been crunching the bottom."

"A difficult place?" Rowland asked, with a sympathetic inflection, looking vaguely at the roughly modeled figure.

"Oh, it 's not the poor clay!" Roderick answered. "The difficult place is here!" And he struck a blow on his heart. "I don't know what 's the matter with me. Nothing comes; all of a sudden I hate things. My old things look ugly; everything looks stupid."

Rowland was perplexed. He was in the situation of a man who has been riding a blood horse at an even, elastic gallop, and of a sudden feels him stumble and balk. As yet, he reflected, he had seen nothing but the sunshine of genius; he had forgotten that it has its storms. Of course it had! And he felt a flood of comradeship rise in his heart which would float them both safely through the worst weather. "Why, you 're tired!" he said. "Of course you 're tired. You have a right to be!"

"Do you think I have a right to be?" Roderick asked, looking at him.

"Unquestionably, after all you have done."

"Well, then, right or wrong, I am tired. I certainly have done a fair winter's work. I want a change."

Rowland declared that it was certainly high time they should be leaving Rome. They would go north and travel. They would go to Switzerland, to Germany, to Holland, to England. Roderick assented, his eye brightened, and Rowland talked of a dozen things they might do. Roderick walked up and down; he seemed to have something to say which he hesitated to bring out.

He hesitated so rarely that Rowland wondered, and at last asked him what was on his mind. Roderick stopped before him, frowning a little.

"I have such unbounded faith in your good-will," he said, "that I believe nothing I can say would offend you."

"Try it," said Rowland.

"Well, then, I think my journey will do me more good if I take it alone. I need n't say I prefer your society to that of any man living. For the last six months it has been everything to me. But I have a perpetual feeling that you are expecting something of me, that you are measuring my doings by a terrifically high standard. You are watching me; I don't want to be watched. I want to go my own way; to work when I choose and to loaf when I choose. It is not that I don't know what I owe you; it is not that we are not friends. It is simply that I want a taste of absolutely unrestricted freedom. Therefore, I say, let us separate."

Rowland shook him by the hand. "Willingly. Do as you desire, I shall miss you, and I venture to believe you 'll pass some lonely hours. But I have only one request to make: that if you get into trouble of any kind whatever, you will immediately let me know."

They began their journey, however, together, and crossed the Alps side by side, muffled in one rug, on the top of the St. Gothard coach. Rowland was going to England to pay some promised visits; his companion had no plan save to ramble through Switzerland and Germany as fancy guided him. He had money, now, that would outlast the summer; when it was spent he would come back to Rome and make another statue. At a little mountain village by the way, Roderick declared that he would stop; he would scramble about a little in the high places and doze in the shade of the pine forests. The coach was changing horses; the two young men walked along the village street, picking their way between dunghills, breathing the light, cool air, and listening to the plash of the fountain and the tinkle of cattle-bells. The coach overtook them, and then Rowland, as he prepared to mount, felt an almost overmastering reluctance.

"Say the word," he exclaimed, "and I will stop too."

Roderick frowned. "Ah, you don't trust me; you don't think I 'm able to take care of myself. That proves that I was right in feeling as if I were watched!"

"Watched, my dear fellow!" said Rowland. "I hope you may never have anything worse to complain of than being watched in the spirit in which I watch you. But I will spare you even that. Good-by!" Standing in his place, as the coach rolled away, he looked back at his friend lingering by the roadside. A great snow-mountain, behind Roderick, was beginning to turn pink in the sunset. The young man waved his hat, still looking grave. Rowland settled himself in his place, reflecting after all that this was a salubrious beginning of independence. He was among forests and glaciers, leaning on the pure bosom of nature. And then—and then—was it not in itself a guarantee against folly to be engaged to Mary Garland?

CHAPTER IV. Experience

Rowland passed the summer in England, staying with several old friends and two or three new ones. On his arrival, he felt it on his conscience to write to Mrs. Hudson and inform her that her son had relieved him of his tutelage. He felt that she considered him an incorruptible Mentor, following Roderick like a shadow, and he wished to let her know the truth. But he made the truth very comfortable, and gave a succinct statement of the young man's brilliant beginnings. He owed it to himself, he said, to remind her that he had not judged lightly, and that Roderick's present achievements were more profitable than his inglorious drudgery at Messrs. Striker & Spooner's. He was now taking a well-earned holiday and proposing to see a little of the world. He would work none the worse for this; every artist needed to knock about and look at things for himself. They had parted company for a couple of months, for Roderick was now a great man and beyond the need of going about with a keeper. But they were to meet again in Rome in the autumn, and then he should be able to send her more good news. Meanwhile, he was very happy in what Roderick had already done—especially happy in the happiness it must have brought to her. He ventured to ask to be kindly commended to Miss Garland.

His letter was promptly answered—to his surprise in Miss Garland's own hand. The same mail brought also an epistle from Cecilia. The latter was voluminous, and we must content ourselves with giving an extract.

"Your letter was filled with an echo of that brilliant Roman world, which made me almost ill with envy. For a week after I got it I thought Northampton really unpardonably tame. But I am drifting back again to my old deeps of resignation, and I rush to the window, when any one passes, with all my old gratitude for small favors. So Roderick Hudson is already a great man, and you turn out to be a great prophet? My compliments to both of you; I never heard of anything working so smoothly. And he takes it all very quietly, and does n't lose his balance nor let it turn his head? You judged him, then, in a day better than I had done in six months, for I really did not expect that he would settle down into such a jog-trot of prosperity. I believed he would do fine things, but I was sure he would intersperse them with a good many follies, and that his beautiful statues would spring up out of the midst of a straggling plantation of wild oats. But from what you tell me, Mr. Striker may now go hang himself..... There is one thing, however, to say as a friend, in the way of warning. That candid soul can keep a secret, and he may have private designs on your equanimity which you don't begin to suspect. What do you think of his being engaged to Miss Garland? The two ladies had given no hint of it all winter, but a fortnight ago, when those big photographs of his statues arrived, they first pinned them up on the wall, and then trotted out into the town, made a dozen calls, and announced the news. Mrs. Hudson did, at least; Miss Garland, I suppose, sat at home writing letters. To me, I confess, the thing was a perfect surprise. I had not a suspicion that all the while he was coming so regularly to make himself agreeable on my veranda, he was quietly preferring his cousin to any one else. Not, indeed, that he was ever at particular pains to make himself agreeable! I suppose he has picked up a few graces in Rome. But he must not acquire too many: if he is too polite when he comes back, Miss Garland will count him as one of the lost. She will be a very good wife for a man of genius, and such a one as they are often shrewd enough to take. She 'll darn his stockings and keep his accounts, and sit at home and trim the lamp and keep up the fire while he studies the Beautiful in pretty neighbors at dinner-parties. The two ladies are evidently very happy, and, to do them justice, very humbly grateful to you. Mrs. Hudson never speaks of you without tears in her eyes, and I am sure she considers you a specially patented agent of Providence. Verily, it 's a good thing for a woman to be in love: Miss Garland has grown almost pretty. I met her the other night at a tea-party; she had a white rose in her hair, and sang a sentimental ballad in a fine contralto voice."

Miss Garland's letter was so much shorter that we may give it entire:—

My dear Sir,—Mrs. Hudson, as I suppose you know, has been for some time unable to use her eyes. She requests me, therefore, to answer your favor of the 22d of June. She thanks you extremely for writing, and wishes me to say that she considers herself in every way under great obligations to you. Your account of her son's progress and the high estimation in which he is held has made her very happy, and she earnestly prays that all may continue well with him. He sent us, a short time ago, several large photographs of his two statues, taken from different points of view. We know little about such things, but they seem to us wonderfully beautiful. We sent them to Boston to be handsomely framed, and the man, on returning them, wrote us that he had exhibited them for a week in his store, and that they had attracted great attention. The frames are magnificent, and the pictures now hang in a row on the parlor wall. Our only quarrel with them is that they make the old papering and the engravings look dreadfully shabby. Mr. Striker stood and looked at them the other day full five minutes, and said, at last, that if Roderick's head was running on such things it was no wonder he could not learn to draw up a deed. We lead here so quiet and monotonous a life that I am afraid I can tell you nothing that will interest you. Mrs. Hudson requests me to say that the little more or less that may happen to us is of small account, as we live in our thoughts and our thoughts are fixed on her dear son. She thanks Heaven he has so good a friend. Mrs. Hudson says that this is too short a letter, but I can say nothing more.

Yours most respectfully,

Mary Garland.

It is a question whether the reader will know why, but this letter gave Rowland extraordinary pleasure. He liked its very brevity and meagreness, and there seemed to him an exquisite modesty in its saying nothing from the young girl herself. He delighted in the formal address and conclusion; they pleased him as he had been pleased by an angular gesture in some expressive girlish figure in an early painting. The letter renewed that impression of strong feeling combined with an almost rigid simplicity, which Roderick's betrothed had personally given him. And its homely stiffness seemed a vivid reflection of a life concentrated, as the young girl had borrowed warrant from her companion to say, in a single devoted idea. The monotonous days of the two women seemed to Rowland's fancy to follow each other like the tick-tick of a great time-piece, marking off the hours which separated them from the supreme felicity of clasping the far-away son and lover to lips sealed with the excess of joy. He hoped that Roderick, now that he had shaken off the oppression of his own importunate faith, was not losing a tolerant temper for the silent prayers of the two women at Northampton.

He was left to vain conjectures, however, as to Roderick's actual moods and occupations. He knew he was no letter-writer, and that, in the young sculptor's own phrase, he had at any time rather build a monument than write a note. But when a month had passed without news of him, he began to be half anxious and half angry, and wrote him three lines, in the care of a Continental banker, begging him at least to give some sign of whether he was alive or dead. A week afterwards came an answer—brief, and dated Baden-Baden. "I know I have been a great brute," Roderick wrote, "not to have sent you a word before; but really I don't know what has got into me. I have lately learned terribly well how to be idle. I am afraid to think how long it is since I wrote to my mother or to Mary. Heaven help them—poor, patient, trustful creatures! I don't know how to tell you what I am doing. It seems all amusing enough while I do it, but it would make a poor show in a narrative intended for your formidable eyes. I found Baxter in Switzerland, or rather he found me, and he grabbed me by the arm and brought me here. I was walking twenty miles a day in the Alps, drinking milk in lonely chalets, sleeping as you sleep, and thinking it was all very good fun; but Baxter told me it would never do, that the Alps were 'd——d rot,' that Baden-Baden was the place, and that if I knew what was good for me I would come along with him. It is a wonderful place, certainly, though, thank the Lord, Baxter departed last week, blaspheming horribly at trente et quarante. But you know all about it and what one does—what one is liable to do. I have succumbed, in a measure, to the liabilities, and I wish I had some one here to give me a thundering good blowing up. Not you, dear friend; you would draw it too mild; you have too much of the milk of human kindness. I have fits of horrible homesickness for my studio, and I shall be devoutly grateful when the summer is over and I can go back and swing a chisel. I feel as if nothing but the chisel would satisfy me; as if I could rush in a rage at a block of unshaped marble. There are a lot of the Roman people here, English and American; I live in the midst of them and talk nonsense from morning till night. There is also some one else; and to her I don't talk sense, nor, thank heaven, mean what I say. I confess, I need a month's work to recover my self-respect."

These lines brought Rowland no small perturbation; the more, that what they seemed to point to surprised him. During the nine months of their companionship Roderick had shown so little taste for dissipation that Rowland had come to think of it as a canceled danger, and it greatly perplexed him to learn that his friend had apparently proved so pliant to opportunity. But Roderick's allusions were ambiguous, and it was possible they might simply mean that he was out of patience with a frivolous way of life and fretting wholesomely over his absent work. It was a very good thing, certainly, that idleness should prove, on experiment, to sit heavily on his conscience. Nevertheless, the letter needed, to Rowland's mind, a key: the key arrived a week later. "In common charity," Roderick wrote, "lend me a hundred pounds! I have gambled away my last franc—I have made a mountain of debts. Send me the money first; lecture me afterwards!" Rowland sent the money by return of mail; then he proceeded, not to lecture, but to think. He hung his head; he was acutely disappointed. He had no right to be, he assured himself; but so it was. Roderick was young, impulsive, unpracticed in stoicism; it was a hundred to one that he was to pay the usual vulgar tribute to folly. But his friend had regarded it as securely gained to his own belief in virtue that he was not as other foolish youths are, and that he would have been capable of looking at folly in the face and passing on his way. Rowland for a while felt a sore sense of wrath. What right had a man who was engaged to that fine girl in Northampton to behave as if his consciousness were a common blank, to be overlaid with coarse sensations? Yes, distinctly, he was disappointed. He had accompanied his missive with an urgent recommendation to leave Baden-Baden immediately, and an offer to meet Roderick at any point he would name. The answer came promptly; it ran as follows: "Send me another fifty pounds! I have been back to the tables. I will leave as soon as the money comes, and meet you at Geneva. There I will tell you everything."

There is an ancient terrace at Geneva, planted with trees and studded with benches, overlooked by gravely aristocratic old dwellings and overlooking the distant Alps. A great many generations have made it a lounging-place, a great many friends and lovers strolled there, a great many confidential talks and momentous interviews gone forward. Here, one morning, sitting on one of the battered green benches, Roderick, as he had promised, told his friend everything. He had arrived late the night before; he looked tired, and yet flushed and excited. He made no professions of penitence, but he practiced an unmitigated frankness, and his self-reprobation might be taken for granted. He implied in every phrase that he had done with it all, and that he was counting the hours till he could get back to work. We shall not rehearse his confession in detail; its main outline will be sufficient. He had fallen in with some very idle people, and had discovered that a little example and a little practice were capable of producing on his own part a considerable relish for their diversions. What could he do? He never read, and he had no studio; in one way or another he had to pass the time. He passed it in dangling about several very pretty women in wonderful Paris toilets, and reflected that it was always something gained for a sculptor to sit under a tree, looking at his leisure into a charming face and saying things that made it smile and play its muscles and part its lips and show its teeth. Attached to these ladies were certain gentlemen who walked about in clouds of perfume, rose at midday, and supped at midnight. Roderick had found himself in the mood for thinking them very amusing fellows. He was surprised at his own taste, but he let it take its course. It led him to the discovery that to live with ladies who expect you to present them with expensive bouquets, to ride with them in the Black Forest on well-looking horses, to come into their opera-boxes on nights when Patti sang and prices were consequent, to propose little light suppers at the Conversation House after the opera or drives by moonlight to the Castle, to be always arrayed and anointed, trinketed and gloved,—that to move in such society, we say, though it might be a privilege, was a privilege with a penalty attached. But the tables made such things easy; half the Baden world lived by the tables. Roderick tried them and found that at first they smoothed his path delightfully. This simplification of matters, however, was only momentary, for he soon perceived that to seem to have money, and to have it in fact, exposed a good-looking young man to peculiar liabilities. At this point of his friend's narrative, Rowland was reminded of Madame de Cruchecassee in The Newcomes, and though he had listened in tranquil silence to the rest of it, he found it hard not to say that all this had been, under the circumstances, a very bad business. Roderick admitted it with bitterness, and then told how much—measured simply financially—it had cost him. His luck had changed; the tables had ceased to back him, and he had found himself up to his knees in debt. Every penny had gone of the solid sum which had seemed a large equivalent of those shining statues in Rome. He had been an ass, but it was not irreparable; he could make another statue in a couple of months.

Rowland frowned. "For heaven's sake," he said, "don't play such dangerous games with your facility. If you have got facility, revere it, respect it, adore it, treasure it—don't speculate on it." And he wondered what his companion, up to his knees in debt, would have done if there had been no good-natured Rowland Mallet to lend a helping hand. But he did not formulate his curiosity audibly, and the contingency seemed not to have presented itself to Roderick's imagination. The young sculptor reverted to his late adventures again in the evening, and this time talked of them more objectively, as the phrase is; more as if they had been the adventures of another person. He related half a dozen droll things that had happened to him, and, as if his responsibility had been disengaged by all this free discussion, he laughed extravagantly at the memory of them. Rowland sat perfectly grave, on principle. Then Roderick began to talk of half a dozen statues that he had in his head, and set forth his design, with his usual vividness. Suddenly, as it was relevant, he declared that his Baden doings had not been altogether fruitless, for that the lady who had reminded Rowland of Madame de Cruchecassee was tremendously statuesque. Rowland at last said that it all might pass if he felt that he was really the wiser for it. "By the wiser," he added, "I mean the stronger in purpose, in will."

"Oh, don't talk about will!" Roderick answered, throwing back his head and looking at the stars. This conversation also took place in the open air, on the little island in the shooting Rhone where Jean-Jacques has a monument. "The will, I believe, is the mystery of mysteries. Who can answer for his will? who can say beforehand that it 's strong? There are all kinds of indefinable currents moving to and fro between one's will and one's inclinations. People talk as if the two things were essentially distinct; on different sides of one's organism, like the heart and the liver. Mine, I know, are much nearer together. It all depends upon circumstances. I believe there is a certain group of circumstances possible for every man, in which his will is destined to snap like a dry twig."

"My dear boy," said Rowland, "don't talk about the will being 'destined.' The will is destiny itself. That 's the way to look at it."

"Look at it, my dear Rowland," Roderick answered, "as you find most comfortable. One conviction I have gathered from my summer's experience," he went on—"it 's as well to look it frankly in the face—is that I possess an almost unlimited susceptibility to the influence of a beautiful woman."

Rowland stared, then strolled away, softly whistling to himself. He was unwilling to admit even to himself that this speech had really the sinister meaning it seemed to have. In a few days the two young men made their way back to Italy, and lingered a while in Florence before going on to Rome. In Florence Roderick seemed to have won back his old innocence and his preference for the pleasures of study over any others. Rowland began to think of the Baden episode as a bad dream, or at the worst as a mere sporadic piece of disorder, without roots in his companion's character. They passed a fortnight looking at pictures and exploring for out the way bits of fresco and carving, and Roderick recovered all his earlier fervor of appreciation and comment. In Rome he went eagerly to work again, and finished in a month two or three small things he had left standing on his departure. He talked the most joyous nonsense about finding himself back in his old quarters. On the first Sunday afternoon following their return, on their going together to Saint Peter's, he delivered himself of a lyrical greeting to the great church and to the city in general, in a tone of voice so irrepressibly elevated that it rang through the nave in rather a scandalous fashion, and almost arrested a procession of canons who were marching across to the choir. He began to model a new statue—a female figure, of which he had said nothing to Rowland. It represented a woman, leaning lazily back in her chair, with her head drooping as if she were listening, a vague smile on her lips, and a pair of remarkably beautiful arms folded in her lap. With rather less softness of contour, it would have resembled the noble statue of Agrippina in the Capitol. Rowland looked at it and was not sure he liked it. "Who is it? what does it mean?" he asked.

"Anything you please!" said Roderick, with a certain petulance. "I call it A Reminiscence."

Rowland then remembered that one of the Baden ladies had been "statuesque," and asked no more questions. This, after all, was a way of profiting by experience. A few days later he took his first ride of the season on the Campagna, and as, on his homeward way, he was passing across the long shadow of a ruined tower, he perceived a small figure at a short distance, bent over a sketch-book. As he drew near, he recognized his friend Singleton. The honest little painter's face was scorched to flame-color by the light of southern suns, and borrowed an even deeper crimson from his gleeful greeting of his most appreciative patron. He was making a careful and charming little sketch. On Rowland's asking him how he had spent his summer, he gave an account of his wanderings which made poor Mallet sigh with a sense of more contrasts than one. He had not been out of Italy, but he had been delving deep into the picturesque heart of the lovely land, and gathering a wonderful store of subjects. He had rambled about among the unvisited villages of the Apennines, pencil in hand and knapsack on back, sleeping on straw and eating black bread and beans, but feasting on local color, rioting, as it were, on chiaroscuro, and laying up a treasure of pictorial observations. He took a devout satisfaction in his hard-earned wisdom and his happy frugality. Rowland went the next day, by appointment, to look at his sketches, and spent a whole morning turning them over. Singleton talked more than he had ever done before, explained them all, and told some quaintly humorous anecdote about the production of each.

"Dear me, how I have chattered!" he said at last. "I am afraid you had rather have looked at the things in peace and quiet. I did n't know I could talk so much. But somehow, I feel very happy; I feel as if I had improved."

"That you have," said Rowland. "I doubt whether an artist ever passed a more profitable three months. You must feel much more sure of yourself."

Singleton looked for a long time with great intentness at a knot in the floor. "Yes," he said at last, in a fluttered tone, "I feel much more sure of myself. I have got more facility!" And he lowered his voice as if he were communicating a secret which it took some courage to impart. "I hardly like to say it, for fear I should after all be mistaken. But since it strikes you, perhaps it 's true. It 's a great happiness; I would not exchange it for a great deal of money."

"Yes, I suppose it 's a great happiness," said Rowland. "I shall really think of you as living here in a state of scandalous bliss. I don't believe it 's good for an artist to be in such brutally high spirits."

Singleton stared for a moment, as if he thought Rowland was in earnest; then suddenly fathoming the kindly jest, he walked about the room, scratching his head and laughing intensely to himself. "And Mr. Hudson?" he said, as Rowland was going; "I hope he is well and happy."

"He is very well," said Rowland. "He is back at work again."

"Ah, there 's a man," cried Singleton, "who has taken his start once for all, and does n't need to stop and ask himself in fear and trembling every month or two whether he is advancing or not. When he stops, it 's to rest! And where did he spend his summer?"

"The greater part of it at Baden-Baden."

"Ah, that 's in the Black Forest," cried Singleton, with profound simplicity. "They say you can make capital studies of trees there."

"No doubt," said Rowland, with a smile, laying an almost paternal hand on the little painter's yellow head. "Unfortunately trees are not Roderick's line. Nevertheless, he tells me that at Baden he made some studies. Come when you can, by the way," he added after a moment, "to his studio, and tell me what you think of something he has lately begun." Singleton declared that he would come delightedly, and Rowland left him to his work.

431

He met a number of his last winter's friends again, and called upon Madame Grandoni, upon Miss Blanchard, and upon Gloriani, shortly after their return. The ladies gave an excellent account of themselves. Madame Grandoni had been taking sea-baths at Rimini, and Miss Blanchard painting wild flowers in the Tyrol. Her complexion was somewhat browned, which was very becoming, and her flowers were uncommonly pretty. Gloriani had been in Paris and had come away in high good-humor, finding no one there, in the artist-world, cleverer than himself. He came in a few days to Roderick's studio, one afternoon when Rowland was present. He examined the new statue with great deference, said it was very promising, and abstained, considerably, from irritating prophecies. But Rowland fancied he observed certain signs of inward jubilation on the clever sculptor's part, and walked away with him to learn his private opinion.

"Certainly; I liked it as well as I said," Gloriani declared in answer to Rowland's anxious query; "or rather I liked it a great deal better. I did n't say how much, for fear of making your friend angry. But one can leave him alone now, for he 's coming round. I told you he could n't keep up the transcendental style, and he has already broken down. Don't you see it yourself, man?"

"I don't particularly like this new statue," said Rowland.

"That 's because you 're a purist. It 's deuced clever, it 's deuced knowing, it 's deuced pretty, but it is n't the topping high art of three months ago. He has taken his turn sooner than I supposed. What has happened to him? Has he been disappointed in love? But that 's none of my business. I congratulate him on having become a practical man."

Roderick, however, was less to be congratulated than Gloriani had taken it into his head to believe. He was discontented with his work, he applied himself to it by fits and starts, he declared that he did n't know what was coming over him; he was turning into a man of moods. "Is this of necessity what a fellow must come to"—he asked of Rowland, with a sort of peremptory flash in his eye, which seemed to imply that his companion had undertaken to insure him against perplexities and was not fulfilling his contract—"this damnable uncertainty when he goes to bed at night as to whether he is going to wake up in a working humor or in a swearing humor? Have we only a season, over before we know it, in which we can call our faculties our own? Six months ago I could stand up to my work like a man, day after day, and never dream of asking myself whether I felt like it. But now, some mornings, it 's the very devil to get going. My statue looks so bad when I come into the studio that I have twenty minds to smash it on the spot, and I lose three or four hours in sitting there, moping and getting used to it."

Rowland said that he supposed that this sort of thing was the lot of every artist and that the only remedy was plenty of courage and faith. And he reminded him of Gloriani's having forewarned him against these sterile moods the year before.

"Gloriani 's an ass!" said Roderick, almost fiercely. He hired a horse and began to ride with Rowland on the Campagna. This delicious amusement restored him in a measure to cheerfulness, but seemed to Rowland on the whole not to stimulate his industry. Their rides were always very long, and Roderick insisted on making them longer by dismounting in picturesque spots and stretching himself in the sun among a heap of overtangled stones. He let the scorching Roman luminary beat down upon him with an equanimity which Rowland found it hard to emulate. But in this situation Roderick talked so much amusing nonsense that, for the sake of his company, Rowland consented to be uncomfortable, and often forgot that, though in these diversions the days passed quickly, they brought forth neither high art nor low. And yet it was perhaps by their help, after all, that Roderick secured several mornings of ardent work on his new figure, and brought it to rapid completion. One afternoon, when it was finished, Rowland went to look at it, and Roderick asked him for his opinion.

"What do you think yourself?" Rowland demanded, not from pusillanimity, but from real uncertainty.

"I think it is curiously bad," Roderick answered. "It was bad from the first; it has fundamental vices. I have shuffled them in a measure out of sight, but I have not corrected them. I can't—I can't—I can't!" he cried passionately. "They stare me in the face—they are all I see!"

Rowland offered several criticisms of detail, and suggested certain practicable changes. But Roderick differed with him on each of these points; the thing had faults enough, but they were not those faults. Rowland, unruffled, concluded by saying that whatever its faults might be, he had an idea people in general would like it.

"I wish to heaven some person in particular would buy it, and take it off my hands and out of my sight!" Roderick cried. "What am I to do now?" he went on. "I have n't an idea. I think of subjects, but they remain mere lifeless names. They are mere words—they are not images. What am I to do?"

Rowland was a trifle annoyed. "Be a man," he was on the point of saying, "and don't, for heaven's sake, talk in that confoundedly querulous voice." But before he had uttered the words, there rang through the studio a loud, peremptory ring at the outer door.

Roderick broke into a laugh. "Talk of the devil," he said, "and you see his horns! If that 's not a customer, it ought to be."

The door of the studio was promptly flung open, and a lady advanced to the threshold—an imposing, voluminous person, who quite filled up the doorway. Rowland immediately felt that he had seen her before, but he recognized her only when she moved forward and disclosed an attendant in the person of a little bright-eyed, elderly gentleman, with a bristling white moustache. Then he remembered that just a year before he and his companion had seen in the Ludovisi gardens a wonderfully beautiful girl, strolling in the train of this conspicuous couple. He looked for her now, and in a moment she appeared, following her companions with the same nonchalant step as before, and leading her great snow-white poodle, decorated with motley ribbons. The elder lady offered the two young men a sufficiently gracious salute; the little old gentleman bowed and smiled with extreme alertness. The young girl, without casting a glance either at Roderick or at Rowland, looked about for a chair, and, on perceiving one, sank into it listlessly, pulled her poodle towards her, and began to rearrange his top-knot. Rowland saw that, even with her eyes dropped, her beauty was still dazzling.

"I trust we are at liberty to enter," said the elder lady, with majesty. "We were told that Mr. Hudson had no fixed day, and that we might come at any time. Let us not disturb you."

Roderick, as one of the lesser lights of the Roman art-world, had not hitherto been subject to incursions from inquisitive tourists, and, having no regular reception day, was not versed in the usual formulas of welcome. He said nothing, and Rowland, looking at him, saw that he was looking amazedly at the young girl and was apparently unconscious of everything else. "By Jove!" he cried precipitately, "it 's that goddess of the Villa Ludovisi!" Rowland in some confusion, did the honors as he could, but the little old gentleman begged him with the most obsequious of smiles to give himself no trouble. "I have been in many a studio!" he said, with his finger on his nose and a strong Italian accent.

"We are going about everywhere," said his companion. "I am passionately fond of art!"

Rowland smiled sympathetically, and let them turn to Roderick's statue. He glanced again at the young sculptor, to invite him to bestir himself, but Roderick was still gazing wide-eyed at the beautiful young mistress of the poodle, who by this time had looked up and was gazing straight at him. There was nothing bold in her look; it expressed a kind of languid, imperturbable indifference. Her beauty was extraordinary; it grew and grew as the young man observed her. In such a face the maidenly custom of averted eyes and ready blushes would have seemed an anomaly; nature had produced it for man's delight and meant that it should surrender itself freely and coldly to admiration. It was not immediately apparent, however, that the young lady found an answering entertainment in the physiognomy of her host; she turned her head after a moment and looked idly round the room, and at last let her eyes rest on the statue of the woman seated. It being left to Rowland to stimulate conversation, he began by complimenting her on the beauty of her dog.

"Yes, he 's very handsome," she murmured. "He 's a Florentine. The dogs in Florence are handsomer than the people." And on Rowland's caressing him: "His name is Stenterello," she added. "Stenterello, give your hand to the gentleman." This order was given in Italian. "Say buon giorno a lei."

Stenterello thrust out his paw and gave four short, shrill barks; upon which the elder lady turned round and raised her forefinger.

"My dear, my dear, remember where you are! Excuse my foolish child," she added, turning to Roderick with an agreeable smile. "She can think of nothing but her poodle."

"I am teaching him to talk for me," the young girl went on, without heeding her mother; "to say little things in society. It will save me a great deal of trouble. Stenterello, love, give a pretty smile and say tanti complimenti!" The poodle wagged his white pate—it looked like one of those little pads in swan's-down, for applying powder to the face—and repeated the barking process.

"He is a wonderful beast," said Rowland.

"He is not a beast," said the young girl. "A beast is something black and dirty—something you can't touch."

"He is a very valuable dog," the elder lady explained. "He was presented to my daughter by a Florentine nobleman."

"It is not for that I care about him. It is for himself. He is better than the prince."

"My dear, my dear!" repeated the mother in deprecating accents, but with a significant glance at Rowland which seemed to bespeak his attention to the glory of possessing a daughter who could deal in that fashion with the aristocracy.

Rowland remembered that when their unknown visitors had passed before them, a year previous, in the Villa Ludovisi, Roderick and he had exchanged conjectures as to their nationality and social quality. Roderick had declared that they were old-world people; but Rowland now needed no telling to feel that he might claim the elder lady as a fellow-countrywoman. She was a person of what is called a great deal of presence, with the faded traces, artfully revived here and there, of once brilliant beauty. Her daughter had come lawfully by her loveliness, but Rowland mentally made the distinction that the mother was silly and that the daughter was not. The mother had a very silly mouth—a mouth, Rowland suspected, capable of expressing an inordinate degree of unreason. The young girl, in spite of her childish satisfaction in her poodle, was not a person of feeble understanding. Rowland received an impression that, for reasons of her own, she was playing a part. What was the part and what were her reasons? She was interesting; Rowland wondered what were her domestic secrets. If her mother was a daughter of the great Republic, it was to be supposed that the young girl was a flower of the American soil; but her beauty had a robustness and tone uncommon in the somewhat facile loveliness of our western maidenhood. She spoke with a vague foreign accent, as if she had spent her life in strange countries. The little Italian apparently divined Rowland's mute imaginings, for he presently stepped forward, with a bow like a master of ceremonies. "I have not done my duty," he said, "in not announcing these ladies. Mrs. Light, Miss Light!"

Rowland was not materially the wiser for this information, but Roderick was aroused by it to the exercise of some slight hospitality. He altered the light, pulled forward two or three figures, and made an apology for not having more to show. "I don't pretend to have anything of an exhibition—I am only a novice."

"Indeed?—a novice! For a novice this is very well," Mrs. Light declared. "Cavaliere, we have seen nothing better than this."

The Cavaliere smiled rapturously. "It is stupendous!" he murmured. "And we have been to all the studios."

"Not to all—heaven forbid!" cried Mrs. Light. "But to a number that I have had pointed out by artistic friends. I delight in studios: they are the temples of the beautiful here below. And if you are a novice, Mr. Hudson," she went on, "you have already great admirers. Half a dozen people have told us that yours were among the things to see." This gracious speech went unanswered; Roderick had already wandered across to the other side of the studio and was revolving about Miss Light. "Ah, he 's gone to look at my beautiful daughter; he is not the first that has had his head turned," Mrs. Light resumed, lowering her voice to a confidential undertone; a favor which, considering the shortness of their acquaintance, Rowland was bound to appreciate. "The artists are all crazy about her. When she goes into a studio she is fatal to the pictures. And when she goes into a ball-room what do the other women say? Eh, Cavaliere?"

"She is very beautiful," Rowland said, gravely.

Mrs. Light, who through her long, gold-cased glass was looking a little at everything, and at nothing as if she saw it, interrupted her random murmurs and exclamations, and surveyed Rowland from head to foot. She looked at him all over; apparently he had not been mentioned to her as a feature of Roderick's establishment. It was the gaze, Rowland felt, which the vigilant and ambitious mamma of a beautiful daughter has always at her command for well-dressed young men of candid physiognomy. Her inspection in this case seemed satisfactory. "Are you also an artist?" she inquired with an almost caressing inflection. It was clear that what she meant was something of this kind: "Be so good as to assure me without delay that you are really the young man of substance and amiability that you appear."

But Rowland answered simply the formal question—not the latent one. "Dear me, no; I am only a friend of Mr. Hudson."

Mrs. Light, with a sigh, returned to the statues, and after mistaking the Adam for a gladiator, and the Eve for a Pocahontas, declared that she could not judge of such things unless she saw them in the marble. Rowland hesitated a moment, and then speaking in the interest of Roderick's renown, said that he was the happy possessor of several of his friend's works and that she was welcome to come and see them at his rooms. She bade the Cavaliere make a note of his address. "Ah, you 're a patron of the arts," she said. "That 's what I should like to be if I had a little money. I delight in beauty in every form. But all these people ask such monstrous prices. One must be a millionaire, to think of such things, eh? Twenty years ago my husband had my portrait painted, here in Rome, by Papucci, who was the great man in those days. I was in a ball dress, with all my jewels, my neck and arms, and all that. The man got six hundred francs, and thought he was very well treated. Those were the days when a family could live like princes in Italy for five thousand scudi a year. The Cavaliere once upon a time was a great dandy—don't blush, Cavaliere; any one can see that, just as any one can see that I was once a pretty woman! Get him to tell you what he made a figure upon. The railroads have brought in the vulgarians. That 's what I call it now—the invasion of the vulgarians! What are poor we to do?"

Rowland had begun to murmur some remedial proposition, when he was interrupted by the voice of Miss Light calling across the room, "Mamma!"

"My own love?"

"This gentleman wishes to model my bust. Please speak to him."

The Cavaliere gave a little chuckle. "Already?" he cried.

Rowland looked round, equally surprised at the promptitude of the proposal. Roderick stood planted before the young girl with his arms folded, looking at her as he would have done at the Medicean Venus. He never paid compliments, and Rowland, though he had not heard him speak, could imagine the startling distinctness with which he made his request.

"He saw me a year ago," the young girl went on, "and he has been thinking of me ever since." Her tone, in speaking, was peculiar; it had a kind of studied inexpressiveness, which was yet not the vulgar device of a drawl.

"I must make your daughter's bust—that 's all, madame!" cried Roderick, with warmth.

"I had rather you made the poodle's," said the young girl. "Is it very tiresome? I have spent half my life sitting for my photograph, in every conceivable attitude and with every conceivable coiffure. I think I have posed enough."

"My dear child," said Mrs. Light, "it may be one's duty to pose. But as to my daughter's sitting to you, sir—to a young sculptor whom we don't know—it is a matter that needs reflection. It is not a favor that 's to be had for the mere asking."

"If I don't make her from life," said Roderick, with energy, "I will make her from memory, and if the thing 's to be done, you had better have it done as well as possible."

"Mamma hesitates," said Miss Light, "because she does n't know whether you mean she shall pay you for the bust. I can assure you that she will not pay you a sou."

"My darling, you forget yourself," said Mrs. Light, with an attempt at majestic severity. "Of course," she added, in a moment, with a change of note, "the bust would be my own property."

"Of course!" cried Roderick, impatiently.

"Dearest mother," interposed the young girl, "how can you carry a marble bust about the world with you? Is it not enough to drag the poor original?"

"My dear, you 're nonsensical!" cried Mrs. Light, almost angrily.

"You can always sell it," said the young girl, with the same artful artlessness.

Mrs. Light turned to Rowland, who pitied her, flushed and irritated. "She is very wicked to-day!"

The Cavaliere grinned in silence and walked away on tiptoe, with his hat to his lips, as if to leave the field clear for action. Rowland, on the contrary, wished to avert the coming storm. "You had better not refuse," he said to Miss Light, "until you have seen Mr. Hudson's things in the marble. Your mother is to come and look at some that I possess."

"Thank you; I have no doubt you will see us. I dare say Mr. Hudson is very clever; but I don't care for modern sculpture. I can't look at it!"

"You shall care for my bust, I promise you!" cried Roderick, with a laugh.

"To satisfy Miss Light," said the Cavaliere, "one of the old Greeks ought to come to life."

"It would be worth his while," said Roderick, paying, to Rowland's knowledge, his first compliment.

"I might sit to Phidias, if he would promise to be very amusing and make me laugh. What do you say, Stenterello? would you sit to Phidias?"

"We must talk of this some other time," said Mrs. Light. "We are in Rome for the winter. Many thanks. Cavaliere, call the carriage." The Cavaliere led the way out, backing like a silver-stick, and Miss Light, following her mother, nodded, without looking at them, to each of the young men.

"Immortal powers, what a head!" cried Roderick, when they had gone. "There 's my fortune!"

"She is certainly very beautiful," said Rowland. "But I 'm sorry you have undertaken her bust."

"And why, pray?"

"I suspect it will bring trouble with it."

"What kind of trouble?"

"I hardly know. They are queer people. The mamma, I suspect, is the least bit of an adventuress. Heaven knows what the daughter is."

"She 's a goddess!" cried Roderick.

"Just so. She is all the more dangerous."

"Dangerous? What will she do to me? She does n't bite, I imagine."

"It remains to be seen. There are two kinds of women—you ought to know it by this time—the safe and the unsafe. Miss Light, if I am not mistaken, is one of the unsafe. A word to the wise!"

"Much obliged!" said Roderick, and he began to whistle a triumphant air, in honor, apparently, of the advent of his beautiful model.

In calling this young lady and her mamma "queer people," Rowland but roughly expressed his sentiment. They were so marked a variation from the monotonous troop of his fellow-country people that he felt much curiosity as to the sources of the change, especially since he doubted greatly whether, on the whole, it elevated the type. For a week he saw the two ladies driving daily in a well-appointed landau, with the Cavaliere and the poodle in the front seat. From Mrs. Light he received a gracious salute, tempered by her native majesty; but the young girl, looking straight before her, seemed profoundly indifferent to observers. Her extraordinary beauty, however, had already made observers numerous and given the habitues of the Pincian plenty to talk about. The echoes of their commentary reached Rowland's ears; but he had little taste for random gossip, and desired a distinctly veracious informant. He had found one in the person of Madame Grandoni, for whom Mrs. Light and her beautiful daughter were a pair of old friends.

"I have known the mamma for twenty years," said this judicious critic, "and if you ask any of the people who have been living here as long as I, you will find they remember her well. I have held the beautiful Christina on my knee when she was a little wizened baby with a very red face and no promise of beauty but those magnificent eyes. Ten years ago Mrs. Light disappeared, and has not since been seen in Rome, except for a few days last winter, when she passed through on her way to Naples. Then it was you met the trio in the Ludovisi gardens. When I first knew her she was the unmarried but very marriageable daughter of an old American painter of very bad landscapes, which people used to buy from charity and use for fire-boards. His name was Savage; it used to make every one laugh, he was such a mild, melancholy, pitiful old gentleman. He had married a horrible wife, an Englishwoman who had been on the stage. It was said she used to beat poor Savage with his mahl-stick and when the domestic finances were low to lock him up in his studio and tell him he should n't come out until he had painted half a dozen of his daubs. She had a good deal of showy beauty. She would then go forth, and, her beauty helping, she would make certain people take the pictures. It helped her at last to make an English lord run away with her. At the time I speak of she had quite disappeared. Mrs. Light was then a very handsome girl, though by no means so handsome as her daughter has now become. Mr. Light was an American consul, newly appointed at one of the Adriatic ports. He was a mild, fair-whiskered young man, with some little property, and my impression is that he had got into bad company at home, and that his family procured him his place to keep him out of harm's way. He came up to Rome on a holiday, fell in love with Miss Savage, and married her on the spot. He had not been married three years when he was drowned in the Adriatic, no one ever knew how. The young widow came back to Rome, to her father, and here shortly afterwards, in the shadow of Saint Peter's, her little girl was born. It might have been supposed that Mrs. Light would marry again, and I know she had opportunities. But she overreached herself. She would take nothing less than a title and a fortune, and they were not forthcoming. She was admired and very fond of admiration; very vain, very worldly, very silly. She remained a pretty widow, with a surprising variety of bonnets and a dozen men always in her train. Giacosa dates from this period. He calls himself a Roman, but I have an impression he came up from Ancona with her. He was l'ami de la maison. He used to hold her bouquets, clean her gloves (I was told), run her errands, get her opera-boxes, and fight her battles with the shopkeepers. For this he needed courage, for she was smothered in debt. She at last left Rome to escape her creditors. Many of them must remember her still, but she seems now to have money to satisfy them. She left her poor old father here alone—helpless, infirm and unable to work. A subscription was shortly afterwards taken up among the foreigners, and he was sent back to America, where, as I afterwards heard, he died in some sort of asylum. From time to time, for several years, I heard vaguely of Mrs. Light as a wandering beauty at French and German watering-places. Once came a rumor that she was going to make a grand marriage in England; then we heard that the gentleman had thought better of it and left her to keep afloat as she could. She was a terribly scatter-brained creature. She pretends to be a great lady, but I consider that old Filomena, my washer-woman, is in essentials a greater one. But certainly, after all, she has been fortunate. She embarked at last on a lawsuit about some property, with her husband's family, and went to America to attend to it. She came back triumphant, with a long purse. She reappeared in Italy, and established herself for a while in Venice. Then she came to Florence, where she spent a couple of years and where I saw her. Last year she passed down to Naples, which I should have said was just the place for her, and this winter she has laid siege to Rome. She seems very prosperous. She has taken a floor in the Palazzo F——, she keeps her carriage, and Christina and she, between them, must have a pretty milliner's bill. Giacosa has turned up again, looking as if he had been kept on ice at Ancona, for her return."

"What sort of education," Rowland asked, "do you imagine the mother's adventures to have been for the daughter?"

"A strange school! But Mrs. Light told me, in Florence, that she had given her child the education of a princess. In other words, I suppose, she speaks three or four languages, and has read several hundred French novels. Christina, I suspect, is very clever. When I saw her, I was amazed at her beauty, and, certainly, if there is any truth in faces, she ought to have the soul of an angel. Perhaps she has. I don't judge her; she 's an extraordinary young person. She has been told twenty times a day by her mother, since she was five years old, that she is a beauty of beauties, that her face is her fortune, and that, if she plays her cards, she may marry a duke. If she has not been fatally corrupted, she is a very superior girl. My own impression is that she is a mixture of good and bad, of ambition and indifference. Mrs. Light, having failed to make her own fortune in matrimony, has transferred her hopes to her daughter, and nursed them till they have become a kind of monomania. She has a hobby, which she rides in secret; but some day she will let you see it. I 'm sure that if you go in some evening unannounced, you will find her scanning the tea-leaves in her cup, or telling her daughter's fortune with a greasy pack of cards, preserved for the purpose. She promises her a prince—a reigning prince. But if Mrs. Light is silly, she is shrewd, too, and, lest considerations of state should deny her prince the luxury of a love-match, she keeps on hand a few common mortals. At the worst she would take a duke, an English lord, or even a young American with a proper number of millions. The poor woman must be rather uncomfortable. She is always building castles and knocking them down again—always casting her nets and pulling them in. If her daughter were less of a beauty, her transparent ambition would be very ridiculous; but there is something in the girl, as one looks at her, that seems to make it very possible she is marked out for one of those wonderful romantic fortunes that history now and then relates. 'Who, after all, was the Empress of the French?' Mrs. Light is forever saying. 'And beside Christina the Empress is a dowdy!'"

"And what does Christina say?"

"She makes no scruple, as you know, of saying that her mother is a fool. What she thinks, heaven knows. I suspect that, practically, she does not commit herself. She is excessively proud, and thinks herself good enough to occupy the highest station in the world; but she knows that her mother talks nonsense, and that even a beautiful girl may look awkward in making unsuccessful advances. So she remains superbly indifferent, and lets her mother take the risks. If the prince is secured, so much the better; if he is not, she need never confess to herself that even a prince has slighted her."

"Your report is as solid," Rowland said to Madame Grandoni, thanking her, "as if it had been prepared for the Academy of Sciences;" and he congratulated himself on having listened to it when, a couple of days later, Mrs. Light and her daughter, attended by the Cavaliere and the poodle, came to his rooms to look at Roderick's statues. It was more comfortable to know just with whom he was dealing.

Mrs. Light was prodigiously gracious, and showered down compliments not only on the statues, but on all his possessions. "Upon my word," she said, "you men know how to make yourselves comfortable. If one of us poor women had half as many easy-chairs and knick-knacks, we should be famously abused. It 's really selfish to be living all alone in such a place as this. Cavaliere, how should you like this suite of rooms and a fortune to fill them with pictures and statues? Christina, love, look at that mosaic table. Mr. Mallet, I could almost beg it from you. Yes, that Eve is certainly very fine. We need n't be ashamed of such a great-grandmother as that. If she was really such a beautiful woman, it accounts for the good looks of some of us. Where is Mr. What 's-his-name, the young sculptor? Why is n't he here to be complimented?"

Christina had remained but for a moment in the chair which Rowland had placed for her, had given but a cursory glance at the statues, and then, leaving her place, had begun to wander round the room—looking at herself in the mirror, touching the ornaments and curiosities, glancing at the books and prints. Rowland's sitting-room was encumbered with bric-a-brac, and she found plenty of occupation. Rowland presently joined her, and pointed out some of the objects he most valued.

"It 's an odd jumble," she said frankly. "Some things are very pretty— some are very ugly. But I like ugly things, when they have a certain look. Prettiness is terribly vulgar nowadays, and it is not every one that knows just the sort of ugliness that has chic. But chic is getting dreadfully common too. There 's a hint of it even in Madame Baldi's bonnets. I like looking at people's things," she added in a moment, turning to Rowland and resting her eyes on him. "It helps you to find out their characters."

"Am I to suppose," asked Rowland, smiling, "that you have arrived at any conclusions as to mine?"

"I am rather muddled; you have too many things; one seems to contradict another. You are very artistic and yet you are very prosaic; you have what is called a 'catholic' taste and yet you are full of obstinate little prejudices and habits of thought, which, if I knew you, I should find very tiresome. I don't think I like you."

"You make a great mistake," laughed Rowland; "I assure you I am very amiable."

"Yes, I am probably wrong, and if I knew you, I should find out I was wrong, and that would irritate me and make me dislike you more. So you see we are necessary enemies."

"No, I don't dislike you."

"Worse and worse; for you certainly will not like me."

"You are very discouraging."

"I am fond of facing the truth, though some day you will deny that. Where is that queer friend of yours?"

"You mean Mr. Hudson. He is represented by these beautiful works."

Miss Light looked for some moments at Roderick's statues. "Yes," she said, "they are not so silly as most of the things we have seen. They have no chic, and yet they are beautiful."

"You describe them perfectly," said Rowland. "They are beautiful, and yet they have no chic. That 's it!"

"If he will promise to put none into my bust, I have a mind to let him make it. A request made in those terms deserves to be granted."

"In what terms?"

"Did n't you hear him? 'Mademoiselle, you almost satisfy my conception of the beautiful. I must model your bust.' That almost should be rewarded. He is like me; he likes to face the truth. I think we should get on together."

The Cavaliere approached Rowland, to express the pleasure he had derived from his beautiful "collection." His smile was exquisitely bland, his accent appealing, caressing, insinuating. But he gave Rowland an odd sense of looking at a little waxen image, adjusted to perform certain gestures and emit certain sounds. It had once contained a soul, but the soul had leaked out. Nevertheless, Rowland reflected, there are more profitless things than mere sound and gesture, in a consummate Italian. And the Cavaliere, too, had soul enough left to desire to speak a few words on his own account, and call Rowland's attention to the fact that he was not, after all, a hired cicerone, but an ancient Roman gentleman. Rowland felt sorry for him; he hardly knew why. He assured him in a friendly fashion that he must come again; that his house was always at his service. The Cavaliere bowed down to the ground. "You do me too much honor," he murmured. "If you will allow me—it is not impossible!"

Mrs. Light, meanwhile, had prepared to depart. "If you are not afraid to come and see two quiet little women, we shall be most happy!" she said. "We have no statues nor pictures—we have nothing but each other. Eh, darling?"

"I beg your pardon," said Christina.

"Oh, and the Cavaliere," added her mother.

"The poodle, please!" cried the young girl.

Rowland glanced at the Cavaliere; he was smiling more blandly than ever.

A few days later Rowland presented himself, as civility demanded, at Mrs. Light's door. He found her living in one of the stately houses of the Via dell' Angelo Custode, and, rather to his surprise, was told she was at home. He passed through half a dozen rooms and was ushered into an immense saloon, at one end of which sat the mistress of the establishment, with a piece of embroidery. She received him very graciously, and then, pointing mysteriously to a large screen which was unfolded across the embrasure of one of the deep windows, "I am keeping guard!" she said. Rowland looked interrogative; whereupon she beckoned him forward and motioned him to look behind the screen. He obeyed, and for some moments stood gazing. Roderick, with his back turned, stood before an extemporized pedestal, ardently shaping a formless mass of clay. Before him sat Christina Light, in a white dress, with her shoulders bare, her magnificent hair twisted into a classic coil, and her head admirably poised. Meeting Rowland's gaze, she smiled a little, only with her deep gray eyes, without moving. She looked divinely beautiful.

CHAPTER V. Christina

The brilliant Roman winter came round again, and Rowland enjoyed it, in a certain way, more deeply than before. He grew at last to feel that sense of equal possession, of intellectual nearness, which it belongs to the peculiar magic of the ancient city to infuse into minds of a cast that she never would have produced. He became passionately, unreasoningly fond of all Roman sights and sensations, and to breathe the Roman atmosphere began to seem a needful condition of being. He could not have defined and explained the nature of his great love, nor have made up the sum of it by the addition of his calculable pleasures. It was a large, vague, idle, half-profitless emotion, of which perhaps the most pertinent thing that may be said is that it enforced a sort of oppressive reconciliation to the present, the actual, the sensuous—to life on the terms that there offered themselves. It was perhaps for this very reason that, in spite of the charm which Rome flings over one's mood, there ran through Rowland's meditations an undertone of melancholy, natural enough in a mind which finds its horizon insidiously limited to the finite, even in very picturesque forms. Whether it is one that tacitly concedes to the Roman Church the monopoly of a guarantee of immortality, so that if one is indisposed to bargain with her for the precious gift, one must do without it altogether; or whether in an atmosphere so heavily weighted with echoes and memories one grows to believe that there is nothing in one's consciousness that is not foredoomed to moulder and crumble and become dust for the feet, and possible malaria for the lungs, of future generations—the fact at least remains that one parts half-willingly with one's hopes in Rome, and misses them only under some very exceptional stress of circumstance. For this reason one may perhaps say that there is no other place in which one's daily temper has such a mellow serenity, and none, at the same time, in which acute attacks of depression are more intolerable. Rowland found, in fact, a perfect response to his prevision that to live in Rome was an education to one's senses and one's imagination, but he sometimes wondered whether this was not a questionable gain in case of one's not being prepared to live wholly by one's imagination and one's senses. The tranquil profundity of his daily satisfaction seemed sometimes to turn, by a mysterious inward impulse, and face itself with questioning, admonishing, threatening eyes. "But afterwards...?" it seemed to ask, with a long reverberation; and he could give no answer but a shy affirmation that there was no such thing as afterwards, and a hope, divided against itself, that his actual way of life would last forever. He often felt heavy-hearted; he was sombre without knowing why; there were no visible clouds in his heaven, but there were cloud-shadows on his mood. Shadows projected, they often were, without his knowing it, by an undue apprehension that things after all might not go so ideally well with Roderick. When he understood his anxiety it vexed him, and he rebuked himself for taking things unmanfully hard. If Roderick chose to follow a crooked path, it was no fault of his; he had given him, he would continue to give him, all that he had offered him—friendship, sympathy, advice. He had not undertaken to provide him with unflagging strength of purpose, nor to stand bondsman for unqualified success.

If Rowland felt his roots striking and spreading in the Roman soil, Roderick also surrendered himself with renewed abandon to the local influence. More than once he declared to his companion that he meant to live and die within the shadow of Saint Peter's, and that he cared little if he never again drew breath in American air. "For a man of my temperament, Rome is the only possible place," he said; "it 's better to recognize the fact early than late. So I shall never go home unless I am absolutely forced."

"What is your idea of 'force'?" asked Rowland, smiling. "It seems to me you have an excellent reason for going home some day or other."

"Ah, you mean my engagement?" Roderick answered with unaverted eyes. "Yes, I am distinctly engaged, in Northampton, and impatiently waited for!" And he gave a little sympathetic sigh. "To reconcile Northampton and Rome is rather a problem. Mary had better come out here. Even at the worst I have no intention of giving up Rome within six or eight years, and an engagement of that duration would be rather absurd."

"Miss Garland could hardly leave your mother," Rowland observed.

"Oh, of course my mother should come. I think I will suggest it in my next letter. It will take her a year or two to make up her mind to it, but if she consents it will brighten her up. It 's too small a life, over there, even for a timid old lady. It is hard to imagine," he added, "any change in Mary being a change for the better; but I should like her to take a look at the world and have her notions stretched a little. One is never so good, I suppose, but that one can improve a little."

"If you wish your mother and Miss Garland to come," Rowland suggested, "you had better go home and bring them."

"Oh, I can't think of leaving Europe, for many a day," Roderick answered. "At present it would quite break the charm. I am just beginning to profit, to get used to things and take them naturally. I am sure the sight of Northampton Main Street would permanently upset me."

It was reassuring to hear that Roderick, in his own view, was but "just beginning" to spread his wings, and Rowland, if he had had any forebodings, might have suffered them to be modified by this declaration. This was the first time since their meeting at Geneva that Roderick had mentioned Miss Garland's name, but the ice being broken, he indulged for some time afterward in frequent allusions to his betrothed, which always had an accent of scrupulous, of almost studied, consideration. An uninitiated observer, hearing him, would have imagined her to be a person of a certain age—possibly an affectionate maiden aunt—who had once done him a kindness which he highly appreciated: perhaps presented him with a check for a thousand dollars. Rowland noted the difference between his present frankness and his reticence during the first six months of his engagement, and sometimes wondered whether it was not rather an anomaly that he should expatiate more largely as the happy event receded. He had wondered over the whole matter, first and last, in a great many different ways, and looked at it in all possible lights. There was something terribly hard to explain in the fact of his having fallen in love with his cousin. She was not, as Rowland conceived her, the sort of girl he would have been likely to fancy, and the operation of sentiment, in all cases so mysterious, was particularly so in this one. Just why it was that Roderick should not logically have fancied Miss Garland, his companion would have been at loss to say, but I think the conviction had its roots in an unformulated comparison between himself and the accepted suitor. Roderick and he were as different as two men could be, and yet Roderick had taken it into his head to fall in love with a woman for whom he himself had been keeping in reserve, for years, a profoundly characteristic passion. That if he chose to conceive a great notion of the merits of Roderick's mistress, the irregularity here was hardly Roderick's, was a view of the case to which poor Rowland did scanty justice. There were women, he said to himself, whom it was every one's business to fall in love with a little—women beautiful, brilliant, artful, easily fascinating. Miss Light, for instance, was one of these; every man who spoke to her did so, if not in the language, at least with something of the agitation, the divine tremor, of a lover. There were other women—they might have great beauty, they might have small; perhaps they were generally to be classified as plain— whose triumphs in this line were rare, but immutably permanent. Such a one preeminently, was Mary Garland. Upon the doctrine of probabilities, it was unlikely that she had had an equal charm for each of them, and was it not possible, therefore, that the charm for Roderick had been simply the charm imagined, unquestioningly accepted: the general charm of youth, sympathy, kindness—of the present feminine, in short—enhanced indeed by several fine facial traits? The charm in this case for Rowland was—the charm!—the mysterious, individual, essential woman. There was an element in the charm, as his companion saw it, which Rowland was obliged to recognize, but which he forbore to ponder; the rather important attraction, namely, of reciprocity. As to Miss Garland being in love with Roderick and becoming charming thereby, this was a point with which his imagination ventured to take no liberties; partly because it would have been indelicate, and partly because it would have been vain. He contented himself with feeling that the young girl was still as vivid an image in his memory as she had been five days after he left her, and with drifting nearer and nearer to the impression that at just that crisis any other girl would have answered Roderick's sentimental needs as well. Any other girl indeed would do so still! Roderick had confessed as much to him at Geneva, in saying that he had been taking at Baden the measure of his susceptibility to female beauty.

His extraordinary success in modeling the bust of the beautiful Miss Light was pertinent evidence of this amiable quality. She sat to him, repeatedly, for a fortnight, and the work was rapidly finished. On one of the last days Roderick asked Rowland to come and give his opinion as to what was still wanting; for the sittings had continued to take place in Mrs. Light's apartment, the studio being pronounced too damp for the fair model. When Rowland presented himself, Christina, still in her white dress, with her shoulders bare, was standing before a mirror, readjusting her hair, the arrangement of which, on this occasion, had apparently not met the young sculptor's approval. He stood beside her, directing the operation with a peremptoriness of tone which seemed to Rowland to denote a considerable advance in intimacy. As Rowland entered, Christina was losing patience. "Do it yourself, then!" she cried, and with a rapid movement unloosed the great coil of her tresses and let them fall over her shoulders.

They were magnificent, and with her perfect face dividing their rippling flow she looked like some immaculate saint of legend being led to martyrdom. Rowland's eyes presumably betrayed his admiration, but her own manifested no consciousness of it. If Christina was a coquette, as the remarkable timeliness of this incident might have suggested, she was not a superficial one.

"Hudson 's a sculptor," said Rowland, with warmth. "But if I were only a painter!"

"Thank Heaven you are not!" said Christina. "I am having quite enough of this minute inspection of my charms."

"My dear young man, hands off!" cried Mrs. Light, coming forward and seizing her daughter's hair. "Christina, love, I am surprised."

"Is it indelicate?" Christina asked. "I beg Mr. Mallet's pardon." Mrs. Light gathered up the dusky locks and let them fall through her fingers, glancing at her visitor with a significant smile. Rowland had never been in the East, but if he had attempted to make a sketch of an old slave-merchant, calling attention to the "points" of a Circassian beauty, he would have depicted such a smile as Mrs. Light's. "Mamma 's not really shocked," added Christina in a moment, as if she had guessed her mother's by-play. "She is only afraid that Mr. Hudson might have injured my hair, and that, per consequenza, I should sell for less."

"You unnatural child!" cried mamma. "You deserve that I should make a fright of you!" And with half a dozen skillful passes she twisted the tresses into a single picturesque braid, placed high on the head, as a kind of coronal.

"What does your mother do when she wants to do you justice?" Rowland asked, observing the admirable line of the young girl's neck.

"I do her justice when I say she says very improper things. What is one to do with such a thorn in the flesh?" Mrs. Light demanded.

"Think of it at your leisure, Mr. Mallet," said Christina, "and when you 've discovered something, let us hear. But I must tell you that I shall not willingly believe in any remedy of yours, for you have something in your physiognomy that particularly provokes me to make the remarks that my mother so sincerely deplores. I noticed it the first time I saw you. I think it 's because your face is so broad. For some reason or other, broad faces exasperate me; they fill me with a kind of rabbia. Last summer, at Carlsbad, there was an Austrian count, with enormous estates and some great office at court. He was very attentive—seriously so; he was really very far gone. Cela ne tenait qu' a moi! But I could n't; he was impossible! He must have measured, from ear to ear, at least a yard and a half. And he was blond, too, which made it worse—as blond as Stenterello; pure fleece! So I said to him frankly, 'Many thanks, Herr Graf; your uniform is magnificent, but your face is too fat.'"

"I am afraid that mine also," said Rowland, with a smile, "seems just now to have assumed an unpardonable latitude."

"Oh, I take it you know very well that we are looking for a husband, and that none but tremendous swells need apply. Surely, before these gentlemen, mamma, I may speak freely; they are disinterested. Mr. Mallet won't do, because, though he 's rich, he 's not rich enough. Mamma made that discovery the day after we went to see you, moved to it by the promising look of your furniture. I hope she was right, eh? Unless you have millions, you know, you have no chance."

"I feel like a beggar," said Rowland.

"Oh, some better girl than I will decide some day, after mature reflection, that on the whole you have enough. Mr. Hudson, of course, is nowhere; he has nothing but his genius and his beaux yeux."

Roderick had stood looking at Christina intently while she delivered herself, softly and slowly, of this surprising nonsense. When she had finished, she turned and looked at him; their eyes met, and he blushed a little. "Let me model you, and he who can may marry you!" he said, abruptly.

Mrs. Light, while her daughter talked, had been adding a few touches to her coiffure. "She is not so silly as you might suppose," she said to Rowland, with dignity. "If you will give me your arm, we will go and look at the bust."

"Does that represent a silly girl?" Christina demanded, when they stood before it.

Rowland transferred his glance several times from the portrait to the original. "It represents a young lady," he said, "whom I should not pretend to judge off-hand."

"She may be a fool, but you are not sure. Many thanks! You have seen me half a dozen times. You are either very slow or I am very deep."

"I am certainly slow," said Rowland. "I don't expect to make up my mind about you within six months."

"I give you six months if you will promise then a perfectly frank opinion. Mind, I shall not forget; I shall insist upon it."

"Well, though I am slow, I am tolerably brave," said Rowland. "We shall see."

Christina looked at the bust with a sigh. "I am afraid, after all," she said, "that there 's very little wisdom in it save what the artist has put there. Mr. Hudson looked particularly wise while he was working; he scowled and growled, but he never opened his mouth. It is very kind of him not to have represented me gaping."

"If I had talked a lot of stuff to you," said Roderick, roundly, "the thing would not have been a tenth so good."

"Is it good, after all? Mr. Mallet is a famous connoisseur; has he not come here to pronounce?"

The bust was in fact a very happy performance, and Roderick had risen to the level of his subject. It was thoroughly a portrait, and not a vague fantasy executed on a graceful theme, as the busts of pretty women, in modern sculpture, are apt to be. The resemblance was deep and vivid; there was extreme fidelity of detail and yet a noble simplicity. One could say of the head that, without idealization, it was a representation of ideal beauty. Rowland, however, as we know, was not fond of exploding into superlatives, and, after examining the piece, contented himself with suggesting two or three alterations of detail.

"Nay, how can you be so cruel?" demanded Mrs. Light, with soft reproachfulness. "It is surely a wonderful thing!"

"Rowland knows it 's a wonderful thing," said Roderick, smiling. "I can tell that by his face. The other day I finished something he thought bad, and he looked very differently from this."

"How did Mr. Mallet look?" asked Christina.

"My dear Rowland," said Roderick, "I am speaking of my seated woman. You looked as if you had on a pair of tight boots."

"Ah, my child, you 'll not understand that!" cried Mrs. Light. "You never yet had a pair that were small enough."

"It 's a pity, Mr. Hudson," said Christina, gravely, "that you could not have introduced my feet into the bust. But we can hang a pair of slippers round the neck!"

"I nevertheless like your statues, Roderick," Rowland rejoined, "better than your jokes. This is admirable. Miss Light, you may be proud!"

"Thank you, Mr. Mallet, for the permission," rejoined the young girl.

"I am dying to see it in the marble, with a red velvet screen behind it," said Mrs. Light.

"Placed there under the Sassoferrato!" Christina went on. "I hope you keep well in mind, Mr. Hudson, that you have not a grain of property in your work, and that if mamma chooses, she may have it photographed and the copies sold in the Piazza di Spagna, at five francs apiece, without your having a sou of the profits."

"Amen!" said Roderick. "It was so nominated in the bond. My profits are here!" and he tapped his forehead.

"It would be prettier if you said here!" And Christina touched her heart.

"My precious child, how you do run on!" murmured Mrs. Light.

"It is Mr. Mallet," the young girl answered. "I can't talk a word of sense so long as he is in the room. I don't say that to make you go," she added, "I say it simply to justify myself."

Rowland bowed in silence. Roderick declared that he must get at work and requested Christina to take her usual position, and Mrs. Light proposed to her visitor that they should adjourn to her boudoir. This was a small room, hardly more spacious than an alcove, opening out of the drawing-room and having no other issue. Here, as they entered, on a divan near the door, Rowland perceived the Cavaliere Giacosa, with his arms folded, his head dropped upon his breast, and his eyes closed.

"Sleeping at his post!" said Rowland with a kindly laugh.

"That 's a punishable offense," rejoined Mrs. Light, sharply. She was on the point of calling him, in the same tone, when he suddenly opened his eyes, stared a moment, and then rose with a smile and a bow.

"Excuse me, dear lady," he said, "I was overcome by the—the great heat."

"Nonsense, Cavaliere!" cried the lady, "you know we are perishing here with the cold! You had better go and cool yourself in one of the other rooms."

"I obey, dear lady," said the Cavaliere; and with another smile and bow to Rowland he departed, walking very discreetly on his toes. Rowland out-stayed him but a short time, for he was not fond of Mrs. Light, and he found nothing very inspiring in her frank intimation that if he chose, he might become a favorite. He was disgusted with himself for pleasing her; he confounded his fatal urbanity. In the court-yard of the palace he overtook the Cavaliere, who had stopped at the porter's lodge to say a word to his little girl. She was a young lady of very tender years and she wore a very dirty pinafore. He had taken her up in his arms and was singing an infantine rhyme to her, and she was staring at him with big, soft Roman eyes. On seeing Rowland he put her down with a kiss, and stepped forward with a conscious grin, an unresentful admission that he was sensitive both to chubbiness and ridicule. 'Rowland began to pity him again; he had taken his dismissal from the drawing-room so meekly.

"You don't keep your promise," said Rowland, "to come and see me. Don't forget it. I want you to tell me about Rome thirty years ago."

"Thirty years ago? Ah, dear sir, Rome is Rome still; a place where strange things happen! But happy things too, since I have your renewed permission to call. You do me too much honor. Is it in the morning or in the evening that I should least intrude?"

"Take your own time, Cavaliere; only come, sometime. I depend upon you," said Rowland.

The Cavaliere thanked him with an humble obeisance. To the Cavaliere, too, he felt that he was, in Roman phrase, sympathetic, but the idea of pleasing this extremely reduced gentleman was not disagreeable to him.

Miss Light's bust stood for a while on exhibition in Roderick's studio, and half the foreign colony came to see it. With the completion of his work, however, Roderick's visits at the Palazzo F—— by no means came to an end. He spent half his time in Mrs. Light's drawing-room, and began to be talked about as "attentive" to Christina. The success of the bust restored his equanimity, and in the garrulity of his good-humor he suffered Rowland to see that she was just now the object uppermost in his thoughts. Rowland, when they talked of her, was rather listener than speaker; partly because Roderick's own tone was so resonant and exultant, and partly because, when his companion laughed at him for having called her unsafe, he was too perplexed to defend himself. The impression remained that she was unsafe; that she was a complex, willful, passionate creature, who might easily engulf a too confiding spirit in the eddies of her capricious temper. And yet he strongly felt her charm; the eddies had a strange fascination! Roderick, in the glow of that renewed admiration provoked by the fixed attention of portrayal, was never weary of descanting on the extraordinary perfection of her beauty.

"I had no idea of it," he said, "till I began to look at her with an eye to reproducing line for line and curve for curve. Her face is the most exquisite piece of modeling that ever came from creative hands. Not a line without meaning, not a hair's breadth that is not admirably finished. And then her mouth! It 's as if a pair of lips had been shaped to utter pure truth without doing it dishonor!" Later, after he had been working for a week, he declared if Miss Light were inordinately plain, she would still be the most fascinating of women. "I 've quite forgotten her beauty," he said, "or rather I have ceased to perceive it as something distinct and defined, something independent of the rest of her. She is all one, and all consummately interesting!"

"What does she do—what does she say, that is so remarkable?" Rowland had asked.

"Say? Sometimes nothing—sometimes everything. She is never the same. Sometimes she walks in and takes her place without a word, without a smile, gravely, stiffly, as if it were an awful bore. She hardly looks at me, and she walks away without even glancing at my work. On other days she laughs and chatters and asks endless questions, and pours out the most irresistible nonsense. She is a creature of moods; you can't count upon her; she keeps observation on the stretch. And then, bless you, she has seen such a lot! Her talk is full of the oddest allusions!"

"It is altogether a very singular type of young lady," said Rowland, after the visit which I have related at length. "It may be a charm, but it is certainly not the orthodox charm of marriageable maidenhood, the charm of shrinking innocence and soft docility. Our American girls are accused of being more knowing than any others, and Miss Light is nominally an American. But it has taken twenty years of Europe to make her what she is. The first time we saw her, I remember you called her a product of the old world, and certainly you were not far wrong."

"Ah, she has an atmosphere," said Roderick, in the tone of high appreciation.

"Young unmarried women," Rowland answered, "should be careful not to have too much!"

"Ah, you don't forgive her," cried his companion, "for hitting you so hard! A man ought to be flattered at such a girl as that taking so much notice of him."

"A man is never flattered at a woman's not liking him."

"Are you sure she does n't like you? That 's to the credit of your humility. A fellow of more vanity might, on the evidence, persuade himself that he was in favor."

"He would have also," said Rowland, laughing, "to be a fellow of remarkable ingenuity!" He asked himself privately how the deuce Roderick reconciled it to his conscience to think so much more of the girl he was not engaged to than of the girl he was. But it amounted almost to arrogance, you may say, in poor Rowland to pretend to know how often Roderick thought of Miss Garland. He wondered gloomily, at any rate, whether for men of his companion's large, easy power, there was not a larger moral law than for narrow mediocrities like himself, who, yielding Nature a meagre interest on her investment (such as it was), had no reason to expect from her this affectionate laxity as to their accounts. Was it not a part of the eternal fitness of things that Roderick, while rhapsodizing about Miss Light, should have it at his command to look at you with eyes of the most guileless and unclouded blue, and to shake off your musty imputations by a toss of his picturesque brown locks? Or had he, in fact, no conscience to speak of? Happy fellow, either way!

Our friend Gloriani came, among others, to congratulate Roderick on his model and what he had made of her. "Devilish pretty, through and through!" he said as he looked at the bust. "Capital handling of the neck and throat; lovely work on the nose. You 're a detestably lucky fellow, my boy! But you ought not to have squandered such material on a simple bust; you should have made a great imaginative figure. If I could only have got hold of her, I would have put her into a statue in spite of herself. What a pity she is not a ragged Trasteverine, whom we might have for a franc an hour! I have been carrying about in my head for years a delicious design for a fantastic figure, but it has always stayed there for want of a tolerable model. I have seen intimations of the type, but Miss Light is the perfection of it. As soon as I saw her I said to myself, 'By Jove, there 's my statue in the flesh!'"

"What is your subject?" asked Roderick.

"Don't take it ill," said Gloriani. "You know I 'm the very deuce for observation. She would make a magnificent Herodias!"

If Roderick had taken it ill (which was unlikely, for we know he thought Gloriani an ass, and expected little of his wisdom), he might have been soothed by the candid incense of Sam Singleton, who came and sat for an hour in a sort of mental prostration before both bust and artist. But Roderick's attitude before his patient little devotee was one of undisguised though friendly amusement; and, indeed, judged from a strictly plastic point of view, the poor fellow's diminutive stature, his enormous mouth, his pimples and his yellow hair were sufficiently ridiculous. "Nay, don't envy our friend," Rowland said to Singleton afterwards, on his expressing, with a little groan of depreciation of his own paltry performances, his sense of the brilliancy of Roderick's talent. "You sail nearer the shore, but you sail in smoother waters. Be contented with what you are and paint me another picture."

"Oh, I don't envy Hudson anything he possesses," Singleton said, "because to take anything away would spoil his beautiful completeness. 'Complete,' that 's what he is; while we little clevernesses are like half-ripened plums, only good eating on the side that has had a glimpse of the sun. Nature has made him so, and fortune confesses to it! He is the handsomest fellow in Rome, he has the most genius, and, as a matter of course, the most beautiful girl in the world comes and offers to be his model. If that is not completeness, where shall we find it?"

461

One morning, going into Roderick's studio, Rowland found the young sculptor entertaining Miss Blanchard—if this is not too flattering a description of his gracefully passive tolerance of her presence. He had never liked her and never climbed into her sky-studio to observe her wonderful manipulation of petals. He had once quoted Tennyson against her:—

"And is there any moral shut Within the bosom of the rose?"

"In all Miss Blanchard's roses you may be sure there is a moral," he had said. "You can see it sticking out its head, and, if you go to smell the flower, it scratches your nose." But on this occasion she had come with a propitiatory gift—introducing her friend Mr. Leavenworth. Mr. Leavenworth was a tall, expansive, bland gentleman, with a carefully brushed whisker and a spacious, fair, well-favored face, which seemed, somehow, to have more room in it than was occupied by a smile of superior benevolence, so that (with his smooth, white forehead) it bore a certain resemblance to a large parlor with a very florid carpet, but no pictures on the walls. He held his head high, talked sonorously, and told Roderick, within five minutes, that he was a widower, traveling to distract his mind, and that he had lately retired from the proprietorship of large mines of borax in Pennsylvania. Roderick supposed at first that, in his character of depressed widower, he had come to order a tombstone; but observing then the extreme blandness of his address to Miss Blanchard, he credited him with a judicious prevision that by the time the tombstone was completed, a monument of his inconsolability might have become an anachronism. But Mr. Leavenworth was disposed to order something.

"You will find me eager to patronize our indigenous talent," he said. "I am putting up a little shanty in my native town, and I propose to make a rather nice thing of it. It has been the will of Heaven to plunge me into mourning; but art has consolations! In a tasteful home, surrounded by the memorials of my wanderings, I hope to take more cheerful views. I ordered in Paris the complete appurtenances of a dining-room. Do you think you could do something for my library? It is to be filled with well-selected authors, and I think a pure white image in this style,"—pointing to one of Roderick's statues,—"standing out against the morocco and gilt, would have a noble effect. The subject I have already fixed upon. I desire an allegorical representation of Culture. Do you think, now," asked Mr. Leavenworth, encouragingly, "you could rise to the conception?"

"A most interesting subject for a truly serious mind," remarked Miss Blanchard.

Roderick looked at her a moment, and then—"The simplest thing I could do," he said, "would be to make a full-length portrait of Miss Blanchard. I could give her a scroll in her hand, and that would do for the allegory."

Miss Blanchard colored; the compliment might be ironical; and there was ever afterwards a reflection of her uncertainty in her opinion of Roderick's genius. Mr. Leavenworth responded that with all deference to Miss Blanchard's beauty, he desired something colder, more monumental, more impersonal. "If I were to be the happy possessor of a likeness of Miss Blanchard," he added, "I should prefer to have it in no factitious disguise!"

Roderick consented to entertain the proposal, and while they were discussing it, Rowland had a little talk with the fair artist. "Who is your friend?" he asked.

"A very worthy man. The architect of his own fortune—which is magnificent. One of nature's gentlemen!"

This was a trifle sententious, and Rowland turned to the bust of Miss Light. Like every one else in Rome, by this time, Miss Blanchard had an opinion on the young girl's beauty, and, in her own fashion, she expressed it epigrammatically. "She looks half like a Madonna and half like a ballerina," she said.

Mr. Leavenworth and Roderick came to an understanding, and the young sculptor good-naturedly promised to do his best to rise to his patron's conception. "His conception be hanged!" Roderick exclaimed, after he had departed. "His conception is sitting on a globe with a pen in her ear and a photographic album in her hand. I shall have to conceive, myself. For the money, I ought to be able to!"

Mrs. Light, meanwhile, had fairly established herself in Roman society. "Heaven knows how!" Madame Grandoni said to Rowland, who had mentioned to her several evidences of the lady's prosperity. "In such a case there is nothing like audacity. A month ago she knew no one but her washerwoman, and now I am told that the cards of Roman princesses are to be seen on her table. She is evidently determined to play a great part, and she has the wit to perceive that, to make remunerative acquaintances, you must seem yourself to be worth knowing. You must have striking rooms and a confusing variety of dresses, and give good dinners, and so forth. She is spending a lot of money, and you 'll see that in two or three weeks she will take upon herself to open the season by giving a magnificent ball. Of course it is Christina's beauty that floats her. People go to see her because they are curious."

"And they go again because they are charmed," said Rowland. "Miss Christina is a very remarkable young lady."

"Oh, I know it well; I had occasion to say so to myself the other day. She came to see me, of her own free will, and for an hour she was deeply interesting. I think she 's an actress, but she believes in her part while she is playing it. She took it into her head the other day to believe that she was very unhappy, and she sat there, where you are sitting, and told me a tale of her miseries which brought tears into my eyes. She cried, herself, profusely, and as naturally as possible. She said she was weary of life and that she knew no one but me she could speak frankly to. She must speak, or she would go mad. She sobbed as if her heart would break. I assure you it 's well for you susceptible young men that you don't see her when she sobs. She said, in so many words, that her mother was an immoral woman. Heaven knows what she meant. She meant, I suppose, that she makes debts that she knows she can't pay. She said the life they led was horrible; that it was monstrous a poor girl should be dragged about the world to be sold to the highest bidder. She was meant for better things; she could be perfectly happy in poverty. It was not money she wanted. I might not believe her, but she really cared for serious things. Sometimes she thought of taking poison!"

"What did you say to that?"

"I recommended her," said Madame Grandoni, "to come and see me instead. I would help her about as much, and I was, on the whole, less

464

unpleasant. Of course I could help her only by letting her talk herself out and kissing her and patting her beautiful hands and telling her to be patient and she would be happy yet. About once in two months I expect her to reappear, on the same errand, and meanwhile to quite forget my existence. I believe I melted down to the point of telling her that I would find some good, quiet, affectionate husband for her; but she declared, almost with fury, that she was sick unto death of husbands, and begged I would never again mention the word. And, in fact, it was a rash offer; for I am sure that there is not a man of the kind that might really make a woman happy but would be afraid to marry mademoiselle. Looked at in that way she is certainly very much to be pitied, and indeed, altogether, though I don't think she either means all she says or, by a great deal, says all that she means. I feel very sorry for her."

Rowland met the two ladies, about this time, at several entertainments, and looked at Christina with a kind of distant attendrissement. He imagined more than once that there had been a passionate scene between them about coming out, and wondered what arguments Mrs. Light had found effective. But Christina's face told no tales, and she moved about, beautiful and silent, looking absently over people's heads, barely heeding the men who pressed about her, and suggesting somehow that the soul of a world-wearied mortal had found its way into the blooming body of a goddess. "Where in the world has Miss Light been before she is twenty," observers asked, "to have left all her illusions behind?" And the general verdict was, that though she was incomparably beautiful, she was intolerably proud. Young ladies to whom the former distinction was not conceded were free to reflect that she was "not at all liked."

It would have been difficult to guess, however, how they reconciled this conviction with a variety of conflicting evidence, and, in especial, with the spectacle of Roderick's inveterate devotion. All Rome might behold that he, at least, "liked" Christina Light. Wherever she appeared he was either awaiting her or immediately followed her. He was perpetually at her side, trying, apparently, to preserve the thread of a disconnected talk, the fate of which was, to judge by her face, profoundly immaterial to the young lady. People in general smiled at the radiant good faith of the handsome young sculptor, and asked each other whether he really supposed that beauties of that quality were meant to wed with poor artists. But although Christina's deportment, as I have said, was one of superb inexpressiveness, Rowland had derived from Roderick no suspicion that he suffered from snubbing, and he was therefore surprised at an incident which befell one evening at a large musical party. Roderick, as usual, was in the field, and, on the ladies taking the chairs which had been arranged for them, he immediately placed himself beside Christina. As most of the gentlemen were standing, his position made him as conspicuous as Hamlet at Ophelia's feet, at the play. Rowland was leaning, somewhat apart, against the chimney-piece. There was a long, solemn pause before the music began, and in the midst of it Christina rose, left her place, came the whole length of the immense room, with every one looking at her, and stopped before him. She was neither pale nor flushed; she had a soft smile.

"Will you do me a favor?" she asked.

"A thousand!"

"Not now, but at your earliest convenience. Please remind Mr. Hudson that he is not in a New England village—that it is not the custom in Rome to address one's conversation exclusively, night after night, to the same poor girl, and that"....

The music broke out with a great blare and covered her voice. She made a gesture of impatience, and Rowland offered her his arm and led her back to her seat.

The next day he repeated her words to Roderick, who burst into joyous laughter. "She 's a delightfully strange girl!" he cried. "She must do everything that comes into her head!"

"Had she never asked you before not to talk to her so much?"

"On the contrary, she has often said to me, 'Mind you now, I forbid you to leave me. Here comes that tiresome So-and-so.' She cares as little about the custom as I do. What could be a better proof than her walking up to you, with five hundred people looking at her? Is that the custom for young girls in Rome?"

"Why, then, should she take such a step?"

"Because, as she sat there, it came into her head. That 's reason enough for her. I have imagined she wishes me well, as they say here—though she has never distinguished me in such a way as that!"

Madame Grandoni had foretold the truth; Mrs. Light, a couple of weeks later, convoked all Roman society to a brilliant ball. Rowland went late, and found the staircase so encumbered with flower-pots and servants that he was a long time making his way into the presence of the hostess. At last he approached her, as she stood making courtesies at the door, with her daughter by her side. Some of Mrs. Light's courtesies were very low, for she had the happiness of receiving a number of the social potentates of the Roman world. She was rosy with triumph, to say nothing of a less metaphysical cause, and was evidently vastly contented with herself, with her company, and with the general promise of destiny. Her daughter was less overtly jubilant, and distributed her greetings with impartial frigidity. She had never been so beautiful. Dressed simply in vaporous white, relieved with half a dozen white roses, the perfection of her features and of her person and the mysterious depth of her expression seemed to glow with the white light of a splendid pearl. She recognized no one individually, and made her courtesy slowly, gravely, with her eyes on the ground. Rowland fancied that, as he stood before her, her obeisance was slightly exaggerated, as with an intention of irony; but he smiled philosophically to himself, and reflected, as he passed into the room, that, if she disliked him, he had nothing to reproach himself with. He walked about, had a few words with Miss Blanchard, who, with a fillet of cameos in her hair, was leaning on the arm of Mr. Leavenworth, and at last came upon the Cavaliere Giacosa, modestly stationed in a corner. The little gentleman's coat-lappet was decorated with an enormous bouquet and his neck encased in a voluminous white handkerchief of the fashion of thirty years ago. His arms were folded, and he was surveying the scene with contracted eyelids, through which you saw the glitter of his intensely dark, vivacious pupil. He immediately embarked on an elaborate apology for not having yet manifested, as he felt it, his sense of the honor Rowland had done him.

"I am always on service with these ladies, you see," he explained, "and that is a duty to which one would not willingly be faithless for an instant."

"Evidently," said Rowland, "you are a very devoted friend. Mrs. Light, in her situation, is very happy in having you."

"We are old friends," said the Cavaliere, gravely. "Old friends. I knew the signora many years ago, when she was the prettiest woman in Rome— or rather in Ancona, which is even better. The beautiful Christina, now, is perhaps the most beautiful young girl in Europe!"

"Very likely," said Rowland.

"Very well, sir, I taught her to read; I guided her little hands to touch the piano keys." And at these faded memories, the Cavaliere's eyes glittered more brightly. Rowland half expected him to proceed, with a little flash of long-repressed passion, "And now—and now, sir, they treat me as you observed the other day!" But the Cavaliere only looked out at him keenly from among his wrinkles, and seemed to say, with all the vividness of the Italian glance, "Oh, I say nothing more. I am not so shallow as to complain!"

Evidently the Cavaliere was not shallow, and Rowland repeated respectfully, "You are a devoted friend."

"That 's very true. I am a devoted friend. A man may do himself justice, after twenty years!"

Rowland, after a pause, made some remark about the beauty of the ball. It was very brilliant.

"Stupendous!" said the Cavaliere, solemnly. "It is a great day. We have four Roman princes, to say nothing of others." And he counted them over on his fingers and held up his hand triumphantly. "And there she stands, the girl to whom I—I, Giuseppe Giacosa—taught her alphabet and her piano-scales; there she stands in her incomparable beauty, and Roman princes come and bow to her. Here, in his corner, her old master permits himself to be proud."

"It is very friendly of him," said Rowland, smiling.

468

The Cavaliere contracted his lids a little more and gave another keen glance. "It is very natural, signore. The Christina is a good girl; she remembers my little services. But here comes," he added in a moment, "the young Prince of the Fine Arts. I am sure he has bowed lowest of all."

Rowland looked round and saw Roderick moving slowly across the room and casting about him his usual luminous, unshrinking looks. He presently joined them, nodded familiarly to the Cavaliere, and immediately demanded of Rowland, "Have you seen her?"

"I have seen Miss Light," said Rowland. "She 's magnificent."

"I 'm half crazy!" cried Roderick; so loud that several persons turned round.

Rowland saw that he was flushed, and laid his hand on his arm. Roderick was trembling. "If you will go away," Rowland said instantly, "I will go with you."

"Go away?" cried Roderick, almost angrily. "I intend to dance with her!"

The Cavaliere had been watching him attentively; he gently laid his hand on his other arm. "Softly, softly, dear young man," he said. "Let me speak to you as a friend."

"Oh, speak even as an enemy and I shall not mind it," Roderick answered, frowning.

"Be very reasonable, then, and go away."

"Why the deuce should I go away?"

"Because you are in love," said the Cavaliere.

"I might as well be in love here as in the streets."

"Carry your love as far as possible from Christina. She will not listen to you—she can't."

"She 'can't'?" demanded Roderick. "She is not a person of whom you may say that. She can if she will; she does as she chooses."

"Up to a certain point. It would take too long to explain; I only beg you to believe that if you continue to love Miss Light you will be very unhappy. Have you a princely title? have you a princely fortune? Otherwise you can never have her."

And the Cavaliere folded his arms again, like a man who has done his duty. Roderick wiped his forehead and looked askance at Rowland; he seemed to be guessing his thoughts and they made him blush a little. But he smiled blandly, and addressing the Cavaliere, "I 'm much obliged to you for the information," he said. "Now that I have obtained it, let me tell you that I am no more in love with Miss Light than you are. Mr. Mallet knows that. I admire her—yes, profoundly. But that 's no one's business but my own, and though I have, as you say, neither a princely title nor a princely fortune, I mean to suffer neither those advantages nor those who possess them to diminish my right."

"If you are not in love, my dear young man," said the Cavaliere, with his hand on his heart and an apologetic smile, "so much the better. But let me entreat you, as an affectionate friend, to keep a watch on your emotions. You are young, you are handsome, you have a brilliant genius and a generous heart, but—I may say it almost with authority—Christina is not for you!"

Whether Roderick was in love or not, he was nettled by what apparently seemed to him an obtrusive negation of an inspiring possibility. "You speak as if she had made her choice!" he cried. "Without pretending to confidential information on the subject, I am sure she has not."

"No, but she must make it soon," said the Cavaliere. And raising his forefinger, he laid it against his under lip. "She must choose a name and a fortune—and she will!"

"She will do exactly as her inclination prompts! She will marry the man who pleases her, if he has n't a dollar! I know her better than you."

The Cavaliere turned a little paler than usual, and smiled more urbanely. "No, no, my dear young man, you do not know her better than I. You have not watched her, day by day, for twenty years. I too have admired her. She is a good girl; she has never said an unkind word to me; the blessed Virgin be thanked! But she must have a brilliant destiny; it has been marked out for her, and she will submit. You had better believe me; it may save you much suffering."

"We shall see!" said Roderick, with an excited laugh.

"Certainly we shall see. But I retire from the discussion," the Cavaliere added. "I have no wish to provoke you to attempt to prove to me that I am wrong. You are already excited."

"No more than is natural to a man who in an hour or so is to dance the cotillon with Miss Light."

"The cotillon? has she promised?"

Roderick patted the air with a grand confidence. "You 'll see!" His gesture might almost have been taken to mean that the state of his relations with Miss Light was such that they quite dispensed with vain formalities.

The Cavaliere gave an exaggerated shrug. "You make a great many mourners!"

"He has made one already!" Rowland murmured to himself. This was evidently not the first time that reference had been made between Roderick and the Cavaliere to the young man's possible passion, and Roderick had failed to consider it the simplest and most natural course to say in three words to the vigilant little gentleman that there was no cause for alarm—his affections were preoccupied. Rowland hoped, silently, with some dryness, that his motives were of a finer kind than they seemed to be. He turned away; it was irritating to look at Roderick's radiant, unscrupulous eagerness. The tide was setting toward the supper-room and he drifted with it to the door. The crowd at this point was dense, and he was obliged to wait for some minutes before he could advance. At last he felt his neighbors dividing behind him, and turning he saw Christina pressing her way forward alone. She was looking at no one, and, save for the fact of her being alone, you would not have supposed she was in her mother's house. As she recognized Rowland she beckoned to him, took his arm, and motioned him to lead her into the supper-room. She said nothing until he had forced a passage and they stood somewhat isolated.

"Take me into the most out-of-the-way corner you can find," she then said, "and then go and get me a piece of bread."

"Nothing more? There seems to be everything conceivable."

"A simple roll. Nothing more, on your peril. Only bring something for yourself."

It seemed to Rowland that the embrasure of a window (embrasures in Roman palaces are deep) was a retreat sufficiently obscure for Miss Light to execute whatever design she might have contrived against his equanimity. A roll, after he had found her a seat, was easily procured. As he presented it, he remarked that, frankly speaking, he was at loss to understand why she should have selected for the honor of a tete-a-tete an individual for whom she had so little taste.

"Ah yes, I dislike you," said Christina. "To tell the truth, I had forgotten it. There are so many people here whom I dislike more, that when I espied you just now, you seemed like an intimate friend. But I have not come into this corner to talk nonsense," she went on. "You must not think I always do, eh?"

"I have never heard you do anything else," said Rowland, deliberately, having decided that he owed her no compliments.

"Very good. I like your frankness. It 's quite true. You see, I am a strange girl. To begin with, I am frightfully egotistical. Don't flatter yourself you have said anything very clever if you ever take it into your head to tell me so. I know it much better than you. So it is, I can't help it. I am tired to death of myself; I would give all I possess to get out of myself; but somehow, at the end, I find myself so vastly more interesting than nine tenths of the people I meet. If a person wished to do me a favor I would say to him, 'I beg you, with tears in my eyes, to interest me. Be strong, be positive, be imperious, if you will; only be something,—something that, in looking at, I can forget my detestable self!' Perhaps that is nonsense too. If it is, I can't help it. I can only apologize for the nonsense I know to be such and that I talk—oh, for more reasons than I can tell you! I wonder whether, if I were to try, you would understand me."

"I am afraid I should never understand," said Rowland, "why a person should willingly talk nonsense."

"That proves how little you know about women. But I like your frankness. When I told you the other day that you displeased me, I had an idea you were more formal,—how do you say it?—more guindé. I am very capricious. To-night I like you better."

"Oh, I am not guindé," said Rowland, gravely.

"I beg your pardon, then, for thinking so. Now I have an idea that you would make a useful friend—an intimate friend—a friend to whom one could tell everything. For such a friend, what would n't I give!"

Rowland looked at her in some perplexity. Was this touching sincerity, or unfathomable coquetry? Her beautiful eyes looked divinely candid; but then, if candor was beautiful, beauty was apt to be subtle. "I hesitate to recommend myself out and out for the office," he said, "but I believe that if you were to depend upon me for anything that a friend may do, I should not be found wanting."

"Very good. One of the first things one asks of a friend is to judge one not by isolated acts, but by one's whole conduct. I care for your opinion—I don't know why."

"Nor do I, I confess," said Rowland with a laugh.

"What do you think of this affair?" she continued, without heeding his laugh.

"Of your ball? Why, it 's a very grand affair."

"It 's horrible—that 's what it is! It 's a mere rabble! There are people here whom I never saw before, people who were never asked. Mamma went about inviting every one, asking other people to invite any one they knew, doing anything to have a crowd. I hope she is satisfied! It is not my doing. I feel weary, I feel angry, I feel like crying. I have twenty minds to escape into my room and lock the door and let mamma go through with it as she can. By the way," she added in a moment, without a visible reason for the transition, "can you tell me something to read?"

Rowland stared, at the disconnectedness of the question.

"Can you recommend me some books?" she repeated. "I know you are a great reader. I have no one else to ask. We can buy no books. We can make debts for jewelry and bonnets and five-button gloves, but we can't spend a sou for ideas. And yet, though you may not believe it, I like ideas quite as well."

"I shall be most happy to lend you some books," Rowland said. "I will pick some out to-morrow and send them to you."

"No novels, please! I am tired of novels. I can imagine better stories for myself than any I read. Some good poetry, if there is such a thing nowadays, and some memoirs and histories and books of facts."

"You shall be served. Your taste agrees with my own."

She was silent a moment, looking at him. Then suddenly—"Tell me something about Mr. Hudson," she demanded. "You are great friends!"

"Oh yes," said Rowland; "we are great friends."

"Tell me about him. Come, begin!"

"Where shall I begin? You know him for yourself."

"No, I don't know him; I don't find him so easy to know. Since he has finished my bust and begun to come here disinterestedly, he has become a great talker. He says very fine things; but does he mean all he says?"

"Few of us do that."

"You do, I imagine. You ought to know, for he tells me you discovered him." Rowland was silent, and Christina continued, "Do you consider him very clever?"

"Unquestionably."

"His talent is really something out of the common way?"

"So it seems to me."

"In short, he 's a man of genius?"

"Yes, call it genius."

"And you found him vegetating in a little village and took him by the hand and set him on his feet in Rome?"

"Is that the popular legend?" asked Rowland.

"Oh, you need n't be modest. There was no great merit in it; there would have been none at least on my part in the same circumstances. Real geniuses are not so common, and if I had discovered one in the wilderness, I would have brought him out into the market-place to see how he would behave. It would be excessively amusing. You must find it so to watch Mr. Hudson, eh? Tell me this: do you think he is going to be a great man—become famous, have his life written, and all that?"

"I don't prophesy, but I have good hopes."

Christina was silent. She stretched out her bare arm and looked at it a moment absently, turning it so as to see—or almost to see—the dimple in her elbow. This was apparently a frequent gesture with her; Rowland had already observed it. It was as coolly and naturally done as if she had been in her room alone. "So he 's a man of genius," she suddenly resumed. "Don't you think I ought to be extremely flattered to have a man of genius perpetually hanging about? He is the first I ever saw, but I should have known he was not a common mortal. There is something strange about him. To begin with, he has no manners. You may say that it 's not for me to blame him, for I have none myself. That 's very true, but the difference is that I can have them when I wish to (and very charming ones too; I 'll show you some day); whereas Mr. Hudson will never have them. And yet, somehow, one sees he 's a gentleman. He seems to have something urging, driving, pushing him, making him restless and defiant. You see it in his eyes. They are the finest, by the way, I ever saw. When a person has such eyes as that you can forgive him his bad manners. I suppose that is what they call the sacred fire."

Rowland made no answer except to ask her in a moment if she would have another roll. She merely shook her head and went on:—

"Tell me how you found him. Where was he—how was he?"

"He was in a place called Northampton. Did you ever hear of it? He was studying law—but not learning it."

"It appears it was something horrible, eh?"

"Something horrible?"

"This little village. No society, no pleasures, no beauty, no life."

"You have received a false impression. Northampton is not as gay as Rome, but Roderick had some charming friends."

"Tell me about them. Who were they?"

"Well, there was my cousin, through whom I made his acquaintance: a delightful woman."

"Young—pretty?"

"Yes, a good deal of both. And very clever."

"Did he make love to her?"

"Not in the least."

"Well, who else?"

"He lived with his mother. She is the best of women."

"Ah yes, I know all that one's mother is. But she does not count as society. And who else?"

Rowland hesitated. He wondered whether Christina's insistence was the result of a general interest in Roderick's antecedents or of a particular suspicion. He looked at her; she was looking at him a little askance, waiting for his answer. As Roderick had said nothing about his engagement to the Cavaliere, it was probable that with this beautiful girl he had not been more explicit. And yet the thing was announced, it was public; that other girl was happy in it, proud of it. Rowland felt a kind of dumb anger rising in his heart. He deliberated a moment intently.

"What are you frowning at?" Christina asked.

"There was another person," he answered, "the most important of all: the young girl to whom he is engaged."

Christina stared a moment, raising her eyebrows. "Ah, Mr. Hudson is engaged?" she said, very simply. "Is she pretty?"

"She is not called a beauty," said Rowland. He meant to practice great brevity, but in a moment he added, "I have seen beauties, however, who pleased me less."

"Ah, she pleases you, too? Why don't they marry?"

"Roderick is waiting till he can afford to marry."

Christina slowly put out her arm again and looked at the dimple in her elbow. "Ah, he 's engaged?" she repeated in the same tone. "He never told me."

Rowland perceived at this moment that the people about them were beginning to return to the dancing-room, and immediately afterwards he saw Roderick making his way toward themselves. Roderick presented himself before Miss Light.

"I don't claim that you have promised me the cotillon," he said, "but I consider that you have given me hopes which warrant the confidence that you will dance with me."

Christina looked at him a moment. "Certainly I have made no promises," she said. "It seemed to me that, as the daughter of the house, I should keep myself free and let it depend on circumstances."

"I beseech you to dance with me!" said Roderick, with vehemence.

Christina rose and began to laugh. "You say that very well, but the Italians do it better."

This assertion seemed likely to be put to the proof. Mrs. Light hastily approached, leading, rather than led by, a tall, slim young man, of an unmistakably Southern physiognomy. "My precious love," she cried, "what a place to hide in! We have been looking for you for twenty minutes; I have chosen a cavalier for you, and chosen well!"

The young man disengaged himself, made a ceremonious bow, joined his two hands, and murmured with an ecstatic smile, "May I venture to hope, dear signorina, for the honor of your hand?"

"Of course you may!" said Mrs. Light. "The honor is for us."

Christina hesitated but for a moment, then swept the young man a courtesy as profound as his own bow. "You are very kind, but you are too late. I have just accepted!"

"Ah, my own darling!" murmured—almost moaned—Mrs. Light.

Christina and Roderick exchanged a single glance—a glance brilliant on both sides. She passed her hand into his arm; he tossed his clustering locks and led her away.

A short time afterwards Rowland saw the young man whom she had rejected leaning against a doorway. He was ugly, but what is called distinguished-looking. He had a heavy black eye, a sallow complexion, a long, thin neck; his hair was cropped en brosse. He looked very young, yet extremely bored. He was staring at the ceiling and stroking an imperceptible moustache. Rowland espied the Cavaliere Giacosa hard by, and, having joined him, asked him the young man's name.

"Oh," said the Cavaliere, "he 's a pezzo grosso! A Neapolitan. Prince Casamassima."

CHAPTER VI. Frascati

One day, on entering Roderick's lodging (not the modest rooms on the Ripetta which he had first occupied, but a much more sumptuous apartment on the Corso), Rowland found a letter on the table addressed to himself. It was from Roderick, and consisted of but three lines: "I am gone to Frascati—for meditation. If I am not at home on Friday, you had better join me." On Friday he was still absent, and Rowland went out to Frascati. Here he found his friend living at the inn and spending his days, according to his own account, lying under the trees of the Villa Mondragone, reading Ariosto. He was in a sombre mood; "meditation" seemed not to have been fruitful. Nothing especially pertinent to our narrative had passed between the two young men since Mrs. Light's ball, save a few words bearing on an incident of that entertainment. Rowland informed Roderick, the next day, that he had told Miss Light of his engagement. "I don't know whether you 'll thank me," he had said, "but it 's my duty to let you know it. Miss Light perhaps has already done so."

Roderick looked at him a moment, intently, with his color slowly rising. "Why should n't I thank you?" he asked. "I am not ashamed of my engagement."

"As you had not spoken of it yourself, I thought you might have a reason for not having it known."

"A man does n't gossip about such a matter with strangers," Roderick rejoined, with the ring of irritation in his voice.

"With strangers—no!" said Rowland, smiling.

Roderick continued his work; but after a moment, turning round with a frown: "If you supposed I had a reason for being silent, pray why should you have spoken?"

"I did not speak idly, my dear Roderick. I weighed the matter before I spoke, and promised myself to let you know immediately afterwards.

It seemed to me that Miss Light had better know that your affections are pledged."

"The Cavaliere has put it into your head, then, that I am making love to her?"

"No; in that case I would not have spoken to her first."

"Do you mean, then, that she is making love to me?"

"This is what I mean," said Rowland, after a pause. "That girl finds you interesting, and is pleased, even though she may play indifference, at your finding her so. I said to myself that it might save her some sentimental disappointment to know without delay that you are not at liberty to become indefinitely interested in other women."

"You seem to have taken the measure of my liberty with extraordinary minuteness!" cried Roderick.

"You must do me justice. I am the cause of your separation from Miss Garland, the cause of your being exposed to temptations which she hardly even suspects. How could I ever face her," Rowland demanded, with much warmth of tone, "if at the end of it all she should be unhappy?"

"I had no idea that Miss Garland had made such an impression on you. You are too zealous; I take it she did n't charge you to look after her interests."

"If anything happens to you, I am accountable. You must understand that."

"That 's a view of the situation I can't accept; in your own interest, no less than in mine. It can only make us both very uncomfortable. I know all I owe you; I feel it; you know that! But I am not a small boy nor an outer barbarian any longer, and, whatever I do, I do with my eyes open. When I do well, the merit 's mine; if I do ill, the fault 's mine! The idea that I make you nervous is detestable. Dedicate your nerves to some better cause, and believe that if Miss Garland and I have a quarrel, we shall settle it between ourselves."

Rowland had found himself wondering, shortly before, whether possibly his brilliant young friend was without a conscience; now it dimly occurred to him that he was without a heart. Rowland, as we have already intimated, was a man with a moral passion, and no small part of it had gone forth into his relations with Roderick. There had been, from the first, no protestations of friendship on either side, but Rowland had implicitly offered everything that belongs to friendship, and Roderick had, apparently, as deliberately accepted it. Rowland, indeed, had taken an exquisite satisfaction in his companion's deep, inexpressive assent to his interest in him. "Here is an uncommonly fine thing," he said to himself: "a nature unconsciously grateful, a man in whom friendship does the thing that love alone generally has the credit of—knocks the bottom out of pride!" His reflective judgment of Roderick, as time went on, had indulged in a great many irrepressible vagaries; but his affection, his sense of something in his companion's whole personality that overmastered his heart and beguiled his imagination, had never for an instant faltered. He listened to Roderick's last words, and then he smiled as he rarely smiled—with bitterness.

"I don't at all like your telling me I am too zealous," he said. "If I had not been zealous, I should never have cared a fig for you."

Roderick flushed deeply, and thrust his modeling tool up to the handle into the clay. "Say it outright! You have been a great fool to believe in me."

"I desire to say nothing of the kind, and you don't honestly believe I do!" said Rowland. "It seems to me I am really very good-natured even to reply to such nonsense."

Roderick sat down, crossed his arms, and fixed his eyes on the floor. Rowland looked at him for some moments; it seemed to him that he had never so clearly read his companion's strangely commingled character—his strength and his weakness, his picturesque personal attractiveness and his urgent egoism, his exalted ardor and his puerile petulance. It would have made him almost sick, however, to think that, on the whole, Roderick was not a generous fellow, and he was so far from having ceased to believe in him that he felt just now, more than ever, that all this was but the painful complexity of genius. Rowland, who had not a grain of genius either to make one say he was an interested reasoner, or to enable one to feel that he could afford a dangerous theory or two, adhered to his conviction of the essential salubrity of genius. Suddenly he felt an irresistible compassion for his companion; it seemed to him that his beautiful faculty of production was a double-edged instrument, susceptible of being dealt in back-handed blows at its possessor. Genius was priceless, inspired, divine; but it was also, at its hours, capricious, sinister, cruel; and men of genius, accordingly, were alternately very enviable and very helpless. It was not the first time he had had a sense of Roderick's standing helpless in the grasp of his temperament. It had shaken him, as yet, but with a half good-humored wantonness; but, henceforth, possibly, it meant to handle him more roughly. These were not times, therefore, for a friend to have a short patience.

"When you err, you say, the fault 's your own," he said at last. "It is because your faults are your own that I care about them."

Rowland's voice, when he spoke with feeling, had an extraordinary amenity. Roderick sat staring a moment longer at the floor, then he sprang up and laid his hand affectionately on his friend's shoulder. "You are the best man in the world," he said, "and I am a vile brute. Only," he added in a moment, "you don't understand me!" And he looked at him with eyes of such radiant lucidity that one might have said (and Rowland did almost say so, himself) that it was the fault of one's own grossness if one failed to read to the bottom of that beautiful soul.

Rowland smiled sadly. "What is it now? Explain."

"Oh, I can't explain!" cried Roderick impatiently, returning to his work. "I have only one way of expressing my deepest feelings—it 's this!" And he swung his tool. He stood looking at the half-wrought clay for a moment, and then flung the instrument down. "And even this half the time plays me false!"

Rowland felt that his irritation had not subsided, and he himself had no taste for saying disagreeable things. Nevertheless he saw no sufficient reason to forbear uttering the words he had had on his conscience from the beginning. "We must do what we can and be thankful," he said. "And let me assure you of this—that it won't help you to become entangled with Miss Light."

Roderick pressed his hand to his forehead with vehemence and then shook it in the air, despairingly; a gesture that had become frequent with him since he had been in Italy. "No, no, it 's no use; you don't understand me! But I don't blame you. You can't!"

"You think it will help you, then?" said Rowland, wondering.

"I think that when you expect a man to produce beautiful and wonderful works of art, you ought to allow him a certain freedom of action, you ought to give him a long rope, you ought to let him follow his fancy and look for his material wherever he thinks he may find it! A mother can't nurse her child unless she follows a certain diet; an artist can't bring his visions to maturity unless he has a certain experience. You demand of us to be imaginative, and you deny us that which feeds the imagination. In labor we must be as passionate as the inspired sibyl; in life we must be mere machines. It won't do. When you have got an artist to deal with, you must take him as he is, good and bad together. I don't say they are pleasant fellows to know or easy fellows to live with; I don't say they satisfy themselves any better than other people. I only say that if you want them to produce, you must let them conceive. If you want a bird to sing, you must not cover up its cage. Shoot them, the poor devils, drown them, exterminate them, if you will, in the interest of public morality; it may be morality would gain—I dare say it would! But if you suffer them to live, let them live on their own terms and according to their own inexorable needs!"

Rowland burst out laughing. "I have no wish whatever either to shoot you or to drown you!" he said. "Why launch such a tirade against a warning offered you altogether in the interest of your freest development? Do you really mean that you have an inexorable need of embarking on a flirtation with Miss Light?—a flirtation as to the felicity of which there may be differences of opinion, but which cannot at best, under the circumstances, be called innocent. Your last summer's adventures were more so! As for the terms on which you are to live, I had an idea you had arranged them otherwise!"

"I have arranged nothing—thank God! I don't pretend to arrange. I am young and ardent and inquisitive, and I admire Miss Light. That 's enough.

I shall go as far as admiration leads me. I am not afraid. Your genuine artist may be sometimes half a madman, but he 's not a coward!"

"Suppose that in your speculation you should come to grief, not only sentimentally but artistically?"

"Come what come will! If I 'm to fizzle out, the sooner I know it the better. Sometimes I half suspect it. But let me at least go out and reconnoitre for the enemy, and not sit here waiting for him, cudgeling my brains for ideas that won't come!"

Do what he would, Rowland could not think of Roderick's theory of unlimited experimentation, especially as applied in the case under discussion, as anything but a pernicious illusion. But he saw it was vain to combat longer, for inclination was powerfully on Roderick's side. He laid his hand on Roderick's shoulder, looked at him a moment with troubled eyes, then shook his head mournfully and turned away.

"I can't work any more," said Roderick. "You have upset me! I 'll go and stroll on the Pincian." And he tossed aside his working-jacket and prepared himself for the street. As he was arranging his cravat before the glass, something occurred to him which made him thoughtful. He stopped a few moments afterward, as they were going out, with his hand on the door-knob. "You did, from your own point of view, an indiscreet thing," he said, "to tell Miss Light of my engagement."

Rowland looked at him with a glance which was partly an interrogation, but partly, also, an admission.

"If she 's the coquette you say," Roderick added, "you have given her a reason the more."

"And that 's the girl you propose to devote yourself to?" cried Rowland.

"Oh, I don't say it, mind! I only say that she 's the most interesting creature in the world! The next time you mean to render me a service, pray give me notice beforehand!"

It was perfectly characteristic of Roderick that, a fortnight later, he should have let his friend know that he depended upon him for society at

Frascati, as freely as if no irritating topic had ever been discussed between them. Rowland thought him generous, and he had at any rate a liberal faculty of forgetting that he had given you any reason to be displeased with him. It was equally characteristic of Rowland that he complied with his friend's summons without a moment's hesitation. His cousin Cecilia had once told him that he was the dupe of his intense benevolence. She put the case with too little favor, or too much, as the reader chooses; it is certain, at least, that he had a constitutional tendency towards magnanimous interpretations. Nothing happened, however, to suggest to him that he was deluded in thinking that Roderick's secondary impulses were wiser than his primary ones, and that the rounded total of his nature had a harmony perfectly attuned to the most amiable of its brilliant parts. Roderick's humor, for the time, was pitched in a minor key; he was lazy, listless, and melancholy, but he had never been more friendly and kindly and appealingly submissive. Winter had begun, by the calendar, but the weather was divinely mild, and the two young men took long slow strolls on the hills and lounged away the mornings in the villas. The villas at Frascati are delicious places, and replete with romantic suggestiveness. Roderick, as he had said, was meditating, and if a masterpiece was to come of his meditations, Rowland was perfectly willing to bear him company and coax along the process. But Roderick let him know from the first that he was in a miserably sterile mood, and, cudgel his brains as he would, could think of nothing that would serve for the statue he was to make for Mr. Leavenworth.

"It is worse out here than in Rome," he said, "for here I am face to face with the dead blank of my mind! There I could n't think of anything either, but there I found things to make me forget that I needed to." This was as frank an allusion to Christina Light as could have been expected under the circumstances; it seemed, indeed, to Rowland surprisingly frank, and a pregnant example of his companion's often strangely irresponsible way of looking at harmful facts. Roderick was silent sometimes for hours, with a puzzled look on his face and a constant fold between his even eyebrows; at other times he talked unceasingly, with a slow, idle, half-nonsensical drawl. Rowland was half a dozen times on the point of asking him what was the matter with him; he was afraid he was going to be ill. Roderick had taken a great fancy to the Villa Mondragone, and used to declaim fantastic compliments to it as they strolled in the winter sunshine on the great terrace which looks toward Tivoli and the iridescent Sabine mountains. He carried his volume of Ariosto in his pocket, and took it out every now and then and spouted half a dozen stanzas to his companion. He was, as a general thing, very little of a reader; but at intervals he would take a fancy to one of the classics and peruse it for a month in disjointed scraps. He had picked up Italian without study, and had a wonderfully sympathetic accent, though in reading aloud he ruined the sense of half the lines he rolled off so sonorously. Rowland, who pronounced badly but understood everything, once said to him that Ariosto was not the poet for a man of his craft; a sculptor should make a companion of Dante. So he lent him the Inferno, which he had brought with him, and advised him to look into it. Roderick took it with some eagerness; perhaps it would brighten his wits. He returned it the next day with disgust; he had found it intolerably depressing.

"A sculptor should model as Dante writes—you 're right there," he said. "But when his genius is in eclipse, Dante is a dreadfully smoky lamp. By what perversity of fate," he went on, "has it come about that I am a sculptor at all? A sculptor is such a confoundedly special genius; there are so few subjects he can treat, so few things in life that bear upon his work, so few moods in which he himself is inclined to it." (It may be noted that Rowland had heard him a dozen times affirm the flat reverse of all this.) "If I had only been a painter—a little quiet, docile, matter-of-fact painter, like our friend Singleton—I should only have to open my Ariosto here to find a subject, to find color and attitudes, stuffs and composition; I should only have to look up from the page at that mouldy old fountain against the blue sky, at that cypress alley wandering away like a procession of priests in couples, at the crags and hollows of the Sabine hills, to find myself grasping my brush. Best of all would be to be Ariosto himself, or one of his brotherhood. Then everything in nature would give you a hint, and every form of beauty be part of your stock. You would n't have to look at things only to say,—with tears of rage half the time,—'Oh, yes, it 's wonderfully pretty, but what the deuce can I do with it?' But a sculptor, now! That 's a pretty trade for a fellow who has got his living to make and yet is so damnably constituted that he can't work to order, and considers that, aesthetically, clock ornaments don't pay!

You can't model the serge-coated cypresses, nor those mouldering old Tritons and all the sunny sadness of that dried-up fountain; you can't put the light into marble—the lovely, caressing, consenting Italian light that you get so much of for nothing. Say that a dozen times in his life a man has a complete sculpturesque vision—a vision in which the imagination recognizes a subject and the subject kindles the imagination. It is a remunerative rate of work, and the intervals are comfortable!"

One morning, as the two young men were lounging on the sun-warmed grass at the foot of one of the slanting pines of the Villa Mondragone, Roderick delivered himself of a tissue of lugubrious speculations as to the possible mischances of one's genius. "What if the watch should run down," he asked, "and you should lose the key? What if you should wake up some morning and find it stopped, inexorably, appallingly stopped? Such things have been, and the poor devils to whom they happened have had to grin and bear it. The whole matter of genius is a mystery. It bloweth where it listeth and we know nothing of its mechanism. If it gets out of order we can't mend it; if it breaks down altogether we can't set it going again. We must let it choose its own pace, and hold our breath lest it should lose its balance. It 's dealt out in different doses, in big cups and little, and when you have consumed your portion it 's as naif to ask for more as it was for Oliver Twist to ask for more porridge. Lucky for you if you 've got one of the big cups; we drink them down in the dark, and we can't tell their size until we tip them up and hear the last gurgle. Those of some men last for life; those of others for a couple of years. Nay, what are you smiling at so damnably?" he went on. "Nothing is more common than for an artist who has set out on his journey on a high-stepping horse to find himself all of a sudden dismounted and invited to go his way on foot. You can number them by the thousand—the people of two or three successes; the poor fellows whose candle burnt out in a night. Some of them groped their way along without it, some of them gave themselves up for blind and sat down by the wayside to beg. Who shall say that I 'm not one of these? Who shall assure me that my credit is for an unlimited sum? Nothing proves it, and I never claimed it; or if I did, I did so in the mere boyish joy of shaking off the dust of Northampton. If you believed so, my dear fellow, you did so at your own risk! What am I, what are the best of us, but an experiment? Do I succeed—do I fail? It does n't depend on me. I 'm prepared for failure. It won't be a disappointment, simply because I shan't survive it. The end of my work shall be the end of my life. When I have played my last card, I shall cease to care for the game. I 'm not making vulgar threats of suicide; for destiny, I trust, won't add insult to injury by putting me to that abominable trouble. But I have a conviction that if the hour strikes here," and he tapped his forehead, "I shall disappear, dissolve, be carried off in a cloud! For the past ten days I have had the vision of some such fate perpetually swimming before my eyes. My mind is like a dead calm in the tropics, and my imagination as motionless as the phantom ship in the Ancient Mariner!"

Rowland listened to this outbreak, as he often had occasion to listen to Roderick's heated monologues, with a number of mental restrictions. Both in gravity and in gayety he said more than he meant, and you did him simple justice if you privately concluded that neither the glow of purpose nor the chill of despair was of so intense a character as his florid diction implied. The moods of an artist, his exaltations and depressions, Rowland had often said to himself, were like the pen-flourishes a writing-master makes in the air when he begins to set his copy. He may bespatter you with ink, he may hit you in the eye, but he writes a magnificent hand. It was nevertheless true that at present poor Roderick gave unprecedented tokens of moral stagnation, and as for genius being held by the precarious tenure he had sketched, Rowland was at a loss to see whence he could borrow the authority to contradict him. He sighed to himself, and wished that his companion had a trifle more of little Sam Singleton's evenness of impulse. But then, was Singleton a man of genius? He answered that such reflections seemed to him unprofitable, not to say morbid; that the proof of the pudding was in the eating; that he did n't know about bringing a genius that had palpably spent its last breath back to life again, but that he was satisfied that vigorous effort was a cure for a great many ills that seemed far gone. "Don't heed your mood," he said, "and don't believe there is any calm so dead that your own lungs can't ruffle it with a breeze. If you have work to do, don't wait to feel like it; set to work and you will feel like it."

"Set to work and produce abortions!" cried Roderick with ire. "Preach that to others. Production with me must be either pleasure or nothing. As

I said just now, I must either stay in the saddle or not go at all. I won't do second-rate work; I can't if I would. I have no cleverness, apart from inspiration. I am not a Gloriani! You are right," he added after a while; "this is unprofitable talk, and it makes my head ache. I shall take a nap and see if I can dream of a bright idea or two."

He turned his face upward to the parasol of the great pine, closed his eyes, and in a short time forgot his sombre fancies. January though it was, the mild stillness seemed to vibrate with faint midsummer sounds. Rowland sat listening to them and wishing that, for the sake of his own felicity, Roderick's temper were graced with a certain absent ductility. He was brilliant, but was he, like many brilliant things, brittle? Suddenly, to his musing sense, the soft atmospheric hum was overscored with distincter sounds. He heard voices beyond a mass of shrubbery, at the turn of a neighboring path. In a moment one of them began to seem familiar, and an instant later a large white poodle emerged into view. He was slowly followed by his mistress. Miss Light paused a moment on seeing Rowland and his companion; but, though the former perceived that he was recognized, she made no bow. Presently she walked directly toward him. He rose and was on the point of waking Roderick, but she laid her finger on her lips and motioned him to forbear. She stood a moment looking at Roderick's handsome slumber.

"What delicious oblivion!" she said. "Happy man! Stenterello"—and she pointed to his face—"wake him up!"

The poodle extended a long pink tongue and began to lick Roderick's cheek.

"Why," asked Rowland, "if he is happy?"

"Oh, I want companions in misery! Besides, I want to show off my dog." Roderick roused himself, sat up, and stared. By this time Mrs. Light had approached, walking with a gentleman on each side of her. One of these was the Cavaliere Giacosa; the other was Prince Casamassima. "I should have liked to lie down on the grass and go to sleep," Christina added. "But it would have been unheard of."

"Oh, not quite," said the Prince, in English, with a tone of great precision. "There was already a Sleeping Beauty in the Wood!"

"Charming!" cried Mrs. Light. "Do you hear that, my dear?"

"When the prince says a brilliant thing, it would be a pity to lose it," said the young girl. "Your servant, sir!" And she smiled at him with a grace that might have reassured him, if he had thought her compliment ambiguous.

Roderick meanwhile had risen to his feet, and Mrs. Light began to exclaim on the oddity of their meeting and to explain that the day was so lovely that she had been charmed with the idea of spending it in the country. And who would ever have thought of finding Mr. Mallet and Mr. Hudson sleeping under a tree!

"Oh, I beg your pardon; I was not sleeping," said Rowland.

"Don't you know that Mr. Mallet is Mr. Hudson's sheep-dog?" asked Christina. "He was mounting guard to keep away the wolves."

"To indifferent purpose, madame!" said Rowland, indicating the young girl.

"Is that the way you spend your time?" Christina demanded of Roderick. "I never yet happened to learn what men were doing when they supposed women were not watching them but it was something vastly below their reputation."

"When, pray," said Roderick, smoothing his ruffled locks, "are women not watching them?"

"We shall give you something better to do, at any rate. How long have you been here? It 's an age since I have seen you. We consider you domiciled here, and expect you to play host and entertain us."

Roderick said that he could offer them nothing but to show them the great terrace, with its view; and ten minutes later the group was assembled there. Mrs. Light was extravagant in her satisfaction; Christina looked away at the Sabine mountains, in silence. The prince stood by, frowning at the rapture of the elder lady.

"This is nothing," he said at last. "My word of honor. Have you seen the terrace at San Gaetano?"

"Ah, that terrace," murmured Mrs. Light, amorously. "I suppose it is magnificent!"

"It is four hundred feet long, and paved with marble. And the view is a thousand times more beautiful than this. You see, far away, the blue, blue sea and the little smoke of Vesuvio!"

"Christina, love," cried Mrs. Light forthwith, "the prince has a terrace four hundred feet long, all paved with marble!"

The Cavaliere gave a little cough and began to wipe his eye-glass.

"Stupendous!" said Christina. "To go from one end to the other, the prince must have out his golden carriage." This was apparently an allusion to one of the other items of the young man's grandeur.

"You always laugh at me," said the prince. "I know no more what to say!"

She looked at him with a sad smile and shook her head. "No, no, dear prince, I don't laugh at you. Heaven forbid! You are much too serious an affair. I assure you I feel your importance. What did you inform us was the value of the hereditary diamonds of the Princess Casamassima?"

"Ah, you are laughing at me yet!" said the poor young man, standing rigid and pale.

"It does n't matter," Christina went on. "We have a note of it; mamma writes all those things down in a little book!"

"If you are laughed at, dear prince, at least it 's in company," said Mrs. Light, caressingly; and she took his arm, as if to resist his possible displacement under the shock of her daughter's sarcasm. But the prince looked heavy-eyed toward Rowland and Roderick, to whom the young girl was turning, as if he had much rather his lot were cast with theirs.

"Is the villa inhabited?" Christina asked, pointing to the vast melancholy structure which rises above the terrace.

"Not privately," said Roderick. "It is occupied by a Jesuits' college, for little boys."

"Can women go in?"

"I am afraid not." And Roderick began to laugh. "Fancy the poor little devils looking up from their Latin declensions and seeing Miss Light standing there!"

"I should like to see the poor little devils, with their rosy cheeks and their long black gowns, and when they were pretty, I should n't scruple to kiss them. But if I can't have that amusement I must have some other. We must not stand planted on this enchanting terrace as if we were stakes driven into the earth. We must dance, we must feast, we must do something picturesque. Mamma has arranged, I believe, that we are to go back to Frascati to lunch at the inn. I decree that we lunch here and send the Cavaliere to the inn to get the provisions! He can take the carriage, which is waiting below."

Miss Light carried out this undertaking with unfaltering ardor. The Cavaliere was summoned, and he stook to receive her commands hat in hand, with his eyes cast down, as if she had been a princess addressing her major-domo. She, however, laid her hand with friendly grace upon his button-hole, and called him a dear, good old Cavaliere, for being always so willing. Her spirits had risen with the occasion, and she talked irresistible nonsense. "Bring the best they have," she said, "no matter if it ruins us! And if the best is very bad, it will be all the more amusing. I shall enjoy seeing Mr. Mallet try to swallow it for propriety's sake! Mr. Hudson will say out like a man that it 's horrible stuff, and that he 'll be choked first! Be sure you bring a dish of maccaroni; the prince must have the diet of the Neapolitan nobility. But I leave all that to you, my poor, dear Cavaliere; you know what 's good! Only be sure, above all, you bring a guitar. Mr. Mallet will play us a tune, I 'll dance with Mr. Hudson, and mamma will pair off with the prince, of whom she is so fond!"

And as she concluded her recommendations, she patted her bland old servitor caressingly on the shoulder. He looked askance at Rowland; his little black eye glittered; it seemed to say, "Did n't I tell you she was a good girl!"

The Cavaliere returned with zealous speed, accompanied by one of the servants of the inn, laden with a basket containing the materials of a rustic luncheon. The porter of the villa was easily induced to furnish a table and half a dozen chairs, and the repast, when set forth, was pronounced a perfect success; not so good as to fail of the proper picturesqueness, nor yet so bad as to defeat the proper function of repasts. Christina continued to display the most charming animation, and compelled Rowland to reflect privately that, think what one might of her, the harmonious gayety of a beautiful girl was the most beautiful sight in nature. Her good-humor was contagious. Roderick, who an hour before had been descanting on madness and suicide, commingled his laughter with hers in ardent devotion; Prince Casamassima stroked his young moustache and found a fine, cool smile for everything; his neighbor, Mrs. Light, who had Rowland on the other side, made the friendliest confidences to each of the young men, and the Cavaliere contributed to the general hilarity by the solemnity of his attention to his plate. As for Rowland, the spirit of kindly mirth prompted him to propose the health of this useful old gentleman, as the effective author of their pleasure. A moment later he wished he had held his tongue, for although the toast was drunk with demonstrative good-will, the Cavaliere received it with various small signs of eager self-effacement which suggested to Rowland that his diminished gentility but half relished honors which had a flavor of patronage. To perform punctiliously his mysterious duties toward the two ladies, and to elude or to baffle observation on his own merits—this seemed the Cavaliere's modest programme. Rowland perceived that Mrs. Light, who was not always remarkable for tact, seemed to have divined his humor on this point. She touched her glass to her lips, but offered him no compliment and immediately gave another direction to the conversation. He had brought no guitar, so that when the feast was over there was nothing to hold the little group together. Christina wandered away with Roderick to another part of the terrace; the prince, whose smile had vanished, sat gnawing the head of his cane, near Mrs. Light, and Rowland strolled apart with the Cavaliere, to whom he wished to address a friendly word in compensation for the discomfort he had inflicted on his modesty. The Cavaliere was a mine of information upon all Roman places and people; he told Rowland a number of curious anecdotes about the old Villa Mondragone. "If history could always be taught in this fashion!" thought Rowland. "It 's the ideal—strolling up and down on the very spot commemorated, hearing sympathetic anecdotes from deeply indigenous lips." At last, as they passed, Rowland observed the mournful physiognomy of Prince Casamassima, and, glancing toward the other end of the terrace, saw that Roderick and Christina had disappeared from view. The young man was sitting upright, in an attitude, apparently habitual, of ceremonious rigidity; but his lower jaw had fallen and was propped up with his cane, and his dull dark eye was fixed upon the angle of the villa which had just eclipsed Miss Light and her companion. His features were grotesque and his expression vacuous; but there was a lurking delicacy in his face which seemed to tell you that nature had been making Casamassimas for a great many centuries, and, though she adapted her mould to circumstances, had learned to mix her material to an extraordinary fineness and to perform the whole operation with extreme smoothness. The prince was stupid, Rowland suspected, but he imagined he was amiable, and he saw that at any rate he had the great quality of regarding himself in a thoroughly serious light. Rowland touched his companion's arm and pointed to the melancholy nobleman.

"Why in the world does he not go after her and insist on being noticed!" he asked.

"Oh, he 's very proud!" said the Cavaliere.

"That 's all very well, but a gentleman who cultivates a passion for that young lady must be prepared to make sacrifices."

"He thinks he has already made a great many. He comes of a very great family—a race of princes who for six hundred years have married none but the daughters of princes. But he is seriously in love, and he would marry her to-morrow."

"And she will not have him?"

"Ah, she is very proud, too!" The Cavaliere was silent a moment, as if he were measuring the propriety of frankness. He seemed to have formed a high opinion of Rowland's discretion, for he presently continued: "It would be a great match, for she brings him neither a name nor a fortune—nothing but her beauty. But the signorina will receive no favors; I know her well! She would rather have her beauty blasted than seem to care about the marriage, and if she ever accepts the prince it will be only after he has implored her on his knees!"

"But she does care about it," said Rowland, "and to bring him to his knees she is working upon his jealousy by pretending to be interested in my friend Hudson. If you said more, you would say that, eh?"

The Cavaliere's shrewdness exchanged a glance with Rowland's. "By no means. Miss Light is a singular girl; she has many romantic ideas. She would be quite capable of interesting herself seriously in an interesting young man, like your friend, and doing her utmost to discourage a splendid suitor, like the prince. She would act sincerely and she would go very far. But it would be unfortunate for the young man," he added, after a pause, "for at the last she would retreat!"

"A singular girl, indeed!"

"She would accept the more brilliant parti. I can answer for it."

"And what would be her motive?"

"She would be forced. There would be circumstances.... I can't tell you more."

"But this implies that the rejected suitor would also come back. He might grow tired of waiting."

"Oh, this one is good! Look at him now." Rowland looked, and saw that the prince had left his place by Mrs. Light and was marching restlessly to and fro between the villa and the parapet of the terrace. Every now and then he looked at his watch. "In this country, you know," said the Cavaliere, "a young lady never goes walking alone with a handsome young man. It seems to him very strange."

"It must seem to him monstrous, and if he overlooks it he must be very much in love."

"Oh, he will overlook it. He is far gone."

"Who is this exemplary lover, then; what is he?"

"A Neapolitan; one of the oldest houses in Italy. He is a prince in your English sense of the word, for he has a princely fortune. He is very young; he is only just of age; he saw the signorina last winter in Naples. He fell in love with her from the first, but his family interfered, and an old uncle, an ecclesiastic, Monsignor B——, hurried up to Naples, seized him, and locked him up. Meantime he has passed his majority, and he can dispose of himself. His relations are moving heaven and earth to prevent his marrying Miss Light, and they have sent us word that he forfeits his property if he takes his wife out of a certain line. I have investigated the question minutely, and I find this is but a fiction to frighten us. He is perfectly free; but the estates are such that it is no wonder they wish to keep them in their own hands. For Italy, it is an extraordinary case of unincumbered property. The prince has been an orphan from his third year; he has therefore had a long minority and made no inroads upon his fortune. Besides, he is very prudent and orderly; I am only afraid that some day he will pull the purse-strings too tight. All these years his affairs have been in the hands of Monsignor B——, who has managed them to perfection—paid off mortagages, planted forests, opened up mines. It is now a magnificent fortune; such a fortune as, with his name, would justify the young man in pretending to any alliance whatsoever. And he lays it all at the feet of that young girl who is wandering in yonder boschetto with a penniless artist."

"He is certainly a phoenix of princes! The signora must be in a state of bliss."

The Cavaliere looked imperturbably grave. "The signora has a high esteem for his character."

"His character, by the way," rejoined Rowland, with a smile; "what sort of a character is it?"

"Eh, Prince Casamassima is a veritable prince! He is a very good young man. He is not brilliant, nor witty, but he 'll not let himself be made a fool of. He 's very grave and very devout—though he does propose to marry a Protestant. He will handle that point after marriage. He 's as you see him there: a young man without many ideas, but with a very firm grasp of a single one—the conviction that Prince Casamassima is a very great person, that he greatly honors any young lady by asking for her hand, and that things are going very strangely when the young lady turns her back upon him. The poor young man, I am sure, is profoundly perplexed. But I whisper to him every day, 'Pazienza, Signor Principe!'"

"So you firmly believe," said Rowland, in conclusion, "that Miss Light will accept him just in time not to lose him!"

"I count upon it. She would make too perfect a princess to miss her destiny."

"And you hold that nevertheless, in the mean while, in listening to, say, my friend Hudson, she will have been acting in good faith?"

The Cavaliere lifted his shoulders a trifle, and gave an inscrutable smile. "Eh, dear signore, the Christina is very romantic!"

"So much so, you intimate, that she will eventually retract, in consequence not of a change of sentiment, but of a mysterious outward pressure?"

"If everything else fails, there is that resource. But it is mysterious, as you say, and you need n't try to guess it. You will never know."

"The poor signorina, then, will suffer!"

"Not too much, I hope."

"And the poor young man! You maintain that there is nothing but disappointment in store for the infatuated youth who loses his heart to her!"

The Cavaliere hesitated. "He had better," he said in a moment, "go and pursue his studies in Florence. There are very fine antiques in the Uffizi!"

Rowland presently joined Mrs. Light, to whom her restless protege had not yet returned. "That 's right," she said; "sit down here; I have something serious to say to you. I am going to talk to you as a friend. I want your assistance. In fact, I demand it; it 's your duty to render it. Look at that unhappy young man."

"Yes," said Rowland, "he seems unhappy."

"He is just come of age, he bears one of the greatest names in Italy and owns one of the greatest properties, and he is pining away with love for my daughter."

"So the Cavaliere tells me."

"The Cavaliere should n't gossip," said Mrs. Light dryly. "Such information should come from me. The prince is pining, as I say; he 's consumed, he 's devoured. It 's a real Italian passion; I know what that means!" And the lady gave a speaking glance, which seemed to coquet for a moment with retrospect. "Meanwhile, if you please, my daughter is hiding in the woods with your dear friend Mr. Hudson. I could cry with rage."

"If things are so bad as that," said Rowland, "it seems to me that you ought to find nothing easier than to dispatch the Cavaliere to bring the guilty couple back."

"Never in the world! My hands are tied. Do you know what Christina would do? She would tell the Cavaliere to go about his business—Heaven forgive her!—and send me word that, if she had a mind to, she would walk in the woods till midnight. Fancy the Cavaliere coming back and delivering such a message as that before the prince! Think of a girl wantonly making light of such a chance as hers! He would marry her to-morrow, at six o'clock in the morning!"

"It is certainly very sad," said Rowland.

"That costs you little to say. If you had left your precious young meddler to vegetate in his native village you would have saved me a world of distress!"

"Nay, you marched into the jaws of danger," said Rowland. "You came and disinterred poor Hudson in his own secluded studio."

"In an evil hour! I wish to Heaven you would talk with him."

"I have done my best."

"I wish, then, you would take him away. You have plenty of money. Do me a favor. Take him to travel. Go to the East—go to Timbuctoo. Then, when Christina is Princess Casamassima," Mrs. Light added in a moment, "he may come back if he chooses."

"Does she really care for him?" Rowland asked, abruptly.

"She thinks she does, possibly. She is a living riddle. She must needs follow out every idea that comes into her head. Fortunately, most of them don't last long; but this one may last long enough to give the prince a chill. If that were to happen, I don't know what I should do! I should be the most miserable of women. It would be too cruel, after all I 've suffered to make her what she is, to see the labor of years blighted by a caprice. For I can assure you, sir," Mrs. Light went on, "that if my daughter is the greatest beauty in the world, some of the credit is mine."

Rowland promptly remarked that this was obvious. He saw that the lady's irritated nerves demanded comfort from flattering reminiscence, and he assumed designedly the attitude of a zealous auditor. She began to retail her efforts, her hopes, her dreams, her presentiments, her disappointments, in the cause of her daughter's matrimonial fortunes. It was a long story, and while it was being unfolded, the prince continued to pass to and fro, stiffly and solemnly, like a pendulum marking the time allowed for the young lady to come to her senses. Mrs. Light evidently, at an early period, had gathered her maternal hopes into a sacred sheaf, which she said her prayers and burnt incense to, and treated like a sort of fetish. They had been her religion; she had none other, and she performed her devotions bravely and cheerily, in the light of day. The poor old fetish had been so caressed and manipulated, so thrust in and out of its niche, so passed from hand to hand, so dressed and undressed, so mumbled and fumbled over, that it had lost by this time much of its early freshness, and seemed a rather battered and disfeatured divinity. But it was still brought forth in moments of trouble to have its tinseled petticoat twisted about and be set up on its altar. Rowland observed that Mrs. Light had a genuine maternal conscience; she considered that she had been performing a sacred duty in bringing up Christina to set her cap for a prince, and when the future looked dark, she found consolation in thinking that destiny could never have the heart to deal a blow at so deserving a person. This conscience upside down presented to Rowland's fancy a real physical image; he was on the point, half a dozen times, of bursting out laughing.

"I don't know whether you believe in presentiments," said Mrs. Light, "and I don't care! I have had one for the last fifteen years. People have laughed at it, but they have n't laughed me out of it. It has been everything to me. I could n't have lived without it. One must believe in something! It came to me in a flash, when Christina was five years old. I remember the day and the place, as if it were yesterday. She was a very ugly baby; for the first two years I could hardly bear to look at her, and I used to spoil my own looks with crying about her. She had an Italian nurse who was very fond of her and insisted that she would grow up pretty. I could n't believe her; I used to contradict her, and we were forever squabbling. I was just a little silly in those days—surely I may say it now—and I was very fond of being amused. If my daughter was ugly, it was not that she resembled her mamma; I had no lack of amusement. People accused me, I believe, of neglecting my little girl; if it was so, I 've made up for it since. One day I went to drive on the Pincio in very low spirits. A trusted friend had greatly disappointed me. While I was there he passed me in a carriage, driving with a horrible woman who had made trouble between us. I got out of my carriage to walk about, and at last sat down on a bench. I can show you the spot at this hour. While I sat there a child came wandering along the path—a little girl of four or five, very fantastically dressed in crimson and orange. She stopped in front of me and stared at me, and I stared at her queer little dress, which was a cheap imitation of the costume of one of these contadine. At last I looked up at her face, and said to myself, 'Bless me, what a beautiful child! what a splendid pair of eyes, what a magnificent head of hair! If my poor Christina were only like that!' The child turned away slowly, but looking back with its eyes fixed on me. All of a sudden I gave a cry, pounced on it, pressed it in my arms, and covered it with kisses. It was Christina, my own precious child, so disguised by the ridiculous dress which the nurse had amused herself in making for her, that her own mother had not recognized her. She knew me, but she said afterwards that she had not spoken to me because I looked so angry. Of course my face was sad. I rushed with my child to the carriage, drove home post-haste, pulled off her rags, and, as I may say, wrapped her in cotton. I had been blind, I had been insane; she was a creature in ten millions, she was to be a beauty of beauties, a priceless treasure! Every day, after that, the certainty grew. From that time I lived only for my daughter. I watched her, I caressed her from morning till night, I worshipped her. I went to see doctors about her, I took every sort of advice. I was determined she should be perfection. The things that have been done for that girl, sir—you would n't believe them; they would make you smile! Nothing was spared; if I had been told that she must have a bath every morning of molten pearls, I would have found means to give it to her. She never raised a finger for herself, she breathed nothing but perfumes, she walked upon velvet. She never was out of my sight, and from that day to this I have never said a sharp word to her. By the time she was ten years old she was beautiful as an angel, and so noticed wherever we went that I had to make her wear a veil, like a woman of twenty. Her hair reached down to her feet; her hands were the hands of a princess. Then I saw that she was as clever as she was beautiful, and that she had only to play her cards. She had masters, professors, every educational advantage. They told me she was a little prodigy. She speaks French, Italian, German, better than most natives. She has a wonderful genius for music, and might make her fortune as a pianist, if it was not made for her otherwise! I traveled all over Europe; every one told me she was a marvel. The director of the opera in Paris saw her dance at a child's party at Spa, and offered me an enormous sum if I would give her up to him and let him have her educated for the ballet. I said, 'No, I thank you, sir; she is meant to be something finer than a princesse de theatre.' I had a passionate belief that she might marry absolutely whom she chose, that she might be a princess out and out. It has never left me till this hour, and I can assure you that it has sustained me in many embarrassments. Financial, some of them; I don't mind confessing it! I have raised money on that girl's face! I 've taken her to the Jews and bade her put up her veil, and asked if the mother of that young lady was not safe! She, of course, was too young to understand me. And yet, as a child, you would have said she knew what was in store for her; before she could read, she had the manners, the tastes, the instincts of a little princess. She would have nothing to do with shabby things or shabby people; if she stained one of her frocks, she was seized with a kind of frenzy and tore it to pieces. At Nice, at Baden, at Brighton, wherever we stayed, she used to be sent for by all the great people to play with their children. She has played at kissing-games with people who now stand on the steps of thrones! I have gone so far as to think at times that those childish kisses were a sign—a symbol—a portent. You may laugh at me if you like, but have n't such things happened again and again without half as good a cause, and does n't history notoriously repeat itself? There was a little Spanish girl at a second-rate English boarding-school thirty years ago!... The Empress certainly is a pretty woman; but what is my Christina, pray? I 've dreamt of it, sometimes every night for a month. I won't tell you I have been to consult those old women who advertise in the newspapers; you 'll call me an old imbecile. Imbecile if you please! I have refused magnificent offers because I believed that somehow or other—if wars and revolutions were needed to bring it about—we should have nothing less than that. There might be another coup d'etat somewhere, and another brilliant young sovereign looking out for a wife! At last, however," Mrs. Light proceeded with incomparable gravity, "since the overturning of the poor king of Naples and that charming queen, and the expulsion of all those dear little old-fashioned Italian grand-dukes, and the dreadful radical talk that is going on all over the world, it has come to seem to me that with Christina in such a position I should be really very nervous. Even in such a position she would hold her head very high, and if anything should happen to her, she would make no concessions to the popular fury. The best thing, if one is prudent, seems to be a nobleman of the highest possible rank, short of belonging to a reigning stock. There you see one striding up and down, looking at his watch, and counting the minutes till my daughter reappears!"

Rowland listened to all this with a huge compassion for the heroine of the tale. What an education, what a history, what a school of character and of morals! He looked at the prince and wondered whether he too had heard Mrs. Light's story. If he had he was a brave man. "I certainly hope you 'll keep him," he said to Mrs. Light. "You have played a dangerous game with your daughter; it would be a pity not to win. But there is hope for you yet; here she comes at last!"

Christina reappeared as he spoke these words, strolling beside her companion with the same indifferent tread with which she had departed. Rowland imagined that there was a faint pink flush in her cheek which she had not carried away with her, and there was certainly a light in Roderick's eyes which he had not seen there for a week.

"Bless my soul, how they are all looking at us!" she cried, as they advanced. "One would think we were prisoners of the Inquisition!" And she paused and glanced from the prince to her mother, and from Rowland to the Cavaliere, and then threw back her head and burst into far-ringing laughter. "What is it, pray? Have I been very improper? Am I ruined forever? Dear prince, you are looking at me as if I had committed the unpardonable sin!"

"I myself," said the prince, "would never have ventured to ask you to walk with me alone in the country for an hour!"

"The more fool you, dear prince, as the vulgar say! Our walk has been charming. I hope you, on your side, have enjoyed each other's society."

"My dear daughter," said Mrs. Light, taking the arm of her predestined son-in-law, "I shall have something serious to say to you when we reach home. We will go back to the carriage."

"Something serious! Decidedly, it is the Inquisition. Mr. Hudson, stand firm, and let us agree to make no confessions without conferring previously with each other! They may put us on the rack first. Mr. Mallet, I see also," Christina added, "has something serious to say to me!"

Rowland had been looking at her with the shadow of his lately-stirred pity in his eyes. "Possibly," he said. "But it must be for some other time."

"I am at your service. I see our good-humor is gone. And I only wanted to be amiable! It is very discouraging. Cavaliere, you, only, look as if you had a little of the milk of human kindness left; from your venerable visage, at least; there is no telling what you think. Give me your arm and take me away!"

The party took its course back to the carriage, which was waiting in the grounds of the villa, and Rowland and Roderick bade their friends farewell.

Christina threw herself back in her seat and closed her eyes; a manoeuvre for which Rowland imagined the prince was grateful, as it enabled him to look at her without seeming to depart from his attitude of distinguished disapproval. Rowland found himself aroused from sleep early the next morning, to see Roderick standing before him, dressed for departure, with his bag in his hand. "I am off," he said. "I am back to work. I have an idea. I must strike while the iron 's hot! Farewell!" And he departed by the first train. Rowland went alone by the next.

CHAPTER VII. Saint Cecilia's

Rowland went often to the Coliseum; he never wearied of it. One morning, about a month after his return from Frascati, as he was strolling across the vast arena, he observed a young woman seated on one of the fragments of stone which are ranged along the line of the ancient parapet. It seemed to him that he had seen her before, but he was unable to localize her face. Passing her again, he perceived that one of the little red-legged French soldiers at that time on guard there had approached her and was gallantly making himself agreeable. She smiled brilliantly, and Rowland recognized the smile (it had always pleased him) of a certain comely Assunta, who sometimes opened the door for Mrs. Light's visitors. He wondered what she was doing alone in the Coliseum, and conjectured that Assunta had admirers as well as her young mistress, but that, being without the same domiciliary conveniencies, she was using this massive heritage of her Latin ancestors as a boudoir. In other words, she had an appointment with her lover, who had better, from present appearances, be punctual. It was a long time since Rowland had ascended to the ruinous upper tiers of the great circus, and, as the day was radiant and the distant views promised to be particularly clear, he determined to give himself the pleasure. The custodian unlocked the great wooden wicket, and he climbed through the winding shafts, where the eager Roman crowds had billowed and trampled, not pausing till he reached the highest accessible point of the ruin. The views were as fine as he had supposed; the lights on the Sabine Mountains had never been more lovely. He gazed to his satisfaction and retraced his steps. In a moment he paused again on an abutment somewhat lower, from which the glance dropped dizzily into the interior. There are chance anfractuosities of ruin in the upper portions of the Coliseum which offer a very fair imitation of the rugged face of an Alpine cliff. In those days a multitude of delicate flowers and sprays of wild herbage had found a friendly soil in the hoary crevices, and they bloomed and nodded amid the antique masonry as freely as they would have done in the virgin rock. Rowland was turning away, when he heard a sound of voices rising up from below. He had but to step slightly forward to find himself overlooking two persons who had seated themselves on a narrow ledge, in a sunny corner. They had apparently had an eye to extreme privacy, but they had not observed that their position was commanded by Rowland's stand-point. One of these airy adventurers was a lady, thickly veiled, so that, even if he had not been standing directly above her, Rowland could not have seen her face. The other was a young man, whose face was also invisible, but who, as Rowland stood there, gave a toss of his clustering locks which was equivalent to the signature—Roderick Hudson. A moment's reflection, hereupon, satisfied him of the identity of the lady. He had been unjust to poor Assunta, sitting patient in the gloomy arena; she had not come on her own errand. Rowland's discoveries made him hesitate. Should he retire as noiselessly as possible, or should he call out a friendly good morning? While he was debating the question, he found himself distinctly hearing his friends' words. They were of such a nature as to make him unwilling to retreat, and yet to make it awkward to be discovered in a position where it would be apparent that he had heard them.

"If what you say is true," said Christina, with her usual soft deliberateness—it made her words rise with peculiar distinctness to Rowland's ear—"you are simply weak. I am sorry! I hoped—I really believed—you were not."

"No, I am not weak," answered Roderick, with vehemence; "I maintain that I am not weak! I am incomplete, perhaps; but I can't help that. Weakness is a man's own fault!"

"Incomplete, then!" said Christina, with a laugh. "It 's the same thing, so long as it keeps you from splendid achievement. Is it written, then, that I shall really never know what I have so often dreamed of?"

"What have you dreamed of?"

"A man whom I can perfectly respect!" cried the young girl, with a sudden flame. "A man, at least, whom I can unrestrictedly admire. I meet one, as I have met more than one before, whom I fondly believe to be cast in a larger mould than most of the vile human breed, to be large in character, great in talent, strong in will! In such a man as that, I say, one's weary imagination at last may rest; or it may wander if it will, yet never need to wander far from the deeps where one's heart is anchored. When I first knew you, I gave no sign, but you had struck me. I observed you, as women observe, and I fancied you had the sacred fire."

"Before heaven, I believe I have!" cried Roderick.

"Ah, but so little! It flickers and trembles and sputters; it goes out, you tell me, for whole weeks together. From your own account, it 's ten to one that in the long run you 're a failure."

"I say those things sometimes myself, but when I hear you say them they make me feel as if I could work twenty years at a sitting, on purpose to refute you!"

"Ah, the man who is strong with what I call strength," Christina replied, "would neither rise nor fall by anything I could say! I am a poor, weak woman; I have no strength myself, and I can give no strength. I am a miserable medley of vanity and folly. I am silly, I am ignorant, I am affected, I am false. I am the fruit of a horrible education, sown on a worthless soil. I am all that, and yet I believe I have one merit! I should know a great character when I saw it, and I should delight in it with a generosity which would do something toward the remission of my sins. For a man who should really give me a certain feeling— which I have never had, but which I should know when it came—I would send Prince Casamassima and his millions to perdition. I don't know what you think of me for saying all this; I suppose we have not climbed up here under the skies to play propriety. Why have you been at such pains to assure me, after all, that you are a little man and not a great one, a weak one and not a strong? I innocently imagined that your eyes declared you were strong. But your voice condemns you; I always wondered at it; it 's not the voice of a conqueror!"

"Give me something to conquer," cried Roderick, "and when I say that I thank you from my soul, my voice, whatever you think of it, shall speak the truth!"

Christina for a moment said nothing. Rowland was too interested to think of moving. "You pretend to such devotion," she went on, "and yet I am sure you have never really chosen between me and that person in America."

"Do me the favor not to speak of her," said Roderick, imploringly.

"Why not? I say no ill of her, and I think all kinds of good. I am certain she is a far better girl than I, and far more likely to make you happy."

"This is happiness, this present, palpable moment," said Roderick; "though you have such a genius for saying the things that torture me!"

"It 's greater happiness than you deserve, then! You have never chosen, I say; you have been afraid to choose. You have never really faced the fact that you are false, that you have broken your faith. You have never looked at it and seen that it was hideous, and yet said, 'No matter, I 'll brave the penalty, I 'll bear the shame!' You have closed your eyes; you have tried to stifle remembrance, to persuade yourself that you were not behaving as badly as you seemed to be, and there would be some way, after all, of compassing bliss and yet escaping trouble. You have faltered and drifted, you have gone on from accident to accident, and I am sure that at this present moment you can't tell what it is you really desire!"

Roderick was sitting with his knees drawn up and bent, and his hands clasped around his legs. He bent his head and rested his forehead on his knees.

Christina went on with a sort of infernal calmness: "I believe that, really, you don't greatly care for your friend in America any more than you do for me. You are one of the men who care only for themselves and for what they can make of themselves. That 's very well when they can make something great, and I could interest myself in a man of extraordinary power who should wish to turn all his passions to account. But if the power should turn out to be, after all, rather ordinary? Fancy feeling one's self ground in the mill of a third-rate talent! If you have doubts about yourself, I can't reassure you; I have too many doubts myself, about everything in this weary world. You have gone up like a rocket, in your profession, they tell me; are you going to come down like the stick? I don't pretend to know; I repeat frankly what I have said before—that all modern sculpture seems to me weak, and that the only things I care for are some of the most battered of the antiques of the Vatican. No, no, I can't reassure you; and when you tell me—with a confidence in my discretion of which, certainly, I am duly sensible—that at times you feel terribly small, why, I can only answer, 'Ah, then, my poor friend, I am afraid you are small.' The language I should like to hear, from a certain person, would be the language of absolute decision."

Roderick raised his head, but he said nothing; he seemed to be exchanging a long glance with his companion. The result of it was to make him fling himself back with an inarticulate murmur. Rowland, admonished by the silence, was on the point of turning away, but he was arrested by a gesture of the young girl. She pointed for a moment into the blue air. Roderick followed the direction of her gesture.

"Is that little flower we see outlined against that dark niche," she asked, "as intensely blue as it looks through my veil?" She spoke apparently with the amiable design of directing the conversation into a less painful channel.

Rowland, from where he stood, could see the flower she meant—a delicate plant of radiant hue, which sprouted from the top of an immense fragment of wall some twenty feet from Christina's place.

Roderick turned his head and looked at it without answering. At last, glancing round, "Put up your veil!" he said. Christina complied. "Does it look as blue now?" he asked.

"Ah, what a lovely color!" she murmured, leaning her head on one side.

"Would you like to have it?"

She stared a moment and then broke into a light laugh.

"Would you like to have it?" he repeated in a ringing voice.

"Don't look as if you would eat me up," she answered. "It 's harmless if I say yes!"

Roderick rose to his feet and stood looking at the little flower. It was separated from the ledge on which he stood by a rugged surface of vertical wall, which dropped straight into the dusky vaults behind the arena. Suddenly he took off his hat and flung it behind him. Christina then sprang to her feet.

"I will bring it you," he said.

She seized his arm. "Are you crazy? Do you mean to kill yourself?"

"I shall not kill myself. Sit down!"

"Excuse me. Not till you do!" And she grasped his arm with both hands.

Roderick shook her off and pointed with a violent gesture to her former place. "Go there!" he cried fiercely.

"You can never, never!" she murmured beseechingly, clasping her hands. "I implore you!"

Roderick turned and looked at her, and then in a voice which Rowland had never heard him use, a voice almost thunderous, a voice which awakened the echoes of the mighty ruin, he repeated, "Sit down!" She hesitated a moment and then she dropped on the ground and buried her face in her hands.

Rowland had seen all this, and he saw more. He saw Roderick clasp in his left arm the jagged corner of the vertical partition along which he proposed to pursue his crazy journey, stretch out his leg, and feel for a resting-place for his foot. Rowland had measured with a glance the possibility of his sustaining himself, and pronounced it absolutely nil. The wall was garnished with a series of narrow projections, the remains apparently of a brick cornice supporting the arch of a vault which had long since collapsed. It was by lodging his toes on these loose brackets and grasping with his hands at certain mouldering protuberances on a level with his head, that Roderick intended to proceed. The relics of the cornice were utterly worthless as a support. Rowland had observed this, and yet, for a moment, he had hesitated. If the thing were possible, he felt a sudden admiring glee at the thought of Roderick's doing it. It would be finely done, it would be gallant, it would have a sort of masculine eloquence as an answer to Christina's sinister persiflage. But it was not possible! Rowland left his place with a bound, and scrambled down some neighboring steps, and the next moment a stronger pair of hands than Christina's were laid upon Roderick's shoulder.

He turned, staring, pale and angry. Christina rose, pale and staring, too, but beautiful in her wonder and alarm. "My dear Roderick," said Rowland, "I am only preventing you from doing a very foolish thing. That 's an exploit for spiders, not for young sculptors of promise."

Roderick wiped his forehead, looked back at the wall, and then closed his eyes, as if with a spasm, of retarded dizziness. "I won't resist you," he said. "But I have made you obey," he added, turning to Christina. "Am I weak now?"

She had recovered her composure; she looked straight past him and addressed Rowland: "Be so good as to show me the way out of this horrible place!"

He helped her back into the corridor; Roderick followed after a short interval. Of course, as they were descending the steps, came questions for Rowland to answer, and more or less surprise. Where had he come from? how happened he to have appeared at just that moment? Rowland answered that he had been rambling overhead, and that, looking out of an aperture, he had seen a gentleman preparing to undertake a preposterous gymnastic feat, and a lady swooning away in consequence. Interference seemed justifiable, and he had made it as prompt as possible. Roderick was far from hanging his head, like a man who has been caught in the perpetration of an extravagant folly; but if he held it more erect than usual Rowland believed that this was much less because he had made a show of personal daring than because he had triumphantly proved to Christina that, like a certain person she had dreamed of, he too could speak the language of decision. Christina descended to the arena in silence, apparently occupied with her own thoughts. She betrayed no sense of the privacy of her interview with Roderick needing an explanation. Rowland had seen stranger things in New York! The only evidence of her recent agitation was that, on being joined by her maid, she declared that she was unable to walk home; she must have a carriage. A fiacre was found resting in the shadow of the Arch of Constantine, and Rowland suspected that after she had got into it she disburdened herself, under her veil, of a few natural tears.

Rowland had played eavesdropper to so good a purpose that he might justly have omitted the ceremony of denouncing himself to Roderick. He preferred, however, to let him know that he had overheard a portion of his talk with Christina.

"Of course it seems to you," Roderick said, "a proof that I am utterly infatuated."

"Miss Light seemed to me to know very well how far she could go," Rowland answered. "She was twisting you round her finger. I don't think she exactly meant to defy you; but your crazy pursuit of that flower was a proof that she could go all lengths in the way of making a fool of you."

"Yes," said Roderick, meditatively; "she is making a fool of me."

"And what do you expect to come of it?"

"Nothing good!" And Roderick put his hands into his pockets and looked as if he had announced the most colorless fact in the world.

"And in the light of your late interview, what do you make of your young lady?"

"If I could tell you that, it would be plain sailing. But she 'll not tell me again I am weak!"

"Are you very sure you are not weak?"

"I may be, but she shall never know it."

Rowland said no more until they reached the Corso, when he asked his companion whether he was going to his studio.

Roderick started out of a reverie and passed his hands over his eyes. "Oh no, I can't settle down to work after such a scene as that. I was not afraid of breaking my neck then, but I feel all in a tremor now. I will go—I will go and sit in the sun on the Pincio!"

"Promise me this, first," said Rowland, very solemnly: "that the next time you meet Miss Light, it shall be on the earth and not in the air."

Since his return from Frascati, Roderick had been working doggedly at the statue ordered by Mr. Leavenworth. To Rowland's eye he had made a very fair beginning, but he had himself insisted, from the first, that he liked neither his subject nor his patron, and that it was impossible to feel any warmth of interest in a work which was to be incorporated into the ponderous personality of Mr. Leavenworth. It was all against the grain; he wrought without love. Nevertheless after a fashion he wrought, and the figure grew beneath his hands. Miss Blanchard's friend was ordering works of art on every side, and his purveyors were in many cases persons whom Roderick declared it was infamy to be paired with. There had been grand tailors, he said, who declined to make you a coat unless you got the hat you were to wear with it from an artist of their own choosing. It seemed to him that he had an equal right to exact that his statue should not form part of the same system of ornament as the "Pearl of Perugia," a picture by an American confrere who had, in Mr. Leavenworth's opinion, a prodigious eye for color. As a customer, Mr. Leavenworth used to drop into Roderick's studio, to see how things were getting on, and give a friendly hint or so. He would seat himself squarely, plant his gold-topped cane between his legs, which he held very much apart, rest his large white hands on the head, and enunciate the principles of spiritual art, as he hoisted them one by one, as you might say, out of the depths of his moral consciousness. His benignant and imperturbable pomposity gave Roderick the sense of suffocating beneath a large fluffy bolster, and the worst of the matter was that the good gentleman's placid vanity had an integument whose toughness no sarcastic shaft could pierce. Roderick admitted that in thinking over the tribulations of struggling genius, the danger of dying of over-patronage had never occurred to him.

The deterring effect of the episode of the Coliseum was apparently of long continuance; if Roderick's nerves had been shaken his hand needed time to recover its steadiness. He cultivated composure upon principles of his own; by frequenting entertainments from which he returned at four o'clock in the morning, and lapsing into habits which might fairly be called irregular. He had hitherto made few friends among the artistic fraternity; chiefly because he had taken no trouble about it, and there was in his demeanor an elastic independence of the favor of his fellow-mortals which made social advances on his own part peculiarly necessary. Rowland had told him more than once that he ought to fraternize a trifle more with the other artists, and he had always answered that he had not the smallest objection to fraternizing: let them come! But they came on rare occasions, and Roderick was not punctilious about returning their visits. He declared there was not one of them whose works gave him the smallest desire to make acquaintance with the insides of their heads. For Gloriani he professed a superb contempt, and, having been once to look at his wares, never crossed his threshold again. The only one of the fraternity for whom by his own admission he cared a straw was little Singleton; but he expressed his regard only in a kind of sublime hilarity whenever he encountered this humble genius, and quite forgot his existence in the intervals. He had never been to see him, but Singleton edged his way, from time to time, timidly, into Roderick's studio, and agreed with characteristic modesty that brilliant fellows like the sculptor might consent to receive homage, but could hardly be expected to render it. Roderick never exactly accepted homage, and apparently did not quite observe whether poor Singleton spoke in admiration or in blame. Roderick's taste as to companions was singularly capricious. There were very good fellows, who were disposed to cultivate him, who bored him to death; and there were others, in whom even Rowland's good-nature was unable to discover a pretext for tolerance, in whom he appeared to find the highest social qualities. He used to give the most fantastic reasons for his likes and dislikes. He would declare he could n't speak a civil word to a man who brushed his hair in a certain fashion, and he would explain his unaccountable fancy for an individual of imperceptible merit by telling you that he had an ancestor who in the thirteenth century had walled up his wife alive. "I like to talk to a man whose ancestor has walled up his wife alive," he would say. "You may not see the fun of it, and think poor P—— is a very dull fellow. It 's very possible; I don't ask you to admire him. But, for reasons of my own, I like to have him about. The old fellow left her for three days with her face uncovered, and placed a long mirror opposite to her, so that she could see, as he said, if her gown was a fit!"

His relish for an odd flavor in his friends had led him to make the acquaintance of a number of people outside of Rowland's well-ordered circle, and he made no secret of their being very queer fish. He formed an intimacy, among others, with a crazy fellow who had come to Rome as an emissary of one of the Central American republics, to drive some ecclesiastical bargain with the papal government. The Pope had given him the cold shoulder, but since he had not prospered as a diplomatist, he had sought compensation as a man of the world, and his great flamboyant curricle and negro lackeys were for several weeks one of the striking ornaments of the Pincian. He spoke a queer jargon of Italian, Spanish, French, and English, humorously relieved with scraps of ecclesiastical Latin, and to those who inquired of Roderick what he found to interest him in such a fantastic jackanapes, the latter would reply, looking at his interlocutor with his lucid blue eyes, that it was worth any sacrifice to hear him talk nonsense! The two had gone together one night to a ball given by a lady of some renown in the Spanish colony, and very late, on his way home, Roderick came up to Rowland's rooms, in whose windows he had seen a light. Rowland was going to bed, but Roderick flung himself into an armchair and chattered for an hour. The friends of the Costa Rican envoy were as amusing as himself, and in very much the same line. The mistress of the house had worn a yellow satin dress, and gold heels to her slippers, and at the close of the entertainment had sent for a pair of castanets, tucked up her petticoats, and danced a fandango, while the gentlemen sat cross-legged on the floor. "It was awfully low," Roderick said; "all of a sudden I perceived it, and bolted. Nothing of that kind ever amuses me to the end: before it 's half over it bores me to death; it makes me sick. Hang it, why can't a poor fellow enjoy things in peace? My illusions are all broken-winded; they won't carry me twenty paces! I can't laugh and forget; my laugh dies away before it begins. Your friend Stendhal writes on his book-covers (I never got farther) that he has seen too early in life la beaute parfaite. I don't know how early he saw it; I saw it before I was born—in another state of being! I can't describe it positively; I can only say I don't find it anywhere now. Not at the bottom of champagne glasses; not, strange as it may seem, in that extra half-yard or so of shoulder that some women have their ball-dresses cut to expose. I don't find it at merry supper-tables, where half a dozen ugly men with pomatumed heads are rapidly growing uglier still with heat and wine; not when I come away and walk through these squalid black streets, and go out into the Forum and see a few old battered stone posts standing there like gnawed bones stuck into the earth. Everything is mean and dusky and shabby, and the men and women who make up this so-called brilliant society are the meanest and shabbiest of all. They have no real spontaneity; they are all cowards and popinjays. They have no more dignity than so many grasshoppers. Nothing is good but one!" And he jumped up and stood looking at one of his statues, which shone vaguely across the room in the dim lamplight.

"Yes, do tell us," said Rowland, "what to hold on by!"

"Those things of mine were tolerably good," he answered. "But my idea was better—and that 's what I mean!"

Rowland said nothing. He was willing to wait for Roderick to complete the circle of his metamorphoses, but he had no desire to officiate as chorus to the play. If Roderick chose to fish in troubled waters, he must land his prizes himself.

"You think I 'm an impudent humbug," the latter said at last, "coming up to moralize at this hour of the night. You think I want to throw dust into your eyes, to put you off the scent. That 's your eminently rational view of the case."

"Excuse me from taking any view at all," said Rowland.

"You have given me up, then?"

"No, I have merely suspended judgment. I am waiting."

"You have ceased then positively to believe in me?"

Rowland made an angry gesture. "Oh, cruel boy! When you have hit your mark and made people care for you, you should n't twist your weapon about at that rate in their vitals. Allow me to say I am sleepy. Good night!"

Some days afterward it happened that Rowland, on a long afternoon ramble, took his way through one of the quiet corners of the Trastevere. He was particularly fond of this part of Rome, though he could hardly have expressed the charm he found in it. As you pass away from the dusky, swarming purlieus of the Ghetto, you emerge into a region of empty, soundless, grass-grown lanes and alleys, where the shabby houses seem mouldering away in disuse, and yet your footstep brings figures of startling Roman type to the doorways. There are few monuments here, but no part of Rome seemed more historic, in the sense of being weighted with a crushing past, blighted with the melancholy of things that had had their day. When the yellow afternoon sunshine slept on the sallow, battered walls, and lengthened the shadows in the grassy courtyards of small closed churches, the place acquired a strange fascination. The church of Saint Cecilia has one of these sunny, waste-looking courts; the edifice seems abandoned to silence and the charity of chance devotion. Rowland never passed it without going in, and he was generally the only visitor. He entered it now, but found that two persons had preceded him. Both were women. One was at her prayers at one of the side altars; the other was seated against a column at the upper end of the nave. Rowland walked to the altar, and paid, in a momentary glance at the clever statue of the saint in death, in the niche beneath it, the usual tribute to the charm of polished ingenuity. As he turned away he looked at the person seated and recognized Christina Light. Seeing that she perceived him, he advanced to speak to her.

She was sitting in a listless attitude, with her hands in her lap; she seemed to be tired. She was dressed simply, as if for walking and escaping observation. When he had greeted her he glanced back at her companion, and recognized the faithful Assunta.

Christina smiled. "Are you looking for Mr. Hudson? He is not here, I am happy to say."

"But you?" he asked. "This is a strange place to find you."

"Not at all! People call me a strange girl, and I might as well have the comfort of it. I came to take a walk; that, by the way, is part of my strangeness. I can't loll all the morning on a sofa, and all the afternoon in a carriage. I get horribly restless. I must move; I must do something and see something.

Mamma suggests a cup of tea. Meanwhile I put on an old dress and half a dozen veils, I take Assunta under my arm, and we start on a pedestrian tour. It 's a bore that I can't take the poodle, but he attracts attention. We trudge about everywhere; there is nothing I like so much. I hope you will congratulate me on the simplicity of my tastes."

"I congratulate you on your wisdom. To live in Rome and not to walk would, I think, be poor pleasure. But you are terribly far from home, and I am afraid you are tired."

"A little—enough to sit here a while."

"Might I offer you my company while you rest?"

"If you will promise to amuse me. I am in dismal spirits."

Rowland said he would do what he could, and brought a chair and placed it near her. He was not in love with her; he disapproved of her; he mistrusted her; and yet he felt it a kind of privilege to watch her, and he found a peculiar excitement in talking to her. The background of her nature, as he would have called it, was large and mysterious, and it emitted strange, fantastic gleams and flashes. Watching for these rather quickened one's pulses. Moreover, it was not a disadvantage to talk to a girl who made one keep guard on one's composure; it diminished one's chronic liability to utter something less than revised wisdom.

Assunta had risen from her prayers, and, as he took his place, was coming back to her mistress. But Christina motioned her away. "No, no; while you are about it, say a few dozen more!" she said. "Pray for me," she added in English. "Pray, I say nothing silly. She has been at it half an hour; I envy her capacity!"

"Have you never felt in any degree," Rowland asked, "the fascination of Catholicism?"

"Yes, I have been through that, too! There was a time when I wanted immensely to be a nun; it was not a laughing matter. It was when I was about sixteen years old. I read the Imitation and the Life of Saint Catherine. I fully believed in the miracles of the saints, and I was dying to have one of my own. The least little accident that could have been twisted into a miracle would have carried me straight into the bosom of the church. I had the real religious passion. It has passed away, and, as I sat here just now, I was wondering what had become of it!"

Rowland had already been sensible of something in this young lady's tone which he would have called a want of veracity, and this epitome of her religious experience failed to strike him as an absolute statement of fact. But the trait was not disagreeable, for she herself was evidently the foremost dupe of her inventions. She had a fictitious history in which she believed much more fondly than in her real one, and an infinite capacity for extemporized reminiscence adapted to the mood of the hour. She liked to idealize herself, to take interesting and picturesque attitudes to her own imagination; and the vivacity and spontaneity of her character gave her, really, a starting-point in experience; so that the many-colored flowers of fiction which blossomed in her talk were not so much perversions, as sympathetic exaggerations, of fact. And Rowland felt that whatever she said of herself might have been, under the imagined circumstances; impulse was there, audacity, the restless, questioning temperament. "I am afraid I am sadly prosaic," he said, "for in these many months now that I have been in Rome, I have never ceased for a moment to look at Catholicism simply from the outside. I don't see an opening as big as your finger-nail where I could creep into it!"

"What do you believe?" asked Christina, looking at him. "Are you religious?"

"I believe in God."

Christina let her beautiful eyes wander a while, and then gave a little sigh. "You are much to be envied!"

"You, I imagine, in that line have nothing to envy me."

"Yes, I have. Rest!"

"You are too young to say that."

"I am not young; I have never been young! My mother took care of that. I was a little wrinkled old woman at ten."

"I am afraid," said Rowland, in a moment, "that you are fond of painting yourself in dark colors."

She looked at him a while in silence. "Do you wish," she demanded at last, "to win my eternal gratitude? Prove to me that I am better than I suppose."

"I should have first to know what you really suppose."

She shook her head. "It would n't do. You would be horrified to learn even the things I imagine about myself, and shocked at the knowledge of evil displayed in my very mistakes."

"Well, then," said Rowland, "I will ask no questions. But, at a venture, I promise you to catch you some day in the act of doing something very good."

"Can it be, can it be," she asked, "that you too are trying to flatter me? I thought you and I had fallen, from the first, into rather a truth-speaking vein."

"Oh, I have not abandoned it!" said Rowland; and he determined, since he had the credit of homely directness, to push his advantage farther. The opportunity seemed excellent. But while he was hesitating as to just how to begin, the young girl said, bending forward and clasping her hands in her lap, "Please tell me about your religion."

"Tell you about it? I can't!" said Rowland, with a good deal of emphasis.

She flushed a little. "Is it such a mighty mystery it cannot be put into words, nor communicated to my base ears?"

"It is simply a sentiment that makes part of my life, and I can't detach myself from it sufficiently to talk about it."

"Religion, it seems to me, should be eloquent and aggressive. It should wish to make converts, to persuade and illumine, to sway all hearts!"

"One's religion takes the color of one's general disposition. I am not aggressive, and certainly I am not eloquent."

"Beware, then, of finding yourself confronted with doubt and despair! I am sure that doubt, at times, and the bitterness that comes of it, can be terribly eloquent. To tell the truth, my lonely musings, before you came in, were eloquent enough, in their way. What do you know of anything but this strange, terrible world that surrounds you? How do you know that your faith is not a mere crazy castle in the air; one of those castles that we are called fools for building when we lodge them in this life?"

"I don't know it, any more than any one knows the contrary. But one's religion is extremely ingenious in doing without knowledge."

"In such a world as this it certainly needs to be!"

Rowland smiled. "What is your particular quarrel with this world?"

"It 's a general quarrel. Nothing is true, or fixed, or permanent. We all seem to be playing with shadows more or less grotesque. It all comes over me here so dismally! The very atmosphere of this cold, deserted church seems to mock at one's longing to believe in something. Who cares for it now? who comes to it? who takes it seriously? Poor stupid Assunta there gives in her adhesion in a jargon she does n't understand, and you and I, proper, passionless tourists, come lounging in to rest from a walk. And yet the Catholic church was once the proudest institution in the world, and had quite its own way with men's souls. When such a mighty structure as that turns out to have a flaw, what faith is one to put in one's poor little views and philosophies? What is right and what is wrong? What is one really to care for? What is the proper rule of life? I am tired of trying to discover, and I suspect it 's not worth the trouble. Live as most amuses you!"

"Your perplexities are so terribly comprehensive," said Rowland, smiling, "that one hardly knows where to meet them first."

"I don't care much for anything you can say, because it 's sure to be half-hearted. You are not in the least contented, yourself."

"How do you know that?"

"Oh, I am an observer!"

"No one is absolutely contented, I suppose, but I assure you I complain of nothing."

"So much the worse for your honesty. To begin with, you are in love."

"You would not have me complain of that!"

"And it does n't go well. There are grievous obstacles. So much I know! You need n't protest; I ask no questions. You will tell no one—me least of all. Why does one never see you?"

"Why, if I came to see you," said Rowland, deliberating, "it would n't be, it could n't be, for a trivial reason—because I had not been in a month, because I was passing, because I admire you. It would be because I should have something very particular to say. I have not come, because I have been slow in making up my mind to say it."

"You are simply cruel. Something particular, in this ocean of inanities? In common charity, speak!"

"I doubt whether you will like it."

"Oh, I hope to heaven it 's not a compliment!"

"It may be called a compliment to your reasonableness. You perhaps remember that I gave you a hint of it the other day at Frascati."

"Has it been hanging fire all this time? Explode! I promise not to stop my ears."

"It relates to my friend Hudson." And Rowland paused. She was looking at him expectantly; her face gave no sign. "I am rather disturbed in mind about him. He seems to me at times to be in an unpromising way." He paused again, but Christina said nothing. "The case is simply this," he went on. "It was by my advice he renounced his career at home and embraced his present one. I made him burn his ships. I brought him to Rome, I launched him in the world, and I stand surety, in a measure, to—to his mother, for his prosperity. It is not such smooth sailing as it might be, and I am inclined to put up prayers for fair winds. If he is to succeed, he must work—quietly, devotedly. It is not news to you, I imagine, that Hudson is a great admirer of yours."

Christina remained silent; she turned away her eyes with an air, not of confusion, but of deep deliberation. Surprising frankness had, as a general thing, struck Rowland as the key-note of her character, but she had more than once given him a suggestion of an unfathomable power of calculation, and her silence now had something which it is hardly extravagant to call portentous. He had of course asked himself how far it was questionable taste to inform an unprotected girl, for the needs of a cause, that another man admired her; the thing, superficially, had an uncomfortable analogy with the shrewdness that uses a cat's paw and lets it risk being singed. But he decided that even rigid discretion is not bound to take a young lady at more than her own valuation, and Christina presently reassured him as to the limits of her susceptibility. "Mr. Hudson is in love with me!" she said.

Rowland flinched a trifle. Then—"Am I," he asked, "from this point of view of mine, to be glad or sorry?"

"I don't understand you."

"Why, is Hudson to be happy, or unhappy?"

She hesitated a moment. "You wish him to be great in his profession? And for that you consider that he must be happy in his life?"

"Decidedly. I don't say it 's a general rule, but I think it is a rule for him."

"So that if he were very happy, he would become very great?"

"He would at least do himself justice."

"And by that you mean a great deal?"

"A great deal."

Christina sank back in her chair and rested her eyes on the cracked and polished slabs of the pavement. At last, looking up, "You have not forgotten, I suppose, that you told me he was engaged?"

"By no means."

"He is still engaged, then?"

"To the best of my belief."

"And yet you desire that, as you say, he should be made happy by something I can do for him?"

"What I desire is this. That your great influence with him should be exerted for his good, that it should help him and not retard him. Understand me. You probably know that your lovers have rather a restless time of it. I can answer for two of them. You don't know your own mind very well, I imagine, and you like being admired, rather at the expense of the admirer. Since we are really being frank, I wonder whether I might not say the great word."

"You need n't; I know it. I am a horrible coquette."

"No, not a horrible one, since I am making an appeal to your generosity. I am pretty sure you cannot imagine yourself marrying my friend."

"There 's nothing I cannot imagine! That is my trouble."

Rowland's brow contracted impatiently. "I cannot imagine it, then!" he affirmed.

Christina flushed faintly; then, very gently, "I am not so bad as you think," she said.

"It is not a question of badness; it is a question of whether circumstances don't make the thing an extreme improbability."

"Worse and worse. I can be bullied, then, or bribed!"

"You are not so candid," said Rowland, "as you pretend to be. My feeling is this. Hudson, as I understand him, does not need, as an artist, the stimulus of strong emotion, of passion. He's better without it; he's emotional and passionate enough when he 's left to himself. The sooner passion is at rest, therefore, the sooner he will settle down to work, and the fewer emotions he has that are mere emotions and nothing more, the better for him. If you cared for him enough to marry him, I should have nothing to say; I would never venture to interfere. But I strongly suspect you don't, and therefore I would suggest, most respectfully, that you should let him alone."

"And if I let him alone, as you say, all will be well with him for ever more?"

"Not immediately and not absolutely, but things will be easier. He will be better able to concentrate himself."

"What is he doing now? Wherein does he dissatisfy you?"

"I can hardly say. He 's like a watch that 's running down. He is moody, desultory, idle, irregular, fantastic."

"Heavens, what a list! And it 's all poor me?"

"No, not all. But you are a part of it, and I turn to you because you are a more tangible, sensible, responsible cause than the others."

Christina raised her hand to her eyes, and bent her head thoughtfully. Rowland was puzzled to measure the effect of his venture; she rather surprised him by her gentleness. At last, without moving, "If I were to marry him," she asked, "what would have become of his fiancee?"

"I am bound to suppose that she would be extremely unhappy."

Christina said nothing more, and Rowland, to let her make her reflections, left his place and strolled away. Poor Assunta, sitting patiently on a stone bench, and unprovided, on this occasion, with military consolation, gave him a bright, frank smile, which might have been construed as an expression of regret for herself, and of sympathy for her mistress. Rowland presently seated himself again near Christina.

"What do you think," she asked, looking at him, "of your friend's infidelity?"

"I don't like it."

"Was he very much in love with her?"

"He asked her to marry him. You may judge."

"Is she rich?"

"No, she is poor."

"Is she very much in love with him?"

"I know her too little to say."

She paused again, and then resumed: "You have settled in your mind, then, that I will never seriously listen to him?"

"I think it unlikely, until the contrary is proved."

"How shall it be proved? How do you know what passes between us?"

"I can judge, of course, but from appearance; but, like you, I am an observer. Hudson has not at all the air of a prosperous suitor."

"If he is depressed, there is a reason. He has a bad conscience. One must hope so, at least. On the other hand, simply as a friend," she continued gently, "you think I can do him no good?"

The humility of her tone, combined with her beauty, as she made this remark, was inexpressibly touching, and Rowland had an uncomfortable sense of being put at a disadvantage. "There are doubtless many good things you might do, if you had proper opportunity," he said. "But you seem to be sailing with a current which leaves you little leisure for quiet benevolence. You live in the whirl and hurry of a world into which a poor artist can hardly find it to his advantage to follow you."

"In plain English, I am hopelessly frivolous. You put it very generously."

"I won't hesitate to say all my thought," said Rowland. "For better or worse, you seem to me to belong, both by character and by circumstance, to what is called the world, the great world. You are made to ornament it magnificently. You are not made to be an artist's wife."

526

"I see. But even from your point of view, that would depend upon the artist. Extraordinary talent might make him a member of the great world!"

Rowland smiled. "That is very true."

"If, as it is," Christina continued in a moment, "you take a low view of me—no, you need n't protest—I wonder what you would think if you knew certain things."

"What things do you mean?"

"Well, for example, how I was brought up. I have had a horrible education. There must be some good in me, since I have perceived it, since I have turned and judged my circumstances."

"My dear Miss Light!" Rowland murmured.

She gave a little, quick laugh. "You don't want to hear? you don't want to have to think about that?"

"Have I a right to? You need n't justify yourself."

She turned upon him a moment the quickened light of her beautiful eyes, then fell to musing again. "Is there not some novel or some play," she asked at last, "in which some beautiful, wicked woman who has ensnared a young man sees his father come to her and beg her to let him go?"

"Very likely," said Rowland. "I hope she consents."

"I forget. But tell me," she continued, "shall you consider—admitting your proposition—that in ceasing to flirt with Mr. Hudson, so that he may go about his business, I do something magnanimous, heroic, sublime—something with a fine name like that?"

Rowland, elated with the prospect of gaining his point, was about to reply that she would deserve the finest name in the world; but he instantly suspected that this tone would not please her, and, besides, it would not express his meaning.

"You do something I shall greatly respect," he contented himself with saying.

She made no answer, and in a moment she beckoned to her maid. "What have I to do to-day?" she asked.

Assunta meditated. "Eh, it 's a very busy day! Fortunately I have a better memory than the signorina," she said, turning to Rowland. She began to count on her fingers. "We have to go to the Pie di Marmo to see about those laces that were sent to be washed. You said also that you wished to say three sharp words to the Buonvicini about your pink dress. You want some moss-rosebuds for to-night, and you won't get them for nothing! You dine at the Austrian Embassy, and that Frenchman is to powder your hair. You 're to come home in time to receive, for the signora gives a dance. And so away, away till morning!"

"Ah, yes, the moss-roses!" Christina murmured, caressingly. "I must have a quantity—at least a hundred. Nothing but buds, eh? You must sew them in a kind of immense apron, down the front of my dress. Packed tight together, eh? It will be delightfully barbarous. And then twenty more or so for my hair. They go very well with powder; don't you think so?" And she turned to Rowland. "I am going en Pompadour."

"Going where?"

"To the Spanish Embassy, or whatever it is."

"All down the front, signorina? Dio buono! You must give me time!" Assunta cried.

"Yes, we'll go!" And she left her place. She walked slowly to the door of the church, looking at the pavement, and Rowland could not guess whether she was thinking of her apron of moss-rosebuds or of her opportunity for moral sublimity. Before reaching the door she turned away and stood gazing at an old picture, indistinguishable with blackness, over an altar. At last they passed out into the court. Glancing at her in the open air, Rowland was startled; he imagined he saw the traces of hastily suppressed tears. They had lost time, she said, and they must hurry; she sent Assunta to look for a fiacre. She remained silent a while, scratching the ground with the point of her parasol, and then at last, looking up, she thanked Rowland for his confidence in her "reasonableness." "It 's really very comfortable to be asked, to be expected, to do something good, after all the horrid things one has been used to doing—instructed, commanded, forced to do! I 'll think over what you have said to me." In that deserted quarter fiacres are rare, and there was some delay in Assunta's procuring one. Christina talked of the church, of the picturesque old court, of that strange, decaying corner of Rome. Rowland was perplexed; he was ill at ease. At last the fiacre arrived, but she waited a moment longer. "So, decidedly," she suddenly asked, "I can only harm him?"

"You make me feel very brutal," said Rowland.

"And he is such a fine fellow that it would be really a great pity, eh?"

"I shall praise him no more," Rowland said.

She turned away quickly, but she lingered still. "Do you remember promising me, soon after we first met, that at the end of six months you would tell me definitely what you thought of me?"

"It was a foolish promise."

"You gave it. Bear it in mind. I will think of what you have said to me. Farewell." She stepped into the carriage, and it rolled away. Rowland stood for some minutes, looking after it, and then went his way with a sigh. If this expressed general mistrust, he ought, three days afterward, to have been reassured. He received by the post a note containing these words:—

"I have done it. Begin and respect me!

"—C. L."

To be perfectly satisfactory, indeed, the note required a commentary. He called that evening upon Roderick, and found one in the information offered him at the door, by the old serving-woman—the startling information that the signorino had gone to Naples.

CHAPTER VIII. Provocation

About a month later, Rowland addressed to his cousin Cecilia a letter of which the following is a portion:—

... "So much for myself; yet I tell you but a tithe of my own story unless I let you know how matters stand with poor Hudson, for he gives me more to think about just now than anything else in the world. I need a good deal of courage to begin this chapter. You warned me, you know, and I made rather light of your warning. I have had all kinds of hopes and fears, but hitherto, in writing to you, I have resolutely put the hopes foremost. Now, however, my pride has forsaken me, and I should like hugely to give expression to a little comfortable despair. I should like to say, 'My dear wise woman, you were right and I was wrong; you were a shrewd observer and I was a meddlesome donkey!' When I think of a little talk we had about the 'salubrity of genius,' I feel my ears tingle. If this is salubrity, give me raging disease! I 'm pestered to death; I go about with a chronic heartache; there are moments when I could shed salt tears. There 's a pretty portrait of the most placid of men! I wish I could make you understand; or rather, I wish you could make me! I don't understand a jot; it 's a hideous, mocking mystery; I give it up! I don't in the least give it up, you know; I 'm incapable of giving it up. I sit holding my head by the hour, racking my brain, wondering what under heaven is to be done. You told me at Northampton that I took the thing too easily; you would tell me now, perhaps, that I take it too hard. I do, altogether; but it can't be helped. Without flattering myself, I may say I 'm sympathetic. Many another man before this would have cast his perplexities to the winds and declared that Mr. Hudson must lie on his bed as he had made it. Some men, perhaps, would even say that I am making a mighty ado about nothing; that I have only to give him rope, and he will tire himself out. But he tugs at his rope altogether too hard for me to hold it comfortably. I certainly never pretended the thing was anything else than an experiment; I promised nothing, I answered for nothing; I only said the case was hopeful, and that it would be a shame to neglect it. I have done my best, and if the machine is running down I have a right to stand aside and let it scuttle. Amen, amen! No, I can write that, but I can't feel it. I can't be just; I can only be generous. I love the poor fellow and I can't give him up. As for understanding him, that 's another matter; nowadays I don't believe even you would. One's wits are sadly pestered over here, I assure you, and I 'm in the way of seeing more than one puzzling specimen of human nature. Roderick and Miss Light, between them!... Have n't I already told you about Miss Light? Last winter everything was perfection. Roderick struck out bravely, did really great things, and proved himself, as I supposed, thoroughly solid. He was strong, he was first-rate; I felt perfectly secure and sang private paeans of joy. We had passed at a bound into the open sea, and left danger behind. But in the summer I began to be puzzled, though I succeeded in not being alarmed. When we came back to Rome, however, I saw that the tide had turned and that we were close upon the rocks. It is, in fact, another case of Ulysses alongside of the Sirens; only Roderick refuses to be tied to the mast. He is the most extraordinary being, the strangest mixture of qualities. I don't understand so much force going with so much weakness— such a brilliant gift being subject to such lapses. The poor fellow is incomplete, and it is really not his own fault; Nature has given him the faculty out of hand and bidden him be hanged with it. I never knew a man harder to advise or assist, if he is not in the mood for listening. I suppose there is some key or other to his character, but I try in vain to find it; and yet I can't believe that Providence is so cruel as to have turned the lock and thrown the key away. He perplexes me, as I say, to death, and though he tires out my patience, he still fascinates me. Sometimes I think he has n't a grain of conscience, and sometimes I think that, in a way, he has an excess. He takes things at once too easily and too hard; he is both too lax and too tense, too reckless and too ambitious, too cold and too passionate. He has developed faster even than you prophesied, and for good and evil alike he takes up a formidable space. There 's too much of him for me, at any rate. Yes, he is hard; there is no mistake about that. He 's inflexible, he 's brittle; and though he has plenty of spirit, plenty of soul, he has n't what I call a heart. He has something that Miss Garland took for one, and I 'm pretty sure she 's a judge. But she judged on scanty evidence. He has something that Christina Light, here, makes believe at times that she takes for one, but she is no judge at all! I think it is established that, in the long run, egotism makes a failure in conduct: is it also true that it makes a failure in the arts?... Roderick's standard is immensely high; I must do him that justice. He will do nothing beneath it, and while he is waiting for inspiration, his imagination, his nerves, his senses must have something to amuse them. This is a highly philosophical way of saying that he has taken to dissipation, and that he has just been spending a month at Naples—a city where 'pleasure' is actively cultivated—in very bad company. Are they all like that, all the men of genius? There are a great many artists here who hammer away at their trade with exemplary industry; in fact I am surprised at their success in reducing the matter to a steady, daily grind: but I really don't think that one of them has his exquisite quality of talent. It is in the matter of quantity that he has broken down. The bottle won't pour; he turns it upside down; it 's no use! Sometimes he declares it 's empty—that he has done all he was made to do. This I consider great nonsense; but I would nevertheless take him on his own terms if it was only I that was concerned. But I keep thinking of those two praying, trusting neighbors of yours, and I feel wretchedly like a swindler. If his working mood came but once in five years I would willingly wait for it and maintain him in leisure, if need be, in the intervals; but that would be a sorry account to present to them. Five years of this sort of thing, moreover, would effectually settle the question. I wish he were less of a genius and more of a charlatan! He 's too confoundedly all of one piece; he won't throw overboard a grain of the cargo to save the rest. Fancy him thus with all his brilliant personal charm, his handsome head, his careless step, his look as of a nervous nineteenth-century Apollo, and you will understand that there is mighty little comfort in seeing him in a bad way. He was tolerably foolish last summer at Baden Baden, but he got on his feet, and for a while he was steady. Then he began to waver again, and at last toppled over. Now, literally, he 's lying prone. He came into my room last night, miserably tipsy. I assure you, it did n't amuse me..... About Miss Light it 's a long story. She is one of the great beauties of all time, and worth coming barefoot to Rome, like the pilgrims of old, to see. Her complexion, her glance, her step, her dusky tresses, may have been seen before in a goddess, but never in a woman. And you may take this for truth, because I 'm not in love with her. On the contrary! Her education has been simply infernal. She is corrupt, perverse, as proud as the queen of Sheba, and an appalling coquette; but she is generous, and with patience and skill you may enlist her imagination in a good cause as well as in a bad one. The other day I tried to manipulate it a little. Chance offered me an interview to which it was possible to give a serious turn, and I boldly broke ground and begged her to suffer my poor friend to go in peace. After a good deal of finessing she consented, and the next day, with a single word, packed him off to Naples to drown his sorrow in debauchery. I have come to the conclusion that she is more dangerous in her virtuous moods than in her vicious ones, and that she probably has a way of turning her back which is the most provoking thing in the world. She 's an actress, she could n't forego doing the thing dramatically, and it was the dramatic touch that made it fatal. I wished her, of course, to let him down easily; but she desired to have the curtain drop on an attitude, and her attitudes deprive inflammable young artists of their reason..... Roderick made an admirable bust of her at the beginning of the winter, and a dozen women came rushing to him to be done, mutatis mutandis, in the same style. They were all great ladies and ready to take him by the hand, but he told them all their faces did n't interest him, and sent them away vowing his destruction."

At this point of his long effusion, Rowland had paused and put by his letter. He kept it three days and then read it over. He was disposed at first to destroy it, but he decided finally to keep it, in the hope that it might strike a spark of useful suggestion from the flint of Cecilia's good sense. We know he had a talent for taking advice. And then it might be, he reflected, that his cousin's answer would throw some light on Mary Garland's present vision of things. In his altered mood he added these few lines:—

"I unburdened myself the other day of this monstrous load of perplexity; I think it did me good, and I let it stand. I was in a melancholy muddle, and I was trying to work myself free. You know I like discussion, in a quiet way, and there is no one with whom I can have it as quietly as with you, most sagacious of cousins! There is an excellent old lady with whom I often chat, and who talks very much to the point. But Madame Grandoni has disliked Roderick from the first, and if I were to take her advice I would wash my hands of him. You will laugh at me for my long face, but you would do that in any circumstances. I am half ashamed of my letter, for I have a faith in my friend that is deeper than my doubts. He was here last evening, talking about the Naples Museum, the Aristides, the bronzes, the Pompeian frescoes, with such a beautiful intelligence that doubt of the ultimate future seemed blasphemy. I walked back to his lodging with him, and he was as mild as midsummer moonlight. He has the ineffable something that charms and convinces; my last word about him shall not be a harsh one."

Shortly after sending his letter, going one day into his friend's studio, he found Roderick suffering from the grave infliction of a visit from Mr. Leavenworth. Roderick submitted with extreme ill grace to being bored, and he was now evidently in a state of high exasperation. He had lately begun a representation of a lazzarone lounging in the sun; an image of serene, irresponsible, sensuous life. The real lazzarone, he had admitted, was a vile fellow; but the ideal lazzarone—and his own had been subtly idealized—was a precursor of the millennium.

Mr. Leavenworth had apparently just transferred his unhurrying gaze to the figure.

"Something in the style of the Dying Gladiator?" he sympathetically observed.

"Oh no," said Roderick seriously, "he 's not dying, he 's only drunk!"

"Ah, but intoxication, you know," Mr. Leavenworth rejoined, "is not a proper subject for sculpture. Sculpture should not deal with transitory attitudes."

"Lying dead drunk is not a transitory attitude! Nothing is more permanent, more sculpturesque, more monumental!"

"An entertaining paradox," said Mr. Leavenworth, "if we had time to exercise our wits upon it. I remember at Florence an intoxicated figure by Michael Angelo which seemed to me a deplorable aberration of a great mind. I myself touch liquor in no shape whatever. I have traveled through Europe on cold water. The most varied and attractive lists of wines are offered me, but I brush them aside. No cork has ever been drawn at my command!"

"The movement of drawing a cork calls into play a very pretty set of muscles," said Roderick. "I think I will make a figure in that position."

"A Bacchus, realistically treated! My dear young friend, never trifle with your lofty mission. Spotless marble should represent virtue, not vice!" And Mr. Leavenworth placidly waved his hand, as if to exorcise the spirit of levity, while his glance journeyed with leisurely benignity to another object—a marble replica of the bust of Miss Light. "An ideal head, I presume," he went on; "a fanciful representation of one of the pagan goddesses—a Diana, a Flora, a naiad or dryad? I often regret that our American artists should not boldly cast off that extinct nomenclature."

"She is neither a naiad nor a dryad," said Roderick, "and her name is as good as yours or mine."

"You call her"—Mr. Leavenworth blandly inquired.

"Miss Light," Rowland interposed, in charity.

"Ah, our great American beauty! Not a pagan goddess—an American, Christian lady! Yes, I have had the pleasure of conversing with Miss Light. Her conversational powers are not remarkable, but her beauty is of a high order. I observed her the other evening at a large party, where some of the proudest members of the European aristocracy were present—duchesses, princesses, countesses, and others distinguished by similar titles. But for beauty, grace, and elegance my fair countrywoman left them all nowhere. What women can compare with a truly refined American lady? The duchesses the other night had no attractions for my eyes; they looked coarse and sensual! It seemed to me that the tyranny of class distinctions must indeed be terrible when such countenances could inspire admiration. You see more beautiful girls in an hour on Broadway than in the whole tour of Europe. Miss Light, now, on Broadway, would excite no particular remark."

"She has never been there!" cried Roderick, triumphantly.

"I 'm afraid she never will be there. I suppose you have heard the news about her."

"What news?" Roderick had stood with his back turned, fiercely poking at his lazzarone; but at Mr. Leavenworth's last words he faced quickly about.

"It 's the news of the hour, I believe. Miss Light is admired by the highest people here. They tacitly recognize her superiority. She has had offers of marriage from various great lords. I was extremely happy to learn this circumstance, and to know that they all had been left sighing. She has not been dazzled by their titles and their gilded coronets. She has judged them simply as men, and found them wanting. One of them, however, a young Neapolitan prince, I believe, has after a long probation succeeded in making himself acceptable. Miss Light has at last said yes, and the engagement has just been announced. I am not generally a retailer of gossip of this description, but the fact was alluded to an hour ago by a lady with whom I was conversing, and here, in Europe, these conversational trifles usurp the lion's share of one's attention. I therefore retained the circumstance. Yes, I regret that Miss Light should marry one of these used-up foreigners. Americans should stand by each other. If she wanted a brilliant match we could have fixed it for her. If she wanted a fine fellow—a fine, sharp, enterprising modern man—I would have undertaken to find him for her without going out of the city of New York. And if she wanted a big fortune, I would have found her twenty that she would have had hard work to spend: money down—not tied up in fever-stricken lands and worm-eaten villas! What is the name of the young man? Prince Castaway, or some such thing!"

It was well for Mr. Leavenworth that he was a voluminous and imperturbable talker; for the current of his eloquence floated him past the short, sharp, startled cry with which Roderick greeted his "conversational trifle." The young man stood looking at him with parted lips and an excited eye.

"The position of woman," Mr. Leavenworth placidly resumed, "is certainly a very degraded one in these countries. I doubt whether a European princess can command the respect which in our country is exhibited toward the obscurest females. The civilization of a country should be measured by the deference shown to the weaker sex. Judged by that standard, where are they, over here?"

Though Mr. Leavenworth had not observed Roderick's emotion, it was not lost upon Rowland, who was making certain uncomfortable reflections upon it. He saw that it had instantly become one with the acute irritation produced by the poor gentleman's oppressive personality, and that an explosion of some sort was imminent. Mr. Leavenworth, with calm unconsciousness, proceeded to fire the mine.

"And now for our Culture!" he said in the same sonorous tones, demanding with a gesture the unveiling of the figure, which stood somewhat apart, muffled in a great sheet.

Roderick stood looking at him for a moment with concentrated rancor, and then strode to the statue and twitched off the cover. Mr. Leavenworth settled himself into his chair with an air of flattered proprietorship, and scanned the unfinished image. "I can conscientiously express myself as gratified with the general conception," he said. "The figure has considerable majesty, and the countenance wears a fine, open expression. The forehead, however, strikes me as not sufficiently intellectual. In a statue of Culture, you know, that should be the great point. The eye should instinctively seek the forehead. Could n't you heighten it up a little?"

Roderick, for all answer, tossed the sheet back over the statue. "Oblige me, sir," he said, "oblige me! Never mention that thing again."

"Never mention it? Why my dear sir"—

"Never mention it. It 's an abomination!"

"An abomination! My Culture!"

"Yours indeed!" cried Roderick. "It 's none of mine. I disown it."

"Disown it, if you please," said Mr. Leavenworth sternly, "but finish it first!"

"I 'd rather smash it!" cried Roderick.

"This is folly, sir. You must keep your engagements."

"I made no engagement. A sculptor is n't a tailor. Did you ever hear of inspiration? Mine is dead! And it 's no laughing matter. You yourself killed it."

"I—I—killed your inspiration?" cried Mr. Leavenworth, with the accent of righteous wrath. "You 're a very ungrateful boy! If ever I encouraged and cheered and sustained any one, I 'm sure I have done so to you."

"I appreciate your good intentions, and I don't wish to be uncivil. But your encouragement is—superfluous. I can't work for you!"

"I call this ill-humor, young man!" said Mr. Leavenworth, as if he had found the damning word.

"Oh, I 'm in an infernal humor!" Roderick answered.

"Pray, sir, is it my infelicitous allusion to Miss Light's marriage?"

"It 's your infelicitous everything! I don't say that to offend you; I beg your pardon if it does. I say it by way of making our rupture complete, irretrievable!"

Rowland had stood by in silence, but he now interfered. "Listen to me," he said, laying his hand on Roderick's arm. "You are standing on the edge of a gulf. If you suffer anything that has passed to interrupt your work on that figure, you take your plunge. It 's no matter that you don't like it; you will do the wisest thing you ever did if you make that effort of will necessary for finishing it. Destroy the statue then, if you like, but make the effort. I speak the truth!"

Roderick looked at him with eyes that still inexorableness made almost tender. "You too!" he simply said.

Rowland felt that he might as well attempt to squeeze water from a polished crystal as hope to move him. He turned away and walked into the adjoining room with a sense of sickening helplessness. In a few moments he came back and found that Mr. Leavenworth had departed—presumably in a manner somewhat portentous. Roderick was sitting with his elbows on his knees and his head in his hands.

Rowland made one more attempt. "You decline to think of what I urge?"

"Absolutely."

"There's one more point—that you shouldn't, for a month, go to Mrs. Light's."

"I go there this evening."

"That too is an utter folly."

"There are such things as necessary follies."

"You are not reflecting; you are speaking in passion."

"Why then do you make me speak?"

Rowland meditated a moment. "Is it also necessary that you should lose the best friend you have?"

Roderick looked up. "That 's for you to settle!"

His best friend clapped on his hat and strode away; in a moment the door closed behind him. Rowland walked hard for nearly a couple of hours. He passed up the Corso, out of the Porta del Popolo and into the Villa Borghese, of which he made a complete circuit. The keenness of his irritation subsided, but it left him with an intolerable weight upon his heart. When dusk had fallen, he found himself near the lodging of his friend Madame Grandoni. He frequently paid her a visit during the hour which preceded dinner, and he now ascended her unilluminated staircase and rang at her relaxed bell-rope with an especial desire for diversion. He was told that, for the moment, she was occupied, but that if he would come in and wait, she would presently be with him. He had not sat musing in the firelight for ten minutes when he heard the jingle of the door-bell and then a rustling and murmuring in the hall. The door of the little saloon opened, but before the visitor appeared he had recognized her voice. Christina Light swept forward, preceded by her poodle, and almost filling the narrow parlor with the train of her dress. She was colored here and there by the flicking firelight.

"They told me you were here," she said simply, as she took a seat.

"And yet you came in? It is very brave," said Rowland.

"You are the brave one, when one thinks of it! Where is the padrona?"

"Occupied for the moment. But she is coming."

"How soon?"

"I have already waited ten minutes; I expect her from moment to moment."

"Meanwhile we are alone?" And she glanced into the dusky corners of the room.

"Unless Stenterello counts," said Rowland.

"Oh, he knows my secrets—unfortunate brute!" She sat silent awhile, looking into the firelight. Then at last, glancing at Rowland, "Come! say something pleasant!" she exclaimed.

"I have been very happy to hear of your engagement."

"No, I don't mean that. I have heard that so often, only since breakfast, that it has lost all sense. I mean some of those unexpected, charming things that you said to me a month ago at Saint Cecilia's."

"I offended you, then," said Rowland. "I was afraid I had."

"Ah, it occurred to you? Why have n't I seen you since?"

"Really, I don't know." And he began to hesitate for an explanation. "I have called, but you have never been at home."

"You were careful to choose the wrong times. You have a way with a poor girl! You sit down and inform her that she is a person with whom a respectable young man cannot associate without contamination; your friend is a very nice fellow, you are very careful of his morals, you wish him to know none but nice people, and you beg me therefore to desist. You request me to take these suggestions to heart and to act upon them as promptly as possible. They are not particularly flattering to my vanity. Vanity, however, is a sin, and I listen submissively, with an immense desire to be just. If I have many faults I know it, in a general way, and I try on the whole to do my best. 'Voyons,' I say to myself, 'it is n't particularly charming to hear one's self made out such a low person, but it is worth thinking over; there 's probably a

540

good deal of truth in it, and at any rate we must be as good a girl as we can. That 's the great point! And then here 's a magnificent chance for humility. If there 's doubt in the matter, let the doubt count against one's self. That is what Saint Catherine did, and Saint Theresa, and all the others, and they are said to have had in consequence the most ineffable joys. Let us go in for a little ineffable joy!' I tried it; I swallowed my rising sobs, I made you my courtesy, I determined I would not be spiteful, nor passionate, nor vengeful, nor anything that is supposed to be particularly feminine. I was a better girl than you made out—better at least than you thought; but I would let the difference go and do magnificently right, lest I should not do right enough. I thought of it a deal for six hours when I know I did n't seem to be, and then at last I did it! Santo Dio!"

"My dear Miss Light, my dear Miss Light!" said Rowland, pleadingly.

"Since then," the young girl went on, "I have been waiting for the ineffable joys. They have n't yet turned up!"

"Pray listen to me!" Rowland urged.

"Nothing, nothing, nothing has come of it. I have passed the dreariest month of my life!"

"My dear Miss Light, you are a very terrible young lady!" cried Rowland.

"What do you mean by that?"

"A good many things. We 'll talk them over. But first, forgive me if I have offended you!"

She looked at him a moment, hesitating, and then thrust her hands into her muff. "That means nothing. Forgiveness is between equals, and you don't regard me as your equal."

"Really, I don't understand!"

Christina rose and moved for a moment about the room. Then turning suddenly, "You don't believe in me!" she cried; "not a grain! I don't know what I would not give to force you to believe in me!"

Rowland sprang up, protesting, but before he had time to go far one of the scanty portieres was raised, and Madame Grandoni came in, pulling her wig straight. "But you shall believe in me yet," murmured Christina, as she passed toward her hostess.

Madame Grandoni turned tenderly to Christina. "I must give you a very solemn kiss, my dear; you are the heroine of the hour. You have really accepted him, eh?"

"So they say!"

"But you ought to know best."

"I don't know—I don't care!" She stood with her hand in Madame Grandoni's, but looking askance at Rowland.

"That 's a pretty state of mind," said the old lady, "for a young person who is going to become a princess."

Christina shrugged her shoulders. "Every one expects me to go into ecstacies over that! Could anything be more vulgar? They may chuckle by themselves! Will you let me stay to dinner?"

"If you can dine on a risotto. But I imagine you are expected at home."

"You are right. Prince Casamassima dines there, en famille. But I 'm not in his family, yet!"

"Do you know you are very wicked? I have half a mind not to keep you."

Christina dropped her eyes, reflectively. "I beg you will let me stay," she said. "If you wish to cure me of my wickedness you must be very patient and kind with me. It will be worth the trouble. You must show confidence in me." And she gave another glance at Rowland. Then suddenly, in a different tone, "I don't know what I 'm saying!" she cried. "I am weary, I am more lonely than ever, I wish I were dead!" The tears rose to her eyes, she struggled with them an instant, and buried her face in her muff; but at last she burst into uncontrollable sobs and flung her arms upon Madame Grandoni's neck. This shrewd woman gave Rowland a significant nod, and a little shrug, over the young girl's beautiful bowed head, and then led Christina tenderly away into the adjoining room. Rowland, left alone, stood there for an instant, intolerably puzzled, face to face with Miss Light's poodle, who had set up a sharp, unearthly cry of sympathy with his mistress. Rowland vented his confusion in dealing a rap with his stick at the animal's unmelodious muzzle, and then rapidly left the house. He saw Mrs. Light's carriage waiting at the door, and heard afterwards that Christina went home to dinner.

A couple of days later he went, for a fortnight, to Florence. He had twenty minds to leave Italy altogether; and at Florence he could at least more freely decide upon his future movements. He felt profoundly, incurably disgusted. Reflective benevolence stood prudently aside, and for the time touched the source of his irritation with no softening side-lights.

It was the middle of March, and by the middle of March in Florence the spring is already warm and deep. He had an infinite relish for the place and the season, but as he strolled by the Arno and paused here and there in the great galleries, they failed to soothe his irritation. He was sore at heart, and as the days went by the soreness deepened rather than healed. He felt as if he had a complaint against fortune; good-natured as he was, his good-nature this time quite declined to let it pass. He had tried to be wise, he had tried to be kind, he had embarked upon an estimable enterprise; but his wisdom, his kindness, his energy, had been thrown back in his face. He was disappointed, and his disappointment had an angry spark in it. The sense of wasted time, of wasted hope and faith, kept him constant company. There were times when the beautiful things about him only exasperated his discontent. He went to the Pitti Palace, and Raphael's Madonna of the Chair seemed, in its soft serenity, to mock him with the suggestion of unattainable repose. He lingered on the bridges at sunset, and knew that the light was enchanting and the mountains divine, but there seemed to be something horribly invidious and unwelcome in the fact. He felt, in a word, like a man who has been cruelly defrauded and who wishes to have his revenge. Life owed him, he thought, a compensation, and he would be restless and resentful until he found it. He knew—or he seemed to know—where he should find it; but he hardly told himself, and thought of the thing under mental protest, as a man in want of money may think of certain funds that he holds in trust. In his melancholy meditations the idea of something better than all this, something that might softly, richly interpose, something that might reconcile him to the future, something that might make one's tenure of life deep and zealous instead of harsh and uneven—the idea of concrete compensation, in a word—shaped itself sooner or later into the image of Mary Garland.

Very odd, you may say, that at this time of day Rowland should still be brooding over a plain girl of whom he had had but the lightest of glimpses two years before; very odd that so deep an impression should have been made by so lightly-pressed an instrument. We must admit the oddity and offer simply in explanation that his sentiment apparently belonged to that species of emotion of which, by the testimony of the poets, the very name and essence is oddity. One night he slept but half an hour; he found his thoughts taking a turn which excited him portentously. He walked up and down his room half the night. It looked out on the Arno; the noise of the river came in at the open window; he felt like dressing and going down into the streets. Toward morning he flung himself into a chair; though he was wide awake he was less excited. It seemed to him that he saw his idea from the outside, that he judged it and condemned it; yet it stood there before him, distinct, and in a certain way imperious. During the day he tried to banish it and forget it; but it fascinated, haunted, at moments frightened him. He tried to amuse himself, paid visits, resorted to several rather violent devices for diverting his thoughts. If on the morrow he had committed a crime, the persons whom he had seen that day would have testified that he had talked strangely and had not seemed like himself. He felt certainly very unlike himself; long afterwards, in retrospect, he used to reflect that during those days he had for a while been literally beside himself. His idea persisted; it clung to him like a sturdy beggar. The sense of the matter, roughly expressed, was this: If Roderick was really going, as he himself had phrased it, to "fizzle out," one might help him on the way—one might smooth the descensus Averno. For forty-eight hours there swam before Rowland's eyes a vision of Roderick, graceful and beautiful as he passed, plunging, like a diver, from an eminence into a misty gulf. The gulf was destruction, annihilation, death; but if death was decreed, why should not the agony be brief? Beyond this vision there faintly glimmered another, as in the children's game of the "magic lantern" a picture is superposed on the white wall before the last one has quite faded. It represented Mary Garland standing there with eyes in which the horror seemed slowly, slowly to expire, and hanging, motionless hands which at last made no resistance when his own offered to take them. When, of old, a man was burnt at the stake it was cruel to have to be present; but if one was present it was kind to lend a hand to pile up the fuel and make the flames do their work quickly and the smoke muffle up the victim. With all deference to your kindness, this was perhaps an obligation you would especially feel if you had a reversionary interest in something the victim was to leave behind him.

One morning, in the midst of all this, Rowland walked heedlessly out of one of the city gates and found himself on the road to Fiesole. It was a completely lovely day; the March sun felt like May, as the English poet of Florence says; the thick-blossomed shrubs and vines that hung over the walls of villa and podere flung their odorous promise into the warm, still air. Rowland followed the winding, climbing lanes; lingered, as he got higher, beneath the rusty cypresses, beside the low parapets, where you look down on the charming city and sweep the vale of the Arno; reached the little square before the cathedral, and rested awhile in the massive, dusky church; then climbed higher, to the Franciscan convent which is poised on the very apex of the mountain. He rang at the little gateway; a shabby, senile, red-faced brother admitted him with almost maudlin friendliness. There was a dreary chill in the chapel and the corridors, and he passed rapidly through them into the delightfully steep and tangled old garden which runs wild over the forehead of the great hill. He had been in it before, and he was very fond of it. The garden hangs in the air, and you ramble from terrace to terrace and wonder how it keeps from slipping down, in full consummation of its bereaved forlornness, into the nakedly romantic gorge beneath. It was just noon when Rowland went in, and after roaming about awhile he flung himself in the sun on a mossy stone bench and pulled his hat over his eyes. The short shadows of the brown-coated cypresses above him had grown very long, and yet he had not passed back through the convent. One of the monks, in his faded snuff-colored robe, came wandering out into the garden, reading his greasy little breviary. Suddenly he came toward the bench on which Rowland had stretched himself, and paused a moment, attentively. Rowland was lingering there still; he was sitting with his head in his hands and his elbows on his knees. He seemed not to have heard the sandaled tread of the good brother, but as the monk remained watching him, he at last looked up. It was not the ignoble old man who had admitted him, but a pale, gaunt personage, of a graver and more ascetic, and yet of a benignant, aspect. Rowland's face bore the traces of extreme trouble. The frate kept his finger in his little book, and folded his arms picturesquely across his breast. It can hardly be determined whether his attitude, as he bent his sympathetic Italian eye upon Rowland, was a happy accident or the result of an exquisite spiritual discernment. To Rowland, at any rate, under the emotion of that moment, it seemed blessedly opportune. He rose and approached the monk, and laid his hand on his arm.

"My brother," he said, "did you ever see the Devil?"

The frate gazed, gravely, and crossed himself. "Heaven forbid!"

"He was here," Rowland went on, "here in this lovely garden, as he was once in Paradise, half an hour ago. But have no fear; I drove him out." And Rowland stooped and picked up his hat, which had rolled away into a bed of cyclamen, in vague symbolism of an actual physical tussle.

"You have been tempted, my brother?" asked the friar, tenderly.

"Hideously!"

"And you have resisted—and conquered!"

"I believe I have conquered."

"The blessed Saint Francis be praised! It is well done. If you like, we will offer a mass for you."

"I am not a Catholic," said Rowland.

The frate smiled with dignity. "That is a reason the more."

"But it 's for you, then, to choose. Shake hands with me," Rowland added; "that will do as well; and suffer me, as I go out, to stop a moment in your chapel."

They shook hands and separated. The frate crossed himself, opened his book, and wandered away, in relief against the western sky. Rowland passed back into the convent, and paused long enough in the chapel to look for the alms-box. He had had what is vulgarly termed a great scare; he believed, very poignantly for the time, in the Devil, and he felt an irresistible need to subscribe to any institution which engaged to keep him at a distance.

The next day he returned to Rome, and the day afterwards he went in search of Roderick. He found him on the Pincian with his back turned to the crowd, looking at the sunset. "I went to Florence," Rowland said, "and I thought of going farther; but I came back on purpose to give you another piece of advice. Once more, you refuse to leave Rome?"

"Never!" said Roderick.

"The only chance that I see, then, of your reviving your sense of responsibility to—to those various sacred things you have forgotten, is in sending for your mother to join you here."

Roderick stared. "For my mother?"

"For your mother—and for Miss Garland."

Roderick still stared; and then, slowly and faintly, his face flushed. "For Mary Garland—for my mother?" he repeated. "Send for them?"

"Tell me this; I have often wondered, but till now I have forborne to ask. You are still engaged to Miss Garland?"

Roderick frowned darkly, but assented.

"It would give you pleasure, then, to see her?"

Roderick turned away and for some moments answered nothing. "Pleasure!" he said at last, huskily. "Call it pain."

"I regard you as a sick man," Rowland continued. "In such a case Miss Garland would say that her place was at your side."

Roderick looked at him some time askance, mistrustfully. "Is this a deep-laid snare?" he asked slowly.

Rowland had come back with all his patience rekindled, but these words gave it an almost fatal chill. "Heaven forgive you!" he cried bitterly. "My idea has been simply this. Try, in decency, to understand it. I have tried to befriend you, to help you, to inspire you with confidence, and I have failed. I took you from the hands of your mother and your betrothed, and it seemed to me my duty to restore you to their hands. That 's all I have to say."

He was going, but Roderick forcibly detained him. It would have been but a rough way of expressing it to say that one could never know how Roderick would take a thing. It had happened more than once that when hit hard, deservedly, he had received the blow with touching gentleness. On the other hand, he had often resented the softest taps. The secondary effect of Rowland's present admonition seemed reassuring. "I beg you to wait," he said, "to forgive that shabby speech, and to let me reflect." And he walked up and down awhile, reflecting. At last he stopped, with a look in his face that Rowland had not seen all winter. It was a strikingly beautiful look.

"How strange it is," he said, "that the simplest devices are the last that occur to one!" And he broke into a light laugh. "To see Mary Garland is just what I want. And my mother—my mother can't hurt me now."

"You will write, then?"

"I will telegraph. They must come, at whatever cost. Striker can arrange it all for them."

In a couple of days he told Rowland that he had received a telegraphic answer to his message, informing him that the two ladies were to sail immediately for Leghorn, in one of the small steamers which ply between that port and New York. They would arrive, therefore, in less than a month. Rowland passed this month of expectation in no very serene frame of mind. His suggestion had had its source in the deepest places of his agitated conscience; but there was something intolerable in the thought of the suffering to which the event was probably subjecting those undefended women. They had scraped together their scanty funds and embarked, at twenty-four hours' notice, upon the dreadful sea, to journey tremulously to shores darkened by the shadow of deeper alarms. He could only promise himself to be their devoted friend and servant. Preoccupied as he was, he was able to observe that expectation, with Roderick, took a form which seemed singular even among his characteristic singularities. If redemption—Roderick seemed to reason—was to arrive with his mother and his affianced bride, these last moments of error should be doubly erratic. He did nothing; but inaction, with him, took on an unwonted air of gentle gayety. He laughed and whistled and went often to Mrs. Light's; though Rowland knew not in what fashion present circumstances had modified his relations with Christina. The month ebbed away and Rowland daily expected to hear from Roderick that he had gone to Leghorn to meet the ship. He heard nothing, and late one evening, not having seen his friend in three or four days, he stopped at Roderick's lodging to assure himself that he had gone at last. A cab was standing in the street, but as it was a couple of doors off he hardly heeded it. The hall at the foot of the staircase was dark, like most Roman halls, and he paused in the street-doorway on hearing the advancing footstep of a person with whom he wished to avoid coming into collision. While he did so he heard another footstep behind him, and turning round found that Roderick in person had just overtaken him. At the same moment a woman's figure advanced from within, into the light of the street-lamp, and a face, half-startled, glanced at him out of the darkness. He gave a cry—it was the face of Mary Garland. Her glance flew past him to Roderick, and in a second a startled exclamation broke from her own lips. It made Rowland turn again. Roderick stood there, pale, apparently trying to speak, but saying nothing. His lips were parted and he was wavering slightly with a strange movement—the movement of a man who has drunk too much. Then Rowland's eyes met Miss Garland's again, and her own, which had rested a moment on Roderick's, were formidable!

CHAPTER IX. Mary Garland

How it befell that Roderick had failed to be in Leghorn on his mother's arrival never clearly transpired; for he undertook to give no elaborate explanation of his fault. He never indulged in professions (touching personal conduct) as to the future, or in remorse as to the past, and as he would have asked no praise if he had traveled night and day to embrace his mother as she set foot on shore, he made (in Rowland's presence, at least) no apology for having left her to come in search of him. It was to be said that, thanks to an unprecedentedly fine season, the voyage of the two ladies had been surprisingly rapid, and that, according to common probabilities, if Roderick had left Rome on the morrow (as he declared that he had intended), he would have had a day or two of waiting at Leghorn. Rowland's silent inference was that Christina Light had beguiled him into letting the time slip, and it was accompanied with a silent inquiry whether she had done so unconsciously or maliciously. He had told her, presumably, that his mother and his cousin were about to arrive; and it was pertinent to remember hereupon that she was a young lady of mysterious impulses. Rowland heard in due time the story of the adventures of the two ladies from Northampton. Miss Garland's wish, at Leghorn, on finding they were left at the mercy of circumstances, had been to telegraph to Roderick and await an answer; for she knew that their arrival was a trifle premature. But Mrs. Hudson's maternal heart had taken the alarm. Roderick's sending for them was, to her imagination, a confession of illness, and his not being at Leghorn, a proof of it; an hour's delay was therefore cruel both to herself and to him. She insisted on immediate departure; and, unskilled as they were in the mysteries of foreign (or even of domestic) travel, they had hurried in trembling eagerness to Rome. They had arrived late in the evening, and, knowing nothing of inns, had got into a cab and proceeded to Roderick's lodging. At the door, poor Mrs. Hudson's frightened anxiety had overcome her, and she had sat quaking and crying in the vehicle, too weak to move. Miss Garland had bravely gone in, groped her way up the dusky staircase, reached Roderick's door, and, with the assistance of such acquaintance with the Italian tongue as she had culled from a phrase-book during the calmer hours of the voyage, had learned from the old woman who had her cousin's household economy in charge that he was in the best of health and spirits, and had gone forth a few hours before with his hat on his ear, per divertirsi.

These things Rowland learned during a visit he paid the two ladies the evening after their arrival. Mrs. Hudson spoke of them at great length and with an air of clinging confidence in Rowland which told him how faithfully time had served him, in her imagination. But her fright was over, though she was still catching her breath a little, like a person dragged ashore out of waters uncomfortably deep. She was excessively bewildered and confused, and seemed more than ever to demand a tender handling from her friends. Before Miss Garland, Rowland was distinctly conscious that he trembled. He wondered extremely what was going on in her mind; what was her silent commentary on the incidents of the night before. He wondered all the more, because he immediately perceived that she was greatly changed since their parting, and that the change was by no means for the worse. She was older, easier, more free, more like a young woman who went sometimes into company. She had more beauty as well, inasmuch as her beauty before had been the depth of her expression, and the sources from which this beauty was fed had in these two years evidently not wasted themselves. Rowland felt almost instantly—he could hardly have said why: it was in her voice, in her tone, in the air—that a total change had passed over her attitude towards himself. She trusted him now, absolutely; whether or no she liked him, she believed he was solid. He felt that during the coming weeks he would need to be solid. Mrs. Hudson was at one of the smaller hotels, and her sitting-room was frugally lighted by a couple of candles. Rowland made the most of this dim illumination to try to detect the afterglow of that frightened flash from Miss Garland's eyes the night before. It had been but a flash, for what provoked it had instantly vanished. Rowland had murmured a rapturous blessing on Roderick's head, as he perceived him instantly apprehend the situation. If he had been drinking, its gravity sobered him on the spot; in a single moment he collected his wits. The next moment, with a ringing, jovial cry, he was folding the young girl in his arms, and the next he was beside his mother's carriage, half smothered in her sobs and caresses. Rowland had recommended a hotel close at hand, and had then discreetly withdrawn. Roderick was at this time doing his part superbly, and Miss Garland's brow was serene. It was serene now, twenty-four hours later; but nevertheless, her alarm had lasted an appreciable moment. What had become of it? It had dropped down deep into her memory, and it was lying there for the present in the shade. But with another week, Rowland said to himself, it would leap erect again; the lightest friction would strike a spark from it. Rowland thought he had schooled himself to face the issue of Mary Garland's advent, casting it even in a tragic phase; but in her personal presence—in which he found a poignant mixture of the familiar and the strange—he seemed to face it and all that it might bring with it for the first time. In vulgar parlance, he stood uneasy in his shoes. He felt like walking on tiptoe, not to arouse the sleeping shadows. He felt, indeed, almost like saying that they might have their own way later, if they would only allow to these first few days the clear light of ardent contemplation. For Rowland at last was ardent, and all the bells within his soul were ringing bravely in jubilee. Roderick, he learned, had been the whole day with his mother, and had evidently responded to her purest trust. He appeared to her appealing eyes still unspotted by the world. That is what it is, thought Rowland, to be "gifted," to escape not only the superficial, but the intrinsic penalties of misconduct. The two ladies had spent the day within doors, resting from the fatigues of travel. Miss Garland, Rowland suspected, was not so fatigued as she suffered it to be assumed. She had remained with Mrs. Hudson, to attend to her personal wants, which the latter seemed to think, now that she was in a foreign land, with a southern climate and a Catholic religion, would forthwith become very complex and formidable, though as yet they had simply resolved themselves into a desire for a great deal of tea and for a certain extremely familiar old black and white shawl across her feet, as she lay on the sofa. But the sense of novelty was evidently strong upon Miss Garland, and the light of expectation was in her eye. She was restless and excited; she moved about the room and went often to the window; she was observing keenly; she watched the Italian servants intently, as they came and went; she had already had a long colloquy with the French chambermaid, who had expounded her views on the Roman question; she noted the small differences in the furniture, in the food, in the sounds that came in from the street. Rowland felt, in all this, that her intelligence, here, would have a great unfolding. He wished immensely he might have a share in it; he wished he might show her Rome. That, of course, would be Roderick's office. But he promised himself at least to take advantage of off-hours.

"It behooves you to appreciate your good fortune," he said to her. "To be young and elastic, and yet old enough and wise enough to discriminate and reflect, and to come to Italy for the first time—that is one of the greatest pleasures that life offers us. It is but right to remind you of it, so that you make the most of opportunity and do not accuse yourself, later, of having wasted the precious season."

Miss Garland looked at him, smiling intently, and went to the window again. "I expect to enjoy it," she said. "Don't be afraid; I am not wasteful."

"I am afraid we are not qualified, you know," said Mrs. Hudson. "We are told that you must know so much, that you must have read so many books. Our taste has not been cultivated. When I was a young lady at school, I remember I had a medal, with a pink ribbon, for 'proficiency in Ancient History'—the seven kings, or is it the seven hills? and Quintus Curtius and Julius Caesar and—and that period, you know. I believe I have my medal somewhere in a drawer, now, but I have forgotten all about the kings. But after Roderick came to Italy we tried to learn something about it. Last winter Mary used to read 'Corinne' to me in the evenings, and in the mornings she used to read another book, to herself. What was it, Mary, that book that was so long, you know,—in fifteen volumes?"

"It was Sismondi's Italian Republics," said Mary, simply.

Rowland could not help laughing; whereupon Mary blushed. "Did you finish it?" he asked.

"Yes, and began another—a shorter one—Roscoe's Leo the Tenth."

"Did you find them interesting?"

"Oh yes."

"Do you like history?"

"Some of it."

"That 's a woman's answer! And do you like art?"

She paused a moment. "I have never seen it!"

"You have great advantages, now, my dear, with Roderick and Mr. Mallet," said Mrs. Hudson. "I am sure no young lady ever had such advantages. You come straight to the highest authorities. Roderick, I suppose, will show you the practice of art, and Mr. Mallet, perhaps, if he will be so good, will show you the theory. As an artist's wife, you ought to know something about it."

"One learns a good deal about it, here, by simply living," said Rowland; "by going and coming about one's daily avocations."

"Dear, dear, how wonderful that we should be here in the midst of it!" murmured Mrs. Hudson. "To think of art being out there in the streets! We did n't see much of it last evening, as we drove from the depot. But the streets were so dark and we were so frightened! But we are very easy now; are n't we, Mary?"

"I am very happy," said Mary, gravely, and wandered back to the window again.

Roderick came in at this moment and kissed his mother, and then went over and joined Miss Garland. Rowland sat with Mrs. Hudson, who evidently had a word which she deemed of some value for his private ear. She followed Roderick with intensely earnest eyes.

"I wish to tell you, sir," she said, "how very grateful—how very thankful—what a happy mother I am! I feel as if I owed it all to you, sir. To find my poor boy so handsome, so prosperous, so elegant, so famous—and ever to have doubted of you! What must you think of me? You 're our guardian angel, sir. I often say so to Mary."

Rowland wore, in response to this speech, a rather haggard brow. He could only murmur that he was glad she found Roderick looking well. He had of course promptly asked himself whether the best discretion dictated that he should give her a word of warning—just turn the handle of the door through which, later, disappointment might enter. He had determined to say nothing, but simply to wait in silence for Roderick to find effective inspiration in those confidently expectant eyes. It was to be supposed that he was seeking for it now; he remained sometime at the window with his cousin. But at last he turned away and came over to the fireside with a contraction of the eyebrows which seemed to intimate that Miss Garland's influence was for the moment, at least, not soothing. She presently followed him, and for an instant Rowland observed her watching him as if she thought him strange. "Strange enough," thought Rowland, "he may seem to her, if he will!" Roderick directed his glance to his friend with a certain peremptory air, which—roughly interpreted—was equivalent to a request to share the intellectual expense of entertaining the ladies. "Good heavens!" Rowland cried within himself; "is he already tired of them?"

"To-morrow, of course, we must begin to put you through the mill," Roderick said to his mother. "And be it hereby known to Mallet that we count upon him to turn the wheel."

"I will do as you please, my son," said Mrs. Hudson. "So long as I have you with me I don't care where I go. We must not take up too much of Mr. Mallet's time."

"His time is inexhaustible; he has nothing under the sun to do. Have you, Rowland? If you had seen the big hole I have been making in it! Where will you go first? You have your choice—from the Scala Santa to the Cloaca Maxima."

"Let us take things in order," said Rowland. "We will go first to Saint Peter's. Miss Garland, I hope you are impatient to see Saint Peter's."

"I would like to go first to Roderick's studio," said Miss Garland.

"It's a very nasty place," said Roderick. "At your pleasure!"

"Yes, we must see your beautiful things before we can look contentedly at anything else," said Mrs. Hudson.

555

"I have no beautiful things," said Roderick. "You may see what there is! What makes you look so odd?"

This inquiry was abruptly addressed to his mother, who, in response, glanced appealingly at Mary and raised a startled hand to her smooth hair.

"No, it 's your face," said Roderick. "What has happened to it these two years? It has changed its expression."

"Your mother has prayed a great deal," said Miss Garland, simply.

"I did n't suppose, of course, it was from doing anything bad! It makes you a very good face—very interesting, very solemn. It has very fine lines in it; something might be done with it." And Rowland held one of the candles near the poor lady's head.

She was covered with confusion. "My son, my son," she said with dignity, "I don't understand you."

In a flash all his old alacrity had come to him. "I suppose a man may admire his own mother!" he cried. "If you please, madame, you 'll sit to me for that head. I see it, I see it! I will make something that a queen can't get done for her."

Rowland respectfully urged her to assent; he saw Roderick was in the vein and would probably do something eminently original. She gave her promise, at last, after many soft, inarticulate protests and a frightened petition that she might be allowed to keep her knitting.

Rowland returned the next day, with plenty of zeal for the part Roderick had assigned to him. It had been arranged that they should go to Saint Peter's. Roderick was in high good-humor, and, in the carriage, was watching his mother with a fine mixture of filial and professional tenderness. Mrs. Hudson looked up mistrustfully at the tall, shabby houses, and grasped the side of the barouche in her hand, as if she were in a sail-boat, in dangerous waters. Rowland sat opposite to Miss Garland. She was totally oblivious of her companions; from the moment the carriage left the hotel, she sat gazing, wide-eyed and absorbed, at the objects about them. If Rowland had felt disposed he might have made a joke of her intense seriousness. From time to time he told her the name of a place or a building, and she nodded, without looking at him. When they emerged into the great square between Bernini's colonnades, she laid her hand on Mrs. Hudson's arm and sank back in the carriage, staring up at the vast yellow facade of the church. Inside the church, Roderick gave his arm to his mother, and Rowland constituted himself the especial guide of Miss Garland. He walked with her slowly everywhere, and made the entire circuit, telling her all he knew of the history of the building. This was a great deal, but she listened attentively, keeping her eyes fixed on the dome. To Rowland himself it had never seemed so radiantly sublime as at these moments; he felt almost as if he had contrived it himself and had a right to be proud of it. He left Miss Garland a while on the steps of the choir, where she had seated herself to rest, and went to join their companions. Mrs. Hudson was watching a great circle of tattered contadini, who were kneeling before the image of Saint Peter. The fashion of their tatters fascinated her; she stood gazing at them in a sort of terrified pity, and could not be induced to look at anything else. Rowland went back to Miss Garland and sat down beside her.

"Well, what do you think of Europe?" he asked, smiling.

"I think it 's horrible!" she said abruptly.

"Horrible?"

"I feel so strangely—I could almost cry."

"How is it that you feel?"

"So sorry for the poor past, that seems to have died here, in my heart, in an hour!"

"But, surely, you 're pleased—you 're interested."

"I am overwhelmed. Here in a single hour, everything is changed. It is as if a wall in my mind had been knocked down at a stroke. Before me lies an immense new world, and it makes the old one, the poor little narrow, familiar one I have always known, seem pitiful."

"But you did n't come to Rome to keep your eyes fastened on that narrow little world. Forget it, turn your back on it, and enjoy all this."

"I want to enjoy it; but as I sat here just now, looking up at that golden mist in the dome, I seemed to see in it the vague shapes of certain people and things at home. To enjoy, as you say, as these things demand of one to enjoy them, is to break with one's past. And breaking is a pain!"

"Don't mind the pain, and it will cease to trouble you. Enjoy, enjoy; it is your duty. Yours especially!"

"Why mine especially?"

"Because I am very sure that you have a mind capable of doing the most liberal justice to everything interesting and beautiful. You are extremely intelligent."

"You don't know," said Miss Garland, simply.

"In that matter one feels. I really think that I know better than you. I don't want to seem patronizing, but I suspect that your mind is susceptible of a great development. Give it the best company, trust it, let it go!"

She looked away from him for some moments, down the gorgeous vista of the great church. "But what you say," she said at last, "means change!"

"Change for the better!" cried Rowland.

"How can one tell? As one stands, one knows the worst. It seems to me very frightful to develop," she added, with her complete smile.

"One is in for it in one way or another, and one might as well do it with a good grace as with a bad! Since one can't escape life, it is better to take it by the hand."

"Is this what you call life?" she asked.

"What do you mean by 'this'?"

"Saint Peter's—all this splendor, all Rome—pictures, ruins, statues, beggars, monks."

"It is not all of it, but it is a large part of it. All these things are impregnated with life; they are the fruits of an old and complex civilization."

"An old and complex civilization: I am afraid I don't like that."

"Don't conclude on that point just yet. Wait till you have tested it. While you wait, you will see an immense number of very beautiful things—things that you are made to understand. They won't leave you as they found you; then you can judge. Don't tell me I know nothing about your understanding. I have a right to assume it."

Miss Garland gazed awhile aloft in the dome. "I am not sure I understand that," she said.

"I hope, at least, that at a cursory glance it pleases you," said Rowland. "You need n't be afraid to tell the truth. What strikes some people is that it is so remarkably small."

"Oh, it's large enough; it's very wonderful. There are things in Rome, then," she added in a moment, turning and looking at him, "that are very, very beautiful?"

"Lots of them."

"Some of the most beautiful things in the world?"

"Unquestionably."

"What are they? which things have most beauty?"

"That is according to taste. I should say the statues."

"How long will it take to see them all? to know, at least, something about them?"

"You can see them all, as far as mere seeing goes, in a fortnight. But to know them is a thing for one's leisure. The more time you spend among them, the more you care for them." After a moment's hesitation he went on: "Why should you grudge time? It 's all in your way, since you are to be an artist's wife."

"I have thought of that," she said. "It may be that I shall always live here, among the most beautiful things in the world!"

"Very possibly! I should like to see you ten years hence."

"I dare say I shall seem greatly altered. But I am sure of one thing."

"Of what?"

"That for the most part I shall be quite the same. I ask nothing better than to believe the fine things you say about my understanding, but even if they are true, it won't matter. I shall be what I was made, what I am now—a young woman from the country! The fruit of a civilization not old and complex, but new and simple."

"I am delighted to hear it: that 's an excellent foundation."

"Perhaps, if you show me anything more, you will not always think so kindly of it. Therefore I warn you."

"I am not frightened. I should like vastly to say something to you: Be what you are, be what you choose; but do, sometimes, as I tell you."

If Rowland was not frightened, neither, perhaps, was Miss Garland; but she seemed at least slightly disturbed. She proposed that they should join their companions.

Mrs. Hudson spoke under her breath; she could not be accused of the want of reverence sometimes attributed to Protestants in the great Catholic temples. "Mary, dear," she whispered, "suppose we had to kiss that dreadful brass toe. If I could only have kept our door-knocker, at Northampton, as bright as that! I think it's so heathenish; but Roderick says he thinks it 's sublime."

Roderick had evidently grown a trifle perverse. "It 's sublimer than anything that your religion asks you to do!" he exclaimed.

"Surely our religion sometimes gives us very difficult duties," said Miss Garland.

560

"The duty of sitting in a whitewashed meeting-house and listening to a nasal Puritan! I admit that 's difficult. But it 's not sublime. I am speaking of ceremonies, of forms. It is in my line, you know, to make much of forms. I think this is a very beautiful one. Could n't you do it?" he demanded, looking at his cousin.

She looked back at him intently and then shook her head. "I think not!"

"Why not?"

"I don't know; I could n't!"

During this little discussion our four friends were standing near the venerable image of Saint Peter, and a squalid, savage-looking peasant, a tattered ruffian of the most orthodox Italian aspect, had been performing his devotions before it. He turned away, crossing himself, and Mrs. Hudson gave a little shudder of horror.

"After that," she murmured, "I suppose he thinks he is as good as any one! And here is another. Oh, what a beautiful person!"

A young lady had approached the sacred effigy, after having wandered away from a group of companions. She kissed the brazen toe, touched it with her forehead, and turned round, facing our friends. Rowland then recognized Christina Light. He was stupefied: had she suddenly embraced the Catholic faith? It was but a few weeks before that she had treated him to a passionate profession of indifference. Had she entered the church to put herself en regle with what was expected of a Princess Casamassima? While Rowland was mentally asking these questions she was approaching him and his friends, on her way to the great altar. At first she did not perceive them.

Mary Garland had been gazing at her. "You told me," she said gently, to Rowland, "that Rome contained some of the most beautiful things in the world. This surely is one of them!"

At this moment Christina's eye met Rowland's and before giving him any sign of recognition she glanced rapidly at his companions. She saw Roderick, but she gave him no bow; she looked at Mrs. Hudson, she looked at Mary

Garland. At Mary Garland she looked fixedly, piercingly, from head to foot, as the slow pace at which she was advancing made possible. Then suddenly, as if she had perceived Roderick for the first time, she gave him a charming nod, a radiant smile. In a moment he was at her side. She stopped, and he stood talking to her; she continued to look at Miss Garland.

"Why, Roderick knows her!" cried Mrs. Hudson, in an awe-struck whisper. "I supposed she was some great princess."

"She is—almost!" said Rowland. "She is the most beautiful girl in Europe, and Roderick has made her bust."

"Her bust? Dear, dear!" murmured Mrs. Hudson, vaguely shocked. "What a strange bonnet!"

"She has very strange eyes," said Mary, and turned away.

The two ladies, with Rowland, began to descend toward the door of the church. On their way they passed Mrs. Light, the Cavaliere, and the poodle, and Rowland informed his companions of the relation in which these personages stood to Roderick's young lady.

"Think of it, Mary!" said Mrs. Hudson. "What splendid people he must know! No wonder he found Northampton dull!"

"I like the poor little old gentleman," said Mary.

"Why do you call him poor?" Rowland asked, struck with the observation.

"He seems so!" she answered simply.

As they were reaching the door they were overtaken by Roderick, whose interview with Miss Light had perceptibly brightened his eye. "So you are acquainted with princesses!" said his mother softly, as they passed into the portico.

"Miss Light is not a princess!" said Roderick, curtly.

"But Mr. Mallet says so," urged Mrs. Hudson, rather disappointed.

"I meant that she was going to be!" said Rowland.

"It 's by no means certain that she is even going to be!" Roderick answered.

"Ah," said Rowland, "I give it up!"

Roderick almost immediately demanded that his mother should sit to him, at his studio, for her portrait, and Rowland ventured to add another word of urgency. If Roderick's idea really held him, it was an immense pity that his inspiration should be wasted; inspiration, in these days, had become too precious a commodity. It was arranged therefore that, for the present, during the mornings, Mrs. Hudson should place herself at her son's service. This involved but little sacrifice, for the good lady's appetite for antiquities was diminutive and bird-like, the usual round of galleries and churches fatigued her, and she was glad to purchase immunity from sight-seeing by a regular afternoon drive. It became natural in this way that, Miss Garland having her mornings free, Rowland should propose to be the younger lady's guide in whatever explorations she might be disposed to make. She said she knew nothing about it, but she had a great curiosity, and would be glad to see anything that he would show her. Rowland could not find it in his heart to accuse Roderick of neglect of the young girl; for it was natural that the inspirations of a capricious man of genius, when they came, should be imperious; but of course he wondered how Miss Garland felt, as the young man's promised wife, on being thus expeditiously handed over to another man to be entertained. However she felt, he was certain he would know little about it. There had been, between them, none but indirect allusions to her engagement, and Rowland had no desire to discuss it more largely; for he had no quarrel with matters as they stood. They wore the same delightful aspect through the lovely month of May, and the ineffable charm of Rome at that period seemed but the radiant sympathy of nature with his happy opportunity. The weather was divine; each particular morning, as he walked from his lodging to Mrs. Hudson's modest inn, seemed to have a blessing upon it. The elder lady had usually gone off to the studio, and he found Miss Garland sitting alone at the open window, turning the leaves of some book of artistic or antiquarian reference that he had given her. She always had a smile, she was always eager, alert, responsive. She might be grave by nature, she might be sad by circumstance, she might have secret doubts and pangs, but she was essentially young and strong and fresh and able to enjoy. Her enjoyment was not especially demonstrative, but it was curiously diligent. Rowland felt that it was not amusement and sensation that she coveted, but knowledge—facts that she might noiselessly lay away, piece by piece, in the perfumed darkness of her serious mind, so that, under this head at least, she should not be a perfectly portionless bride. She never merely pretended to understand; she let things go, in her modest fashion, at the moment, but she watched them on their way, over the crest of the hill, and when her fancy seemed not likely to be missed it went hurrying after them and ran breathless at their side, as it were, and begged them for the secret. Rowland took an immense satisfaction in observing that she never mistook the second-best for the best, and that when she was in the presence of a masterpiece, she recognized the occasion as a mighty one. She said many things which he thought very profound—that is, if they really had the fine intention he suspected. This point he usually tried to ascertain; but he was obliged to proceed cautiously, for in her mistrustful shyness it seemed to her that cross-examination must necessarily be ironical. She wished to know just where she was going—what she would gain or lose. This was partly on account of a native intellectual purity, a temper of mind that had not lived with its door ajar, as one might say, upon the high-road of thought, for passing ideas to drop in and out at their pleasure; but had made much of a few long visits from guests cherished and honored—guests whose presence was a solemnity. But it was even more because she was conscious of a sort of growing self-respect, a sense of devoting her life not to her own ends, but to those of another, whose life would be large and brilliant. She had been brought up to think a great deal of "nature" and nature's innocent laws; but now Rowland had spoken to her ardently of culture; her strenuous fancy had responded, and she was pursuing culture into retreats where the need for some intellectual effort gave a noble severity to her purpose. She wished to be very sure, to take only the best, knowing it to be the best. There was something exquisite in this labor of pious self-adornment, and Rowland helped it, though its fruits were not for him. In spite of her lurking rigidity and angularity, it was very evident that a nervous, impulsive sense of beauty was constantly at play in her soul, and that her actual experience of beautiful things moved her in some very deep places. For all that she was not demonstrative, that her manner was simple, and her small-talk of no very ample flow; for all that, as she had said, she was a young woman from the country, and the country was West Nazareth, and West Nazareth was in its way a stubborn little fact, she was feeling the direct influence of the great amenities of the world, and they were shaping her with a divinely intelligent touch. "Oh exquisite virtue of circumstance!" cried Rowland to himself, "that takes us by the hand and leads us forth out of corners where, perforce, our attitudes are a trifle contracted, and beguiles us into testing mistrusted faculties!" When he said to Mary Garland that he wished he might see her ten years hence, he was paying mentally an equal compliment to circumstance and to the girl herself. Capacity was there, it could be freely trusted; observation would have but to sow its generous seed. "A superior woman"—the idea had harsh associations, but he watched it imaging itself in the vagueness of the future with a kind of hopeless confidence.

They went a great deal to Saint Peter's, for which Rowland had an exceeding affection, a large measure of which he succeeded in infusing into his companion. She confessed very speedily that to climb the long, low, yellow steps, beneath the huge florid facade, and then to push the ponderous leathern apron of the door, to find one's self confronted with that builded, luminous sublimity, was a sensation of which the keenness renewed itself with surprising generosity. In those days the hospitality of the Vatican had not been curtailed, and it was an easy and delightful matter to pass from the gorgeous church to the solemn company of the antique marbles. Here Rowland had with his companion a great deal of talk, and found himself expounding aesthetics a perte de vue. He discovered that she made notes of her likes and dislikes in a new-looking little memorandum book, and he wondered to what extent she reported his own discourse. These were charming hours. The galleries had been so cold all winter that Rowland had been an exile from them; but now that the sun was already scorching in the great square between the colonnades, where the twin fountains flashed almost fiercely, the marble coolness of the long, image-bordered vistas made them a delightful refuge. The great herd of tourists had almost departed, and our two friends often found themselves, for half an hour at a time, in sole and tranquil possession of the beautiful Braccio Nuovo. Here and there was an open window, where they lingered and leaned, looking out into the warm, dead air, over the towers of the city, at the soft-hued, historic hills, at the stately shabby gardens of the palace, or at some sunny, empty, grass-grown court, lost in the heart of the labyrinthine pile. They went sometimes into the chambers painted by Raphael, and of course paid their respects to the Sistine Chapel; but Mary's evident preference was to linger among the statues. Once, when they were standing before that noblest of sculptured portraits, the so-called Demosthenes, in the Braccio Nuovo, she made the only spontaneous allusion to her projected marriage, direct or indirect, that had yet fallen from her lips. "I am so glad," she said, "that Roderick is a sculptor and not a painter."

The allusion resided chiefly in the extreme earnestness with which the words were uttered. Rowland immediately asked her the reason of her gladness.

"It 's not that painting is not fine," she said, "but that sculpture is finer. It is more manly."

Rowland tried at times to make her talk about herself, but in this she had little skill. She seemed to him so much older, so much more pliant to social uses than when he had seen her at home, that he had a desire to draw from her some categorical account of her occupation and thoughts. He told her his desire and what suggested it. "It appears, then," she said, "that, after all, one can grow at home!"

"Unquestionably, if one has a motive. Your growth, then, was unconscious? You did not watch yourself and water your roots?"

She paid no heed to his question. "I am willing to grant," she said, "that Europe is more delightful than I supposed; and I don't think that, mentally, I had been stingy. But you must admit that America is better than you have supposed."

"I have not a fault to find with the country which produced you!" Rowland thought he might risk this, smiling.

"And yet you want me to change—to assimilate Europe, I suppose you would call it."

"I have felt that desire only on general principles. Shall I tell you what I feel now? America has made you thus far; let America finish you! I should like to ship you back without delay and see what becomes of you. That sounds unkind, and I admit there is a cold intellectual curiosity in it."

She shook her head. "The charm is broken; the thread is snapped! I prefer to remain here."

Invariably, when he was inclined to make of something they were talking of a direct application to herself, she wholly failed to assist him; she made no response. Whereupon, once, with a spark of ardent irritation, he told her she was very "secretive." At this she colored a little, and he said that in default of any larger confidence it would at least be a satisfaction to make her confess to that charge. But even this satisfaction she denied him, and his only revenge was in making, two or three times afterward, a softly ironical allusion to her slyness. He told her that she was what is called in French a sournoise. "Very good," she answered, almost indifferently, "and now please tell me again—I have forgotten it—what you said an 'architrave' was."

It was on the occasion of her asking him a question of this kind that he charged her, with a humorous emphasis in which, also, if she had been curious in the matter, she might have detected a spark of restless ardor, with having an insatiable avidity for facts. "You are always snatching at information," he said; "you will never consent to have any disinterested conversation."

She frowned a little, as she always did when he arrested their talk upon something personal. But this time she assented, and said that she knew she was eager for facts. "One must make hay while the sun shines," she added. "I must lay up a store of learning against dark days. Somehow, my imagination refuses to compass the idea that I may be in Rome indefinitely."

He knew he had divined her real motives; but he felt that if he might have said to her—what it seemed impossible to say—that fortune possibly had in store for her a bitter disappointment, she would have been capable of answering, immediately after the first sense of pain, "Say then that I am laying up resources for solitude!"

But all the accusations were not his. He had been watching, once, during some brief argument, to see whether she would take her forefinger out of her Murray, into which she had inserted it to keep a certain page. It would have been hard to say why this point interested him, for he had not the slightest real apprehension that she was dry or pedantic. The simple human truth was, the poor fellow was jealous of science. In preaching science to her, he had over-estimated his powers of self-effacement. Suddenly, sinking science for the moment, she looked at him very frankly and began to frown. At the same time she let the Murray slide down to the ground, and he was so charmed with this circumstance that he made no movement to pick it up.

"You are singularly inconsistent, Mr. Mallet," she said.

"How?"

"That first day that we were in Saint Peter's you said things that inspired me. You bade me plunge into all this. I was all ready; I only wanted a little push; yours was a great one; here I am in mid-ocean! And now, as a reward for my bravery, you have repeatedly snubbed me."

"Distinctly, then," said Rowland, "I strike you as inconsistent?"

"That is the word."

"Then I have played my part very ill."

"Your part? What is your part supposed to have been?"

He hesitated a moment. "That of usefulness, pure and simple."

"I don't understand you!" she said; and picking up her Murray, she fairly buried herself in it.

That evening he said something to her which necessarily increased her perplexity, though it was not uttered with such an intention. "Do you remember," he asked, "my begging you, the other day, to do occasionally as I told you? It seemed to me you tacitly consented."

"Very tacitly."

"I have never yet really presumed on your consent. But now I would like you to do this: whenever you catch me in the act of what you call inconsistency, ask me the meaning of some architectural term. I will know what you mean; a word to the wise!"

One morning they spent among the ruins of the Palatine, that sunny desolation of crumbling, over-tangled fragments, half excavated and half identified, known as the Palace of the Caesars. Nothing in Rome is more interesting, and no locality has such a confusion of picturesque charms. It is a vast, rambling garden, where you stumble at every step on the disinterred bones of the past; where damp, frescoed corridors, relics, possibly, of Nero's Golden House, serve as gigantic bowers, and where, in the springtime, you may sit on a Latin inscription, in the shade of a flowering almond-tree, and admire the composition of the Campagna. The day left a deep impression on Rowland's mind, partly owing to its intrinsic sweetness, and partly because his companion, on this occasion, let her Murray lie unopened for an hour, and asked several questions irrelevant to the Consuls and the Caesars. She had begun by saying that it was coming over her, after all, that Rome was a ponderously sad place. The sirocco was gently blowing, the air was heavy, she was tired, she looked a little pale.

"Everything," she said, "seems to say that all things are vanity. If one is doing something, I suppose one feels a certain strength within one to contradict it. But if one is idle, surely it is depressing to live, year after year, among the ashes of things that once were mighty. If I were to remain here I should either become permanently 'low,' as they say, or I would take refuge in some dogged daily work."

"What work?"

"I would open a school for those beautiful little beggars; though I am sadly afraid I should never bring myself to scold them."

"I am idle," said Rowland, "and yet I have kept up a certain spirit."

"I don't call you idle," she answered with emphasis.

569

"It is very good of you. Do you remember our talking about that in Northampton?"

"During that picnic? Perfectly. Has your coming abroad succeeded, for yourself, as well as you hoped?"

"I think I may say that it has turned out as well as I expected."

"Are you happy?"

"Don't I look so?"

"So it seems to me. But"—and she hesitated a moment—"I imagine you look happy whether you are so or not."

"I 'm like that ancient comic mask that we saw just now in yonder excavated fresco: I am made to grin."

"Shall you come back here next winter?"

"Very probably."

"Are you settled here forever?"

"'Forever' is a long time. I live only from year to year."

"Shall you never marry?"

Rowland gave a laugh. "'Forever'—'never!' You handle large ideas. I have not taken a vow of celibacy."

"Would n't you like to marry?"

"I should like it immensely."

To this she made no rejoinder: but presently she asked, "Why don't you write a book?"

Rowland laughed, this time more freely. "A book! What book should I write?"

"A history; something about art or antiquities."

"I have neither the learning nor the talent."

She made no attempt to contradict him; she simply said she had supposed otherwise. "You ought, at any rate," she continued in a moment, "to do something for yourself."

"For myself? I should have supposed that if ever a man seemed to live for himself"—

"I don't know how it seems," she interrupted, "to careless observers. But we know—we know that you have lived—a great deal—for us."

Her voice trembled slightly, and she brought out the last words with a little jerk.

"She has had that speech on her conscience," thought Rowland; "she has been thinking she owed it to me, and it seemed to her that now was her time to make it and have done with it."

She went on in a way which confirmed these reflections, speaking with due solemnity. "You ought to be made to know very well what we all feel. Mrs. Hudson tells me that she has told you what she feels. Of course Roderick has expressed himself. I have been wanting to thank you too; I do, from my heart."

Rowland made no answer; his face at this moment resembled the tragic mask much more than the comic. But Miss Garland was not looking at him; she had taken up her Murray again.

In the afternoon she usually drove with Mrs. Hudson, but Rowland frequently saw her again in the evening. He was apt to spend half an hour in the little sitting-room at the hotel-pension on the slope of the Pincian, and Roderick, who dined regularly with his mother, was present on these occasions. Rowland saw him little at other times, and for three weeks no observations passed between them on the subject of Mrs. Hudson's advent. To Rowland's vision, as the weeks elapsed, the benefits to proceed from the presence of the two ladies remained shrouded in mystery. Roderick was peculiarly inscrutable. He was preoccupied with his work on his mother's portrait, which was taking a very happy turn; and often, when he sat silent, with his hands in his pockets, his legs outstretched, his head thrown back, and his eyes on vacancy, it was to be supposed that his fancy was hovering about the half-shaped image in his studio, exquisite even in its immaturity. He said little, but his silence did not of necessity imply disaffection, for he evidently found it a deep personal luxury to lounge away the hours in an atmosphere so charged with feminine tenderness. He was not alert, he suggested nothing in the way of excursions (Rowland was the prime mover in such as were attempted), but he conformed passively at least to the tranquil temper of the two women, and made no harsh comments nor sombre allusions. Rowland wondered whether he had, after all, done his friend injustice in denying him the sentiment of duty. He refused invitations, to Rowland's knowledge, in order to dine at the jejune little table-d'hote; wherever his spirit might be, he was present in the flesh with religious constancy. Mrs. Hudson's felicity betrayed itself in a remarkable tendency to finish her sentences and wear her best black silk gown. Her tremors had trembled away; she was like a child who discovers that the shaggy monster it has so long been afraid to touch is an inanimate terror, compounded of straw and saw-dust, and that it is even a safe audacity to tickle its nose. As to whether the love-knot of which Mary Garland had the keeping still held firm, who should pronounce? The young girl, as we know, did not wear it on her sleeve. She always sat at the table, near the candles, with a piece of needle-work. This was the attitude in which Rowland had first seen her, and he thought, now that he had seen her in several others, it was not the least becoming.

CHAPTER X. The Cavaliere

There befell at last a couple of days during which Rowland was unable to go to the hotel. Late in the evening of the second one Roderick came into his room. In a few moments he announced that he had finished the bust of his mother.

"And it 's magnificent!" he declared. "It 's one of the best things I have done."

"I believe it," said Rowland. "Never again talk to me about your inspiration being dead."

"Why not? This may be its last kick! I feel very tired. But it 's a masterpiece, though I do say it. They tell us we owe so much to our parents. Well, I 've paid the filial debt handsomely!" He walked up and down the room a few moments, with the purpose of his visit evidently still undischarged. "There 's one thing more I want to say," he presently resumed. "I feel as if I ought to tell you!" He stopped before Rowland with his head high and his brilliant glance unclouded. "Your invention is a failure!"

"My invention?" Rowland repeated.

"Bringing out my mother and Mary."

"A failure?"

"It 's no use! They don't help me."

Rowland had fancied that Roderick had no more surprises for him; but he was now staring at him, wide-eyed.

"They bore me!" Roderick went on.

"Oh, oh!" cried Rowland.

"Listen, listen!" said Roderick with perfect gentleness. "I am not complaining of them; I am simply stating a fact. I am very sorry for them; I am greatly disappointed."

"Have you given them a fair trial?"

"Should n't you say so? It seems to me I have behaved beautifully."

"You have done very well; I have been building great hopes on it."

"I have done too well, then. After the first forty-eight hours my own hopes collapsed. But I determined to fight it out; to stand within the temple; to let the spirit of the Lord descend! Do you want to know the result? Another week of it, and I shall begin to hate them. I shall want to poison them."

"Miserable boy!" cried Rowland. "They are the loveliest of women!"

"Very likely! But they mean no more to me than a Bible text to an atheist!"

"I utterly fail," said Rowland, in a moment, "to understand your relation to Miss Garland."

Roderick shrugged his shoulders and let his hands drop at his sides. "She adores me! That 's my relation." And he smiled strangely.

"Have you broken your engagement?"

"Broken it? You can't break a ray of moonshine."

"Have you absolutely no affection for her?"

Roderick placed his hand on his heart and held it there a moment. "Dead—dead—dead!" he said at last.

"I wonder," Rowland asked presently, "if you begin to comprehend the beauty of Miss Garland's character. She is a person of the highest merit."

"Evidently—or I would not have cared for her!"

"Has that no charm for you now?"

"Oh, don't force a fellow to say rude things!"

"Well, I can only say that you don't know what you are giving up."

Roderick gave a quickened glance. "Do you know, so well?"

"I admire her immeasurably."

Roderick smiled, we may almost say sympathetically. "You have not wasted time."

Rowland's thoughts were crowding upon him fast. If Roderick was resolute, why oppose him? If Mary was to be sacrificed, why, in that way, try to save her? There was another way; it only needed a little presumption to make it possible. Rowland tried, mentally, to summon presumption to his aid; but whether it came or not, it found conscience there before it. Conscience had only three words, but they were cogent. "For her sake—for her sake," it dumbly murmured, and Rowland resumed his argument. "I don't know what I would n't do," he said, "rather than that Miss Garland should suffer."

"There is one thing to be said," Roderick answered reflectively. "She is very strong."

"Well, then, if she 's strong, believe that with a longer chance, a better chance, she will still regain your affection."

"Do you know what you ask?" cried Roderick. "Make love to a girl I hate?"

"You hate?"

"As her lover, I should hate her!"

"Listen to me!" said Rowland with vehemence.

"No, listen you to me! Do you really urge my marrying a woman who would bore me to death? I would let her know it in very good season, and then where would she be?"

Rowland walked the length of the room a couple of times and then stopped suddenly. "Go your way, then! Say all this to her, not to me!"

"To her? I am afraid of her; I want you to help me."

"My dear Roderick," said Rowland with an eloquent smile, "I can help you no more!"

Roderick frowned, hesitated a moment, and then took his hat. "Oh, well," he said, "I am not so afraid of her as all that!" And he turned, as if to depart.

"Stop!" cried Rowland, as he laid his hand on the door.

Roderick paused and stood waiting, with his irritated brow.

"Come back; sit down there and listen to me. Of anything you were to say in your present state of mind you would live most bitterly to repent. You don't know what you really think; you don't know what you really feel. You don't know your own mind; you don't do justice to Miss Garland. All this is impossible here, under these circumstances. You 're blind, you 're deaf, you 're under a spell. To break it, you must leave Rome."

"Leave Rome! Rome was never so dear to me."

"That 's not of the smallest consequence. Leave it instantly."

"And where shall I go?"

"Go to some place where you may be alone with your mother and Miss Garland."

"Alone? You will not come?"

"Oh, if you desire it, I will come."

Roderick inclining his head a little, looked at his friend askance. "I don't understand you," he said; "I wish you liked Miss Garland either a little less, or a little more."

Rowland felt himself coloring, but he paid no heed to Roderick's speech. "You ask me to help you," he went on. "On these present conditions I can do nothing. But if you will postpone all decision as to the continuance of your engagement a couple of months longer, and meanwhile leave Rome, leave Italy, I will do what I can to 'help you,' as you say, in the event of your still wishing to break it."

"I must do without your help then! Your conditions are impossible. I will leave Rome at the time I have always intended—at the end of June. My

576

rooms and my mother's are taken till then; all my arrangements are made accordingly. Then, I will depart; not before."

"You are not frank," said Rowland. "Your real reason for staying has nothing to do with your rooms."

Roderick's face betrayed neither embarrassment nor resentment. "If I 'm not frank, it 's for the first time in my life. Since you know so much about my real reason, let me hear it! No, stop!" he suddenly added, "I won't trouble you. You are right, I have a motive. On the twenty-fourth of June Miss Light is to be married. I take an immense interest in all that concerns her, and I wish to be present at her wedding."

"But you said the other day at Saint Peter's that it was by no means certain her marriage would take place."

"Apparently I was wrong: the invitations, I am told, are going out."

Rowland felt that it would be utterly vain to remonstrate, and that the only thing for him was to make the best terms possible. "If I offer no further opposition to your waiting for Miss Light's marriage," he said, "will you promise, meanwhile and afterwards, for a certain period, to defer to my judgment—to say nothing that may be a cause of suffering to Miss Garland?"

"For a certain period? What period?" Roderick demanded.

"Ah, don't drive so close a bargain! Don't you understand that I have taken you away from her, that I suffer in every nerve in consequence, and that I must do what I can to restore you?"

"Do what you can, then," said Roderick gravely, putting out his hand. "Do what you can!" His tone and his hand-shake seemed to constitute a promise, and upon this they parted.

Roderick's bust of his mother, whether or no it was a discharge of what he called the filial debt, was at least a most admirable production. Rowland, at the time it was finished, met Gloriani one evening, and this unscrupulous genius immediately began to ask questions about it. "I am told our high-flying friend has come down," he said. "He has been doing a queer little old woman."

"A queer little old woman!" Rowland exclaimed. "My dear sir, she is Hudson's mother."

"All the more reason for her being queer! It is a bust for terra-cotta, eh?"

"By no means; it is for marble."

"That's a pity. It was described to me as a charming piece of quaintness: a little demure, thin-lipped old lady, with her head on one side, and the prettiest wrinkles in the world—a sort of fairy godmother."

"Go and see it, and judge for yourself," said Rowland.

"No, I see I shall be disappointed. It 's quite the other thing, the sort of thing they put into the campo-santos. I wish that boy would listen to me an hour!"

But a day or two later Rowland met him again in the street, and, as they were near, proposed they should adjourn to Roderick's studio. He consented, and on entering they found the young master. Roderick's demeanor to Gloriani was never conciliatory, and on this occasion supreme indifference was apparently all he had to offer. But Gloriani, like a genuine connoisseur, cared nothing for his manners; he cared only for his skill. In the bust of Mrs. Hudson there was something almost touching; it was an exquisite example of a ruling sense of beauty. The poor lady's small, neat, timorous face had certainly no great character, but Roderick had reproduced its sweetness, its mildness, its minuteness, its still maternal passion, with the most unerring art. It was perfectly unflattered, and yet admirably tender; it was the poetry of fidelity. Gloriani stood looking at it a long time most intently. Roderick wandered away into the neighboring room.

"I give it up!" said the sculptor at last. "I don't understand it."

"But you like it?" said Rowland.

"Like it? It 's a pearl of pearls. Tell me this," he added: "is he very fond of his mother; is he a very good son?" And he gave Rowland a sharp look.

"Why, she adores him," said Rowland, smiling.

"That 's not an answer! But it 's none of my business. Only if I, in his place, being suspected of having—what shall I call it?—a cold heart, managed to do that piece of work, oh, oh! I should be called a pretty lot of names. Charlatan, poseur, arrangeur! But he can do as he chooses! My dear young man, I know you don't like me," he went on, as Roderick came back. "It 's a pity; you are strong enough not to care about me at all. You are very strong."

"Not at all," said Roderick curtly. "I am very weak!"

"I told you last year that you would n't keep it up. I was a great ass. You will!"

"I beg your pardon—I won't!" retorted Roderick.

"Though I 'm a great ass, all the same, eh? Well, call me what you will, so long as you turn out this sort of thing! I don't suppose it makes any particular difference, but I should like to say now I believe in you."

Roderick stood looking at him for a moment with a strange hardness in his face. It flushed slowly, and two glittering, angry tears filled his eyes. It was the first time Rowland had ever seen them there; he saw them but once again. Poor Gloriani, he was sure, had never in his life spoken with less of irony; but to Roderick there was evidently a sense of mockery in his profession of faith. He turned away with a muttered, passionate imprecation. Gloriani was accustomed to deal with complex problems, but this time he was hopelessly puzzled. "What 's the matter with him?" he asked, simply.

Rowland gave a sad smile, and touched his forehead. "Genius, I suppose."

Gloriani sent another parting, lingering look at the bust of Mrs. Hudson. "Well, it 's deuced perfect, it 's deuced simple; I do believe in him!" he said. "But I 'm glad I 'm not a genius. It makes," he added with a laugh, as he looked for Roderick to wave him good-by, and saw his back still turned, "it makes a more sociable studio."

Rowland had purchased, as he supposed, temporary tranquillity for Mary Garland; but his own humor in these days was not especially peaceful. He was attempting, in a certain sense, to lead the ideal life, and he found it, at the least, not easy. The days passed, but brought with them no official invitation to Miss Light's wedding. He occasionally met her, and he occasionally met Prince Casamassima; but always separately, never together. They were apparently taking their happiness in the inexpressive manner proper to people of social eminence. Rowland continued to see Madame Grandoni, for whom he felt a confirmed affection. He had always talked to her with frankness, but now he made her a confidant of all his hidden dejection. Roderick and Roderick's concerns had been a common theme with him, and it was in the natural course to talk of Mrs. Hudson's arrival and Miss Garland's fine smile. Madame Grandoni was an intelligent listener, and she lost no time in putting his case for him in a nutshell. "At one moment you tell me the girl is plain," she said; "the next you tell me she 's pretty. I will invite them, and I shall see for myself. But one thing is very clear: you are in love with her."

Rowland, for all answer, glanced round to see that no one heard her.

"More than that," she added, "you have been in love with her these two years. There was that certain something about you!... I knew you were a mild, sweet fellow, but you had a touch of it more than was natural. Why did n't you tell me at once? You would have saved me a great deal of trouble. And poor Augusta Blanchard too!" And herewith Madame Grandoni communicated a pertinent fact: Augusta Blanchard and Mr. Leavenworth were going to make a match. The young lady had been staying for a month at Albano, and Mr. Leavenworth had been dancing attendance. The event was a matter of course. Rowland, who had been lately reproaching himself with a failure of attention to Miss Blanchard's doings, made some such observation.

"But you did not find it so!" cried his hostess. "It was a matter of course, perhaps, that Mr. Leavenworth, who seems to be going about Europe with the sole view of picking up furniture for his 'home,' as he calls it, should think Miss Blanchard a very handsome piece; but it was not a matter of course—or it need n't have been—that she should be willing to become a sort of superior table-ornament. She would have accepted you if you had tried."

"You are supposing the insupposable," said Rowland. "She never gave me a particle of encouragement."

"What would you have had her do? The poor girl did her best, and I am sure that when she accepted Mr. Leavenworth she thought of you."

"She thought of the pleasure her marriage would give me."

"Ay, pleasure indeed! She is a thoroughly good girl, but she has her little grain of feminine spite, like the rest. Well, he 's richer than you, and she will have what she wants; but before I forgive you I must wait and see this new arrival—what do you call her?—Miss Garland. If I like her, I will forgive you; if I don't, I shall always bear you a grudge."

Rowland answered that he was sorry to forfeit any advantage she might offer him, but that his exculpatory passion for Miss Garland was a figment of her fancy. Miss Garland was engaged to another man, and he himself had no claims.

"Well, then," said Madame Grandoni, "if I like her, we 'll have it that you ought to be in love with her. If you fail in this, it will be a double misdemeanor. The man she 's engaged to does n't care a straw for her. Leave me alone and I 'll tell her what I think of you."

As to Christina Light's marriage, Madame Grandoni could make no definite statement. The young girl, of late, had made her several flying visits, in the intervals of the usual pre-matrimonial shopping and dress-fitting; she had spoken of the event with a toss of her head, as a matter which, with a wise old friend who viewed things in their essence, she need not pretend to treat as a solemnity. It was for Prince Casamassima to do that. "It is what they call a marriage of reason," she once said. "That means, you know, a marriage of madness!"

"What have you said in the way of advice?" Rowland asked.

"Very little, but that little has favored the prince. I know nothing of the mysteries of the young lady's heart. It may be a gold-mine, but at any rate it 's a mine, and it 's a long journey down into it. But the marriage in itself is an excellent marriage. It 's not only brilliant, but it 's safe. I think Christina is quite capable of making it a means of misery; but there is no position that would be sacred to her. Casamassima is an irreproachable young man;

there is nothing against him but that he is a prince. It is not often, I fancy, that a prince has been put through his paces at this rate. No one knows the wedding-day; the cards of invitation have been printed half a dozen times over, with a different date; each time Christina has destroyed them. There are people in Rome who are furious at the delay; they want to get away; they are in a dreadful fright about the fever, but they are dying to see the wedding, and if the day were fixed, they would make their arrangements to wait for it. I think it very possible that after having kept them a month and produced a dozen cases of malaria, Christina will be married at midnight by an old friar, with simply the legal witnesses."

"It is true, then, that she has become a Catholic?"

"So she tells me. One day she got up in the depths of despair; at her wit's end, I suppose, in other words, for a new sensation. Suddenly it occurred to her that the Catholic church might after all hold the key, might give her what she wanted! She sent for a priest; he happened to be a clever man, and he contrived to interest her. She put on a black dress and a black lace veil, and looking handsomer than ever she rustled into the Catholic church. The prince, who is very devout, and who had her heresy sorely on his conscience, was thrown into an ecstasy. May she never have a caprice that pleases him less!"

Rowland had already asked Madame Grandoni what, to her perception, was the present state of matters between Christina and Roderick; and he now repeated his question with some earnestness of apprehension. "The girl is so deucedly dramatic," he said, "that I don't know what coup de theatre she may have in store for us. Such a stroke was her turning Catholic; such a stroke would be her some day making her courtesy to a disappointed world as Princess Casamassima, married at midnight, in her bonnet. She might do— she may do—something that would make even more starers! I 'm prepared for anything."

"You mean that she might elope with your sculptor, eh?"

"I 'm prepared for anything!"

"Do you mean that he 's ready?"

"Do you think that she is?"

"They 're a precious pair! I think this. You by no means exhaust the subject when you say that Christina is dramatic. It 's my belief that in the course of her life she will do a certain number of things from pure disinterested passion. She 's immeasurably proud, and if that is often a fault in a virtuous person, it may be a merit in a vicious one. She needs to think well of herself; she knows a fine character, easily, when she meets one; she hates to suffer by comparison, even though the comparison is made by herself alone; and when the estimate she may have made of herself grows vague, she needs to do something to give it definite, impressive form. What she will do in such a case will be better or worse, according to her opportunity; but I imagine it will generally be something that will drive her mother to despair; something of the sort usually termed 'unworldly.'"

Rowland, as he was taking his leave, after some further exchange of opinions, rendered Miss Light the tribute of a deeply meditative sigh. "She has bothered me half to death," he said, "but somehow I can't manage, as I ought, to hate her. I admire her, half the time, and a good part of the rest I pity her."

"I think I most pity her!" said Madame Grandoni.

This enlightened woman came the next day to call upon the two ladies from Northampton. She carried their shy affections by storm, and made them promise to drink tea with her on the evening of the morrow. Her visit was an era in the life of poor Mrs. Hudson, who did nothing but make sudden desultory allusions to her, for the next thirty-six hours. "To think of her being a foreigner!" she would exclaim, after much intent reflection, over her knitting; "she speaks so beautifully!" Then in a little while, "She was n't so much dressed as you might have expected. Did you notice how easy it was in the waist? I wonder if that 's the fashion?" Or, "She 's very old to wear a hat; I should never dare to wear a hat!" Or, "Did you notice her hands?—very pretty hands for such a stout person. A great many rings, but nothing very handsome. I suppose they are hereditary." Or, "She 's certainly not handsome, but she 's very sweet-looking. I wonder why she does n't have something done to her teeth." Rowland also received a summons to Madame Grandoni's tea-drinking, and went betimes, as he had been requested. He was eagerly desirous to lend his mute applause to Mary Garland's debut in the Roman social world. The two ladies had arrived, with Roderick, silent and careless, in attendance. Miss Blanchard was also present, escorted by Mr. Leavenworth, and the party was completed by a dozen artists of both sexes and various nationalities. It was a friendly and easy assembly, like all Madame Grandoni's parties, and in the course of the evening there was some excellent music. People played and sang for Madame Grandoni, on easy terms, who, elsewhere, were not to be heard for the asking. She was herself a superior musician, and singers found it a privilege to perform to her accompaniment. Rowland talked to various persons, but for the first time in his life his attention visibly wandered; he could not keep his eyes off Mary Garland. Madame Grandoni had said that he sometimes spoke of her as pretty and sometimes as plain; to-night, if he had had occasion to describe her appearance, he would have called her beautiful. She was dressed more than he had ever seen her; it was becoming, and gave her a deeper color and an ampler presence. Two or three persons were introduced to her who were apparently witty people, for she sat listening to them with her brilliant natural smile. Rowland, from an opposite corner, reflected that he had never varied in his appreciation of Miss Blanchard's classic contour, but that somehow, to-night, it impressed him hardly more than an effigy stamped upon a coin of low value. Roderick could not be accused of rancor, for he had approached Mr. Leavenworth with unstudied familiarity, and, lounging against the wall, with hands in pockets, was discoursing to him with candid serenity. Now that he had done him an impertinence, he evidently found him less intolerable. Mr. Leavenworth stood stirring his tea and silently opening and shutting his mouth, without looking at the young sculptor, like a large, drowsy dog snapping at flies. Rowland had found it disagreeable to be told Miss Blanchard would have married him for the asking, and he would have felt some embarrassment in going to speak to her if his modesty had not found incredulity so easy. The facile side of a union with Miss Blanchard had never been present to his mind; it had struck him as a thing, in all ways, to be compassed with a great effort. He had half an hour's talk with her; a farewell talk, as it seemed to him—a farewell not to a real illusion, but to the idea that for him, in that matter, there could ever be an acceptable pis-aller. He congratulated Miss Blanchard upon her engagement, and she received his compliment with a touch of primness. But she was always a trifle prim, even when she was quoting Mrs. Browning and George Sand, and this harmless defect did not prevent her responding on this occasion that Mr. Leavenworth had a "glorious heart." Rowland wished to manifest an extreme regard, but toward the end of the talk his zeal relaxed, and he fell a-thinking that a certain natural ease in a woman was the most delightful thing in the world. There was Christina Light, who had too much, and here was Miss Blanchard, who had too little, and there was Mary Garland (in whom the quality was wholly uncultivated), who had just the right amount.

He went to Madame Grandoni in an adjoining room, where she was pouring out tea.

"I will make you an excellent cup," she said, "because I have forgiven you."

He looked at her, answering nothing; but he swallowed his tea with great gusto, and a slight deepening of his color; by all of which one would have known that he was gratified. In a moment he intimated that, in so far as he had sinned, he had forgiven himself.

"She is a lovely girl," said Madame Grandoni. "There is a great deal there. I have taken a great fancy to her, and she must let me make a friend of her."

"She is very plain," said Rowland, slowly, "very simple, very ignorant."

"Which, being interpreted, means, 'She is very handsome, very subtle, and has read hundreds of volumes on winter evenings in the country.'"

"You are a veritable sorceress," cried Rowland; "you frighten me away!" As he was turning to leave her, there rose above the hum of voices in the drawing-room the sharp, grotesque note of a barking dog. Their eyes met in a glance of intelligence.

"There is the sorceress!" said Madame Grandoni. "The sorceress and her necromantic poodle!" And she hastened back to the post of hospitality.

Rowland followed her, and found Christina Light standing in the middle of the drawing-room, and looking about in perplexity. Her poodle, sitting on his haunches and gazing at the company, had apparently been expressing a sympathetic displeasure at the absence of a welcome. But in a moment Madame Grandoni had come to the young girl's relief, and Christina had tenderly kissed her.

"I had no idea," said Christina, surveying the assembly, "that you had such a lot of grand people, or I would not have come in. The servant said nothing; he took me for an invitee. I came to spend a neighborly half-hour; you know I have n't many left! It was too dismally dreary at home. I hoped I should find you alone, and I brought Stenterello to play with the cat. I don't know that if I had known about all this I would have dared to come in; but since I 've stumbled into the midst of it, I beg you 'll let me stay. I am not dressed, but am I very hideous? I will sit in a corner and no one will notice me. My dear, sweet lady, do let me stay. Pray, why did n't you ask me? I never have been to a little party like this. They must be very charming. No dancing—tea and conversation? No tea, thank you; but if you could spare a biscuit for Stenterello; a sweet biscuit, please. Really, why did n't you ask me? Do you have these things often? Madame Grandoni, it 's very unkind!" And the young girl, who had delivered herself of the foregoing succession of sentences in her usual low, cool, penetrating voice, uttered these last words with a certain tremor of feeling. "I see," she went on, "I do very well for balls and great banquets, but when people wish to have a cosy, friendly, comfortable evening, they leave me out, with the big flower-pots and the gilt candlesticks."

"I 'm sure you 're welcome to stay, my dear," said Madame Grandoni, "and at the risk of displeasing you I must confess that if I did n't invite you, it was because you 're too grand. Your dress will do very well, with its fifty flounces, and there is no need of your going into a corner. Indeed, since you 're here, I propose to have the glory of it. You must remain where my people can see you."

586

"They are evidently determined to do that by the way they stare. Do they think I intend to dance a tarantella? Who are they all; do I know them?" And lingering in the middle of the room, with her arm passed into Madame Grandoni's, she let her eyes wander slowly from group to group. They were of course observing her. Standing in the little circle of lamplight, with the hood of an Eastern burnous, shot with silver threads, falling back from her beautiful head, one hand gathering together its voluminous, shimmering folds, and the other playing with the silken top-knot on the uplifted head of her poodle, she was a figure of radiant picturesqueness. She seemed to be a sort of extemporized tableau vivant. Rowland's position made it becoming for him to speak to her without delay. As she looked at him he saw that, judging by the light of her beautiful eyes, she was in a humor of which she had not yet treated him to a specimen. In a simpler person he would have called it exquisite kindness; but in this young lady's deportment the flower was one thing and the perfume another. "Tell me about these people," she said to him. "I had no idea there were so many people in Rome I had not seen. What are they all talking about? It 's all beyond me, I suppose. There is Miss Blanchard, sitting as usual in profile against a dark object. She is like a head on a postage-stamp. And there is that nice little old lady in black, Mrs. Hudson. What a dear little woman for a mother! Comme elle est proprette! And the other, the fiancee, of course she 's here. Ah, I see!" She paused; she was looking intently at Miss Garland. Rowland measured the intentness of her glance, and suddenly acquired a firm conviction. "I should like so much to know her!" she said, turning to Madame Grandoni. "She has a charming face; I am sure she 's an angel. I wish very much you would introduce me. No, on second thoughts, I had rather you did n't. I will speak to her bravely myself, as a friend of her cousin." Madame Grandoni and Rowland exchanged glances of baffled conjecture, and Christina flung off her burnous, crumpled it together, and, with uplifted finger, tossing it into a corner, gave it in charge to her poodle. He stationed himself upon it, on his haunches, with upright vigilance. Christina crossed the room with the step and smile of a ministering angel, and introduced herself to Mary Garland. She had once told Rowland that she would show him, some day, how gracious her manners could be; she was now redeeming her promise. Rowland, watching her, saw Mary Garland rise slowly, in response to her greeting, and look at her with serious deep-gazing eyes. The almost dramatic opposition of these two keenly interesting girls touched Rowland with a nameless apprehension, and after a moment he preferred to turn away. In doing so he noticed Roderick. The young sculptor was standing planted on the train of a lady's dress, gazing across at Christina's movements with undisguised earnestness. There were several more pieces of music; Rowland sat in a corner and listened to them. When they were over, several people began to take their leave, Mrs. Hudson among the number. Rowland saw her come up to Madame Grandoni, clinging shyly to Mary Garland's arm. Miss Garland had a brilliant eye and a deep color in her cheek. The two ladies looked about for Roderick, but Roderick had his back turned. He had approached Christina, who, with an absent air, was sitting alone, where she had taken her place near Miss Garland, looking at the guests pass out of the room. Christina's eye, like Miss Garland's, was bright, but her cheek was pale. Hearing Roderick's voice, she looked up at him sharply; then silently, with a single quick gesture, motioned him away. He obeyed her, and came and joined his mother in bidding good night to Madame Grandoni. Christina, in a moment, met Rowland's glance, and immediately beckoned him to come to her. He was familiar with her spontaneity of movement, and was scarcely surprised. She made a place for him on the sofa beside her; he wondered what was coming now. He was not sure it was not a mere fancy, but it seemed to him that he had never seen her look just as she was looking then. It was a humble, touching, appealing look, and it threw into wonderful relief the nobleness of her beauty. "How many more metamorphoses," he asked himself, "am I to be treated to before we have done?"

"I want to tell you," said Christina. "I have taken an immense fancy to Miss Garland. Are n't you glad?"

"Delighted!" exclaimed poor Rowland.

"Ah, you don't believe it," she said with soft dignity.

"Is it so hard to believe?"

"Not that people in general should admire her, but that I should. But I want to tell you; I want to tell some one, and I can't tell Miss Garland herself. She thinks me already a horrid false creature, and if I were to express to her frankly what I think of her, I should simply disgust her. She would be quite right; she has repose, and from that point of view I and my doings must seem monstrous. Unfortunately, I have n't repose. I am trembling now; if I could ask you to feel my arm, you would see! But I want to tell you that I admire Miss Garland more than any of the people who call themselves her friends—except of course you. Oh, I know that! To begin with, she is extremely handsome, and she does n't know it."

"She is not generally thought handsome," said Rowland.

"Evidently! That 's the vulgarity of the human mind. Her head has great character, great natural style. If a woman is not to be a supreme beauty in the regular way, she will choose, if she 's wise, to look like that. She 'll not be thought pretty by people in general, and desecrated, as she passes, by the stare of every vile wretch who chooses to thrust his nose under her bonnet; but a certain number of superior people will find it one of the delightful things of life to look at her. That lot is as good as another! Then she has a beautiful character!"

"You found that out soon!" said Rowland, smiling.

"How long did it take you? I found it out before I ever spoke to her. I met her the other day in Saint Peter's; I knew it then. I knew it—do you want to know how long I have known it?"

"Really," said Rowland, "I did n't mean to cross-examine you."

"Do you remember mamma's ball in December? We had some talk and you then mentioned her—not by name. You said but three words, but I saw you admired her, and I knew that if you admired her she must have a beautiful character. That 's what you require!"

"Upon my word," cried Rowland, "you make three words go very far!"

"Oh, Mr. Hudson has also spoken of her."

"Ah, that 's better!" said Rowland.

"I don't know; he does n't like her."

"Did he tell you so?" The question left Rowland's lips before he could stay it, which he would have done on a moment's reflection.

Christina looked at him intently. "No!" she said at last. "That would have been dishonorable, would n't it? But I know it from my knowledge of him. He does n't like perfection; he is not bent upon being safe, in his likings; he 's willing to risk something! Poor fellow, he risks too much!"

Rowland was silent; he did not care for the thrust; but he was profoundly mystified. Christina beckoned to her poodle, and the dog marched stiffly across to her. She gave a loving twist to his rose-colored top-knot, and bade him go and fetch her burnous. He obeyed, gathered it up in his teeth, and returned with great solemnity, dragging it along the floor.

"I do her justice. I do her full justice," she went on, with soft earnestness. "I like to say that, I like to be able to say it. She 's full of intelligence and courage and devotion. She does n't do me a grain of justice; but that is no harm. There is something so fine in the aversions of a good woman!"

"If you would give Miss Garland a chance," said Rowland, "I am sure she would be glad to be your friend."

"What do you mean by a chance? She has only to take it. I told her I liked her immensely, and she frowned as if I had said something disgusting. She looks very handsome when she frowns." Christina rose, with these words, and began to gather her mantle about her. "I don't often like women," she went on. "In fact I generally detest them. But I should like to know Miss Garland well. I should like to have a friendship with her; I have never had one; they must be very delightful. But I shan't have one now, either—not if she can help it! Ask her what she thinks of me; see what she will say. I don't want to know; keep it to yourself. It 's too sad. So we go through life. It 's fatality—that 's what they call it, is n't it? We please the people we don't care for, we displease those we do! But I appreciate her, I do her justice; that 's the more important thing. It 's because I have imagination. She has none. Never mind; it 's her only fault. I do her justice; I understand very well." She kept softly murmuring and looking about for Madame Grandoni. She saw the good lady near the door, and put out her hand to Rowland for good night. She held his hand an instant, fixing him with her eyes, the living splendor of which, at this moment, was something transcendent. "Yes, I do her justice," she repeated. "And you do her more; you would lay down your life for her." With this she turned away, and before he could answer, she left him. She went to Madame Grandoni, grasped her two hands, and held out her forehead to be kissed. The next moment she was gone.

"That was a happy accident!" said Madame Grandoni. "She never looked so beautiful, and she made my little party brilliant."

"Beautiful, verily!" Rowland answered. "But it was no accident."

"What was it, then?"

"It was a plan. She wished to see Miss Garland. She knew she was to be here."

"How so?"

"By Roderick, evidently."

"And why did she wish to see Miss Garland?"

"Heaven knows! I give it up!"

"Ah, the wicked girl!" murmured Madame Grandoni.

"No," said Rowland; "don't say that now. She 's too beautiful."

"Oh, you men! The best of you!"

"Well, then," cried Rowland, "she 's too good!"

The opportunity presenting itself the next day, he failed not, as you may imagine, to ask Mary Garland what she thought of Miss Light. It was a Saturday afternoon, the time at which the beautiful marbles of the Villa Borghese are thrown open to the public. Mary had told him that Roderick had promised to take her to see them, with his mother, and he joined the party in the splendid Casino. The warm weather had left so few strangers in Rome that they had the place almost to themselves. Mrs. Hudson had confessed to an invincible fear of treading, even with the help of her son's arm, the polished marble floors, and was sitting patiently on a stool, with folded hands, looking shyly, here and there, at the undraped paganism around her. Roderick had sauntered off alone, with an irritated brow, which seemed to betray the conflict between the instinct of observation and the perplexities of circumstance. Miss Garland was wandering in another direction, and though she was consulting her catalogue, Rowland fancied it was from habit; she too was preoccupied. He joined her, and she presently sat down on a divan, rather wearily, and closed her Murray. Then he asked her abruptly how Christina had pleased her.

She started the least bit at the question, and he felt that she had been thinking of Christina.

"I don't like her!" she said with decision.

"What do you think of her?"

"I think she 's false." This was said without petulance or bitterness, but with a very positive air.

"But she wished to please you; she tried," Rowland rejoined, in a moment.

"I think not. She wished to please herself!"

Rowland felt himself at liberty to say no more. No allusion to Christina had passed between them since the day they met her at Saint Peter's, but he knew that she knew, by that infallible sixth sense of a woman who loves, that this strange, beautiful girl had the power to injure her. To what extent she had the will, Mary was uncertain; but last night's interview, apparently, had not reassured her. It was, under these circumstances, equally unbecoming for Rowland either to depreciate or to defend Christina, and he had to content himself with simply having verified the girl's own assurance that she had made a bad impression. He tried to talk of indifferent matters—about the statues and the frescoes; but to-day, plainly, aesthetic curiosity, with Miss Garland, had folded its wings. Curiosity of another sort had taken its place. Mary was longing, he was sure, to question him about Christina; but she found a dozen reasons for hesitating. Her questions would imply that Roderick had not treated her with confidence, for information on this point should properly have come from him. They would imply that she was jealous, and to betray her jealousy was intolerable to her pride. For some minutes, as she sat scratching the brilliant pavement with the point of her umbrella, it was to be supposed that her pride and her anxiety held an earnest debate. At last anxiety won.

"A propos of Miss Light," she asked, "do you know her well?"

"I can hardly say that. But I have seen her repeatedly."

"Do you like her?"

"Yes and no. I think I am sorry for her."

Mary had spoken with her eyes on the pavement. At this she looked up. "Sorry for her? Why?"

"Well—she is unhappy."

"What are her misfortunes?"

"Well—she has a horrible mother, and she has had a most injurious education."

For a moment Miss Garland was silent. Then, "Is n't she very beautiful?" she asked.

"Don't you think so?"

"That 's measured by what men think! She is extremely clever, too."

"Oh, incontestably."

"She has beautiful dresses."

"Yes, any number of them."

"And beautiful manners."

"Yes—sometimes."

"And plenty of money."

"Money enough, apparently."

"And she receives great admiration."

"Very true."

"And she is to marry a prince."

"So they say."

Miss Garland rose and turned to rejoin her companions, commenting these admissions with a pregnant silence. "Poor Miss Light!" she said at last, simply. And in this it seemed to Rowland there was a touch of bitterness.

Very late on the following evening his servant brought him the card of a visitor. He was surprised at a visit at such an hour, but it may be said that when he read the inscription—Cavaliere Giuseppe Giacosa—his surprise declined. He had had an unformulated conviction that there was to be a sequel to the apparition at Madame Grandoni's; the Cavaliere had come to usher it in.

He had come, evidently, on a portentous errand. He was as pale as ashes and prodigiously serious; his little cold black eye had grown ardent, and he had left his caressing smile at home. He saluted Rowland, however, with his usual obsequious bow.

"You have more than once done me the honor to invite me to call upon you," he said. "I am ashamed of my long delay, and I can only say to you, frankly, that my time this winter has not been my own." Rowland assented, ungrudgingly fumbled for the Italian correlative of the adage "Better late than never," begged him to be seated, and offered him a cigar. The Cavaliere sniffed imperceptibly the fragrant weed, and then declared that, if his kind host would allow him, he would reserve it for consumption at another time. He apparently desired to intimate that the solemnity of his errand left him no breath for idle smoke-puffings. Rowland stayed himself, just in time, from an enthusiastic offer of a dozen more cigars, and, as he watched the Cavaliere stow his treasure tenderly away in his pocket-book, reflected that only an Italian could go through such a performance with uncompromised dignity. "I must confess," the little old man resumed, "that even now I come on business not of my own—or my own, at least, only in a secondary sense. I have been dispatched as an ambassador, an envoy extraordinary, I may say, by my dear friend Mrs. Light."

"If I can in any way be of service to Mrs. Light, I shall be happy," Rowland said.

"Well then, dear sir, Casa Light is in commotion. The signora is in trouble—in terrible trouble." For a moment Rowland expected to hear that the signora's trouble was of a nature that a loan of five thousand francs would assuage. But the Cavaliere continued: "Miss Light has committed a great crime; she has plunged a dagger into the heart of her mother."

"A dagger!" cried Rowland.

The Cavaliere patted the air an instant with his finger-tips. "I speak figuratively. She has broken off her marriage."

"Broken it off?"

"Short! She has turned the prince from the door." And the Cavaliere, when he had made this announcement, folded his arms and bent upon Rowland his intense, inscrutable gaze. It seemed to Rowland that he detected in the polished depths of it a sort of fantastic gleam of irony or of triumph; but superficially, at least, Giacosa did nothing to discredit his character as a presumably sympathetic representative of Mrs. Light's affliction.

Rowland heard his news with a kind of fierce disgust; it seemed the sinister counterpart of Christina's preternatural mildness at Madame Grandoni's tea-party. She had been too plausible to be honest. Without being able to trace the connection, he yet instinctively associated her present rebellion with her meeting with Mary Garland. If she had not seen Mary, she would have let things stand. It was monstrous to suppose that she could have sacrificed so brilliant a fortune to a mere movement of jealousy, to a refined instinct of feminine deviltry, to a desire to frighten poor Mary from her security by again appearing in the field. Yet Rowland remembered his first impression of her; she was "dangerous," and she had measured in each direction the perturbing effect of her rupture. She was smiling her sweetest smile at it! For half an hour Rowland simply detested her, and longed to denounce her to her face. Of course all he could say to Giacosa was that he was extremely sorry. "But I am not surprised," he added.

"You are not surprised?"

"With Miss Light everything is possible. Is n't that true?"

Another ripple seemed to play for an instant in the current of the old man's irony, but he waived response. "It was a magnificent marriage," he said, solemnly. "I do not respect many people, but I respect Prince Casamassima."

"I should judge him indeed to be a very honorable young man," said Rowland.

"Eh, young as he is, he 's made of the old stuff. And now, perhaps he 's blowing his brains out. He is the last of his house; it 's a great house. But Miss Light will have put an end to it!"

"Is that the view she takes of it?" Rowland ventured to ask.

This time, unmistakably, the Cavaliere smiled, but still in that very out-of-the-way place. "You have observed Miss Light with attention," he said, "and this brings me to my errand. Mrs. Light has a high opinion of your wisdom, of your kindness, and she has reason to believe you have influence with her daughter."

"I—with her daughter? Not a grain!"

"That is possibly your modesty. Mrs. Light believes that something may yet be done, and that Christina will listen to you. She begs you to come and see her before it is too late."

"But all this, my dear Cavaliere, is none of my business," Rowland objected. "I can't possibly, in such a matter, take the responsibility of advising Miss Light."

The Cavaliere fixed his eyes for a moment on the floor, in brief but intense reflection. Then looking up, "Unfortunately," he said, "she has no man near her whom she respects; she has no father!"

"And a fatally foolish mother!" Rowland gave himself the satisfaction of exclaiming.

The Cavaliere was so pale that he could not easily have turned paler; yet it seemed for a moment that his dead complexion blanched. "Eh, signore, such as she is, the mother appeals to you. A very handsome woman—disheveled, in tears, in despair, in dishabille!"

Rowland reflected a moment, not on the attractions of Mrs. Light under the circumstances thus indicated by the Cavaliere, but on the satisfaction he would take in accusing Christina to her face of having struck a cruel blow.

"I must add," said the Cavaliere, "that Mrs. Light desires also to speak to you on the subject of Mr. Hudson."

"She considers Mr. Hudson, then, connected with this step of her daughter's?"

"Intimately. He must be got out of Rome."

"Mrs. Light, then, must get an order from the Pope to remove him. It 's not in my power."

The Cavaliere assented, deferentially. "Mrs. Light is equally helpless. She would leave Rome to-morrow, but Christina will not budge. An order from the Pope would do nothing. A bull in council would do nothing."

"She 's a remarkable young lady," said Rowland, with bitterness.

But the Cavaliere rose and responded coldly, "She has a great spirit." And it seemed to Rowland that her great spirit, for mysterious reasons, gave him more pleasure than the distressing use she made of it gave him pain. He was on the point of charging him with his inconsistency, when Giacosa resumed: "But if the marriage can be saved, it must be saved. It 's a beautiful marriage. It will be saved."

597

"Notwithstanding Miss Light's great spirit to the contrary?"

"Miss Light, notwithstanding her great spirit, will call Prince Casamassima back."

"Heaven grant it!" said Rowland.

"I don't know," said the Cavaliere, solemnly, "that heaven will have much to do with it."

Rowland gave him a questioning look, but he laid his finger on his lips. And with Rowland's promise to present himself on the morrow at Casa Light, he shortly afterwards departed. He left Rowland revolving many things: Christina's magnanimity, Christina's perversity, Roderick's contingent fortune, Mary Garland's certain trouble, and the Cavaliere's own fine ambiguities.

Rowland's promise to the Cavaliere obliged him to withdraw from an excursion which he had arranged with the two ladies from Northampton. Before going to Casa Light he repaired in person to Mrs. Hudson's hotel, to make his excuses.

He found Roderick's mother sitting with tearful eyes, staring at an open note that lay in her lap. At the window sat Miss Garland, who turned her intense regard upon him as he came in. Mrs. Hudson quickly rose and came to him, holding out the note.

"In pity's name," she cried, "what is the matter with my boy? If he is ill, I entreat you to take me to him!"

"He is not ill, to my knowledge," said Rowland. "What have you there?"

"A note—a dreadful note. He tells us we are not to see him for a week. If I could only go to his room! But I am afraid, I am afraid!"

"I imagine there is no need of going to his room. What is the occasion, may I ask, of his note?"

"He was to have gone with us on this drive to—what is the place?—to Cervara. You know it was arranged yesterday morning. In the evening he was to have dined with us. But he never came, and this morning arrives this awful thing. Oh dear, I 'm so excited! Would you mind reading it?"

Rowland took the note and glanced at its half-dozen lines. "I cannot go to Cervara," they ran; "I have something else to do. This will occupy me perhaps for a week, and you 'll not see me. Don't miss me—learn not to miss me. R. H."

"Why, it means," Rowland commented, "that he has taken up a piece of work, and that it is all-absorbing. That 's very good news." This explanation was not sincere; but he had not the courage not to offer it as a stop-gap. But he found he needed all his courage to maintain it, for Miss Garland had left her place and approached him, formidably unsatisfied.

"He does not work in the evening," said Mrs. Hudson. "Can't he come for five minutes? Why does he write such a cruel, cold note to his poor mother—to poor Mary? What have we done that he acts so strangely? It 's this wicked, infectious, heathenish place!" And the poor lady's suppressed mistrust of the Eternal City broke out passionately. "Oh, dear Mr. Mallet," she went on, "I am sure he has the fever and he 's already delirious!"

"I am very sure it 's not that," said Miss Garland, with a certain dryness.

She was still looking at Rowland; his eyes met hers, and his own glance fell. This made him angry, and to carry off his confusion he pretended to be looking at the floor, in meditation. After all, what had he to be ashamed of? For a moment he was on the point of making a clean breast of it, of crying out, "Dearest friends, I abdicate: I can't help you!" But he checked himself; he felt so impatient to have his three words with Christina. He grasped his hat.

"I will see what it is!" he cried. And then he was glad he had not abdicated, for as he turned away he glanced again at Mary and saw that, though her eyes were full of trouble, they were not hard and accusing, but charged with appealing friendship.

He went straight to Roderick's apartment, deeming this, at an early hour, the safest place to seek him. He found him in his sitting-room, which had been closely darkened to keep out the heat. The carpets and rugs had been removed, the floor of speckled concrete was bare and lightly sprinkled with water. Here and there, over it, certain strongly perfumed flowers had been scattered. Roderick was lying on his divan in a white dressing-gown, staring up at the frescoed ceiling. The room was deliciously cool, and filled with the moist, sweet odor of the circumjacent roses and violets. All this seemed highly fantastic, and yet Rowland hardly felt surprised.

"Your mother was greatly alarmed at your note," he said, "and I came to satisfy myself that, as I believed, you are not ill." Roderick lay motionless, except that he slightly turned his head toward his friend. He was smelling a large white rose, and he continued to present it to his nose. In the darkness of the room he looked exceedingly pale, but his handsome eyes had an extraordinary brilliancy. He let them rest for some time on Rowland, lying there like a Buddhist in an intellectual swoon, whose perception should be slowly ebbing back to temporal matters. "Oh, I 'm not ill," he said at last. "I have never been better."

"Your note, nevertheless, and your absence," Rowland said, "have very naturally alarmed your mother. I advise you to go to her directly and reassure her."

"Go to her? Going to her would be worse than staying away. Staying away at present is a kindness." And he inhaled deeply his huge rose, looking up over it at Rowland. "My presence, in fact, would be indecent."

"Indecent? Pray explain."

"Why, you see, as regards Mary Garland. I am divinely happy! Does n't it strike you? You ought to agree with me. You wish me to spare her feelings; I spare them by staying away. Last night I heard something"—

"I heard it, too," said Rowland with brevity. "And it 's in honor of this piece of news that you have taken to your bed in this fashion?"

"Extremes meet! I can't get up for joy."

"May I inquire how you heard your joyous news?—from Miss Light herself?"

"By no means. It was brought me by her maid, who is in my service as well."

"Casamassima's loss, then, is to a certainty your gain?"

"I don't talk about certainties. I don't want to be arrogant, I don't want to offend the immortal gods. I 'm keeping very quiet, but I can't help being happy. I shall wait a while; I shall bide my time."

"And then?"

"And then that transcendent girl will confess to me that when she threw overboard her prince she remembered that I adored her!"

"I feel bound to tell you," was in the course of a moment Rowland's response to this speech, "that I am now on my way to Mrs. Light's."

"I congratulate you, I envy you!" Roderick murmured, imperturbably.

"Mrs. Light has sent for me to remonstrate with her daughter, with whom she has taken it into her head that I have influence. I don't know to what extent I shall remonstrate, but I give you notice I shall not speak in your interest."

Roderick looked at him a moment with a lazy radiance in his eyes. "Pray don't!" he simply answered.

"You deserve I should tell her you are a very shabby fellow."

"My dear Rowland, the comfort with you is that I can trust you. You 're incapable of doing anything disloyal."

"You mean to lie here, then, smelling your roses and nursing your visions, and leaving your mother and Miss Garland to fall ill with anxiety?"

"Can I go and flaunt my felicity in their faces? Wait till I get used to it a trifle. I have done them a palpable wrong, but I can at least forbear to add insult to injury. I may be an arrant fool, but, for the moment, I have taken it into my head to be prodigiously pleased. I should n't be able to conceal it; my pleasure would offend them; so I lock myself up as a dangerous character."

"Well, I can only say, 'May your pleasure never grow less, or your danger greater!'"

Roderick closed his eyes again, and sniffed at his rose. "God's will be done!"

On this Rowland left him and repaired directly to Mrs. Light's. This afflicted lady hurried forward to meet him. Since the Cavaliere's report of her condition she had somewhat smoothed and trimmed the exuberance of her distress, but she was evidently in extreme tribulation, and she clutched Rowland by his two hands, as if, in the shipwreck of her hopes, he were her single floating spar. Rowland greatly pitied her, for there is something respectable in passionate grief, even in a very bad cause; and as pity is akin to love, he endured her rather better than he had done hitherto.

"Speak to her, plead with her, command her!" she cried, pressing and shaking his hands. "She 'll not heed us, no more than if we were a pair of clocks a-ticking. Perhaps she will listen to you; she always liked you."

"She always disliked me," said Rowland. "But that does n't matter now. I have come here simply because you sent for me, not because I can help you. I cannot advise your daughter."

"Oh, cruel, deadly man! You must advise her; you shan't leave this house till you have advised her!" the poor woman passionately retorted. "Look at me in my misery and refuse to help me! Oh, you need n't be afraid, I know I 'm a fright, I have n't an idea what I have on. If this goes on, we may both as well turn scarecrows. If ever a woman was desperate, frantic, heart-broken, I am that woman. I can't begin to tell you. To have nourished a serpent, sir, all these years! to have lavished one's self upon a viper that turns and stings her own poor mother! To have toiled and prayed, to have pushed and struggled, to have eaten the bread of bitterness, and all the rest of it, sir—and at the end of all things to find myself at this pass. It can't be, it 's too cruel, such things don't happen, the Lord don't allow it. I 'm a religious woman, sir, and the Lord all about me. With his own hand he had given me his reward! I would have lain down in the dust and let her walk over me; I would have given her the eyes out of my head, if she had taken a fancy to them. No, she 's a cruel, wicked, heartless, unnatural girl! I speak to you, Mr. Mallet, in my dire distress, as to my only friend. There is n't a creature here that I can look to—not one of them all that I have faith in. But I always admired you. I said to Christina the first time I saw you that there at last was a real gentleman. Come, don't disappoint me now! I feel so terribly alone, you see; I feel what a nasty, hard, heartless world it is that has come and devoured my dinners and danced to my fiddles, and yet that has n't a word to throw to me in my agony! Oh, the money, alone, that I have put into this thing, would melt the heart of a Turk!"

During this frenzied outbreak Rowland had had time to look round the room, and to see the Cavaliere sitting in a corner, like a major-domo on the divan of an antechamber, pale, rigid, and inscrutable.

"I have it at heart to tell you," Rowland said, "that if you consider my friend Hudson"—

Mrs. Light gave a toss of her head and hands. "Oh, it 's not that. She told me last night to bother her no longer with Hudson, Hudson! She did n't care a button for Hudson. I almost wish she did; then perhaps one might understand it. But she does n't care for anything in the wide world, except to do her own hard, wicked will, and to crush me and shame me with her cruelty."

"Ah, then," said Rowland, "I am as much at sea as you, and my presence here is an impertinence. I should like to say three words to Miss Light on my own account. But I must absolutely and inexorably decline to urge the cause of Prince Casamassima. This is simply impossible."

Mrs. Light burst into angry tears. "Because the poor boy is a prince, eh? because he 's of a great family, and has an income of millions, eh? That 's why you grudge him and hate him. I knew there were vulgar people of that way of feeling, but I did n't expect it of you. Make an effort, Mr. Mallet; rise to the occasion; forgive the poor fellow his splendor. Be just, be reasonable! It 's not his fault, and it 's not mine. He 's the best, the kindest young man in the world, and the most correct and moral and virtuous! If he were standing here in rags, I would say it all the same. The man first—the money afterwards: that was always my motto, and always will be. What do you take me for? Do you suppose I would give Christina to a vicious person? do you suppose I would sacrifice my precious child, little comfort as I have in her, to a man against whose character one word could be breathed? Casamassima is only too good, he 's a saint of saints, he 's stupidly good! There is n't such another in the length and breadth of Europe. What he has been through in this house, not a common peasant would endure. Christina has treated him as you would n't treat a dog. He has been insulted, outraged, persecuted! He has been driven hither and thither till he did n't know where he was. He has stood there where you stand—there, with his name and his millions and his devotion—as white as your handkerchief, with hot tears in his eyes, and me ready to go down on my knees to him and say, 'My own sweet prince, I could kiss the ground you tread on, but it is n't decent that I should allow you to enter my house and expose yourself to these horrors again.' And he would come back, and he would come back, and go through it all again, and take all that was given him, and only want the girl the more! I was his confidant; I know everything. He used to beg my forgiveness for Christina. What do you say to that? I seized him once and kissed him, I did! To find that and to find all the rest with it, and to believe it was a gift straight from the pitying angels of heaven, and then to see it dashed away before your eyes and to stand here helpless—oh, it 's a fate I hope you may ever be spared!"

"It would seem, then, that in the interest of Prince Casamassima himself I ought to refuse to interfere," said Rowland.

Mrs. Light looked at him hard, slowly drying her eyes. The intensity of her grief and anger gave her a kind of majesty, and Rowland, for the moment, felt ashamed of the ironical ring of his observation. "Very good, sir," she said. "I 'm sorry your heart is not so tender as your conscience. My compliments to your conscience! It must give you great happiness. Heaven help me! Since you fail us, we are indeed driven to the wall. But I have fought my own battles before, and I have never lost courage, and I don't see why I should break down now. Cavaliere, come here!"

Giacosa rose at her summons and advanced with his usual deferential alacrity. He shook hands with Rowland in silence.

"Mr. Mallet refuses to say a word," Mrs. Light went on. "Time presses, every moment is precious. Heaven knows what that poor boy may be doing.

If at this moment a clever woman should get hold of him she might be as ugly as she pleased! It 's horrible to think of it."

The Cavaliere fixed his eyes on Rowland, and his look, which the night before had been singular, was now most extraordinary. There was a nameless force of anguish in it which seemed to grapple with the young man's reluctance, to plead, to entreat, and at the same time to be glazed over with a reflection of strange things.

Suddenly, though most vaguely, Rowland felt the presence of a new element in the drama that was going on before him. He looked from the Cavaliere to Mrs. Light, whose eyes were now quite dry, and were fixed in stony hardness on the floor.

"If you could bring yourself," the Cavaliere said, in a low, soft, caressing voice, "to address a few words of solemn remonstrance to Miss Light, you would, perhaps, do more for us than you know. You would save several persons a great pain. The dear signora, first, and then Christina herself. Christina in particular. Me too, I might take the liberty to add!"

There was, to Rowland, something acutely touching in this humble petition. He had always felt a sort of imaginative tenderness for poor little unexplained Giacosa, and these words seemed a supreme contortion of the mysterious obliquity of his life. All of a sudden, as he watched the Cavaliere, something occurred to him; it was something very odd, and it stayed his glance suddenly from again turning to Mrs. Light. His idea embarrassed him, and to carry off his embarrassment, he repeated that it was folly to suppose that his words would have any weight with Christina.

The Cavaliere stepped forward and laid two fingers on Rowland's breast. "Do you wish to know the truth? You are the only man whose words she remembers."

Rowland was going from surprise to surprise. "I will say what I can!" he said. By this time he had ventured to glance at Mrs. Light. She was looking at him askance, as if, upon this, she was suddenly mistrusting his motives.

"If you fail," she said sharply, "we have something else! But please to lose no time."

She had hardly spoken when the sound of a short, sharp growl caused the company to turn. Christina's fleecy poodle stood in the middle of the vast saloon, with his muzzle lowered, in pompous defiance of the three conspirators against the comfort of his mistress. This young lady's claims for him seemed justified; he was an animal of amazingly delicate instincts. He had preceded Christina as a sort of van-guard of defense, and she now slowly advanced from a neighboring room.

"You will be so good as to listen to Mr. Mallet," her mother said, in a terrible voice, "and to reflect carefully upon what he says. I suppose you will admit that he is disinterested. In half an hour you shall hear from me again!" And passing her hand through the Cavaliere's arm, she swept rapidly out of the room.

Christina looked hard at Rowland, but offered him no greeting. She was very pale, and, strangely enough, it at first seemed to Rowland that her beauty was in eclipse. But he very soon perceived that it had only changed its character, and that if it was a trifle less brilliant than usual, it was admirably touching and noble. The clouded light of her eyes, the magnificent gravity of her features, the conscious erectness of her head, might have belonged to a deposed sovereign or a condemned martyr. "Why have you come here at this time?" she asked.

"Your mother sent for me in pressing terms, and I was very glad to have an opportunity to speak to you."

"Have you come to help me, or to persecute me?"

"I have as little power to do one as I have desire to do the other. I came in great part to ask you a question. First, your decision is irrevocable?"

Christina's two hands had been hanging clasped in front of her; she separated them and flung them apart by an admirable gesture.

"Would you have done this if you had not seen Miss Garland?"

She looked at him with quickened attention; then suddenly, "This is interesting!" she cried. "Let us have it out." And she flung herself into a chair and pointed to another.

"You don't answer my question," Rowland said.

"You have no right, that I know of, to ask it. But it 's a very clever one; so clever that it deserves an answer. Very likely I would not."

"Last night, when I said that to myself, I was extremely angry," Rowland rejoined.

"Oh, dear, and you are not angry now?"

"I am less angry."

"How very stupid! But you can say something at least."

"If I were to say what is uppermost in my mind, I would say that, face to face with you, it is never possible to condemn you."

"Perche?"

"You know, yourself! But I can at least say now what I felt last night. It seemed to me that you had consciously, cruelly dealt a blow at that poor girl. Do you understand?"

"Wait a moment!" And with her eyes fixed on him, she inclined her head on one side, meditatively. Then a cold, brilliant smile covered her face, and she made a gesture of negation. "I see your train of reasoning, but it 's quite wrong. I meant no harm to Miss Garland; I should be extremely sorry to make her suffer. Tell me you believe that."

This was said with ineffable candor. Rowland heard himself answering, "I believe it!"

"And yet, in a sense, your supposition was true," Christina continued. "I conceived, as I told you, a great admiration for Miss Garland, and I frankly confess I was jealous of her. What I envied her was simply her character! I said to myself, 'She, in my place, would n't marry Casamassima.' I could not help saying it, and I said it so often that I found a kind of inspiration in it. I hated the idea of being worse than she—of doing something that she would n't do. I might be bad by nature, but I need n't be by volition. The end of it all was that I found it impossible not to tell the prince that I was his very humble servant, but that I could not marry him."

"Are you sure it was only of Miss Garland's character that you were jealous, not of—not of"—

"Speak out, I beg you. We are talking philosophy!"

"Not of her affection for her cousin?"

"Sure is a good deal to ask. Still, I think I may say it! There are two reasons; one, at least, I can tell you: her affection has not a shadow's weight with Mr. Hudson! Why then should one fear it?"

"And what is the other reason?"

"Excuse me; that is my own affair."

Rowland was puzzled, baffled, charmed, inspired, almost, all at once. "I have promised your mother," he presently resumed, "to say something in favor of Prince Casamassima."

She shook her head sadly. "Prince Casamassima needs nothing that you can say for him. He is a magnificent parti. I know it perfectly."

"You know also of the extreme affliction of your mother?"

"Her affliction is demonstrative. She has been abusing me for the last twenty-four hours as if I were the vilest of the vile." To see Christina sit there in the purity of her beauty and say this, might have made one bow one's head with a kind of awe. "I have failed of respect to her at other times, but I have not done so now. Since we are talking philosophy," she pursued with a gentle smile, "I may say it 's a simple matter! I don't love him. Or rather, perhaps, since we are talking philosophy, I may say it 's not a simple matter. I spoke just now of inspiration. The inspiration has been great, but—I frankly confess it—the choice has been hard. Shall I tell you?" she demanded, with sudden ardor; "will you understand me? It was on the one side the world, the splendid, beautiful, powerful, interesting world. I know what that is; I have tasted of the cup, I know its sweetness. Ah, if I chose, if I let myself go, if I flung everything to the winds, the world and I would be famous friends! I know its merits, and I think, without vanity, it would see mine. You would see some fine things! I should like to be a princess, and I think I should be a very good one; I would play my part well. I am fond of luxury, I am fond of a great society, I am fond of being looked at. I am corrupt, corruptible, corruption! Ah, what a pity that could n't be, too! Mercy of Heaven!" There was a passionate tremor in her voice; she covered her face with her hands and sat motionless. Rowland saw that an intense agitation, hitherto successfully repressed, underlay her calmness, and he could easily believe that her battle had been fierce. She rose quickly and turned away, walked a few paces, and stopped. In a moment she was facing him again, with tears in her eyes and a flush in her cheeks. "But you need n't think I 'm afraid!" she said. "I have chosen, and I shall hold to it. I have something here, here, here!" and she patted her heart. "It 's my own. I shan't part with it. Is it what you call an ideal? I don't know; I don't care! It is brighter than the Casamassima diamonds!"

"You say that certain things are your own affair," Rowland presently rejoined; "but I must nevertheless make an attempt to learn what all this means—what it promises for my friend Hudson. Is there any hope for him?"

"This is a point I can't discuss with you minutely. I like him very much."

"Would you marry him if he were to ask you?"

"He has asked me."

"And if he asks again?"

"I shall marry no one just now."

"Roderick," said Rowland, "has great hopes."

"Does he know of my rupture with the prince?"

"He is making a great holiday of it."

Christina pulled her poodle towards her and began to smooth his silky fleece. "I like him very much," she repeated; "much more than I used to. Since you told me all that about him at Saint Cecilia's, I have felt a great friendship for him. There 's something very fine about him; he 's not afraid of anything. He is not afraid of failure; he is not afraid of ruin or death."

"Poor fellow!" said Rowland, bitterly; "he is fatally picturesque."

"Picturesque, yes; that 's what he is. I am very sorry for him."

"Your mother told me just now that you had said that you did n't care a straw for him."

"Very likely! I meant as a lover. One does n't want a lover one pities, and one does n't want—of all things in the world—a picturesque husband! I should like Mr. Hudson as something else. I wish he were my brother, so that he could never talk to me of marriage. Then I could adore him. I would nurse him, I would wait on him and save him all disagreeable rubs and shocks. I am much stronger than he, and I would stand between him and the world. Indeed, with Mr. Hudson for my brother, I should be willing to live and die an old maid!"

"Have you ever told him all this?"

"I suppose so; I 've told him five hundred things! If it would please you, I will tell him again."

"Oh, Heaven forbid!" cried poor Rowland, with a groan.

He was lingering there, weighing his sympathy against his irritation, and feeling it sink in the scale, when the curtain of a distant doorway was lifted and Mrs. Light passed across the room. She stopped half-way, and gave the young persons a flushed and menacing look. It found apparently little to reassure her, and she moved away with a passionate toss of her drapery. Rowland thought with horror of the sinister compulsion to which the young girl was to be subjected. In this ethereal flight of hers there was a certain painful effort and tension of wing; but it was none the less piteous to imagine her being rudely jerked down to the base earth she was doing her adventurous utmost to spurn. She would need all her magnanimity for her own trial, and it seemed gross to make further demands upon it on Roderick's behalf.

Rowland took up his hat. "You asked a while ago if I had come to help you," he said. "If I knew how I might help you, I should be particularly glad."

She stood silent a moment, reflecting. Then at last, looking up, "You remember," she said, "your promising me six months ago to tell me what you finally thought of me? I should like you to tell me now."

He could hardly help smiling. Madame Grandoni had insisted on the fact that Christina was an actress, though a sincere one; and this little speech seemed a glimpse of the cloven foot. She had played her great scene, she had made her point, and now she had her eye at the hole in the curtain and she was watching the house! But she blushed as she perceived his smile, and her blush, which was beautiful, made her fault venial.

"You are an excellent girl!" he said, in a particular tone, and gave her his hand in farewell.

There was a great chain of rooms in Mrs. Light's apartment, the pride and joy of the hostess on festal evenings, through which the departing visitor passed before reaching the door. In one of the first of these Rowland found himself waylaid and arrested by the distracted lady herself.

"Well, well?" she cried, seizing his arm. "Has she listened to you—have you moved her?"

"In Heaven's name, dear madame," Rowland begged, "leave the poor girl alone! She is behaving very well!"

"Behaving very well? Is that all you have to tell me? I don't believe you said a proper word to her. You are conspiring together to kill me!"

Rowland tried to soothe her, to remonstrate, to persuade her that it was equally cruel and unwise to try to force matters. But she answered him only with harsh lamentations and imprecations, and ended by telling him that her daughter was her property, not his, and that his interference was most insolent and most scandalous. Her disappointment seemed really to have crazed her, and his only possible rejoinder was to take a summary departure.

A moment later he came upon the Cavaliere, who was sitting with his elbows on his knees and his head in his hands, so buried in thought that Rowland had to call him before he roused himself. Giacosa looked at him a moment keenly, and then gave a shake of the head, interrogatively.

Rowland gave a shake negative, to which the Cavaliere responded by a long, melancholy sigh. "But her mother is determined to force matters," said Rowland.

"It seems that it must be!"

"Do you consider that it must be?"

"I don't differ with Mrs. Light!"

"It will be a great cruelty!"

The Cavaliere gave a tragic shrug. "Eh! it is n't an easy world."

"You should do nothing to make it harder, then."

"What will you have? It 's a magnificent marriage."

"You disappoint me, Cavaliere," said Rowland, solemnly. "I imagined you appreciated the great elevation of Miss Light's attitude. She does n't love the prince; she has let the matter stand or fall by that."

The old man grasped him by the hand and stood a moment with averted eyes. At last, looking at him, he held up two fingers.

"I have two hearts," he said, "one for myself, one for the world. This one opposes Miss Light, the other adores her! One suffers horribly at what the other does."

"I don't understand double people, Cavaliere," Rowland said, "and I don't pretend to understand you. But I have guessed that you are going to play some secret card."

"The card is Mrs. Light's, not mine," said the Cavaliere.

"It 's a menace, at any rate?"

"The sword of Damocles! It hangs by a hair. Christina is to be given ten minutes to recant, under penalty of having it fall. On the blade there is something written in strange characters. Don't scratch your head; you will not make it out."

"I think I have guessed it," Rowland said, after a pregnant silence. The Cavaliere looked at him blankly but intently, and Rowland added, "Though there are some signs, indeed, I don't understand."

"Puzzle them out at your leisure," said the Cavaliere, shaking his hand. "I hear Mrs. Light; I must go to my post. I wish you were a Catholic; I would beg you to step into the first church you come to, and pray for us the next half-hour."

"For 'us'? For whom?"

"For all of us. At any rate remember this: I worship the Christina!"

Rowland heard the rustle of Mrs. Light's dress; he turned away, and the Cavaliere went, as he said, to his post. Rowland for the next couple of days pondered his riddle.

CHAPTER XI. Mrs. Hudson

Of Roderick, meanwhile, Rowland saw nothing; but he immediately went to Mrs. Hudson and assured her that her son was in even exceptionally good health and spirits. After this he called again on the two ladies from Northampton, but, as Roderick's absence continued, he was able neither to furnish nor to obtain much comfort. Miss Garland's apprehensive face seemed to him an image of his own state of mind. He was profoundly depressed; he felt that there was a storm in the air, and he wished it would come, without more delay, and perform its ravages. On the afternoon of the third day he went into Saint Peter's, his frequent resort whenever the outer world was disagreeable. From a heart-ache to a Roman rain there were few importunate pains the great church did not help him to forget. He had wandered there for half an hour, when he came upon a short figure, lurking in the shadow of one of the great piers. He saw it was that of an artist, hastily transferring to his sketch-book a memento of some fleeting variation in the scenery of the basilica; and in a moment he perceived that the artist was little Sam Singleton.

Singleton pocketed his sketch-book with a guilty air, as if it cost his modesty a pang to be detected in this greedy culture of opportunity. Rowland always enjoyed meeting him; talking with him, in these days, was as good as a wayside gush of clear, cold water, on a long, hot walk. There was, perhaps, no drinking-vessel, and you had to apply your lips to some simple natural conduit; but the result was always a sense of extreme moral refreshment. On this occasion he mentally blessed the ingenuous little artist, and heard presently with keen regret that he was to leave Rome on the morrow. Singleton had come to bid farewell to Saint Peter's, and he was gathering a few supreme memories. He had earned a purse-full of money, and he was meaning to take a summer's holiday; going to Switzerland, to Germany, to Paris. In the autumn he was to return home; his family—composed, as Rowland knew, of a father who was cashier in a bank and five unmarried sisters, one of whom gave lyceum-lectures on woman's rights, the whole resident at Buffalo, New York—had been writing him peremptory letters and appealing to him as a son, brother, and fellow-citizen. He would have been grateful for another year in Rome, but what must be must be, and he had laid up treasure which, in Buffalo, would seem infinite. They talked some time; Rowland hoped they might meet in Switzerland, and take a walk or two together. Singleton seemed to feel that Buffalo had marked him for her own; he was afraid he should not see Rome again for many a year.

"So you expect to live at Buffalo?" Rowland asked sympathetically.

"Well, it will depend upon the views—upon the attitude—of my family," Singleton replied. "Oh, I think I shall get on; I think it can be done. If I find it can be done, I shall really be quite proud of it; as an artist of course I mean, you know. Do you know I have some nine hundred sketches? I shall live in my portfolio. And so long as one is not in Rome, pray what does it matter where one is? But how I shall envy all you Romans—you and Mr. Gloriani, and Mr. Hudson, especially!"

"Don't envy Hudson; he has nothing to envy."

Singleton grinned at what he considered a harmless jest. "Yes, he 's going to be the great man of our time! And I say, Mr. Mallet, is n't it a mighty comfort that it 's we who have turned him out?"

"Between ourselves," said Rowland, "he has disappointed me."

Singleton stared, open-mouthed. "Dear me, what did you expect?"

"Truly," said Rowland to himself, "what did I expect?"

"I confess," cried Singleton, "I can't judge him rationally. He fascinates me; he 's the sort of man one makes one's hero of."

"Strictly speaking, he is not a hero," said Rowland.

Singleton looked intensely grave, and, with almost tearful eyes, "Is there anything amiss—anything out of the way, about him?" he timidly asked. Then, as Rowland hesitated to reply, he quickly added, "Please, if there is, don't tell me! I want to know no evil of him, and I think I should hardly believe it. In my memories of this Roman artist-life, he will be the central figure. He will stand there in radiant relief, as beautiful and unspotted as one of his own statues!"

"Amen!" said Rowland, gravely. He remembered afresh that the sea is inhabited by big fishes and little, and that the latter often find their way down the throats of the former. Singleton was going to spend the afternoon in taking last looks at certain other places, and Rowland offered to join him on his sentimental circuit. But as they were preparing to leave the church, he heard himself suddenly addressed from behind. Turning, he beheld a young woman whom he immediately recognized as Madame Grandoni's maid. Her mistress was present, she said, and begged to confer with him before he departed.

This summons obliged Rowland to separate from Singleton, to whom he bade farewell. He followed the messenger, and presently found Madame Grandoni occupying a liberal area on the steps of the tribune, behind the great altar, where, spreading a shawl on the polished red marble, she had comfortably seated herself. He expected that she had something especial to impart, and she lost no time in bringing forth her treasure.

"Don't shout very loud," she said, "remember that we are in church; there 's a limit to the noise one may make even in Saint Peter's. Christina Light was married this morning to Prince Casamassima."

Rowland did not shout at all; he gave a deep, short murmur: "Married—this morning?"

"Married this morning, at seven o'clock, le plus tranquillement du monde, before three or four persons. The young couple left Rome an hour afterwards."

For some moments this seemed to him really terrible; the dark little drama of which he had caught a glimpse had played itself out. He had believed that Christina would resist; that she had succumbed was a proof that the pressure had been cruel. Rowland's imagination followed her forth with an irresistible tremor into the world toward which she was rolling away, with her detested husband and her stifled ideal; but it must be confessed that if the first impulse of his compassion was for Christina, the second was for Prince Casamassima. Madame Grandoni acknowledged an extreme curiosity as to the secret springs of these strange doings: Casamassima's sudden dismissal, his still more sudden recall, the hurried private marriage. "Listen," said Rowland, hereupon, "and I will tell you something." And he related, in detail, his last visit to Mrs. Light and his talk with this lady, with Christina, and with the Cavaliere.

"Good," she said; "it 's all very curious. But it 's a riddle, and I only half guess it."

"Well," said Rowland, "I desire to harm no one; but certain suppositions have taken shape in my mind which serve as a solvent to several ambiguities."

"It is very true," Madame Grandoni answered, "that the Cavaliere, as he stands, has always needed to be explained."

"He is explained by the hypothesis that, three-and-twenty years ago, at Ancona, Mrs. Light had a lover."

"I see. Ancona was dull, Mrs. Light was lively, and—three-and-twenty years ago—perhaps, the Cavaliere was fascinating. Doubtless it would be fairer to say that he was fascinated. Poor Giacosa!"

"He has had his compensation," Rowland said. "He has been passionately fond of Christina."

"Naturally. But has Christina never wondered why?"

"If she had been near guessing, her mother's shabby treatment of him would have put her off the scent. Mrs. Light's conscience has apparently told her that she could expiate an hour's too great kindness by twenty years' contempt. So she kept her secret. But what is the profit of having a secret unless you can make some use of it? The day at last came when she could turn hers to account; she could let the skeleton out of the closet and create a panic."

"I don't understand."

"Neither do I morally," said Rowland. "I only conceive that there was a horrible, fabulous scene. The poor Cavaliere stood outside, at the door, white as a corpse and as dumb. The mother and daughter had it out together. Mrs. Light burnt her ships. When she came out she had three lines of writing in her daughter's hand, which the Cavaliere was dispatched with to the prince. They overtook the young man in time, and, when he reappeared, he was delighted to dispense with further waiting. I don't know what he thought of the look in his bride's face; but that is how I roughly reconstruct history."

"Christina was forced to decide, then, that she could not afford not to be a princess?"

"She was reduced by humiliation. She was assured that it was not for her to make conditions, but to thank her stars that there were none made for her. If she persisted, she might find it coming to pass that there would be conditions, and the formal rupture—the rupture that the world would hear of and pry into—would then proceed from the prince and not from her."

"That 's all nonsense!" said Madame Grandoni, energetically.

"To us, yes; but not to the proudest girl in the world, deeply wounded in her pride, and not stopping to calculate probabilities, but muffling her shame, with an almost sensuous relief, in a splendor that stood within her grasp and asked no questions. Is it not possible that the late Mr. Light had made an outbreak before witnesses who are still living?"

"Certainly her marriage now," said Madame Grandoni, less analytically, "has the advantage that it takes her away from her—parents!"

This lady's farther comments upon the event are not immediately pertinent to our history; there were some other comments of which Rowland had a deeply oppressive foreboding. He called, on the evening of the morrow upon Mrs. Hudson, and found Roderick with the two ladies. Their companion had apparently but lately entered, and Rowland afterwards learned that it was his first appearance since the writing of the note which had so distressed his mother. He had flung himself upon a sofa, where he sat with his chin upon his breast, staring before him with a sinister spark in his eye. He fixed his gaze on Rowland, but gave him no greeting. He had evidently been saying something to startle the women; Mrs. Hudson had gone and seated herself, timidly and imploringly, on the edge of the sofa, trying to take his hand. Miss Garland was applying herself to some needlework with conscious intentness.

Mrs. Hudson gave Rowland, on his entrance, a touching look of gratitude. "Oh, we have such blessed news!" she said. "Roderick is ready to leave Rome."

"It 's not blessed news; it 's most damnable news!" cried Roderick.

"Oh, but we are very glad, my son, and I am sure you will be when you get away. You 're looking most dreadfully thin; is n't he, Mr. Mallet? It 's plain enough you need a change. I 'm sure we will go wherever you like. Where would you like to go?"

Roderick turned his head slowly and looked at her. He had let her take his hand, which she pressed tenderly between her own. He gazed at her for some time in silence. "Poor mother!" he said at last, in a portentous tone.

"My own dear son!" murmured Mrs. Hudson in all the innocence of her trust.

"I don't care a straw where you go! I don't care a straw for anything!"

"Oh, my dear boy, you must not say that before all of us here—before Mary, before Mr. Mallet!"

"Mary—Mr. Mallet?" Roderick repeated, almost savagely. He released himself from the clasp of his mother's hand and turned away, leaning his elbows on his knees and holding his head in his hands. There was a silence; Rowland said nothing because he was watching Miss Garland. "Why should I stand on ceremony with Mary and Mr. Mallet?" Roderick presently added. "Mary pretends to believe I 'm a fine fellow, and if she believes it as she ought to, nothing I can say will alter her opinion. Mallet knows I 'm a hopeless humbug; so I need n't mince my words with him."

"Ah, my dear, don't use such dreadful language!" said Mrs. Hudson. "Are n't we all devoted to you, and proud of you, and waiting only to hear what you want, so that we may do it?"

Roderick got up, and began to walk about the room; he was evidently in a restless, reckless, profoundly demoralized condition. Rowland felt that it was literally true that he did not care a straw for anything, but he observed with anxiety that Mrs. Hudson, who did not know on what delicate ground she was treading, was disposed to chide him caressingly, as a mere expression of tenderness. He foresaw that she would bring down the hovering thunderbolt on her head.

"In God's name," Roderick cried, "don't remind me of my obligations! It 's intolerable to me, and I don't believe it 's pleasant to Mallet. I know they 're tremendous—I know I shall never repay them. I 'm bankrupt! Do you know what that means?"

The poor lady sat staring, dismayed, and Rowland angrily interfered. "Don't talk such stuff to your mother!" he cried. "Don't you see you 're frightening her?"

"Frightening her? she may as well be frightened first as last. Do I frighten you, mother?" Roderick demanded.

"Oh, Roderick, what do you mean?" whimpered the poor lady. "Mr. Mallet, what does he mean?"

"I mean that I 'm an angry, savage, disappointed, miserable man!" Roderick went on. "I mean that I can't do a stroke of work nor think a profitable thought! I mean that I 'm in a state of helpless rage and grief and shame! Helpless, helpless—that 's what it is. You can't help me, poor mother—not with kisses, nor tears, nor prayers! Mary can't help me—not for all the honor she does me, nor all the big books on art that she pores over. Mallet can't help me—not with all his money, nor all his good example, nor all his friendship, which I 'm so profoundly well aware of: not with it all multiplied a thousand times and repeated to all eternity! I thought you would help me, you and Mary; that 's why I sent for you. But you can't, don't think it! The sooner you give up the idea the better for you. Give up being proud of me, too; there 's nothing left of me to be proud of! A year ago I was a mighty fine fellow; but do you know what has become of me now? I have gone to the devil!"

There was something in the ring of Roderick's voice, as he uttered these words, which sent them home with convincing force. He was not talking for effect, or the mere sensuous pleasure of extravagant and paradoxical utterance, as had often enough been the case ere this; he was not even talking viciously or ill-humoredly. He was talking passionately, desperately, and from an irresistible need to throw off the oppressive burden of his mother's confidence. His cruel eloquence brought the poor lady to her feet, and she stood there with clasped hands, petrified and voiceless. Mary Garland quickly left her place, came straight to Roderick, and laid her hand on his arm, looking at him with all her tormented heart in her eyes. He made no movement to disengage himself; he simply shook his head several times, in dogged negation of her healing powers. Rowland had been living for the past month in such intolerable expectancy of disaster that now that the ice was broken, and the fatal plunge taken, his foremost feeling was almost elation; but in a moment his orderly instincts and his natural love of superficial smoothness overtook it.

"I really don't see, Roderick," he said, "the profit of your talking in just this way at just this time. Don't you see how you are making your mother suffer?"

"Do I enjoy it myself?" cried Roderick. "Is the suffering all on your side and theirs? Do I look as if I were happy, and were stirring you up with a stick for my amusement? Here we all are in the same boat; we might as well understand each other! These women must know that I 'm not to be counted on. That sounds remarkably cool, no doubt, and I certainly don't deny your right to be utterly disgusted with me."

"Will you keep what you have got to say till another time," said Mary, "and let me hear it alone?"

"Oh, I 'll let you hear it as often as you please; but what 's the use of keeping it? I 'm in the humor; it won't keep! It 's a very simple matter. I 'm a failure, that 's all; I 'm not a first-rate man. I 'm second-rate, tenth-rate, anything you please. After that, it 's all one!"

Mary Garland turned away and buried her face in her hands; but Roderick, struck, apparently, in some unwonted fashion with her gesture, drew her towards him again, and went on in a somewhat different tone. "It 's hardly worth while we should have any private talk about this, Mary," he said. "The thing would be comfortable for neither of us. It 's better, after all, that it be said once for all and dismissed. There are things I can't talk to you about. Can I, at least? You are such a queer creature!"

"I can imagine nothing you should n't talk to me about," said Mary.

"You are not afraid?" he demanded, sharply, looking at her.

She turned away abruptly, with lowered eyes, hesitating a moment. "Anything you think I should hear, I will hear," she said. And then she returned to her place at the window and took up her work.

"I have had a great blow," said Roderick. "I was a great ass, but it does n't make the blow any easier to bear."

"Mr. Mallet, tell me what Roderick means!" said Mrs. Hudson, who had found her voice, in a tone more peremptory than Rowland had ever heard her use.

"He ought to have told you before," said Roderick. "Really, Rowland, if you will allow me to say so, you ought! You could have given a much better account of all this than I myself; better, especially, in that it would have been more lenient to me. You ought to have let them down gently; it would have saved them a great deal of pain. But you always want to keep things so smooth! Allow me to say that it 's very weak of you."

"I hereby renounce such weakness!" said Rowland.

"Oh, what is it, sir; what is it?" groaned Mrs. Hudson, insistently.

"It 's what Roderick says: he 's a failure!"

Mary Garland, on hearing this declaration, gave Rowland a single glance and then rose, laid down her work, and walked rapidly out of the room. Mrs. Hudson tossed her head and timidly bristled. "This from you, Mr. Mallet!" she said with an injured air which Rowland found harrowing.

But Roderick, most characteristically, did not in the least resent his friend's assertion; he sent him, on the contrary, one of those large, clear looks of his, which seemed to express a stoical pleasure in Rowland's frankness, and which set his companion, then and there, wondering again, as he had so often done before, at the extraordinary contradictions of his temperament. "My dear mother," Roderick said, "if you had had eyes that were not blinded by this sad maternal vanity, you would have seen all this for yourself; you would have seen that I 'm anything but prosperous."

"Is it anything about money?" cried Mrs. Hudson. "Oh, do write to Mr. Striker!"

"Money?" said Roderick. "I have n't a cent of money; I 'm bankrupt!"

"Oh, Mr. Mallet, how could you let him?" asked Mrs. Hudson, terribly.

"Everything I have is at his service," said Rowland, feeling ill.

"Of course Mr. Mallet will help you, my son!" cried the poor lady, eagerly.

"Oh, leave Mr. Mallet alone!" said Roderick. "I have squeezed him dry; it 's not my fault, at least, if I have n't!"

"Roderick, what have you done with all your money?" his mother demanded.

"Thrown it away! It was no such great amount. I have done nothing this winter."

"You have done nothing?"

"I have done no work! Why in the world did n't you guess it and spare me all this? Could n't you see I was idle, distracted, dissipated?"

"Dissipated, my dear son?" Mrs. Hudson repeated.

"That 's over for the present! But could n't you see—could n't Mary see—that I was in a damnably bad way?"

"I have no doubt Miss Garland saw," said Rowland.

"Mary has said nothing!" cried Mrs. Hudson.

"Oh, she 's a fine girl!" Rowland said.

"Have you done anything that will hurt poor Mary?" Mrs. Hudson asked.

"I have only been thinking night and day of another woman!"

Mrs. Hudson dropped helplessly into her seat again. "Oh dear, dear, had n't we better go home?"

"Not to get out of her way!" Roderick said. "She has started on a career of her own, and she does n't care a straw for me. My head was filled with her; I could think of nothing else; I would have sacrificed everything to her—you, Mary, Mallet, my work, my fortune, my future, my honor! I was in a fine state, eh? I don't pretend to be giving you good news; but I 'm telling the simple, literal truth, so that you may know why I have gone to the dogs. She pretended to care greatly for all this, and to be willing to make any sacrifice in return; she had a magnificent chance, for she was being forced into a mercenary marriage with a man she detested. She led me to believe that she would give this up, and break short off, and keep herself free and sacred and pure for me. This was a great honor, and you may believe that I valued it. It turned my head, and I lived only to see my happiness come to pass. She did everything to encourage me to hope it would; everything that her infernal coquetry and falsity could suggest."

"Oh, I say, this is too much!" Rowland broke out.

"Do you defend her?" Roderick cried, with a renewal of his passion. "Do you pretend to say that she gave me no hopes?" He had been speaking with growing bitterness, quite losing sight of his mother's pain and bewilderment in the passionate joy of publishing his wrongs. Since he was hurt, he must cry out; since he was in pain, he must scatter his pain abroad. Of his never thinking of others, save as they spoke and moved from his cue, as it were, this extraordinary insensibility to the injurious effects of his eloquence was a capital example; the more so as the motive of his eloquence was never an appeal for sympathy or compassion, things to which he seemed perfectly indifferent and of which he could make no use. The great and characteristic point with him was the perfect absoluteness of his own emotions and experience. He never saw himself as part of a whole; only as the clear-cut, sharp-edged, isolated individual, rejoicing or raging, as the case might be, but needing in any case absolutely to affirm himself. All this, to Rowland, was ancient history, but his perception of it stirred within him afresh, at the sight of Roderick's sense of having been betrayed. That he, under the circumstances, should not in fairness be the first to lodge a complaint of betrayal was a point to which, at his leisure, Rowland was of course capable of rendering impartial justice; but Roderick's present desperation was so peremptory that it imposed itself on one's sympathies. "Do you pretend to say," he went on, "that she did n't lead me along to the very edge of fulfillment and stupefy me with all that she suffered me to believe, all that she sacredly promised? It amused her to do it, and she knew perfectly well what she really meant. She never meant to be sincere; she never dreamed she could be. She 's a ravenous flirt, and why a flirt is a flirt is more than I can tell you. I can't understand playing with those matters; for me they 're serious, whether I take them up or lay them down. I don't see what 's in your head, Rowland, to attempt to defend Miss Light; you were the first to cry out against her! You told me she was dangerous, and I pooh-poohed you. You were right; you 're always right. She 's as cold and false and heartless as she 's beautiful, and she has sold her heartless beauty to the highest bidder. I hope he knows what he gets!"

"Oh, my son," cried Mrs. Hudson, plaintively, "how could you ever care for such a dreadful creature?"

"It would take long to tell you, dear mother!"

Rowland's lately-deepened sympathy and compassion for Christina was still throbbing in his mind, and he felt that, in loyalty to it, he must say a word for her. "You believed in her too much at first," he declared, "and you believe in her too little now."

Roderick looked at him with eyes almost lurid, beneath lowering brows. "She is an angel, then, after all?—that 's what you want to prove!" he cried. "That 's consoling for me, who have lost her! You 're always right, I say; but, dear friend, in mercy, be wrong for once!"

"Oh yes, Mr. Mallet, be merciful!" said Mrs. Hudson, in a tone which, for all its gentleness, made Rowland stare. The poor fellow's stare covered a great deal of concentrated wonder and apprehension—a presentiment of what a small, sweet, feeble, elderly lady might be capable of, in the way of suddenly generated animosity. There was no space in Mrs. Hudson's tiny maternal mind for complications of feeling, and one emotion existed only by turning another over flat and perching on top of it. She was evidently not following Roderick at all in his dusky aberrations. Sitting without, in dismay, she only saw that all was darkness and trouble, and as Roderick's glory had now quite outstripped her powers of imagination and urged him beyond her jurisdiction, so that he had become a thing too precious and sacred for blame, she found it infinitely comfortable to lay the burden of their common affliction upon Rowland's broad shoulders. Had he not promised to make them all rich and happy? And this was the end of it! Rowland felt as if his trials were, in a sense, only beginning. "Had n't you better forget all this, my dear?" Mrs. Hudson said. "Had n't you better just quietly attend to your work?"

"Work, madame?" cried Roderick. "My work 's over. I can't work—I have n't worked all winter. If I were fit for anything, this sentimental collapse would have been just the thing to cure me of my apathy and break the spell of my idleness. But there 's a perfect vacuum here!" And he tapped his forehead. "It 's bigger than ever; it grows bigger every hour!"

"I 'm sure you have made a beautiful likeness of your poor little mother," said Mrs. Hudson, coaxingly.

"I had done nothing before, and I have done nothing since! I quarreled with an excellent man, the other day, from mere exasperation of my nerves, and threw away five thousand dollars!"

"Threw away—five thousand dollars!" Roderick had been wandering among formidable abstractions and allusions too dark to penetrate. But here was a concrete fact, lucidly stated, and poor Mrs. Hudson, for a moment, looked it in the face. She repeated her son's words a third time with a gasping murmur, and then, suddenly, she burst into tears. Roderick went to her, sat down beside her, put his arm round her, fixed his eyes coldly on the floor, and waited for her to weep herself out. She leaned her head on his shoulder and sobbed broken-heartedly. She said not a word, she made no attempt to scold; but the desolation of her tears was overwhelming. It lasted some time—too long for Rowland's courage. He had stood silent, wishing simply to appear very respectful; but the elation that was mentioned a while since had utterly ebbed, and he found his situation intolerable. He walked away—not, perhaps, on tiptoe, but with a total absence of bravado in his tread.

The next day, while he was at home, the servant brought him the card of a visitor. He read with surprise the name of Mrs. Hudson, and hurried forward to meet her. He found her in his sitting-room, leaning on the arm of her son and looking very pale, her eyes red with weeping, and her lips tightly compressed. Her advent puzzled him, and it was not for some time that he began to understand the motive of it. Roderick's countenance threw no light upon it; but Roderick's countenance, full of light as it was, in a way, itself, had never thrown light upon anything. He had not been in Rowland's rooms for several weeks, and he immediately began to look at those of his own works that adorned them. He lost himself in silent contemplation. Mrs. Hudson had evidently armed herself with dignity, and, so far as she might, she meant to be impressive. Her success may be measured by the fact that Rowland's whole attention centred in the fear of seeing her begin to weep. She told him that she had come to him for practical advice; she begged to remind him that she was a stranger in the land. Where were they to go, please? what were they to do? Rowland glanced at Roderick, but Roderick had his back turned and was gazing at his Adam with the intensity with which he might have examined Michael Angelo's Moses.

"Roderick says he does n't know, he does n't care," Mrs. Hudson said; "he leaves it entirely to you."

Many another man, in Rowland's place, would have greeted this information with an irate and sarcastic laugh, and told his visitors that he thanked them infinitely for their confidence, but that, really, as things stood now, they must settle these matters between themselves; many another man might have so demeaned himself, even if, like Rowland, he had been in love with Mary Garland and pressingly conscious that her destiny was also part of the question. But Rowland swallowed all hilarity and all sarcasm, and let himself seriously consider Mrs. Hudson's petition. His wits, however, were but indifferently at his command; they were dulled by his sense of the inexpressible change in Mrs. Hudson's attitude. Her visit was evidently intended as a formal reminder of the responsiblities Rowland had worn so lightly. Mrs. Hudson was doubtless too sincerely humble a person to suppose that if he had been recreant to his vows of vigilance and tenderness, her still, small presence would operate as a chastisement. But by some diminutive logical process of her own she had convinced herself that she had been weakly trustful, and that she had suffered Rowland to think too meanly, not only of her understanding, but of her social consequence. A visit in her best gown would have an admonitory effect as regards both of these attributes; it would cancel some favors received, and show him that she was no such fool! These were the reflections of a very shy woman, who, determining for once in her life to hold up her head, was perhaps carrying it a trifle extravagantly.

"You know we have very little money to spend," she said, as Rowland remained silent. "Roderick tells me that he has debts and nothing at all to pay them with. He says I must write to Mr. Striker to sell my house for what it will bring, and send me out the money. When the money comes I must give it to him. I 'm sure I don't know; I never heard of anything so dreadful! My house is all I have. But that is all Roderick will say. We must be very economical."

Before this speech was finished Mrs. Hudson's voice had begun to quaver softly, and her face, which had no capacity for the expression of superior wisdom, to look as humbly appealing as before. Rowland turned to Roderick and spoke like a school-master. "Come away from those statues, and sit down here and listen to me!"

Roderick started, but obeyed with the most graceful docility.

"What do you propose to your mother to do?" Rowland asked.

"Propose?" said Roderick, absently. "Oh, I propose nothing."

The tone, the glance, the gesture with which this was said were horribly irritating (though obviously without the slightest intention of being so), and for an instant an imprecation rose to Rowland's lips. But he checked it, and he was afterwards glad he had done so. "You must do something," he said. "Choose, select, decide!"

"My dear Rowland, how you talk!" Roderick cried. "The very point of the matter is that I can't do anything. I will do as I 'm told, but I don't call that doing. We must leave Rome, I suppose, though I don't see why. We have got no money, and you have to pay money on the railroads."

Mrs. Hudson surreptitiously wrung her hands. "Listen to him, please!" she cried. "Not leave Rome, when we have staid here later than any Christians ever did before! It 's this dreadful place that has made us so unhappy."

"That 's very true," said Roderick, serenely. "If I had not come to Rome, I would n't have risen, and if I had not risen, I should n't have fallen."

"Fallen—fallen!" murmured Mrs. Hudson. "Just hear him!"

"I will do anything you say, Rowland," Roderick added. "I will do anything you want. I have not been unkind to my mother—have I, mother? I was unkind yesterday, without meaning it; for after all, all that had to be said. Murder will out, and my low spirits can't be hidden. But we talked it over and made it up, did n't we? It seemed to me we did. Let Rowland decide it, mother; whatever he suggests will be the right thing." And Roderick, who had hardly removed his eyes from the statues, got up again and went back to look at them.

Mrs. Hudson fixed her eyes upon the floor in silence. There was not a trace in Roderick's face, or in his voice, of the bitterness of his emotion of the day before, and not a hint of his having the lightest weight upon his conscience. He looked at Rowland with his frank, luminous eye as if there had never been a difference of opinion between them; as if each had ever been for both, unalterably, and both for each.

Rowland had received a few days before a letter from a lady of his acquaintance, a worthy Scotswoman domiciled in a villa upon one of the olive-covered hills near Florence. She held her apartment in the villa upon a long lease, and she enjoyed for a sum not worth mentioning the possession of an extraordinary number of noble, stone-floored rooms, with ceilings vaulted and frescoed, and barred windows commanding the loveliest view in the world. She was a needy and thrifty spinster, who never hesitated to declare that the lovely view was all very well, but that for her own part she lived in the villa for cheapness, and that if she had a clear three hundred pounds a year she would go and really enjoy life near her sister, a baronet's lady, at Glasgow. She was now proposing to make a visit to that exhilarating city, and she desired to turn an honest penny by sub-letting for a few weeks her historic Italian chambers. The terms on which she occupied them enabled her to ask a rent almost jocosely small, and she begged Rowland to do what she called a little genteel advertising for her. Would he say a good word for her rooms to his numerous friends, as they left Rome? He said a good word for them now to Mrs. Hudson, and told her in dollars and cents how cheap a summer's lodging she might secure. He dwelt upon the fact that she would strike a truce with tables-d'hote and have a cook of her own, amenable possibly to instruction in the Northampton mysteries. He had touched a tender chord; Mrs. Hudson became almost cheerful. Her sentiments upon the table-d'hote system and upon foreign household habits generally were remarkable, and, if we had space for it, would repay analysis; and the idea of reclaiming a lost soul to the Puritanic canons of cookery quite lightened the burden of her depression. While Rowland set forth his case Roderick was slowly walking round the magnificent Adam, with his hands in his pockets. Rowland waited for him to manifest an interest in their discussion, but the statue seemed to fascinate him and he remained calmly heedless. Rowland was a practical man; he possessed conspicuously what is called the sense of detail. He entered into Mrs. Hudson's position minutely, and told her exactly why it seemed good that she should remove immediately to the Florentine villa. She received his advice with great frigidity, looking hard at the floor and sighing, like a person well on her guard against an insidious optimism. But she had nothing better to propose, and Rowland received her permission to write to his friend that he had let the rooms.

Roderick assented to this decision without either sighs or smiles. "A Florentine villa is a good thing!" he said. "I am at your service."

"I 'm sure I hope you 'll get better there," moaned his mother, gathering her shawl together.

Roderick laid one hand on her arm and with the other pointed to Rowland's statues. "Better or worse, remember this: I did those things!" he said.

Mrs. Hudson gazed at them vaguely, and Rowland said, "Remember it yourself!"

"They are horribly good!" said Roderick.

Rowland solemnly shrugged his shoulders; it seemed to him that he had nothing more to say. But as the others were going, a last light pulsation of the sense of undischarged duty led him to address to Roderick a few words of parting advice. "You 'll find the Villa Pandolfini very delightful, very comfortable," he said. "You ought to be very contented there. Whether you work or whether you loaf, it 's a place for an artist to be happy in. I hope you will work."

"I hope I may!" said Roderick with a magnificent smile.

"When we meet again, have something to show me."

"When we meet again? Where the deuce are you going?" Roderick demanded.

"Oh, I hardly know; over the Alps."

"Over the Alps! You 're going to leave me?" Roderick cried.

Rowland had most distinctly meant to leave him, but his resolution immediately wavered. He glanced at Mrs. Hudson and saw that her eyebrows were lifted and her lips parted in soft irony. She seemed to accuse him of a craven shirking of trouble, to demand of him to repair his cruel havoc in her life by a solemn renewal of zeal. But Roderick's expectations were the oddest! Such as they were, Rowland asked himself why he should n't make a bargain with them. "You desire me to go with you?" he asked.

"If you don't go, I won't—that 's all! How in the world shall I get through the summer without you?"

"How will you get through it with me? That 's the question."

"I don't pretend to say; the future is a dead blank. But without you it 's not a blank—it 's certain damnation!"

"Mercy, mercy!" murmured Mrs. Hudson.

Rowland made an effort to stand firm, and for a moment succeeded. "If I go with you, will you try to work?"

Roderick, up to this moment, had been looking as unperturbed as if the deep agitation of the day before were a thing of the remote past. But at these words his face changed formidably; he flushed and scowled, and all his passion returned. "Try to work!" he cried. "Try—try! work—work! In God's name don't talk that way, or you 'll drive me mad! Do you suppose I 'm trying not to work? Do you suppose I stand rotting here for the fun of it? Don't you suppose I would try to work for myself before I tried for you?"

"Mr. Mallet," cried Mrs. Hudson, piteously, "will you leave me alone with this?"

Rowland turned to her and informed her, gently, that he would go with her to Florence. After he had so pledged himself he thought not at all of the pain of his position as mediator between the mother's resentful grief and the son's incurable weakness; he drank deep, only, of the satisfaction of not separating from Mary Garland. If the future was a blank to Roderick, it was hardly less so to himself. He had at moments a lively foreboding of impending calamity. He paid it no especial deference, but it made him feel indisposed to take the future into his account. When, on his going to take leave of Madame Grandoni, this lady asked at what time he would come back to Rome, he answered that he was coming back either never or forever. When she asked him what he meant, he said he really could n't tell her, and parted from her with much genuine emotion; the more so, doubtless, that she blessed him in a quite loving, maternal fashion, and told him she honestly believed him to be the best fellow in the world.

The Villa Pandolfini stood directly upon a small grass-grown piazza, on the top of a hill which sloped straight from one of the gates of Florence. It offered to the outer world a long, rather low facade, colored a dull, dark yellow, and pierced with windows of various sizes, no one of which, save those on the ground floor, was on the same level with any other. Within, it had a great, cool, gray cortile, with high, light arches around it, heavily-corniced doors, of majestic altitude, opening out of it, and a beautiful mediaeval well on one side of it. Mrs. Hudson's rooms opened into a small garden supported on immense substructions, which were planted on the farther side of the hill, as it sloped steeply away. This garden was a charming place. Its south wall was curtained with a dense orange vine, a dozen fig-trees offered you their large-leaved shade, and over the low parapet the soft, grave Tuscan landscape kept you company. The rooms themselves were as high as chapels and as cool as royal sepulchres. Silence, peace, and security seemed to abide in the ancient house and make it an ideal refuge for aching hearts. Mrs. Hudson had a stunted, brown-faced Maddalena, who wore a crimson handkerchief passed over her coarse, black locks and tied under her sharp, pertinacious chin, and a smile which was as brilliant as a prolonged flash of lightning. She smiled at everything in life, especially the things she did n't like and which kept her talent for mendacity in healthy exercise. A glance, a word, a motion was sufficient to make her show her teeth at you like a cheerful she-wolf. This inexpugnable smile constituted her whole vocabulary in her dealings with her melancholy mistress, to whom she had been bequeathed by the late occupant of the apartment, and who, to Rowland's satisfaction, promised to be diverted from her maternal sorrows by the still deeper perplexities of Maddalena's theory of roasting, sweeping, and bed-making.

Rowland took rooms at a villa a trifle nearer Florence, whence in the summer mornings he had five minutes' walk in the sharp, black, shadow-strip projected by winding, flower-topped walls, to join his friends. The life at the Villa Pandolfini, when it had fairly defined itself, was tranquil and monotonous, but it might have borrowed from exquisite circumstance an absorbing charm. If a sensible shadow rested upon it, this was because it had an inherent vice; it was feigning a repose which it very scantily felt. Roderick had lost no time in giving the full measure of his uncompromising chagrin, and as he was the central figure of the little group, as he held its heart-strings all in his own hand, it reflected faithfully the eclipse of his own genius. No one had ventured upon the cheerful commonplace of saying that the change of air and of scene would restore his spirits; this would have had, under the circumstances, altogether too silly a sound. The change in question had done nothing of the sort, and his companions had, at least, the comfort of their perspicacity. An essential spring had dried up within him, and there was no visible spiritual law for making it flow again. He was rarely violent, he expressed little of the irritation and ennui that he must have constantly felt; it was as if he believed that a spiritual miracle for his redemption was just barely possible, and was therefore worth waiting for. The most that one could do, however, was to wait grimly and doggedly, suppressing an imprecation as, from time to time, one looked at one's watch. An attitude of positive urbanity toward life was not to be expected; it was doing one's duty to hold one's tongue and keep one's hands off one's own windpipe, and other people's. Roderick had long silences, fits of profound lethargy, almost of stupefaction. He used to sit in the garden by the hour, with his head thrown back, his legs outstretched, his hands in his pockets, and his eyes fastened upon the blinding summer sky. He would gather a dozen books about him, tumble them out on the ground, take one into his lap, and leave it with the pages unturned. These moods would alternate with hours of extreme restlessness, during which he mysteriously absented himself. He bore the heat of the Italian summer like a salamander, and used to start off at high noon for long walks over the hills. He often went down into Florence, rambled through her close, dim streets, and lounged away mornings in the churches and galleries. On many of these occasions Rowland bore him company, for they were the times when he was most like his former self. Before Michael Angelo's statues and the pictures of the early Tuscans, he quite forgot his own infelicities, and picked up the thread of his old aesthetic loquacity. He had a particular fondness for Andrea del Sarto, and affirmed that if he had been a painter he would have taken the author of the Madonna del Sacco for his model. He found in Florence some of his Roman friends, and went down on certain evenings to meet them. More than once he asked Mary Garland to go with him into town, and showed her the things he most cared for. He had some modeling clay brought up to the villa and deposited in a room suitable for his work; but when this had been done he turned the key in the door and the clay never was touched. His eye was heavy and his hand cold, and his mother put up a secret prayer that he might be induced to see a doctor. But on a certain occasion, when her prayer became articulate, he had a great outburst of anger and begged her to know, once for all, that his health was better than it had ever been. On the whole, and most of the time, he was a sad spectacle; he looked so hopelessly idle. If he was not querulous and bitter, it was because he had taken an extraordinary vow not to be; a vow heroic, for him, a vow which those who knew him well had the tenderness to appreciate. Talking with him was like skating on thin ice, and his companions had a constant mental vision of spots designated "dangerous."

This was a difficult time for Rowland; he said to himself that he would endure it to the end, but that it must be his last adventure of the kind. Mrs. Hudson divided her time between looking askance at her son, with her hands tightly clasped about her pocket-handkerchief, as if she were wringing it dry of the last hour's tears, and turning her eyes much more directly upon Rowland, in the mutest, the feeblest, the most intolerable reproachfulness. She never phrased her accusations, but he felt that in the unillumined void of the poor lady's mind they loomed up like vaguely-outlined monsters. Her demeanor caused him the acutest suffering, and if, at the outset of his enterprise, he had seen, how dimly soever, one of those plaintive eye-beams in the opposite scale, the brilliancy of Roderick's promises would have counted for little. They made their way to the softest spot in his conscience and kept it chronically aching. If Mrs. Hudson had been loquacious and vulgar, he would have borne even a less valid persecution with greater fortitude. But somehow, neat and noiseless and dismally lady-like, as she sat there, keeping her grievance green with her soft-dropping tears, her displeasure conveyed an overwhelming imputation of brutality. He felt like a reckless trustee who has speculated with the widow's mite, and is haunted with the reflection of ruin that he sees in her tearful eyes. He did everything conceivable to be polite to Mrs. Hudson, and to treat her with distinguished deference. Perhaps his exasperated nerves made him overshoot the mark, and rendered his civilities a trifle peremptory. She seemed capable of believing that he was trying to make a fool of her;

she would have thought him cruelly recreant if he had suddenly departed in desperation, and yet she gave him no visible credit for his constancy. Women are said by some authorities to be cruel; I don't know how true this is, but it may at least be pertinent to remark that Mrs. Hudson was very much of a woman. It often seemed to Rowland that he had too decidedly forfeited his freedom, and that there was something positively grotesque in a man of his age and circumstances living in such a moral bondage.

But Mary Garland had helped him before, and she helped him now—helped him not less than he had assured himself she would when he found himself drifting to Florence. Yet her help was rendered in the same unconscious, unacknowledged fashion as before; there was no explicit change in their relations. After that distressing scene in Rome which had immediately preceded their departure, it was of course impossible that there should not be on Miss Garland's part some frankness of allusion to Roderick's sad condition. She had been present, the reader will remember, during only half of his unsparing confession, and Rowland had not seen her confronted with any absolute proof of Roderick's passion for Christina Light. But he knew that she knew far too much for her happiness; Roderick had told him, shortly after their settlement at the Villa Pandolfini, that he had had a "tremendous talk" with his cousin. Rowland asked no questions about it; he preferred not to know what had passed between them. If their interview had been purely painful, he wished to ignore it for Miss Garland's sake; and if it had sown the seeds of reconciliation, he wished to close his eyes to it for his own—for the sake of that unshaped idea, forever dismissed and yet forever present, which hovered in the background of his consciousness, with a hanging head, as it were, and yet an unshamed glance, and whose lightest motions were an effectual bribe to patience. Was the engagement broken? Rowland wondered, yet without asking. But it hardly mattered, for if, as was more than probable, Miss Garland had peremptorily released her cousin, her own heart had by no means recovered its liberty. It was very certain to Rowland's mind that if she had given him up she had by no means ceased to care for him passionately, and that, to exhaust her charity for his weaknesses, Roderick would have, as the phrase is, a long row to hoe. She spoke of Roderick as she might have done of a person suffering from a serious malady which demanded much tenderness; but if Rowland had found it possible to accuse her of dishonesty he would have said now that she believed appreciably less than she pretended to in her victim's being an involuntary patient. There are women whose love is care-taking and patronizing, and who rather prefer a weak man because he gives them a comfortable sense of strength. It did not in the least please Rowland to believe that Mary Garland was one of these; for he held that such women were only males in petticoats, and he was convinced that Miss Garland's heart was constructed after the most perfect feminine model. That she was a very different woman from Christina Light did not at all prove that she was less a woman, and if the Princess Casamassima had gone up into a high place to publish her disrelish of a man who lacked the virile will, it was very certain that Mary Garland was not a person to put up, at any point, with what might be called the princess's leavings. It was Christina's constant practice to remind you of the complexity of her character, of the subtlety of her mind, of her troublous faculty of seeing everything in a dozen different lights. Mary Garland had never pretended not to be simple; but Rowland had a theory that she had really a more multitudinous sense of human things, a more delicate imagination, and a finer instinct of character. She did you the honors of her mind with a grace far less regal, but was not that faculty of quite as remarkable an adjustment? If in poor Christina's strangely commingled nature there was circle within circle, and depth beneath depth, it was to be believed that Mary Garland, though she did not amuse herself with dropping stones into her soul, and waiting to hear them fall, laid quite as many sources of spiritual life under contribution. She had believed Roderick was a fine fellow when she bade him farewell beneath the Northampton elms, and this belief, to her young, strenuous, concentrated imagination, had meant many things. If it was to grow cold, it would be because disenchantment had become total and won the battle at each successive point.

Miss Garland had even in her face and carriage something of the preoccupied and wearied look of a person who is watching at a sick-bed; Roderick's broken fortunes, his dead ambitions, were a cruel burden to the heart of a girl who had believed that he possessed "genius," and supposed that genius was to one's spiritual economy what full pockets were to one's domestic. And yet, with her, Rowland never felt, as with Mrs. Hudson, that undercurrent of reproach and bitterness toward himself, that impertinent implication that he had defrauded her of happiness. Was this justice, in Miss Garland, or was it mercy? The answer would have been difficult, for she had almost let Rowland feel before leaving Rome that she liked him well enough to forgive him an injury. It was partly, Rowland fancied, that there were occasional lapses, deep and sweet, in her sense of injury. When, on arriving at Florence, she saw the place Rowland had brought them to in their trouble, she had given him a look and said a few words to him that had seemed not only a remission of guilt but a positive reward. This happened in the court of the villa—the large gray quadrangle, overstretched, from edge to edge of the red-tiled roof, by the soft Italian sky. Mary had felt on the spot the sovereign charm of the place; it was reflected in her deeply intelligent glance, and Rowland immediately accused himself of not having done the villa justice. Miss Garland took a mighty fancy to Florence, and used to look down wistfully at the towered city from the windows and garden. Roderick having now no pretext for not being her cicerone, Rowland was no longer at liberty, as he had been in Rome, to propose frequent excursions to her. Roderick's own invitations, however, were not frequent, and Rowland more than once ventured to introduce her to a gallery or a church. These expeditions were not so blissful, to his sense, as the rambles they had taken together in Rome, for his companion only half surrendered herself to her enjoyment, and seemed to have but a divided attention at her command. Often, when she had begun with looking intently at a picture, her silence, after an interval, made him turn and glance at her. He usually found that if she was looking at the picture still, she was not seeing it. Her eyes were fixed, but her thoughts were wandering, and an image more vivid than any that Raphael or Titian had drawn had superposed itself upon the canvas. She asked fewer questions than before, and seemed to have lost heart for consulting guide-books and encyclopaedias. From time to time, however, she uttered a deep, full murmur of gratification. Florence in midsummer was perfectly void of travelers, and the dense little city gave forth its aesthetic aroma with a larger frankness, as the nightingale sings when the listeners have departed. The churches were deliciously cool, but the gray streets were stifling, and the great, dove-tailed polygons of pavement as hot to the tread as molten lava. Rowland, who suffered from intense heat, would have found all this uncomfortable in solitude; but Florence had never charmed him so completely as during these midsummer strolls with his preoccupied companion. One evening they had arranged to go on the morrow to the Academy. Miss Garland kept her appointment, but as soon as she appeared, Rowland saw that something painful had befallen her. She was doing her best to look at her ease, but her face bore the marks of tears. Rowland told her that he was afraid she was ill, and that if she preferred to give up the visit to Florence he would submit with what grace he might. She hesitated a moment, and then said she preferred to adhere to their plan. "I am not well," she presently added, "but it 's a moral malady, and in such cases I consider your company beneficial."

"But if I am to be your doctor," said Rowland, "you must tell me how your illness began."

"I can tell you very little. It began with Mrs. Hudson being unjust to me, for the first time in her life. And now I am already better!"

I mention this incident because it confirmed an impression of Rowland's from which he had derived a certain consolation. He knew that Mrs. Hudson considered her son's ill-regulated passion for Christina Light a very regrettable affair, but he suspected that her manifest compassion had been all for Roderick, and not in the least for Mary Garland. She was fond of the young girl, but she had valued her primarily, during the last two years, as a kind of assistant priestess at Roderick's shrine. Roderick had honored her by asking her to become his wife, but that poor Mary had any rights in consequence Mrs. Hudson was quite incapable of perceiving. Her sentiment on the subject was of course not very vigorously formulated, but she was unprepared to admit that Miss Garland had any ground for complaint. Roderick was very unhappy; that was enough, and Mary's duty was to join her patience and her prayers to those of his doting mother. Roderick might fall in love with whom he pleased; no doubt that women trained in the mysterious Roman arts were only too proud and too happy to make it easy for him; and it was very presuming in poor, plain Mary to feel any personal resentment. Mrs. Hudson's philosophy was of too narrow a scope to suggest that a mother may forgive where a mistress cannot, and she thought herself greatly aggrieved that Miss Garland was not so disinterested as herself. She was ready to drop dead in Roderick's service, and she was quite capable of seeing her companion falter and grow faint, without a tremor of compassion. Mary, apparently, had given some intimation of her belief that if constancy is the flower of devotion, reciprocity is the guarantee of constancy, and Mrs. Hudson had rebuked her failing faith and called it cruelty. That Miss Garland had found it hard to reason with Mrs. Hudson, that she suffered deeply from the elder lady's softly bitter imputations, and that, in short, he had companionship in misfortune—all this made Rowland find a certain luxury in his discomfort.

The party at Villa Pandolfini used to sit in the garden in the evenings, which Rowland almost always spent with them. Their entertainment was in the heavily perfumed air, in the dim, far starlight, in the crenelated tower of a neighboring villa, which loomed vaguely above them in the warm darkness, and in such conversation as depressing reflections allowed. Roderick, clad always in white, roamed about like a restless ghost, silent for the most part, but making from time to time a brief observation, characterized by the most fantastic cynicism. Roderick's contributions to the conversation were indeed always so fantastic that, though half the time they wearied him unspeakably, Rowland made an effort to treat them humorously. With Rowland alone Roderick talked a great deal more; often about things related to his own work, or about artistic and aesthetic matters in general. He talked as well as ever, or even better; but his talk always ended in a torrent of groans and curses. When this current set in, Rowland straightway turned his back or stopped his ears, and Roderick now witnessed these movements with perfect indifference. When the latter was absent from the star-lit circle in the garden, as often happened, Rowland knew nothing of his whereabouts; he supposed him to be in Florence, but he never learned what he did there. All this was not enlivening, but with an even, muffled tread the days followed each other, and brought the month of August to a close. One particular evening at this time was most enchanting; there was a perfect moon, looking so extraordinarily large that it made everything its light fell upon seem small; the heat was tempered by a soft west wind, and the wind was laden with the odors of the early harvest. The hills, the vale of the Arno, the shrunken river, the domes of Florence, were vaguely effaced by the dense moonshine; they looked as if they were melting out of sight like an exorcised vision. Rowland had found the two ladies alone at the villa, and he had sat with them for an hour. He felt absolutely hushed by the solemn splendor of the scene, but he had risked the remark that, whatever life might yet have in store for either of them, this was a night that they would never forget.

"It 's a night to remember on one's death-bed!" Miss Garland exclaimed.

"Oh, Mary, how can you!" murmured Mrs. Hudson, to whom this savored of profanity, and to whose shrinking sense, indeed, the accumulated loveliness of the night seemed to have something shameless and defiant.

They were silent after this, for some time, but at last Rowland addressed certain idle words to Miss Garland. She made no reply, and he turned to look at her. She was sitting motionless, with her head pressed to Mrs. Hudson's shoulder, and the latter lady was gazing at him through the silvered dusk with a look which gave a sort of spectral solemnity to the sad, weak meaning of her eyes. She had the air, for the moment, of a little old malevolent fairy. Miss Garland, Rowland perceived in an instant, was not absolutely motionless; a tremor passed through her figure. She was weeping, or on the point of weeping, and she could not trust herself to speak. Rowland left his place and wandered to another part of the garden, wondering at the motive of her sudden tears. Of women's sobs in general he had a sovereign dread, but these, somehow, gave him a certain pleasure. When he returned to his place Miss Garland had raised her head and banished her tears. She came away from Mrs. Hudson, and they stood for a short time leaning against the parapet.

"It seems to you very strange, I suppose," said Rowland, "that there should be any trouble in such a world as this."

"I used to think," she answered, "that if any trouble came to me I would bear it like a stoic. But that was at home, where things don't speak to us of enjoyment as they do here. Here it is such a mixture; one does n't know what to choose, what to believe. Beauty stands there—beauty such as this night and this place, and all this sad, strange summer, have been so full of—and it penetrates to one's soul and lodges there, and keeps saying that man was not made to suffer, but to enjoy. This place has undermined my stoicism, but— shall I tell you? I feel as if I were saying something sinful—I love it!"

"If it is sinful, I absolve you," said Rowland, "in so far as I have power. We are made, I suppose, both to suffer and to enjoy. As you say, it 's a mixture. Just now and here, it seems a peculiarly strange one. But we must take things in turn."

His words had a singular aptness, for he had hardly uttered them when Roderick came out from the house, evidently in his darkest mood. He stood for a moment gazing hard at the view.

"It 's a very beautiful night, my son," said his mother, going to him timidly, and touching his arm.

He passed his hand through his hair and let it stay there, clasping his thick locks. "Beautiful?" he cried; "of course it 's beautiful! Everything is beautiful; everything is insolent, defiant, atrocious with beauty. Nothing is ugly but me—me and my poor dead brain!"

"Oh, my dearest son," pleaded poor Mrs. Hudson, "don't you feel any better?"

Roderick made no immediate answer; but at last he spoke in a different voice. "I came expressly to tell you that you need n't trouble yourselves any longer to wait for something to turn up. Nothing will turn up! It 's all over! I said when I came here I would give it a chance. I have given it a chance. Have n't I, eh? Have n't I, Rowland? It 's no use; the thing 's a failure! Do with me now what you please. I recommend you to set me up there at the end of the garden and shoot me."

"I feel strongly inclined," said Rowland gravely, "to go and get my revolver."

"Oh, mercy on us, what language!" cried Mrs. Hudson.

"Why not?" Roderick went on. "This would be a lovely night for it, and I should be a lucky fellow to be buried in this garden. But bury me alive, if you prefer. Take me back to Northampton."

"Roderick, will you really come?" cried his mother.

"Oh yes, I 'll go! I might as well be there as anywhere—reverting to idiocy and living upon alms. I can do nothing with all this; perhaps I should really like Northampton. If I 'm to vegetate for the rest of my days, I can do it there better than here."

"Oh, come home, come home," Mrs. Hudson said, "and we shall all be safe and quiet and happy. My dearest son, come home with your poor mother!"

"Let us go, then, and go quickly!"

Mrs. Hudson flung herself upon his neck for gratitude. "We 'll go to-morrow!" she cried. "The Lord is very good to me!"

Mary Garland said nothing to this; but she looked at Rowland, and her eyes seemed to contain a kind of alarmed appeal. Rowland noted it with exultation, but even without it he would have broken into an eager protest.

"Are you serious, Roderick?" he demanded.

"Serious? of course not! How can a man with a crack in his brain be serious? how can a muddlehead reason? But I 'm not jesting, either; I can no more make jokes than utter oracles!"

"Are you willing to go home?"

"Willing? God forbid! I am simply amenable to force; if my mother chooses to take me, I won't resist. I can't! I have come to that!"

"Let me resist, then," said Rowland. "Go home as you are now? I can't stand by and see it."

It may have been true that Roderick had lost his sense of humor, but he scratched his head with a gesture that was almost comical in its effect. "You are a queer fellow! I should think I would disgust you horribly."

"Stay another year," Rowland simply said.

"Doing nothing?"

"You shall do something. I am responsible for your doing something."

"To whom are you responsible?"

Rowland, before replying, glanced at Miss Garland, and his glance made her speak quickly. "Not to me!"

"I 'm responsible to myself," Rowland declared.

"My poor, dear fellow!" said Roderick.

"Oh, Mr. Mallet, are n't you satisfied?" cried Mrs. Hudson, in the tone in which Niobe may have addressed the avenging archers, after she had seen her eldest-born fall. "It 's out of all nature keeping him here. When we 're in a poor way, surely our own dear native land is the place for us. Do leave us to ourselves, sir!"

This just failed of being a dismissal in form, and Rowland bowed his head to it. Roderick was silent for some moments; then, suddenly, he covered his face with his two hands. "Take me at least out of this terrible Italy," he cried, "where everything mocks and reproaches and torments and eludes me! Take me out of this land of impossible beauty and put me in the midst of ugliness. Set me down where nature is coarse and flat, and men and manners are vulgar. There must be something awfully ugly in Germany. Pack me off there!"

Rowland answered that if he wished to leave Italy the thing might be arranged; he would think it over and submit a proposal on the morrow. He suggested to Mrs. Hudson, in consequence, that she should spend the autumn in Switzerland, where she would find a fine tonic climate, plenty of fresh milk, and several pensions at three francs and a half a day. Switzerland, of course, was not ugly, but one could not have everything.

Mrs. Hudson neither thanked him nor assented; but she wept and packed her trunks. Rowland had a theory, after the scene which led to these preparations, that Mary Garland was weary of waiting for Roderick to come to his senses, that the faith which had bravely borne his manhood company hitherto, on the tortuous march he was leading it, had begun to believe it had gone far enough. This theory was not vitiated by something she said to him on the day before that on which Mrs. Hudson had arranged to leave Florence.

"Cousin Sarah, the other evening," she said, "asked you to please leave us. I think she hardly knew what she was saying, and I hope you have not taken offense."

"By no means; but I honestly believe that my leaving you would contribute greatly to Mrs. Hudson's comfort. I can be your hidden providence, you know; I can watch you at a distance, and come upon the scene at critical moments."

Miss Garland looked for a moment at the ground; and then, with sudden earnestness, "I beg you to come with us!" she said.

It need hardly be added that after this Rowland went with them.

CHAPTER XII. The Princess Casamassima

Rowland had a very friendly memory of a little mountain inn, accessible with moderate trouble from Lucerne, where he had once spent a blissful ten days. He had at that time been trudging, knapsack on back, over half Switzerland, and not being, on his legs, a particularly light weight, it was no shame to him to confess that he was mortally tired. The inn of which I speak presented striking analogies with a cow-stable; but in spite of this circumstance, it was crowded with hungry tourists. It stood in a high, shallow valley, with flower-strewn Alpine meadows sloping down to it from the base of certain rugged rocks whose outlines were grotesque against the evening sky. Rowland had seen grander places in Switzerland that pleased him less, and whenever afterwards he wished to think of Alpine opportunities at their best, he recalled this grassy concave among the mountain-tops, and the August days he spent there, resting deliciously, at his length, in the lee of a sun-warmed boulder, with the light cool air stirring about his temples, the wafted odors of the pines in his nostrils, the tinkle of the cattle-bells in his ears, the vast progression of the mountain shadows before his eyes, and a volume of Wordsworth in his pocket. His face, on the Swiss hill-sides, had been scorched to within a shade of the color nowadays called magenta, and his bed was a pallet in a loft, which he shared with a German botanist of colossal stature—every inch of him quaking at an open window. These had been drawbacks to felicity, but Rowland hardly cared where or how he was lodged, for he spent the livelong day under the sky, on the crest of a slope that looked at the Jungfrau. He remembered all this on leaving Florence with his friends, and he reflected that, as the midseason was over, accommodations would be more ample, and charges more modest. He communicated with his old friend the landlord, and, while September was yet young, his companions established themselves under his guidance in the grassy valley.

He had crossed the Saint Gothard Pass with them, in the same carriage. During the journey from Florence, and especially during this portion of it, the cloud that hung over the little party had been almost dissipated, and they had looked at each other, in the close contiguity of the train and the posting-carriage, without either accusing or consoling glances. It was impossible not to enjoy the magnificent scenery of the Apennines and the Italian Alps, and there was a tacit agreement among the travelers to abstain from sombre allusions. The effect of this delicate compact seemed excellent; it ensured them a week's intellectual sunshine. Roderick sat and gazed out of the window with a fascinated stare, and with a perfect docility of attitude. He concerned himself not a particle about the itinerary, or about any of the wayside arrangements; he took no trouble, and he gave none. He assented to everything that was proposed, talked very little, and led for a week a perfectly contemplative life. His mother rarely removed her eyes from him; and if, a while before, this would have extremely irritated him, he now seemed perfectly unconscious of her observation and profoundly indifferent to anything that might befall him. They spent a couple of days on the Lake of Como, at a hotel with white porticoes smothered in oleander and myrtle, and the terrace-steps leading down to little boats with striped awnings. They agreed it was the earthly paradise, and they passed the mornings strolling through the perfumed alleys of classic villas, and the evenings floating in the moonlight in a circle of outlined mountains, to the music of silver-trickling oars. One day, in the afternoon, the two young men took a long stroll together. They followed the winding footway that led toward Como, close to the lake-side, past the gates of villas and the walls of vineyards, through little hamlets propped on a dozen arches, and bathing their feet and their pendant tatters in the gray-green ripple; past frescoed walls and crumbling campaniles and grassy village piazzas, and the mouth of soft ravines that wound upward, through belts of swinging vine and vaporous olive and splendid chestnut, to high ledges where white chapels gleamed amid the paler boskage, and bare cliff-surfaces, with their sun-cracked lips, drank in the azure light. It all was confoundingly picturesque; it was the Italy that we know from the steel engravings in old keepsakes and annuals, from the vignettes on music-sheets and the drop-curtains at theatres; an Italy that we can never confess to ourselves—in spite of our own changes and of Italy's—that we have ceased to believe in. Rowland and Roderick turned aside from the little paved footway that clambered and dipped and wound and doubled beside the lake, and stretched themselves idly beneath a fig-tree, on a grassy promontory. Rowland had never known anything so divinely soothing as the dreamy softness of that early autumn afternoon. The iridescent mountains shut him in; the little waves, beneath him, fretted the white pebbles at the laziest intervals; the festooned vines above him swayed just visibly in the all but motionless air.

Roderick lay observing it all with his arms thrown back and his hands under his head. "This suits me," he said; "I could be happy here and forget everything. Why not stay here forever?" He kept his position for a long time and seemed lost in his thoughts. Rowland spoke to him, but he made vague answers; at last he closed his eyes. It seemed to Rowland, also, a place to stay in forever; a place for perfect oblivion of the disagreeable. Suddenly Roderick turned over on his face, and buried it in his arms. There had been something passionate in his movement; but Rowland was nevertheless surprised, when he at last jerked himself back into a sitting posture, to perceive the trace of tears in his eyes. Roderick turned to his friend, stretching his two hands out toward the lake and mountains, and shaking them with an eloquent gesture, as if his heart was too full for utterance.

"Pity me, sir; pity me!" he presently cried. "Look at this lovely world, and think what it must be to be dead to it!"

"Dead?" said Rowland.

"Dead, dead; dead and buried! Buried in an open grave, where you lie staring up at the sailing clouds, smelling the waving flowers, and hearing all nature live and grow above you! That 's the way I feel!"

"I am glad to hear it," said Rowland. "Death of that sort is very near to resurrection."

"It 's too horrible," Roderick went on; "it has all come over me here tremendously! If I were not ashamed, I could shed a bushel of tears. For one hour of what I have been, I would give up anything I may be!"

"Never mind what you have been; be something better!"

"I shall never be anything again: it 's no use talking! But I don't know what secret spring has been touched since I have lain here. Something in my heart seemed suddenly to open and let in a flood of beauty and desire. I know what I have lost, and I think it horrible! Mind you, I know it, I feel it! Remember that hereafter. Don't say that he was stupefied and senseless; that his perception was dulled and his aspiration dead. Say that he trembled in every nerve with a sense of the beauty and sweetness of life; that he rebelled and protested and shrieked; that he was buried alive, with his eyes open, and his heart beating to madness; that he clung to every blade of grass and every way-side thorn as he passed; that it was the most horrible spectacle you ever witnessed; that it was an outrage, a murder, a massacre!"

"Good heavens, man, are you insane?" Rowland cried.

"I never have been saner. I don't want to be bad company, and in this beautiful spot, at this delightful hour, it seems an outrage to break the charm. But I am bidding farewell to Italy, to beauty, to honor, to life! I only want to assure you that I know what I lose. I know it in every pulse of my heart! Here, where these things are all loveliest, I take leave of them. Farewell, farewell!"

During their passage of the Saint Gothard, Roderick absented himself much of the time from the carriage, and rambled far in advance, along the huge zigzags of the road. He displayed an extraordinary activity; his light weight and slender figure made him an excellent pedestrian, and his friends frequently saw him skirting the edge of plunging chasms, loosening the stones on long, steep slopes, or lifting himself against the sky, from the top of rocky pinnacles. Mary Garland walked a great deal, but she remained near the carriage to be with Mrs. Hudson. Rowland remained near it to be with Miss Garland. He trudged by her side up that magnificent ascent from Italy, and found himself regretting that the Alps were so low, and that their trudging was not to last a week. She was exhilarated; she liked to walk; in the way of mountains, until within the last few weeks, she had seen nothing greater than Mount Holyoke, and she found that the Alps amply justified their reputation. Rowland knew that she loved nature, but he was struck afresh with the vivacity of her observation of it, and with her knowledge of plants and stones. At that season the wild flowers had mostly departed, but a few of them lingered, and Miss Garland never failed to espy them in their outlying corners. They interested her greatly; she was charmed when they were old friends, and charmed even more when they were new. She displayed a very light foot in going in quest of them, and had soon covered the front seat of the carriage with a tangle of strange vegetation. Rowland of course was alert in her service, and he gathered for her several botanical specimens which at first seemed inaccessible. One of these, indeed, had at first appeared easier of capture than his attempt attested, and he had paused a moment at the base of the little peak on which it grew, measuring the risk of farther pursuit. Suddenly, as he stood there, he remembered Roderick's defiance of danger and of Miss Light, at the Coliseum, and he was seized with a strong desire to test the courage of his companion. She had just scrambled up a grassy slope near him, and had seen that the flower was out of reach. As he prepared to approach it, she called to him eagerly to stop; the thing was impossible! Poor Rowland, whose passion had been terribly starved, enjoyed immensely the thought of having her care, for three minutes, what became of him. He was the least brutal of men, but for a moment he was perfectly indifferent to her suffering.

"I can get the flower," he called to her. "Will you trust me?"

"I don't want it; I would rather not have it!" she cried.

"Will you trust me?" he repeated, looking at her.

She looked at him and then at the flower; he wondered whether she would shriek and swoon, as Miss Light had done. "I wish it were something better!" she said simply; and then stood watching him, while he began to clamber. Rowland was not shaped for an acrobat, and his enterprise was difficult; but he kept his wits about him, made the most of narrow foot-holds and coigns of vantage, and at last secured his prize. He managed to stick it into his buttonhole and then he contrived to descend. There was more than one chance for an ugly fall, but he evaded them all. It was doubtless not gracefully done, but it was done, and that was all he had proposed to himself. He was red in the face when he offered Miss Garland the flower, and she was visibly pale. She had watched him without moving. All this had passed without the knowledge of Mrs. Hudson, who was dozing beneath the hood of the carriage. Mary Garland's eyes did not perhaps display that ardent admiration which was formerly conferred by the queen of beauty at a tournament; but they expressed something in which Rowland found his reward. "Why did you do that?" she asked, gravely.

He hesitated. He felt that it was physically possible to say, "Because I love you!" but that it was not morally possible. He lowered his pitch and answered, simply, "Because I wanted to do something for you."

"Suppose you had fallen," said Miss Garland.

"I believed I would not fall. And you believed it, I think."

"I believed nothing. I simply trusted you, as you asked me."

"Quod erat demonstrandum!" cried Rowland. "I think you know Latin."

When our four friends were established in what I have called their grassy valley, there was a good deal of scrambling over slopes both grassy and stony, a good deal of flower-plucking on narrow ledges, a great many long walks, and, thanks to the lucid mountain air, not a little exhilaration. Mrs. Hudson was obliged to intermit her suspicions of the deleterious atmosphere of the old world, and to acknowledge the edifying purity of the breezes of Engelthal. She was certainly more placid than she had been in Italy; having always lived in the country, she had missed in Rome and Florence that social solitude mitigated by bushes and rocks which is so dear to the true New England temperament. The little unpainted inn at Engelthal, with its plank partitions, its milk-pans standing in the sun, its "help," in the form of angular young women of the country-side, reminded her of places of summer sojourn in her native land; and the beautiful historic chambers of the Villa Pandolfini passed from her memory without a regret, and without having in the least modified her ideal of domiciliary grace. Roderick had changed his sky, but he had not changed his mind; his humor was still that of which he had given Rowland a glimpse in that tragic explosion on the Lake of Como. He kept his despair to himself, and he went doggedly about the ordinary business of life; but it was easy to see that his spirit was mortally heavy, and that he lived and moved and talked simply from the force of habit. In that sad half-hour among the Italian olives there had been such a fierce sincerity in his tone, that Rowland began to abdicate the critical attitude. He began to feel that it was essentially vain to appeal to the poor fellow's will; there was no will left; its place was an impotent void. This view of the case indeed was occasionally contravened by certain indications on Roderick's part of the power of resistance to disagreeable obligations: one might still have said, if one had been disposed to be didactic at any hazard, that there was a method in his madness, that his moral energy had its sleeping and its waking hours, and that, in a cause that pleased it, it was capable of rising with the dawn. But on the other hand, pleasure, in this case, was quite at one with effort; evidently the greatest bliss in life, for Roderick, would have been to have a plastic idea. And then, it was impossible not to feel tenderly to a despair which had so ceased to be aggressive—not to forgive a great deal of apathy to a temper which had so unlearned its irritability. Roderick said frankly that Switzerland made him less miserable than Italy, and the Alps seemed less to mock at his enforced leisure than the Apennines. He indulged in long rambles, generally alone, and was very fond of climbing into dizzy places, where no sound could overtake him, and there, flinging himself on the never-trodden moss, of pulling his hat over his eyes and lounging away the hours in perfect immobility. Rowland sometimes walked with him; though Roderick never invited him, he seemed duly grateful for his society. Rowland now made it a rule to treat him like a perfectly sane man, to assume that all things were well with him, and never to allude to the prosperity he had forfeited or to the work he was not doing. He would have still said, had you questioned him, that Roderick's condition was a mood—certainly a puzzling one. It might last yet for many a weary hour; but it was a long lane that had no turning. Roderick's blues would not last forever. Rowland's interest in Miss Garland's relations with her cousin was still profoundly attentive, and perplexed as he was on all sides, he found nothing transparent here. After their arrival at Engelthal, Roderick appeared to seek the young girl's society more than he had done hitherto, and this revival of ardor could not fail to set his friend a-wondering. They sat together and strolled together, and Miss Garland often read aloud to him. One day, on their coming to dinner, after he had been lying half the morning at her feet, in the shadow of a rock, Rowland asked him what she had been reading.

"I don't know," Roderick said, "I don't heed the sense." Miss Garland heard this, and Rowland looked at her. She looked at Roderick sharply and with a little blush. "I listen to Mary," Roderick continued, "for the sake of her voice. It 's distractingly sweet!" At this Miss Garland's blush deepened, and she looked away.

Rowland, in Florence, as we know, had suffered his imagination to wander in the direction of certain conjectures which the reader may deem unflattering to Miss Garland's constancy. He had asked himself whether her faith in Roderick had not faltered, and that demand of hers which had brought about his own departure for Switzerland had seemed almost equivalent to a confession that she needed his help to believe. Rowland was essentially a modest man, and he did not risk the supposition that Miss Garland had contrasted him with Roderick to his own advantage; but he had a certain consciousness of duty resolutely done which allowed itself to fancy, at moments, that it might be not illogically rewarded by the bestowal of such stray grains of enthusiasm as had crumbled away from her estimate of his companion. If some day she had declared, in a sudden burst of passion, that she was outwearied and sickened, and that she gave up her recreant lover, Rowland's expectation would have gone half-way to meet her. And certainly if her passion had taken this course no generous critic would utterly condemn her. She had been neglected, ignored, forsaken, treated with a contempt which no girl of a fine temper could endure. There were girls, indeed, whose fineness, like that of Burd Helen in the ballad, lay in clinging to the man of their love through thick and thin, and in bowing their head to all hard usage. This attitude had often an exquisite beauty of its own, but Rowland deemed that he had solid reason to believe it never could be Mary Garland's. She was not a passive creature; she was not soft and meek and grateful for chance bounties. With all her reserve of manner she was proud and eager; she asked much and she wanted what she asked; she believed in fine things and she never could long persuade herself that fine things missed were as beautiful as fine things achieved. Once Rowland passed an angry day. He had dreamed—it was the most insubstantial of dreams—that she had given him the right to believe that she looked to him to transmute her discontent. And yet here she was throwing herself back into Roderick's arms at his lightest overture, and playing with his own half fearful, half shameful hopes! Rowland declared to himself that his position was essentially detestable, and that all the philosophy he could bring to bear upon it would make it neither honorable nor comfortable. He would go away and make an end of it. He did not go away; he simply took a long walk, stayed away from the inn all day, and on his return found Miss Garland sitting out in the moonlight with Roderick.

Rowland, communing with himself during the restless ramble in question, had determined that he would at least cease to observe, to heed, or to care for what Miss Garland and Roderick might do or might not do together. Nevertheless, some three days afterward, the opportunity presenting itself, he deliberately broached the subject with Roderick. He knew this was inconsistent and faint-hearted; it was indulgence to the fingers that itched to handle forbidden fruit. But he said to himself that it was really more logical to be inconsistent than the reverse; for they had formerly discussed these mysteries very candidly. Was it not perfectly reasonable that he should wish to know the sequel of the situation which Roderick had then delineated? Roderick had made him promises, and it was to be expected that he should ascertain how the promises had been kept. Rowland could not say to himself that if the promises had been extorted for Mary Garland's sake, his present attention to them was equally disinterested; and so he had to admit that he was indeed faint-hearted. He may perhaps be deemed too narrow a casuist, but we have repeated more than once that he was solidly burdened with a conscience.

"I imagine," he said to Roderick, "that you are not sorry, at present, to have allowed yourself to be dissuaded from making a final rupture with Miss Garland."

Roderick eyed him with the vague and absent look which had lately become habitual to his face, and repeated "Dissuaded?"

"Don't you remember that, in Rome, you wished to break your engagement, and that I urged you to respect it, though it seemed to hang by so slender a thread? I wished you to see what would come of it? If I am not mistaken, you are reconciled to it."

"Oh yes," said Roderick, "I remember what you said; you made it a kind of personal favor to yourself that I should remain faithful. I consented,

654

but afterwards, when I thought of it, your attitude greatly amused me. Had it ever been seen before?—a man asking another man to gratify him by not suspending his attentions to a pretty girl!"

"It was as selfish as anything else," said Rowland. "One man puts his selfishness into one thing, and one into another. It would have utterly marred my comfort to see Miss Garland in low spirits."

"But you liked her—you admired her, eh? So you intimated."

"I admire her profoundly."

"It was your originality then—to do you justice you have a great deal, of a certain sort—to wish her happiness secured in just that fashion. Many a man would have liked better himself to make the woman he admired happy, and would have welcomed her low spirits as an opening for sympathy. You were awfully queer about it."

"So be it!" said Rowland. "The question is, Are you not glad I was queer? Are you not finding that your affection for Miss Garland has a permanent quality which you rather underestimated?"

"I don't pretend to say. When she arrived in Rome, I found I did n't care for her, and I honestly proposed that we should have no humbug about it. If you, on the contrary, thought there was something to be gained by having a little humbug, I was willing to try it! I don't see that the situation is really changed. Mary Garland is all that she ever was—more than all. But I don't care for her! I don't care for anything, and I don't find myself inspired to make an exception in her favor. The only difference is that I don't care now, whether I care for her or not. Of course, marrying such a useless lout as I am is out of the question for any woman, and I should pay Miss Garland a poor compliment to assume that she is in a hurry to celebrate our nuptials."

"Oh, you 're in love!" said Rowland, not very logically. It must be confessed, at any cost, that this assertion was made for the sole purpose of hearing Roderick deny it.

But it quite failed of its aim. Roderick gave a liberal shrug of his shoulders and an irresponsible toss of his head. "Call it what you please! I am past caring for names."

Rowland had not only been illogical, he had also been slightly disingenuous. He did not believe that his companion was in love; he had argued the false to learn the true. The true was that Roderick was again, in some degree, under a charm, and that he found a healing virtue in Mary's presence, indisposed though he was to admit it. He had said, shortly before, that her voice was sweet to his ear; and this was a promising beginning. If her voice was sweet it was probable that her glance was not amiss, that her touch had a quiet magic, and that her whole personal presence had learned the art of not being irritating. So Rowland reasoned, and invested Mary Garland with a still finer loveliness.

It was true that she herself helped him little to definite conclusions, and that he remained in puzzled doubt as to whether these happy touches were still a matter of the heart, or had become simply a matter of the conscience. He watched for signs that she rejoiced in Roderick's renewed acceptance of her society; but it seemed to him that she was on her guard against interpreting it too largely. It was now her turn—he fancied that he sometimes gathered from certain nameless indications of glance and tone and gesture—it was now her turn to be indifferent, to care for other things. Again and again Rowland asked himself what these things were that Miss Garland might be supposed to care for, to the injury of ideal constancy; and again, having designated them, he divided them into two portions. One was that larger experience, in general, which had come to her with her arrival in Europe; the vague sense, borne in upon her imagination, that there were more things one might do with one's life than youth and ignorance and Northampton had dreamt of; the revision of old pledges in the light of new emotions. The other was the experience, in especial, of Rowland's—what? Here Rowland always paused, in perfect sincerity, to measure afresh his possible claim to the young girl's regard. What might he call it? It had been more than civility and yet it had been less than devotion. It had spoken of a desire to serve, but it had said nothing of a hope of reward. Nevertheless, Rowland's fancy hovered about the idea that it was recompensable, and his reflections ended in a reverie which perhaps did not define it, but at least, on each occasion, added a little to its volume. Since Miss Garland had asked him as a sort of favor to herself to come also to Switzerland, he thought it possible she might let him know whether he seemed to have effectively served her. The days passed without her doing so, and at last Rowland walked away to an isolated eminence some five miles from the inn and murmured to the silent rocks that she was ungrateful. Listening nature seemed not to contradict him, so that, on the morrow, he asked the young girl, with an infinitesimal touch of irony, whether it struck her that his deflection from his Florentine plan had been attended with brilliant results.

"Why, we are delighted that you are with us!" she answered.

He was anything but satisfied with this; it seemed to imply that she had forgotten that she had solemnly asked him to come. He reminded her of her request, and recalled the place and time. "That evening on the terrace, late, after Mrs. Hudson had gone to bed, and Roderick being absent."

She perfectly remembered, but the memory seemed to trouble her. "I am afraid your kindness has been a great charge upon you," she said. "You wanted very much to do something else."

"I wanted above all things to oblige you, and I made no sacrifice. But if I had made an immense one, it would be more than made up to me by any assurance that I have helped Roderick into a better mood."

She was silent a moment, and then, "Why do you ask me?" she said. "You are able to judge quite as well as I."

Rowland blushed; he desired to justify himself in the most veracious manner. "The truth is," he said, "that I am afraid I care only in the second place for Roderick's holding up his head. What I care for in the first place is your happiness."

"I don't know why that should be," she answered. "I have certainly done nothing to make you so much my friend. If you were to tell me you intended to leave us to-morrow, I am afraid that I should not venture to ask you to stay. But whether you go or stay, let us not talk of Roderick!"

"But that," said Rowland, "does n't answer my question. Is he better?"

"No!" she said, and turned away.

He was careful not to tell her that he intended to leave them. One day, shortly after this, as the two young men sat at the inn-door watching the sunset, which on that evening was very striking and lurid, Rowland made an attempt to sound his companion's present sentiment touching Christina Light. "I wonder where she is," he said, "and what sort of a life she is leading her prince."

Roderick at first made no response. He was watching a figure on the summit of some distant rocks, opposite to them. The figure was apparently descending into the valley, and in relief against the crimson screen of the western sky, it looked gigantic. "Christina Light?" Roderick at last repeated, as if arousing himself from a reverie. "Where she is? It 's extraordinary how little I care!"

"Have you, then, completely got over it?"

To this Roderick made no direct reply; he sat brooding a while. "She 's a humbug!" he presently exclaimed.

"Possibly!" said Rowland. "But I have known worse ones."

"She disappointed me!" Roderick continued in the same tone.

"Had she, then, really given you hopes?"

"Oh, don't recall it!" Roderick cried. "Why the devil should I think of it? It was only three months ago, but it seems like ten years." His friend said nothing more, and after a while he went on of his own accord. "I believed there was a future in it all! She pleased me—pleased me; and when an artist—such as I was—is pleased, you know!" And he paused again. "You never saw her as I did; you never heard her in her great moments. But there is no use talking about that! At first she would n't regard me seriously; she chaffed me and made light of me. But at last I forced her to admit I was a great man. Think of that, sir! Christina Light called me a great man. A great man was what she was looking for, and we agreed to find our happiness for life in each other. To please me she promised not to marry till I gave her leave. I was not in a marrying way myself, but it was damnation to think of another man possessing her. To spare my sensibilities, she promised to turn off her prince, and the idea of her doing so made me as happy as to see a perfect statue shaping itself in the block. You have seen how she kept her promise! When I learned it, it was as if the statue had suddenly cracked and turned hideous. She died for me, like that!" And he snapped his fingers. "Was it wounded vanity, disappointed desire, betrayed confidence? I am sure I don't know; you certainly have some name for it."

"The poor girl did the best she could," said Rowland.

"If that was her best, so much the worse for her! I have hardly thought of her these two months, but I have not forgiven her."

"Well, you may believe that you are avenged. I can't think of her as happy."

"I don't pity her!" said Roderick. Then he relapsed into silence, and the two sat watching the colossal figure as it made its way downward along the jagged silhouette of the rocks. "Who is this mighty man," cried Roderick at last, "and what is he coming down upon us for? We are small people here, and we can't undertake to keep company with giants."

"Wait till we meet him on our own level," said Rowland, "and perhaps he will not overtop us."

"For ten minutes, at least," Roderick rejoined, "he will have been a great man!" At this moment the figure sank beneath the horizon line and became invisible in the uncertain light. Suddenly Roderick said, "I would like to see her once more—simply to look at her."

"I would not advise it," said Rowland.

"It was her beauty that did it!" Roderick went on. "It was all her beauty; in comparison, the rest was nothing. What befooled me was to think of it as my property! And I had made it mine—no one else had studied it as I had, no one else understood it. What does that stick of a Casamassima know about it at this hour? I should like to see it just once more; it 's the only thing in the world of which I can say so."

"I would not advise it," Rowland repeated.

"That 's right, dear Rowland," said Roderick; "don't advise! That 's no use now."

The dusk meanwhile had thickened, and they had not perceived a figure approaching them across the open space in front of the house. Suddenly it stepped into the circle of light projected from the door and windows, and they beheld little Sam Singleton stopping to stare at them. He was the giant whom they had seen descending along the rocks. When this was made apparent Roderick was seized with a fit of intense hilarity—it was the first time he had laughed in three months. Singleton, who carried a knapsack and walking-staff, received from Rowland the friendliest welcome. He was in the serenest possible humor, and if in the way of luggage his knapsack contained nothing but a comb and a second shirt, he produced from it a dozen admirable sketches. He had been trudging over half Switzerland and making everywhere the most vivid pictorial notes. They were mostly in a box at Interlaken, and in gratitude for Rowland's appreciation, he presently telegraphed for his box, which, according to the excellent Swiss method, was punctually delivered by post. The nights were cold, and our friends, with three or four other chance sojourners, sat in-doors over a fire of logs. Even with Roderick sitting moodily in the outer shadow they made a sympathetic little circle, and they turned over Singleton's drawings, while he perched in the chimney-corner, blushing and grinning, with his feet on the rounds of his chair. He had been pedestrianizing for six weeks, and he was glad to rest awhile at Engelthal. It was an economic repose, however, for he sallied forth every morning, with his sketching tools on his back, in search of material for new studies. Roderick's hilarity, after the first evening, had subsided, and he watched the little painter's serene activity with a gravity that was almost portentous. Singleton, who was not in the secret of his personal misfortunes, still treated him with timid frankness as the rising star of American art. Roderick had said to Rowland, at first, that Singleton reminded him of some curious little insect with a remarkable mechanical instinct in its antennae; but as the days went by it was apparent that the modest landscapist's unflagging industry grew to have an oppressive meaning for him. It pointed a moral, and Roderick used to sit and con the moral as he saw it figured in Singleton's bent back, on the hot hill-sides, protruding from beneath his white umbrella. One day he wandered up a long slope and overtook him as he sat at work; Singleton related the incident afterwards to Rowland, who, after giving him in Rome a hint of Roderick's aberrations, had strictly kept his own counsel.

"Are you always like this?" said Roderick, in almost sepulchral accents.

"Like this?" repeated Singleton, blinking confusedly, with an alarmed conscience.

"You remind me of a watch that never runs down. If one listens hard one hears you always—tic-tic, tic-tic."

"Oh, I see," said Singleton, beaming ingenuously. "I am very equable."

"You are very equable, yes. And do you find it pleasant to be equable?"

Singleton turned and grinned more brightly, while he sucked the water from his camel's-hair brush. Then, with a quickened sense of his indebtedness to a Providence that had endowed him with intrinsic facilities, "Oh, delightful!" he exclaimed.

Roderick stood looking at him a moment. "Damnation!" he said at last, solemnly, and turned his back.

One morning, shortly after this, Rowland and Roderick took a long walk. They had walked before in a dozen different directions, but they had not yet crossed a charming little wooded pass, which shut in their valley on one side and descended into the vale of Engelberg. In coming from Lucerne they had approached their inn by this path, and, feeling that they knew it, had hitherto neglected it in favor of untrodden ways. But at last the list of these was exhausted, and Rowland proposed the walk to Engelberg as a novelty. The place is half bleak and half pastoral; a huge white monastery rises abruptly from the green floor of the valley and complicates its picturesqueness with an element rare in Swiss scenery. Hard by is a group of chalets and inns, with the usual appurtenances of a prosperous Swiss resort—lean brown guides in baggy homespun, lounging under carved wooden galleries, stacks of alpenstocks in every doorway, sun-scorched Englishmen without shirt-collars. Our two friends sat a while at the door of an inn, discussing a pint of wine, and then Roderick, who was indefatigable, announced his intention of climbing to a certain rocky pinnacle which overhung the valley, and, according to the testimony of one of the guides, commanded a view of the Lake of Lucerne. To go and come back was only a matter of an hour, but Rowland, with the prospect of his homeward trudge before him, confessed to a preference for lounging on his bench, or at most strolling a trifle farther and taking a look at the monastery. Roderick went off alone, and his companion after a while bent his steps to the monasterial church. It was remarkable, like most of the churches of Catholic Switzerland, for a hideous style of devotional ornament; but it had a certain cold and musty picturesqueness, and Rowland lingered there with some tenderness for Alpine piety. While he was near the high-altar some people came in at the west door; but he did not notice them, and was presently engaged in deciphering a curious old German epitaph on one of the mural tablets. At last he turned away, wondering whether its syntax or its theology was the more uncomfortable, and, to this infinite surprise, found himself confronted with the Prince and Princess Casamassima.

The surprise on Christina's part, for an instant, was equal, and at first she seemed disposed to turn away without letting it give place to a greeting. The prince, however, saluted gravely, and then Christina, in silence, put out her hand. Rowland immediately asked whether they were staying at Engelberg, but Christina only looked at him without speaking. The prince answered his questions, and related that they had been making a month's tour in Switzerland, that at Lucerne his wife had been somewhat obstinately indisposed, and that the physician had recommended a week's trial of the tonic air and goat's milk of Engelberg. The scenery, said the prince, was stupendous, but the life was terribly sad—and they had three days more! It was a blessing, he urbanely added, to see a good Roman face.

Christina's attitude, her solemn silence and her penetrating gaze seemed to Rowland, at first, to savor of affectation; but he presently perceived that she was profoundly agitated, and that she was afraid of betraying herself. "Do let us leave this hideous edifice," she said; "there are things here that set one's teeth on edge." They moved slowly to the door, and when they stood outside, in the sunny coolness of the valley, she turned to Rowland and said, "I am extremely glad to see you." Then she glanced about her and observed, against the wall of the church, an old stone seat. She looked at Prince Casamassima a moment, and he smiled more intensely, Rowland thought, than the occasion demanded. "I wish to sit here," she said, "and speak to Mr. Mallet—alone."

"At your pleasure, dear friend," said the prince.

The tone of each was measured, to Rowland's ear; but that of Christina was dry, and that of her husband was splendidly urbane. Rowland remembered that the Cavaliere Giacosa had told him that Mrs. Light's candidate was thoroughly a prince, and our friend wondered how he relished a peremptory accent. Casamassima was an Italian of the undemonstrative type, but Rowland nevertheless divined that, like other princes before him, he had made the acquaintance of the thing called compromise. "Shall I come back?" he asked with the same smile.

"In half an hour," said Christina.

In the clear outer light, Rowland's first impression of her was that she was more beautiful than ever. And yet in three months she could hardly have changed; the change was in Rowland's own vision of her, which that last interview, on the eve of her marriage, had made unprecedentedly tender.

"How came you here?" she asked. "Are you staying in this place?"

"I am staying at Engelthal, some ten miles away; I walked over."

"Are you alone?"

"I am with Mr. Hudson."

"Is he here with you?"

"He went half an hour ago to climb a rock for a view."

"And his mother and that young girl, where are they?"

"They also are at Engelthal."

"What do you do there?"

"What do you do here?" said Rowland, smiling.

"I count the minutes till my week is up. I hate mountains; they depress me to death. I am sure Miss Garland likes them."

"She is very fond of them, I believe."

"You believe—don't you know? But I have given up trying to imitate Miss Garland," said Christina.

"You surely need imitate no one."

"Don't say that," she said gravely. "So you have walked ten miles this morning? And you are to walk back again?"

"Back again to supper."

"And Mr. Hudson too?"

"Mr. Hudson especially. He is a great walker."

"You men are happy!" Christina cried. "I believe I should enjoy the mountains if I could do such things. It is sitting still and having them scowl down at you! Prince Casamassina never rides. He only goes on a mule. He was carried up the Faulhorn on a litter."

"On a litter?" said Rowland.

"In one of those machines—a chaise a porteurs—like a woman."

Rowland received this information in silence; it was equally unbecoming to either relish or deprecate its irony.

"Is Mr. Hudson to join you again? Will he come here?" Christina asked.

"I shall soon begin to expect him."

"What shall you do when you leave Switzerland?" Christina continued. "Shall you go back to Rome?"

"I rather doubt it. My plans are very uncertain."

"They depend upon Mr. Hudson, eh?"

"In a great measure."

"I want you to tell me about him. Is he still in that perverse state of mind that afflicted you so much?"

Rowland looked at her mistrustfully, without answering. He was indisposed, instinctively, to tell her that Roderick was unhappy; it was possible she might offer to help him back to happiness. She immediately perceived his hesitation.

"I see no reason why we should not be frank," she said. "I should think we were excellently placed for that sort of thing. You remember that formerly I cared very little what I said, don't you? Well, I care absolutely not at all now. I say what I please, I do what I please! How did Mr. Hudson receive the news of my marriage?"

"Very badly," said Rowland.

"With rage and reproaches?" And as Rowland hesitated again—"With silent contempt?"

"I can tell you but little. He spoke to me on the subject, but I stopped him. I told him it was none of his business, or of mine."

"That was an excellent answer!" said Christina, softly. "Yet it was a little your business, after those sublime protestations I treated you to. I was really very fine that morning, eh?"

"You do yourself injustice," said Rowland. "I should be at liberty now to believe you were insincere."

"What does it matter now whether I was insincere or not? I can't conceive of anything mattering less. I was very fine—is n't it true?"

"You know what I think of you," said Rowland. And for fear of being forced to betray his suspicion of the cause of her change, he took refuge in a commonplace. "Your mother, I hope, is well."

"My mother is in the enjoyment of superb health, and may be seen every evening at the Casino, at the Baths of Lucca, confiding to every new-comer that she has married her daughter to a pearl of a prince."

Rowland was anxious for news of Mrs. Light's companion, and the natural course was frankly to inquire about him. "And the Cavaliere Giacosa is well?" he asked.

Christina hesitated, but she betrayed no other embarrassment. "The Cavaliere has retired to his native city of Ancona, upon a pension, for the rest of his natural life. He is a very good old man!"

"I have a great regard for him," said Rowland, gravely, at the same time that he privately wondered whether the Cavaliere's pension was paid by Prince Casamassima for services rendered in connection with his marriage. Had the Cavaliere received his commission? "And what do you do," Rowland continued, "on leaving this place?"

"We go to Italy—we go to Naples." She rose and stood silent a moment, looking down the valley. The figure of Prince Casamassima appeared in the distance, balancing his white umbrella. As her eyes rested upon it, Rowland imagined that he saw something deeper in the strange expression which had lurked in her face while he talked to her. At first he had been dazzled by her blooming beauty, to which the lapse of weeks had only added splendor; then he had seen a heavier ray in the light of her eye—a sinister intimation of sadness and bitterness. It was the outward mark of her sacrificed ideal. Her eyes grew cold as she looked at her husband, and when, after a moment, she turned them upon Rowland, they struck him as intensely tragical. He felt a singular mixture of sympathy and dread; he wished to give her a proof of friendship, and yet it seemed to him that she had now turned her face in a direction where friendship was impotent to interpose. She half read his feelings, apparently, and she gave a beautiful, sad smile. "I hope we may never meet again!" she said. And as Rowland gave her a protesting look—"You have seen me at my best. I wish to tell you solemnly, I was sincere! I know appearances are against me," she went on quickly. "There is a great deal I can't tell you. Perhaps you have guessed it; I care very little. You know, at any rate,

I did my best. It would n't serve; I was beaten and broken; they were stronger than I. Now it 's another affair!"

"It seems to me you have a large chance for happiness yet," said Rowland, vaguely.

"Happiness? I mean to cultivate rapture; I mean to go in for bliss ineffable! You remember I told you that I was, in part, the world's and the devil's. Now they have taken me all. It was their choice; may they never repent!"

"I shall hear of you," said RZowland.

"You will hear of me. And whatever you do hear, remember this: I was sincere!"

Prince Casamassima had approached, and Rowland looked at him with a good deal of simple compassion as a part of that "world" against which Christina had launched her mysterious menace. It was obvious that he was a good fellow, and that he could not, in the nature of things, be a positively bad husband; but his distinguished inoffensiveness only deepened the infelicity of Christina's situation by depriving her defiant attitude of the sanction of relative justice. So long as she had been free to choose, she had esteemed him: but from the moment she was forced to marry him she had detested him. Rowland read in the young man's elastic Italian mask a profound consciousness of all this; and as he found there also a record of other curious things—of pride, of temper, of bigotry, of an immense heritage of more or less aggressive traditions—he reflected that the matrimonial conjunction of his two companions might be sufficiently prolific in incident.

"You are going to Naples?" Rowland said to the prince by way of conversation.

"We are going to Paris," Christina interposed, slowly and softly. "We are going to London. We are going to Vienna. We are going to St. Petersburg."

Prince Casamassima dropped his eyes and fretted the earth with the point of his umbrella. While he engaged Rowland's attention Christina turned away. When Rowland glanced at her again he saw a change pass over her face; she was observing something that was concealed from his own eyes by the angle of the church-wall. In a moment Roderick stepped into sight.

He stopped short, astonished; his face and figure were jaded, his garments dusty. He looked at Christina from head to foot, and then, slowly, his cheek flushed and his eye expanded. Christina returned his gaze, and for some moments there was a singular silence. "You don't look well!" Christina said at last.

Roderick answered nothing; he only looked and looked, as if she had been a statue. "You are no less beautiful!" he presently cried.

She turned away with a smile, and stood a while gazing down the valley; Roderick stared at Prince Casamassima. Christina then put out her hand to Rowland. "Farewell," she said. "If you are near me in future, don't try to see me!" And then, after a pause, in a lower tone, "I was sincere!" She addressed herself again to Roderick and asked him some commonplace about his walk. But he said nothing; he only looked at her. Rowland at first had expected an outbreak of reproach, but it was evident that the danger was every moment diminishing. He was forgetting everything but her beauty, and as she stood there and let him feast upon it, Rowland was sure that she knew it. "I won't say farewell to you," she said; "we shall meet again!" And she moved gravely away. Prince Casamassima took leave courteously of Rowland; upon Roderick he bestowed a bow of exaggerated civility. Roderick appeared not to see it; he was still watching Christina, as she passed over the grass. His eyes followed her until she reached the door of her inn. Here she stopped and looked back at him.

CHAPTER XIII. Switzerland

On the homeward walk, that evening, Roderick preserved a silence which Rowland allowed to make him uneasy. Early on the morrow Roderick, saying nothing of his intentions, started off on a walk; Rowland saw him striding with light steps along the rugged path to Engelberg. He was absent all day and he gave no account of himself on his return. He said he was deadly tired, and he went to bed early. When he had left the room Miss Garland drew near to Rowland.

"I wish to ask you a question," she said. "What happened to Roderick yesterday at Engelberg?"

"You have discovered that something happened?" Rowland answered.

"I am sure of it. Was it something painful?"

"I don't know how, at the present moment, he judges it. He met the Princess Casamassima."

"Thank you!" said Miss Garland, simply, and turned away.

The conversation had been brief, but, like many small things, it furnished Rowland with food for reflection. When one is looking for symptoms one easily finds them. This was the first time Mary Garland had asked Rowland a question which it was in Roderick's power to answer, the first time she had frankly betrayed Roderick's reticence. Rowland ventured to think it marked an era.

The next morning was sultry, and the air, usually so fresh at those altitudes, was oppressively heavy. Rowland lounged on the grass a while, near Singleton, who was at work under his white umbrella, within view of the house; and then in quest of coolness he wandered away to the rocky ridge whence you looked across at the Jungfrau. To-day, however, the white summits were invisible; their heads were muffled in sullen clouds and the valleys beneath them curtained in dun-colored mist. Rowland had a book in his pocket, and he took it out and opened it. But his page remained unturned; his own thoughts were more importunate. His interview with Christina Light had made a great impression upon him, and he was haunted with the memory of her almost blameless bitterness, and of all that was tragic and fatal in her latest transformation. These things were immensely appealing, and Rowland thought with infinite impatience of Roderick's having again encountered them. It required little imagination to apprehend that the young sculptor's condition had also appealed to Christina. His consummate indifference, his supreme defiance, would make him a magnificent trophy, and Christina had announced with sufficient distinctness that she had said good-by to scruples. It was her fancy at present to treat the world as a garden of pleasure, and if, hitherto, she had played with Roderick's passion on its stem, there was little doubt that now she would pluck it with an unfaltering hand and drain it of its acrid sweetness. And why the deuce need Roderick have gone marching back to destruction? Rowland's meditations, even when they began in rancor, often brought him peace; but on this occasion they ushered in a quite peculiar quality of unrest. He felt conscious of a sudden collapse in his moral energy; a current that had been flowing for two years with liquid strength seemed at last to pause and evaporate. Rowland looked away at the stagnant vapors on the mountains; their dreariness seemed a symbol of the dreariness which his own generosity had bequeathed him. At last he had arrived at the uttermost limit of the deference a sane man might pay to other people's folly; nay, rather, he had transgressed it; he had been befooled on a gigantic scale. He turned to his book and tried to woo back patience, but it gave him cold comfort and he tossed it angrily away. He pulled his hat over his eyes, and tried to wonder, dispassionately, whether atmospheric conditions had not something to do with his ill-humor. He remained for some time in this attitude, but was finally aroused from it by a singular sense that, although he had heard nothing, some one had approached him. He looked up and saw Roderick standing before him on the turf. His mood made the spectacle unwelcome, and for a moment he felt like uttering an uncivil speech. Roderick stood looking at him with an expression of countenance which had of late become rare. There was an unfamiliar spark in his eye and a certain imperious alertness in his carriage. Confirmed habit, with Rowland, came speedily to the front. "What is it now?" he asked himself, and invited Roderick to sit down. Roderick had evidently something particular to say, and if he remained silent for a time it was not because he was ashamed of it.

"I would like you to do me a favor," he said at last. "Lend me some money."

"How much do you wish?" Rowland asked.

"Say a thousand francs."

Rowland hesitated a moment. "I don't wish to be indiscreet, but may I ask what you propose to do with a thousand francs?"

"To go to Interlaken."

"And why are you going to Interlaken?"

Roderick replied without a shadow of wavering, "Because that woman is to be there."

Rowland burst out laughing, but Roderick remained serenely grave. "You have forgiven her, then?" said Rowland.

"Not a bit of it!"

"I don't understand."

"Neither do I. I only know that she is incomparably beautiful, and that she has waked me up amazingly. Besides, she asked me to come."

"She asked you?"

"Yesterday, in so many words."

"Ah, the jade!"

"Exactly. I am willing to take her for that."

"Why in the name of common sense did you go back to her?"

"Why did I find her standing there like a goddess who had just stepped out of her cloud? Why did I look at her? Before I knew where I was, the harm was done."

Rowland, who had been sitting erect, threw himself back on the grass and lay for some time staring up at the sky. At last, raising himself, "Are you perfectly serious?" he asked.

"Deadly serious."

"Your idea is to remain at Interlaken some time?"

"Indefinitely!" said Roderick; and it seemed to his companion that the tone in which he said this made it immensely well worth hearing.

"And your mother and cousin, meanwhile, are to remain here? It will soon be getting very cold, you know."

"It does n't seem much like it to-day."

"Very true; but to-day is a day by itself."

"There is nothing to prevent their going back to Lucerne. I depend upon your taking charge of them."

At this Rowland reclined upon the grass again; and again, after reflection, he faced his friend. "How would you express," he asked, "the character of the profit that you expect to derive from your excursion?"

"I see no need of expressing it. The proof of the pudding is in the eating! The case is simply this. I desire immensely to be near Christina Light, and it is such a huge refreshment to find myself again desiring something, that I propose to drift with the current. As I say, she has waked me up, and it is possible something may come of it. She makes me feel as if I were alive again. This," and he glanced down at the inn, "I call death!"

"That I am very grateful to hear. You really feel as if you might do something?"

"Don't ask too much. I only know that she makes my heart beat, makes me see visions."

"You feel encouraged?"

"I feel excited."

"You are really looking better."

"I am glad to hear it. Now that I have answered your questions, please to give me the money."

Rowland shook his head. "For that purpose, I can't!"

"You can't?"

"It 's impossible. Your plan is rank folly. I can't help you in it."

Roderick flushed a little, and his eye expanded. "I will borrow what money I can, then, from Mary!" This was not viciously said; it had simply the ring of passionate resolution.

Instantly it brought Rowland to terms. He took a bunch of keys from his pocket and tossed it upon the grass. "The little brass one opens my dressing-case," he said. "You will find money in it."

Roderick let the keys lie; something seemed to have struck him; he looked askance at his friend. "You are awfully gallant!"

"You certainly are not. Your proposal is an outrage."

"Very likely. It 's a proof the more of my desire."

"If you have so much steam on, then, use it for something else. You say you are awake again. I am delighted; only be so in the best sense. Is n't it very plain? If you have the energy to desire, you have also the energy to reason and to judge. If you can care to go, you can also care to stay, and staying being the more profitable course, the inspiration, on that side, for a man who has his self-confidence to win back again, should be greater."

Roderick, plainly, did not relish this simple logic, and his eye grew angry as he listened to its echo. "Oh, the devil!" he cried.

Rowland went on. "Do you believe that hanging about Christina Light will do you any good? Do you believe it won't? In either case you should keep away from her. If it won't, it 's your duty; and if it will, you can get on without it."

"Do me good?" cried Roderick. "What do I want of 'good'—what should I do with 'good'? I want what she gives me, call it by what name you will. I want to ask no questions, but to take what comes and let it fill the impossible hours! But I did n't come to discuss the matter."

"I have not the least desire to discuss it," said Rowland. "I simply protest."

Roderick meditated a moment. "I have never yet thought twice of accepting a favor of you," he said at last; "but this one sticks in my throat."

"It is not a favor; I lend you the money only under compulsion."

"Well, then, I will take it only under compulsion!" Roderick exclaimed. And he sprang up abruptly and marched away.

His words were ambiguous; Rowland lay on the grass, wondering what they meant. Half an hour had not elapsed before Roderick reappeared, heated with rapid walking, and wiping his forehead. He flung himself down and looked at his friend with an eye which expressed something purer than bravado and yet baser than conviction.

"I have done my best!" he said. "My mother is out of money; she is expecting next week some circular notes from London. She had only ten francs in her pocket. Mary Garland gave me every sou she possessed in the world. It makes exactly thirty-four francs. That 's not enough."

"You asked Miss Garland?" cried Rowland.

"I asked her."

"And told her your purpose?"

"I named no names. But she knew!"

"What did she say?"

"Not a syllable. She simply emptied her purse."

Rowland turned over and buried his face in his arms. He felt a movement of irrepressible elation, and he barely stifled a cry of joy. Now, surely, Roderick had shattered the last link in the chain that bound Mary to him, and after this she would be free!... When he turned about again, Roderick was still sitting there, and he had not touched the keys which lay on the grass.

"I don't know what is the matter with me," said Roderick, "but I have an insurmountable aversion to taking your money."

"The matter, I suppose, is that you have a grain of wisdom left."

"No, it 's not that. It 's a kind of brute instinct. I find it extremely provoking!" He sat there for some time with his head in his hands and his eyes on the ground. His lips were compressed, and he was evidently, in fact, in a state of profound irritation. "You have succeeded in making this thing excessively unpleasant!" he exclaimed.

"I am sorry," said Rowland, "but I can't see it in any other way."

"That I believe, and I resent the range of your vision pretending to be the limit of my action. You can't feel for me nor judge for me, and there are certain things you know nothing about. I have suffered, sir!" Roderick went on with increasing emphasis. "I have suffered damnable torments. Have I been such a placid, contented, comfortable man this last six months, that when I find a chance to forget my misery, I should take such pains not to profit by it? You ask too much, for a man who himself has no occasion to play the hero. I don't say that invidiously; it 's your disposition, and you can't help it. But decidedly, there are certain things you know nothing about."

Rowland listened to this outbreak with open eyes, and Roderick, if he had been less intent upon his own eloquence, would probably have perceived that he turned pale. "These things—what are they?" Rowland asked.

"They are women, principally, and what relates to women. Women for you, by what I can make out, mean nothing. You have no imagination—no sensibility!"

"That 's a serious charge," said Rowland, gravely.

"I don't make it without proof!"

"And what is your proof?"

Roderick hesitated a moment. "The way you treated Christina Light. I call that grossly obtuse."

"Obtuse?" Rowland repeated, frowning.

"Thick-skinned, beneath your good fortune."

"My good fortune?"

"There it is—it 's all news to you! You had pleased her. I don't say she was dying of love for you, but she took a fancy to you."

"We will let this pass!" said Rowland, after a silence.

"Oh, I don't insist. I have only her own word for it."

"She told you this?"

"You noticed, at least, I suppose, that she was not afraid to speak. I never repeated it, not because I was jealous, but because I was curious to see how long your ignorance would last if left to itself."

"I frankly confess it would have lasted forever. And yet I don't consider that my insensibility is proved."

"Oh, don't say that," cried Roderick, "or I shall begin to suspect—what I must do you the justice to say that I never have suspected—that you are a trifle conceited. Upon my word, when I think of all this, your protest, as you call it, against my following Christina Light seems to me thoroughly offensive. There is something monstrous in a man's pretending to lay down the law to a sort of emotion with which he is quite unacquainted—in his asking a fellow to give up a lovely woman for conscience' sake, when he has never had the impulse to strike a blow for one for passion's!"

"Oh, oh!" cried Rowland.

"All that 's very easy to say," Roderick went on; "but you must remember that there are such things as nerves, and senses, and imagination, and a restless demon within that may sleep sometimes for a day, or for six months, but that sooner or later wakes up and thumps at your ribs till you listen to him! If you can't understand it, take it on trust, and let a poor imaginative devil live his life as he can!"

Roderick's words seemed at first to Rowland like something heard in a dream; it was impossible they had been actually spoken—so supreme an expression were they of the insolence of egotism. Reality was never so consistent as that! But Roderick sat there balancing his beautiful head, and the echoes of his strident accent still lingered along the half-muffled mountain-side. Rowland suddenly felt that the cup of his chagrin was full to overflowing, and his long-gathered bitterness surged into the simple, wholesome passion of anger for wasted kindness. But he spoke without violence, and Roderick was probably at first far from measuring the force that lay beneath his words.

"You are incredibly ungrateful," he said. "You are talking arrogant nonsense. What do you know about my sensibilities and my imagination? How do you know whether I have loved or suffered? If I have held my tongue and not troubled you with my complaints, you find it the most natural thing in the world to put an ignoble construction on my silence. I loved quite as well as you; indeed, I think I may say rather better. I have been constant. I have been willing to give more than I received. I have not forsaken one mistress because I thought another more beautiful, nor given up the other and believed all manner of evil about her because I had not my way with her. I have been a good friend to Christina Light, and it seems to me my friendship does her quite as much honor as your love!"

"Your love—your suffering—your silence—your friendship!" cried Roderick. "I declare I don't understand!"

677

"I dare say not. You are not used to understanding such things—you are not used to hearing me talk of my feelings. You are altogether too much taken up with your own. Be as much so as you please; I have always respected your right. Only when I have kept myself in durance on purpose to leave you an open field, don't, by way of thanking me, come and call me an idiot."

"Oh, you claim then that you have made sacrifices?"

"Several! You have never suspected it?"

"If I had, do you suppose I would have allowed it?" cried Roderick.

"They were the sacrifices of friendship and they were easily made; only I don't enjoy having them thrown back in my teeth."

This was, under the circumstances, a sufficiently generous speech; but Roderick was not in the humor to take it generously. "Come, be more definite," he said. "Let me know where it is the shoe has pinched."

Rowland frowned; if Roderick would not take generosity, he should have full justice. "It 's a perpetual sacrifice," he said, "to live with a perfect egotist."

"I am an egotist?" cried Roderick.

"Did it never occur to you?"

"An egotist to whom you have made perpetual sacrifices?" He repeated the words in a singular tone; a tone that denoted neither exactly indignation nor incredulity, but (strange as it may seem) a sudden violent curiosity for news about himself.

"You are selfish," said Rowland; "you think only of yourself and believe only in yourself. You regard other people only as they play into your own hands. You have always been very frank about it, and the thing seemed so mixed up with the temper of your genius and the very structure of your mind, that often one was willing to take the evil with the good and to be thankful that, considering your great talent, you were no worse. But if one believed in you, as I have done, one paid a tax upon it."

678

Roderick leaned his elbows on his knees, clasped his hands together, and crossed them, shadewise, over his eyes. In this attitude, for a moment, he sat looking coldly at his friend. "So I have made you very uncomfortable?" he went on.

"Extremely so."

"I have been eager, grasping, obstinate, vain, ungrateful, indifferent, cruel?"

"I have accused you, mentally, of all these things, with the exception of vanity."

"You have often hated me?"

"Never. I should have parted company with you before coming to that."

"But you have wanted to part company, to bid me go my way and be hanged!"

"Repeatedly. Then I have had patience and forgiven you."

"Forgiven me, eh? Suffering all the while?"

"Yes, you may call it suffering."

"Why did you never tell me all this before?"

"Because my affection was always stronger than my resentment; because I preferred to err on the side of kindness; because I had, myself, in a measure, launched you in the world and thrown you into temptations; and because nothing short of your unwarrantable aggression just now could have made me say these painful things."

Roderick picked up a blade of long grass and began to bite it; Rowland was puzzled by his expression and manner. They seemed strangely cynical; there was something revolting in his deepening calmness. "I must have been hideous," Roderick presently resumed.

"I am not talking for your entertainment," said Rowland.

"Of course not. For my edification!" As Roderick said these words there was not a ray of warmth in his brilliant eye.

"I have spoken for my own relief," Rowland went on, "and so that you need never again go so utterly astray as you have done this morning."

"It has been a terrible mistake, then?" What his tone expressed was not willful mockery, but a kind of persistent irresponsibility which Rowland found equally exasperating. He answered nothing.

"And all this time," Roderick continued, "you have been in love? Tell me the woman."

Rowland felt an immense desire to give him a visible, palpable pang. "Her name is Mary Garland," he said.

Apparently he succeeded. The surprise was great; Roderick colored as he had never done. "Mary Garland? Heaven forgive us!"

Rowland observed the "us;" Roderick threw himself back on the turf. The latter lay for some time staring at the sky. At last he sprang to his feet, and Rowland rose also, rejoicing keenly, it must be confessed, in his companion's confusion.

"For how long has this been?" Roderick demanded.

"Since I first knew her."

"Two years! And you have never told her?"

"Never."

"You have told no one?"

"You are the first person."

"Why have you been silent?"

"Because of your engagement."

"But you have done your best to keep that up."

"That 's another matter!"

"It 's very strange!" said Roderick, presently. "It 's like something in a novel."

"We need n't expatiate on it," said Rowland. "All I wished to do was to rebut your charge that I am an abnormal being."

But still Roderick pondered. "All these months, while I was going on! I wish you had mentioned it."

"I acted as was necessary, and that 's the end of it."

"You have a very high opinion of her?"

"The highest."

"I remember now your occasionally expressing it and my being struck with it. But I never dreamed you were in love with her. It 's a pity she does n't care for you!"

Rowland had made his point and he had no wish to prolong the conversation; but he had a desire to hear more of this, and he remained silent.

"You hope, I suppose, that some day she may?"

"I should n't have offered to say so; but since you ask me, I do."

"I don't believe it. She idolizes me, and if she never were to see me again she would idolize my memory."

This might be profound insight, and it might be profound fatuity. Rowland turned away; he could not trust himself to speak.

"My indifference, my neglect of her, must have seemed to you horrible. Altogether, I must have appeared simply hideous."

"Do you really care," Rowland asked, "what you appeared?"

"Certainly. I have been damnably stupid. Is n't an artist supposed to be a man of perceptions? I am hugely disgusted."

"Well, you understand now, and we can start afresh."

"And yet," said Roderick, "though you have suffered, in a degree, I don't believe you have suffered so much as some other men would have done."

"Very likely not. In such matters quantitative analysis is difficult."

Roderick picked up his stick and stood looking at the ground. "Nevertheless, I must have seemed hideous," he repeated—"hideous." He turned away, scowling, and Rowland offered no contradiction.

They were both silent for some time, and at last Roderick gave a heavy sigh and began to walk away. "Where are you going?" Rowland then asked.

"Oh, I don't care! To walk; you have given me something to think of." This seemed a salutary impulse, and yet Rowland felt a nameless perplexity. "To have been so stupid damns me more than anything!" Roderick went on. "Certainly, I can shut up shop now."

Rowland felt in no smiling humor, and yet, in spite of himself, he could almost have smiled at the very consistency of the fellow. It was egotism still: aesthetic disgust at the graceless contour of his conduct, but never a hint of simple sorrow for the pain he had given. Rowland let him go, and for some moments stood watching him. Suddenly Mallet became conscious of a singular and most illogical impulse—a desire to stop him, to have another word with him—not to lose sight of him. He called him and Roderick turned. "I should like to go with you," said Rowland.

"I am fit only to be alone. I am damned!"

"You had better not think of it at all," Rowland cried, "than think in that way."

"There is only one way. I have been hideous!" And he broke off and marched away with his long, elastic step, swinging his stick. Rowland watched him and at the end of a moment called to him. Roderick stopped and looked at him in silence, and then abruptly turned, and disappeared below the crest of a hill.

Rowland passed the remainder of the day uncomfortably. He was half irritated, half depressed; he had an insufferable feeling of having been placed in the wrong, in spite of his excellent cause. Roderick did not come home to dinner; but of this, with his passion for brooding away the hours on far-off mountain sides, he had almost made a habit. Mrs. Hudson appeared at the noonday repast with a face which showed that Roderick's demand for money had unsealed the fountains of her distress. Little Singleton consumed an enormous and well-earned dinner. Miss Garland, Rowland observed, had not contributed her scanty assistance to her kinsman's pursuit of the Princess Casamassima without an effort. The effort was visible in her pale face and her silence; she looked so ill that when they left the table Rowland felt almost bound to remark upon it. They had come out upon the grass in front of the inn.

"I have a headache," she said. And then suddenly, looking about at the menacing sky and motionless air, "It 's this horrible day!"

Rowland that afternoon tried to write a letter to his cousin Cecilia, but his head and his heart were alike heavy, and he traced upon the paper but a single line. "I believe there is such a thing as being too reasonable. But when once the habit is formed, what is one to do?" He had occasion to use his keys and he felt for them in his pocket; they were missing, and he remembered that he had left them lying on the hill-top where he had had his talk with Roderick. He went forth in search of them and found them where he had thrown them. He flung himself down in the same place again; he felt indisposed to walk. He was conscious that his mood had vastly changed since the morning; his extraordinary, acute sense of his rights had been replaced by the familiar, chronic sense of his duties. Only, his duties now seemed impracticable; he turned over and buried his face in his arms. He lay so a long time, thinking of many things; the sum of them all was that Roderick had beaten him. At last he was startled by an extraordinary sound; it took him a moment to perceive that it was a portentous growl of thunder. He roused himself and saw that the whole face of the sky had altered. The clouds that had hung motionless all day were moving from their stations, and getting into position, as it were, for a battle. The wind was rising; the sallow vapors were turning dark and consolidating their masses. It was a striking spectacle, but Rowland judged best to observe it briefly, as a storm was evidently imminent. He took his way down to the inn and found Singleton still at his post, profiting by the last of the rapidly-failing light to finish his study, and yet at the same time taking rapid notes of the actual condition of the clouds.

"We are going to have a most interesting storm," the little painter gleefully cried. "I should like awfully to do it."

Rowland adjured him to pack up his tools and decamp, and repaired to the house. The air by this time had become portentously dark, and the thunder was incessant and tremendous; in the midst of it the lightning flashed and vanished, like the treble shrilling upon the bass. The innkeeper and his servants had crowded to the doorway, and were looking at the scene with faces which seemed a proof that it was unprecedented. As Rowland approached, the group divided, to let some one pass from within, and Mrs. Hudson came forth, as white as a corpse and trembling in every limb.

"My boy, my boy, where is my boy?" she cried. "Mr. Mallet, why are you here without him? Bring him to me!"

"Has no one seen Mr. Hudson?" Rowland asked of the others. "Has he not returned?"

Each one shook his head and looked grave, and Rowland attempted to reassure Mrs. Hudson by saying that of course he had taken refuge in a chalet.

"Go and find him, go and find him!" she cried, insanely. "Don't stand there and talk, or I shall die!" It was now as dark as evening, and Rowland could just distinguish the figure of Singleton scampering homeward with his box and easel. "And where is Mary?" Mrs. Hudson went on; "what in mercy's name has become of her? Mr. Mallet, why did you ever bring us here?"

There came a prodigious flash of lightning, and the limitless tumult about them turned clearer than midsummer noonday. The brightness lasted long enough to enable Rowland to see a woman's figure on the top of an eminence near the house. It was Mary Garland, questioning the lurid darkness for Roderick. Rowland sprang out to interrupt her vigil, but in a moment he encountered her, retreating. He seized her hand and hurried her to the house, where, as soon as she stepped into the covered gallery, Mrs. Hudson fell upon her with frantic lamentations.

"Did you see nothing,—nothing?" she cried. "Tell Mr. Mallet he must go and find him, with some men, some lights, some wrappings. Go, go, go, sir! In mercy, go!"

Rowland was extremely perturbed by the poor lady's vociferous folly, for he deemed her anxiety superfluous. He had offered his suggestion with sincerity; nothing was more probable than that Roderick had found shelter in a herdsman's cabin. These were numerous on the neighboring mountains, and the storm had given fair warning of its approach. Miss Garland stood there very pale, saying nothing, but looking at him. He expected that she would check her cousin's importunity. "Could you find him?" she suddenly asked. "Would it be of use?"

The question seemed to him a flash intenser than the lightning that was raking the sky before them. It shattered his dream that he weighed in the scale! But before he could answer, the full fury of the storm was upon them; the rain descended in sounding torrents. Every one fell back into the house. There had been no time to light lamps, and in the little uncarpeted parlor, in the unnatural darkness, Rowland felt Mary's hand upon his arm. For a moment it had an eloquent pressure; it seemed to retract her senseless challenge, and to say that she believed, for Roderick, what he believed. But nevertheless, thought Rowland, the cry had come, her heart had spoken; her first impulse had been to sacrifice him. He had been uncertain before; here, at least, was the comfort of certainty!

It must be confessed, however, that the certainty in question did little to enliven the gloom of that formidable evening. There was a noisy crowd about him in the room—noisy even with the accompaniment of the continual thunder-peals; lodgers and servants, chattering, shuffling, and bustling, and annoying him equally by making too light of the tempest and by vociferating their alarm. In the disorder, it was some time before a lamp was lighted, and the first thing he saw, as it was swung from the ceiling, was the white face of Mrs. Hudson, who was being carried out of the room in a swoon by two stout maid-servants, with Mary Garland forcing a passage. He rendered what help he could, but when they had laid the poor woman on her bed, Miss Garland motioned him away.

"I think you make her worse," she said.

Rowland went to his own chamber. The partitions in Swiss mountain-inns are thin, and from time to time he heard Mrs. Hudson moaning, three rooms off. Considering its great fury, the storm took long to expend itself; it was upwards of three hours before the thunder ceased. But even then the rain continued to fall heavily, and the night, which had come on, was impenetrably black. This lasted till near midnight. Rowland thought of Mary Garland's challenge in the porch, but he thought even more that, although the fetid interior of a high-nestling chalet may offer a convenient refuge from an Alpine tempest, there was no possible music in the universe so sweet as the sound of Roderick's voice. At midnight, through his dripping window-pane, he saw a star, and he immediately went downstairs and out into the gallery. The rain had ceased, the cloud-masses were dissevered here and there, and several stars were visible. In a few minutes he heard a step behind him, and, turning, saw Miss Garland. He asked about Mrs. Hudson and learned that she was sleeping, exhausted by her fruitless lamentations. Miss Garland kept scanning the darkness, but she said nothing to cast doubt on Roderick's having found a refuge. Rowland noticed it. "This also have I guaranteed!" he said to himself. There was something that Mary wished to learn, and a question presently revealed it.

"What made him start on a long walk so suddenly?" she asked. "I saw him at eleven o'clock, and then he meant to go to Engelberg, and sleep."

"On his way to Interlaken?" Rowland said.

"Yes," she answered, under cover of the darkness.

"We had some talk," said Rowland, "and he seemed, for the day, to have given up Interlaken."

"Did you dissuade him?"

"Not exactly. We discussed another question, which, for the time, superseded his plan."

Miss Garland was silent. Then—"May I ask whether your discussion was violent?" she said.

"I am afraid it was agreeable to neither of us."

"And Roderick left you in—in irritation?"

"I offered him my company on his walk. He declined it."

Miss Garland paced slowly to the end of the gallery and then came back. "If he had gone to Engelberg," she said, "he would have reached the hotel before the storm began."

Rowland felt a sudden explosion of ferocity. "Oh, if you like," he cried, "he can start for Interlaken as soon as he comes back!"

But she did not even notice his wrath. "Will he come back early?" she went on.

"We may suppose so."

"He will know how anxious we are, and he will start with the first light!"

Rowland was on the point of declaring that Roderick's readiness to throw himself into the feelings of others made this extremely probable; but he checked himself and said, simply, "I expect him at sunrise."

Miss Garland bent her eyes once more upon the irresponsive darkness, and then, in silence, went into the house. Rowland, it must be averred, in spite of his resolution not to be nervous, found no sleep that night. When the early dawn began to tremble in the east, he came forth again into the open air. The storm had completely purged the atmosphere, and the day gave promise of cloudless splendor. Rowland watched the early sun-shafts slowly reaching higher, and remembered that if Roderick did not come back to breakfast, there were two things to be taken into account. One was the heaviness of the soil on the mountain-sides, saturated with the rain; this would make him walk slowly: the other was the fact that, speaking without irony, he was not remarkable for throwing himself into the sentiments of others. Breakfast, at the inn, was early, and by breakfast-time Roderick had not appeared. Then Rowland admitted that he was nervous. Neither Mrs. Hudson nor Miss Garland had left their apartment; Rowland had a mental vision of them sitting there praying and listening; he had no desire to see them more directly. There were a couple of men who hung about the inn as guides for the ascent of the Titlis; Rowland sent each of them forth in a different direction, to ask the news of Roderick at every chalet door within a morning's walk. Then he called Sam Singleton, whose peregrinations had made him an excellent mountaineer, and whose zeal and sympathy were now unbounded, and the two started together on a voyage of research. By the time they had lost sight of the inn, Rowland was obliged to confess that, decidedly, Roderick had had time to come back.

He wandered about for several hours, but he found only the sunny stillness of the mountain-sides. Before long he parted company with Singleton, who, to his suggestion that separation would multiply their resources, assented with a silent, frightened look which reflected too vividly his own rapidly-dawning thought. The day was magnificent; the sun was everywhere; the storm had lashed the lower slopes into a deeper flush of autumnal color, and the snow-peaks reared themselves against the near horizon in glaring blocks and dazzling spires. Rowland made his way to several chalets, but most of them were empty. He thumped at their low, foul doors with a kind of nervous, savage anger; he challenged the stupid silence to tell him something about his friend. Some of these places had evidently not been open in months. The silence everywhere was horrible; it seemed to mock at his impatience and to be a conscious symbol of calamity. In the midst of it, at the door of one of the chalets, quite alone, sat a hideous cretin, who grinned at Rowland over his goitre when, hardly knowing what he did, he questioned him. The creature's family was scattered on the mountain-sides; he could give Rowland no help to find them. Rowland climbed into many awkward places, and skirted, intently and peeringly, many an ugly chasm and steep-dropping ledge. But the sun, as I have said, was everywhere; it illumined the deep places over which, not knowing where to turn next, he halted and lingered, and showed him nothing but the stony Alpine void—nothing so human even as death. At noon he paused in his quest and sat down on a stone; the conviction was pressing upon him that the worst that was now possible was true. He suspended his search; he was afraid to go on. He sat there for an hour, sick to the depths of his soul. Without his knowing why, several things, chiefly trivial, that had happened during the last two years and that he had quite forgotten, became vividly present to his mind. He was aroused at last by the sound of a stone dislodged near by, which rattled down the mountain. In a moment, on a steep, rocky slope opposite to him, he beheld a figure cautiously descending—a figure which was not Roderick. It was Singleton, who had seen him and began to beckon to him.

"Come down—come down!" cried the painter, steadily making his own way down. Rowland saw that as he moved, and even as he selected his foothold and watched his steps, he was looking at something at the bottom of the cliff. This was a great rugged wall which had fallen backward from the perpendicular, and the descent, though difficult, was with care sufficiently practicable.

"What do you see?" cried Rowland.

Singleton stopped, looked across at him and seemed to hesitate; then, "Come down—come down!" he simply repeated.

Rowland's course was also a steep descent, and he attacked it so precipitately that he afterwards marveled he had not broken his neck. It was a ten minutes' headlong scramble. Half-way down he saw something that made him dizzy; he saw what Singleton had seen. In the gorge below them a vague white mass lay tumbled upon the stones. He let himself go, blindly, fiercely. Singleton had reached the rocky bottom of the ravine before him, and had bounded forward and fallen upon his knees. Rowland overtook him and his own legs collapsed. The thing that yesterday was his friend lay before him as the chance of the last breath had left it, and out of it Roderick's face stared upward, open-eyed, at the sky.

He had fallen from a great height, but he was singularly little disfigured. The rain had spent its torrents upon him, and his clothes and hair were as wet as if the billows of the ocean had flung him upon the strand. An attempt to move him would show some hideous fracture, some horrible physical dishonor; but what Rowland saw on first looking at him was only a strangely serene expression of life. The eyes were dead, but in a short time, when Rowland had closed them, the whole face seemed to awake. The rain had washed away all blood; it was as if Violence, having done her work, had stolen away in shame. Roderick's face might have shamed her; it looked admirably handsome.

"He was a beautiful man!" said Singleton.

They looked up through their horror at the cliff from which he had apparently fallen, and which lifted its blank and stony face above him, with no care now but to drink the sunshine on which his eyes were closed, and then Rowland had an immense outbreak of pity and anguish. At last they spoke of carrying him back to the inn. "There must be three or four men," Rowland said, "and they must be brought here quickly. I have not the least idea where we are."

"We are at about three hours' walk from home," said Singleton. "I will go for help; I can find my way."

"Remember," said Rowland, "whom you will have to face."

"I remember," the excellent fellow answered. "There was nothing I could ever do for him in life; I will do what I can now."

He went off, and Rowland stayed there alone. He watched for seven long hours, and his vigil was forever memorable. The most rational of men was for an hour the most passionate. He reviled himself with transcendent bitterness, he accused himself of cruelty and injustice, he would have lain down there in Roderick's place to unsay the words that had yesterday driven him forth on his lonely ramble. Roderick had been fond of saying that there are such things as necessary follies, and Rowland was now proving it. At last he grew almost used to the dumb exultation of the cliff above him. He saw that Roderick was a mass of hideous injury, and he tried to understand what had happened. Not that it helped him; before that confounding mortality one hypothesis after another faltered and swooned away. Roderick's passionate walk had carried him farther and higher than he knew; he had outstayed, supposably, the first menace of the storm, and perhaps even found a defiant entertainment in watching it. Perhaps he had simply lost himself. The tempest had overtaken him, and when he tried to return, it was too late. He had attempted to descend the cliff in the darkness, he had made the inevitable slip, and whether he had fallen fifty feet or three hundred little mattered. The condition of his body indicated the shorter fall. Now that all was over, Rowland understood how exclusively, for two years, Roderick had filled his life. His occupation was gone.

Singleton came back with four men—one of them the landlord of the inn. They had formed a sort of rude bier of the frame of a chaise a porteurs, and by taking a very round-about course homeward were able to follow a tolerably level path and carry their burden with a certain decency. To Rowland it seemed as if the little procession would never reach the inn; but as they drew near it he would have given his right hand for a longer delay. The people of the inn came forward to meet them, in a little silent, solemn convoy. In the doorway, clinging together, appeared the two bereaved women. Mrs. Hudson tottered forward with outstretched hands and the expression of a blind person; but before she reached her son, Mary Garland had rushed past her, and, in the face of the staring, pitying, awe-stricken crowd, had flung herself, with the magnificent movement of one whose rights were supreme, and with a loud, tremendous cry, upon the senseless vestige of her love.

That cry still lives in Rowland's ears. It interposes, persistently, against the reflection that when he sometimes—very rarely—sees her, she is unreservedly kind to him; against the memory that during the dreary journey back to America, made of course with his assistance, there was a great frankness in her gratitude, a great gratitude in her frankness. Miss Garland lives with Mrs. Hudson, at Northampton, where Rowland visits his cousin Cecilia more frequently than of old. When he calls upon Miss Garland he never sees Mrs.

Hudson. Cecilia, who, having her shrewd impression that he comes to see Miss Garland as much as to see herself, does not feel obliged to seem unduly flattered, calls him, whenever he reappears, the most restless of mortals. But he always says to her in answer, "No, I assure you I am the most patient!"

About Author

Henry James OM (15 April 1843 – 28 February 1916) was an American-British author regarded as a key transitional figure between literary realism and literary modernism, and is considered by many to be among the greatest novelists in the English language. He was the son of Henry James Sr. and the brother of renowned philosopher and psychologist William James and diarist Alice James.

He is best known for a number of novels dealing with the social and marital interplay between émigré Americans, English people, and continental Europeans. Examples of such novels include The Portrait of a Lady, The Ambassadors, and The Wings of the Dove. His later works were increasingly experimental. In describing the internal states of mind and social dynamics of his characters, James often made use of a style in which ambiguous or contradictory motives and impressions were overlaid or juxtaposed in the discussion of a character's psyche. For their unique ambiguity, as well as for other aspects of their composition, his late works have been compared to impressionist painting.

His novella The Turn of the Screw has garnered a reputation as the most analysed and ambiguous ghost story in the English language and remains his most widely adapted work in other media. He also wrote a number of other highly regarded ghost stories and is considered one of the greatest masters of the field.

James published articles and books of criticism, travel, biography, autobiography, and plays. Born in the United States, James largely relocated to Europe as a young man and eventually settled in England, becoming a British subject in 1915, one year before his death. James was nominated for the Nobel Prize in Literature in 1911, 1912 and 1916.

Life

Early years, 1843–1883

James was born at 2 Washington Place in New York City on 15 April 1843. His parents were Mary Walsh and Henry James Sr. His father was intelligent and steadfastly congenial. He was a lecturer and philosopher who had inherited independent means from his father, an Albany banker and investor. Mary came from a wealthy family long settled in New York City. Her sister Katherine lived with her adult family for an extended period of time. Henry Jr. had three brothers, William, who was one year his senior, and younger brothers Wilkinson (Wilkie) and Robertson. His younger sister was Alice. Both of his parents were of Irish and Scottish descent.

The family first lived in Albany, at 70 N. Pearl St., and then moved to Fourteenth Street in New York City when James was still a young boy. His education was calculated by his father to expose him to many influences, primarily scientific and philosophical; it was described by Percy Lubbock, the editor of his selected letters, as "extraordinarily haphazard and promiscuous." James did not share the usual education in Latin and Greek classics. Between 1855 and 1860, the James' household traveled to London, Paris, Geneva, Boulogne-sur-Mer and Newport, Rhode Island, according to the father's current interests and publishing ventures, retreating to the United States when funds were low. Henry studied primarily with tutors and briefly attended schools while the family traveled in Europe. Their longest stays were in France, where Henry began to feel at home and became fluent in French. He was afflicted with a stutter, which seems to have manifested itself only when he spoke English; in French, he did not stutter.

In 1860 the family returned to Newport. There Henry became a friend of the painter John La Farge, who introduced him to French literature, and in particular, to Balzac. James later called Balzac his "greatest master," and said that he had learned more about the craft of fiction from him than from anyone else.

In the autumn of 1861 Henry received an injury, probably to his back, while fighting a fire. This injury, which resurfaced at times throughout his life, made him unfit for military service in the American Civil War.

In 1864 the James family moved to Boston, Massachusetts to be near William, who had enrolled first in the Lawrence Scientific School at Harvard and then in the medical school. In 1862 Henry attended Harvard Law School, but realised that he was not interested in studying law. He pursued his interest in literature and associated with authors and critics William Dean Howells and Charles Eliot Norton in Boston and Cambridge, formed lifelong friendships with Oliver Wendell Holmes Jr., the future Supreme Court Justice, and with James and Annie Fields, his first professional mentors.

His first published work was a review of a stage performance, "Miss Maggie Mitchell in Fanchon the Cricket," published in 1863. About a year later, A Tragedy of Error, his first short story, was published anonymously. James's first payment was for an appreciation of Sir Walter Scott's novels, written for the North American Review. He wrote fiction and non-fiction pieces for The Nation and Atlantic Monthly, where Fields was editor. In 1871 he published his first novel, Watch and Ward, in serial form in the Atlantic Monthly. The novel was later published in book form in 1878.

During a 14-month trip through Europe in 1869–70 he met Ruskin, Dickens, Matthew Arnold, William Morris, and George Eliot. Rome impressed him profoundly. "Here I am then in the Eternal City," he wrote to his brother William. "At last—for the first time—I live!" He attempted to support himself as a freelance writer in Rome, then secured a position as Paris correspondent for the New York Tribune, through the influence of its editor John Hay. When these efforts failed he returned to New York City. During 1874 and 1875 he published Transatlantic Sketches, A Passionate Pilgrim, and Roderick Hudson. During this early period in his career he was influenced by Nathaniel Hawthorne.

In 1869 he settled in London. There he established relationships with Macmillan and other publishers, who paid for serial installments that they would later publish in book form. The audience for these serialized novels was largely made up of middle-class women, and James struggled to fashion serious literary work within the strictures imposed by editors' and publishers' notions of what was suitable for young women to read. He lived in rented rooms but was able to join gentlemen's clubs that had libraries and where he could entertain male friends. He was introduced to English society by Henry Adams and Charles Milnes Gaskell, the latter introducing him to the Travellers' and the Reform Clubs.

In the fall of 1875 he moved to the Latin Quarter of Paris. Aside from two trips to America, he spent the next three decades—the rest of his life—in Europe. In Paris he met Zola, Alphonse Daudet, Maupassant, Turgenev, and others. He stayed in Paris only a year before moving to London.

In England he met the leading figures of politics and culture. He continued to be a prolific writer, producing The American (1877), The Europeans (1878), a revision of Watch and Ward (1878), French Poets and Novelists (1878), Hawthorne (1879), and several shorter works of fiction. In 1878 Daisy Miller established his fame on both sides of the Atlantic. It drew notice perhaps mostly because it depicted a woman whose behavior is outside the social norms of Europe. He also began his first masterpiece, The Portrait of a Lady, which would appear in 1881.

In 1877 he first visited Wenlock Abbey in Shropshire, home of his friend Charles Milnes Gaskell whom he had met through Henry Adams. He was much inspired by the darkly romantic Abbey and the surrounding countryside, which features in his essay Abbeys and Castles. In particular the gloomy monastic fishponds behind the Abbey are said to have inspired the lake in The Turn of the Screw.

While living in London, James continued to follow the careers of the "French realists", Émile Zola in particular. Their stylistic methods influenced his own work in the years to come. Hawthorne's influence on him faded during this period, replaced by George Eliot and Ivan Turgenev. 1879–1882 saw the publication of The Europeans, Washington Square, Confidence, and The Portrait of a Lady. He visited America in 1882–1883, then returned to London.

The period from 1881 to 1883 was marked by several losses. His mother died in 1881, followed by his father a few months later, and then by his brother Wilkie. Emerson, an old family friend, died in 1882. His friend Turgenev died in 1883.

Middle years, 1884–1897

In 1884 James made another visit to Paris. There he met again with Zola, Daudet, and Goncourt. He had been following the careers of the French "realist" or "naturalist" writers, and was increasingly influenced by them. In 1886, he published The Bostonians and The Princess Casamassima, both influenced by the French writers he'd studied assiduously. Critical reaction and sales were poor. He wrote to Howells that the books had hurt his career rather than helped because they had "reduced the desire, and demand, for my productions to zero". During this time he became friends with Robert Louis Stevenson, John Singer Sargent, Edmund Gosse, George du Maurier, Paul Bourget, and Constance Fenimore Woolson. His third novel from the 1880s was The Tragic Muse. Although he was following the precepts of Zola in his novels of the '80s, their tone and attitude are closer to the fiction of Alphonse Daudet. The lack of critical and financial success for his novels during this period led him to try writing for the theatre. (His dramatic works and his experiences with theatre are discussed below.)

In the last quarter of 1889, he started translating "for pure and copious lucre" Port Tarascon, the third volume of Alphonse Daudet adventures of Tartarin de Tarascon. Serialized in Harper's Monthly Magazine from June 1890, this translation praised as "clever" by The Spectator was published in January 1891 by Sampson Low, Marston, Searle & Rivington.

After the stage failure of Guy Domville in 1895, James was near despair and thoughts of death plagued him. The years spent on dramatic works were not entirely a loss. As he moved into the last phase of his career he found ways to adapt dramatic techniques into the novel form.

In the late 1880s and throughout the 1890s James made several trips through Europe. He spent a long stay in Italy in 1887. In that year the short novel The Aspern Papers and The Reverberator were published.

Late years, 1898–1916

In 1897–1898 he moved to Rye, Sussex, and wrote The Turn of the Screw. 1899–1900 saw the publication of The Awkward Age and The Sacred

Fount. During 1902–1904 he wrote The Ambassadors, The Wings of the Dove, and The Golden Bowl.

In 1904 he revisited America and lectured on Balzac. In 1906–1910 he published The American Scene and edited the "New York Edition", a 24-volume collection of his works. In 1910 his brother William died; Henry had just joined William from an unsuccessful search for relief in Europe on what then turned out to be his (Henry's) last visit to the United States (from summer 1910 to July 1911), and was near him, according to a letter he wrote, when he died.

In 1913 he wrote his autobiographies, A Small Boy and Others, and Notes of a Son and Brother. After the outbreak of the First World War in 1914 he did war work. In 1915 he became a British subject and was awarded the Order of Merit the following year. He died on 28 February 1916, in Chelsea, London. As he requested, his ashes were buried in Cambridge Cemetery in Massachusetts.

Biographers

James regularly rejected suggestions that he should marry, and after settling in London proclaimed himself "a bachelor". F. W. Dupee, in several volumes on the James family, originated the theory that he had been in love with his cousin Mary ("Minnie") Temple, but that a neurotic fear of sex kept him from admitting such affections: "James's invalidism ... was itself the symptom of some fear of or scruple against sexual love on his part." Dupee used an episode from James's memoir A Small Boy and Others, recounting a dream of a Napoleonic image in the Louvre, to exemplify James's romanticism about Europe, a Napoleonic fantasy into which he fled.

Dupee had not had access to the James family papers and worked principally from James's published memoir of his older brother, William, and the limited collection of letters edited by Percy Lubbock, heavily weighted toward James's last years. His account therefore moved directly from James's childhood, when he trailed after his older brother, to elderly invalidism. As more material became available to scholars, including the diaries of contemporaries and hundreds of affectionate and sometimes erotic letters written by James to younger men, the picture of neurotic celibacy gave way to a portrait of a closeted homosexual.

Between 1953 and 1972, Leon Edel authored a major five-volume biography of James, which accessed unpublished letters and documents after Edel gained the permission of James's family. Edel's portrayal of James included the suggestion he was celibate. It was a view first propounded by critic Saul Rosenzweig in 1943. In 1996 Sheldon M. Novick published Henry James: The Young Master, followed by Henry James: The Mature Master (2007). The first book "caused something of an uproar in Jamesian circles" as it challenged the previous received notion of celibacy, a once-familiar paradigm in biographies of homosexuals when direct evidence was non-existent. Novick also criticised Edel for following the discounted Freudian interpretation of homosexuality "as a kind of failure." The difference of opinion erupted in a series of exchanges between Edel and Novick which were published by the online magazine Slate, with the latter arguing that even the suggestion of celibacy went against James's own injunction "live!"—not "fantasize!"

A letter James wrote in old age to Hugh Walpole has been cited as an explicit statement of this. Walpole confessed to him of indulging in "high jinks", and James wrote a reply endorsing it: "We must know, as much as possible, in our beautiful art, yours & mine, what we are talking about — & the only way to know it is to have lived & loved & cursed & floundered & enjoyed & suffered — I don't think I regret a single 'excess' of my responsive youth".

The interpretation of James as living a less austere emotional life has been subsequently explored by other scholars. The often intense politics of Jamesian scholarship has also been the subject of studies. Author Colm Tóibín has said that Eve Kosofsky Sedgwick's Epistemology of the Closet made a landmark difference to Jamesian scholarship by arguing that he be read as a homosexual writer whose desire to keep his sexuality a secret shaped his layered style and dramatic artistry. According to Tóibín such a reading "removed James from the realm of dead white males who wrote about posh people. He became our contemporary."

James's letters to expatriate American sculptor Hendrik Christian Andersen have attracted particular attention. James met the 27-year-old Andersen in Rome in 1899, when James was 56, and wrote letters to Andersen that are intensely emotional: "I hold you, dearest boy, in my innermost love, & count on your feeling me—in every throb of your soul". In a letter of 6 May 1904, to his brother William, James referred to himself as "always your hopelessly celibate even though sexagenarian Henry". How accurate that description might have been is the subject of contention among James's biographers,   but the letters to Andersen were occasionally quasi-erotic: "I put, my dear boy, my arm around you, & feel the pulsation, thereby, as it were, of our excellent future & your admirable endowment." To his homosexual friend Howard Sturgis, James could write: "I repeat, almost to indiscretion, that I could live with you. Meanwhile I can only try to live without you."

His numerous letters to the many young gay men among his close male friends are more forthcoming. In a letter to Howard Sturgis, following a long visit, James refers jocularly to their "happy little congress of two" and in letters to Hugh Walpole he pursues convoluted jokes and puns about their relationship, referring to himself as an elephant who "paws you oh so benevolently" and winds about Walpole his "well meaning old trunk". His letters to Walter Berry printed by the Black Sun Press have long been celebrated for their lightly veiled eroticism.

He corresponded in almost equally extravagant language with his many female friends, writing, for example, to fellow novelist Lucy Clifford: "Dearest Lucy! What shall I say? when I love you so very, very much, and see you nine times for once that I see Others! Therefore I think that—if you want it made clear to the meanest intelligence—I love you more than I love Others." To his New York friend Mary Cadwalader Jones: "Dearest Mary Cadwalader. I yearn over you, but I yearn in vain; & your long silence really breaks my heart, mystifies, depresses, almost alarms me, to the point even of making me wonder if poor unconscious & doting old Célimare [Jones's pet name for James] has 'done' anything, in some dark somnambulism of the spirit, which has ... given you a bad moment, or a wrong impression, or a 'colourable pretext' ... However these things may be, he loves you as tenderly as ever;

nothing, to the end of time, will ever detach him from you, & he remembers those Eleventh St. matutinal intimes hours, those telephonic matinées, as the most romantic of his life ..." His long friendship with American novelist Constance Fenimore Woolson, in whose house he lived for a number of weeks in Italy in 1887, and his shock and grief over her suicide in 1894, are discussed in detail in Edel's biography and play a central role in a study by Lyndall Gordon. (Edel conjectured that Woolson was in love with James and killed herself in part because of his coldness, but Woolson's biographers have objected to Edel's account.)

Works

Style and themes

James is one of the major figures of trans-Atlantic literature. His works frequently juxtapose characters from the Old World (Europe), embodying a feudal civilisation that is beautiful, often corrupt, and alluring, and from the New World (United States), where people are often brash, open, and assertive and embody the virtues—freedom and a more highly evolved moral character—of the new American society. James explores this clash of personalities and cultures, in stories of personal relationships in which power is exercised well or badly. His protagonists were often young American women facing oppression or abuse, and as his secretary Theodora Bosanquet remarked in her monograph Henry James at Work:

> When he walked out of the refuge of his study and into the world and looked around him, he saw a place of torment, where creatures of prey perpetually thrust their claws into the quivering flesh of doomed, defenseless children of light ... His novels are a repeated exposure of this wickedness, a reiterated and passionate plea for the fullest freedom of development, unimperiled by reckless and barbarous stupidity.

Critics have jokingly described three phases in the development of James's prose: "James I, James II, and The Old Pretender." He wrote short stories and plays. Finally, in his third and last period he returned to the long, serialised novel. Beginning in the second period, but most noticeably in the third, he increasingly abandoned direct statement in favour of frequent

703

double negatives, and complex descriptive imagery. Single paragraphs began to run for page after page, in which an initial noun would be succeeded by pronouns surrounded by clouds of adjectives and prepositional clauses, far from their original referents, and verbs would be deferred and then preceded by a series of adverbs. The overall effect could be a vivid evocation of a scene as perceived by a sensitive observer. It has been debated whether this change of style was engendered by James's shifting from writing to dictating to a typist, a change made during the composition of What Maisie Knew.

In its intense focus on the consciousness of his major characters, James's later work foreshadows extensive developments in 20th century fiction. Indeed, he might have influenced stream-of-consciousness writers such as Virginia Woolf, who not only read some of his novels but also wrote essays about them. Both contemporary and modern readers have found the late style difficult and unnecessary; his friend Edith Wharton, who admired him greatly, said that there were passages in his work that were all but incomprehensible. James was harshly portrayed by H. G. Wells as a hippopotamus laboriously attempting to pick up a pea that had got into a corner of its cage. The "late James" style was ably parodied by Max Beerbohm in "The Mote in the Middle Distance".

More important for his work overall may have been his position as an expatriate, and in other ways an outsider, living in Europe. While he came from middle-class and provincial beginnings (seen from the perspective of European polite society) he worked very hard to gain access to all levels of society, and the settings of his fiction range from working class to aristocratic, and often describe the efforts of middle-class Americans to make their way in European capitals. He confessed he got some of his best story ideas from gossip at the dinner table or at country house weekends. He worked for a living, however, and lacked the experiences of select schools, university, and army service, the common bonds of masculine society. He was furthermore a man whose tastes and interests were, according to the prevailing standards of Victorian era Anglo-American culture, rather feminine, and who was shadowed by the cloud of prejudice that then and later accompanied suspicions of his homosexuality. Edmund Wilson famously compared James's objectivity to Shakespeare's:

One would be in a position to appreciate James better if one compared him with the dramatists of the seventeenth century—Racine and Molière, whom he resembles in form as well as in point of view, and even Shakespeare, when allowances are made for the most extreme differences in subject and form. These poets are not, like Dickens and Hardy, writers of melodrama—either humorous or pessimistic, nor secretaries of society like Balzac, nor prophets like Tolstoy: they are occupied simply with the presentation of conflicts of moral character, which they do not concern themselves about softening or averting. They do not indict society for these situations: they regard them as universal and inevitable. They do not even blame God for allowing them: they accept them as the conditions of life.

It is also possible to see many of James's stories as psychological thought-experiments. In his preface to the New York edition of The American he describes the development of the story in his mind as exactly such: the "situation" of an American, "some robust but insidiously beguiled and betrayed, some cruelly wronged, compatriot..." with the focus of the story being on the response of this wronged man. The Portrait of a Lady may be an experiment to see what happens when an idealistic young woman suddenly becomes very rich. In many of his tales, characters seem to exemplify alternative futures and possibilities, as most markedly in "The Jolly Corner", in which the protagonist and a ghost-doppelganger live alternative American and European lives; and in others, like The Ambassadors, an older James seems fondly to regard his own younger self facing a crucial moment.

Major novels

The first period of James's fiction, usually considered to have culminated in The Portrait of a Lady, concentrated on the contrast between Europe and America. The style of these novels is generally straightforward and, though personally characteristic, well within the norms of 19th-century fiction. Roderick Hudson (1875) is a Künstlerroman that traces the development of the title character, an extremely talented sculptor. Although the book shows some signs of immaturity—this was James's first serious attempt at a full-length novel—it has attracted favourable comment due to the vivid realisation of the three major characters: Roderick Hudson, superbly gifted but unstable and unreliable; Rowland Mallet, Roderick's limited but much more mature friend and patron; and Christina Light, one of James's most enchanting and maddening femmes fatales. The pair of Hudson and Mallet has been seen as representing the two sides of James's own nature: the wildly imaginative artist and the brooding conscientious mentor.

In The Portrait of a Lady (1881) James concluded the first phase of his career with a novel that remains his most popular piece of long fiction. The story is of a spirited young American woman, Isabel Archer, who "affronts her destiny" and finds it overwhelming. She inherits a large amount of money and subsequently becomes the victim of Machiavellian scheming by two American expatriates. The narrative is set mainly in Europe, especially in England and Italy. Generally regarded as the masterpiece of his early phase, The Portrait of a Lady is described as a psychological novel, exploring the minds of his characters, and almost a work of social science, exploring the differences between Europeans and Americans, the old and the new worlds.

The second period of James's career, which extends from the publication of The Portrait of a Lady through the end of the nineteenth century, features less popular novels including The Princess Casamassima, published serially in The Atlantic Monthly in 1885–1886, and The Bostonians, published serially in The Century Magazine during the same period. This period also featured James's celebrated Gothic novella, The Turn of the Screw.

The third period of James's career reached its most significant achievement in three novels published just around the start of the 20th century: The Wings of the Dove (1902), The Ambassadors (1903), and The Golden Bowl (1904). Critic F. O. Matthiessen called this "trilogy" James's major phase, and these novels have certainly received intense critical study. It was the second-written of the books, The Wings of the Dove (1902) that was the first published because it attracted no serialization. This novel tells the story of Milly Theale, an American heiress stricken with a serious disease, and her impact on the people around her. Some of these people befriend Milly with honourable motives, while others are more self-interested. James stated in his autobiographical books that Milly was based on Minny Temple, his beloved cousin who died at an early age of tuberculosis. He said that he attempted in the novel to wrap her memory in the "beauty and dignity of art".

Shorter narratives

James was particularly interested in what he called the "beautiful and blest nouvelle", or the longer form of short narrative. Still, he produced a number of very short stories in which he achieved notable compression of sometimes complex subjects. The following narratives are representative of James's achievement in the shorter forms of fiction.

- "A Tragedy of Error" (1864), short story
- "The Story of a Year" (1865), short story
- A Passionate Pilgrim (1871), novella
- Madame de Mauves (1874), novella
- Daisy Miller (1878), novella
- The Aspern Papers (1888), novella
- The Lesson of the Master (1888), novella
- The Pupil (1891), short story
- "The Figure in the Carpet" (1896), short story
- The Beast in the Jungle (1903), novella
- An International Episode (1878)
- Picture and Text
- Four Meetings (1885)
- A London Life, and Other Tales (1889)
- The Spoils of Poynton (1896)

- Embarrassments (1896)

- The Two Magics: The Turn of the Screw, Covering End (1898)

- A Little Tour of France (1900)

- The Sacred Fount (1901)

- Views and Reviews (1908)

- The Wings of the Dove, Volume I (1902)

- The Wings of the Dove, Volume II (1909)

- The Finer Grain (1910)

- The Outcry (1911)

- Lady Barbarina: The Siege of London, An International Episode and Other Tales (1922)

- The Birthplace (1922)

Plays

At several points in his career James wrote plays, beginning with one-act plays written for periodicals in 1869 and 1871 and a dramatisation of his popular novella Daisy Miller in 1882. From 1890 to 1892, having received a bequest that freed him from magazine publication, he made a strenuous effort to succeed on the London stage, writing a half-dozen plays of which only one, a dramatisation of his novel The American, was produced. This play was performed for several years by a touring repertory company and had a respectable run in London, but did not earn very much money for James. His other plays written at this time were not produced.

In 1893, however, he responded to a request from actor-manager George Alexander for a serious play for the opening of his renovated St. James's Theatre, and wrote a long drama, Guy Domville, which Alexander produced. There was a noisy uproar on the opening night, 5 January 1895, with hissing from the gallery when James took his bow after the final curtain, and the author was upset. The play received moderately good reviews and had a modest run of four weeks before being taken off to make way for Oscar Wilde's The Importance of Being Earnest, which Alexander thought would have better prospects for the coming season.

After the stresses and disappointment of these efforts James insisted that he would write no more for the theatre, but within weeks had agreed to write a curtain-raiser for Ellen Terry. This became the one-act "Summersoft", which he later rewrote into a short story, "Covering End", and then expanded into a full-length play, The High Bid, which had a brief run in London in 1907, when James made another concerted effort to write for the stage. He wrote three new plays, two of which were in production when the death of Edward VII on 6 May 1910 plunged London into mourning and theatres closed. Discouraged by failing health and the stresses of theatrical work, James did not renew his efforts in the theatre, but recycled his plays as successful novels. The Outcry was a best-seller in the United States when it was published in 1911. During the years 1890–1893 when he was most engaged with the theatre, James wrote a good deal of theatrical criticism and assisted Elizabeth Robins and others in translating and producing Henrik Ibsen for the first time in London.

Leon Edel argued in his psychoanalytic biography that James was traumatised by the opening night uproar that greeted Guy Domville, and that it plunged him into a prolonged depression. The successful later novels, in Edel's view, were the result of a kind of self-analysis, expressed in fiction, which partly freed him from his fears. Other biographers and scholars have not accepted this account, however; the more common view being that of F.O. Matthiessen, who wrote: "Instead of being crushed by the collapse of his hopes [for the theatre]... he felt a resurgence of new energy."

Non-fiction

Beyond his fiction, James was one of the more important literary critics in the history of the novel. In his classic essay The Art of Fiction (1884), he argued against rigid prescriptions on the novelist's choice of subject and method of treatment. He maintained that the widest possible freedom in content and approach would help ensure narrative fiction's continued vitality.

James wrote many valuable critical articles on other novelists; typical is his book-length study of Nathaniel Hawthorne, which has been the subject of critical debate. Richard Brodhead has suggested that the study was emblematic of James's struggle with Hawthorne's influence, and constituted an effort to place the elder writer "at a disadvantage." Gordon Fraser, meanwhile, has suggested that the study was part of a more commercial effort by James to introduce himself to British readers as Hawthorne's natural successor.

When James assembled the New York Edition of his fiction in his final years, he wrote a series of prefaces that subjected his own work to searching, occasionally harsh criticism.

At 22 James wrote The Noble School of Fiction for The Nation's first issue in 1865. He would write, in all, over 200 essays and book, art, and theatre reviews for the magazine.

For most of his life James harboured ambitions for success as a playwright. He converted his novel The American into a play that enjoyed modest returns in the early 1890s. In all he wrote about a dozen plays, most of which went unproduced. His costume drama Guy Domville failed disastrously on its opening night in 1895. James then largely abandoned his efforts to conquer the stage and returned to his fiction. In his Notebooks he maintained that his theatrical experiment benefited his novels and tales by helping him dramatise his characters' thoughts and emotions. James produced a small but valuable amount of theatrical criticism, including perceptive appreciations of Henrik Ibsen.

With his wide-ranging artistic interests, James occasionally wrote on the visual arts. Perhaps his most valuable contribution was his favourable assessment of fellow expatriate John Singer Sargent, a painter whose critical status has improved markedly in recent decades. James also wrote sometimes charming, sometimes brooding articles about various places he visited and lived in. His most famous books of travel writing include Italian Hours (an example of the charming approach) and The American Scene (most definitely on the brooding side).

James was one of the great letter-writers of any era. More than ten thousand of his personal letters are extant, and over three thousand have been published in a large number of collections. A complete edition of James's letters began publication in 2006, edited by Pierre Walker and Greg Zacharias. As of 2014, eight volumes have been published, covering the period from 1855 to 1880. James's correspondents included celebrated contemporaries like Robert Louis Stevenson, Edith Wharton and Joseph Conrad, along with many others in his wide circle of friends and acquaintances. The letters range from the "mere twaddle of graciousness" to serious discussions of artistic, social and personal issues.

Very late in life James began a series of autobiographical works: A Small Boy and Others, Notes of a Son and Brother, and the unfinished The Middle Years. These books portray the development of a classic observer who was passionately interested in artistic creation but was somewhat reticent about participating fully in the life around him.

Reception

Criticism, biographies and fictional treatments

James's work has remained steadily popular with the limited audience of educated readers to whom he spoke during his lifetime, and has remained firmly in the canon, but, after his death, some American critics, such as Van Wyck Brooks, expressed hostility towards James for his long expatriation and eventual naturalisation as a British subject. Other critics such as E. M. Forster complained about what they saw as James's squeamishness in the treatment of sex and other possibly controversial material, or dismissed his late style as difficult and obscure, relying heavily on extremely long sentences and excessively latinate language. Similarly Oscar Wilde criticised him for writing "fiction as if it were a painful duty". Vernon Parrington, composing a canon of American literature, condemned James for having cut himself off from America. Jorge Luis Borges wrote about him, "Despite the scruples and delicate complexities of James, his work suffers from a major defect: the absence of life." And Virginia Woolf, writing to Lytton Strachey, asked, "Please tell me what you find in Henry James. ... we have his works here, and

711

I read, and I can't find anything but faintly tinged rose water, urbane and sleek, but vulgar and pale as Walter Lamb. Is there really any sense in it?" The novelist W. Somerset Maugham wrote, "He did not know the English as an Englishman instinctively knows them and so his English characters never to my mind quite ring true," and argued "The great novelists, even in seclusion, have lived life passionately. Henry James was content to observe it from a window." Maugham nevertheless wrote, "The fact remains that those last novels of his, notwithstanding their unreality, make all other novels, except the very best, unreadable." Colm Tóibín observed that James "never really wrote about the English very well. His English characters don't work for me."

Despite these criticisms, James is now valued for his psychological and moral realism, his masterful creation of character, his low-key but playful humour, and his assured command of the language. In his 1983 book, The Novels of Henry James, Edward Wagenknecht offers an assessment that echoes Theodora Bosanquet's:

> "To be completely great," Henry James wrote in an early review, "a work of art must lift up the heart," and his own novels do this to an outstanding degree ... More than sixty years after his death, the great novelist who sometimes professed to have no opinions stands foursquare in the great Christian humanistic and democratic tradition. The men and women who, at the height of World War II, raided the secondhand shops for his out-of-print books knew what they were about. For no writer ever raised a braver banner to which all who love freedom might adhere.

William Dean Howells saw James as a representative of a new realist school of literary art which broke with the English romantic tradition epitomised by the works of Charles Dickens and William Makepeace Thackeray. Howells wrote that realism found "its chief exemplar in Mr. James... A novelist he is not, after the old fashion, or after any fashion but his own." F.R. Leavis championed Henry James as a novelist of "established pre-eminence" in The Great Tradition (1948), asserting that The Portrait of a Lady and The Bostonians were "the two most brilliant novels in the language." James is now prized as a master of point of view who moved literary fiction forward by insisting in showing, not telling, his stories to the reader. (Source: Wikipedia)

NOTABLE WORKS

NOVELS

Watch and Ward (1871)

Roderick Hudson (1875)

The American (1877)

The Europeans (1878)

Confidence (1879)

Washington Square (1880)

The Portrait of a Lady (1881)

The Bostonians (1886)

The Princess Casamassima (1886)

The Reverberator (1888)

The Tragic Muse (1890)

The Other House (1896)

The Spoils of Poynton (1897)

What Maisie Knew (1897)

The Awkward Age (1899)

The Sacred Fount (1901)

The Wings of the Dove (1902)

The Ambassadors (1903)

The Golden Bowl (1904)

The Whole Family (collaborative novel with eleven other authors, 1908)

The Outcry (1911)

The Ivory Tower (unfinished, published posthumously 1917)

The Sense of the Past (unfinished, published posthumously 1917)

SHORT STORIES AND NOVELLAS

A Tragedy of Error (1864)

The Story of a Year (1865)

A Landscape Painter (1866)

A Day of Days (1866)

My Friend Bingham (1867)

Poor Richard (1867)

The Story of a Masterpiece (1868)

A Most Extraordinary Case (1868)

A Problem (1868)

De Grey: A Romance (1868)

Osborne's Revenge (1868)

The Romance of Certain Old Clothes (1868)

A Light Man (1869)

Gabrielle de Bergerac (1869)

Travelling Companions (1870)

A Passionate Pilgrim (1871)

At Isella (1871)

Master Eustace (1871)

Guest's Confession (1872)

The Madonna of the Future (1873)

The Sweetheart of M. Briseux (1873)

The Last of the Valerii (1874)

Madame de Mauves (1874)

Adina (1874)

Professor Fargo (1874)

Eugene Pickering (1874)

Benvolio (1875)

Crawford's Consistency (1876)

The Ghostly Rental (1876)

Four Meetings (1877)

Rose-Agathe (1878, as Théodolinde)

Daisy Miller (1878)

Longstaff's Marriage (1878)

An International Episode (1878)

The Pension Beaurepas (1879)

A Diary of a Man of Fifty (1879)

A Bundle of Letters (1879)

The Point of View (1882)

The Siege of London (1883)

Impressions of a Cousin (1883)

Lady Barberina (1884)

Pandora (1884)

The Author of Beltraffio (1884)

Georgina's Reasons (1884)

A New England Winter (1884)

The Path of Duty (1884)

Mrs. Temperly (1887)

Louisa Pallant (1888)

The Aspern Papers (1888)

The Liar (1888)

The Modern Warning (1888, originally published as The Two Countries)

A London Life (1888)

The Patagonia (1888)

The Lesson of the Master (1888)

The Solution (1888)

The Pupil (1891)

Brooksmith (1891)

The Marriages (1891)

The Chaperon (1891)

Sir Edmund Orme (1891)

Nona Vincent (1892)

The Real Thing (1892)

The Private Life (1892)

Lord Beaupré (1892)

The Visits (1892)

Sir Dominick Ferrand (1892)

Greville Fane (1892)

Collaboration (1892)

Owen Wingrave (1892)

The Wheel of Time (1892)

The Middle Years (1893)

The Death of the Lion (1894)

The Coxon Fund (1894)

The Next Time (1895)

Glasses (1896)

The Altar of the Dead (1895)

The Figure in the Carpet (1896)

The Way It Came (1896, also published as The Friends of the Friends)

The Turn of the Screw (1898)

Covering End (1898)

In the Cage (1898)

John Delavoy (1898)

The Given Case (1898)

Europe (1899)

The Great Condition (1899)

The Real Right Thing (1899)

Paste (1899)

The Great Good Place (1900)

Maud-Evelyn (1900)

Miss Gunton of Poughkeepsie (1900)

The Tree of Knowledge (1900)

The Abasement of the Northmores (1900)

The Third Person (1900)

The Special Type (1900)

The Tone of Time (1900)

Broken Wings (1900)

The Two Faces (1900)

Mrs. Medwin (1901)

The Beldonald Holbein (1901)

The Story in It (1902)

Flickerbridge (1902)

The Birthplace (1903)

The Beast in the Jungle (1903)

The Papers (1903)

Fordham Castle (1904)

Julia Bride (1908)

The Jolly Corner (1908)

The Velvet Glove (1909)

Mora Montravers (1909)

Crapy Cornelia (1909)

The Bench of Desolation (1909)

A Round of Visits (1910)

OTHER

Transatlantic Sketches (1875)

French Poets and Novelists (1878)

Hawthorne (1879)

Portraits of Places (1883)

A Little Tour in France (1884)

Partial Portraits (1888)

Essays in London and Elsewhere (1893)

Picture and Text (1893)

Terminations (1893)

Theatricals (1894)

Theatricals: Second Series (1895)

Guy Domville (1895)

The Soft Side (1900)

William Wetmore Story and His Friends (1903)

The Better Sort (1903)

English Hours (1905)

The Question of our Speech; The Lesson of Balzac. Two Lectures (1905)

The American Scene (1907)

Views and Reviews (1908)

Italian Hours (1909)

A Small Boy and Others (1913)

Notes on Novelists (1914)

Notes of a Son and Brother (1914)

Within the Rim (1918)

Travelling Companions (1919)

Notebooks (various, published posthumously)

The Middle Years (unfinished, published posthumously 1917)

A Most Unholy Trade (1925, published posthumously)

The Art of the Novel : Critical Prefaces (1934)

CPSIA information can be obtained
at www.ICGtesting.com
Printed in the USA
LVHW092117021120
670493LV00003B/141

9 781662 716379